Loosening the Grip

A HANDBOOK OF ALCOHOL INFORMATION

Loosening the Grip

A HANDBOOK OF ALCOHOL INFORMATION

Eleventh Edition

JEAN KINNEY, MSW
Lecturer, Community and Family Medicine
Giesel School of Medicine at Dartmouth College

Illustrations by
Stuart A. Copans, MD

Mc
Graw
Hill
Education

LOOSENING THE GRIP: A HANDBOOK OF ALCOHOL INFORMATION, ELEVENTH EDITION

Published by McGraw-Hill Education, 2 Penn Plaza, New York, NY 10121.

This book is printed on acid-free paper.

1 2 3 4 5 6 7 8 9 0 DOC/DOC 1 0 9 8 7 6 5 4

ISBN 978-0-07-802855-7
MHID 0-07-802855-8

Senior Vice President, Products & Markets: *Kurt L. Strand*
Vice President, General Manager, Products & Markets: *Michael Ryan*
Vice President, Content Production & Technology Services: *Kimberly Meriwether David*
Lead Product Developer: *Lisa Pinto*
Product Development Coordinator: *Adina Lonn*
Associate Marketing Manager: *Alexandra Schultz*
Director, Content Production: *Terri Schiesl*
Lead Content Project Manager: *Jane Mohr*
Buyer: *Susan K. Culbertson*
Cover Designer: *Studio Montage, St. Louis, MO.*
Cover Image: Cover art and text cartoon art copyright © Stuart A. Copans, M.D.
Media Project Manager: *Jennifer Bartell*
Compositor: *Laserwords Private Limited*
Typeface: *10/12 Times Lt Std*
Printer: *R. R. Donnelley*

All credits appearing on page or at the end of the book are considered to be an extension of the copyright page.

Library of Congress Cataloging-in-Publication Data

Kinney, Jean, 1943- author.
Loosening the grip: a handbook of alcohol information.—Eleventh edition/Jean Kinney, MSW, lecturer, Community and Family Medicine, Geisel Medical School at Dartmouth; illustrations by Stuart A. Copans, MD.
pages cm
Includes bibliographical references and index.
ISBN 978-0-07-802855-7 (alk. paper)
1. Alcoholism—United States—Handbooks, manuals, etc. 2. Alcoholism—Treatment—United States—Handbooks, manuals, etc. I. Title.
HV5292.K53 2015
362.292—dc23

2013050731

www.mhhe.com

Contributors

Stuart A. Copans, MD *Illustrator*

Dr. Copans, a child psychiatrist, was a lecturer in an alcohol counselor training program, discussing the effects of alcohol abuse on the family—the early sign of what became a major professional interest. He has directed a residential adolescent substance abuse program, in a Dartmouth-affiliated teaching hospital, and provides consultation to private and public programs as well as schools in Massachusetts.

Andrew Horrigan, MD *Chapter 12, Other Psychiatric Conditions; Chapter 13, Drugs of Abuse Other Than Alcohol*

Dr. Horrigan, a psychiatrist with an interest in addiction medicine, is one of a long line of Dartmouth-affiliated contributors recruited early in their careers. He had been involved in community mental health and substance abuse services in northern New England before moving to New Zealand, where he is a psychiatrist with the Wellington and Wairarrapa Health District. (And yes, he's still involved in addiction medicine.)

Jean Kinney, MSW

Jean Kinney, lecturer in Community and Family Medicine at Geisel School of Medicine at Dartmouth was the associate director of the Alcohol Counselor Training Program at Dartmouth conducted between 1972 and 1978, the program that was the impetus for this text. Upon completion of the training program, she joined Project Cork, a program established to develop and implement a model curriculum for medical student education on alcohol. In 1999, she was the first recipient of the NIAAA's Senator Harold Hughes Award, in recognition of her professional efforts in translating scientific work into clinical practice. She publishes a substance abuse website for health care professionals.

Trevor R. P. Price, MD *Chapter 3, Alcohol and the Body; Chapter 6, Medical Complications*

Dr. Price entered psychiatry after training in internal medicine. His interest in alcohol was sparked during his tenure at Dartmouth Medical School, when he was a member of the faculty for the Alcohol Counselor Training Program. Dr. Price has been on the faculty of Dartmouth Medical School, the University of Pennsylvania School of Medicine, and the Medical College of Pennsylvania and Drexel University College of Medicine. He has traded being a department chair for private practice and the opportunity to once again provide patient care.

By the time a text has reached its eleventh edition, it becomes difficult to sort out and separate the particular contributions of individual people. Those listed above assumed responsibility for revising and updating material for this edition. Much of what remains incorporated here is, however, the product of others who contributed to earlier editions and whose work remains.

Frederick Burkle Jr., MD, MPH, FAAP, FACEP *Chapter 11, Adolescents, early editions*

Dr. Burkle, a lecturer to the counselor trainees at Dartmouth Medical School, came to a psychiatry residency program at Dartmouth Medical School after a practice in pediatrics. He has long since left chilly New England and joined the faculty of the University of Hawaii's School of Medicine and School of Public Health. He has been central in worldwide efforts around refugee health care.

Hugh MacNamee, MD *Chapter 11, Adolescents, earliest editions*

Dr. MacNamee was an associate professor of clinical psychiatry in the Division of Child Psychiatry at Dartmouth until his death. His eminently practical stance and uncommon common sense were always much in evidence. Some things really cannot be improved on. His influence continues, too, through other contributors who trained under him.

Fred C. Osher, MD *Chapter 12, Other Psychiatric Considerations: Suicide, Co-Occurring Psychiatric Illness*

Dr. Osher entered the field of psychiatry at Dartmouth Medical School after serving as the medical director of a detoxification center in Detroit, a setting that sparked a lifelong interest in substance abuse issues, care for disadvantaged populations, and public policy. He was an early member of the New Hampshire Psychiatric Research Center, a leader in the area of the care of those with psychiatric illness and co-occurring substance use problems. Dr. Osher is now the Director of the Center for Behavioral Health, Justice, and Public Policy at the University of Maryland School of Medicine.

Donald West, MD *Chapter 12, Other Psychiatric Considerations: Co-Occurring Psychiatric Illness; Chapter 13, Drugs of Abuse Other Than Alcohol*

Dr. West, associate professor of psychiatry at Dartmouth is the director of the short-term psychiatric unit at the Medical Center and involved in substance abuse services. He originally came to Dartmouth from the University of New Mexico on a half-year sabbatical, which he spent with the substance abuse treatment team, and the area apparently began to look like home.

for each of us

and those who nurture us

God of Compassion, if anyone has come to Thine altar troubled in spirit, depressed and apprehensive, expecting to go away as she came, with the same haunting heaviness of heart; if anyone is deeply wounded of soul, hardly daring to hope that anything can afford her the relief she seeks, so surprised by the ill that life can do that she is half afraid to pray; O God, surprise her, we beseech Thee, by the graciousness of Thy help; and enable her to take from thy bounty as ungrudgingly as Thou givest, that she may leave her sorrow and take a song away.

AUTHOR UNKNOWN

Brief Contents

Contents

Preface

> Material on alcohol and alcoholism is mushrooming. There are books, articles, scientific reports, pamphlets. On present use, past use, abuse. Around prevention, efforts at early detection, effects on the family, effects on the body. When, where, why.
>
> And yet, if you are in the helping business and reasonably bright and conscientious and can find an occasional half hour to read but don't have all day to search library stacks, then it's probably hard for you to lay your hands on the information you need when it would be most helpful.
>
> This handbook is an attempt to partially remedy the situation. It contains what we believe is the basic information an alcohol counselor or other professional confronted with alcohol problems needs to know and would like to have handy. The work here isn't original. It is an effort to synthesize, organize, and sometimes "translate" the information from medicine, psychology, psychiatry, anthropology, sociology, and counseling that applies to alcohol use and alcoholism treatment. This handbook isn't the last word. But we hope it is a starting point.
>
> Preface, *Loosening the Grip*, First Edition, 1978

In the period since publication of the first edition of this handbook, what was then described as rapid growth in the literature has become a veritable deluge. Consequently, the demands on those in the helping professions are even greater. To be current would entail not only scanning the literature from the disciplines mentioned, but also looking at the many journals of the alcohol and substance abuse fields.

Since the first edition of *Loosening the Grip,* there have been many changes in the alcohol field. Perhaps most notably, there is no longer a distinct alcohol field in the way there was in the 1970s. Today the field is substance abuse, which represents a merging of the previously separate worlds of alcohol treatment and drug treatment.

Ever since the first edition of this book, people have asked about the title. Yes, there is a story behind it. When Gwen Leaton, my coauthor for the first five editions, and I were preparing the original text, an apt title did not leap forth. Somewhere along the line, in casual conversation someone recounted a comment made by an alcoholic struggling to get sober. This person, discussing her drinking in a rather defiant and belligerent fashion, said, "If God didn't want me to drink, He'd knock the glass out of my hand!" One of us jokingly commented that we hoped whoever was present had supplied the obviously perfect retort, "He will; all you have to do is loosen your grip." Somehow that metaphor caught the simplicity and the complexity, the ease and the difficulty, the "holding on" and "being held" that are a part of alcohol problems.

An almost mandatory conclusion for book prefaces is an exhaustive listing of "all the persons whose support and assistance. . . ." Trusting that family, friends, and professional colleagues know who they are, you will find here a slight departure from that tradition. In fact, many of the most significant contributions to this work have been made by individuals whose names and identities, such as the woman in the example just given, are unknown—substance abuse clinicians, those in the twelve-step groups, members of the clergy, school counselors, the medical profession—all those who have been responsible for the strides in our collective understanding and clinical practice, all those whose efforts in their professional and private lives make loosening the grip possible.

Jean Kinney

Premises Underpinning This Book

Three simple assumptions lie at the heart of this book.

One. Textbooks need not lead to terminal boredom, nor put you to sleep. The writing style as well as the illustrations in this book aim to keep you awake. Of course, it's OK if the illustrations make you smile. Typically each also serves as a visual exclamation point, a non-traditional way of emphasizing key points and an alternative to underlining. Similarly, while many of the marginal annotations provide historical or scientific information, others capture, in just a few words, a basic point.

Two. Anyone who is going to muck around in someone else's life had better be knowledgeable about what is likely to be encountered. Those in the helping professions are guaranteed to have clients with alcohol and other drug problems. Being informed about alcohol and other drugs isn't optional; it's a requisite. And "informed" means not "sort-of-familiar-with" but knowledgeable.

Three. The task of mastering essential information on alcohol can be formidable. There are two seemingly contradictory challenges. To a large extent, everyone "knows" about alcohol and other drugs,

IT'S A SHAME SOME OF THE DRAWINGS ARE FOR THE BIRDS.
PART OF WHAT MAKES THIS BOOK SO GOOD IS THE CARTOONS

> and everyone has an opinion. Go to a party, and when someone asks what you do, say you work in the substance abuse field. You can almost bet that this person will then proceed to inform you that "what really needs to be done is . . ." or some variant. Now, imagine what would happen if you say you are in theoretical physics with a particular interest in nanoparticles. In this case, you'd hear "oh," and the conversation would rapidly move on to something else. Because alcohol is a topic on which we all consider ourselves experts of a sort, one challenge of this text is prompting readers to reflect on what they presume they know, be it about drinking patterns, what motivates drinking, or the causes of alcohol problems.
>
> Then there is the opposite problem, that a portion of the knowledge base for alcohol is drawn from the biological and medical sciences. This portion includes information that for most of us is not part of our fund of knowledge. Even the vocabulary is foreign to us. If we were to eavesdrop on a conversation of experts, we might suspect they were speaking Klingon.
>
> This doesn't mean you can't *ever* get it. It does mean that a text such as this has to work hard not only at identifying the essential basic knowledge but also at providing a good translation of scientific information with which readers are not familiar. A translation is not a matter of spewing out facts or distributing a list of vocabulary terms. A good translation involves selecting the right metaphor or calling upon just the right analogy to demonstrate the concept. It involves drawing upon things with which students are familiar and pointing out parallels to demonstrate the way in which a particular concept works.

In writing about the history of medicine, Jonathan Miller made an interesting observation. The big breakthroughs in understanding how the body works have occurred only *after* the invention or creation of something in our external world that provides an example. It was only after the invention of the pump that the heart's function became obvious. It isn't coincidence that the rapid strides in understanding the brain's function followed the introduction of the computer. The contributors hope that this book provides some of these "ah hah!" moments for readers.

To a remarkable degree this book does succeed in conveying how a host of phenomena unfold—whether it's how alcohol is metabolized by the body, the etiology of serious alcohol problems, or the basis for cultural differences. This is a testimony to the contributors to this book who see being a teacher as a significant part of their professional work, whether it is education of patients, medical students, or other professionals. For readers who become clinicians, an inevitable and important part of your efforts will be education.

Other Drug Use, and How This Book Fits In

The title of this book suggests that it is only about alcohol. Indeed, the first edition was published in 1978 when there was a sharp distinction between "alcohol" and "drugs." What did we think alcohol was?

Alcohol is clearly only one of a number of substances that are used for their mood-altering properties. The person in trouble with alcohol often uses other drugs, as those who use drugs often use alcohol, and so clinicians need to be informed about other substances. And while the focus here is on alcohol, it is discussed too as a prototypical drug of abuse. In the process of examining alcohol's effects and the associated problems, the book also points out similarities and differences between alcohol and other drugs. Thus it provides a framework and tools useful in considering the different drugs of abuse. While not providing the last word on other drug use and the attendant problems, this work can be a starting point.

Only a minority of you reading this text will have ever used heroin or tried crystal meth or used bath salts for something other than bathing. However, the odds are good that you have had firsthand experience with alcohol. Beyond having had a drink, it is also likely that you have had at least one experience of intoxication and have experienced or witnessed negative consequences associated with drinking—the kind of thing that makes you cringe the next day. As you reflect on what you learn from this book and rethink what is familiar to you, you will better understand other drugs of abuse and the experiences of those who use them.

FEATURES OF THIS TEXT

Demographic Influences on Alcohol Use

No single factor predicts either alcohol use or the potential problems that may emerge. Drawing on the public health model, *Loosening the Grip* considers the interplay of the multiple significant factors that need to be considered. It reviews the effects of the drug, alcohol, which invite its use. It examines individual characteristics, drawing on our rapidly growing understanding of genetic influences alongside demographic characteristics, be it age, gender, minority status whether based on race, ethnicity, or sexual orientation, being economically advantaged or disadvantaged, religious affiliation, education, and regional differences. Equal attention is directed to the family, the neighborhood, and the immediate community, as well as to larger cultural and social influences. This becomes the basis for later discussion of prevention, treatment, and policy, as well as comparing and contrasting alcohol and other drugs of abuse.

Special Populations

This edition continues to focus on the impact of alcohol and other drug use among adolescents, those in college, women, the elderly, and those in the workplace. In addition there is attention to another special population, persons involved with the criminal justice system for drug-related offenses. This theme is woven throughout the book and examines the disparities in sentencing practices, plea bargains, and the disproportionate impact on people of color.

Drugs Other Than Alcohol

The chapter dedicated to Drugs of Abuse Other Than Alcohol surveys the major drug classes, discussing their acute and chronic effects. It also examines the patterns and social costs of drug use and offers an overview of treatment and screening for drug use.

Clinical Approaches

This edition continues to address the range of clinical interventions, from prevention to screening, assessment, harm reduction, and formal alcohol/substance abuse treatment. It also describes specific treatment techniques—individual counseling, group work, the use of specific evidence-based therapies, and the use of self-help. The edition also features an expanded discussion of evidence-based treatments and their importance in the spectrum of addiction treatment.

Readable Style

With a writing style that is conversational and easy to follow, this text draws readers in and leads them through its broad coverage of the topic in terms of age groups, social institutions, and counseling options. By synthesizing information from medicine, psychology, psychiatry, anthropology, sociology, and counseling, this text presents a broad view of alcohol use and treatment of alcohol-related problems.

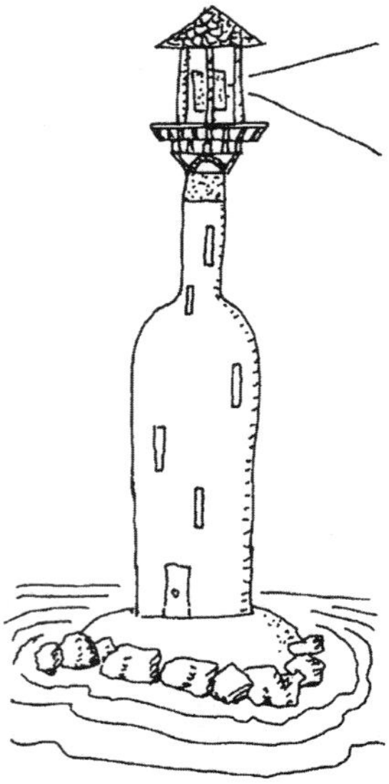

NEW TO THE ELEVENTH EDITION

From an author's perspective, trying to identify specific points that distinguish a new edition from the previous one is pointless. The risk isn't that you'll not see the forest for the trees. The danger is that you may become wholly preoccupied with the leaves.

A good textbook is far more than the information generated by several hundred Google searches. What distinguishes a text is the way in which it draws all the snippets of information together. It offers a way to view a topic, provides a map, and gives guidance as you explore the material, even pointing out the possible shoals.

The changes in this Eleventh edition reflect two significant events. One is the publication a year ago of the fifth edition of the American

Psychiatric Association's *Diagnostic and Statistical Manual.* This *Manual* addresses the spectrum of psychiatric disorders. It notably redefines the nature of alcohol and other drug problems—now termed substance use problems. Beyond introducing new terminology, this has broad implications for diagnosis, treatment and prevention. Another significant societal event is related to the ever-changing legal status of marijuana, and the potential impact it may have for individuals, communities, as well as the drug trade. This edition too addresses topics which may have been percolating for awhile, but have been gathering more attention. These include the conditions described as "behavioral addictions" ranging from internet use, to gambling, to sexual addiction. Interestingly, caffeine has been in the spotlight, on the basis of its being an additive to energy drinks. The discussion of performance-enhancing drugs now goes beyond athletes, steroids, and physical capacity. The newest twist is the use of cognitive performance-enhancing drugs, not only for students, but also air traffic controllers and surgeons. As might be expected this new edition updates the array of statistics. But going beyond that, it points to various trends, such as adolescent drinking patterns, as well as pointing out data which either supports or refutes many commonly held perceptions.

There too is discussion of the ever-increasing number and variety of drugs available. One group is designer drugs, manufactured to mimic illicit drugs, and with names such as Meow-Meow and Molly, drugs not yet deemed illicit. Another group are drugs long used in African and Asian countries, but only now becoming popular in the United States, drugs such as betel nut, salvia, and khat, and how these are related to alcohol use.

SUPPLEMENTS

An Online Learning Center with instructor resources can be found at **www.mhhe.com/kinney11e.**

Resources for Instructors

Instructor's Manual

The instructor's manual offers information for use in the classroom and for further exploration by students. It also provides related links in the following areas: medicine, alcohol, other drugs of abuse, patterns of substance abuse, clinical guides, curricula, policy and white papers, and international data.

Test Bank

This downloadable test bank is provided for instructors to use as a basis for their own exams.

PowerPoint Presentation

The chapter-by-chapter PowerPoint presentations are helpful teaching aids that can be modified to meet the needs of individual instructors and their courses.

Contact your McGraw-Hill sales representative to obtain a password to access the instructor's side of the website.

ACKNOWLEDGMENTS

The editor and the publisher would like to thank the following instructors for reviewing *Loosening the Grip* for the eleventh edition. Their comments and suggestions have been very helpful.

David S. Anderson
George Mason University

Roy Kammer
Minnesota State University, Mankato

Thomas Lipa
Tompkins Cortland Community College

Kathryn Judkins Miller
San Antonio College

CourseSmart
Learn Smart. Choose Smart.

This text is available as an eTextbook from CourseSmart, a new way for faculty to find and review eTextbooks. It's also a great option for students who are interested in accessing their course materials digitally and saving money. CourseSmart offers thousands of the most commonly adopted textbooks across hundreds of courses from a wide variety of higher education publishers. It is the only place for faculty to review and compare the full text of a textbook online, providing immediate access without the environmental impact of requesting a print exam copy. At CourseSmart, students can save up to 50% off the cost of a print book, reduce their impact on the environment, and gain access to powerful Web tools for learning including full text search, notes and highlighting, and e-mail tools for sharing notes between classmates. For further details, contact your sales representative or go to www.coursesmart.com.

McGraw Hill create

Craft your teaching resources to match the way you teach! With McGraw-Hill Create you can easily rearrange chapters, combine material from other content sources, and quickly upload content you have written, such as your course syllabus or teaching notes. Find the content you need in Create by searching through thousands of leading McGraw-Hill textbooks. Arrange your book to fit your teaching style. Create even allows you to personalize your book's appearance by selecting the cover and adding your name, school, and course information. Order a Create book and you'll receive a complimentary print review copy in three to five business days or a complimentary electronic review copy (eComp) via e-mail in about one hour. Go to www.mcgrawhillcreate.com today and register. Experience how McGraw-Hill Create empowers you to teach *your* students *your* way.

CHAPTER 1

Alcohol

ONCE UPON A TIME . . .

Imagine yourself at an archeology site in Clairvaux, high in the Swiss hills. Stone pots found there, dating from the Old Stone Age, almost certainly contained a mild beer or wine. Over 10,000 years ago, the earliest humans probably discovered alcohol much as they did fire, as a gift of nature uncovered by human curiosity. If any watery mixture of sugars or starches, such as berries or barley or honey, is allowed to stand long enough in a warm place, alcohol will make itself.

Ramses III distributed beer to his subjects and then told them the tingling they felt radiated from him.

No one knows what kind of alcoholic beverage came first—wine, beer, or mead—but by the Neolithic Age it was everywhere. Tales of liquor abound in folklore. One story relates that at the beginning of time the forces of good and evil contested with each other for domination of the earth. Eventually the forces for good won out. But a great many of them were killed in the process, and wherever they fell, a vine sprouted from the ground—so it seems some felt wine to be a good force. Other myths depict the powers of alcohol as gifts from the gods. Some civilizations worshiped specific gods of wine. The Egyptians' god was Osiris; the Greeks', Dionysius; and the Romans', Bacchus. Wine was used in early rituals as libations (poured out on the ground, altar, and so on). Priests often drank it as part of the rituals. The Bible, too, is full of references to sacrifices, including wine.

From ritual uses the drinking of wine expanded to convivial uses, and drinking customs developed. Alcohol was a regular part of meals, viewed as a staple in the diet, even before ovens were invented for baking bread. The Assyrians received a daily portion from their masters of a "gallon" of bread and a gallon of fermented brew (probably a barley beer). Bread and wine were offered by the Hebrews on their successful return from battle. In Greece and Rome, wine was essential at every kind of gathering. Alcohol was found to contribute to fun and games at

Persia. *Malcolm, in his "History of Persia," relates that wine was discovered in that kingdom in the reign of Janisheed. He attempted to preserve grapes in a large vessel. Fermentation occurred, and the king believed that the juice was poison and labeled it as such. A lady of the palace, wishing to commit suicide, drank from it. She was pleased with the stupor that followed and repeated the experiment until the supply was exhausted. She imparted the secret to the king and a new quantity was made. Hence wine in Persia is called "delightful poison."*

—William W. Spooner

The Cyclopaedia of Temperance and Prohibition. New York: Funk & Wagnalls, 1891.

a party—for example, the Roman orgy. Certainly it was a safer beverage than water, but surely its effects also had something to do with its popularity. It is hard to imagine drinking water at an orgy or welcoming a victorious army with lemonade. By the Middle Ages, alcohol was an integral part of life, accompanying birth, marriage, death, the crowning of kings, diplomatic exchanges, treaty signings, and councils. The monasteries became the taverns and inns of the times, and travelers received the benefit of the grape.

The ancients figured that what was good in these instances might be good in others, and alcohol came into use as a medicine. It was an antiseptic and an anesthetic and was used in combinations to form salves and tonics. It was used to treat a host of problems, from black jaundice to knee pain and even hiccups. St. Paul advised Timothy, "No longer drink only water, but use a little wine for the sake of your stomach and your frequent ailments." Liquor was a recognized mood changer, nature's tranquilizer. In the Bible, King Lemuel's mother advised, "Give wine to them that be of heavy hearts." The Bible also refers to wine as stimulating and cheering: "praise to God, that He hath brought forth fruit out of the earth, and wine that maketh glad the heart of man."

Fermentation and Discovery of Distillation

Nature alone cannot produce stronger stuff than 15% alcohol. Fermentation is a natural process that occurs when yeasts combine with plants, be they potatoes, fruit, or grains. The sugar in the plants, exposed either to wild yeasts from the air or to commercial yeasts, produces an enzyme, which in turn converts sugar into alcohol. Fermentive yeast very rarely survives in solutions stronger than 15% alcohol. When that level is reached, the yeast ceases to produce and dies.

In the tenth century, a Persian physician and alchemist, Rhazes, discovered distilled spirits. Actually, he was looking for a way to release "the spirit of the wine," which was welcomed at the time as the "true water of life." European scientists rejoiced in their long-sought "philosopher's stone," or perfect element. A mystique developed, and alcohol was called the fountain of youth, eau-de-vie, aqua vitae. *Usequebaugh,* from the Gaelic *usige beath,* meaning "breath of life," is the source of the word "whiskey." The word "alcohol" itself is derived from the Arabic *al kohl.* It originally referred to a fine powder of antimony used for staining the eyelids and gives rise to speculation on the expression "Here's mud in your eye." The word evolved to describe any finely ground substance, then the essence of a thing; eventually it came to mean "finely divided spirit," or the essential spirit of the wine. Nineteenth-century temperance advocates tried to prove that the word "alcohol" is derived from the Arabic *alghul,* meaning "ghost or evil spirit."

It may not cure you, but it will make you feel better
Rhazes discovers distilling

Distilled liquor wasn't a popular drink until about the sixteenth century. Before that, it was used as the basic medicine and cure for all human ailments. Distillation is a simple process that can produce an alcohol content of almost 93%. Remember, nature stops at 15%. Start with a fermented brew. When it is boiled, the alcohol separates from the liquid as steam. Alcohol boils at a lower temperature than the other liquid. The escaping steam is caught in a cooling tube and turns into a liquid again, leaving the juice, water, and so on behind. Voilà—stronger stuff—about 50% alcohol.

Proof as a way of measuring the strength of a given liquor came from a practice used by the early American settlers to test their brews. They saturated gunpowder with alcohol and ignited it: too strong, it flared up; too weak, it sputtered. A strong blue flame was considered the sign of proper strength. Almost straight alcohol was diluted with water to gain the desired flame. Half and half was considered 100 proof. Thus, 86-proof bourbon is 43% alcohol. Because alcohol dilutes itself with water from the air, 200-proof, or 100%, alcohol is not possible. The U.S. standards for spirits are between 195 and 198 proof.

Alcohol Use in America

Alcohol came to America with the European explorers and colonists. Alcohol was known in Mexico and the southernmost parts of the southwestern United States, but not considered a beverage. Use was restricted to rituals and special celebrations. In 1620, the *Mayflower* landed at Plymouth because, as it says in the ship's log, "We could not now take time for further search or consideration, our victuals having been much spent, especially our bere." The Spanish missionaries brought grapevines, and before the United States was yet a nation, there was wine making in California. The Dutch opened the first distillery on Staten Island in 1640. In the Massachusetts Bay Colony, brewing ranked next in importance after milling and baking. The Puritans did not disdain the use of alcohol, as is sometimes supposed. A federal law passed in 1790 provided each soldier a daily ration of one-fourth pint of brandy, rum, or whiskey. The colonists imported wine and malt beverages and planted vineyards, but it was Jamaican rum that became the answer to the thirst of the new nation. For its sake, New Englanders became the bankers of the slave trade that supplied the molasses needed to produce rum. Eventually whiskey, the backwoods substitute for rum, superseded rum in popularity. Sour-mash bourbon became the great American drink.

This is a very brief view of alcohol's history. The extent of its uses, the ways in which it has been viewed, and even the amount of writing about it give witness to the value placed on this strange substance. Alcohol has been everywhere, connected to everything that is a part of everyday life. Growing the grapes or grains to produce it may have prompted the development of agriculture. Whether making it, using it as a medicine, drinking it, or writing about it, people from early times have devoted much time and energy to alcohol.

WHY BOTHER?

Our society's values are being corrupted by advertising's insistence on the equation: Youth equals popularity, popularity equals success, success equals happiness.
—John Fisher
The Plot to Make You Buy

So alcohol happened. Why didn't it go the way of the dinosaurs? Think about the first time you ever tasted alcohol. Some people were exposed early. Some may have been allowed a taste of Dad's beer while sharing his pretzels when he watched *Monday Night Football*. Some sneaked sips at the first big wedding or party they attended. For some, alcohol was served at home as part of special meals, with kids getting a small glass of wine. For others, alcohol was seen very infrequently at home, if at all. They may not have tried alcohol until middle school or high school, whether at a friend's house or a party.

A significant part of our introduction to alcohol occurs through movies, as well as ads on television or in magazines. In addition to any firsthand early experience, these sources also mold our understanding of what alcohol is and how it is a part of adult life.

When you tried that first sip of Dad's beer, you didn't like the taste. But you took a sip every time it was offered. As the ads tell you—*as you're fighting your way to the top, it helps to have a taste of what's up there.*

In middle school, too often you found that parties were as much torture as fun. You felt awkward; conversation didn't come easily; you never felt comfortable. Then one time, someone brought some orange juice spiked with vodka. That went down easily; the effects were nice. The ads have it right. *To keep the party going, keep the best on hand.*

By the time you got your driver's license, you and your folks had had more discussions than you could begin to count about drinking. They were particularly concerned about the dangers of drinking and driving. Your friends, too, had all heard the same spiel. You knew your parents were concerned and what they said made sense. But still, it seemed that there must be *some* reasonable exceptions. After all, you were all together at Zarah's house; no one was going to be driving. There might have been a brief flash of guilt, but "really," nothing was going to happen. *On your night of nights, add that sophisticated touch.*

Or perhaps your family didn't drink. Maybe they *just* didn't, and it really wasn't that much a part of the community you lived in. Or rather than being neutral or uninterested, they may have been opposed to alcohol. They gave you lots of reasons: "people who drink get into trouble" or even "God's against it." You looked up to your folks, or were scared of them, or really believed that part about God's stand. Among your friends, as odd as it may sound, the issue never really came up. Then came college, the army, or a job and your own apartment. Suddenly it seemed as if everyone drank something, sometime, somewhere.

They weren't dropping dead at the first sip or getting into too much trouble that you could see. There may have been a few "incidents," but people mostly laughed and brushed it off with "Aaah, he was trashed." Lightning didn't strike. You didn't see the devil popping out of the bottle. Just the opposite—everyone seemed to be having a lot of fun. *When the gang gets together . . . bowling, fishing, sailing, hiking, swimming, everywhere.*

It could be that you grew up with wine being served at meals. At some time you were initiated into the process as a matter of course. You never gave it a second thought. You might have had a religious background that introduced you to wine as a part of your ritual acceptance into adulthood or as a part of your particular church's worship.

With time, age, and social mobility, the reasons for continuing to drink become more complex. It is not unusual to drink a bit more than one can handle at some point. After one experience of being drunk, sick, or hung over, some people decide never to touch the stuff again. For most, however, something they are getting or think they are getting out of alcohol makes them try it again. Despite alcohol's effects on us, most of us search for an experience we have had with it, want to have with it, or have been led to believe that we can have with its use. *As an essential part of the Good Life, _______ cannot be excelled.*

Theories of Alcohol Use
It's an attempt to recapture the security of feeding at the breast.

Theories to Explain Alcohol Use

Those trying to explain drinking behavior have always been more interested in heavy drinking, what we now term "alcohol dependence," than in explaining alcohol use per se. Nonetheless, various theories were advanced in the past to explain the basic *why* behind alcohol use. Probably all contain some truth. They are included here to provide a historical perspective. They resurface from time to time as "new" ideas and may be assumed by the uninformed to explain alcohol dependence.

"It calms me down, helps my nerves. It helps me unwind after a hard day." This explanation can be thought of as the anxiety thesis. In part it is derived from Sigmund Freud's work. Freud concluded that in times of *anxiety and stress* people fall back on things that have worked for them in the past. In theory, the behaviors you will choose to relieve anxiety are those you used when you last felt most secure. That lovely, secure time might last have been at Mom's breast. It has been downhill ever since. In this case, use of the mouth (eating, smoking, drinking) is chosen to ease stressful situations.

It is an attempt to deal with the anxiety of an un stable environment.

Another version of the anxiety thesis came from Donald Horton's anthropological studies. He observed that alcohol was used by indigenous peoples either ritually or socially to relieve the anxiety caused by an unstable environment. Drunken acts are acceptable and not punished. The greater the environmental stress, the heavier the drinking. Accordingly, in this view, alcohol's anxiety-reducing property is the one universal key to why people drink alcohol. This theory has by and large been rejected as the sole reason for drinking. Indeed, with the advances in biological research on alcohol's effects, it is now realized that alcohol does not, in fact, reduce anxiety. At best it partially masks it.

Another theory that surfaced was based on the need for a *feeling of power* over oneself or one's environment. Most people don't talk about this, but take a look at the heavy reliance of the liquor industry on macho models, executive types, and beautiful women surrounded by adoring males. People in ads celebrate winning anything with a drink of some sort.

The power theory was explored by researchers in the early 1970s, under the direction of David McClelland. They examined folktales from both heavy- and light-drinking societies. Their research indicated that concern with relief from tension or anxiety was no greater in heavy-drinking societies than in those that consumed less. To look at this further they conducted a study with college men over a period of 10 years. Without revealing the reasons for the study, they asked the students to write down their fantasies before, during, and after drinking. The stories revealed that the more the students drank, the more they felt bigger, stronger, more influential, more aggressive, and more capable of great sexual conquest. The conclusion was that people drink to experience a feeling of power—exhibited in two different patterns. What was called *p-power* is a personal powerfulness, uninhibited and carried out at the expense of others. Social power, or *s-power,* is a more altruistic powerfulness, power to help others. This s-power was found to predominate after two or three drinks; heavier drinking produced a predominance of p-power.

Another theory arose during the late 1960s at the height of the counterculture, with its wave of drug use, particularly psychedelic drugs. This approach, as discussed by Andrew Weil, before he became a health guru, claimed that people *have a need for transcendent experiences.* People will try anything that suggests itself as a way to fulfill this need—for instance, alcohol, drugs, yoga, or meditation. Some drugs were then commonly said to "blow your mind" or were designated as "mind-expanding drugs." Evidence cited for seeking altered states of consciousness begins with very young children, who whirl, hyperventilate, or attempt in other ways to produce a change in their experience. When they are older, people learn that chemicals can produce different states. Alcohol is often used in pursuit of these states because it is the one intoxicant we make legally available. The "drug scene" was viewed as another answer to the same search.

Another perspective on factors that may contribute to alcohol use focuses on stresses associated with modern, everyday life—be they finding a job in a tight economy, a move to a new city, or changes in family structure. Use of alcohol is seen as one response to stress. Other responses to stress include hypertension, ulcer disease, and migraine headaches. Accordingly, stress management has become popular as a technique to help people develop alternative, less destructive means of *coping with stress.*

There's one other connection between stress and alcohol. We all know people who are "worriers," always able to imagine something that might go wrong. Then there are those who are their exact opposites, who couldn't be more laid back. Interestingly, our genetic makeup plays a role in how prone we are to experiencing stress. Wholly independently, our genetic makeup also influences the extent to which alcohol helps to defuse stress. Either alone or in combination, these traits will not cause an alcohol problem, but they may up the odds.

If all be true that I do think,
There are five reasons we should drink;
Good wine—a friend—or being dry—
Or lest we should be by and by—
Or any other reason why.
—DEAN OF CHRIST CHURCH, OXFORD
Reasons for Drinking, 1689

More recently a factor that has been considered to shed light on reasons for drinking is the role of *expectations*—that is, what individuals believe alcohol will do to or for them. (In the research literature this is referred to as "expectancies.") For the most part, researchers now are less interested in identifying factors within the individual that motivate alcohol use. More attention is being directed toward the social setting in which people find themselves, to identify factors associated with patterns of use. For example, attention is turning to the role of peers in determining adolescents' decisions to use alcohol, the influence of parental standards in setting norms for their teenagers' drinking, and the impact of legislative approaches.

One inescapable fact is that, from the very earliest recorded times, alcohol has been important to people. Selden Bacon, an early head of the Rutgers School of Alcohol Studies, made a point worth keeping in mind. He called attention to the original needs that alcohol might have served: to satisfy hunger and thirst, to medicate or anesthetize, or to foster religious ecstasy. Our modern, complex society has virtually eliminated all these earlier functions. Now all that is left is alcohol the depressant, the mood-altering drug, the possible, or believed, reliever of tension, inhibition, and guilt. Contemporary society has had to create new needs for alcohol to meet.

Myths

In thinking about alcohol use, remember that myths, a variant of expectancies, are equally important to people. Many think that alcohol makes them warm when they are cold (not so), sexier (in the courting, maybe; in the execution, not so), more manly, more womanly, cured of their ills (not usually), less scared of people (possibly), and better able to function (only if very little is taken). Ask people what a drink does for them, and you will find that many of their reasons are based on myths. Whether factually based or not, myths often influence people's experience of alcohol use. Whatever the truth in the mixture of theory and myth, enough people in the United States must expect alcohol to do *something*, to have spent $175 billion for alcoholic beverages in 2012 a $600 billion industry.

ALCOHOL PROBLEMS: THE FLY IN THE OINTMENT

To alcohol! The cause of, and solution to, all of life's problems.
—MATT GROENING
The Simpsons

Alcohol is many-faceted. Along with its ritual, medicinal, dietary, and pleasurable uses, alcohol can leave in its wake confusion, pain, disorder, and tragedy. The use and abuse of alcohol have gone hand in hand in all cultures. With the notable exceptions of Muslims and Buddhists, whose religions forbid drinking, temperance and abstinence have been the exception rather than the rule among most peoples of the world.

Problems as Sin or Moral Failing

Societies have come to grips with alcohol problems in a variety of ways. One approach regards drunkenness as a sin or a moral failing and the drunk as a moral weakling. The Greek word for *drunk,* for example, means literally to "misbehave at the wine." An Egyptian writer admonished his drunken friend with the slightly contemptuous "Thou art like a little child." Noah, who undoubtedly had reason to seek relief in alcohol after getting all those creatures safely through the flood, was not looked on kindly by his children as he lay in his drunken stupor.

The complaints have continued through time. A Dutch physician of the sixteenth century criticized the heavy use of alcohol in Germany and Flanders by saying, "That freelier than is profitable to health, they take it and drink it." Some of the most forceful sanctions have come from the temperance movements. An early U.S. temperance leader wrote that "alcohol is preeminently a destroyer in every department of life." As late as the 1970s, the New Hampshire Christian Civic League devoted an entire issue of its monthly newspaper to a polemic against the idea that alcoholism is a disease. In its view, the disease concept gives reprieve to the "odious alcohol sinner."

Problems as a Legal Issue

Many see the use of alcohol as a legislative issue and believe misuse can be solved by laws. Total prohibition is one of the methods used by those who believe that legislation can sober people up. Most legal approaches throughout history have been piecemeal affairs invoked to deal with specific situations. Excessive drinking was so bad in ancient Greece that "drinking captains" were appointed to supervise drinking. Elaborate rules were devised for drinking at parties. Another perennial favorite has been control of supply. In 81 C.E., a Roman emperor ordered the destruction of half the British vineyards.

The views of drunkenness as a sin or as a legislative matter often go hand in hand. The common denominator is the idea that the drunk chooses to be drunk and is therefore either a sinner or a ne'er-do-well, who can be handled by making it illegal to drink. In 1606, intoxication was made a statutory offense in England by an "Act for Repressing the Odious and Loathsome Sin of Drunkenness." In the reign of Charles I, laws were passed to suppress liquor altogether.

America's Response to Alcohol Problems

Those who settled a new world did not escape the problems resulting from alcohol use. The traditional methods of dealing with these problems continued. From the 1600s to the 1800s, attitudes toward alcohol were low-key. Laws were passed in various colonies and states to deal with liquor use, such as an early Connecticut law forbidding drinking for more than half an hour at a time. Another law in Virginia in 1760 prohibited ministers from "drinking to excess and inciting riot." But there were no temperance societies, no large-scale prohibitions, and no religious bodies arguing about alcohol use.

Drinking in the colonies was largely a family affair and remained so until the beginning of the nineteenth century. With increasing immigration, industrialization, and greater social freedoms, drinking became less family centered. Alcohol abuse became more open and more destructive.

The opening of the West brought the saloon into prominence. The old, stable social and family patterns began to change. The frontier hero took to gulping his drinks with his foot on a bar rail. Attitudes regarding the use of alcohol began to intensify. These developments hold the key to many modern attitudes toward alcohol, the stigma of inebriation, and the wet-dry controversy. Differing views of alcohol began to polarize America. The legal and moral approaches reached their apex in the United States with the growth of the temperance movement and the passage of the Eighteenth Amendment, enacting Prohibition in 1919.

Temperance and Prohibition

The American temperance movement did not begin as a prohibition movement. The temperance movement coincided with the rise of social consciousness, a belief in the efficacy of law to resolve human problems. It was part and parcel of the humanitarian movement, which included child labor and prison reform, women's rights, abolition, and social welfare and poverty legislation. Originally it condemned only excessive drinking and the drinking of distilled liquor, not all alcoholic beverages nor all drinking. It was believed that the evils connected with the abuse of alcohol could be remedied through proper legislation. The aims of the original temperance movement were largely moral, uplifting, and rehabilitative.

Passions grow, however, and before long those who had condemned only the excessive use of distilled liquor were condemning all alcohol. Those genial, well-meaning physicians, business owners, and farmers began to organize their social lives around their crusade. Fraternal orders, such as the Independent Order of Good Templars of 1850, grew and proliferated. In a short span of time it had branches all over the United States, with churches, missions, and hospitals—all dedicated to the idea that society's evils were caused by liquor. This particular group influenced the growth of the Woman's Christian Temperance Union (WCTU) and the Anti-Saloon League. By 1869, it had become the National Prohibition Party, the spearhead of political action, which advocated the complete suppression of liquor by law.

People who had no experience at all with drinking got involved in the crusade. In 1874, Frances Willard founded the WCTU in Cleveland. Women became interested in the movement, which simultaneously advocated social reform, prayer, prevention, education, and legislation in the field of alcohol. Mass meetings were organized, to which thousands went. Journals were published; fear and hatred of alcohol were

Equal Suffrage. *The probable influence of Women's Suffrage upon the temperance reform can be no better indicated than by the following words of the Brewer's Congress held in Chicago in 1881: Resolved, That we oppose always and everywhere the ballot in the hands of woman, for woman's vote is the last hope of the prohibitionists.*

–William W. Spooner

The Cyclopaedia of Temperance and Prohibition. New York: Funk & Wagnalls, 1891.

taught in children's programs; libraries were established. The WCTU was responsible for the first laws requiring alcohol education in the schools, some of which remain on the books. All alcohol use—moderate, light, heavy, and excessive—was condemned. All users were one and the same. Bacon, in describing the classic temperance movement, says there was "one word for the action—DRINK. One word for the category of people—DRINKER."

By 1895, many smaller local groups had joined the Anti-Saloon League, which had become the most influential of the temperance groups. It was nonpartisan politically and supported any prohibitionist candidate. It pressured Congress and state legislatures and was backed by church groups in "action against the saloon." Political pressure mounted. The major thrust of all these activities was that the only real problem was alcohol and the only real solution was prohibition.

Prohibition

At the beginning of Prohibition, the Reverend Billy Sunday stirred audiences with this optimistic prediction: "The reign of tears is over. The slums will soon be a memory. We will turn our prisons into factories and our jails into storehouses and corncribs. Men will walk upright now, women will smile and children will laugh. Hell will be forever for rent."

In 1919, Congress passed the Volstead Act, the Eighteenth Amendment, ushering in Prohibition. What exactly did Prohibition prohibit? This act made the commercial manufacture, sale, and transportation of alcoholic beverages illegal. It did not ban the possession of alcoholic beverages nor make it illegal to produce either beer or wine for personal consumption. The act had 60 provisions, was messy and complicated, and no precedent had been set to force the public cooperation required to make it work. Prohibition remained in effect from 1920 to 1933.

Prohibition shaped much of the country's economic, social, and underground life. Its repeal under the Twenty-First Amendment in 1933 did not remedy the situation. Although there was a decline in alcohol dependence under Prohibition, as indicated by a decline in deaths from cirrhosis, it had failed nonetheless. The real problems created by alcohol were obscured or ignored by the false wet-dry controversy. The quarrel raged between the manufacturers, retailers, and consumers on one side and the temperance people, many churches, and women on the other. Those with alcohol problems or dependent on alcohol were ignored in the furor. When Prohibition was repealed, the problem of abuse was still there, and those dependent on alcohol were still there, along with the associated stigma of alcoholism. Possibly the major legacy of Prohibition was the development of underground crime syndicates. When no longer needed to provide alcohol, they took on other illicit activities—gambling, prostitution, and later, drug trafficking.

The front door of the Boston Licensing Board was ripped down by the crush to get beer licenses the day Prohibition ended.

A Different Perspective

As far back as the third century there are vague references that distinguish between being merely intoxicated and being a "drunkard." In a commentary on imperial law, a Roman jurist of that era suggested that inveterate drunkenness be considered a medical matter rather than a legal one. In the thirteenth century, James I of Aragon issued an edict providing for hospitalization of conspicuously active drunks. In 1655, Younge, an English journalist, wrote a pamphlet in which he seemed to discern the difference between one who drinks and one who has a chronic condition related to alcohol. He says, "He that will be drawn to drink when he hath neither need of it nor mind to it is a drunkard."

In vino veritas.
—Pliny

The word "alcoholism" was first introduced in 1849. Magnus Huss, a prominent Swedish physician, wrote a book on the physical problems associated with drinking distilled spirits, titled *Chronic Alcoholic Illness: A Contribution to the Study of Dyscasias Based on My Personal Experience and the Experience of Others.* (The term "dyscasias" is no longer used. Even when this work was published, the meaning of the term was a bit vague, covering a combination of maladies and generally used to describe those thought to have a "poor constitution.") In using the term "alcoholism," Huss was following the common scientific practice of using "ism" as a description of a disease, especially those associated with poisonings. While recognizing the host of medical complications, he thought that the culprit was distilled spirits, not fermented beverages.

A Comment on Terminology

Over the years there has been an evolution in terminology. In the past year "alcohol use disorders" replaced "alcohol dependence" and "alcohol abuse," which had replaced "alcoholism." Alcohol use disorders will be the framework generally used throughout this book; with a few exceptions. The terms "abuse" and "dependence" will be used if these are used in a survey or research being discussed. "Alcoholism" is used in discussions of historical periods when it was the commonly used term. The word "alcoholic" too can be troublesome. In everyday conversations, "alcoholic" can be used in a way that seems to reduce individuals to nothing more than a disease. In referring to anyone in terms of a single characteristic—be it race, gender, ethnicity, sexual orientation, or a disease state—there is the danger of reducing individuals to stereotypes.

History of Alcohol Treatment

In the United States, too, there have been those who have seen the inebriate, the drunkard, the alcoholic in a different way—as having a condition that rightfully belongs in the domain of medicine.

Early Views

The first serious medical considerations of the problem of inebriety, as it was then called, came in the eighteenth and nineteenth centuries. Two famous writings addressed the problem in what seemed to be a new light. Although their work on the physical aspects of alcohol became fodder for the temperance zealots, both Dr. Benjamin Rush and Dr. Thomas Trotter seriously considered the effects of alcohol in a scientific way. Rush, a signer of the Declaration of Independence and the first surgeon general, wrote a lengthy treatise with a nearly equally lengthy title, *An Inquiry into the Effects of Ardent Spirits on the Human Body and Mind, with an Account of the Means of Preventing and the Remedies of Curing Them.* Rush's book is a compendium of the attitudes of the time, given weight by scholarly treatment. The more important of the two is the classic work of Trotter, an Edinburgh physician. In 1804, he wrote *An Essay, Medical, Philosophical, and Chemical, on Drunkenness and Its Effects on the Human Body.* He states: "In the writings of medicine, we find drunkenness only cursorily mentioned among the powers that injure health. The priesthood

Wine is a bad thing,
It makes you quarrel with your neighbor.
It makes you shoot at your landlord,
It makes you—miss him.
—Mark Twain

Temperate temperance is best. Intemperate temperance injures the cause of temperance.
—Mark Twain

hath poured forth its anathemas from the pulpit; and the moralist, no less severe, hath declaimed against it as a vice degrading to our nature." He then gets down to the heart of the matter: "In medical language, I consider drunkenness, strictly speaking, to be a disease, produced by a remote cause, and giving birth to actions and movements in the living body that disorder the functions of health." Trotter did not gain many adherents to his position, but small efforts were also being made at that time in the United States and elsewhere.

Early Treatment Efforts

Around the 1830s, in Massachusetts, Connecticut, and New York, small groups were forming to reform "intemperate persons" by hospitalizing them, instead of sending them to jail or the workhouse. The new groups, started by the medical superintendent of Worcester, Massachusetts, Dr. Samuel Woodward, and Dr. Eli Todd, did not see inebriates in the same class with criminals, the indigent, or the insane. Between 1841 and 1874, 11 nonprofit hospitals and houses were set up. In 1876, *The Journal of Inebriety* started publication to advance these reformers' views and findings. These efforts were taking place against the background of the temperance movement. Consequently, there was tremendous popular opposition from both the church and the legislative chambers. The journal was not prestigious by the standards of the medical journals of that time, and before Prohibition the hospitals were closed and the journal folded.

Another group briefly flourished. The Washington Temperance Society began in Chase's Tavern in Baltimore in 1840. Six drinking buddies were the founders, and they each agreed to bring a friend to the next meeting. Within a few months, parades and public meetings were being held to spread the message: "Drunkard! Come up here! You can reform. We don't slight the drunkard. We love him!" At the peak of its success in 1844, the membership consisted of 100,000 "reformed common drunkards" and 300,000 "common tipplers." A women's auxiliary group, the Martha Washington Society, was dedicated to feeding and clothing the poor. Based on the promise of religious salvation, the Washington Temperance Society was organized in much the same way as the ordinary temperance groups, but with a difference. It was founded on the basis of one drunkard's helping another, of drunks telling their story in public. The society prospered all over the East Coast as far north as New Hampshire. A hospital, the Home for the Fallen, was established in Boston and still exists under a different name. There are many similarities between the Washington Society and Alcoholics Anonymous (AA): people helping each other, regular meetings, sharing experiences, fellowship, reliance on a Higher Power, and total abstention from alcohol. The society was, however, caught up in the frenzies of the total temperance movement, including the controversies, power struggles, religious fights, and competition among the leaders. By 1848, just eight short years after being founded, it was absorbed into the total prohibition movement. The treatment of the inebriate became unimportant in the heat of the argument.

Emergence of Modern Treatment

Following the failure of Prohibition, there was a reemergence of the view that the alcoholic, the chronic inebriated, the drunkard—whatever the label—was a sick person. The founding of the Laboratory of Applied Psychology at Yale University and the founding of Alcoholics Anonymous, both occurring in the 1930s, were instrumental in bringing this about. Also in the 1930s, a recovering Bostonian, Richard Peabody, first began to apply psychological methods to the treatment of what he termed alcoholism. He replaced the terms "drunk" and "drunkenness" with the more scientific and less judgmental "alcoholic" and "alcoholism." At Yale, Yandell Henderson, Howard Haggard, Leon Greenberg, and later E. M. Jellinek founded the *Quarterly Journal of Studies on Alcohol.* The journal continues publication, but the name was changed in 2007 to the *Journal of Studies on Alcohol and Drugs.* Unlike the earlier *Journal of Inebriety,* the *Quarterly Journal* had a sound scientific footing and became the vehicle for disseminating alcohol research.

Starting with Haggard's work on alcohol metabolism, these efforts marked the first modern attempt to put the study of alcohol and alcohol problems in a scientific framework. Jellinek's influential work, *The Disease Concept of Alcoholism,* was a product of the Yale experience. The Yale Center of Alcohol Studies and the Classified Abstract Archive of the Alcohol Literature were established. The Yale Plan Clinic was also set up to diagnose and treat alcoholism. The Yale Summer School of Alcohol Studies, now the Rutgers School, educated professionals and laypeople from all walks of life. Yale's prestigious influence had far-reaching effects. A voluntary organization, the National Council on Alcoholism (NCA)—now renamed the National Council on Alcohol and Other Drug Dependence (NCADD)—also grew out of the Yale School. It was founded in 1944 to provide public information and education about alcohol, through the joint efforts of Jellinek and Marty Mann, a recovering woman who became the Council's first president.

On the other side of the coin, Alcoholics Anonymous was having more success in treating alcoholics than was any other group. AA grew, with a current estimated membership of over 2 million worldwide. Its members became influential in removing the stigma that had so long accompanied alcoholism. Lawyers, businesspeople, teachers—people from every sector of society—began to recover. They could be seen leading useful, normal lives without alcohol. (More will be said in Chapter 10 on the origins and program of AA.) The successful recoveries of its members helped lay to rest the earlier attitude that alcoholism was essentially untreatable.

Report to Temperance Union Statistics of Intemperance

A regular meeting of the Temperance Union was held yesterday [September 7, 1876]. The main feature was a report on the number of crimes and casualties produced in this City by the use of intoxicating liquors. . . . The total number of arrests in the City for the quarter was 18,493. Of these it is stated that the following were directly caused by the use of intoxicating liquors:

Disorderly conduct	*3,591*
Delirium tremens	*5*
Habitual drunkards	*17*
Intoxication	*5,697*
Drunk and disorderly	*2,157*
Reckless driving	*106*
Vagrancy	*1,131*

Add to these, the crimes probably caused by drink, such as assault and battery (1,219); cruelty to children (11); felonious assault (114); homicide (11) and 131 cases of insanity—it makes the total of arrests caused by liquor 15,090. This only leaves 4,303 as the total number of arrests from all other causes.

New York Times, September 10, 1876

Growth of a Profession and System of Care

With the growth in alcohol services, a new professional emerged, the alcohol counselor. These counselors form the backbone of treatment efforts. With increasing professionalism, the term "counselor" is being replaced by the term "therapist" or "clinician." Alcohol counselors' associations were formed in many states. The early distinction of separating alcohol and drug counselors has gone by the boards. In some instances, alcohol-drug counselor associations certify alcohol counselors; in others, state licensing boards have been established. To promote uniformity of standards as well as facilitate recognition of credentials between states and across different certification groups, a voluntary organization—the National Certification Reciprocity Consortium—was established in the 1980s. Since that time other substance abuse specialists have emerged—tobacco addiction counselors, prevention specialists, and clinical supervisors, as well as those with special expertise in co-occurring disorders. In addition, credentials for counselors have been modified to recognize different levels of expertise and experience. In light of these developments, efforts are under way to merge the different credentialing groups to create uniform standards.

All excess is ill, but drunkenness is the worst sort.
—William Penn

Interest in counselor credentialing began in the mid-1970s. A decade later, physicians in the substance abuse field began to examine the same questions. What qualifications should a physician have to work in the field? Is personal experience, the initial impetus for many physicians to enter this area of medicine, sufficient? The question was answered, just as it had been with substance abuse counselors, with a clear no. Professional organizations for physicians were formed to develop a credentialing process, as well as to establish a medical specialty, addiction medicine, that would be analogous to other medical specialties, such as orthopedics, pediatrics, or family practice. Similar groups have emerged in nursing.

Concern about professional education and standards has not been restricted to those whose primary professional involvement is in substance abuse. It has been increasingly recognized that a core knowledge base and associated clinical skills need to be part of any helping professional's training. Thus there has been a proliferation of workshops, special conferences, courses, and degree programs for the range of helping professions. The federal alcohol and drug institutes and the Center for Substance Abuse Treatment (CSAT) have initiated programs to improve professional education among physicians, nurses, and social workers.

A diplomat's life is made up of three ingredients: protocol, Geritol and alcohol.
—Adlai E. Stevenson
New York Times, November 5, 1986

With the emergence of alcohol-drug treatment as a new health care service, efforts were initiated to develop standards, not only for treatment personnel but also for treatment agencies. In 1984, the Joint Commission on the Accreditation of Health Care Organizations first established minimal standards for alcohol rehabilitation programs. Other groups, such as the Commission on Accreditation of Rehabilitation Facilities (CARF), also began to accredit substance abuse services.

These efforts have resulted from, and at the same time have contributed to, our society's response to alcohol and other drug use as a major public health concern.

Public Policy

Changing perceptions of alcohol problems have become the foundation for public policy. Alcohol dependence and alcohol abuse are now recognized as major public health problems. At the center of federal efforts has been the National Institute on Alcohol Abuse and Alcoholism (NIAAA). It was established with the passage in 1970 of the Comprehensive Alcohol Abuse and Alcoholism Prevention, Treatment, and Rehabilitation Act, sponsored by a freshman senator from Iowa, the late Senator Harold Hughes, himself a recovering person. With its founding, the Institute became a major sponsor of research, training, public education, and alcohol treatment services. The legislation also created what might be called a bill of rights for those with alcohol dependence. It recognized that they suffer from a "disease that requires treatment"; it also provided some protections against discrimination in the hiring of recovering individuals. That protection was further extended through passage of the Americans with Disabilities Act of 1990, designed to protect those with disabilities from discrimination.

PORTRAIT OF A MAN WHO
SWears He will never
HAve another drink

In a similar vein, the Uniform Alcoholism and Intoxication Treatment Act, passed by Congress in 1971 and dealing with the issue of public intoxication, was recommended for enactment by the states. This act mandated treatment rather than punishment. With it, public inebriation was no longer a crime. These legislative acts incorporated the emerging new views of alcohol dependence and alcohol abuse: it is a problem; it is treatable.

The National Institute on Drug Abuse (NIDA) was founded in 1974, four years after NIAAA. That two separate institutes were established, one for alcohol and the other for drugs, says a great deal about the thinking at that time. Over the years there has been talk about whether they should be merged. This led to serious deliberation within the National Institute of Health (NIH) beginning in 2011. Part of the proposed reorganization involved relocating some of NIAAA's and NIDA's activities to other institutes within the NIH. For example, programs dealing with smoking moved to the National Cancer Institute. There were a range of responses to the suggestion of merger. Those supporting it felt economic savings would obviously occur. Too, it was felt that there could be real payoffs from the two institutes working together more closely. On the con side were those concerned that by moving programs elsewhere, these efforts might be diluted and less visible. While hardly a major player, the Distilled Spirits Council, the trade group for liquor manufacturers, voiced opposition to the merger, not welcoming its products being tied to the likes of cocaine or heroin. In late 2012, the head of the NIH announced things would stay as they had been. In large part the issue was more complicated than had been appreciated, and it was no longer clear that advantages would outweigh the disadvantages.

Treatment Services

On the heels of this legislation there was a rapid increase in alcohol treatment services, public and private, both residential and outpatient. In addition, each state mandated alcohol and other drug abuse services that focused on public information and education as well as treatment. Similarly, community mental health centers that received federal support were required to provide alcohol services. Also, health insurance coverage began to include rather than exclude alcohol treatment services for its subscribers.

In the 1990s, concern about rising health care costs, increases that consistently exceeded the rate of inflation, brought about efforts to limit coverage for many medical services. Alcohol and other drug abuse services covered by insurance disproportionately felt the ax. Insurance providers became reluctant to cover residential care. Thus, the most common form of treatment, the 28-day residential program, ceased to be the dominant treatment model. Many inpatient treatment programs closed because of empty beds. There was a corresponding increase in outpatient treatment. Professionals recognize that inpatient care need not be the universal standard. However, it is critical for some patients. In recognition that more intensive treatment is required for many people, intensive outpatient treatment programs have since emerged. In 2010, a federal law went into effect, The Mental Health Parity and Addiction Equity Act. This law requires that health insurance plans provide benefits for substance abuse and mental health treatment that are comparable to the benefits provided for all other medical problems. This includes the level of co-payments required, the number of visits allowed, and lifetime payment limits. Simply put, insurance plans cannot establish different levels of benefits for different medical conditions. The Affordable Care Act, beginning in 2014, will introduce further changes. Most importantly, this law extends substance abuse treatment services to an estimated 30 million persons and prompts the integration of these services within the health care system.

Harm Reduction

Whether talking about addiction, taxation [on cigarettes] or education [about smoking], there is always at the center of the conversation an essential conundrum: How come we're selling this deadly stuff anyway?
—Anna Quindlen, columnist

The central goal of alcohol policy is to reduce harm to the individual and society. Gradually the focus on alcohol dependence broadened to include the larger issues of alcohol problems and alcohol use. Previously, the public's attitude could have been summarized as "The only real alcohol problem is alcoholism and that wouldn't happen to me." Alcohol problems are no longer seen as so far removed from the average person. Driving while intoxicated has captured public attention. This alcohol-related problem can touch anyone, for there is generally "another" car. The concern about driving while intoxicated seems to have spilled over to intoxication in general. Intoxication has become less acceptable and is as likely to elicit disgust as to be considered funny or amusing.

What has been termed dependence is only one of the many health consequences of drinking. The International Classification of Diseases has identified over 60 different conditions that appear to be caused by drinking. Of these, half have alcohol in their name, indicating that they would not be present except for drinking. Alcohol problems can occur in the absence of a diagnosable alcohol disorder. The potential health consequences resulting from drinking, even in modest amounts, are increasingly recognized. This goes beyond the issues of driving while intoxicated. Warning labels on alcoholic beverages were introduced in 1989. The possible dangers of drinking during pregnancy are now broadly recognized. Patient education on both alcohol and tobacco is generally part of prenatal care.

Regulation

Regulation is the main vehicle for implementing alcohol policy. Whole books have been written about the laws and regulations that apply to alcohol. Every level of government is involved—federal, state, and local. The majority of laws controlling alcohol use are state laws. These address what beverages can be sold, the location of outlets, requirements for liquor licenses, hours of operation, and legal drinking age. The legal drinking age became 21 nationally because the federal government threatened the states with the loss of federal highway funds if a state's drinking age was under 21. Levels of taxes vary considerably. Federal taxes are uniform across states; tax rates at the state level vary and vary by the type of beverage. In addition, some towns and counties are dry, others in the same state are not. Some states don't allow alcohol sales on a Sunday, others do. Where alcohol can be sold varies widely. Sixteen states allow the sale of beer, wine, and spirits in supermarkets, drugstores, convenience stores, gas stations, and liquor stores. Others are far more restrictive. The most restrictive sell wine and spirits only in liquor stores, and beer separately in another store. Restaurants in some states and towns don't sell wine, but they can serve you wine if you bring your own bottle. There are other possibilities most couldn't even imagine. Several states allow alcohol sales at a bar's drive-up window. A Burger King in a tourist area of Florida opened a beer garden. So it's burger, fries, and a beer, but no take-out.

The partner of regulation is enforcement. States and local communities vary in the level and type of enforcement, whether it's sobriety checkpoints, or endeavoring to reduce underage sales, or checks on licensed establishments,

Evidence-Based Guides to Policy

In the United States, there is tension between two different approaches to alcohol problems and alcohol treatment. Is alcohol dependence better considered a medical condition or a behavioral disorder? There is also a tension in treatment goals. Is the goal to reduce harm or to achieve abstinence? Or is abstinence better considered as a means? Increasingly it is recognized that this is not a matter of "either–or"; rather, it is a matter of "which–when." A large body of research has considered the effectiveness of different approaches. Evidence-based practices can serve as a guide to action.

An article by Rehm and Greenfield reviewed different policy initiatives and summarized the evidence of their effectiveness. Four types of interventions were examined:

- *Legislative intervention.* This includes taxation on alcohol, drinking-driving laws, licensing practices, and control of advertising. In brief, alcohol taxes have an impact on patterns of consumption and the levels of problems resulting from drinking. As taxes go up, negative outcomes go down. Younger people are those most at risk for injury and disability from drinking; enforcement of a minimal legal drinking age reduces the rate of these problems. Some states have a government monopoly on alcohol sales, with alcohol available in state liquor stores. In other states, alcohol is sold through private retail outlets. Government monopolies are better able to control underage purchases, as well as to avoid sales to intoxicated persons. State monopolies, as organized systems, are more successful in controlling hours of sales, price, and the density of sales outlets. Restricting availability, whether through limiting the hours of sales or the concentration of sales outlets, reduces consumption and negative outcomes, particularly injuries from violence.
- *Law enforcement.* The effectiveness of legislative interventions depends on the presence of enforcement. For example, the legal level of alcohol for driving has an impact, but only to the extent that there is visible enforcement, which is best accomplished by frequent random breath tests.
- *Treatment systems.* There are two major concerns. One is the size of the untreated population. A number of factors are seen as accounting for this, including denial of problems and stigma. But there are also barriers to care, such as a lack of transportation or child care, a lack of services in the person's area, and inadequate insurance coverage. The other concern is to enhance treatment efforts. One important component is creating a rational integrated system of care. For example, all too often people are admitted to hospitals for detoxification and then discharged without follow-up or referral for treatment. Data indicates that intensive outpatient treatment, as well as brief interventions, is cost effective. Medications, such as naltrexone and acamprosate, are effective and underutilized. AA by itself is less effective than alcohol treatment. However, alcohol treatment in combination with AA has better results than alcohol treatment alone. A challenge is to mesh self-help with formal treatment. Efforts are required to promote screening, brief intervention, and treatment referrals by primary care physicians—the family doctors, pediatricians, and obstetricians—as these are effective in reducing alcohol problems.

- *Media and awareness campaigns.* Evidence suggests that media campaigns are only marginally effective in reducing harm resulting from drinking or reducing consumption. However, they may be effective in providing support for the passage and implementation of legislative initiatives.

ALCOHOL BEVERAGE INDUSTRY

Any discussion of alcohol, alcohol use, alcohol problems, and alcohol policy needs to include a look at the alcohol beverage industry. Public policy is directed toward reducing alcohol problems through regulation, but the clear goal of the beverage industry is to sell alcohol through advertising.

Advertising—The Basics

In 2010, the alcohol industry's advertising budget was $1.7 billion. However, what one thinks of as advertising is literally less than half of it. These reported advertising costs refer to what the Federal Trade Commission (FTC) terms "measured" media—TV, magazines, newspapers, and outdoor billboards. Other forms of advertising are termed "promotional expenses." For "well-promoted brands," traditional advertising represents only one-third of the total advertising/promotion budget, so the total promotional *and* advertising budget for alcohol in reality is over $5.0 billion. Promotional efforts include:

Advertising is the greatest art form of the 20th century.
—MARSHALL MCLUHAN
Advertising Age, September 3, 1976

- Sponsorship of cultural, musical, and sporting events
- Internet advertising
  There are two basic approaches for targeting internet ads. One approach involves specifying characteristics of the desired audience, characteristics known to the website host. Check out the "targeting options" available on Facebook. Most of these include data people provide when they sign-up for Facebook. Another approach for targeting advertising is making "informed guesses" based on a particular user's search history. This is information that is gathered by search engines. The particular characteristics would be those expected to be associated with an interest in the service/product being advertised. So if someone wants to sell wine online, it might be wise to limit the placement of the ads to those who've searched for wine more than once in the past six months! What distinguishes internet ads from the traditional media is the absence of any third party that can validate the claims made in respect to strategic placement. You only have Facebook's word or a search engine's word about the quality of the data it assembles.
- Displays for retail outlets
  Window and interior displays for stores, bars, and restaurants are a significant expense. These costs are not restricted to printing expenses. The retailers and bar owners are also paid to display these materials.

The business of the advertiser is to see that we go about our business with some magic spell or tune or slogan throbbing quietly in the background of our minds.
—Marshall McLuhan
Commonweal

- Distribution of items with brand logos
  One of the lesser known jobs available to a college student is as a beer company's representative. The job includes passing out all manner of things with the beer company's logo—from posters to beer mugs, backpacks, T-shirts, hats, and Frisbees. The list goes on and on. Students don't have to read a magazine or watch TV to be exposed to advertisements; they only have to walk down the hallways of their schools. For example, one study on tobacco involved a survey of middle and high school students in rural New England. One-third reported owning a promotional item for cigarettes. While only 4.5% reported taking such an item to school that day, 45% reported seeing such an item on the day of the survey.
- Product placements in movies and TV shows
  That beer in a movie doesn't have a made-up generic logo; the Bud Lite, Corona, or Sam Adams doesn't get there because the prop department selected it at random. Special companies exist to promote the use of products in entertainment productions, be they smartphones, cars, or alcoholic beverages.
- Catalogs and other direct mail communications
- Price promotions, such as sales, coupons, and rebates
- Trade promotions directed at wholesalers and retailers
  More than one small convenience store owner has paid for a child's college education from the special payments that come from placing advertising materials prominently.

The alcohol industry's expenditures for advertising, not including promotion, are virtually equivalent to what is spent on advertising for all other beverages combined—from milk to fruit drinks. This raises the suspicion that, contrary to the industry's claims, advertising does not simply represent companies' efforts to capture a larger share of the existing market by encouraging drinkers to switch brands. Rather, advertising is also directed at increasing the market size. That means promoting use among those who are nondrinkers, very light drinkers, or drinkers in the making. Two-thirds of the advertising dollars are spent on ads for beer, and two companies account for 4 out of every 5 advertising dollars spent on beer.

Targeting Underage Youth

Of special concern is targeting young people. Advertisers pay attention to adolescents' interests and the latest things attracting their attention.

Animated Characters

The use of animated characters in media ads is just one case in point. The classic example was the introduction of the Budweiser frogs during the 1994 Super Bowl, an event known as a showcase for advertisers. Were the Budweiser frogs an effort to prime the pump for future consumers? Although the frogs were dropped from Budweiser's website in 1997, they live on in cyberspace.

Placement of Advertising

Decisions about where to place advertisements are carefully considered by manufacturers or businesses. Magazines and television shows can provide very detailed information about their readers or viewers, with a breakdown by age, income, education, geographic region, and ethnicity. This allows advertisers to target very specific populations.

In response to lobbying from a variety of groups, and the fear of government action, in 2003 the liquor and beer trade organizations joined the wine industry in adopting a "30% threshold" as a guide for the placement of beverage ads. This means that beverage manufacturers were encouraged—compliance is voluntary—not to place ads in print media or on television shows whose underage audience exceeds 30%. At the same time the National Academy of Medicine was recommending a 15% threshold. Has this altered advertising practices? Several reports indicate the answer is yes, followed by a "but." Progress has been made; the proportion of TV ads above the 30% threshold was cut in half between 2001 and 2007. Of the ads that remain, all are found on cable networks. For the first four years of that period, print ads virtually disappeared, declining by 90%. Now for the "buts." As the beverage companies have made efforts to avoid TV programs with an underage audience above 30%, they have also worked at placing ads on the programs that are under the threshold, but not by very much. As magazine ads declined, the TV ads increased. Of all the alcohol brands advertised in the larger than 30% youth market, 20 different beverages accounted for the majority of these. The major brewers—Anheuser-Bush, Heineken, Miller, and Molson Coors—were at the top of this list. During this period, the Distilled Spirits Council modified its voluntary marketing guidelines to allow television ads. Thus the return of liquor ads on television, though the industry restricted airing these before 11 PM. However, from 9 PM onward teens are an ever increasing percentage of the viewing audience. At 11 PM they haven't all been tucked into bed or remain up merely to finish homework.

Social Media

If the television advertising restrictions have been a handicap, this has been offset by new avenues for industry advertising. For a significant portion of the population, the traditional media, whether print or network TV, are now far less central than they were for their parents and grandparents. Facebook, launched in 2004, has close to a billion users worldwide, as many as a third of these under age 21. Facebook includes ads from alcoholic beverage groups. There is ostensibly a policy to prevent underage people from accessing alcohol-related material. However, it relies solely on users entering their birthdate, to prove they are 21 or older. Beyond ads for which there is a charge, companies are encouraged to use other Facebook features for free. These include Facebook pages, Facebook applications, and Facebook events. What might be

Advertising is a racket . . . its constructive contribution to humanity is exactly minus zero.
—F. SCOTT FITZGERALD
The Crack-Up

found there? One ad announced, "Want to drink FREE? Click here for your chance at winning an open bar party for you and 100 of your closest friends." Do a Facebook search for "beer" and see how many pages come up. There are links to free phone apps so you can easily keep a journal to rate the different brews you imbibe. There is an app to help you out with an emergency, when you don't have a bottle opener for that beer. It lists common household items that can do the job. How many pages include photos of the latest party, with glasses raised or, in some instances, Joe or Jill passed out? In 2010, Facebook briefly reset its default so far more people could view other people's pages. What may seem irrelevant when someone's in high school or college becomes an issue when that person hits the job market.

One alcohol beverage company has created a new special corporate position devoted to using Twitter and other social media to promote its product. Another has decided to devote its entire advertising budget to digital sources for one of its brands.

New Zealand National Guidelines on the Naming, Packaging, and Merchandising of Alcoholic Beverages

Manufacturers' and retailers' point-of-sale promotions and practices should not:

- *have the appearance of special appeal to minors via designs, motifs, cartoon characters, or other devices that predominantly appeal to children;*
- *lead to confusion with confectionery or soft drinks;*
- *lead to confusion as to the alcoholic nature and/or alcohol strength of the product;*
- *draw any association with drug culture, narcotics, or illegal drugs;*
- *encourage immoderate, illegal, or irresponsible alcohol consumption;*
- *suggest an association with violent, aggressive, dangerous, or antisocial imagery or behavior;*
- *suggest that mental or physical capabilities, especially sexual success or prowess, can be enhanced by alcohol;*
- *run counter to Host Responsibility guidelines; or*
- *mimic containers or shapes that are predominantly associated with antisocial or dangerous behavior (for example, hypodermic needles and syringes and explosive devices).*

Size of the Underage Market

These young viewers and readers are not the only ones envisioning alcoholic beverages in their future; the size of the underage market cannot have totally escaped the beverage industry. A report issued a decade ago pointed out that underage drinking represents 19.2% of all alcohol consumption. Of the estimated total of 50.52 billion drinks then consumed annually in the United States, 9.7 billion drinks went to those under age 21. That translates into 26.6 million drinks *daily* by those not legally old enough to consume alcohol. The annual bar tab for underage drinking?—$22.5 billion. Other estimates of the underage market are a bit lower, but no one would say it is insignificant.

New Beverages

Of concern to those in the substance abuse field is the creation of beverages that are seen as appealing to younger people. The first of these were the wine coolers introduced in the 1980s. Fruit juice and carbonated beverage are added to the wine, basically masking the wine's flavor. Next came drinks designed to mimic old-fashioned nonalcoholic beverages. First introduced in England, they have crossed the Atlantic, ranging from Two Dogs Alcoholic Lemonade to TGI Friday's Lemon Drop Drink, with its 40% alcohol content. The next arrival was "alcopops," neon-colored single servings, packaged in test-tube-style plastic vials. Or how about six-packs of "Jello-shots"—plastic tumblers of gelatin, fruit-flavored and laced with vodka? These hit the U.S. market and were stocked on grocery shelves with packaging that resembled their traditional nonalcoholic counterparts. Labels included cartoon characters or resembled the design of old favorites, such as Kool-Aid. Restrictions on Jello-shots were enacted on a state-by-state basis. If

You can fool all the people all the time if the advertising is right and the budget is big enough.

—Joseph E. Levine, film producer

anyone were to become dismayed by decreased access, there is always the internet, with the instructions and equipment to make your own.

The next innovation was the first generation of alcoholic energy drinks. Among the first was Spykes, marketed by Anheuser-Busch, "to give your beer a kick." Spykes was a 2-oz bottle of flavored malt beverage, 12% alcohol, meant to be mixed with beer or other drinks or consumed as a shot. Packaged in colorful bottles, it sold for less than a dollar, came in four flavors, and was uncannily similar to energy drinks popular with teens. Though it was supposedly part of "an effort to respond to adults looking for innovative alcoholic beverages," in announcing that it was being pulled, the Anheuser-Busch president attributed the decision to limited volume potential and unfounded criticism. More than two dozen state attorneys general and a broad range of community groups had protested its production. Apparently at least 27 other manufacturers were not similarly concerned about "limited" markets.

The next version of energy drinks was caffeinated alcoholic beverages. Caffeine masks the subjective sense of intoxication, thus increasing overconsumption and contributing to risky behavior. As their popularity and potency grew, so too did efforts to ban them. Four Loko was a special concern. A 23.5-ounce container of Four Loco had as much alcohol as four "standard" beers and about four times the caffeine of a coke. In November 2010 the Food and Drug Administration ruled caffeine added to alcoholic drinks to be "an unsafe food additive." All caffeinated alcoholic beverages had to be removed from shelves by December. In response to the claim that these weren't really being targeted to younger drinkers, someone observed, there are not too many adults who want their beer to taste like cocoa or mangos.[1]

Probably the most outrageous effort to introduce nontraditional beverages occurred in Australia. The offering was Moo Joose—alcoholic milk. The manufacturer, Wicked Holdings Pty Ltd., envisioned a beverage containing more than 5% alcohol by volume, to be available in flavors of chocolate, banana, strawberry, and coffee and to mimic flavored milk. The following were set forth as positive features: (a) "Milk with its component proteins is likely to produce feelings of satiation that may limit the amount consumed"; (b) "It is possible that the milk content may reduce the rate of absorption of alcohol into the

[1] "Straight" energy drinks have suddenly hit the limelight. The problem is the dangers associated with a common additive, carnitine. Identified as L-carnitine on the product label, it is included for its supposed energy boosting properties, although those effects are unproven. Why is carnitine a concern? Research published in March 2013 identifies it as being as significant as cholesterol and fat in linking consumption of red meat to heart disease. While this connection was long attributed to cholesterol and fat, there was the recognition that something else was involved. The something else is now known. Caritine is the "transportation system" instrumental in distributing fat and cholesterol throughout the body. Significantly, the level of carnitine in one energy drink is equivalent to eating an 8 oz. porterhouse steak. So if you have two energy drinks a day at least 4 days a week, you've ingested the same amount of carnitine as you'd get eating 8 steaks in a single week.

walls of the stomach and small intestine and act like food in delaying the rate of absorption"; (c) "The fact that the fat content is low is likely to make more attractive [*sic*] to young women. . . . Low sugar levels are also an attraction to young women in the 18+ age group." Another positive feature was its proposed four-pack packaging, which would supposedly foster moderation, as well as narrow-necked bottles with screw tops that would minimize the chances of other persons spiking the drink.

We grew up founding our dreams on the infinite promise of American advertising. I still believe that one can learn to play the piano by mail and that mud will give you a perfect complexion.
—ZELDA FITZGERALD
Save Me the Waltz

Among those speaking on Moo Joose's behalf was a major Australian substance abuse group. The Alcohol and Drug Foundation (Queensland) in explaining its support for Moo Joose noted that any incidental alcohol problems would be more than offset by declines in drinking resulting from its anticipated prevention campaign conducted jointly with the beverage industry. The licensing group was unconvinced by these arguments, and the application was denied on the basis that it represented an unacceptable risk to the health and well-being of young people. This particular case is an instance of concerns that have been expressed about the potential for problems in *any* beverage industry and substance abuse field collaboration. (See Chapter 14 for further discussion.)

Now, jump ahead to the future. How about a machine that lets you inhale your "drink"? Imagine the possible advertising slogans, "Tired of sipping or gulping your drink?" or "Go green with gas. No paper cups, no glasses to wash." or "Go AWOL!" AWOL stands for **A**lcohol **W**ith**o**ut **L**iquid and was introduced at a trendy New York bar in the summer of 2004. It involved a contraption resembling an oversized asthma inhaler attached to an oxygen tank. Turn it on, and it disperses liquor as a vapor in an oxygen mist. There's no worry about inhaling too rapidly; a dial can be set to regulate the rate of alcohol vapor dispensed. So far, the future of AWOL is up in the air, stymied by fine print in the liquor licensing regulations, such as alcohol having to be dispensed from its original container.

Everything that can be invented has been invented.
Commissioner, U.S. Office of Patents, 1899

Targeting Women and Minority Groups

Beyond targeting the youth market, some companies have created advertising campaigns directed toward women and minority groups. The content of the ads is another source of concern. Even by advertising standards, many are blatantly sexist, depicting women in a demeaning manner and promoting the stereotypes of male behavior that contribute to sexual harassment.

The tobacco industry operates in the same fashion. In early 2007, R. J. Reynolds introduced a new cigarette, Camel No. 9. Does this conjure up references of being "dressed to the nines" or being on "cloud nine"? This new cigarette was packaged in a black and pink box with matching pink tin foil and described as "light and luscious." In addition to placing large ads in women's magazines such as *Vogue, Cosmopolitan,* and *Glamour,* R. J. Reynolds hosted "launching parties" in 15 cities. These affairs, promoted as a girls' night out, included loud music, bars, massages, hair styling, and gift bags with makeup, jewelry, and sample packages of Camel No. 9. All of this was happening just as Congress was considering more stringent limits on advertising that would have banned such events.

The same people who tell us that smoking doesn't cause cancer are now telling us that advertising cigarettes doesn't cause smoking.

—ELLEN GOODMAN, COLUMNIST

Newsweek, July 28, 1986, page 17

Communities with large African American and Hispanic populations are more likely to see alcohol advertising on a daily basis. Outdoor billboards promoting alcohol are more common. Similarly, convenience and neighborhood stores in these communities have more alcohol ads prominently placed in store windows.

Targeting Developing Countries

Another concern is the alcohol beverage industry's (especially the distillers') sales promotions in developing countries. With a declining domestic market, one way to maintain profits is to increase foreign sales. Hand in hand with economic development, many countries have begun to experience a significant increase in alcohol-related problems. Western patterns of alcohol use, now being introduced, are often very different from traditional practices (see Chapter 5). One question raised by efforts to increase sales in developing countries is an ethical one. Is there any justification for introducing alcohol problems into countries already struggling with the problems of poverty, malnutrition, inadequate health care, high rates of maternal and infant mortality, and illiteracy?

Another, even more basic, question arises in response to breweries now being built in developing countries, usually financed by international brewers. Here the concern is not a future rise in alcohol problems. The brewing process itself requires significant amounts of scarce resources—water and grain. Any diversion of water from agricultural use or community water supplies or any activities that reduce the amount of grain for food can have an immediate and devastating impact on people's health and well-being. This concern is all the more pressing with the increasing severity and frequency of drought.

Alcohol and the Media

There is a counterbalance, sort of, for the alcohol industry's efforts to have its product appear in the hands of Justin Timberlake or Jennifer Lawrence. These are the public service announcements that promote responsible use. However, adolescents and young adults would have to watch 22 ads for an alcoholic beverage before seeing a spot promoting responsible drinking. The expenditures for responsibility ads represent a little more than 2% of the industry's advertising budgets.

A number of years ago there were efforts to work with movie and television writers, directors, and producers to change the way drinking and alcohol problems are depicted. Of concern was the way drinking was often glamorized and its consequences either trivialized or ignored. Indeed there have been changes. Characters in recovery are featured, as well as those struggling with alcohol abuse or dependence.

From the vantage point of the twenty-first century, it is hard to imagine that a campaign was ever necessary to have alcohol problems incorporated in television programming. Seemingly, it is now everywhere. It has become a staple of talk shows. No one is surprised if Dr. Phil deals with substance abuse problems or any other popular form of addiction, be it compulsive shopping or sexual addiction. And now, too, there is reality TV. Read the end of this sentence, as if you were standing behind a podium and had just opened the envelope—"The winner of the 2014 Emmy for Reality Programming (pause)—*Intervention.*" Go to the show's website and there is even the opportunity to suggest a friend or family member as "the star" for a future episode.

China: World's Leading Brewer

In 2010, China produced 4.8 billion liters of beer, representing 25.3% of world beer production. The United States, in the number 2 position, produced 13.7% of the world output, with 22.9 billion liters.

Barth Haas Group, July 2011

Finally, consider the cable news channels. What is presented as "news" at times closely resembles what in another era might have been considered material for a gossip column. The viewer sees the mug shot taken at the point of booking of a celebrity DWI or the exterior shot of the treatment program a celebrity has recently entered. Yet something is missing in all of these discussions. The "problem" as discussed is not an individual's pain; more likely, it is the public relations challenges and whether the celebrity's image can be salvaged and rehabilitated.

Nor are these events used as teachable moments. By way of contrast, consider the response to former first lady Betty Ford's surgery for breast cancer. The *New York Times* described a "deluge of inquiries" for information on screening; the American Cancer Society was "swamped" with requests for informational pamphlets; and there was a dramatic rise in the number of women getting mammograms. Thus women were motivated to take action in accordance with the health guidelines of the time. Were this to occur now, one wonders how much of the discussion might be on the possibilities for reconstructive breast surgery from a cosmetic perspective.

OTHER DRUG USE

After caffeine, alcohol is the psychoactive substance most widely used in the United States.[2] Even though alcohol arrived along with the first European colonists, it is not the oldest psychoactive drug used in North America. That honor goes to tobacco, a plant native to North America and introduced to the rest of the world through trade between the Virginia colony and England.

[2]The patterns of alcohol and other drug use are described in Chapters 2 and 13.

Tobacco

Early Use

Among Europeans, the earliest use of tobacco was as snuff—powdered tobacco that was sniffed—the preferred form of tobacco among the upper classes. Though not as fashionable, tobacco was also smoked, by breaking the leaves and stuffing them into a pipe. From Europe these forms of tobacco use were transported to the American colonists. By the early 1800s, other forms of tobacco were becoming more popular; for example, chewing tobacco gradually began to replace snuff. By the end of the century, the annual per capita consumption of chewing tobacco was 2.8 pounds. In terms of tobacco smoking, cigars came to replace pipes. Imported from Europe, cigars were rather expensive and were a status symbol, a hallmark of the upper class. A cigar is still the mark of a tycoon. Consider the cartoons depicting the well-to-do, portly, bushy-mustached, white-haired businessman wearing a suit, complete with vest and pocket watch, and smoking a large cigar. Or consider the characters long associated with the Monopoly game.

There are a vast number of things and customs . . . which do not contribute . . . the slightest to mental, moral, or physical advancement, and which serve only as a diversion, a relaxation, an amusement, or a consolation. Why destroy them?
—A TOBACCO LOBBYIST, 1919

When they first appeared in the 1850s, cigarettes were viewed with disdain and considered "the smoke" of the lower classes. Cigarettes were first adopted by urban immigrants and particularly adolescent boys. Initially sold individually, not in packs, cigarettes were far less expensive than cigars. That the cigarette wasn't the choice of any "real" man was made clear by its name, formed by adding the feminine suffix "ette" to "cigar." Despite the stigma, circumstances made cigarette use more common. The Civil War battlefields were not well suited to leisurely smoking a cigar; a quick smoke was the safer option. In the latter part of the 1800s, periods of economic depression placed cigars out of reach, and many smokers switched to cigarettes. The invention of the Bonsack cigarette manufacturing machine and innovations in marketing promoted the adoption of cigarettes.

During the Depression, the average family spent as much as 6.9% of its income on tobacco.

Advertising and Promotion

With the possible exception of Super Bowl hoopla, it is almost impossible for those living in the twenty-first century to appreciate the impact of the earliest cigarette marketing. Surely a first-rate textbook on marketing could be written drawing on nothing other than the efforts of the tobacco industry over the years. Much of what we now think of as advertising was introduced by the tobacco companies.

They were the first to place full-page spreads in magazines that reached virtually every household in the way that broadband does now. Of course, tobacco companies had the example of the patent medicine manufacturers to build upon. The potential for mass production, coupled with aggressive marketing to create demand, very rapidly catapulted cigarettes into becoming the primary route for nicotine administration. How successful? Over a 60-year period, production didn't just double or triple. Between 1889 and 1949, it grew by an astronomical 2,000%.

Beyond advertising, the tobacco companies used other promotional techniques successfully. They were among the first to give away cards featuring entertainment figures, the predecessor of the next century's baseball cards. In a stroke of genius, in both World War I and World War II, cigarettes were provided free to soldiers as part of their basic rations. This promotion to young men clearly succeeded; in the 1950s, 80% of all men were smokers. Marketing to women began in the 1920s and 1930s. The number of women who smoked doubled in a decade.

During WWII tobacco farmers were exempt from military service because they were considered essential workers.

Undoubtedly a self-reinforcing cycle was set in motion. The more people who smoked, the more acceptable the behavior and, in turn, the more smoking was interwoven into public life in ways large and small. In the public's mind, smoking was defined as a behavior that denotes a host of desirable traits—being part of the "in crowd," macho, liberated, sexy, athletic, or any of the other attributes depicted in cigarette ads.

Concerns

As there were anti-alcohol voices, so too there were some opposed to tobacco. But there were some significant differences. For one, tobacco products were sold in a wide variety of places—from general stores to candy stores to cigar stores—and most of these settings were well integrated into community life. So there wasn't the equivalent of the bar or saloon as a target for attack. In fact, many at the time considered cigar stores as wholesome alternatives to saloons. Interestingly, too, distinctions were made between different tobacco products. The tobacco prohibition movement typically focused exclusively on cigarettes. In the 1890s, several states banned cigarette sales, but these first laws did not apply to cigars or chewing tobacco. Whether these bans could have been maintained in light of the subsequent heavy advertising campaigns is doubtful. But the return of a generation of World War I veterans who had become addicted to their daily ration of nicotine significantly redefined the image of the smoker.

Isn't it rather too bad that an organization [the WCTU] which undoubtedly did so much good in the fight against the saloon should . . . fly off on such a tangent? The liquor and tobacco problems are as different as the sun and the moon.

Tobacco Industry editorial, 1921

The military continues to make special allowances for tobacco products. If cigarettes are not free, at least they are a bargain. Regulations dictate that a military base can only sell cigarettes at 5¢ below the going price in the area. This is never enforced. A pack of cigarettes purchased on a military base may be 25% lower than the price off-base.

Although some of the opposition to smoking was based on health concerns, until the mid–twentieth century, these were generally dismissed as having no foundation. Then the solid scientific basis for these health concerns became evident. In 1964, the landmark *Surgeon General's Report on Smoking and Health* painstakingly laid out the health problems associated with smoking. Along with public health efforts, such as education and promotion of smoking cessation, government efforts were made to restrict the tobacco industry's promotional activities. For example, in 1963, with the *Surgeon General's Report* clearly on the horizon, the tobacco industry had to curtail advertising to the youth market; and in the following year it agreed to cease other media advertising. In some instances these limitations were ignored; in other instances, alternative marketing methods were adopted. In addition, the tobacco companies followed a duplicitous course. In public they challenged the scientific evidence for health problems and the addictive nature of nicotine, while at the same time withholding information from their own studies of health effects. Companies also went through the motions of creating "safer" cigarettes, while simultaneously manipulating nicotine content, which was the ingredient that hooked smokers and kept them coming back for more.

Legal Action

In 1994 the state of Minnesota filed the first in what became a set of complicated lawsuits against the major tobacco manufacturers, involving both the federal and state governments. These cases raised a host of questions pertaining to product safety, the role of government in regulation, and manufacturers' responsibility for liabilities. The goal of the states was to recover costs for their health care expenditures for smoking-related illnesses. In 1998, the Master Settlement Agreement (MSA) was signed between 46 states and the tobacco industry. It involved billions of dollars to be allocated to the states; the states pledged to commit at least half of these monies to prevention and smoking cessation. Sadly this has not been the case. In late 2012, a group of nationally recognized public health groups, including the American Cancer Society and the American Heart Association, issued a public statement on what has actually occurred. Of the $25.7 billion dollars provided to the states over a 25-year period, less than 2% was used for prevention and smoking cessation. The remainder went into the state coffers. The publicity these cases received certainly was a source of public education, further diminishing public acceptance of smoking and promoting acceptance of further regulation. At the same time, it's hard not to wonder what else might have been.

In later chapters the acute and chronic effects of drinking and other drug use are discussed. However, two differences between alcohol and nicotine—the addictive ingredient of tobacco—warrant mention here. Nicotine has a much greater risk of addiction than alcohol (see Chapter 13).

On the other hand, nicotine does not have an intoxicating effect similar to that of alcohol. An evening of heavy smoking may make someone reek, but that isn't comparable to drunkenness. Cognitive function isn't impaired by smoking: for years smoking in the workplace was common. If as many people had been drinking at their desks as were then smoking there, the business community would have screeched to a halt! Probably the single behavioral change associated with smoking is the edginess and tension of short-term abstinence that is a sign of physical dependence. It is what prompts the smoker to announce, "I'm going out for a cigarette." The significant problems associated with smoking develop over the long haul. Of course, the hook with tobacco is that the highly addictive nature of nicotine assures that smoking continues long enough for the smoker to develop health problems.

Earliest Physical Evidence of Cannabis

The Yanghai Tombs near Turpan, China, have recently been excavated to reveal the 2700-year-old grave of a Caucasoid shaman whose accoutrements included a large cache of cannabis, superbly preserved by climatic and burial conditions. A multidisciplinary international team demonstrated [with multiple tests that] . . . the material contained tetrahydrocannabinol, the psychoactive component of cannabis . . . these investigations provide the oldest documentation of cannabis as a pharmacologically active agent.

E. B. Russo, *Journal of Experimental Botany,* 2008

Marijuana

History

Unlike nicotine and alcohol, which have been part of the American landscape since colonial times, marijuana is a far more recent arrival. Derived from the plant *cannabis sativa,* marijuana is native to central Asia. Anthropologists and historians have traced its spread throughout the world. It was known in China as early as 3000 B.C.E. The conventional wisdom is that it was never widely used for its psychoactive effects, and it was considered an inferior medicine. The response in India, a millennium later, was more enthusiastic. Cannabis was adopted both as a sacred plant and as a medicine capable of curing all major ills while also promoting vital energy.

From India, cannabis spread to Persia in the eighth century B.C.E. While it was known in both ancient Greece and Rome, records suggest that the major interest was for its fiber to manufacture rope. Apparently, in terms of pleasure, it was dismissed as a poor substitute for wine or beer. The reception of cannabis in the Middle East was more positive, especially as the rise of Islam had led to a ban on alcohol. The term "cannabis" comes from the Persian *kanabas.* The extract from the plant was called hashish, which is Arabic for "grass."

Medicinal Uses

After the fall of Rome, Persia was the center of learning and the sciences. Writings from that period speak of marijuana's therapeutic uses. It was recommended for diverse problems ranging from earaches to epilepsy and flatulence. It was also recommended for stimulating appetite and producing a craving for sweets. For literally centuries, Islamic scholars and clerics debated whether it was appropriate to use hashish for pleasure. Finally the answer came in the seventeenth century: no. The thinking was that its psychoactive properties were similar to those of wine; it too clouds the mind and interferes with prayer. This resulting prohibition continues—except for medical uses—and in most Islamic countries is incorporated into law.

Over several centuries, Arab incursions introduced cannabis into North Africa and Europe. In Europe cannabis was never particularly popular for its psychoactive properties. Interest was largely restricted to its use as a medicine. But as a medicine, it was deemed lacking. In England, physicians found that the compounds imported from India had widely varying strengths and thus were unreliable. Overall they were considered less effective than other available medications, such as opium and its derivatives.

American physicians, following the example of British colleagues, imported cannabis extracts from India and were a bit more inclined to use them for an array of conditions. Cannabis was incorporated into the many available patent medicines sold in an array of stores, by traveling salesmen, or by mail order. Compared to other ingredients—such as coca, alcohol, opium, morphine, and later heroin—in these various tonics, pills, balms, powders, elixirs, and extracts, cannabis was virtually an inert ingredient! In the later efforts to ban patent medicines and control drug use, cannabis was not one of the ingredients primarily targeted. While prescribed with declining frequency, it wasn't until 1942 that cannabis was removed from the list of drugs approved for medical purposes. This stance toward marijuana is now being challenged at the state level. Despite this federal statute, since 1996, 17 states and the District of Columbia passed laws providing for medical marijuana. Of note, in 2010, the U.S. Attorney General indicated that prosecuting those who have been provided medical marijuana under state law is not a federal priority. Attitudes toward marijuana use are changing rapidly. Two states, Colorado and Washington, have taken the next step, legalizing the use of marijuana by adults for any purpose. Other states are conducting hearings on the issue and some are likely to follow suit. The results of a national survey show how dramatically public attitudes are changing. In 2013, for the first time the majority of those polled approved of legalizing marijuana. Admittedly it was just barely a majority (52%) voicing approval. But that was an 11% increase from just three years earlier. In addition over 7 of every 10 people said efforts to enforce marijuana laws "cost more than it's worth."

Marijuana is American hasheesh. . . . You can grow enough marijuana in a window-box to drive the whole population of the United States stark, staring, raving mad.
—WILFRED BLACK

Dope: The Story of the Living Dead. New York: Star & Co., 1928

Mexican Family Goes Insane

A widow and her four children have been driven insane by eating the marihuana plant, according to doctors, who say there is no hope of saving the children's lives and that the mother will be insane for the rest of her life.

The mother was without money to buy other food for the children, whose ages range from 3 to 15, so they gathered some herbs and vegetables growing in the yard for their dinner. Two hours after mother and children had eaten the plants, they were stricken. Neighbors, hearing outbursts of crazed laughter, rushed to the house to find the entire family insane. Examination revealed that the narcotic marihuana was growing among the garden vegetables.

New York Times, July 6, 1927

Recreational Use

Although hemp had been grown from colonial times, recreational or nonmedical cannabis use was largely unknown in the United States until the last century. Cannabis as a psychoactive substance was introduced to the American continent in the 1600s by slaves from West Africa brought to Brazil. However, it was never adopted by either the Portuguese colonialists or native peoples of Brazil. Nonetheless, use continued and, over time, gradually spread along the coasts. In the early 1900s, cannabis, under the name marijuana, indicating its Latin American roots, was introduced into the American Southwest by Mexican settlers and into New Orleans by sailors from Mexican and Caribbean ports. From the first, marijuana was suspect and aroused concerns. In part this was consistent with the efforts to control patent medicines, restrict the use of opiates and cocaine, and ban alcohol. It was consistent, too, with international conferences and treaties in the early 1900s directed at curtailing international trade in opiates. However, the major factor at work was racism. As portrayed by the press, law enforcement, and other public officials, marijuana was exceedingly dangerous and highly addictive, prompting uncontrolled violence and causing insanity, along with virtually every social ill one could imagine. This was the era that introduced phrases such as "drug fiend" into our vocabulary. In light of this clear marijuana "threat," by 1932 more than 10 states had enacted laws to ban its use. Despite the fact that marijuana was used primarily by the marginalized and by racial and ethnic groups, there was a sense of urgency to protect the broader society. Beyond the perceived dangers associated with its use, another factor was at work—the fear that marijuana, if it remained legal, might fill the niche left by the prohibition of alcohol and ban on narcotics. With the passage of the Harrison Act in 1914, narcotics and cocaine had been classified as controlled substances available only for medical purposes and by prescription. (See Chapter 13 for further discussion of drug control.)

The subsequent movement of marijuana into the mainstream of American culture might be seen as having occurred in two stages. The first was its association with the blues and jazz and the bohemian scene. The second was its adoption by the 1960s counterculture. Ironically, the earlier success in defining marijuana as deviant and unacceptable, along with the exaggerations about its effects, probably helped make it the psychoactive substance of choice for a movement with the mantra "Don't trust anyone over 30."

Rethinking Prohibition

Prohibitionists wanted and expected people to switch their spending from alcohol to dairy products, modern appliances, life insurance, savings, and education. That simply did not happen. Prohibition may actually have increased drinking. During Prohibition, spending on alcohol increased. Beyond bootleg alcohol, people purchased patent medicines (which contained high concentrations of alcohol), medicinal alcohol, and even sacramental alcohol. The amount of alcoholic liquors sold by physicians and hospitals doubled between 1923 and 1931. The amount of medicinal alcohol (95 percent pure alcohol) sold increased by 400 percent during the same time. There were more new drinking spots established, such as the speak-easies, than there were bars or saloons closed down. There was also spending on substitutes for alcohol. Some consumers turned to narcotics, hashish, tobacco, and marijuana.

The Other Side of Prohibition. Cato Policy Analysis No. 157. Washington DC: The Cato Institute, July 1991

Points for Reflection

Classifying psychoactive substances as either *licit* or *illicit* is not based exclusively or even primarily on their pharmacological properties. It is as much, if not more, a matter of class, race, and economic issues. During the course of your readings and study, consider several questions: If it were possible to erase all previous history and attitudes and start afresh, and you were asked to designate classes of drugs to be licit, which would you choose? What factors would you consider to be important in making these assignments? Which things would you see as important in defining harm? And harm to whom? Are there harms that are introduced or avoided by the legal or illicit status of a substance? To what extent can these be diminished? In which column would alcohol, tobacco, and caffeine be found, your licit or illicit list?

REFERENCES AND FURTHER READINGS

Alcohol History Database. <www.scc.rutgers.edu/alcohol_history> Note: Contains bibliographic records for over 600 monographs, pamphlets, and journals from the nineteenth and early twentieth centuries dealing primarily with the American Temperance and Prohibition movements.

Alcoholics Anonymous. *Alcoholics Anonymous Comes of Age.* New York: AA World Service, 1957.

Alexander M. *The New Jim Crow: Mass Incarceration in the Age of Colorblindness.* New York: The New Press, 2012. (paperback)

Austin G. *Alcohol in Western Society from Antiquity to 1800.* Oxford UK: Santa ABC-Clio Information Services, 1985.

Bacon S. The classical temperance movement in the U.S.A. *British Journal of Addiction* 62:5–18, 1967.

Burnham JC. *Bad Habits. Drinking, Smoking, Taking Drugs, Gambling, Sexual Misbehavior, and Swearing in American History.* New York: New York University Press, 1993.

Center on Alcohol Marketing and Youth. *Youth Exposure to Alcohol Advertising on Television, 2001–2007.* Washington DC: Georgetown University, June 2008. (20 refs.) <www.camy.org>

DP: The Washingtonians. *AA Grapevine* 27(9):16–22, 1971.

Foster SE, Vaughan RD, Foster WH, Califano JA. Alcohol consumption and expenditures for underage drinking and adult excessive drinking. *Journal of the American Medical Association* 289(8):989–995, 2003. (46 refs.)

Grier SA, Kumanyika S. Targeted marketing and public health. (review) *Annual Review of Public Health* 31:349–369, 2010. (136 refs.)

Gunja N, Brown JA. Energy drinks: Health risks and toxicity. *Medical Journal of Australia.* 196(1):46–49, 2012. (29 refs.)

Grenard JL, Dent CW, Stacy AW. Exposure to alcohol advertisements and teenage alcohol-related problems. *Pediatrics* 131(2):369–379, 2013. (51 refs.)

Hemphill TA. Alcoholic beverage industry self-regulation and youth advertising: The Federal Trade Commission Report. *Business and Society Review* 110(3):321–329, 2005. (20 refs.) Note: An update of this Federal Trade Commission report was scheduled for publication in late fall 2013.

Horton D. Alcohol use in primitive societies. In Pittman DJ, White HR, eds: *Society, Culture, and Drinking Patterns Reexamined.* New Brunswick NJ: Rutgers Center of Alcohol Studies, 1991.

Jernigan DH, Ostroff J, Ross CS, Naimi TS, Brewer RD. Youth exposure to alcohol advertising in magazines—United States, 2001–2005. *MMWR. Morbidity and Mortality Weekly Report* 56(30):763–767, 2007. (10 refs.)

Lender ME, Kamchanappe KR. Temperance tales, anti-liquor fiction and American attitudes toward alcoholics in the late 19th and early 20th centuries. *Journal of Studies on Alcohol* 38(7):1347–1370, 1979.

Mart S, Mergendoller J, Simon M. Alcohol promotion on Facebook. *The Journal of Global Drug Policy and Practice* 3(3), 2009. (55 refs.) <www.globaldrugpolicy.org/3/3/1.php>

McClelland D, et al. *The Drinking Man.* New York: The Free Press, 1972.

Munro G. An addiction agency's collaboration with the drinks industry: Moo Joose as a case study. *Addiction* 99(11): 1370–1374, 2004. (31 refs.)

Munro G, Learmonth A. "An unacceptable risk": The problem of alcoholic milk. *Drug & Alcohol Review* 23(3):345–349, 2004. (26 refs.)

National Institute on Alcohol Abuse and Alcoholism. *Tenth Special Report to U.S. Congress on Alcohol and Health.* Washington DC: U.S. Government Printing Office, 2000.

Rehm J, Greenfield TK. Public alcohol policy: Current directions and new opportunities. *Clinical Pharmacology and Therapeutics* 83(4):640–643, 2008. (31 refs.)

Schaffer A. Vaporize me. Is inhalable alcohol a good idea? *Slate.* September 2004. <www.slate.com/id/2106393>

Smith EA, Malone RE. "Everywhere the soldier will be": Wartime tobacco promotion in the US military. *American Journal of Public Health* 99(9):1595–1602, 2009. (99 refs.)

Sournia JC. *A History of Alcoholism.* Cambridge MA: Basil Blackwell, 1990.

Warner J, Riviere J. Why abstinence matters to Americans. (editorial) *Addiction* 102(4):502–505, 2007. (23 refs.)

Weil A. Man's innate need: Getting high. In: *Dealing with Drug Abuse.* New York: Ford Foundation, 1972.

CHAPTER 2

Alcohol and Its Costs

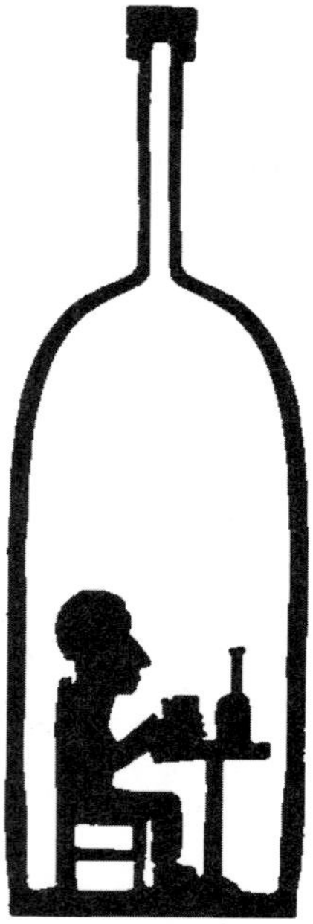

In the United States, statistics on who drinks—what, where, and when—have been kept since 1850. However, it's difficult to make comparisons between different periods. One reason is that only since 1950 have statistics been gathered methodically and impartially. Another reason is that there have been changes in the way the basic information is organized and reported. A century ago, reports included numbers of "inebriates" or "drunkards." In the 1940s through the 1960s, "alcoholics" became a designated subgroup. Then came the 1970s and another change. "Heavy drinkers" began to replace "alcoholics" as a category in reporting statistical information. In the 1980s, government surveys of alcohol use adopted formal medical diagnostic terminology to designate those whose alcohol use is problematic. Thus "alcohol dependence" replaced "alcoholism." Plus, "alcohol abuse" was introduced as an additional category of problem drinking. Very recently, there was yet another change in terminology. Alcohol abuse and alcohol dependence were combined into a single category, "Alcohol Use Disorder" with several levels of severity. This is discussed in detail in Chapter 4. For the purpose of this chapter, it is sufficient to view an alcohol use disorder as a medically recognized condition warranting evaluation and treatment.

For over 30 years, the federal government has conducted an annual survey of drinking patterns and related problems. For many years a separate parallel drug use survey was conducted. Now, the *National Survey on Drug Use and Health* gathers information on alcohol and other drugs, including nicotine.[1] It is a primary source for the information presented

[1]Two things of note: The National Survey includes those age 12 and older. Also, while the results of political polls or marketing polls are available virtually overnight, the same is not true of scientific polls. The findings from the 2012 National Survey were published in early fall 2013. However, much of the finer detail only became available a number of months later.

here. A major focus of this survey is drinking frequency—whether at some point during the respondent's life, or during the past year, or in the past month, or never. If someone has had a drink in the past month, he or she is considered a *current drinker.* For current drinkers there are also questions about the amount consumed. Those who report having had five or more drinks on any one occasion during the past month are termed *binge drinkers.* If someone has had five or more drinks on at least five occasions in the past month, he or she is categorized as a *heavy drinker.*

WHO DRINKS WHAT, WHEN, AND WHERE

Out of the maze of statistics available on how much Americans drink, where they drink, and with what consequences, some are important to note. It is now estimated that 71% of men and 63% of women are drinkers, having had a drink at some point in the past year. They constitute about 67% of the adult population. The proportion of current drinkers, those who have had a drink in the past month, is smaller, a bit more than half of the population (52%).

Historically, per capita consumption rose dramatically in the decade following Prohibition, increasing by more than 50%. While less dramatic and despite some modest ups and downs, overall consumption continued to rise through the 1970s, peaking in the early 1980s. Since then, alcohol consumption has declined. Consumption in 1997 declined to 2.14 gallons of ethanol (the chemical name of the type of alcohol we consume) per person, the lowest level since 1962. Since then consumption has been inching upward, but it still remains relatively low. Part of the decline in per capita consumption is due to changes in the age distribution in the general population. As a country, we are growing older, and older people drink less. In Canada it has been estimated that as much as 7% to 17% of its decline in per capita consumption is due simply to changes in the age distribution.

In 2011, the statistically average American consumed the equivalent of 2.26 gallons of pure ethanol. The alcohol content varies by type of beverage. Accordingly, of the total alcohol consumed, 33% of the alcohol came from liquor, 17% from wine, and the remaining 50% from beer.

A word of caution. All of these figures describe the statistically average American. However, it is important to realize that the average American is a statistical myth. It isn't as if we all awake each New Year's Day to find our annual allotment for alcohol sitting on the doorstep. The typical American does not, in fact, drink his or her "statistical quota." First of all, recall that approximately 30% of Americans do not use alcohol at all. Of those who drink, there is a wide variation

in drinking patterns. Seventy percent of the drinking population consumes only 20% of all the alcohol. The remaining 30% of the drinkers consumes 80% of the alcohol. Most significantly, one-third of that heavy-drinking 30%, or less than 7% of the total population, consumes 50% of all alcohol. Picture what that means. Imagine having 10 beers to serve to a group of 10 people. If you served these to represent the actual consumption pattern described, you'd have the following: Three people would sit empty-handed. Five people would share two beers. That leaves two people to divide up eight beers. Of those two people, one person would take two and the other person would get a whole six-pack!

I have very poor and unhappy brains for drinking. I could well wish courtesy would invent some other custom of entertainment.
—William Shakespeare
Othello

The same pattern holds for underage drinkers. As someone who examined the data on adolescent drinking noted, there is "the myth that 'all' youth drink" and the impression that "many are binge drinkers." In 2011, for those under age 21, slightly over a quarter (26%) had used alcohol in the previous month. Among all those under the legal drinking age, 17% had consumed five or more drinks on at least one occasion in the previous month, the definition of binge drinking. However, it is the 18- to 20-year-olds who had the highest rate and accounted for about two-thirds of the underage binge drinking. Equally important, this group of binge drinkers accounted for more than 85% of all alcohol consumed by this age group.

The description of drinking patterns in this section represents a snapshot of drinking in the year 2012. This kind of data is called cross-sectional; it compares individuals with different characteristics whether by age, gender, or residence, at the same moment in time. A caution. A common error is to use this type of data to think about differences over time. However, as makes sense if you think about it, it is an error to presume the drinking of this year's 20-year-olds can predict the drinking of future 20-year-olds. Nor is today's 40-year-old a good predictor of how today's 20-year-old will drink two decades from now. Any group's alcohol or drug use is influenced by the particular era in which its members grew up as well as the situation at the time. For example, the elderly of a generation ago had a higher rate of lifetime abstinence than today's elderly. This is attributed to the fact that the previous generation grew up in the era of Prohibition.

Drinking Patterns

Patterns of alcohol consumption vary by almost any characteristic you can imagine, be it age, type of community, employment status, or type of occupation, to name just a few. There are also changes over time, in terms of the amount of alcohol consumed and the particular beverages that are in or out of favor.

Historical Trends

The earliest figures on drinking go back to shortly before the Civil War. In fact, per capita consumption now is close to the level reported for 1850. However, tastes have clearly changed.

Year	Per Capita Consumption	Beer	Wine	Liquor
1850	2.10 gal	7%	4%	89%
2010	2.26	50	17	33

Age

Patterns of alcohol consumption vary with age. Although 21 may be the legal drinking age, current drinking starts far sooner. The rate of current drinking typically peaks in the early 20s and then gradually declines with age; the same is true of heavy drinking.

Age(yrs)	12–13	14–15	16–17	18–20	21–25	26–34	35 or Older
Drinkers	2%	11%	25%	46%	69%	65%	54%
Binge drinking	1	5	15	31	45	36	19

Gender

Women are more likely to be nondrinkers than are men. Furthermore, they drink less frequently than men. When they do drink, they typically consume less. Among late adolescents and young adults, patterns for women more closely resemble those of men.

	Lifelong Abstinence	Past Year Abstinence	Past Year Drinking	Current Drinking	Binge Drinking
Men	15%	16%	69%	57%	30%
Women	21	17	63	47	16

In addition, beverage preference changes with age. Among younger people, beer has long been the favorite beverage. While still in front place, liquor and particularly flavored drinks are becoming more popular. With age, individuals tend to drink more of their alcohol quota in the form of wine.

Race and Ethnicity

In examining drinking patterns by racial and ethnic group membership, including those who identify themselves as multiracial, several things stand out. Whites as a group have the largest proportion of lifetime drinkers. The proportion of lifetime nondrinkers is not a good predictor of the proportion of heavy drinkers or the proportion with an alcohol use disorder. Asian Americans are the single exception. (Chapter 5 considers factors that can help explain what at first glance seem to be inconsistencies.)

Racial Group	Lifelong Abstainers	Current Drinking	Binge Drinking	Heavy Drinking	Abuse or Dependence
Whites	13%	57%	24%	8%	7%
African Americans	24	43	21	5	6
Native Americans or Alaska Natives	22	42	30	9	17
Hispanic/Latinos	28	42	23	5	7
Asian Americans	34	37	13	2	3
2 or more races	19	52	25	7	7

Education

In looking at the drinking patterns for those 26 and older, among both men and women, the proportion of drinkers increases with years of education. However the reverse is true for heavy drinkers, with higher rates of heavier drinking found among those with less than a college education.

	Lifelong Abstinence	Past Year Abstinence	Past Year Drinking	Current Drinking	Binge Drinking	Heavy Drinking
Not HS graduate	41%	17%	42%	35%	%	%
HS graduate	14	20	66	51	26	9
1–3 yrs college	9	15	76	60	27	8
4+ yrs college	7	13	80	68	22	6

Employment Status

Patterns of alcohol use are known to vary with employment. Among those 18 and older, individuals working full-time are more likely to use alcohol (65%) than are those working part-time (59%) or those who are unemployed (55%). The lowest rate of drinking is found among those not in the labor market, such as the retirees, stay-at-home moms, and the disabled. On the other hand, heavy drinking is more common among those unemployed (13%) versus those who are working (9%). Binge drinking is slightly higher among the unemployed (33%) than those with a job (30%).

In comparing drinking between those who are employed and those who are unemployed, a common interpretation is that problem drinking causes unemployment. With the country in a serious economic downturn, the opposite question has now been asked. Does job loss affect alcohol use? The answer is yes. Being laid off from either a full- or part-time job in the past year is associated with drinking more on any given day, higher levels of binge drinking, and increased rates of alcohol abuse or dependence.

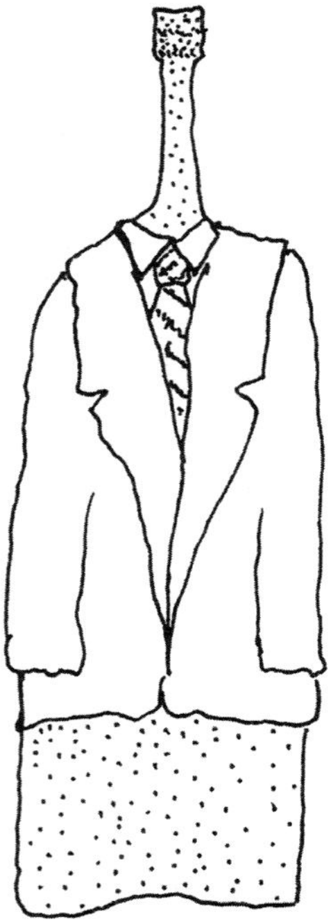

Family Income

Typically, the proportion of drinkers rises with family income; the opposite is true of heavy drinking. Several years ago a survey found that the proportion of heavy drinking was twice as high among those whose household income was below the national median income than those with income above that level.

Geographic Region

Historically, there have been differences in drinking patterns based on where people lived. The usual measure is per capita consumption, which is used to compare regions as well as changes in consumption over time. Typically, per capita consumption is calculated by dividing all the alcohol consumed by the size of the "drinking age" population. In the United States, the drinking population is everyone age 14 and above. The West has the highest level of per capita consumption and the South the lowest. However, there is an interesting twist. Remember the tale of 10 beers. If people are nondrinkers, their "alcohol quota" is consumed by others. Some regions have a higher population of nondrinkers than do others; if per capita consumption is based only on those who drink, the picture looks quite different. Similarly if consumption levels are calculated based on current drinkers, the picture again looks quite different.

	Northeast	Midwest	South	West
Per capita consumption (total drinking age population)	2.30 gal.	2.28 gal.	2.18 gal.	2.34 gal.
Per capita consumption (based on past-year drinkers)	2.79	2.88	2.94	3.04
Per capita consumption (based on past-month drinkers)	3.40	3.61	5.79	4.73

Past-year drinkers include some who are very light drinkers—it's the glass of champagne on New Year's Eve or a beer while watching the deciding game in the World Series. What if per capita consumption were based on the portion of the population defined as current drinkers, those having had a drink in the past month? The proportions then range from 57.1% of those in the Northeast to under half of those in the South (48.7%), and the per capita consumption reflects these differences. Again, the picture changes.

Beyond absolute differences, regions differ by whether their levels of consumption are dropping, rising, or remaining unchanged. From year to year these changes are relatively minor and are related to patterns of migration. With younger people, who tend to drink more than older people, now moving south, the average age of the population in the South is declining and the level of alcohol consumption is rising accordingly. For the regions with a decline in younger people, there is a decline in per capita consumption.

Type of Community

Additional differences in drinking patterns are seen in terms of the type of community in which people live. In 2012, the rates of past month alcohol use in large and small metropolitan areas (54% and 52%, respectively) were higher than in rural areas (44%). Binge drinking was equally prevalent in large and small metropolitan areas (both 23%, but was less prevalent in rural areas). Large metropolitan areas in 2012 had the highest rate of individuals who had a drink in the past month (54%). The lowest rate of current drinking was among those who live in rural areas (44%). The rates of binge drinking were about the same in the metropolitan areas, whether large or small (23%), but a bit lower in rural communities (20%). In terms of underage drinking, the differences based on the type of community are growing smaller.

Marital Status

The lowest rate of current drinking is found among those who are widowed, with only a third having had a drink in the past month. The rate is around 55% for all others. This is probably related to age. The widowed generally are older and, thus, in the age group with the lowest proportion of drinkers.

The proportion of drinkers is similar for all others, whether married, separated or divorced, or never married. However, the picture is different when one looks at heavy drinking and the presence of an alcohol problem (alcohol abuse and dependence), both of which are markedly higher for those who have never married or are divorced.

Religion

Religion influences drinking in two ways. One is the stance of different religious groups toward drinking. Some are strongly opposed to any drinking, while drinking per se is not a concern of others. The second way is the extent to which people consider religion as important to them. Conservative Protestant denominations, which typically disapprove of drinking, have the lowest percentage of members who drink, slightly over 50%. The religious groups with the highest proportion of members who use alcohol are Jews, at close to 90%, followed by Catholics and liberal Protestant groups in which approximately three-quarters of members drink. Although Jews have the biggest proportion of drinkers, less than 1% are heavy drinkers. Both drinking and rates of heavy drinking vary according to the importance placed upon religion. Only half of those who consider religion very important drink, only a third are weekly drinkers, and under 2% report occasions of heavy drinking. Among those for whom religion is "not at all" or "not really" important, about 53% are weekly drinkers and 9% are heavy drinkers.

We take a drink only for the sake of the benediction.
—PERETZ

Association with Other Drug Use

There is a relationship between the use of alcohol, tobacco products, and illicit drugs. Heavy drinkers have higher rates of tobacco use and illicit drug use.

	Past Month Alcohol Use			
Other Drug Use	None	Drinking (no binges)	Binge Drinking	Heavy Drinking
Tobacco use	19%	21%	46%	64%
Illicit drug use	4	7	19	31

International Comparisons

How do drinking patterns in the United States compare to those in other countries? Globally there is remarkable variety. Countries differ in terms of the *quantities* consumed and the *beverages* that are preferred (whether wine, spirits, or home brew); *who* drinks, in terms of age and gender;

and the *occasions* when drinking occurs. Countries also differ in terms of their relative proportion of drinkers and nondrinkers, as is evident from the most recent United Nations *Global Status Report on Alcohol 2011.*

	Per Capita Consumption			Abstainers		
	Recorded	Unrecorded	Total	Total	Men	Women
Algeria	0.66 liters	0.30 liters	0.96 liters	89%	80%	98%
Costa Rica	4.15	1.40	5.55	60	45	75
Kenya	1.71	2.50	4.21	55	45	65
Uganda	10.93	1.00	11.93	54	48	60
United States	8.44	1.00	9.44	33	29	36
Russia	11.03	4.73	15.76	23	9	35
Canada	7.77	2.00	9.77	22	18	26
Ireland	13.39	1.00	14.39	22	17	26
Lithuania	12.03	3.00	15.03	20	10	28
France	13.30	0.36	13.66	6	4	9
Norway	6.21	1.60	7.81	6	6	6
Denmark	11.37	2.00	13.37	3	2	4

Source: World Health Organization. *Global Status Report on Alcohol 2011.* Geneva: WHO, 2011.

Comparisons of drinking patterns between countries are difficult to make without taking several factors into account. For example, about a tenth of men and over a third of women in Russia are nondrinkers. On the other hand, in Denmark 98% of men and 94% of women drink, so the alcohol consumed within a country is spread over very different portions of the population.

THE SCREAMER
...Experience the ups and downs of problem drinking.

Although the data are limited, there seems to be a convergence of drinking patterns around the globe. Internationally, alcohol consumption in industrialized countries is declining. For example, over a two-decade period between 1970 and 1990, per capita consumption in Italy virtually halved. At the same time, consumption in economically underdeveloped countries is rising. Hence, differences in drinking patterns are less pronounced.

ALCOHOL PROBLEMS

Generally all problems related to drinking can be considered as falling into one of two categories. There are the problems that arise from long-term heavy drinking. Then there are the problems that can occur for anyone on any drinking occasion, typically in the presence of intoxication.

Alcohol Use Disorders

The most recent federal estimate (2012) is that 8.8% of all Americans age 12 or older have a serious alcohol or drug problem, consistent with a diagnosis of dependence or abuse. This rate is essentially unchanged since 2000. The majority of these (68%) represent an alcohol problem. The remainder have an alcohol and drug problem (13%) or drug problem but not an alcohol problem (19%). While drugs often get more attention than alcohol, serious alcohol problems are far more common than illicit drug problems. For each person having a problem with illicit drugs, there are four with an alcohol problem. Thus, in the United States, an estimated 18 million people have a serious problem with alcohol. Also of significance is that the vast majority of these people will go untreated.

For every person with an alcohol problem, it is estimated that four family members are directly affected, which means that approximately 72.4 million family members are touched by alcohol. In terms of which families are affected, those who are separated or divorced are more likely to report a family member with an alcohol problem. Those separated or divorced are three times more likely to report having had an alcoholic spouse. Younger adults are also more likely to report having an alcoholic family member than are older adults. The proportions are 42% for those under age 45 versus 26% for those over age 65. These figures represent a family member's assessment. The numbers probably include the person with a long-standing alcohol use disorder as well as the problem drinker or the one-time drunken traffic offender who appears in court, or the person who, when drunk for the one and only time in his or her life, ends up in a hospital emergency room. But the suspicion is that, when reporting "troubles," people are not referring to those who miss work after a particularly festive New Year's Eve. It is important to appreciate that persons beyond the family may also be negatively affected by another's drinking. A large study conducted in Australia found that over half those surveyed mentioned being affected by drinking of someone outside the family—be it a college roommate, a coworker, or a stranger at a bar.

Among those who are alcohol dependent, under 5% are among the homeless, the modern counterpart of what was at one time termed "skid row." At least 95% of problem drinkers are employed or employable; they are estimated to constitute 10% of the nation's workforce. Most of them are living with their families. The vast majority live in respectable neighborhoods and are homemakers, bankers, physicians, salespeople, farmers, teachers, computer programmers, and clergy. They try to raise decent children, go to football games, shop for their groceries, go to work, and rake the leaves.

Economic Costs Versus Economic Benefits

Although they constitute only a small portion of the drinking population, those with alcohol use disorders cost the United States a huge amount

TABLE 2.1 Social Costs of Alcohol Use, 2010*

	$ (in billions)	% of costs
Reduced productivity in the workplace	$124.0	48%
Reduced productivity in the home	21.0	8.1
Motor vehicle crashes	29.3	11.3
Co-morbidities (related illnesses)	22.4	8.7
Unintentional injuries (excluding auto)	24.7	9.6
Crime	10.1	3.9
Fetal alcohol syndrome	15.7	6.1
Treatment for alcoholism	11.9	4.6
Total	258.0	

*1998 figures adjusted for inflation through 2010

Source: National Institute on Alcohol Abuse and Alcoholism. *Tenth Special Report to U.S. Congress on Alcohol and Health.* Washington DC: U.S. Government Printing Office, 2000.

of money each year. In assessing these costs, government statistics rely heavily on data gathered during the census, conducted every 10 years. The quantity of information generated may take several years to analyze. When dealing with national counts of anything, from population figures to the numbers of licensed drivers to the quantity of alcohol sold, the data are almost always estimates. The figures are derived from the most recent data available or are inferred from other sources. The most recent estimates of the economic costs of alcohol problems are presented in Table 2.1, using 1998 data adjusted for inflation.

The other side of the cost coin is revenue. In 2010 alcohol taxes collected by the federal and state governments totaled $25.4 billion. Historically alcohol taxes provided close to 40% of federal revenues. Now they account for only a half of 1% (0.5%). To a significant degree this is attributable to the failure to raise taxes to even keep pace with inflation. Over the past half century the federal taxes on beer have declined by 41%. In 1987, federal tax rates on distilled spirits were raised for the first time in 34 years. Alcoholic beverages have become so inexpensive that their prices are essentially the same as those of nonalcoholic drinks. The net effect of all this is that the typical American can drink more but can spend less of the total family income to do it.

Beer ranks fourth, behind soft drinks, coffee, and bottled water, in terms of total beverage consumption in the United States.

How do the social benefits of alcohol use compare with its social costs? Social benefits include tax revenues, wages, salaries, and income generated directly by the manufacture and sales of alcohol or indirectly via the hospitality industry plus philanthropic contributions by the alcohol beverage industry. These social benefits have not

How could you spend our grocery money on liquor again? How?
I'm economizing. Groceries are 42% more expensive and liquor is only up 12%.

been systematically calculated, unlike the social costs associated with drinking. Nor have there been efforts to calculate alcohol's benefits to individuals. A rough calculation of the cost-benefits of alcohol can be made by comparing the figures for social costs, $258 billion in 2010, and for social benefits—that is, the alcohol-generated tax revenues, $25.4 billion. Thus, for each dollar of taxes generated, there is a corresponding cost to society of $10.16. In examining the impact of tax rates, using 2006 figures, the author noted that the social costs which accrued were almost half the size of the federal budget deficit for that year.

Other attempts have been made to consider the social costs of alcohol use, especially with respect to health care costs. A classic study with the provocative title "The Taxes of Sin: Do Smokers and Drinkers Pay Their Way?" was concerned with just that question. A variety of costs related to drinking and smoking were examined—for example, the monetary impact of early death due to smoking and heavy drinking. The study found that if smokers and drinkers die early, the amount of money they have paid into retirement plans and Social Security in part becomes available to subsidize the benefits of others. The conclusion was that smokers do pay their way, but those with alcohol problems do not. At best, taxes on alcohol were found to only cover about half of the expenses generated by those who drink heavily.

Only recently have there been efforts to quantify the economic costs of underage drinking. Generally the studies of benefits and costs are unconcerned with the age of the drinkers involved. A study that looked at data from 2001 estimated that underage drinkers consumed about 16% of all alcohol. It examined a range of costs associated with underage drinking—accidents, violence, crime, high-risk sex, poisoning, suicide, burns, and also treatment costs. The total cost was estimated to be in the range of $62 billion. A significant portion of this total represents costs that are paid over time. These are referred to as "quality-of-life costs"; an example might be costs for medical and nursing care for the person paralyzed after an alcohol-related auto accident. The social cost is in the vicinity of $3 per *each* drink consumed by an underage drinker; the taxes, or societal benefit, from that drink are 10¢.

Obituary

He passed away Monday, April 14, 2008, at the local community hospital, age 48 years.

An intelligent, perceptive, artistic, and kind man, [he] none the less drank himself to death. He is survived by family and friends, and assorted drinking buddies who should consider his death a glimpse into their own possible futures.

Obituary, *New London* (CT) *Day*, 2008

Personal Costs

The personal cost of alcohol problems is tremendous. It is estimated that alcohol-related deaths may run as high as 10% of all deaths annually. This represents the nation's third leading cause of preventable deaths. Heavy drinking significantly reduces life expectancy. The mortality rate of those with alcohol dependence is more than twice that of the general population. Those with alcohol dependence also have a higher rate of violent deaths. Drinking figures prominently in both accidental and violent death whether or not alcohol dependence is present. As many as 75% of all unintentional injuries are alcohol-related, including motor fatalities, falls, drownings, fires, and burns.

Injuries

Alcohol use is implicated in injuries. Studies have repeatedly shown that those who have been drinking have a greater likelihood of landing in an emergency room. This is true of all age groups. One statewide study of trauma center patients found that, of those 12–17 years old, 12.8% were alcohol positive; of those 18–20 years old, 47.0% were alcohol positive; of those 21–25 years old, 64% were alcohol positive. Another large study drew on the insurance records of more than 1.5 million people covered by the health insurance plans of 70 large corporations. For those with a history of an alcohol problem, 46% had been hospitalized as the result of injury in the prior three years. When a history of other drug use was added to the alcohol use, the risk for injury rose to 58%.

The risk of injury increases with rising blood alcohol levels, indicated as BAC (blood alcohol concentrations). Thus, for bicyclists, the risk of injury is five times greater for those with a BAC higher than 0.02. At a BAC of 0.08 or higher—the level set by law for driving while intoxicated—the chances of injury are 20 times higher.

Another factor related to the risk of injury is the age at which people start drinking. For those who started drinking before age 14, as opposed to those who delay drinking until age 21, there is a five times greater risk of having an alcohol-related injury and a more than three times greater likelihood of an alcohol injury in the past year.

It is the upheaval of prior norms by a society that has finally recognized that it must change its habits and do whatever is required, whether it means a small change or a significant one, in order to stop the senseless loss inflicted by drunken drivers.

—Robert N Wilentz, Chief Justice

New Jersey Supreme Court

Majority opinion in 6-1 ruling that a host may be held liable for serving alcohol to persons later involved in drunk-driving incidents, June 27, 1984.

Motor Vehicle Fatalities

The figure for alcohol-related traffic fatalities includes deaths not only of drivers but also of passengers, pedestrians, and bicyclists. The 2010 figure represents a 35-year low. The rate of decline has been highest among younger drivers, for whom the level of alcohol fatalities has essentially been halved. In some states the number of deaths from prescription drug painkillers exceeds the number associated with drinking and driving. Alcohol-related fatalities are not evenly spread across all drivers. Approximately two-thirds of alcohol-related fatalities occur among those between the ages of 21 and 34. Women have always had far fewer alcohol-related fatalities than men. In 2010, they accounted for 20% of all alcohol fatalities. Over the past 10 years, the rate of DWI arrests among women has risen by 29%. Also warranting comment is that the majority of children killed in alcohol-related accidents are passengers in the drinking driver's car.

For accidents that occur after drinking, the chances of fatality rise with the blood alcohol level. The severity of injuries and the associated length of a hospital stay are also related to the level of intoxication. Drivers with a blood alcohol level of between 0.05 and 0.08 (the legal level for intoxication) have a nine times greater risk of a fatal accident than do drivers who have not been drinking. In fatal motor vehicle accidents involving a pedestrian or bicyclist, the odds are greater that it will be the bicyclist or pedestrian, not the motorist, who has been drinking; alcohol at intoxicating levels has been found in 63% of pedestrian deaths and a third of cyclist deaths.

Annually in the United States there are over 82 million drinking-driving trips, at BACs of 0.08 percent and higher, the legal level for intoxication. However, there are 1.5 million arrests for drinking and driving each year.

Alcohol and the outcome of an accident are related in several other ways. Drinking is likely to decrease the use of protective devices, such as seat belts and motorcycle safety helmets. With intoxicating levels of alcohol, the use of helmets declines by one-third. In a major urban area, in which bicycle use is rising, fully 70% of riders who had been drinking prior to an accident were not wearing helmets. Also, medical care for those who have been drinking and sustain injuries is likely to be more complicated. For accident victims with a similar severity of injuries, those who had been drinking had lower blood pressure and lower PCO_2 (the latter is a measure of blood gases, and both are indexes for shock). Thus, their medical condition was more fragile and likely to lead to problems if resuscitation and/or emergency care were delayed.

Falls

Drinking increases the risk of both death and injury from falls. A review of all studies of deaths from falls showed alcohol involved in 15% to 63% of them. As blood alcohol rises, the risk of falls increases. Compared with those who have not been drinking, those with a 0.10 blood alcohol content (BAC) have a 3 times greater risk of a fall; with a BAC of 0.16 or above, the risk is 60 times higher. Of the injuries commonly associated with falls, fractures of the ribs and vertebrae are 16 times higher for people who are heavy chronic drinkers than for nonproblematic, or "social," drinkers. One study following people over a decade found that the likelihood of a fatal fall increased in proportion to the number of drinks an individual had reportedly consumed on a "typical" drinking occasion. Among the elderly, already vulnerable to falls, having two or more drinks per day further increases the risk of falls by 25%.

Presentation to Medical Conference . . .

The attention of the civilized world has been called to the conspicuous fact of the accuracy of the fire of gunners of our battleships in the recent war with Spain. The contrast between fire of the men of our navy and that of Spain was chiefly to be attributed, no doubt, to the custom that prevails on the ships of the latter, where daily rations of grog are given at all times, and when an action is going on or anticipated double rations of grog are furnished to the men; while, since 1862, when that custom was abolished by our government, no rations of grog are allowed at any time on board our ships.

New York Times, October 21, 1898, page 12
Talk by Dr. J. M. Farrington to New York Medical Society on why physicians should not promote or approve use of alcohol

Burns

Drinking increases the risk of injury and death by burns and fires. Four out of five fire deaths occur in homes. Smoking is the leading cause, and alcohol a significant contributor. Up to 40% of the people who die in house fires have high BACs. Approximately one-quarter of burn injuries involve people who have been drinking. Alcohol use also appears to have an impact on the outcome of burn injuries. Among burn victims, those with a positive BAC had virtually twice the proportion of fatalities. The likelihood of death increases with higher BACs. In addition, it has been found that those diagnosed with alcohol dependence had a three times higher rate of mortality and died with less extensive burns. Independently, both the blood alcohol level at the time of the fire and the presence of alcohol dependence influence survival rates. For home fires involving cigarette smoking, alcohol, too, is likely to be a factor.

Water Mishaps

Drinking is involved in up to 50% of deaths from drowning. In boating-related drownings, one study found 45% of the victims had a positive BAC, and 22% were legally intoxicated. Studies have shown that boat operators who are suffering from fatigue due to sun, wind, glare, and wave motion are 10 times as likely to miss course correction signals if they are also legally intoxicated. Furthermore, those legally intoxicated (with a 0.08 BAC) are at a 10 times greater risk of death in boating accidents. Boat passengers who have been drinking are at increased risk also. Alcohol similarly plays a role in diving accidents, many of which result in spinal cord injury and paralysis. Diving injuries that result in spinal cord injury are four times as likely to involve intoxicated divers. Not surprisingly, blood alcohol levels as low as 0.012 impair divers' judgment and, at levels of 0.04, impair the ability to perform dives.

Bacchus has drowned more men than Neptune.
—THOMAS FULLER

Air Traffic Safety

No alcohol-related accidents have occurred among the major commercial airlines, but alcohol use has been a factor in a small percentage of other aviation accidents. Experimental studies show that alcohol levels as low as 0.025 reduce a pilot's ability to perform essential tasks. Not unexpectedly, one of the predictors is having a history of other alcohol-related offenses, such as a DWI.

The Workplace

Alcohol has been implicated in injuries in the workplace in a variety of settings. An Australian study found that, among fatal workplace injuries, 65% of those injured had a BAC of 0.05 or higher, and another 16% had measurable blood alcohol levels. In addition, drinking outside work also has an impact on the workplace. Higher overall levels of drinking (14 or more drinks per week) are associated with higher numbers of workers' compensation claims.

Suicide

Alcohol plays a significant role in suicide. Studies indicate that, in one-third of suicide attempts, the individual had been drinking. In slightly over one-third of successful suicides, the individual had a positive

BAC. Drinking is also associated with more lethal means of suicide—particularly the use of firearms. Alcohol is associated more often with impulsive suicides than it is with premeditated suicides. Among adolescents, a pattern of binge drinking is associated with suicide. Finally, there is a clear association between alcohol abuse and alcohol dependence and rates of suicide. The risk increases with other drug use and the presence of psychiatric disorders. For adolescents seen in emergency departments following a suicide attempt, if drugs are involved, virtually all also include alcohol.

If once a man indulges himself in murder, very soon he comes to think little of robbing; and from robbing he comes next to drinking and Sabbath-breaking, and from that to incivility and procrastination.
—Thomas De Quincey, 1839

Violence

There is a clear link between alcohol and violence. Of the estimated 11.1 million incidents of violent crime each year, close to one out of three perpetrators was reported to have been drinking. By comparison and despite popular myths to the contrary, in only 1 out of 20 cases were other drugs involved. Drinking also increases the likelihood of being the victim of violence. In as many as two-thirds of all homicides, the victim, the assailant, or both had been drinking. Alcohol is involved in both attempted and completed rapes. For 50% of the rapists and for 30% of the victims, alcohol is a prominent feature. The more serious the crime and the more serious the injuries, the more likely that alcohol is involved.

Drinking is a major factor in family violence. Incidents of violence against partners are twice as likely to involve alcohol as are incidents of violence committed against strangers. In couples whose relationships have included aggressive episodes, physical aggression is four times more likely to involve alcohol than is verbal aggression. Alcohol is also a precipitating factor in child abuse, beatings, and other family violence. It is estimated that alcohol is implicated in two-thirds of all cases of family violence. In cases of domestic violence, the likelihood of severe physical aggression is more than 11 times higher on days when men have been drinking than on days when there is no drinking. Fifty percent of patients treated in emergency rooms as a result of violence-related injuries had been drinking in the six hours before the incident.

The passage of the Volstead Act to enforce Prohibition had an immediate impact on crime. A study of 30 major U.S. cities found the number of crimes increased 24 percent between 1920 and 1921. It revealed that during that period more money was spent on police (11.4%) and more people were arrested for violating Prohibition laws (102%). But increased law enforcement efforts did not appear to reduce drinking: arrests for drunkenness and disorderly conduct increased 41 percent, and arrests of drunken drivers increased 81 percent.
—Charles Hanson Towne
The Rise and Fall of Prohibition, 1932

Crime

Alcohol use is reflected in national crime statistics. Its role in homicide, family violence, and violent offenses has been noted. The current estimate of the total national bill for alcohol-related crimes and misdemeanors is over $10 billion. Alcohol is also a prominent part of the picture for those in local jails. A survey conducted by the U.S. Department of Justice found that virtually two-thirds of community jail inmates met criteria for alcohol or drug abuse/dependence, with the proportion for drugs slightly higher than for alcohol.

The relationship between alcohol and crime is evident, too, in where crimes occur. City blocks with bars have been found to have higher rates of assaults, robberies, and rapes than city blocks without bars. The relationship between crime and alcohol use is not wholly clear. For example, one question raised is whether those who have been drinking are simply more likely to be apprehended. Or does the alcohol–crime relationship possibly reflect patterns of law enforcement? The current thinking is that a variety of interacting factors play a role, such as expectancies, personality factors, the social context, and the pharmacological properties of alcohol.

Best while you have it use your breath
There is no drinking after death.
—JOHN FLETCHER, C. 1616
English playwright

Health Care and Alcohol

Alcohol has a significant impact on both health care delivery and health care costs. The following list summarizes some significant points:

- Studies have consistently shown that a minimum of 20% of all hospitalized persons have a significant alcohol problem, whatever the presenting problem or admitting diagnosis. That is an absolute minimum. In some institutions, the proportion is apt to be higher. Several years ago the Veterans Administration (VA) estimated that 50% of all VA hospital beds were filled by veterans with alcohol problems.
- Some people incur a disproportionate share of health care costs. One large-scale study of hospital costs found that a small proportion of patients, only 13%, had hospital bills equal to the remaining 87%. The distinguishing characteristic of the high-cost group was not age, gender, economic status, or ethnicity. The distinguishing characteristic of high-cost users was that they were heavy drinkers and/or heavy smokers. A follow-up study found that high-cost users also had multiple hospitalizations. In general, patients with a history of alcohol dependence have significantly more repeated hospitalizations than do those without such a history.
- When health care costs for those with untreated alcohol dependence and their families were compared to costs for families where alcohol is not in the picture, the difference is striking. The families with an alcohol-dependent member have 100% greater medical costs. In the one-year period prior to alcohol treatment, the health care costs are over 300% of those of the general public. Such a pattern of increasing medical care immediately prior to diagnosis is true for many chronic diseases, including diabetes, heart disease, and respiratory illnesses.
- Following alcohol treatment, there is a rapid decline in the total family's health care costs.
- As alcohol problems contribute to health care costs, so too does the failure to diagnose them. For example, interventions among hospitalized patients reduce readmissions. Every dollar spent on brief interventions leads to a savings of $19 in future costs for rehospitalization. In

a single military hospital it was estimated that one year's missed diagnoses generated an additional $10 million in hospital expenditures.

It is unfortunate and ironic that, of all these health care costs, only a small proportion—approximately 15%—represents expenditures for rehabilitation or treatment of the primary alcohol problem. The bulk of the medical cost is for treatment of alcohol-induced illness and trauma. The NIAAA estimates that nationally 85% of those with alcohol dependence or alcohol abuse are not receiving any formal treatment. Even if one were to factor in those who enter AA and who have had no involvement in formal treatment (approximately 60% of the 2 million members of AA), that reduces the untreated portion by only another 5%. In an economically developed country, one is hard-pressed to consider any other serious, potentially life-threatening medical condition that is untreated in 85% of those affected.

A more recently recognized health care cost is the expenditures that result from fetal alcohol syndrome (FAS) and fetal alcohol effects (FAE). It has been estimated that the costs for treatment and the special education, training, and required support services for those with FAS add over $10 billion to the nation's annual health care costs. These infants grow to become children and eventually adults who continue to require care.

DRUGS OTHER THAN ALCOHOL

Patterns of Use and Risk Alcohol and the other socially legal drugs, nicotine and caffeine, are used far more widely than any other drugs. To put this into perspective, in the past month, over half the population (52%) used alcohol, a little over half of that used nicotine (28%), and 8% used an illicit drug, with three-quarters of all illicit drug use being marijuana. Only 2% of people used any other illicit drug, be it methamphetamine, heroin, or a prescription drug used for nonmedical purposes.

To approach this from a different angle, in the past month for every person using heroin, there were 5,200 people using alcohol. For each person who used marijuana, there were 21 people who used alcohol. Picture yourself at an Ohio State home football game. If the stands are filled in proportion to those who've used different drugs in the past month, the 52,000 drinkers would fill over half of the stadium. The 1,000 people who've used heroin in the past month don't even fill all the seats in an end zone. There would still be empty seats there, even if you included those who used any illicit drug other than marijuana.

Drugs vary in the likelihood that use will lead to abuse or addiction; this is called *abuse potential*. The majority of those using alcohol can be termed "social drinkers"; however, you don't find a similar proportion of "social smokers" or "social 'smack' [heroin] users."

Illicit Drugs as a Commodity Many of the social and personal costs related to the use of illicit drugs flow not from their pharmacological effects but from their legal status. This has an impact on individuals and society. Drugs have become *a commodity*, manufactured, sold, and purchased as are other consumer goods. The manufacture and distribution of drugs is a multi-billion-dollar business. It is a mistake to think of illicit drug production as small independent efforts, such as a small marijuana plot to supply the grower and his or her friends or methamphetamine being "cooked" in a farmhouse kitchen out on the Great Plains. Drug operations are of sufficient size to threaten the stability of national governments. In Latin America, it's the drug cartels. Poppy cultivation in Afghanistan representing over 90% of the world's heroin supply bankrolls a government insurgency. These are simply the most dramatic examples. The list can be extended to such things as corruption of government officials or usurping national parks for marijuana production (see Chapter 11). Also of importance, within an illicit drug market there is no such thing as "quality control." Substances sold are of unknown purity and of unknown strength. Thus there may be deaths from overdoses or medical problems that arise from contaminants in the drugs purchased.

In some cases something may be deliberately added to dilute a drug being sold. Same volume, same price, less drug. Historically this was the work of street dealers. Worldwide, much of the cocaine now sold contains levamisol, a veterinary drug used to deworm farm animals. In the United States close to 80% of the supply contains levamisol, which can cause serious medical problems. Apparently it is added at the point of processing, which is "managed" by the South American drug cartels.

Social Costs Within the United States, the largest, most easily measured social cost of illicit drugs is the expenditures by the *criminal justice system* resulting from drug-related crimes, including possession. The United States has the largest prison population in the world. The state prison systems include 57% of all those incarcerated; local jails house 34%. So the costs fall to the states and local communities. Between 1980 and 2007, the number incarcerated for drug-related crime, including possession, grew by 550%. Of drug arrests, over half were for possession only. The budget for incarcerating drug offenders in 2010 was estimated at $10.3 billion. African Americans comprise 13% of the total U.S. population, but accounted for 53% of sentenced drug offenders in state prisons. This disparity cannot be explained by significantly different rates of use or abuse/dependence.

The costs of incarceration also fall on the family. Between 1991 and 2007, in state and federal prisons, the number of inmates with children under age 18 increased by 79%. Over half of all prisoners (52%) have a child under age 18; among women who are incarcerated, 75% are mothers. Over 1.75 million children have an incarcerated parent. In most of

Applying Cost-Benefit Analysis to Cannabis

Cost-benefit analysis has led some in Australia to openly muse about the impact of regulating and taxing cannabis. The cannabis industry in Australia is the same financial size as its gold industry, twice the size of its wine industry, and three-quarters the size of the nation's beer industry. An obvious question is "Why leave a $5 billion industry off the books and in the hands of criminal elements?" Beyond the loss of revenue, there is another issue. Despite all the drug control efforts, most Australians say marijuana is easy to get. Furthermore, of the 50,000 cannabis arrests in 2001–2002, approximately three-quarters were for simple possession. So, scarce law enforcement resources are diverted from violent and other serious crimes; and the fines generated do not cover law enforcement costs. Furthermore, the current one-stop-shopping system, meaning a single illicit drug market, combines marijuana with more serious drugs such as heroin, amphetamines, and cocaine, raising the question of whether this has the effect of making these other drugs more accessible.

Wodak A, Cooney A. Should cannabis be taxed and regulated? *Drug and Alcohol Review* 23(2):139–141, 2004 these instances, that parent was the primary source of financial support for his or her children. Drug-related offenses account for at least a quarter of these incarcerations.

Other Drugs in Combination with Alcohol It is important to remember that for alcohol and other drugs, it is not an "either–or" situation. Those who use drugs and those who use alcohol are not distinct populations. The use of alcohol and drugs in combination increases the risk for a range of problems, including driving under the influence, accidents, medical problems, and risk of overdose. If daily smoking, which represents 30% of all adults, is included in the "other drug" category, beyond injury there are also significant long-term health problems.

REFERENCES AND FURTHER READINGS

Alcohol Epidemiologic Data System, LaVallee RA, Yi H-y. *Apparent Per Capita Consumption: National, State, and Regional Trends, 1977–2007. Surveillance Report No. 95.* Bethesda MD: National Institute on Alcohol Abuse and Alcoholism, 2012. (21 refs.)

Alcohol Epidemiologic Data System, Chen CM, Yi H-y, Faden VB. *Trends in Underage Drinking in the United States, 1991–2011. Surveillance Report No. 96.* Bethesda MD: National Institute on Alcohol Abuse and Alcoholism, 2013. (46 refs.)

Alcohol Epidemiologic Data System, Yi H-y, Hoy AK, Chen MC, Williams GD. *Trends in Alcohol-Related Fatal Traffic Crashes, United States, 1982–2004. Surveillance Report No. 76.* Bethesda MD: National Institute on Alcohol Abuse and Alcoholism, 2006. (9 refs.)

Baumberg B. The global economic burden of alcohol: A review and some suggestions. *Drug and Alcohol Review* 25(6):537–551, 2006. (109 refs.)

Botch SR, Johnson RD. Civilian aviation fatalities involving pilot ethanol and a previous record of substance abuse. *Aviation, Space, and Environmental Medicine* 80(10):841–844, 2009. (19 refs.)

Boyd R, Kresnow MJ, Dellinger AM. Alcohol-impaired driving and children in the household. *Family & Community Health* 33(2):167–174, 2009. (22 refs.)

Bureau of Justice Statistics, Glaze LE, Maruschak LM. *Special Report: Parents in Prison and Their Minor Children.* Washington DC: Department of Justice, August 2008. (revised January 2009.) NCJ Publication No. 222984.

Cherpitel C, Borges GLG, Wilcox HC. Acute alcohol use and suicidal behavior: A review of the literature. *Alcoholism: Clinical and Experimental Research* 28(5 Supplement 1):18S–28S, 2004. (87 refs.)

Driscoll TR, Harrison JA, Steenkamp M. Review of the role of alcohol in drowning associated with recreational aquatic activity (review). *Injury Prevention* 10(2):107–113, 2004. (66 refs.)

Flowers NT, Naimi TS, Brewer RD, Elder RW, Shults RA, Jiles R. Patterns of alcohol consumption and alcohol impaired driving in the United States. *Alcoholism: Clinical and Experimental Research* 32(4):639–644, 2009. (46 refs.)

Foster SE, Vaughan RD, Foster WH, Califano JA. Alcohol consumption and expenditures for underage drinking and adult excessive drinking. *Journal of the American Medical Association* 289(8):989–995, 2003. (46 refs.)

Holt JB, Miller JW, Naimi TS, Sui DZ. Religious affiliation and alcohol consumption in the United States. *Geographical Review* 96(4):523–542, 2006. (68 refs.)

Johnston LD, O'Malley PM, Bachman JG, Schulenberg JE. *Monitoring the Future, National Results on Adolescent Drug Use. Overview of Key Findings, 2012.* Bethesda MD: National Institute on Drug Abuse, 2013.

Linakis JG, Chun CH, Mello J, Baird J. Alcohol-related visits to the emergency department by injured adolescents: A national perspective. *Journal of Adolescent Health* 45(1):84–90, 2009. (32 refs)

Manning WG, Keeler EB, Newhouse JP, Sloss EM, Wasserman J. The taxes of sin: Do smokers and drinkers pay their way? *Journal of the American Medical Association* 261(11):1604–1609, 1989.

Michalak L, Trocki K, Bond J. Religion and alcohol in the U.S. National Alcohol Survey: How important is religion for abstention and drinking? *Drug and Alcohol Dependence* 87(2/3): 268–280, 2007. (52 refs.)

Mukamal KJ, Mittleman MA, Longstreth WT, Newman AB, Fried LP, Siscovick DS. Self-reported alcohol consumption and falls in older adults: Cross-sectional and longitudinal analyses of the Cardiovascular Health Study. *Journal of the American Geriatrics Society* 52(7):1174–1179, 2004. (27 refs.)

Naimi TS. The cost of alcohol and its corresponding taxes in the U.S.: A massive public subsidy of excessive drinking and alcohol industries. *American Journal of Preventive Medicine* 41(5): 546–547, 2011. (8 refs.)

National Highway Traffic Safety Agency, Center for Statistics and Analysis. *Traffic Safety Facts. State Alcohol-Impaired-Driving Estimates by State, 2010 Data.* Washington DC: National Highway Traffic Safety Agency, April 2012. (Publication No. DOT HS 811 612.)

Petteruti A, Walsh N, Velázquez T. *Pruning Prisons: How Cutting Corrections Can Save Money and Protect Public Safety.* Washington, DC: Justice Policy Institute, 2009. (70 refs.)

Popovici I, French MT. Does unemployment lead to greater alcohol consumption? *Industrial Relations* 52(2):444–466, 2013. (74 refs.)

Rehm J, Mathers C, Popova S, Thavorncharoensap M, Teerawattananon Y, Patra J. Alcohol and Global Health: 1. Global burden of disease and injury and economic cost attributable to alcohol use and alcohol-use disorders. *Lancet* 373(9682): 2223–2233, 2009. (65 refs.)

Reid TR. Caffeine: It's the world's most popular psychoactive drug. *National Geographic Magazine* 207(1):2+, 2005.

Silver GM, Albright JM, Schermer CR, Halerz M, Conrad P, Ackerman PD, et al. Adverse clinical outcomes associated with elevated blood alcohol levels at the time of burn injury. *Journal of Burn Care & Research* 29(5):784–789, 2008. (34 refs.)

Substance Abuse and Mental Health Services Administration. *Results from the 2012 National Survey on Drug Use and Health. Summary of National Findings.* Rockville MD: Substance Abuse and Mental Health Services Administration, 2013. NSDUH Series H-46, DHHS Publication No. SMA 13-4795.

Taylor B, Irving HM, Kanteres F, Room R, Borges G, Cherpitel C, et al. The more you drink, the harder you fall: A systematic review and meta-analysis of how acute alcohol consumption and injury or collision risk increase together. *Drug and Alcohol Dependence* 110(1–2):108–116, 2010. (63 refs.)

Wagenaar AC, Tobler AL, Komro KA. Effects of alcohol tax and price policies on morbidity and mortality: A systematic review. *American Journal of Public Health* 100(11):2270-2278, 2010. (70 refs.)

World Health Organization. *Global Status Report on Alcohol 2011.* Geneva: WHO 2011.

Yoon YH, Stinson FS, Yi H-y, Dufour MC. Accidental alcohol poisoning mortality in the United States, 1996–1998. *Alcohol Research & Health* 27(1):110–118, 2003. (38 refs.)

Alcohol and the Body

I'm on an 1800 calorie diet... 10 beers and 25 pretzel sticks.

	Calories
Beer, 12-oz can	*173*
Martini, 3 oz, 3:1	*145*
Olive, 1 large	*20*
Rum, 1 oz	*73*
Sherry, sweet, 3 oz	*150*
Fortified wines	*120–160*
Scotch, 1 oz	*73*
Cola, 8 oz	*105*
Pretzels, 5 small sticks	*20*

Joy of Cooking

It is widely recognized that alcohol is more than a beverage. Alcohol is a drug. When ingested, it has specific and predictable physiological effects on the body—any body, every body. The physical impact of chronic use or what happens with excessive use is what grabs the public's attention. Often overlooked are the normal, routine effects on anyone who uses alcohol. Let us examine what happens to alcohol in the body—how it is taken in, how it is broken down, and how it thereby alters body functioning.

☐ INGESTION AND ABSORPTION

The human body is well engineered to change the foods ingested into substances needed to maintain life and provide energy. Despite occasional upsets from too much spice or too much food, in general, this process goes on without a hitch. The first part of this transformation is called digestion. *Digestion* is like a carpenter who dismantles an old building, salvages the materials, and uses them in new construction. Digestion is the body's way of dismantling food to get raw materials required by the body. Whether alcohol can be called a food was at one time a big point of controversy. Alcohol does have calories. One ounce of pure alcohol contains 210 calories. To translate that into drinks, an ounce of whiskey contains 75 calories, and a 12-ounce can of beer contains 150 calories. Alcohol's usefulness as a food is limited, however. Sometimes alcohol is described as providing empty calories. It does not contain vitamins, minerals, or other essential nutrients. Also, alcohol can interfere with the body's ability to use other sources of energy. As a food, alcohol is unique, in that it requires no digestion. Since alcohol is a liquid, no mechanical action by the teeth is required to break it down. No digestive juices need be added to transform it into a form that can be absorbed by the bloodstream and transported to all parts of the body.

What happens to alcohol in the body? Surprisingly, *absorption* of alcohol begins almost immediately with a very small amount taken up into the bloodstream through the tiny blood vessels in the mouth. But the majority goes the route of all food when swallowed—into the stomach. If other food is present in the stomach, the alcohol mixes with it. Here, too, some alcohol seeps into the bloodstream. Up to 20% can be absorbed directly from the stomach, and another small portion is metabolized in the stomach. The remainder passes into the small intestine to be absorbed. The amount of food in the stomach when drinking takes place has important ramifications. Alcohol is an irritant. It increases the flow of hydrochloric acid, a digestive juice secreted by cells of the stomach lining. Anyone who has an ulcer and takes a drink can readily confirm this. This phenomenon explains the feeling of warmth as the drink goes down. The presence of food dilutes the alcohol and tends to diminish its irritant properties.

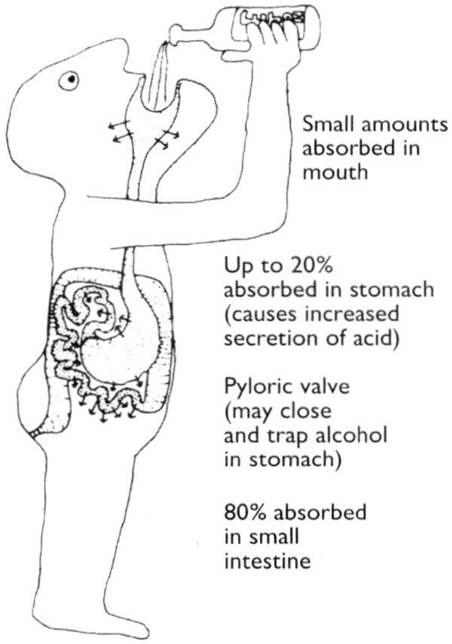

ABSORPTION OF ALCOHOL

The amount of food in the stomach is an important factor in determining the speed with which the alcohol is absorbed by the bloodstream. A rapid rate of absorption is largely responsible for the subjective feeling of being intoxicated—thus, the basis for the advice, "Don't drink on an empty stomach." How much and how quickly alcohol is absorbed depends both on the total amount of alcohol in the stomach's contents and on the relative proportion of alcohol to food. The greater the amount of alcohol and the smaller the amount of food in the stomach, the more rapidly the alcohol is absorbed into the bloodstream and the higher the resulting blood alcohol level. A sex-based difference also seems to influence blood alcohol levels. This is related to differing amounts of an enzyme, gastric *a*lcohol *deh*ydrogenate (ADH), produced by the stomach lining that promotes the breakdown of alcohol. Because women have significantly lower levels of this enzyme, more of the alcohol they drink remains available to enter the small intestine and be taken up by the blood. Therefore, when women and men consume equivalent amounts of alcohol, women have a higher blood alcohol concentration.

In addition to the impact of food in the stomach, the rate of absorption varies with the type of beverage. The higher the concentration of alcohol in a beverage (up to 50%, or 100 proof), the more quickly the alcohol is absorbed. This partially explains why distilled spirits, with their higher alcohol content, have more apparent "kick" than wine or beer. In addition, wine and beer contain some food substances that slow absorption. On the other hand, carbon dioxide, which hastens the passage of alcohol from the stomach, may increase the speed of absorption. As a result, champagne, sparkling wines, and drinks mixed with carbonated soda may give a sense of "bubbles in the head."

Now, on from the stomach to the pyloric valve. This valve controls the passage of the stomach's contents into the small intestine. It is sensitive to the presence of alcohol. With high concentrations of alcohol, it tends to get "stuck" in the closed position—a condition called *pylorospasm.* When pylorospasm occurs, the alcohol trapped in the stomach may cause sufficient irritation and distress to induce vomiting. This is what accounts for much of the nausea and vomiting that may accompany too much drinking. A stuck pylorus valve also may serve as a self-protective mechanism. It may prevent the passage into the small intestine of what might otherwise be life-threatening doses of alcohol.

BLOOD ALCOHOL CONCENTRATION

In considering the effects of alcohol, several questions come to mind. How much alcohol and in how large a person? How fast did the alcohol get there? Is the blood alcohol level rising or declining? Let us consider each of these in turn.

First, let's consider the concentration of alcohol in the blood. One tablespoon of sugar mixed in a cup of water yields a much sweeter solution than a tablespoon of sugar diluted in a gallon of water. Similarly, consuming a drink with 1 ounce of alcohol results in a higher blood alcohol level in a 100-pound woman than in a 200-pound man. In fact, it is virtually twice as high. Her body contains less water than his. Even if they are of the same weight, the amount of water in the woman's body is less than in the man's. For that reason, when they consume the same amount of alcohol, her blood alcohol level will be higher than his. The second factor is rate of absorption, which depends both on the amount and concentration of alcohol in the stomach and on how rapidly it is ingested. So, if you quickly drink a scotch on the rocks on an empty stomach, you will probably be more giddy than if you drink more alcohol more slowly—say, in the form of beer after a meal. Even with a given blood alcohol level, there is greater impairment the faster the level has been achieved. Impairment is based on both the amount absorbed and the rate of absorption. The rate of absorption determines how fast the alcohol reaches the brain. Finally, on any drinking occasion, there are different effects for a particular blood alcohol level, depending on whether the blood alcohol level is going up or coming down.

Once in the small intestine, the remainder of the alcohol (at least 80% of that ingested) is very rapidly absorbed into the bloodstream. The bloodstream is the body's transportation system. It delivers the oxygen and nutrients that the cells require for energy and picks up wastes produced by cell metabolism. By this route, too, alcohol is carried to all parts of the body.

Although blood alcohol levels are almost universally used as the measure of alcohol in the body, this does not mean that alcohol merely rides around in the bloodstream until the liver is able to break it down. Alcohol is both highly soluble in water and able to pass rapidly through cell walls. Therefore, it is distributed uniformly throughout the water content of all body tissues and cells. For a given blood alcohol level, the alcohol content of the tissues and cells varies in proportion to the amount of water they contain. The alcohol content of liver tissue is 64% of that in the blood; of muscle tissue, 84%; of brain tissue, 75%. It takes very little time for the tissues to absorb the alcohol circulating in the blood. Within two minutes, brain tissues will accurately reflect the blood alcohol level.

BREAKDOWN AND REMOVAL

It is better to hide ignorance, but it is hard to do this when we relax over wine.
—HERACLITUS
On the Universe

The removal of alcohol from the body begins as soon as the alcohol is absorbed by the bloodstream. Small amounts leave unmetabolized through sweat, urine, and breath. The proportion of alcohol in exhaled air has a constant and predictable relationship to the blood alcohol concentration—which is the basis for the use of breathalyzers. These routes, at most, account for the elimination of only 5% of the alcohol consumed. The rest has to be changed chemically and metabolized to be removed from the body.

About a quarter century ago, a joint Italian-U.S. research group, headed by Mario Frezza and Charles Lieber, published new findings on *metabolism*. This was front page news, particularly because they identified differences between men and women. The breakdown, or metabolism, of alcohol occurs in a multistep process. The first step is its biochemical conversion to acetaldehyde. The enzyme that accomplishes this is called *alcohol dehydrogenase,* referred to as ADH. Before Frezza and Lieber's work, this enzyme was thought to be present and active only in the liver. They, however, identified a gastric form of ADH. The breakdown of alcohol that occurs in the stomach is termed "first-pass metabolism." In the absence of alcohol dependence, for men, the amount of alcohol that can be metabolized by the stomach may be as great as 30% of the alcohol consumed. Women will metabolize only half that amount in the stomach. Therefore, greater proportions of alcohol enter the bloodstream of women.[1] For both sexes at all ages, a history of chronic heavy alcohol use leads to a significant decrease in first-pass metabolism.

The acetaldehyde that is formed is itself acted on in the second step of metabolism, by still another enzyme called *aldehyde dehydrogenase* (ALDH). Aldehyde dehydrogenase, too, is present in both the stomach and the liver. Then, very rapidly the acetaldehyde produced is further metabolized into acetic acid. This is dispersed throughout the body,

[1]Some research suggests that this sex-based difference may be apparent only among young adults and then may reverse in later life.

where it is broken down in cells and tissues to become carbon dioxide and water. The following diagram illustrates the chain of events:

alcohol → acetaldehyde[2] → acetic acid → carbon dioxide and water

Almost any cell or organ can break down the acetic acid that is formed. But only the liver or the stomach can handle the first two steps. These first steps depend upon the availability of a substance known as NAD^+, which must be present for the enzyme ADH to do its job. This essential substance, or cofactor, is present only in the liver and stomach. The rate of metabolism—that is, how quickly metabolism takes place—is determined by the availability of this cofactor. It is not in infinite supply or immediately present in sufficient quantities to accomplish the metabolism of alcohol in one fell swoop.

As alcohol is oxidized to acetaldehyde, the cofactor NAD^+ is changed; it is converted to NADH. As this occurs, the proportion of NADH to NAD^+ increases. The change in the relative amounts of these two substances has a number of important biochemical ramifications, which are discussed in Chapter 6.

Generally the rate at which food is metabolized depends on the energy requirements of the body. Experience will confirm this, especially for anyone who has taken a stab at dieting. Chopping wood burns up more calories than watching movies. Eat too much food, and a storehouse of fat begins to accumulate around the middle. By balancing our caloric intake with exercise, we can avoid accumulating a fat roll. Alcohol is unique in that it is metabolized at a constant rate irrespective of the amount present or the body's metabolic needs. The presence of large amounts of alcohol at a particular moment does not prompt the liver to work faster. Despite alcohol's potential as a fine source of calories, increased exercise (and hence raising the body's need for calories) does not increase the speed of metabolism. This is probably not news to anyone who has tried to sober up someone who is drunk. It is simply a matter of time. Exercise may mean only that you have to contend with a wide-awake drunk rather than a sleeping one. He or she is still intoxicated.

The rate at which alcohol is metabolized may vary a little between people. It will also increase somewhat after an extended drinking career. Yet the average rate is around 0.5 ounce of pure alcohol per hour—roughly equivalent to one mixed drink of 86-proof whiskey, or a 4-ounce

Outox Doesn't Beat Time

A fructose soft drink, Outox, claims to noticeably increase the alcohol elimination rate. Theories to explain this "fructose effect" are based on the assumption that NAD^+ is regenerated faster in the presence of fructose. Indeed, research shows that the soft drink may decrease the blood alcohol concentration by about 10%. However, the lower BAC is not a consequence of increasing the elimination rate. Rather, it is the result of slower absorption due to the presence of the stomach contents.

—M Pavlic, K Libiseller, et al.

Wiener Klinische Wochenschrift, 2007

[2]It is at this point that disulfiram (Antabuse), a drug used in alcohol treatment, acts. Disulfiram stops the breakdown of acetaldehyde by blocking acetaldehyde dehydrogenase. Thus, acetaldehyde starts to accumulate in the system. It is very toxic, and its effects are those associated with an Antabuse reaction. A better term would be "acetaldehyde reaction." The toxicity of acetaldehyde usually isn't a problem because it breaks down faster than it is formed. But disulfiram does not allow this to take place so rapidly—thus the nausea, flushing, and heart palpitations. It has been observed that Asians often have such symptoms when drinking. These are seemingly based on genetically determined metabolic differences. In effect, some Asians may have a genetically determined built-in Antabuse-like response.

glass of wine, or one 12-ounce can of beer. The unmetabolized alcohol remains circulating in the bloodstream, "waiting in line." The presence of not-yet-metabolized alcohol in the blood, and hence the brain, is responsible for its intoxicating effects.

ALCOHOL'S ACUTE EFFECTS ON THE BODY

What is the immediate effect of alcohol on the various body organs and functions?

Digestive System

Alcohol is an irritant. This explains the burning sensation as it goes down. Alcohol in the stomach promotes the flow of gastric juices. A glass of wine before dinner may thereby promote digestion by priming the stomach for food. But with intoxicating amounts, alcohol impedes or stops digestion. It can be irritating to the lining of the stomach and small intestine.

What is man, when you come to think upon him, but a minutely set, ingenious machine for turning, with infinite artfulness, the red wine of Shiraz into urine?
—ISAK DINESEN, 1934

Circulatory System

In general, acute use of alcohol has relatively minor effects on the circulatory system in healthy individuals. In moderate amounts, alcohol is a vasodilator of the surface blood vessels. The vessels near the skin surface expand, which accounts for the sensation of warmth and flush to the skin that accompany drinking. Despite the subjective feeling of warmth, body heat is lost. Thus, whoever sends out the St. Bernard with a brandy cask to aid the cold, snow-stranded traveler is misguided. Despite the illusion of warmth, a good belt of alcohol will likely further cool off the body.

The reason I don't drink and drive is simple. I hate having to stop at every gas station to go to the bathroom.

Kidneys

Anyone who has had a couple of drinks may well spend some time traipsing back and forth to the bathroom. The increased urine output is not caused by alcohol's direct action on the kidneys, nor is it due simply to the amount of liquid consumed. This phenomenon is related to the effect of alcohol on the posterior portion of the pituitary gland, located at the base of the brain. The pituitary secretes a hormone, called ADH (*a*nti*d*iuretic *h*ormone), that regulates the amount of water the kidneys excrete. When the pituitary is affected by alcohol, its functioning is depressed. Therefore, too little of the hormone is released, and the kidneys produce a larger than normal amount of dilute urine. This effect is most pronounced when alcohol is being absorbed and the blood alcohol level is rising.

Liver

The liver is very sensitive to the acute effects of alcohol. (See Chapter 6 for more information about the long-term effects of alcohol on the liver.) It has been demonstrated that for any drinker, not just heavy drinkers, even relatively small amounts of alcohol (1 to 2 ounces) can lead to rapid accumulation of fat in liver cells.

The liver performs an incredible number of metabolic functions—a very important one is its role in maintaining a proper blood sugar level. Sugar (the body's variety, called glucose) is the only source of energy that brain cells can use. Because the brain is the master control center of the body, an inadequate supply of glucose in the brain can have far-reaching consequences.

When alcohol is present in the body, the liver preferentially devotes its "attention," so to speak, to metabolizing it. This may interfere with the normal liver function of maintaining a steady, adequate supply of blood sugar. In the liver there is a stored form of glucose (glycogen) that usually is readily available to be converted to glucose. However, if one has had an inadequate diet, or has not eaten much for a day or two, glycogen may not be adequate. At such times the liver normally would employ a more complicated biochemical process to transform other nutrients, such as protein, into glucose. This process is called gluconeogenesis. However, in the presence of alcohol this complicated maneuver is blocked. In such cases hypoglycemia can result. In a hypoglycemic state the concentration of sugar in the blood is abnormally low. As a result, the brain is deprived of its proper nourishment. Symptoms include hunger, weakness, nervousness, sweating, headache, and tremor. If the blood sugar level is sufficiently depressed, coma can occur. Hypoglycemia may be more likely to occur and may be more severe in individuals who already have liver damage from chronic alcohol use. But it can occur in otherwise normal people with healthy livers who have been drinking heavily and have not been eating properly for as little as 48 to 72 hours.

In individuals with adequate diets, other metabolic effects of alcohol may cause abnormally high levels of blood glucose. This is called hyperglycemia, which is a state similar to that occurring in diabetics. In view of its potentially significant effect on blood sugar levels, the possible dangers posed by alcohol for the diabetic are obvious.

The liver also plays an important role in the metabolism of other drugs. The presence of alcohol can interfere with this role and be responsible for some alcohol-drug interactions. The liver enzyme ADH is essential to the metabolism of alcohol. Quantitatively, it is the liver's major means of metabolizing alcohol. The liver does have a "backup" system, however. This secondary system is called the cytochrome P450 system, previously referred to as MEOS (**M**icrosomal **E**thanol **O**xidization **S**ystem). It is located in intracellular structures called microsomes. While termed a backup system for metabolizing alcohol, it is believed that this secondary system begins to help out significantly in removing alcohol only after long-term heavy drinking. It is mentioned here because it is a major system in metabolizing other drugs, including many prescription drugs. Thus alcohol's effects on this system may affect the ways in which many drugs are metabolized by the liver, which can have clinical importance.

Acutely, the cytochrome P450 system activity is inhibited dramatically by the presence of alcohol. Therefore, other drugs may not be broken down at their usual rates. If other drugs in the system have depressant effects similar to that of alcohol, the central nervous system (CNS) will be subjected to both simultaneously. However, with some drugs there are additional potential problems. Suppose someone is taking a prescription drug, such as phenytoin (Dilantin) or warfarin sodium (Coumadin), at set intervals. The presence of alcohol may acutely interfere with the metabolism of such medications; thus, when the next scheduled dose is taken, substantial amounts of the earlier dose may remain and cumulative toxic effects may occur. With chronic alcohol use, the activity of the cytochrome P450 system is speeded up. In this instance various drugs are broken down faster, so higher doses must be administered to achieve a given therapeutic effect. (Alcohol and drug interactions are discussed in more detail later in this chapter.)

Central Nervous System

The major acute effect of alcohol on the central nervous system is that of a depressant. The common misconception that alcohol is a stimulant comes from the fact that its depressant action disinhibits many higher cortical functions, which place a brake on various actions. It does this in a somewhat paradoxical fashion. Through the depressant effects of alcohol, parts of the brain are released from their normal inhibitory restraints. Thus behavior that would ordinarily be censured and inhibited can occur. Acute alcohol intoxication, in fact, induces a mild delirium, which is a fully reversible acute brain dysfunction. Thinking becomes fuzzy; orientation, recent memory, and other higher mental functions, notably impulse control, are altered. An electroencephalogram (EEG) taken when someone is high typically shows a diffuse slowing of normal brain waves associated with this mild state of delirium. For the light and even relatively heavy occasional drinker, these acute effects are, of course, completely reversible. Regular heavy use over time presents a substantially different story.

Precisely how alcohol affects the brain and thereby influences behavior is not fully understood. Research indicates that alcohol exerts a major effect on the physical structure of nerve cell membranes, an effect that alters their functioning. These changes may be transient with acute alcohol intake, may persist with chronic use, or may lead to other changes in the structure and function of nerve cells as they compensate and adapt to the continued presence of high levels of alcohol. These effects on nerve cells, directly caused by the presence of alcohol, are presumed to play a major role in causing the behaviors seen with acute intoxication. They are also believed to be the basis for the phenomena of craving, tolerance, withdrawal, and loss of control that are the key features defining alcohol dependence.

Alcohol significantly affects the production and activity of many different neurotransmitters, which act as chemical messengers in the brain. Neurotransmitters allow the cells in the brain to send messages from one cell to another. Thus they are the basis of the brain's communication system. Neurotransmitters allow messages to cross the spaces between cells, called synapses, and activate the receptors on the "receiving" nerve cells.

Several neurotransmitter systems are believed to be particularly important in mediating the effects of alcohol. Alcohol decreases the levels of one of the brain's major inhibitory transmitters, *GABA*. This causes changes in the communication across the synapse. The effects of alcohol on GABA may contribute to the disinhibition of behavior. Alcohol also hastens the breakdown and removal of the noradrenergic neurotransmitter, *norepinephrine*. This chemical is known to be involved with activation and stimulation of the nervous system and the fight-or-flight response to threats. The removal of this stimulating neurotransmitter may help explain the calming or relaxing effects of alcohol.

In addition, alcohol depresses the activity of *serotonin* in some regions of the brain. Decreased levels of serotonin have been linked to behaviors associated with intoxicated states, depression, anxiety, poor impulse control, aggressiveness, and occasionally suicidal behavior. Finally, the presence of alcohol increases the level of endogenous (meaning naturally and normally occurring) opiate-like substances, known as endorphins. This in turn may lead to increased dopamine activity, especially in the parts of the brain known to be involved in generating feelings of pleasure and well-being. Recent research indicates that other brain receptors—particularly the nicotinic and cholinergic receptors—may contribute to alcohol's reinforcing properties. To further complicate this, alcohol appears to affect neurotransmitters in some sections of the brain more than those in other sections.

The wine urges me on, the bewitching wine, which sets even a wise man to singing and to laughing gently and rouses him up to dance and brings forth words which were better unspoken.
—Homer
The Odyssey

Without question, the brain is the organ that is most sensitive to the acute effects of alcohol. This sensitivity is what being "high," drunk, intoxicated, or impaired is all about. The neurophysiological basis of intoxication is not yet fully understood. Without a doubt the intensity of the effect is directly related to the concentration of alcohol in the blood and hence the brain, but even here several other factors need to be considered.

The degree of intoxication is dependent on whether the blood alcohol level is rising, falling, or constant. It is known that the CNS and behavioral effects of a given blood alcohol concentration (BAC) are greater when the blood alcohol level is rising. This is called the *Mellanby effect*. It is almost as if there were a small "practice effect," the development of a short-term adaptation or tolerance by the nervous system to alcohol's presence acutely. Thus, for a given BAC, there is *more* impairment when the blood level is rising than when the level of alcohol in the blood is falling. Another possible effect of ingesting a large amount of alcohol is disturbances in memory. With BACs in the range of 0.20 or above, the ability to form memories of events is impaired. The person may have absolutely no memory of events, or memories may be partial and spotty. Although commonly referred to as alcohol blackouts, the medical term is anterograde amnesia involving short-term memory. Women are more likely than men to experience these disturbances in memory. (See Chapter 6 for further discussion of blackouts.)

The drug alcohol is a CNS depressant. It interferes with the activity of various brain centers and neurochemical systems—sometimes with seemingly paradoxical results. A high BAC can suppress CNS function across the board, even to the point of causing respiratory arrest and death. At lower doses it may lead to the activated, giddy, poorly controlled, and disinhibited behaviors that are typical of intoxication. This is not due to stimulation of CNS centers that mediate such behavior. Rather, it is attributable to the indirect effect of the selective suppression of inhibitory systems that normally keep such impulsive behaviors in check.

Watch or recall someone becoming intoxicated and see the progression of effects. The following examples refer to the CNS effects in a hypothetical "average" male. Of course, the observed effects of differing numbers of drinks over an hour in any given person may vary considerably. However, the type and severity of behavioral effects that do occur are a direct function of the amount of alcohol consumed; they progress in a fairly predictable fashion.

The drinks used in the following examples are a little under one-half ounce of pure alcohol, the equivalent of a 12-ounce beer, a 4-ounce glass of wine, or an ounce of 86-proof whiskey. Many generous hosts and hostesses mix drinks with more than 1 ounce of alcohol, even in the context of a quite proper cocktail party. Then there are college fraternity parties. They often ladle out large quantities of spiked punch of unknown—but usually high—alcohol content. Or there are the adolescents living in rural New England who, at an impromptu party out in the woods, simply pass the bottle around. So, as you read on, don't shrug off the "Ten Drinks" section as an impossibility.

In the scientific literature, several different units are used in reporting blood alcohol levels. The following measures are equivalents:
0.01%
0.01 g/dl
100 mg%
10 mg/dl
0.01 g%

One Drink

With 1 drink, the drinker will be a bit more relaxed, possibly loosened up a little. Unless he chugged it rapidly, thus getting a rapid rise in blood alcohol, his behavior will be little changed. If he is of average height and weighs 160 pounds, by the end of an hour his blood alcohol level will be 0.02. (The actual measurement is grams %, or grams/100 milliliters. For example, 0.02 g% = 200 mg%.) An hour later all traces of alcohol will be gone.

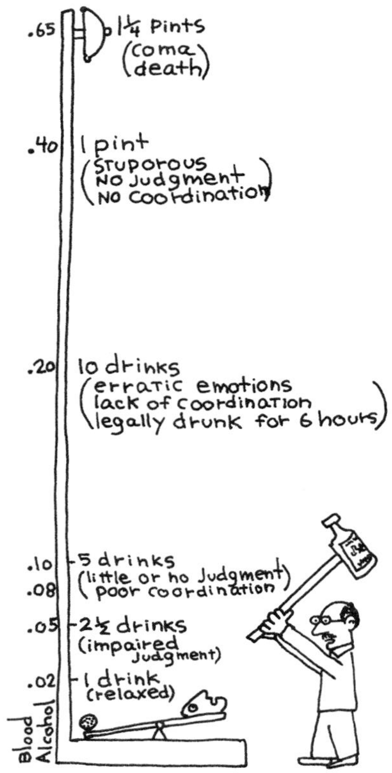

.08 = legally drunk

It takes only one drink to get me drunk. The trouble is, I can't remember if it's the thirteenth or the fourteenth.
—George Burns

Two and One-Half Drinks

With 2½ drinks in an hour's time, the partygoer will have a 0.05 blood alcohol level. He's high. The "newer" parts of the brain, those controlling judgment, will have been affected. That our friend has been drinking is apparent. He may be loud, boisterous, and making passes. Disinhibited, he is saying and doing things he might usually censor. These are the effects that mistakenly cause people to think of alcohol as a stimulant. The system isn't really hyped up. Rather, the inhibitions have been suspended, due to the alcohol's depression of the parts of the brain that normally put the brakes on. At this time our friend is entering the danger zone for driving. With $2^1/_2$ drinks in an hour, two and a half hours will be required to completely metabolize the alcohol.

Five Drinks

With 5 drinks in an hour, there is no question you have a drunk on your hands, and the law would agree. A blood alcohol level of 0.10 is now more than sufficient to issue a DWI in any state. By this time the drinker's judgment is nil ("Off coursh I can drive!"). In addition to the frontal regions of the brain controlling judgment, the cerebellar centers controlling muscle coordination are also impaired. There's a stagger to the walk and a slur to the speech. Even though the loss of dexterity and reaction time can be measured, the drinker, now with altered perception and judgment, may claim he has never functioned better. For all traces of alcohol to disappear from the system, five hours will be required.

Ten Drinks

This quantity of alcohol in the system yields a blood alcohol content of 0.20. More areas of the brain than just the judgment, perceptual, and motor centers are affected. Emotions are probably very erratic—rapidly ranging from laughter to tears to rage. Even if your guest could remember he had a coat—which he may not because of memory impairment—he'd never be able to put it on. For all the alcohol to be metabolized, 10 hours will be required. He'll still be legally drunk after 6 hours.

Sixteen Drinks—2 Six-Packs and 4 Beers

With this amount of alcohol the drinker is stuporous. Though not passed out, nothing the senses take in actually registers. Judgment is gone, coordination wiped out, and sensory perception almost nil. With the liver handling roughly 1 ounce of alcohol per hour, it will be 16 hours, well into tomorrow, before all the alcohol is gone.

Twenty Drinks—Not Quite a Fifth of Whiskey

At this point the person is in a coma and dangerously close to death. The vital brain centers that send out instructions to the heart and breathing apparatus are partially anesthetized. At a blood alcohol level of

0.40 to 0.50, a person is in a deep coma and entirely unresponsive. At a BAC of 0.60 to 0.70, breathing ceases and death occurs.

ACUTE OVERDOSE AND TOXICITY

With alcohol, as with many other drugs, an acute overdose may be fatal. Usually this occurs when very large doses of alcohol are consumed within a very short period of time. Rapid absorption of the ingested alcohol leads to a rapid and steep rise in BAC. In a relatively brief period, this may lead to loss of consciousness, coma, progressive respiratory depression, and death. Thus a "chugging" contest can be a fatal game.

In general, the acute lethal dose of alcohol is considered to be from 5 to 8 mg/kg of body weight—the equivalent of about a fifth to a fifth and a half of 86-proof liquor for the typical 160-pound male. Acute doses of this amount of alcohol can be expected to result in BACs in the range of 0.35 to 0.70. Alcohol overdoses with fatal outcomes are consistently associated with BACs in this range, which is not at all surprising. It is known that a BAC above 0.40 often severely and, all too commonly, lethally depresses respiratory function.

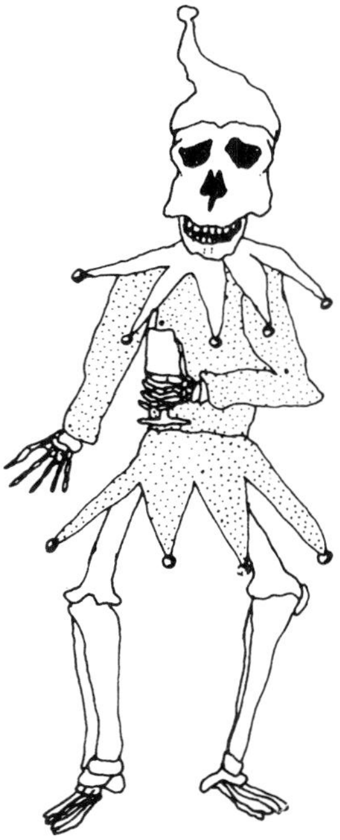

Of course, the exact lethal dose and BAC in any individual will vary with age, sex, general physical health, and degree of tolerance to alcohol. All things being equal, a very large, healthy, young adult male will tolerate a dose of alcohol that might be fatal for a small, medically ill, elderly female. This is true, only more so, for an alcohol-dependent person who has established a high level of tolerance, compared to the alcohol-naive novice drinker.

The alcohol-dependent person may tolerate an acute dose of alcohol that would kill an otherwise comparable non-dependent individual. Although chronic heavy drinking and a high tolerance to alcohol may provide the alcohol-dependent person with some margin of safety, this protection has limits. Even the most severely dependent person may do him- or herself in by consuming enough alcohol in one drinking bout to raise the BAC to the upper end of the lethal range. Therefore, it is probably fair to say that a BAC of 0.70 or higher is virtually certain to be lethal to anyone. The higher the level within the 0.35 to 0.70 range, the greater the risk of death.

DIFFERENCES IN WOMEN

Substitute a 120-pound woman in the previous scenarios, and the weight differential will dramatically speed up the process. A woman and a man who have identical body weights and who both drink the same amount of alcohol will have different blood alcohol levels. Hers will be higher. Women and men differ in their relative amounts of body fat and water.

Women have a higher proportion of fat and correspondingly lower amounts of water. This difference is highly relevant since alcohol is not very fat soluble. Her body contains less water than his with which to dilute the ingested alcohol, which results in her having a higher concentration of alcohol in her blood.

Simply on that basis, let's contrast a 120-pound woman to our hypothetical 160-pound male drinker. With 1 drink in one hour, she would have a BAC of 0.04; 2½ drinks, and her BAC would be slightly over 0.10. By 5 drinks, she'd have a 0.21 reading. Should she make it through 11 drinks, she'd be in a coma with a blood alcohol level of 0.45 and potentially at risk of dying.

Beyond body weight and differences in the proportions of fat and water, there are other important differences between men and women with respect to how they handle alcohol. A significant one is their differing levels of gastric alcohol dehydrogenase. Gastric ADH may account for the metabolism of up to 30% of alcohol in males. This means that, for men, nearly one-third of the alcohol consumed will be metabolized in the stomach and never pass into the small intestine to be absorbed into the bloodstream. This is not true for women, who have lower levels of gastric ADH. Because of this, significantly less alcohol is metabolized in the stomach, and, consequently, more alcohol is available to enter the circulatory system when the alcohol passes from the stomach to the small intestine. Therefore, when consuming identical amounts of alcohol, women will have higher blood alcohol concentrations than men, even if one takes into account the differences in weight and relative proportions of body fat and water.

There are also apparent differences in the metabolism of alcohol in both male and female heavy drinkers. In both men and women with a history of heavy drinking, there is less gastric ADH. Since women have less gastric ADH to start with, and because it declines with heavy alcohol use, there is a virtual absence of gastric ADH among women who drink heavily. Thus, for women who have a history of heavy drinking, the amount of alcohol that reaches the bloodstream will be virtually identical to that resulting from a dose of alcohol administered intravenously. These differences in metabolism and the resulting demands on the liver to metabolize larger amounts of alcohol may be one of the mechanisms accounting for women's recognized greater vulnerability to liver disease.

Quite possibly other important biological differences in alcohol's effects may exist between men and women. Most of the older research on the physiological effects of alcohol was conducted on men, and researchers had assumed that the findings were equally true for women. Though the basic differences between the absorption rates in men and women were reported as early as 1932, they were largely forgotten or ignored until the mid-1970s. The impact of the menstrual cycle was not recognized or reported until 1976! Given these failures to examine the effects of the primary and obvious difference between men and women, who knows what more subtle areas have not yet been considered. Women have gotten short shrift not only in terms of alcohol research, but in all areas of medical investigation. In light of this, the National Institutes of Health has made considerable efforts to promote equal inclusion of women as subjects in biomedical research studies and in clinical trials of new drugs.

Despite individual biological differences, virtually all people react to alcohol in basically the same way. This is true despite the fact that, for a given blood alcohol level, a very heavy drinker who has developed tolerance to alcohol may show somewhat less impairment in function than an inexperienced drinker would. This uniform, well-documented response enables the law to set a specific and standard blood alcohol level for defining intoxication in both men and women and across all age groups. The blood alcohol level can be easily measured by taking blood samples or a breathalyzer test. The breathalyzer is able to measure blood alcohol levels because, just as carbon dioxide in the blood diffuses across small capillaries in the lungs to be eliminated in exhaled air, so does alcohol. The amount of carbon dioxide in exhaled air is directly proportionate to that circulating in the bloodstream. The same is true for alcohol. The breathalyzer measures the concentration of alcohol in the exhaled air. From that measurement, the exact concentration of alcohol in the blood can be determined.

TOLERANCE

The immediate effects of consumption of alcohol have been described. With continued regular alcohol use over an extended period, predictable changes take place in the body. Tolerance develops, and any drinker, not only the alcohol-dependent individual, can testify to this. The first few times someone tries alcohol, one drink is enough to cause a tipsy feeling. With some drinking experience, one drink no longer has that effect. In part this may reflect greater wisdom. The veteran drinker has learned "how to drink" to avoid feeling intoxicated. The experienced drinker has learned to sip, not gulp, a drink and avoids drinking on an empty stomach. The other reason is that, with repeated exposures to alcohol, the central nervous system (CNS) adapts to its presence in increasing amounts. It can tolerate more alcohol and still maintain normal functioning. This is one of the properties that defines alcohol as an addictive drug. Over the long haul the body requires a larger dose to induce the effects previously produced by smaller doses.

Not only does tolerance develop over relatively long spans of time, but there are also rapid adaptive changes in the CNS on each drinking occasion. A drinker is more out of commission when the blood alcohol level is climbing than when it is falling. In a testing situation, if someone

Origin of Breathalyzer

"When is a man intoxicated? What are the symptoms of intoxication? How do human beings behave under the influence of liquor?" Physicians at the University of Cincinnati came up with an innovative method to answer these questions. With the "tremendous increase of automobile traffic and the difficulties in enforcing the Eighteenth Amendment," physicians found themselves with "infinitely increased responsibility in the diagnosis of acute intoxication." Some scientific evidence was needed to support the charge of intoxication.

Testing blood or spinal fluid was too cumbersome. A technique used to test for acetate in diabetics was adapted. It involved blowing into a football. The air was then passed through a solution containing potassium dichromate and sulphuric acid. Changes in color denoted differing alcohol concentrations. The unit of measure was mg/cubit centimeter equivalent of what is now termed (0.01 BAC).

When the researchers reported their findings, the following categories were identified:

Dry and Decent under 1 mg/per
Delinquent and Disgusting (2–3 mg);
Dizzy and Delirious (3–4 mg);
Dazed and Dejected (4–5 mg); and
Dead Drunk (more than 5 mg).)46

—Emil Bogen, MD

Scientific tests tell when a man is drunk. *New York Times,* June 5, 1927

The Poisoning Program

During Prohibition, the major source of alcohol was through bootleggers re-distilling stolen industrial alcohol—the alcohol used in paints and solvents, fuels and medical supplies. Some 60 million gallons of industrial alcohol were stolen annually to supply the country's drinkers.

To combat this, the government turned to chemistry. In 1906, the government required that chemicals be added to industrial alcohol, to prevent its use as beverage alcohol. During Prohibition, these laws were changed. Rather than industrial alcohol simply being foul-smelling, and vile tasting, manufacturers were required to also make it deadly. Among the new additives were poisons—kerosene, gasoline, benzene, cadmium, iodine, zinc, mercury, nicotine, ether, formaldehyde, chloroform, and acetone. The Treasury Department also demanded more methyl alcohol be added—up to 10% of total product—the most deadly new ingredient.

On Christmas Eve 1926, the first of over 60 desperately ill people showed up at hospitals in New York City. By the end of the following day, half of them had died. The New York medical examiner described this as "our national experiment in extermination." The Chicago Tribune *editorialized "Normally, no American government would engage in such business. . . . It is only in the fanaticism of Prohibition that any means, however barbarous, are considered justified.*

By the end of Prohibition it is estimated at least 10,000 people died as a result of the poisoning program.
—DEBORAH SOLOMON

The Chemist's War: The little-told story of how the U.S. government poisoned alcohol during Prohibition with deadly consequences, *Slate*, February 2010

is given alcohol to drink and then asked to perform certain tasks, the results are predictable. Impairment is greater on the ascending limb—the rising side of the blood alcohol concentration curve, the absorption phase. As the blood alcohol level drops during the elimination phase, the individual, when similarly tested, will be able to function better with the same blood alcohol content. It is as if one learns to function better in the presence of alcohol after "practice." In fact, what probably has happened is that the brain has made some subtle adjustments in the way it functions in the presence of alcohol. Here, too, there are differences between men and women. Both show greater impairment as alcohol levels rise, but there are differences in the kinds of impairment. When intoxicated, women appear to have greater impairment than men for tasks that require motor coordination. Yet they are superior to men in tasks that require attention. Since driving requires both skills, neither appears the better bet on the highway.

ALCOHOL AS AN ANESTHETIC

Alcohol is an anesthetic. By modern standards, it is not a very good one. The dose of alcohol required to produce anesthesia is very close to the lethal amount. When the vital centers have been depressed enough by alcohol to produce unconsciousness, it takes only a wee bit more to cause respiratory cessation and put someone permanently to sleep. Sadly, several times a year almost every newspaper obituary column documents a death from alcohol. Usually the tragedy involves young people. It may follow chugging a fifth of liquor on a dare or as a prank; or it may involve coerced drinking as part of a college fraternity initiation, following which the drinker passes out and, if left alone and unattended, dies in his sleep.

OTHER TYPES OF ALCOHOL

In this discussion of alcohol, it is clear that we have been referring to "booze," "suds," "the sauce," "brew," or any of the other colloquial terms for beverage alcohol. To be scientifically accurate, this kind of alcohol is called ethanol, ethyl alcohol, or grain alcohol. "Alcohol," if one is precise, is a term used to refer to a family of substances. What all alcohols have in common is a particular grouping of carbon, hydrogen, and oxygen atoms to form the alcohol molecule. They differ only in the number of carbon atoms and associated hydrogen atoms. Each alcohol is named according to the number of carbons it has. Ethanol has two carbon atoms.

One other kind of alcohol with which everyone is familiar is *methanol*, also known as wood alcohol, or methyl alcohol. It has one carbon atom and is an ingredient of antifreeze, paint thinners, and

Sterno. Another is *isopropanol,* commonly known as rubbing alcohol or isopropyl alcohol, comprised of three carbons. It is a common ingredient in perfumes and aftershave, for example.

Most commonly these types of alcohols are consumed if ethanol is unavailable, often with severe consequences. Due to their different chemical makeup, these other alcohols cause big problems if taken into the body. The difficulty lies in the differences in rates of metabolism and the kinds of by-products formed. For example, it takes nine times longer for methanol to be eliminated than it does ethanol. Although methanol itself is not especially toxic, when the liver enzyme ADH acts on it, formaldehyde instead of acetaldehyde is formed. Formaldehyde causes tissue damage, especially in the eyes. The formaldehyde is then broken down into formic acid, which is also not as innocent as the acetic acid produced by ethanol metabolism and can cause severe states of acidosis. Ingestion of methyl alcohol can lead to blindness and can be fatal; it requires prompt and vigorous medical attention. In addition to administration of ethanol, treatment may include renal dialysis.

The treatment of acute methanol poisoning is one of a handful of situations in clinical medicine where ethanol has a legitimate and important therapeutic role. Administering ethanol to a methanol-poisoned patient slows the rate of methanol metabolism, which results in a reduction of the levels of toxic by-products formed. Why? Because ethanol successfully competes with methanol for the limited amount of the liver enzyme ADH, which is required for the metabolism of either variety of alcohol. Rapidly administering ethyl alcohol, while at the same time treating acidosis and correcting the body's acid-base imbalance, may ameliorate or even entirely eliminate serious complications. The U.S. Food and Drug Administration has approved a new drug to treat poisoning from ethylene glycol, also known as glycol alcohol, a major constituent of antifreeze. This drug, called Fomepizole, inhibits alcohol dehydrogenase, thereby slowing the ethylene glycol's metabolism.

Poisonings from non-beverage alcohols don't happen only to those alcohol-dependent persons who in desperation will drink anything. Several years ago there was an Italian wine scandal in which table wines were laced with methanol, resulting in more than 100 deaths. A far more common accident involves the toddler who gets into the medicine cabinet or the teenager or adult who doesn't know that all alcohols are not the same chemically and that some may have very dangerous effects.

THE INFLUENCE OF EXPECTATIONS

The focus in this chapter has been on the pharmacological properties of alcohol. The physical changes described, especially alcohol's effects on the CNS, are directly tied to the amount of alcohol consumed and the rapidity with which it is ingested. Pharmacologists refer to these phenomena as dose- and rate-related effects. However, the human psyche also enters into the equation. Although one's beliefs, wishes, or attitudes cannot negate alcohol's actions, they can have an impact. A person's expectations influence the experience of drinking and how a drinking episode is interpreted. There is increasing literature on this phenomenon. Some of these studies involve research situations in which people think they are getting alcohol when, in fact, the drink they consume has none. The explanation for this interaction between pharmacological effects and beliefs is that beliefs are likely to influence what in your surroundings you notice and tune in to when drinking. Thus the person who expects that drinking makes people more aggressive is likely to see others as "asking" for a fight, whereas the person who thinks that drinking enhances sexuality may be attuned to "invitations" for intimacy.

Quickly, bring me a beaker of wine, so that I may wet my mind and say something clever.
—ARISTOPHANES

ADVICE FOR THE MODERATE DRINKER

Although this section offers suggestions to "the moderate drinker," it's worth mentioning that the term is falling out of favor. A report on alcohol, commissioned by the European Union, addressed "ill-defined terms not recommended for use"; the list includes "social drinking," "moderate drinking," "sensible drinking," and "responsible drinking." Indeed there are probably as many definitions for these terms as there are drinkers. That's not the only objection. Such terms have moralistic overtones not appropriate in discussion of health issues. The World Health Organization, in its directory of alcohol-related terms, points out that such terms suggest that all drinking is one of two types; it is either "OK" or "not OK." The language used ought to better characterize the reality, that drinking can have varying levels of risk. Accordingly, the WHO suggests that "hazardous use" replace "excessive use." It is also suggested that "lower-risk use" become the phrase to characterize the drinking style attributed to social or moderate drinkers.

Medical Declarations on the Alcohol Question. The third and final English medical declaration written in 1871. *"As it is believed that the inconsiderate prescription of large quantities of alcoholic liquids by medical men for their patients has given rise in many instances to the formation of intemperate habits, the undersigned are of the opinion that no medical practitioner should prescribe it without a sense of grave responsibility. They believe that alcohol, in whatever form, should be prescribed with as much care as any powerful drug. The directions for its use should be so framed as not to be interpreted as a sanction for use to excess, or necessarily for the continuance of its use when the occasion is past."*

—WALTER W. SPOONER

The Cyclopaedia of Temperance and Prohibition, 1891

Medically, "moderate use" denotes a pattern of regular use of no more than one to two drinks per day for men or one for women. Drinking at this level has been shown to have beneficial preventive effects in relation to a number of medical illnesses. These include coronary artery disease and ischemic heart disease; stroke; the development of gallstones and associated gallbladder disease; Type II diabetes; chronic bronchitis; certain types of lymphoma; hypercholesterolemia; and benign prostatic hypertrophy. Accompanying this is the fact that light to moderate drinkers have lower mortality than others in their age group who are either teetotalers or heavy drinkers.

In considering these reported benefits of regular moderate alcohol use, it is important to emphasize the significance of the operative word, "moderate." There are some other caveats. For one, this doesn't mean an average of one to two drinks and thus saving up several days' quota for a blowout on a Saturday night. Equally important, this beneficial effect is not universal, either. While it probably comes as no great surprise that excessive use of alcohol over a long period can lead to serious problems, what is unfortunately less recognized and appreciated is that, even in moderate amounts, alcohol use can present substantial medical risks for some individuals. There is no set "dose" of alcohol that reliably can be considered safe for people in general or even for any single individual throughout his or her life.

Contraindications to Moderate Use

For some people, in some circumstances, at particular times, what is usually considered moderate alcohol use is too much. The most striking example is the caution against alcohol use during pregnancy. It is becoming more widely appreciated that drinking during pregnancy can cause abnormalities in the infant, a condition called *fetal alcohol syndrome* (FAS), or a less severe condition termed *fetal alcohol effects* (FAE). Sometimes these conditions in combination are termed *fetal alcohol spectrum disorder* (FASD). A woman wishing to conceive should be thoughtful about her drinking. Since many pregnancies are not confirmed until the middle of the first trimester, she might ingest harmful levels of alcohol before being aware of her pregnancy. There are other possible adverse consequences of alcohol use during pregnancy. Moderate alcohol use has been linked to an increase in spontaneous abortions. Drinking as little as one drink per day, for a total of 1 ounce of alcohol per day, doubles the risk of spontaneous abortion during the second trimester. Nursing mothers, too, are advised to refrain from alcohol use because alcohol can pass to the infant through breast milk. Though maternal alcohol use while nursing does not appear to affect mental development, infants whose mothers consumed one or more drinks per day have been found to have slower rates of motor development.

I don't use drugs, my dreams are frightening enough.
—M. C. ESCHER

Even relatively modest alcohol use can create problems for those with cardiac and circulatory problems, such as coronary artery disease and/or congestive heart failure, as well as hypertension. High blood pressure in up to 10% of all cases is believed to be the direct result of alcohol use. For those with established hypertension, alcohol use can make the management and adequate control of blood pressure more difficult. It may also increase the risk for stroke. Moderate drinking also has been found to elevate the level of certain blood fats in individuals with Type IV hyperlipoproteinemia.

Others for whom moderate drinking may be unwise include individuals with seizure disorders, diabetes mellitus, gout, osteoporosis, and various skin conditions, including psoriasis, as well as those with gastric and duodenal ulcers. The ways in which alcohol may aggravate these conditions are discussed in Chapter 6. Although none of these medical conditions may constitute an absolute contraindication to using alcohol, all fall into the category of relative contraindications. A glass of wine with meals once or twice a week may present no problem, but several drinks before dinner plus wine with the meal or an evening on the town is ill advised. As a general rule, anyone being treated for an acute medical condition ought to inquire about the need to modify temporarily what may be very moderate drinking. In addition to the possibility of alcohol's complicating medical conditions, there is the possibility of its interacting with the medications prescribed to treat them.

When will I learn? The answer to life's problems aren't at the bottom of a bottle, they're on TV!
—Matt Groening
The Simpsons

Alcohol-Drug Interactions

Alcohol-drug interactions may be the area in which the moderate drinker is potentially most vulnerable to medical problems arising from alcohol use. Alcohol is a drug. When alcohol is taken in combination with many prescribed medications or over-the-counter drugs or alternative/herbal preparations, there can be undesirable and quite possibly dangerous alcohol-drug interactions.

The Basis of Alcohol-Drug Interactions

Though these interactions can vary from individual to individual, they depend primarily on the amount of alcohol and type of medication consumed, as well as the person's drinking history. The moderate drinker who has not developed tolerance to alcohol will have a very different response from that of the habitual heavier drinker. In fact, the consequences may be far more serious. Two basic mechanisms discussed below explain virtually all alcohol-drug interactions.

Liver's Role in Metabolism One such factor is that the presence of alcohol alters the liver's capacity to metabolize other drugs. Recall that the cytochrome P450 system metabolizes a variety of other drugs as well as alcohol. Commonly it may be significantly inhibited, or slowed down, in the presence of alcohol. Therefore, drugs ordinarily metabolized by the liver's cytochrome P450 system will not be removed as rapidly or as completely as usual. The result is that these medications will then be present in the body in higher than expected levels. This can result in unexpected toxic effects.

On the other hand, for those with a long history of heavy drinking, alcohol has the opposite effect on the cytochrome P450 system. The activation of this system is enhanced, or speeded up, through a process known as enzyme induction. Thus certain drugs are removed, or metabolized, more quickly. The medication is removed more rapidly, so its levels in the body are lower than expected or desired. The net effect is that the individual is very likely not receiving the intended therapeutic effects of a given dose of a medication. To compensate for this, it may be necessary to increase the dose of the drug administered to achieve the intended therapeutic effect.

Nature of Drug Effects The other major source of difficulty results from so-called *additive* as well as *synergistic* effects. Alcohol is a CNS depressant. Other medications may also depress CNS functions. When two depressant drugs are present simultaneously, their combined effects may be equal to or often far greater than would be expected with the sum of the two. It is important to be aware that drugs and alcohol are not metabolized instantaneously. Recall that it takes the body approximately one hour to handle 1 drink (whether the drink is a 12-ounce bottle of beer or a mixed drink with a shot of 80-proof liquor). Therefore, if someone has had several drinks, an hour or two later alcohol will still be in the system. As long as alcohol remains in the body, the potential exists for significant additive effects, even though the other depressant drugs are taken several hours later, or vice versa.

Common Interactions of Medications and Alco[illegible]

Many of the potential interactions of alcohol wit[illegible]nonly prescribed medications are outlined in the appen[illegible] the table in the appendix is not all-inclusive. If a drug is [illegible]'t assume that it has no interaction with alcohol. Anyone [illegible]cohol and is taking other medications is advised to ask [illegible]ysician or pharmacist specifically about potential alcoho[illegible]ug-drug interactions.

Problems Associated with Drinking and Intoxication

Accidents and Injury

Along with alcohol-drug interactions, the other common medical problems associated with alcohol use are accidents and injuries. These are more likely to occur during an intoxicated state because of the nature of alcohol-induced impairment. Judgment is impaired, placing individuals in situations that invite danger. Diminished judgment, along with decreased reaction and response time and poorer coordination and motor skills, leads to a lessened ability to cope with whatever may occur. In addition to injuries being more common with intoxication, their severity has also been found to rise with the level of impairment. Similarly, other

Potato Alcohol vs. Standard Oil

While the German government is doing all in its power to encourage prospectors for petroleum—of which not a barrel is produced within the Empire—in order that the monopoly of the Standard Oil Company . . . may be checked, there is quietly coming into markets of the empire, a substitute for oil, which, by the best informed and most disinterested is looked upon as the source of the final solution of the oil problem and the means by which the grasp of the great monopoly will be broken. The output of the new substance is capable of almost limitless expansion, its sources of supply, as infallible as time, and the product itself will be most difficult if not impossible to monopolize, since every farmer may, in a sense, dig it, from his own soil. It is called potato alcohol, or more commonly, spirit.

—T. BYARD COLLINS

Potato alcohol vs Standard Oil, *New York Times*, June 18, 1905

Note: In the United States, among the prohibitionists, there too was considerable interest in promoting ethanol for fuel. It was seen as providing the liquor industry with an alternative outlet for its product.

psychoactive substances that affect judgment and motor skills can be contributing factors in alcohol-related accidents.

HIV/AIDS

In the minds of the general public as well as health care and substance abuse professionals, AIDS is clearly linked with those who use drugs intravenously, a group for whom AIDS is becoming virtually endemic. The dramatic rise of AIDS among intravenous drug users is not based primarily on the pharmacological properties of the drugs but, rather, on the route of administration. Among intravenous drug users, HIV infection is readily transmitted by the common and dangerous practice of sharing needles. Given the multiple problems that accompany chronic drug use, those who are actively using drugs are difficult to influence by informational and preventive efforts.

This is the great fault of wine; it first trips up the feet: it is a cunning wrestler.
—Titus Maccius Plautus

Within the rapidly growing body of research on AIDS, the relationship of alcohol use and AIDS has also been examined. The ability of chronic alcohol use to suppress the immune system has been clearly established. Even the effects of acute use among those who generally drink moderately have become evident. Pilot experiments with healthy volunteers suggest that a single administration of alcohol equivalent to 0.7 to 3.1 liters of beer (two to eight 12-ounce cans) can have a negative impact on the immune system. Furthermore, these effects may persist for up to four days after ingestion. The question this raises is whether casual alcohol consumption can either increase the vulnerability to infection or enhance the progression of latent HIV infection. On behavioral grounds alone, there is a link between intoxication and an increased risk of HIV infection. With intoxication, sexual activity is likely to be more casual and less considered, with sexual partners determined by their availability rather than the presence of an emotional relationship, and is less likely to involve contraception or safe-sex practices to reduce the risk of sexually transmitted diseases, including HIV infection.

Sexual Assault

The role of alcohol and other drugs in sexual assault and date rape is receiving increasing attention. Despite some media accounts to the contrary, *the* drug most commonly involved is alcohol. The risk of sexual assault or coerced sex increases along with a woman's BAC on the particular occasion. Another study, again of college students, surveyed women and men. During the last three months, the following were attributed to drinking, by women and men: unprotected sex (11% and 15%); sex they were not happy with at the time (6% and 7%); sex later regretted (16% and 19%). In addition, 34% of women and 25% of men reported unwanted sexual advances in the past four weeks as a result of other people's drinking.

Unexpected and Sudden Natural Deaths

The association between intoxication and unnatural causes of death, such as accident, suicide, and homicide, is described in Chapter 2. Equally as significant is the finding of the high prevalence of positive BACs among people who have died suddenly and unexpectedly from natural causes. This finding is based on the determination of the blood alcohol concentration as part of medico-legal autopsies conducted for all natural out-of-hospital deaths occurring during a one-year period in a large Finnish metropolitan area. For this group of sudden and unexpected deaths, 36% of males and 15% of females had positive blood alcohol levels. The blood alcohol concentration for approximately half of these men and women was 0.15 or greater. Acute consumption of alcohol in people not dependent on alcohol was certified as being a significant contributor in 23% of male and 8% of female sudden, unexpected deaths. For men, acute alcohol use was a contributing factor for 11% of deaths from coronary artery disease, 40% of other heart disease, and 7% for all other diseases. For both sexes the most vulnerable individuals are those in middle age.

Alcohol Use and Exercise

With the increasing interest in fitness and exercise, what are the recommendations for drinking in relation to sports and exercise? Alcohol can affect performance and be the source of potential problems if used immediately before, during, or immediately after exercise. Athletes who release pregame tension with a "few beers" before competition to take care of the jitters may slow reaction time and impair coordination, thus reducing their performance and increasing the risk of injury. Before competition, endurance athletes sometimes "carbohydrate load"—that is, eat extra carbohydrates to increase the glycogen stored in muscles, which serves as a source of energy. They may include beer as part of their precompetition meal. However, beer is a poor source of carbohydrates compared to juices or soda. As for calories, two-thirds of the calories in beer come from the alcohol. Thus they represent "empty calories" with little nutritional value and therefore are a poor energy source. These calories are used to generate heat and are not available for energy. Besides being a poor source of nutritionally useful carbohydrates, the alcohol can affect heat tolerance and lead to dehydration because of alcohol's inhibition of antidiuretic hormone. Athletes who consume alcohol before a performance are at risk for significant fluid loss. Cardiac arrhythmias, including atrial fibrillation (described in Chapter 6), have been reported in otherwise healthy athletes following consumption of unusually large amounts of alcohol. Hence, the recommendation of sports physicians is not to consume alcohol for 24 hours before competition.

DRUG-ALCOHOL COMPARISONS

A number of factors account for a drug's effects, whether it's sold in a liquor store, convenience store, a drugstore, or on a street corner, whether commercially produced or harvested from a plot in the woods. Several of the most important are described here.

Route of Administration

The route of administration—how a drug is introduced into the body—has significance. Consider prescribed medications. They may be taken *orally*. Often there are further instructions, such as "Take with 8 ounces of water" or "Take on an empty stomach" or "Take with meals." Some pills have coatings and others are gel capsules because the medication has to navigate the digestive system. Some medications may be administered via *inhalers*—for example, asthma or allergy medications. Also drugs may be *injected*. Here as well there are variations—just under the skin or into a large muscle (usually the arm or the buttock) or intravenously. Finally, drugs can be *absorbed through the skin* via patches, as in some pain medications or the nicotine patch. Unlike alcohol, which is taken by mouth, other drugs may have multiple routes of administration.

Great people talk about ideas, average people talk about things, and small people talk about wine.
—Fran Lebowitz

Why It Matters

With prescription drugs, the particular route of administration is selected to assure that drugs are delivered efficiently and effectively. The particular formulation is selected so that a drug is not removed from the body before it can do its job and so that a drug is delivered at the proper rate.

Drugs of abuse do *not* come with a product insert describing how to take the drug. Nonetheless the same issues of *efficiency* and *effectiveness* are operative. Consider marijuana. When marijuana is smoked in a joint, approximately 30% of the active ingredient that provides the desired effect, the THC[3], is destroyed by the heat involved with smoking. In addition, another 20 to 40% is lost in sidestream smoke, the amount released in the smoke between puffs. So this route of administration might be considered very inefficient. In total, 50 to 70% of the active ingredient never reaches the user.

I don't know. I never smoked AstroTurf.
—Tug McGraw
BASEBALL PLAYER, 1974
When asked if he preferred grass or artificial turf

For drugs of abuse, the target organ from the user's perspective is the brain. The bloodstream is the body's transportation system for delivering the drug to the brain. The most efficient delivery system is the

[3]Sixty-one substances found only in marijuana are called cannabinoids. One of these cannabinoids accounts for virtually all of marijuana's effects; it is delta-9-tetrahydrocannabinol. The abbreviation is THC.

one that gets the drug into the bloodstream the most rapidly. Drugs that are inhaled or smoked enter the bloodstream through the lungs; forget the slow journey through the stomach and small intestine as is required with alcohol. If you compare drugs that are inhaled or snorted to alcohol, it's like cruising along on the interstate compared to wending your way along some rural, scenic route. The most efficient route, intravenous administration, places the drug directly into the bloodstream. That is like sailing down the interstate in a Porsche.

How rapidly a drug reaches the brain determines not only when the effects begin to occur, but also how the effects are experienced. With injected drugs, the time to reach the brain can be measured in seconds. With alcohol, it's a matter of minutes. With injection, the entire dose is available at once. There is no way to get all of the alcohol from a drink in one fell swoop. A "rush" is how the effects of heroin are described. Wham. It's a feeling of intense pleasure. Even if people were to chug a drink, clearly not recommended, its effects are never described in the terms used for heroin or opiates taken intravenously.

Pharmaceuticals: A Special Case Frequently, the route of administration associated with prescription drug abuse is different from what the manufacturer intended when formulating the drug for medical use. A good example is OxyContin, a pain medication. It is prescribed for chronic, severe pain. Its active ingredient is oxycodone, the basis of other pain medications, such as Percodan. OxyContin differs from these other pain medications in one significant respect. It is formulated in a time-release form. So patients only need to take it twice a day instead of as many as six times per day. Therefore, a single tablet is equivalent to several doses of these other pain drugs. (OxyContin may have 2 to 30 times as much oxycodone as the amount found in a Percocet.) When used as a drug of abuse, it is first crushed and then ingested, sometimes orally, but more commonly it is snorted or diluted in water and injected. Crushing disarms the time-release actions. The full amount of the drug is immediately available. The result is a rush similar to that associated with heroin, rather than a slow, steady, less dramatic effect.

Potential Problems

The route of administration has significance in terms of the kinds of problems that can result from use. For some substances, the dangers that come from the route of administration are greater than the effects of the drug itself. Nicotine is a prime example. Many long-term health problems are tied to *smoking,* not to nicotine. Injection, while very efficient, presents significant problems, such as the risks of infection that accompany nonsterile techniques. The common practice of sharing needles is also very dangerous as it is a very efficient way of transferring bloodborne viruses, such as HIV/AIDS and hepatitis B and C.

By-Products of Metabolism

We have already seen how alcohol is broken down and removed from the body. Alcohol is first broken down into acetaldehyde, which, although toxic, is rapidly broken down into acetic acid. Acetic acid is essentially diluted vinegar. These by-products are rather tame and don't have any mood-altering properties. For some drugs this is not the case. When heroin is metabolized, it is first transformed into morphine, itself an opiate. Morphine might be thought of as heroin-lite, a far cry from vinegar.

Recall that the danger from drinking non-beverage alcohols is due to the toxicity of substances formed when they are metabolized. In addition, problems can arise if the by-products formed by a drug interact with other drugs that may be simultaneously present. Alcohol and cocaine is such a case.[4] In the presence of alcohol, in addition to the two usual by-products formed when cocaine is broken down, a third by-product is produced. This by-product, very similar to cocaine, is called coca-ethylene. It remains in circulation and needs to be metabolized by the same enzymes involved in metabolizing the cocaine itself. By analogy, cocaine's transformation into coca-ethylene is a bit like the person who is recycling at home, throwing a portion of stuff gathered up back into the recycling bin, which means only having to re-handle it later. This by-product makes drinking while taking cocaine more attractive but also problem-ridden. Coca-ethylene, while having properties very similar to cocaine, in fact may be more toxic to the heart and liver.

In considering the interaction of alcohol and cocaine, at least two physiological factors are at play. In the presence of alcohol, cocaine levels increase by as much as 30%. Presumably this is because both alcohol and cocaine are competing for a finite supply of some of the enzymes required for metabolism. (If the cocaine is taken a half-hour after drinking, there is no such effect.) Second, alcohol does not merely delay the metabolism of cocaine, it alters the process. In the presence of alcohol, approximately 20% of the cocaine—rather than being metabolized into inert products that are removed from the body—is diverted and transformed into coca-ethylene.

The high associated with coca-ethylene is indistinguishable from a pure cocaine high. However, it is metabolized more slowly than cocaine, so it remains in the body longer. The pleasurable effects associated with cocaine persist, due to the continuing presence of coca-ethylene, even

[4]**Metabolism of cocaine.** In the absence of alcohol, cocaine is broken down into two major products. Two versions of the enzyme carboxyl esterase accomplish this. One of the metabolic products is benzoylecgonine, and the other is ecgonine methyl ester. These in turn are excreted by the kidneys. The enzymes involved in this process are not exclusively devoted to the metabolism of cocaine. Rather they are involved in the metabolism of a family of compounds known as esters—found in the heart, stomach, kidney, and colon—but most abundantly in the liver. These enzymes are involved in the metabolism of an array of esters; they can be considered as providing the body protection by assisting in the elimination of a number of substances taken in through the diet or other routes.

after the cocaine itself has been eliminated. In a laboratory setting, there is increased "liking" reported for cocaine when combined with alcohol, even when the actual level of cocaine in the blood is the same. People also report that when alcohol is present, coming down from a cocaine high is less uncomfortable. In tandem with this, people say they feel less impaired than they feel with an equivalent blood alcohol but without cocaine in the body.

Cocaine and alcohol interact in other ways. Independently each raises heart rate and blood pressure. Together there is even a greater rise. However, coca-ethylene has an even greater effect on heart rate. It has been estimated that over half a million people annually are evaluated in hospital emergency rooms for possible heart attacks in the wake of cocaine use. The risk of sudden death is up to 20 times greater for those using alcohol and cocaine than if the person is using alcohol alone.

Actions in the Brain

The preceding discussion considers how drugs get to the brain. What happens then? What accounts for the different effects among drugs? A number of things come into play. To oversimplify, much of it comes down to the ways in which drugs affect the neurotransmitters, as described earlier in discussing alcohol's effects.

Neurotransmitters—The Body's E-mail

In this discussion, think of neurotransmitters as being the body's version of e-mail. There has to be a cell that sends the e-mail, and another cell with an "in-box" to receive it (receptor). Generally, the in-boxes are quite specialized. Each accepts only one type of e-mail. Say, one in-box is dedicated to e-mail from Mom. In that case, if the e-mail doesn't have "From: Mom" in the header, it's ignored. Typically receptor cells are similarly specialized, responding to a particular neurotransmitter. Drugs too can alter the flow of e-mail. They can act as a spam filter and not allow the usual messages through. No messages from Mom make it to the in-box. Or there may be instances when a drug causes the cells to put out far more e-mails than the in-box can handle. So the messages from Mom are just hanging around.

How is education supposed to make me feel smarter? Besides, every time I learn something new, it pushes some old stuff out of my brain. Remember when I took that home winemaking course, and I forgot how to drive?

—MATT GROENING

The Simpsons

The effects of drugs of abuse have an uncanny resemblance to those associated with naturally occurring neurotransmitters. Actually, that is backward! Without a doubt, the substances we use and think of as "drugs" got that status for the very reason that their effects *do* so closely parallel those of the natural neurotransmitters.

Site of Action

Drug effects on specific neurotransmitter system(s) include action on the levels of the neurotransmitters themselves, as well as the receptor sites, where the neurotransmitters have their effects. There are certain kinds of predictable ways that substances of abuse can affect neurotransmitter systems. The drugs may prevent a neurotransmitter from breaking down, leading to a buildup of the neurotransmitter. Alternatively, it can prevent amounts of a neurotransmitter secreted into the space between nerve cells from being reabsorbed (which normally occurs), resulting in more of the neurotransmitter being available. Also, taking a drug can lower the production of a particular neurotransmitter, thus leading to a lower than normal level of that transmitter. Or the drug may block the site where the neurotransmitter acts and thus prevent it from having its usual effects despite the normal amount being present. The impact of either a buildup or shortage depends on the function of that neurotransmitter. (Given that the body is always trying to maintain a balance, over the longer term, if drug use continues, the nerve cells will make adjustments caused by the effects of drugs.) In some cases, drugs will not only affect the chemical signaling system overseen by neurotransmitters but will also have a generalized effect on the nerve cells, acting as a toxin, or making them simply more sluggish.

Interestingly, there are no special alcohol receptors, but alcohol affects a variety of neurotransmitters. Compared to other drugs, alcohol is a very small molecule. This means it can readily pass through cell walls. Recall, it is water soluble and is distributed to all cells of the body, in proportion to the amount of water present. In this sense in part it doesn't have to send a message; it just "shows up," entering cells and having its effect.

Distribution of Neurotransmitters

Beyond the fact that drugs affect neurotransmitters, of equal importance is the site in the brain where the various neurotransmitters are located. Two parts of the brain are of particular significance. One is the brainstem, which controls the basic body functions. Whether particular neurotransmitters affected by a drug are or are not present in the brainstem explains the potential life-threatening effects of a drug.

Compare alcohol or heroin with marijuana. Unlike alcohol or heroin, there are no known deaths resulting from marijuana use. Marijuana alters perception and judgment and thus may be implicated in a driving fatality. However, there is no marijuana blood level that is lethal. Essentially this is because the brainstem does not contain neurotransmitters that are affected by marijuana in any significant way. To borrow a line from a book titled *Everything You Wanted to Know About Drugs but Were Afraid to Ask Your Children*—"The lethal dose of cannabis is a 2 kilo block dropped on your head from the 25th floor of a high-rise building."

Another section of the brain is referred to either as the "pleasure center" or the "reward center." The function of this part of the brain is virtually self-explanatory. The closely connected segments of brain that comprise the pleasure center let us know when something is enjoyable, through the release of neurotransmitters associated with experiences of pleasure. Equally important, the process is set up to increase the likelihood of repeating the behavior that evokes pleasure. This is accomplished by alerting other parts of the brain to pay attention to what is going on so that it is easier to perform the same act again. This has survival value. Encouraging us to eat or to have sex are always the first examples given. But these centers are also associated with listening to music or seeing a dramatic sunset or whatever it is that causes us to laugh or to smile. And guess what? Neurotransmitters affected by drugs of abuse are very plentiful and active in the pleasure center of the brain.

Neurotransmitters Associated with Substance Use

In addition to the neurotransmitters noted above, others are also closely linked to substance use. The major ones and their functions include

- GABA: inhibitory, slows communication, reduces anxiety
- Norepinephrine: activating; enhances communication
- Dopamine: associated with feelings of pleasure and attentional processes
- Serotonin: associated with anxiety, depression, impulsivity, aggression, and suicidal behavior
- Glutamate: the major excitatory neurotransmitter
- Endorphins: pleasure, feeling of well-being

Solubility in Fat or Water

Drugs differ in whether they are soluble in water or fat or both water and fat. Recall how the gender differences in the body's relative proportions of water and fat affects blood alcohol concentrations. All else being equal, being of the same weight, with equivalent doses of alcohol, women—who have proportionately more body fat and less muscle mass and tissue water than males—have a higher blood alcohol level.

Whether a drug is fat or water soluble determines how it is distributed in the body, plus where and how long it is stored. For most people, the most practical significance of this is its implications for drug testing. Many a college health service has gotten a call from a student who has a job interview scheduled, which may include a drug test, who was just wondering . . . Drugs that are fat soluble leave long-lasting traces in tissues in a way that alcohol does not. Thus detectable amounts of a drug may be present in blood samples due to their slow release from fat stores, long after the last intake of the drug. One can also test hair samples and fingernails to identify prior use of a drug.

For alcohol, once the blood alcohol drops to zero, there is no similar continuing evidence of recent use. (There are some biological tests that can measure changes that were likely caused by recent drinking.) The active ingredient in marijuana, on the other hand, is very fat soluble and is released slowly from fat. It may therefore be present in urine drug screens of somewhat regular users for weeks after the last use.

Setting the Stage for Dependence

There are changes in the brain that result from alcohol and other drug use that have long-term consequences. It is presumed that these changes in part constitute the biological basis of craving that is a hallmark of dependence, as well as the continuing use of alcohol or drugs despite a host of negative consequences. These are not changes that only occur with long periods of drinking or other drug use. Indeed, these changes also explain social drinking—the drink taken to relax or the drink taken to celebrate.

Let's draw upon what may seem like an odd analogy. Suppose you have an iPhone. And suppose you have an app that alerts you to things that you are likely to enjoy. In many ways this app functions in the same way that some websites alert you to a book you may want to buy or music you might want to download. These alerts are based on your past behavior, by what you've ordered on sites you've visited in the past. So this iPhone things-you-enjoy-app knows your preferences. Who knows how—by scanning e-mail or by keeping track of text messages, online purchases, or things on your calendar. Based on this information, it automatically informs you that such and such a group is performing down at the Dirt Cowboy, or the movie down at the mall stars Johnny Depp, or there is a sale at the boutique of those shirts you adore, . . . or they have a two for one special at the bar you love. This app is wonderful; it keeps you posted on things you like to do.

NATIONAL LIQUOR ASSOCIATION
We are giving away a new SmartPhone APP That whispers "have a drink" whenever it passes a Bar or a liquor Store.

However, there's one significant quirk. You can't ever remove the app. It's there forever. Get a new phone, and the app comes with it. In fact, if you do try to disable it, it doesn't turn off. Instead, it goes into a default emergency mode. Feeling a bit down, and not wanting to do anything? The app is there to help out. Working in emergency mode, rather than providing you with an array of choices, it limits itself to the things that *really* make you feel good, the things that are fail-proof. Suppose one of the things is alcohol or drugs? The app points out how close you are to the liquor store, or reminds you that there is a Happy Hour tonight beginning in 46 minutes, or draws your thoughts to a page on Facebook with the posting of photos from last weekend's party, or reminds you if you stop by your folks' house you could raid the medicine cabinet, and on and on.

Something very similar occurs with alcohol and drugs. In thinking about their effects on the brain's chemical messengers, the neurotransmitters, it is easy to focus on those that induce feelings of pleasure, that evoke that nice "high." However, there are other neurotransmitters that are involved in an equally important, if seemingly more mundane, task. These are the chemical messengers that signal other portions of the brain—"Pay attention." "Keep track of what is going on." This is essential if a pleasurable activity is to be repeated.

An important question being raised is the significance, if any, of an individual's age when alcohol or other drug use begins. It is known, for example, that an adolescent brain is not fully mature. It is also recognized that those who begin drinking at an earlier age are at increased risk of alcohol dependence in later life. The question is whether this early substance use has a disproportionate impact down the road.

IN CONCLUSION

Any substance taken into the body may have significant effects. All too often we have discovered these effects to be more harmful than we had previously thought. Chemical additives, fertilizers, pesticides, antibiotics given to livestock destined for the table, or chemicals such as BPA and phthalates found in plastics. If only as much attention were paid to alcohol and other drug use as is paid to other products, health would be significantly improved. Many of the devastating yet largely avoidable problems our society encounters as a result of substance use—including accidents, traffic fatalities, domestic violence, suicide, and homicides—may be lessened if uninformed and ill-considered use is replaced by greater knowledge about the effects of the drugs we use, and in particular the legal drug we drink and the legal drug we smoke.

REFERENCES AND FURTHER READINGS

Abramson S, Singh AK. Treatment of the alcohol intoxications: Ethylene glycol, methanol and isopropanol (review). *Current Opinion in Nephrology and Hypertension* 9(6):695–701, 2000. (32 refs.)

Anderson P, Baumberg B. *Alcohol in Europe. A Public Health Perspective.* London: Institute of Alcohol Studies, June 2006.

Brick J, Erickson CK. Intoxication is not always visible: An unrecognized prevention challenge (review). *Alcoholism: Clinical and Experimental Research* 33(9):1489–1507, 2009. (97 refs.)

Bullers S, Ennis M. Effects of blood-alcohol concentration (BAC) feedback on BAC estimates over time. *Journal of Alcohol and Drug Education* 50(2):66–87, 2006. (24 refs.)

Center for Behavioral Health Statistics and Quality, Substance Abuse and Mental Health Services Administration. *The NSDUH Report: State Estimates of Drunk and Drugged Driving (May 31, 2012).* Rockville, MD: Substance Abuse and Mental Health Services Administration, 2012. (9 refs.)

Chamberlain E, Solomon R. The case for a 0.05% criminal law blood alcohol concentration limit for driving (review). *Injury Prevention* 8(Supplement 3):1–17, 2003. (109 refs.)

Chikritzhs TN, Jonas HA, Stockwell TR, Heale PF, Dietze PM. Mortality and life-years lost due to alcohol: A comparison of acute and chronic causes. *Medical Journal of Australia* 174(6):281–284, 2001. (15 refs.)

Correa CL, Oga S. Effects of the menstrual cycle of white women on ethanol toxicokinetics. *Journal of Studies on Alcohol* 65(2):227–231, 2004. (19 refs.)

Eaton DL. Scientific judgment and toxic torts: A primer in toxicology for judges and lawyers. *Journal of Law and Policy* 12:5–42, 2003. (50 refs.)

Editor. Papers on absorption, distribution, and elimination of alcohol in non-alcoholics. *Alcoholism: Clinical and Experimental Research* 24(4):244–257, 2000.

Filmore MT, Blackburn J, Harrison ELR. Acute disinhibiting effects of alcohol as a factor in risky driving behavior. *Drug and Alcohol Dependence* 95(1/2):97–106, 2008. (52 refs.)

Frezza M, diPadova C, Pozzato G, Terpin M, Baraona E, Lieber CS. High blood alcohol levels in women: The role of decreased gastric alcohol dehydrogenase activity and first-pass metabolism. *New England Journal of Medicine* 322(2):95–99, 1990. (31 refs.)

Gibbons B. Alcohol: The legal drug. *National Geographic* 181(Feb):2–35, 1992.

Gutjahr E, Gmel G, Rehm J. Relation between average alcohol consumption and disease: An overview (review). *European Addiction Research* 7(3):117–127, 2001. (161 refs.)

Harris DS, Everhart ET, Mendelson J, Jones RT. The pharmacology of cocaethylene in humans following cocaine and ethanol administration. *Drug and Alcohol Dependence* 72(2):169–182, 2003. (41 refs.)

Hawton K, van Heeringen K. Suicide. *Lancet* 373(9672): 1372–1381, 2009. (141 refs.)

Kerr WC, Greenfield TK, Midanik LT. How many drinks does it take you to feel drunk? Trends and predictors for subjective drunkenness. *Addiction* 101(10):1428–1437, 2006. (31 refs.)

Krautt JA, Kurtztt I. Toxic alcohol ingestions: Clinical features, diagnosis, and management (review). *Clinical Journal of the American Society of Nephrology* 3(1):208–225, 2008. (129 refs.)

Lieber CS. The discovery of the microsomal ethanol oxidizing system and its physiologic and pathologic role (review). *Drug Metabolism Reviews* 36(3/4):511–529, 2004. (117 refs.)

Lovinger DM. Communication networks in the brain neurons, receptors, neurotransmitters, and alcohol (review). *Alcohol Research & Health* 31(3):196–214, 2008. (141 refs.)

Parlesak A, Billinger MHU, Bode C, Bode C. Gastric alcohol dehydrogenase activity in man: Influence of gender, age, alcohol consumption and smoking in a Caucasian population. *Alcohol and Alcoholism* 37(4):388–393, 2002. (32 refs.)

Pennings EJM, Leccese AP, de Wolf FA. Effects of concurrent use of alcohol and cocaine (review). *Addiction* 97(7):773–783, 2002. (81 refs.)

Quertemont E, Didone V. Role of acetaldehyde in mediating the pharmacological and behavioral effects of alcohol. *Alcohol Research & Health* 29(4):258–265, 2006,

Standridge JB, Zylstra RG, Adams SM. Alcohol consumption: An overview of benefits and risk (review). *Southern Medical Journal* 97(7):664–672, 2004. (73 refs.)

Tanaka E. Toxicological interactions involving psychiatric drugs and alcohol: An update. *Journal of Clinical Pharmacy and Therapeutics* 28(2):81–95, 2003. (133 refs.)

Verster JC. The alcohol hangover: A puzzling phenomenon (review). *Alcohol and Alcoholism* 43(2):124–126, 2008. (17 refs.)

White AM. What happened? Alcohol, memory blackouts, and the brain. *Alcohol Research & Health* 27(2):186–196, 2003. (80 refs.)

Whitfield JB. Acute reactions to alcohol (review). *Addiction Biology* 2(4):377–386, 1997. (70 refs.)

CHAPTER 4

Alcohol Use Disorders

DEFINITIONS

AND WHAT GIVES YOU THE RIGHT TO CALL ME AN ALCOHOLIC?

Thanks be to God, since my leaving drinking of wine, I do find myself much better, and do my business better, and do spend less money, and less time in idle company.
—SAMUEL PEPYS
Diary, January 2, 1662

The social problems associated with alcohol use were described in Chapter 2. Even if there were no such phenomena as alcohol use disorders, beverage alcohol would lead to social disruption and considerable social costs—a fact society now recognizes. For too long the statistics on dented fenders caused by impaired drivers, the dollars lost by industry, or even the percentage of alcohol-related hospital admissions were ignored. Seen merely as the product of many people's single, uninformed encounters with alcohol, they were dismissed as the cost a drinking culture has to pay.

Attitudes, however, have changed dramatically. Today, those who choose to drink are recognized as potentially endangering others as well as themselves. Drinkers are not seen as having a right to get drunk, unwind, or get hammered indiscriminately. Drinkers are not given amnesty for things that happen when they are intoxicated. These individual decisions can have an impact on public safety and public life; in recognition of this, attitudes about what constitutes acceptable and unacceptable drinking have changed. Increasingly, intoxicated behavior is not overlooked or tolerated. Direct expressions of disapproval are more common. The one seeming exception is college students and binge drinking. Yet even there, the days of *Animal House* are gone. Being a college student does not confer immunity from the larger society's expectations and laws.

There are, however, those whose drinking behavior will not be touched by admonitions to drink responsibly. There are those whose behavior will not be altered by public service announcements that urge friends to select a designated driver. There are those whose behavior will not respond to friends' suggestions to "take it easy" or friends' expressions of disapproval. The special problem that besets these 18.2 million individuals is that, for them, alcohol is no longer the servant, but the master. The chances are quite good that people we know or have known fall into this category. There are also the estimated 72 million family members who live directly in the shadow of someone's alcohol disorder.

What constitutes an alcohol use disorder? This question confronts substance abuse clinicians daily. A physician may request assistance in determining whether an alcohol problem exists. A client or a spouse may challenge a diagnosis: "Why, she can't be an alcoholic because . . ." Even in nonworking hours the question crops up during conversation with good friends or casual acquaintances. Before considering definitions that have been set forth, consider the word "alcoholic," which is the term most commonly used by the general public. The word itself provides some clues. The suffix *-ic* has a special meaning. According to *Merriam-Webster's Collegiate Dictionary:*[1]

> -ic n suffix: One having the character or nature of; one belonging to or associated with; one exhibiting or affected by

Attaching *-ic* to alcohol forms a word to denote the person linked with alcohol. That's a start. Clearly, not all drinkers are linked with alcohol, just as not all baseball players are linked with the Boston Red Sox. Why the link, or association? The basis is probably frequency of alcohol use, pattern of use, quantity used, or frequency of indications that the person has been drinking. "Belonging to" has several connotations, including "an individual being possessed by or under the control of." The Chinese have a saying: "The man takes a drink, the drink takes a drink, and then the drink takes the man." This final step closely approximates what the word "alcohol-ic" means. In a few words this proverb captures the essence of a serious alcohol use disorder.

It is worth noting that the discussion or debate on who has, or what constitutes, a serious alcohol use disorder is relatively recent. This doesn't mean that society had not previously noticed those in trouble with alcohol. But whatever debate there was, it centered on the purported cause, as well as ways of handling these individuals. Essentially two basic approaches prevailed. One view held that "obviously" these individuals were morally inferior: after all, the vast majority of people who drank did so moderately without presenting problems for themselves or their communities. The other view held that "obviously" such individuals were possessed: would people in their right minds drink like that of their own volition?

[1]From *Merriam-Webster's Collegiate® Dictionary, 11th Edition* © 2010 by Merriam-Webster, Incorporated <www.Merriam-Webster.com>. Used by permission.

With increasing scientific study and understanding of the "drink taking the man" phenomenon, the task of definition became more complicated. It became clear that some people are distinctly different from those able to drink moderately. Also it became evident that individuals with a serious alcohol use disorder are not all alike. Not all develop DTs (delirium tremens) when they stop drinking. There are big differences in the quantity of alcohol consumed and the number of years of drinking before family problems arise. Many chronic heavy drinkers develop cirrhosis, but more do not. Given the range of differences among those with alcohol dependence, what is the basic core, the shared characteristics? An answer to this question is fundamental to any attempt to define the condition.

Drunkenness is nothing but voluntary madness.
—SENECA

Early Definitions of Alcoholism

It was during the middle of the twentieth century that the view of alcoholism as a disease or medical condition gradually took hold. And viewing alcoholism as a disease required defining it. What follows is a cross section of the early definitions:

- *1940s, Alcoholics Anonymous (AA).* AA has never had an official definition. The concept of Dr. William Silkworth, one of AA's early friends, is still cited by AA members: "an obsession of the mind and an allergy of the body. The obsession or compulsion guarantees that the sufferer will drink against his own will and interest. The allergy guarantees that the sufferer will either die or go insane." Another operative definition frequently heard among AA members is "an alcoholic is a person who cannot predict with accuracy what will happen when he takes a drink."
- *1946, E. M. Jellinek, a pioneer in modern alcohol studies.* "Alcoholism is any use of alcoholic beverages that causes any damage to the individual or to society or both."
- *1950, World Health Organization (WHO).* The WHO's Alcoholism Subcommittee defined alcoholism as "any form of drinking which in extent goes beyond the tradition and customary 'dietary' use, or the ordinary compliance with the social drinking customs of the community concerned, irrespective of etiological factors leading to such behavior, and irrespective also of the extent to which such etiological factors are dependent upon heredity, constitution, or acquired physiopathological and metabolic influences."
- *1968, American Psychiatric Association, Committee on Nomenclature and Statistics.* "Alcoholism: this category is for patients whose alcohol intake is great enough to damage their physical health, or their personal or social functioning, or when it has become a prerequisite to normal functioning." Three subtypes of alcoholism were further identified: episodic excessive drinking, habitual excessive drinking, and alcohol addiction.

- *1977, American Medical Association (AMA).* From the *Manual on Alcoholism,* edited by the AMA Panel on Alcoholism: "Alcoholism is an illness characterized by significant impairment that is directly associated with persistent and excessive use of alcohol. Impairment may involve physiological, psychological, or social dysfunction."

One swallow doesn't make a summer but too many swallows make a fall.
–G. D. PRENTICE

In examining these early definitions, we find that each, although not necessarily conflicting with the others, tends to have a particular focus. Some are purely descriptive. Others attempt to speak to the origins of the condition. Several concentrate on the unfortunate consequences associated with alcohol use. Others zero in on hallmark signs or symptoms, especially loss of control or frequency of intoxication.

Add to these expert definitions all of the definitions that have been used casually by each of us and our neighbors. These have varied from "alcoholism is an illness" to "it's the number one drug problem" to "when someone's hammered all the time" to "when someone drinks in the morning." Note that, generally, laypeople have had far more permissive criteria and have adopted definitions that would exclude themselves and most people they know as candidates for the condition.

Toward Uniformity in Terminology

Actions taken by the World Health Organization in 1977 and the American Psychiatric Association (APA) two years later were important in clarifying and promoting greater consensus as to the definition of alcoholism. The WHO prepares and publishes the *International Classification of Diseases,* known as the *ICD.* It provides a comprehensive list of all injuries, diseases, and disorders and is used worldwide. The APA publishes a manual restricted to psychiatric disorders, known as the *Diagnostic and Statistical Manual (DSM).* The changes by the WHO and the APA introduced greater consistency across the various drug classes. Ironically, for the sake of clarification, both groups abandoned use of the term "alcoholism."

Neither group disputed the existence of the condition; however, for medical and scientific purposes, both the WHO and the APA substituted "alcohol dependence syndrome" for what had been discussed as alcoholism. This was done because of the multiple definitions abounding in the professional community. Equally, this change was prompted by the general public's widespread everyday use of "alcoholic" and the variants that were being coined, such as "work-aholic." When the same term is shared, but used differently, by laypeople and the medical community, confusion is likely. So, paradoxically, it was, in part, the very success in educating the public about alcoholism as a disease that necessitated the change in terminology. Although there was agreement about dropping the word "alcoholism," there wasn't consensus about the term to replace it. "Addiction" was one suggestion, but was rejected because it had negative connotations—hence, the term "dependence." The APA adopted "alcohol abuse" for other alcohol use problems; the WHO selected the term "harmful use."

Standardizing Terminology

When it comes to clinical interactions with colleagues and other professionals, the day is past when each clinician has the luxury of defining a condition according to individual biases and preferences. In the United States, the APA's *Diagnostic and Statistical Manual* provides the approved terminology for psychiatric illness. The 1980 version of the *Diagnostic and Statistical Manual,* the third edition *(DSM-III)*, was noteworthy in several respects. It was the first to distinguish between two separate alcohol-related syndromes: alcohol abuse and alcohol dependence. Both conditions entail impairment in social and occupational functioning. The essential distinguishing feature of dependence was the presence of tolerance and withdrawal. There is always room to quibble with definitions, and that operational definition did have its critics. The major criticism was that physical dependence was required to make the diagnosis of dependence. This is never a black-and-white situation. Some drinkers may not show marked physical dependence although their lives are in utter chaos because of alcohol use. Though the definition was not perfect, even a flawed definition was preferable to having none.

An alcoholic is someone you don't like who drinks as much as you do.
—DYLAN THOMAS

With the inclusion of alcohol dependence in both the APA and the WHO manuals, and alcohol abuse and harmful use in the APA and the WHO manuals, it seemed that the experts had spoken and that further discussion of definitions wasn't really necessary. However, the topic was rekindled in the 1990s, during efforts to enact national health care reform. The discussions focused on what would and would not be covered by health insurance. It was in this context, in 1993, that the American Society of Addiction Medicine (ASAM), a professional association of physician specialists in the substance abuse field, issued a policy statement defining alcoholism:

> Alcoholism is a *primary,* chronic *disease* with genetic, psychological and environmental factors influencing its development and manifestations. The disease is often *progressive* and *fatal.* It is characterized by continuous or periodic *impaired control* over drinking, preoccupation with the drug alcohol, use of alcohol despite adverse consequences, and distortions in thinking, most notably *denial.*

The statement then proceeded to define each of the words in italics. Interestingly, ASAM makes an explicit statement about the meaning of the word "disease." It emphasized that a disease represents an "involuntary disability."

Although alcohol dependence then became the approved term according to the American Psychiatric Association and the World Health Organization, that doesn't mean the term "alcoholism" has been wholly banished. Several journals in the substance use field continue to use "alcoholism" in their titles. Alcoholism continues to be used in articles in medical and academic journals. And yes, "alcoholism" is the word used by the federal agency dealing with alcohol use and alcohol problems, the National Institute on Alcohol Abuse and Alcoholism.

disease *(dĭˇz-ez) [Eng. dis-priv. + ease]. 1. morbus, illness, sickness; an interruption; cessation; or disordering of body functions, systems, or organs. 2. A pathological entity characterized usually by at least two of these criteria: a recognized etiologic agent(s), an identifiable group of signs and symptoms, or consistent anatomical alterations. See also syndrome.*

syndrome *(sĭˇn'drom) [G. syn, together, + dromas, a running]. The aggregate of signs and symptoms associated with any morbid process and constituting together the picture of the disease.*

sign *(sin) [L. signum, mark]. 1. Any abnormality indicative of disease, discoverable by examination; an objective symptom of disease. 2. In psychology, any object or artifact that represents a specific thing or conveys a specific idea to the person who perceives it.*

(Note: What the clinician can observe.)

symptom *(sĭˇmp'tom) [G. symptoma]. Any morbid phenomenon or departure from the normal in function, appearance or sensation which is experienced by the patient and indicative of disease. See also, sign.*

(Note: What the patient reports.)

Webster's New World/Stedman's Concise Medical Dictionary. New York: Prentice Hall, 1997

A DISEASE?

Anyone who is sufficiently interested in alcohol problems to have read this far is probably accustomed to hearing alcoholism referred to as an illness, a disease, or a medical condition. This has not always been the case. The work of E. M. Jellinek, often called a father of alcohol studies, was largely responsible for the shift from a defect to an illness model. Through his research and writings, Jellinek in essence said that alcoholism had been mislabeled.

Implications of Disease Classification

Whether alcoholism is or is not a disease is, to use researchers' terminology, *not* an empirical question. No test or experiment can be conducted to prove or disprove that alcoholism is an illness. But, clearly, how we label something is very important. It provides clues about how to feel and think, what to expect, and how to act. For instance, whether a particular bulb is tagged as a tulip or garlic will make a big difference. Depending on which you think it is, you'll either plant and water or chop and sauté. Very different behaviors are associated with each. An error may lead to strangely flavored spaghetti sauce and a less colorful flower bed next spring.

For both laypeople and professionals, the recognition that alcohol disorders properly belong in the category of illness has had a dramatic impact. Society generally bestows sympathy on sick people. We accept the notion that sick people do not choose to be sick. We agree to provide care to restore health. During a period of illness, we don't expect people to fill their usual roles or meet their responsibilities. We give them a special designation—that of patient. Furthermore, we don't criticize sick people for manifesting the symptoms of their illness. To demand that a person with the flu stop running a fever would be pointless and unkind. As alcoholism has come to be perceived as an illness, society has come to see that much of the bizarre, associated behavior is not willful but symptomatic. We see these individuals as requiring care.

Although Jellinek's efforts may have triggered this shift, a number of other events added impetus. The National Council on Alcoholism put its efforts into lobbying and public education. The American Medical Association and American Hospital Association published various committee reports. State agencies created treatment programs.

Medical societies and other professional associations assumed responsibility for their members' education and addressed the ethical responsibility to treat alcohol problems. It is suspected that the single biggest push came from recovering alcoholics, especially through the work of AA. Virtually everyone today has personal knowledge of an apparently hopeless alcoholic who stopped drinking and now seems a new, different person.

The formulation of alcoholism as an illness opened up possibilities for treatment that were formerly nonexistent. It brought into the helping arena the resources of medicine, nursing, social work, psychology, and other professions that before had no mandate to be involved. Viewing alcoholism as a disease was important in reducing the stigma associated with the condition. In turn, this improved the likelihood that individuals and families would seek help rather than be encumbered by shame or burdened by a sense of hopelessness, trying to keep the condition a family secret. Finally, the resources of the federal government were focused on alcohol problems as a major public health issue, and treatment and educational programs were created.

Criticisms of the Disease Concept

The disease concept of alcoholism has had its critics. There was a period, several decades ago, when "Is alcoholism a disease?" was sure to stir debate. Interestingly it was psychiatry that was among the first to express discomfort with considering alcoholism a "disease." In the view of psychiatry, alcoholism was a "symptom"; it was evidence of an underlying neurosis. Accordingly, the goal was to involve the patient in psychoanalysis to deal with the "real" problem, the neurosis. If successful, then the symptom, the compulsive drinking, would go away.

In addition, there were those who considered alcoholism to represent an absence of willpower, or a disregard for society's rules and expectations. For those folks, to term alcoholism a disease was to let people off the hook.

The controversy has by and large faded away. Two authors, Herbert Fingarette and Stanton Peele, who discounted the disease concept, were long the major remaining voices in a debate that has largely disappeared.

Peele, in his writings, raised an interesting question, whether the disease concept of alcoholism was simply part of a larger social phenomenon, which he described as "the diseasing of America." He questioned whether as a society we too readily accept the notion of disease (or victimhood) to account for an expanding array of behaviors. This argument does have some merit. Peele pointed to the proliferation of "recovery literature," according to which everyone is seemingly a victim of some sort, and the burgeoning discussions of "co-dependency,"

"adult children of fill in the blank," and "dysfunctional families." In addition, "traditional" addiction terminology has been applied to other compulsive or excessive behaviors. Thus, one hears of workaholism, food addiction, shopping addiction, exercise addiction, sexual addiction, and, computer or internet addiction.[2] These questions warrant reflection. However, one can think about them and quite possibly come to different conclusions in respect to alcohol and other drug use problems.

As noted, the debate has faded away. When alcohol or other drug dependence is now discussed as a disease or medical condition, it is almost always characterized as a *chronic disease*. One hallmark of a chronic illness is that treatment requires the active participation of the patient. With any chronic condition the key word is not "cure" but "management." The management of chronic disease commonly involves six elements: (1) treatment of acute flare-ups; (2) emotional support; (3) education to enable the individual to actively participate in care; (4) rehabilitative measures to prompt the life changes necessary to live with the limitations imposed by the illness; (5) family involvement; and (6) regular monitoring. (See Chapter 9 for further discussion of the nature of chronic disease and its implications for treatment.)

☐ NATURAL HISTORY

The "natural history" of an illness refers to the typical progression of signs and symptoms as the disease unfolds in the absence of treatment. Jellinek was one of the first to speak of alcoholism as a disease and to describe its progression. Thus, he was seeing the condition in a new light and considering it from a perspective that was quite different from the views that then prevailed. It has been suggested that drawing upon a scientific and medical framework, and the supposed neutral perspective that is part of science, was a way of moving past the wet-dry controversy that had long framed thinking about alcohol and alcohol problems.

Jellinek's Phases of Alcoholism

How did Jellinek arrive at his disease formulation of alcoholism? A trained biostatistician, he was understandably fascinated by statistics—the pictures they portray and the questions they raise. Much of his work was descriptive, defining the turf of alcoholism: who, when, where. One of his first studies, published in 1952, charted the signs and symptoms associated with alcoholism. This work was based on a survey of more than 2,000 members of AA. Although differences certainly existed

[2]Although beyond the scope of this discussion, there is ongoing research into the biological basis of the "behavioral" addictions, those that do not involve use of alcohol or other drugs.

among individuals, to him it was the similarities that were striking. He saw a pattern in the appearance of the symptoms, and he saw a progression of the condition in terms of increasing dysfunction. The symptoms and signs tended to cluster together. On the basis of these observations, Jellinek developed the idea of four phases in the emergence of alcoholism: prealcoholic, prodromal, crucial, and chronic. Although many in the field may not be aware of their origins, these phases have been widely used in alcohol treatment as a part of patient education: the four phases are portrayed graphically on the following page.

Prealcoholic

In Jellinek's formulation, during the *prealcoholic phase,* the individual's use of alcohol is socially motivated. However, the prospective alcoholic soon experiences psychological relief in the drinking situation. Possibly his or her tensions are greater than other people's, or possibly the individual has no other way of handling tensions that arise. It does not matter. Either way, the individual learns to seek out occasions where drinking will occur—at some point connecting drinking with psychological relief. Drinking then becomes the individual's standard means of handling stress, although the drinking behavior will not look different to an outsider. This phase can extend from several months to two or more years. An increase in tolerance gradually develops.

Prodromal

Suddenly there is the emergence of the *prodromal phase.* "Prodromal" means "warning or signaling disease." According to Jellinek, the behavior that heralds the change is the occurrence of "alcoholic palimpsests," or blackouts.[3] Blackouts are amnesia-like periods that occur while drinking. The drinker seems to be functioning normally but later has no memory of what happened. Other behaviors emerge during this phase that testify to alcohol's no longer being just a beverage, but a "need." Among the warning signs Jellinek noted were sneaking extra drinks before or during parties, gulping the first drink or two, and feeling guilt about the drinking behavior. At this point, consumption is heavy but not necessarily conspicuous. To look "OK" requires conscious effort by the drinker. Jellinek thought this period could last from six months to four or five years, depending on the drinker's circumstances.

Crucial

The third phase is the *crucial phase.* The key symptom that ushers in this phase is loss of control. Taking a drink sets up a chain reaction. The drinker can no longer control the amount consumed after the first drink, yet the drinker can control whether or not to take that first drink. So it is possible to stop drinking for a time. With loss of control, the drinking is now clearly different. It requires explanation, so rationalizations begin. Simultaneously, the individual adopts strategies to regain control. The thinking can go as follows: "If I just _______, then it will be OK." Tactics commonly adopted are deliberate periods of abstinence, changes in drinking patterns, or geographical changes to escape/avoid/be relieved of stress;

[3]This is a description of Jellinek's work. A discussion of blackouts and the more recent findings about them appears in Chapter 6.

Signs of Developing Alcoholism
derived from E. M. Jellinek

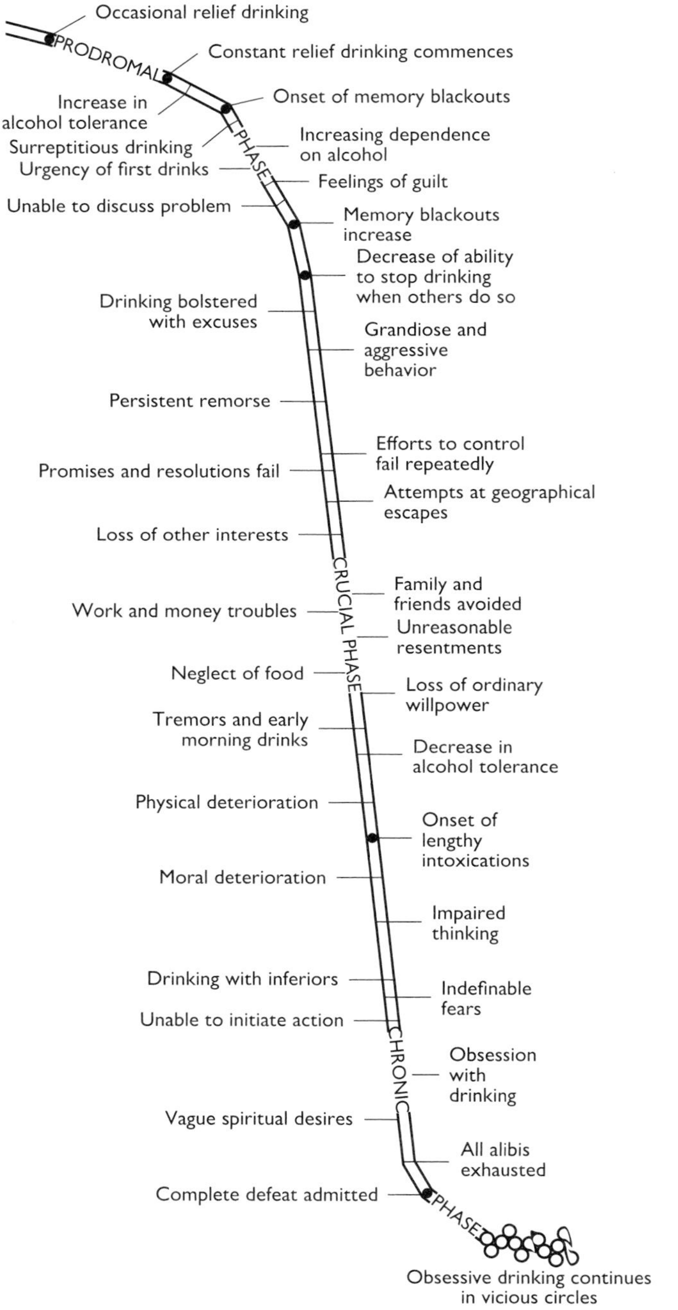

From: Jellinek EM. Phases of alcohol addiction. *Quarterly Journal of Studies on Alcohol* 13:673–684, 1952.

Note: This diagram has been popularized through a handout, often called the "Valley Chart," that is widely used by treatment programs. In these handouts, a corresponding upward slope depicts the process of recovery. This recovery arm is *not* based on Jellinek's work, but was added in 1952 by Marcus Glatt, an English alcohol researcher.

similarly, job changes occur. All these attempts were thought doomed to fail. The individual responds to these failures by being alternately resentful, remorseful, and aggressive. Life becomes alcohol centered. Family life and friendships deteriorate. The first alcohol-related hospitalization is likely to occur. Morning drinking may begin to creep in, foreshadowing the next phase.

He is a drunkard who takes more than three glasses though he be not drunk.
—EPICTETUS

The final phase in the process is the *chronic phase.* In the preceding crucial phase, drinkers may have been somewhat successful in maintaining a job and their social footing. Now, as drinking begins earlier in the day, intoxication is an almost daily, daylong phenomenon. "Benders" are more frequent. The individual may also go to dives and drink with persons outside the normal peer group. Not unexpectedly, at this stage the person finds him- or herself on the fringes of society. When ethanol is unavailable, poisonous substitutes become a possible alternative.

Can you spare $1.29 for a cup of coffee?
Chronic

During the chronic phase, marked physical changes occur. Tolerance for alcohol drops sharply; the individual becomes stuporous after a few drinks. Tremors develop. Many simple tasks are impossible in the sober state. The individual is beset by indefinable fears. Finally, the rationalization system fails. The long-used excuses are revealed as just that—excuses—and the individual is seen as spontaneously open to treatment. Often, however, drinking is likely to continue, because the alcohol-dependent person can imagine no way out of his or her circumstances. Jellinek did emphasize that individuals need not reach the chronic phase before successful treatment can occur.

Natural History of Alcoholism

In 1983 George Vaillant published *The Natural History of Alcoholism.* In effect it was an update of Jellinek's work. This book set forth the results of several studies that have been invaluable in confirming and, in many instances, amplifying our understanding of alcoholism as a disease. Vaillant's work was based on two groups of men who at that point had been followed for approximately 50 years, from their adolescence into their 60s. (He inherited an ongoing research effort.) The major goal of the research had been to study adult development through the life cycle. There was an interesting side benefit for the alcohol field. Not unexpectedly, during the course of the study, members from both groups developed alcohol problems. Thus for the first time it became possible to begin to separate "the chicken from the egg." The question could be asked, "What are the factors that distinguish those who develop alcohol dependence from those who do not?"

A HARVARD ALCOHOLIC

A CORE CITY ALCOHOLIC

One group in the study, the college sample, was officially described as "students from an Eastern university." In fact, it was composed of Harvard undergraduates from the classes of 1942 to 1944. The other group, referred to as "the core city sample," was composed of

I only drink to make other people seem more interesting.
—George Jean Nathan

adolescents from high-crime, inner-city neighborhoods. They were initially selected to participate in the study when they were about 14 years old, primarily because they were not known to be seriously delinquent. At the beginning of these studies, members of both groups were extensively interviewed. A variety of psychological tests were administered, detailed family histories were obtained, and measures of the subjects' personal functioning were made. At regular intervals these men were re-contacted to collect detailed information on the progress of their lives.

In brief, Vaillant determined that those who developed alcohol dependence were *not* more likely to have had impoverished childhoods or to have had preexisting personality or psychological problems. Therefore, it was his conclusion that such problems, which are often cited as evidence of an "alcoholic personality," do not predate the emergence of the disease. On the contrary, they are the symptoms or consequences of alcohol dependence. As for predictors of alcoholism, the significant determinants were found to be having a family history of alcoholism and having been raised in a culture with a high rate of alcoholism.

Several other findings are worth noting. Vaillant compared the various diagnostic classifications, or diagnostic approaches. He discovered a high overlap between those people diagnosed as alcohol dependent (using *DSM-III* criteria) and those identified as "problem drinkers" with a high "problem index"—then a sociological classification system. Also he recognized that by the time an individual had experienced four or more negative consequences as a result of drinking, it was almost assured that a formal diagnosis of alcohol dependence could be made. The specific negative consequences seemed to be of little importance. Virtually no one had had four or more alcohol-related problems through mere "bad luck."

Also, as dependence progressed over time, the number of problems tended to increase and the overall life situation—psychological adjustment, economic functioning, social and family relationships—deteriorated. Vaillant observed that studies that point to the contrary usually report on persons who have been in treatment and contacted later on a single occassion. He speculated that these studies have not followed the individuals for a sufficient length of time. Dependence has a downward course, but during the slide there will be both ups and downs. Presumably, people who enter treatment facilities do so at a low point. Therefore, at follow-up, even if they continue to be actively drinking, it should not be surprising to find their situation somewhat improved. However, if follow-ups were conducted at several points, over a long enough period, the full ravages of untreated alcohol dependence would become apparent. As Vaillant notes, paraphrasing an AA saying, "Alcoholism is baffling, cunning, powerful, . . . and patient."

Vaillant concluded that there is indeed a progression in alcoholism. However, there is not the orderliness in symptoms' emergence that

Jellinek had described. As a result of the progression, there are only two likely outcomes. The men in the study either died or recovered through abstinence. The proportion who either returned to nonproblematic drinking or whose alcoholism stabilized was very small. Again, over time this small middle ground continued to shrink.

Types of Alcoholism

Were the same research that underpins Jellinek's formulation conducted today, people would be quick to point out a number of limitations. For example, all of those studied were members of AA. This would raise the immediate question of whether they were representative of all those dependent on alcohol. Indeed, Jellinek himself asked that question.

Jellinek's Species of Alcoholism

Jellinek continued his study of alcohol, focusing on how alcohol problems appear in other countries. He found differences that could not be accounted for simply by the phases of alcohol dependence. They seemed to be differences of kind, rather than simply the degree of dependence. As a result, he expanded his classification system to include species, meaning categories, of alcoholism. He proposed five different categories and named each of these with a Greek letter. *Alpha Alcoholism* was seen as a purely psychological dependence, without loss of control or an inability to abstain. Jellinek noted that others might call this species "problem drinking." *Beta Alcoholism* involved physical problems, such as cirrhosis or gastritis, but neither psychological nor physical dependence. Jellinek thought this species was possibly most common in societies where widespread heavy drinking was coupled with an inadequate diet. *Gamma Alcoholism,* which was considered the most prominent type in the United States, is the variety depicted in the chart on page 94. *Delta Alcoholism* was seen as similar to the Gamma, but with one important difference. Although it is characterized by psychological and physical dependence, there is no loss of control. Therefore, on any occasion the drinker can control the amount consumed. The individual, however, cannot stop drinking for even a day without suffering withdrawal. The last variety Jellinek described was *Epsilon Alcoholism,* which he dubbed *periodic alcoholism,* marked by bouts of heavy drinking interspersed with sober periods, and which he considered significantly different from the other types.

In *The Disease Concept of Alcoholism,* Jellinek concluded that perhaps not all of these species can be considered a disease. He speculated that Alpha and Epsilon varieties might be symptoms of other disorders. By more adequately classifying and categorizing the phenomenon of alcoholism, he brought a scientific approach to a field that had been dominated by beliefs. That was no modest contribution.

A Caution

When faced with a construct such as Jellinek's phases, outlining a sequence of behaviors based "on research," it is natural to consider it established fact, the definitive explanation. The instinct is to discount the possibility or likelihood of variation. This is an error. Such presentations are better considered as a model, or framework. Jellinek's phases at best provide a tool for organizing our thinking, not rules for how people either "will" or "ought to" act. Inevitably, there will be variation. It's a bit like setting forth the progression of a cross-country trip from New York to California. Several things are certain. There will be an ocean at the point of departure and at the conclusion of the trip. At some point you will cross the Mississippi River. There will be sections of flat terrain; there will be sections with large mountains. However, you don't have to take Interstate 80 for it to qualify as a cross-country journey.

Current Thinking

A considerable portion of the research now being undertaken addresses questions that concerned Jellinek. As noted earlier, although there are common features in alcohol dependence, there are differences too. For this reason, alcohol dependence is sometimes described as a *heterogeneous disease*. These differences need to be explained and may represent factors that have important implications for treatment, prevention, or early diagnosis. By way of comparison, consider that there are different types of pneumonia and different types of diabetes. Distinguishing among them is necessary to determine appropriate treatment; in the case of pneumonia, the type dictates the class of antibiotic that will be prescribed.

Over the past few decades there have been efforts to identify different types of alcohol dependence, in effect updating Jellinek's species. Several subtypes of alcohol dependence have been proposed. Among the features used in creating typologies are age of onset, personality traits (such as the presence or absence of impulsiveness), the presence or absence of major psychiatric illness, the presence or absence of antisocial personality disorder and criminality, as well as a positive or negative family history of alcohol dependence. The most serious symptoms and earliest onset tend to be seen in those with the following features: positive family history, history of antisocial personality disorder, and personality traits that include impulsivity and risk taking.

An important reason for identifying types of alcohol dependence is the possibility that different types might respond differently to different treatments. Identifying different types is a necessary part of exploring treatment matching. *Project MATCH*, discussed in Chapter 10, was a large national multisite clinical research effort sponsored by the NIAAA to take on this challenge. One of the early research efforts explored the impact of medication in addition to the usual psychosocial treatments on two subtypes of alcohol dependence, referred to as *Type A* and *Type B*. The results showed that those with Type A alcohol dependence (which is distinguished by later onset, fewer childhood risk factors, fewer alcohol-related problems, less severe dependence, and less psychiatric illness) had better outcomes when treated by serotonergic drug therapy than when treated with a placebo. However, this pharmacological treatment had no such benefit for Type B dependence.

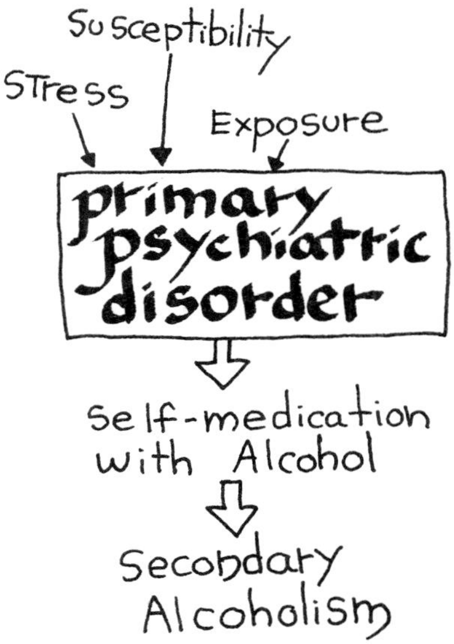

Another set of distinctions sometimes made is between *primary alcoholism* and *secondary, reactive, alcoholism*. The secondary type is seen as alcohol dependence that grows out of or is superimposed on a psychiatric illness or major psychological problem. This is not to imply that researchers think this alcohol problem need not be treated in its own right. However, it does mean that, in such cases, the individual requires treatment for the condition(s) that spawned or facilitated the development of dependence in addition to active treatment for alcohol dependence.

GUIDES FOR DIAGNOSIS

National Council on Alcoholism Criteria

Once the perspective of alcoholism as a disease had been introduced, the next major task was to establish guidelines for diagnosis. The first step was taken in the 1970s, with the publication of a paper titled "Criteria for the Diagnosis of Alcoholism." It was prepared by a committee of the National Council on Alcoholism (NCA) and published in two major medical journals. The goal was to provide guidelines for use by physicians in diagnosing the condition. The committee compiled a comprehensive list of signs and symptoms of alcohol dependence that could be ascertained through physical examination, medical history, social history, laboratory tests, and clinical observations. These were then arranged in a rather complicated scheme, with some items being given more weight than others.

Sometimes too much drink is barely enough.
—MARK TWAIN

There were many similarities between these criteria and the symptoms of alcohol dependence developed by Jellinek 20 years earlier. However, Jellinek's formulation was not a useful tool for physicians or other clinicians. Jellinek's list was based on the self-reports of recovering persons, so the symptoms were from their point of view. A good number of the symptoms involved efforts to deceive and attempts to appear normal. When a patient withholds information, or provides an edited version, the physician is seriously handicapped.

Wine is a turncoat; first a friend and then an enemy.
—HENRY FIELDING

In addition to the diagnostic criteria listed, the committee discussed the nature of the condition and commented on its treatment. Alcoholism was characterized as a chronic, progressive disease. It was noted

that, although the condition is incurable, it is highly treatable. Because it is a chronic disease, the diagnosis once made never can be dropped. Therefore, an individual successfully involved in a treatment program would have his or her diagnosis amended to "alcoholism: arrested" or "alcoholism: in remission." Criteria were provided to determine when this change in diagnosis is appropriate.

The NCA criteria never had a significant impact on medicine as a whole and were known primarily to those in the substance abuse field. However, they clearly influenced the thinking of the American Psychiatric Association (APA) and served as a model for the changes adopted by the APA in the following decade.

Diagnostic Criteria of the American Psychiatric Association

DSM-III Criteria

Although definitely on the right track, the NCA criteria were cumbersome. The publication in 1980 of the APA's *Diagnostic and Statistical Manual of Mental Disorders, Third Edition*, known as the *DSM-III,* was a significant step forward, a milestone not only for alcohol dependence but for other psychiatric conditions as well. It represented a major departure from previous diagnostic schemes in several ways. For one, this edition set forth very specific diagnostic criteria, explicitly specifying what signs and symptoms must be present to make a diagnosis for a particular condition. The goal was to make the diagnosis of psychiatric conditions more uniform. Diagnosis was no longer based on what the clinician thought was the underlying reason for the condition—for example, whether it was a psychological maladjustment or a physiological abnormality.

In addition, *DSM-III* involved a reorganization, as well as a renaming of major groups of psychiatric illnesses. For the first time *substance use disorders,* which includes alcohol dependence and alcohol abuse, became a separate major diagnostic category. Previously these conditions had been assigned to the category of personality disorders. This earlier assignment had reflected the common notion that substance abuse is the result of psychological problems. With the creation of the new category, the *DSM-III* no longer implied any particular etiology.

The APA's diagnostic manual and its counterpart, *International Classification of Diseases (ICD)*, are routinely updated and revised to reflect new knowledge. In response to clinicians' concerns and clinical research, in subsequent editions some modifications were made in the way alcohol dependence was defined.

DSM-IV Criteria

Revision of the APA's diagnostic manual is a complex process. It entails convening study groups of experts who not only review the literature but also conduct pilot tests to determine the impact of any changes being considered. During development of the *Fourth Edition,* several issues were of particular importance to those preparing the section on substance use. The group felt it was important to devise a single set of criteria that would be applicable to all psychoactive substances. For example, evidence of withdrawal might be a common feature of dependence, even though the symptoms would depend on the particular substance. Another area of concern was the relationship of any proposed criteria to the World Health Organization's classification system, *ICD-10.* Indeed, pilot research showed that there was a high degree of overlap between the two classification systems. If a person is diagnosed as alcohol dependent by one system, odds are that he or she will be diagnosed as dependent by the other.

One of the biggest issues with which the task force struggled while drafting the *DSM-IV*'s section on substance-related disorders was whether to keep or drop the category of abuse. There were those who questioned whether abuse is a separate condition or whether it is really just "early" dependence. Some of the same criteria, such as "use despite negative social consequences," were being used to diagnose both conditions, introducing confusion. In making diagnoses, the idea is to find the features that distinguish between illnesses, not the features that are common among them. Here research findings were able to offer some guidance. A follow-up study had been conducted of individuals who were diagnosed with alcohol abuse four years previously. The results showed that alcohol abuse did not inevitably blossom into dependence. That was true in only 30% of those reexamined. For the remaining 70%, either their problems remitted or a pattern of abuse continued without escalating. Thus the natural history of alcohol abuse was seen to differ from that of alcohol dependence. The task force decided to retain abuse as a category distinct from dependence. The counterpart to abuse in the *ICD-10* schema is "harmful use."

DSM-5 Criteria

The newest set of diagnostic criteria, the *DSM-5* was published in early summer 2013. This was the first revision of the *Manual* in 20 years. Although the discussion here is on *alcohol* use disorders, it is but one in the larger category of substance use disorders. The *DSM-5* made important changes for all substance use disorders.

Changes Introduced The *DSM-5* views substance use disorders as falling along a spectrum, with different levels of severity. Three levels of severity are specified—mild, moderate, or severe—depending on the number of positive symptoms. A total of 11 symptoms are identified as criteria for making a diagnosis. (See Box 4.1.) The diagnosis is determined simply by the number of symptoms that were present in a 12-month period. The diagnosis does not require the presence of any

BOX 4.1 *DSM-5* Diagnostic Criteria

Alcohol use disorder is a problematic pattern of alcohol use leading to significant impairment or distress, as evidenced by two of the following symptoms occurring within a 12-month period:

1. Alcohol is often taken in larger amounts or over a longer period than was intended.
2. There is a persistent desire or unsuccessful efforts to cut down or control alcohol use.
3. A great deal of time is spent in activities necessary to obtain alcohol, use alcohol, or recover from its effects.
4. Craving, or a strong desire or urge to use alcohol.
5. Recurrent alcohol use resulting in a failure to fulfill major role obligations at work, school, or home.
6. Continued alcohol use despite having persistent or recurrent social or interpersonal problems caused or exacerbated by alcohol's effects.
7. Important social, occupational, or recreational activities are given up or reduced because of alcohol use.
8. Recurrent alcohol use in situations in which it is physically hazardous.
9. Alcohol use is continued even when it is known that physical or psychological problems are caused by or aggravated by continued use.
10. Tolerance, as defined by either (a) need for markedly increased amounts of alcohol to achieve intoxication or desired effect; or (b) markedly diminished effect with continued use of the same amount of alcohol.
11. Withdrawal, as evidenced by either the characteristic withdrawal syndrome for alcohol; or the use of alcohol (or a closely related substance, such as a benzodiazepine) to relieve or avoid withdrawal symptoms.

particular symptoms. Alcohol Use Disorder (Mild) is defined as the presences of 2 or 3 symptoms in a 12-month period, Alcohol Use Disorder (Moderate), by the presence of 4 or 5, and Alcohol Use Disorder (Severe), by the presence of 6 or more. There are no longer the diagnostic categories of abuse or dependence.

I really don't need alcohol. I'd just rather have a glass of sherry than a tranquilizer.

The *DSM-5* criteria for a substance use disorder incorporate all but one of the symptoms used in the earlier diagnostic criteria for abuse and dependence. One new criterion was added. The item which was dropped was "recurring legal problems." Certainly, it seems as if it "should" be a clear marker of a substance use problem. Interestingly, it is not. A number of studies have found that legal problems are actually rare among those with a substance use disorder. This is true whatever the substance. For cannabis (marijuana) disorders, it was 3%; for alcohol, 6%, for heroin and other opiates, 8%; and cocaine, 12%. To include a symptom that is so uncommon isn't particularly useful. It was also recognized that legal problems include a high degree of chance. That alone makes it a questionable "symptom" of a medical condition. The presence of craving is the symptom that was added as a new criterion. While certainly reported by many people, there were some who questioned whether it was needed. The feeling was that it didn't really add further information because there was substantial overlap with other items. However, there were two reasons for doing so. One, it is a criterion from the WHO's Classification System and is used worldwide, and also there are medications that can be effective in reducing cravings in some people.

Changes Not Made As mentioned, there is growing discussion of *behavioral addictions*, compulsive behaviors that do not involve substance use. However, only pathological gambling is included in the *DSM-5*. It was felt that not enough is yet known about other behavioral compulsions. Nonetheless, as mentioned earlier there is an increasing body of research into the biological basis of behavioral addictions, in terms of brain function and various neurotransmitters. While an oversimplification, many of the changes associated with behavioral addictions mirror those seen in substance-based addictions, as shown by brain imaging. Thus, some people experience "a high," or significant degree of excitement, which leads to changes in brain neurochemistry that invite the behavior to be repeated.

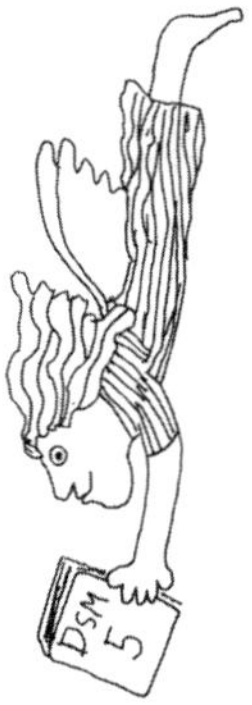

Comparison of DSM-IV and DSM-5 Diagnoses Studies have looked at how a diagnosis would differ depending upon which criteria are used. Multiple studies have found that the overwhelming majority of those with alcohol dependence (over 90%) would now be diagnosed with a severe alcohol use disorder. At the other end of the spectrum, of those who were diagnosed with alcohol abuse, only 2% would no longer meet the criteria for an alcohol disorder using the *DSM-5* criteria. The differences that exist tend to be how persons with a diagnosis of abuse are distributed between the categories of mild or moderate disorders. If anything, the total number with an alcohol use disorder is a bit higher using the newly adopted criteria.

Other Aspects In making a diagnosis, it is necessary to note whether there is or is not physiological dependence, indicated by the presence of tolerance (the need for increased amounts to achieve intoxication or the desired effects) or withdrawal. This is the only instance in which the term dependence is used. Notice the specified time frame is "a 12-month period"; it is not the past 12 months. A diagnosis once made does not go away. It is a significant part of someone's medical history. There may be a change in the level of severity, with an increase in symptoms or a decline. If someone has stopped—or dramatically reduced—drinking, for at least three months, so that there are no longer symptoms, with the exception of craving, the alcohol use disorder is in remission. Early remission is used to identify those who have none of the symptoms for the past 3 to 12 months; the absence of symptoms for a period longer than a year is characterized as stable remission. Both categories include those we think of as "in recovery." However, if someone is living in a controlled environment which dramatically limits access to alcohol, be it a halfway house or a correctional facility, this is not viewed as remission.

The *DSM* is not merely a book filled with countless lists of psychiatric conditions and bulleted lists of their symptoms. For each condition there is also a summary of information useful in formulating a diagnosis, such as the prevalence of the disorder; any common related medical conditions; the natural history; both culture- and gender-related factors; the availability of any diagnostic markers such as laboratory tests; the associated suicide risk; the impact on functioning; and any common co-occurring psychiatric conditions.

In *The Disease Concept of Alcoholism,* Jellinek noted that a disease is "simply anything the medical profession agrees to call a disease." By that standard, an alcohol disorder has been a disease for some time. However, with the refinement of diagnostic criteria there is now far clearer guidance in identifying those who suffer from it.

There's nothing wrong with being an alcoholic, if you are doing something about it.

billboard on the Boston skyline

REFERENCES AND FURTHER READINGS

The primary, original sources for the major historical pieces of work discussed in this chapter were deliberately selected. Because this chapter reviews the evolution of the disease framework as well as approaches to diagnosis, there is considerable value in examining the original articles. Beyond allowing the authors to speak for themselves, these classic works offer instructive insights into the views of alcoholism that then prevailed.

American Psychiatric Association. *Diagnostic and Statistical Manual,* 5th ed. Washington, DC: American Psychiatric Association, 2013.

Caetano R. There is potential for cultural and social bias in DSM-5. (editorial) *Addiction* 106(5):885–887, 2011. (9 refs.)

Criteria Committee, National Council on Alcoholism. Criteria for the diagnosis of alcoholism. *American Journal of Psychiatry* 129(2):41–49, 1972.

Dundon W, Lynch KG, Pettinati HM, Lipkin C. Treatment outcomes in Type A and B alcohol dependence 6 months after serotonergic pharmacotherapy. *Alcoholism: Clinical and Experimental Research* 28(7):1065–1073, 2004. (33 refs.)

Finch E, Welch S. Classification of alcohol and drug problems. *Psychiatry* 5(12):423–426, 2006. (16 refs.)

Frascella J, Potenza MN, Brown LL, Childress AR. Shared brain vulnerabilities open the way for nonsubstance addictions: Carving addiction at a new joint? *Annals of the New York Academy of Sciences. Addiction Reviews* 2 1187:294–315, 2010. (254 refs.)

Glatt M. Group therapy in alcoholism. *British Journal of Addiction* 54(2):133+, 1958.

Grove R, McBride O, Slade T. Towards DSM-5: Exploring diagnostic thresholds for alcohol dependence and abuse. *Alcohol and Alcoholism* 45(1):45–52, 2010. (70 refs.)

Hasin DS, Fenton MC, Beseler C, Park JY, Wall MM. Analyses related to the development of DSM-5 criteria for substance use related disorders: 2. Proposed DSM-5 criteria for alcohol, cannabis, cocaine and heroin disorders in 663 substance abuse patients. *Drug and Alcohol Dependence* 122(1-2):28–37, 2012. (78 refs.)

Hasin DS, Grant B, Endicott J. The natural history of alcohol abuse: Implications for definitions of alcohol use disorders. *American Journal of Psychiatry* 147(11):1537–1541, 1990.

Hasin DS, Liu XH, Alderson D, Grant BF. *DSM-IV* alcohol dependence: A categorical or dimensional phenotype. *Psychological Medicine* 36(12):1695–1705, 2006. (37 refs.)

International Advisory Group of the Revision ICD-10. A conceptual framework for the revision of the ICD-10 classification of mental and behavioural disorders. *World Psychiatry* 10(2):86–92, 2011. (31 refs.)

Jellinek EM. Phases of alcohol addiction. *Quarterly Journal of Studies on Alcohol* 13:673–684, 1952.

Jellinek EM. *The Disease Concept of Alcoholism.* New Haven, CT: Hill House Press, 1960.

Johnson BA, Cloninger CR, Roache JD, Bordnick PS, Ruiz P. Age of onset as a discriminator between alcoholic subtypes in a treatment-seeking outpatient population. *American Journal on Addictions* 9(1):17–27, 2000. (40 refs.)

Moss HB, Chen CM, Yi H-y. Subtypes of alcohol dependence in a nationally representative sample. *Drug and Alcohol Dependence* 91(2/3):149–158, 2007. (29 refs.)

Newlin DB. Are "physiological" and "psychological" addiction really different? Well, no! . . . um, er, yes? *Substance Use & Misuse* 43(7):967–971, 2008. (16 refs.)

Peele S. *How We Allowed Recovery Zealots and the Treatment Industry to Convince Us We Are Out of Control.* New York: Lexington/Jossey-Bass, 1995.

Olsen CM. Natural rewards, neuroplasticity, and non-drug addictions (review). *Neuropharmacology* 61(7, special issue): 1109–1122, 2011. (345 refs.)

Rinaldi RC, Steindler EM, Wilford BB, Goodwin D. Clarification and standardization of substance abuse terminology. *Journal of the American Medical Association* 259(4):555–557, 1988.

Room R. Substance use disorders: A conceptual and terminological muddle. (editorial). *Addiction* 106(5):879–882, 2011. (18 refs.)

Saunders JB, Schuckit MA, eds. Diagnostic issues in substance use disorders. *Addiction* 101(Supplement 1):entire issue, 2006.

Vaillant GE. *The Natural History of Alcoholism, Revisited.* Cambridge, MA: Harvard University Press, 1996.

Wakefield JC. DSM-5: An overview of changes and controversies. *Clinical Social Work Journal* 41(2, special issue):139–154, 2013.

Woody G, Schuckit M, Weinrieb R, Yu E. A review of the substance use disorder section of the *DSM-IV. Psychiatric Clinics of North America* 16(1):21–32, 1993.

CHAPTER 5

Etiology of Alcohol Use Disorders

What are the causes of alcohol dependence? As we gain more knowledge, the answers become more complex. A comparison to the common cold may be useful. Once you have "it," there isn't much question. The sneezing, the runny nose, the stuffed-up feeling that the cold tablet manufacturers describe so well leave little doubt. But why you? Because "it" was going around. Your resistance was down. Others in the family have "it." The guy at Starbucks didn't cover his mouth when he coughed. You became chilled when caught in the rain. You forgot your vitamin C. Everyone has a pet theory and usually chalks it up to a number of factors working in combination against you. Some chance factor does seem to be involved. There are times when we do not catch colds that are going around. The phenomenon cannot be explained with precision. It is more a matter of figuring out the odds and probabilities as the possible contributing factors are considered.

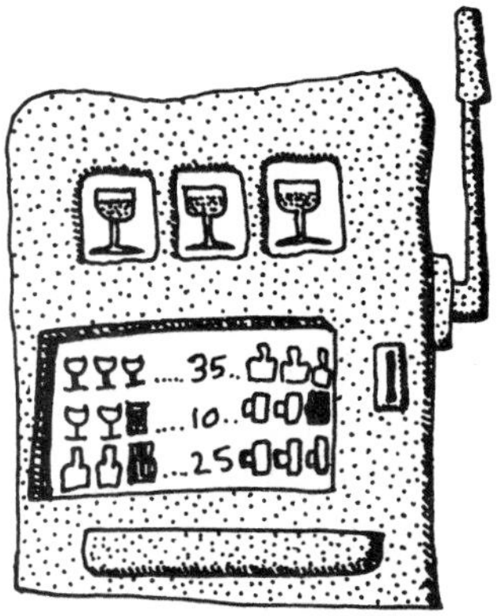

PUBLIC HEALTH MODEL

Members of the public health field have developed a systematic way of tackling the problem of disease, its causes, and the risks of contracting it. First, they look at the agent, the "thing" that causes the disease. Next, they consider the host, the person who has the illness, to find characteristics that may have made him or her a likely target. Finally, they examine the environment, the setting in which the agent and host come together. A thorough look at these three aspects ensures that no major influences are overlooked.

With respect to alcohol, each of these areas is significant. Accordingly, alcohol dependence is often termed a biopsychosocial illness, reflecting the fact that causality is seen as an interplay of *bio*logical, *psycho*logical, and *social* factors. Alcohol dependence qualifies as a public health problem. It is among the leading causes of death in the United States, afflicting 1 out of every 10 adults. It touches the lives of 1 out of every 8 children. The response to alcohol dependence is, unfortunately, pale compared with its impact.

From the public health viewpoint, the first sphere to be examined as a possible cause is the *agent.* For alcohol dependence, the agent is the substance, alcohol. This is such an obvious fact that it might seem silly to dwell on it. No one can be alcohol dependent without an exposure to alcohol. The substance must be used before the possibility of dependence exists. Alcohol is an addictive substance. With sufficient quantities over a long enough time, the body undergoes physical changes. When this has occurred and the substance is withdrawn, there is a physiological response, withdrawal. For alcohol, a well-defined set of symptoms accompanies cessation of drinking in an addicted person.

Any person can be addicted to alcohol, but to use this fact alone to explain alcohol dependence represents untidy thinking. That alcohol is addicting does not explain why anyone would drink enough to reach the point of addiction. Temperance literature tried to paint a picture of an evil demon in the bottle. Take a sip, and he's got you. This is no longer a convincing metaphor. It is obvious that drinking need not lead inevitably to a life of drunkenness. Let's look at the action of the drug itself. What invites its use and makes it a candidate for use sufficient to cause addiction? Then let's move to the individual: What is it in the individual's physiological and psychological makeup that may place him or her at risk? For the sake of discussion, physiology and psychology are separated, but in reality they are closely intertwined. Finally, let's turn to the larger social scene, the culture, and all of the attitudes, the spoken and unspoken rules about alcohol use and what is OK or not OK, as well as what is and is not legally available.

THE AGENT

Candy is dandy
But liquor is quicker.
—Ogden Nash

We take any number of substances into our bodies, from meats to sweets, as solids or liquids. Although everyone overeats occasionally, considering habitual overeating as a form of "substance abuse," or the associated craving as just as powerful as that associated with drugs, is a very recent concept. A physiological basis for this is only now being explored. However, in the case of alcohol, the physiological effects themselves suggest some of the reasons it is such a likely candidate for heavy chronic use. First, alcohol is a depressant drug. One of its first effects is on the central nervous system, the "higher" centers related to judgment, inhibition, and the like. What is more important is what this feels like, how it is experienced. With mild intoxication comes relaxation, a more carefree feeling, generally experienced as pleasant, a high. Preexisting tensions are relieved. A good mood can be accentuated. We experience alcohol as changing our mood for the better. This capacity of alcohol is one factor to remember in trying to understand use sufficient for dependence.

A common expression is "I sure could use a drink now." We might say it after a hard day at work, after a round of good physical exercise, or after a period of chaos and emotional stress. This expression certainly includes the awareness that alcohol can influence our emotional state. Equally as important is the word "now." We recognize that the effects are immediate. Alcohol not only makes a difference, it does so very rapidly. If alcohol had a delayed reaction time—say, three days, three weeks, or even three hours—it wouldn't be a useful method to alter mood states. The unpredictability of people's lives makes drinking now for what may happen later seem quite pointless. So its speed in altering emotional states is another characteristic of the drug alcohol that enhances its likelihood for overuse.

Alcohol has another characteristic common to all depressant drugs. With mild inebriation, behavior is less inhibited; there are feelings of relaxation. However, at the same time there is a gradual increase of psychomotor activity. While feeling the initial glow, the drinker is unaware of this. As the warm glow subsides, the increased psychomotor activity becomes apparent, often experienced as a wound-up and edgy feeling, similar to that caused by too many cups of coffee or caffeinated soft drinks. The increase in psychomotor activity builds up gradually. Since it is delayed and its onset is masked, the drinker is not very likely to recognize the feeling as a product of the alcohol use. This phenomenon is akin to a mini-hangover. Possibly some people, including those not dependent on alcohol, have a second or third drink "to relax" and, in fact, to get rid of the very feelings created by the first drink.

What we are considering here is the *abuse potential* of the drug alcohol—the likelihood that individuals will choose to re-administer a drug. There are ways of studying the abuse potential of a drug in a laboratory setting. For example, given a choice of two substances, both of which have already been sampled, which one will people choose? If there is a marked preference for drug A rather than drug B, then A is the one with more likelihood for abuse. Another approach is to compare a new drug with one that has a known level of abuse, again by determining which one people will choose. Sometimes people are given two choices, with one being a drug and the other a placebo—a substance that is inert, without any psychoactive properties. If the drug is not selected more frequently than the "non-drug," it has a very low abuse potential. In essence people don't feel any different than if they'd taken nothing. Another method is to ask people to rate the effects of a drug: "How does it make you feel? Is it pleasant? Would you want to take it again?" In addition, they can be asked to rate the drug in comparison with other substances. If someone's eyes light up and a smile appears when describing his or her response to the drug, watch out. The drug has a greater likelihood of abuse than if the individual is unimpressed by its effects or finds it unpleasant.

Beyond the immediate effects of the drug, other related factors influence abuse potential. As a general rule, the quicker the effects are felt, the greater the likelihood of abuse. And at the same time, the more rapidly the drug effects disappear, the greater its abuse potential. Typically the drugs with the highest abuse potential are those whose desired effects are strong and immediate. It's truly magic. The effects of a drug are also related to the way it is taken into the body. The most rapid response occurs with inhaling or injecting, methods that deliver the drug to the brain quickly. But the speed of delivery is only part of the story.

The peculiar charm of alcohol lies in the sense of careless well-being and bodily comfort which it creates. It unburdens the individual of his cares and fears. Under such conditions it is easy to laugh or to weep, to love or to hate, not wisely but too well.
—DR. HAVEN EMERSON
Alcohol and Man, New York: Macmillan, 1932

The other factor that influences abuse potential is how rapidly the desired effects fade. If drugs have a dramatic impact but only a short duration, this invites re-administration. What further increases the odds of re-administration and increases the likelihood of abuse is when the drug has unpleasant effects as it wears off. To use an example from other drugs, in terms of abuse potential, cocaine ranks right up there on all counts. Forget the half hour or so that may be needed to feel alcohol's effects; with the ingestion of cocaine, it is literally seconds. This is clearly captured by the language used to describe cocaine's effects. It is described as a "rush," not as a "warm glow" or a "buzz," the phrases heard with alcohol. However, the euphoria fades quickly. The effects dissipate within 10 to 30 minutes, depending on whether the cocaine was snorted or injected. As the effects wane, there is the inevitable "crash," characterized as dysphoria, having negative feelings. Among drinkers, the vast majority are properly described as social drinkers; among those who use cocaine regularly, there are proportionately far fewer "social snorters."

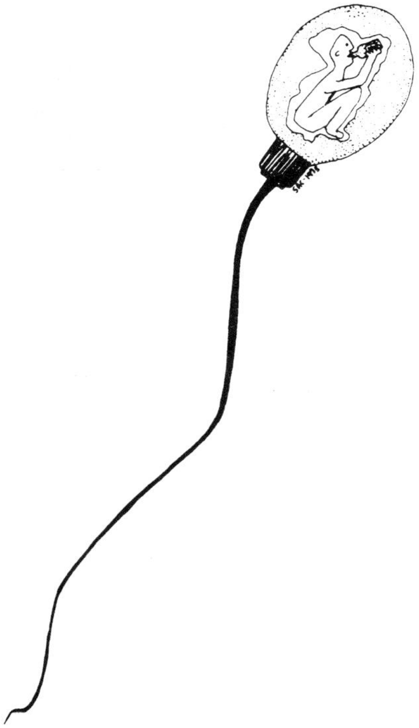

THE HOST—GENETIC FACTORS

The belief that alcohol dependence runs in families has long been a part of the folk wisdom. If not in your childhood, then certainly in your parents', a great-aunt may well have explained away the town drunk with "He's his father's son." No further comment was presumed necessary. The obvious truth was clear: many of life's misfortunes are the result of "bad" genes. Historically just such an understanding of genetics, supported by warped theological views, led to statutes that authorized the sterilization of the feebleminded, the hopelessly insane, and the chronically drunk.

Such an approach has fallen into disrepute. It is now clear that heredity is not as simple as it seemed. Each individual, at the point of conception, receives a unique set of genetic material. This material is like a set of internal instructions that guide the individual's growth and development. In many instances, the genetic endowment simply sets down limits, or predispositions. The final outcome will depend on the life situation and environment in which the person finds, or places, him- or herself. Thus, some people tend to be slim and some tend to put on weight easily. Such a tendency is probably genetic. In large measure, however, whether people are fat, thin, or just right depends on them.

Nature and Nurture

Drunkards beget drunkards.
—PLUTARCH

What are the facts about the role of heredity in alcohol dependence? Actually, alcohol dependence does run in families. The child of an alcohol-dependent parent is more likely to have problems with alcohol. One study tracing family trees found that 50% of the descendants of alcoholics were themselves also alcoholic. Though that figure is a bit higher than what similar studies show, it is a dramatic example of the typical finding that the offspring of those who are alcohol dependent have a four times greater risk of developing the disease.

The observations of those working in the area of alcohol rehabilitation and treatment lend anecdotal support to the view of a constitutional vulnerability. Some clients report a major alcohol problem very early in life, often by the time of adolescence, which progressed rapidly in the absence of any unique, identifiable psychological stress. Similarly, at AA meetings attendees often hear, "I was an alcoholic from my first drink." Usually this means that for seemingly idiosyncratic reasons the speaker never drank "normally," as did peers, but used, and was affected by, alcohol differently. Interestingly, back in 1940, Jellinek recognized a possible hereditary factor and suggested a distinguishable familial type of alcoholism.

However, something running in families is not proof that it is inherited. After all, speaking French runs in families—in France. Separating nature from nurture is a complex but necessary task. Certainly, an alcohol-dependent, actively drinking parent would be expected to have an impact on a growing child. It is not unreasonable to expect that in the family lies the soil of addiction. Yet again, the simple fact that this sounds reasonable does not make it true.

The current understanding is that heredity plays a significant role in the development of alcohol dependence in some people. Research is exploding in this arena, and much has been learned since the early 1970s. Different types of research shed light on this question from different angles. These different types of studies are described in the following sections.

Twin and Adoption Studies

Ultimately, if heredity is a factor, there must be some basic biological differences between those who are prone to develop alcohol dependence and those who are not. But the initial task of researchers was simply to establish the extent to which alcohol dependence does or does not run in families. Several approaches are used to examine this.

We can't design an experiment to separate human nature from nurture. We can't ask some families to raise children one way and other families to raise their children differently so that the differences can be determined. Human research requires locating individuals with particular life experiences or characteristics and then comparing them with those who have other backgrounds. Twin studies and adoption studies are the two classic methods of such research. Donald Goodwin, a clinician researcher, conducted some of the important initial work on the topic of alcoholism and the role of genetics. Many of his (and others') studies have used data from Scandinavian countries because they keep very complete records of marriages, births, and so on. This makes tracing families easier.

One early study was based on a large sample of male twins raised together. In each set, one twin was alcoholic. The researchers determined whether the twins were identical or fraternal. Then they interviewed the twin of the known alcoholic. The prediction was that, if alcohol dependence has a hereditary basis, the other twin of identical sets would be more likely to be alcohol dependent than if he were a fraternal twin. This assumption was made because identical twins share the same genetic material. The assumption proved true. However, hereditary factors do not totally dictate the development of alcohol dependence, because not all the identical twins were both alcoholic. The researchers further discovered that an apparent predisposition exists toward having, or being spared, the social deterioration associated with dependence. If both twins were alcoholic, the best predictor of the other twin's life situation was not how much or how long he had been drinking. The life situation of the first twin was more reliable. So there appears to be a hereditary predisposition to both alcohol dependence and the social problems associated with it.

An adoption study conducted by Goodwin, using Danish subjects, further supported the influence of heredity. He traced children born to an alcohol-dependent parent. These children had been adopted by the age of six weeks. He compared them with adopted children of biological parents without alcohol problems. The adoptive families of both groups were essentially the same. He discovered that those who had a biological parent who was alcoholic were themselves more likely to develop alcohol dependence in adulthood. Thus, dependence cannot be attributed simply to the home environment. Although these earliest studies involved only males, subsequent research suggests that there is a similar genetic predisposition among females.

Half-Sibling Studies

Further studies have helped separate the relative influence of genetic makeup and home environment. These studies have used half-siblings. Of the half-siblings, one had an alcoholic parent, but the other did not. Thus, some of the children had a biological predisposition, while the others did not. These half-brothers and half-sisters were raised together in the same home. In some cases both were reared in a non-alcoholic family. In other cases, both grew up in a home with an alcoholic parent. As expected, those with a genetic background positive for dependence were themselves more likely to develop alcoholism as adults. Of equal significance was the finding that being reared in a home with an active alcoholic did not further increase the chances of developing dependence. This was true for both the biologically at-risk children and their half-brothers and half-sisters who did not have a biological predisposition. This finding has been confirmed by other studies. Such findings provided strong support for the importance of the genetic predisposition in some cases of alcoholism.

Studies of Non-alcoholic Blood Relatives

Once researchers had determined the presence of a genetic factor, their next step was to understand the nature of this genetic predisposition. The National Institute on Alcohol Abuse and Alcoholism (NIAAA) established a major research effort, the Collaborative Study on the Genetics of Alcoholism, to explore these questions. Any genetic difference between those biologically prone to alcohol dependence and those who are not will be manifested in some biological differences, and scientists are trying to identify these. They hypothesize that there are differences in the way our bodies handle alcohol and in how our brains experience its effects. The differences could conceivably be differences of metabolism, differences in response to chronic exposure to ethanol, or possibly a unique response to a single dose. For example, those at high risk may experience greater pleasure and those at low risk more discomfort.

One group of studies looked at how alcohol's effects are experienced. These studies used young men who exhibited no symptoms of alcohol dependence but who had a blood relative with alcohol dependence. Those having an alcohol-dependent family member typically described a *lesser response to a single dose of alcohol* than did those with no alcohol-dependent blood relative. To translate this—those with a family history of alcohol dependence don't feel as "high" as those who have no family history of dependence. So think about it: if feeling alcohol's effects is a significant part of drinking, then those with a family history will need to drink more than their peers. This may increase their risks for dependence.

A difference in response to alcohol proved to be important. Follow-up studies eight years later found that those who had a markedly reduced response to alcohol were four times more likely themselves to be alcohol dependent. Fifty-six percent of the subjects with a low alcohol response had developed dependence versus only 14% of those with high levels of sensitivity. Notice that the comparison was no longer on the basis of having or not having an alcohol-dependent relative. The comparison was the response to alcohol's effects. But having alcohol dependence in the family stacked the deck in terms of the chances of being a high or low responder.

In a similar vein, some studies have explored *other responses to alcohol*. One such study determined that those with a family history of dependence have greater muscle relaxation with a single dose of alcohol than those without such a family background. After drinking, those at high risk are more likely to have brain alpha-wave activity, as measured by electroencephalogram (EEG). Such brain waves are associated with feelings of relaxation.

High-risk subjects, those with a family history of alcohol dependence, perform less well on portions of standard neuropsychological tests. Such tests measure a variety of *cognitive functions*. This finding is noteworthy because it long has been recognized that those who are alcohol dependent do poorly on some of these tests, such as a test for abstracting ability. However, researchers had always presumed that this diminished performance was the result of brain damage from heavy drinking. Now the question is whether this condition predates the dependence.

Finally, studies have revealed a *difference in metabolism*. In one study, a group of presently non-alcohol-dependent young men with an alcohol-dependent father or brother showed greater acetaldehyde levels during alcohol metabolism than did another similar group who did not have an alcohol-dependent family member. Much higher levels of acetaldehyde often accompany drinking in Asians. These higher levels produce a disulfiram-like reaction, which discourages alcohol consumption and thereby provides some protection against the development of alcohol dependence. Paradoxically, though, with just a modest increase of acetaldehyde, the addiction process may be facilitated.

These differences have often been considered as deficiencies. It is now being recognized that what is inherited may not necessarily be a deficiency but might, paradoxically, be described as a strength. In other words, some people might inherit an ability to handle alcohol too well. They may be more immune to negative physical consequences of drinking, such as nausea and hangovers, or they may be able to function better than the average person when alcohol is ingested. If so, those who are at risk for alcohol dependence are deprived of the very cues that, for others, keep drinking in check.

Genetic Markers

The earliest genetic marker studies, before the emergence of molecular biology, were relatively straightforward. They attempted to link alcohol dependence to other traits that were known to be inherited. If such associations could be identified, they would point to the gene responsible. Some of the characteristics first examined for an association with alcohol dependence were blood type, an inherited type of color blindness, and the ability to taste or not to taste particular chemicals.

Research in genetics has become increasingly sophisticated. Accordingly it has become possible not merely to examine genes directly but also to manipulate them. Scientists have developed techniques that allow them to alter portions of genes. We speak of "gene therapy" or "genetic engineering." The massive national research program, the Human Genome Project, succeeded in charting human genetic material, a challenge similar in scope to landing a person on the moon or going to Mars. This achievement opened the door for treating illnesses known to be caused by a specific genetic abnormality. Such genetic-based treatments will be able to go beyond the therapies currently available, because the source of the disease is totally removed.

Heredity. *The heredity of form and the heredity of mental traits and character are unquestioned. Inebriety belongs to the same class, and has been recognized as hereditary for all ages. On one of the monuments of Egypt there is a drawing of a drunkard father and several drunken children, and the grouping conveys the idea that the inebriety of the parent was the direct cause of the children's disgrace.*

—Walter W. Spooner

The Cyclopædia of Temperance and Prohibition, 1891

If there were ever the thought that addiction might be the result of a single gene, that hope has been abandoned. As one researcher noted wistfully, the size of a tomato is determined by three different genes, so it is improbable that a single gene could explain the origins of alcohol or drug disorders.

Animal Studies

Animal studies can offer valuable insights into human biology. The findings cannot be directly generalized to humans; however, work with chimpanzees, baboons, and rats can shed light on promising areas for human investigation and can provide clues. Among the more interesting early animal studies was the discovery of "drinking rats." Different strains of rats were given a choice of water or water spiked with alcohol of differing concentrations. Inevitably, they sampled each and usually opted for plain water. They drank the alcohol-water solution only when it was the sole liquid available. However, several strains of rats were important exceptions. They preferred alcohol and water solutions of around 5%, which translates to 10 proof. These drinking rats could be inbred to produce offspring that preferred even higher alcohol concentrations.

But do these rats develop a condition that appears to resemble alcohol dependence? Seemingly they do—some strains consistently choose to drink alcohol and reach a BAC of 0.5 to 0.20. These rats will work (press a bar in their cages) to obtain alcohol. In addition, the alcohol's attraction is not merely its taste or smell. They select it over other favorite foods or drinks; they will even self-administer alcohol directly into the stomach. These rats seek alcohol for its pharmacological properties. Furthermore, there is evidence of tolerance as well as differences in initial sensitivity to alcohol.

Other behaviors among the drinking rats distinguished them from their non-drinking counterparts, and several of the observed differences seemingly have parallels to human behaviors. These differences may shed some light on factors that give impetus to drinking. For example, the drinking rats were described as having an innately higher level of activity when presented with a new environment. They are more inclined to explore. They are also described as more anxious. They seemingly have temperaments that are similar to those associated with higher levels of drinking in humans.

While drinking rats indicate that genetics plays a role, a more recent animal model allows examining the role of specific genes. So in addition to drinking rats, there are now "knockout mice." Recent developments in genetic engineering make it possible to turn off (i.e., knock out) individual genes. Differences in behavior that arise when a gene is inactivated allow researchers to identify its impact on function and behavior.

The Central Question The basic question remains: What is the inherited "something"? Ultimately the difference lies somewhere in brain chemistry. Recall the one way in which alcohol is different from other drugs: no one single receptor in the brain is uniquely linked to alcohol. By contrast, we know that special sites in the brain—such as opiate receptors, nicotine receptors, and benzodiazepine receptors—are responsible for a significant portion of those drugs' effects. So in the absence of a special alcohol receptor, we assume that alcohol must affect or alter the function of a wide range of the usual receptors and neurotransmitters that serve as the communications system for the central nervous system. The neurotransmitters of particular interest are dopamine, serotonin, GABA, and the naturally occurring internal opioid systems.

Here, too, animal studies have been helpful. The drinking and nondrinking rats differ with respect to their brain chemistry. In some instances there are greater or lesser amounts of a particular enzyme. Or there can be more or fewer receptors available to respond to these chemicals. Also, differences exist in the concentration of these receptors in different parts of the brain. The range of possible factors in combination can boggle the mind. By current count, for serotonin, just one of the many different neurotransmitters, there are seven variants of receptor cells. Quite conceivably, each could respond differently to the presence of alcohol.

Human Studies

A study published in 1990, involving human subjects, caused considerable excitement because it seemed a major breakthrough in understanding the genetic basis of alcohol dependence. With hindsight, we can appreciate our naiveté in believing a genetic breakthrough could be so easy. The research involved an examination of genetic material in the brain tissue of persons with alcohol dependence and a comparison to the brain tissue of non-dependent individuals. Of particular interest was a gene, known as D_2, that is associated with the brain's receptors for dopamine, a neurotransmitter. Dopamine is one of the neurochemicals in the brain involved with the sensation of pleasure. The receptor is the site where this neurochemical acts. Researchers found that there are two forms (or alleles) of this gene. As a point for comparison, think of the gene for eye color as having different alleles. One allele corresponds to brown eyes, another to blue eyes, and so on. In the shorthand that geneticists use, the variations for the dopamine receptor gene are referred to as A_1 and A_2. Of special interest was whether or not dependence is associated with a particular form of the gene. Indeed, that was found to be so. Among those with alcohol dependence, 69% had the A_1 allele. Only 20% of those without dependence had that version. This kind of association suggested that the A_1 gene may increase the susceptibility to dependence. Its presence does not make alcohol dependence inevitable, or one would expect a 100% association. Likewise, its absence does not offer immunity.

Other researchers had difficulty in reproducing the findings of this study. This raised the question of whether the first results were just a fluke, a matter of chance. (It's sort of like winning the lottery—statistically improbable, but it does happen.) A decade later, the answer seems to be "No it wasn't, but . . ." The "but" referred to the way the two groups were selected. The group of alcoholics in the initial study had very severe forms of alcohol dependence. This is the variety of dependence that is now seen as most likely to have a genetic component. Equally important, the comparison group was carefully selected for the absence of alcohol dependence. This comparison population was described as being "super normal." Because alcohol dependence is so common, unless one makes a clear point of excluding alcoholics, the chances are that within a random assortment of people some will be alcohol dependent. Indeed, later research that restricted the characteristics of the populations it studied did find associations between the A_1 gene and alcohol dependence.

Research on the D_2 gene has suggested other relationships. It has been found that D_2 plays a role in how alcohol is metabolized. One form of the D_2 gene is associated with the flushing that is common in some Asians and promotes the faster metabolism of aldehyde dehydrogenase (see Chapter 3). The D_2 gene also seems to be implicated in the differences in cognitive style and neuropsychological functioning that were found in looking at people at risk for alcohol dependence.

What is evident, too, is that to understand alcohol's effects one must think in terms of a cascade effect, with one reaction leading to another, which in turns sparks another, which has an impact on something else, and so on. The following excerpt from a scientific article captures this complexity:

> The dopaminergic system, and in particular the dopamine D_2 receptor, has been implicated in reward mechanisms. The net effect of neurotransmitter interaction at the mesolimbic brain region induces "reward" when dopamine is released from the neuron at the nucleus accumbens and interacts with a dopamine D_2 receptor. "The reward cascade" involves the release of serotonin, which in turn at the hypothalamus stimulates enkephalin, which in turn inhibits GABA at the substania nigra, which in turn fine-tunes the amount of dopamine released at the nucleus accumbens or "reward site." It is well known that under normal conditions in the reward site dopamine works to maintain our normal drives. In fact, it has come to be known as the "pleasure molecule" and/or the "antistress molecule." . . . A consensus of the literature suggests that when there is a dysfunction in the brain reward cascade, which could be caused by certain genetic variants, especially in the dopamine system causing a hypodopaminergic trait, the brain of that person requires a dopamine fix to feel good. This trait leads to drug-seeking behavior.[1]

The nature of the changes in this process led the researchers to describe addiction as a "reward deficiency syndrome." As seen in the above passage, an array of neurotransmitters is identified as involved in this process. The normal function of any one of them may be altered by the presence of alcohol or another drug.

[1]Blum K, Braverman ER, Holder JM, Lubar JF, Monastra VJ, Miller D, et al. Reward deficiency syndrome: A biogenetic model for the diagnosis and treatment of impulsive, addictive and compulsive behaviors. *Journal of Psychoactive Drugs* 32(Supplement):1–112 (entire issue), 2000.

Genetics plays a role in another way. Genetic makeup seems to determine our susceptibility not just to alcohol dependence but also to organ damage associated with heavy drinking and the severity of withdrawal, as well as determining our susceptibility to other drug dependencies and some co-occurring psychiatric disorders.

Familial Versus Non-familial Alcohol Dependence: So What?

Given the strong evidence for the role of a genetic factor in some cases of alcohol dependence, experts suggest thinking in terms of at least two types of alcohol dependence: familial and non-familial. The familial form is characterized by a positive family history of alcohol dependence, an earlier age of onset, and more destructive symptoms. This necessitates and leads to treatment at a relatively young age. This form involves no increased likelihood of other psychiatric illness. On the other hand, the non-familial type is seen as having a later onset and is characterized by less virulent symptoms.

With a genetic vulnerability clearly established, how might this information be used clinically? Certainly the issue is relevant to prevention efforts. But how might it be useful in treating alcohol dependence? In what is clearly a very preliminary and pilot effort, there has been some exploration of the impact of medications that affect dopamine activity. In one study alcohol-dependent persons with the D_2 gene associated with dopamine deficiency who received such medication reported less craving, less anxiety, and less depression. They were less likely to drop out of treatment. This medication certainly does not cure alcohol dependence. It has the promise to address biological underpinnings, which, if attended to, make it possible for people to participate in treatment and decrease the likelihood of relapse.

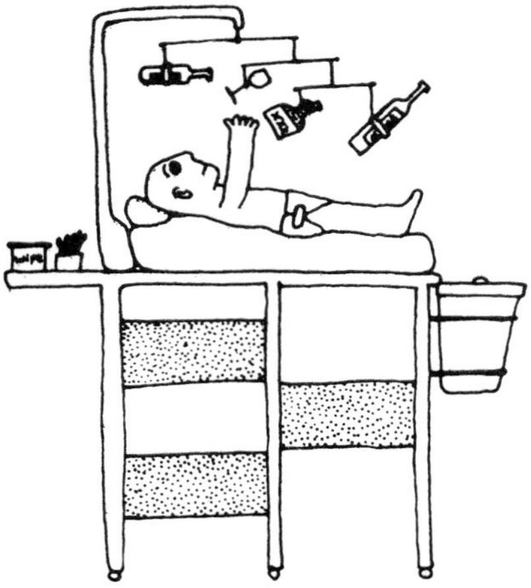

Epigenetics: The Interaction of Genes and the Environment

Commonly we think of genetics as defining characteristics that are set at birth. The obvious example is eye color. Stress in our lives doesn't change eye color, nor does our diet, nor does how much we exercise. Short of getting contact lens to cover up what our "real" eye color is, eye color is set. Now it is being recognized that in many instances there is far more to it. Yes, our genetic endowment is set. However, there are what we might think of as "on and off" switches attached to genes. These "switches" *can* be triggered by environmental influences. A single event will not change the setting, but the continued presence of environmental factors might. This interaction between the environment and our genetic make-up is referred to as epigenetics.

Environmental influences are not limited to things that we think of as "external" factors. We also do things that directly change our internal environment. An obvious example is the drugs we take. An important and growing area of research is exploring the role of epigenetics in the emergence and unfolding of substance use disorders. Though still in its infancy such research may provide insights and information useful in treatment. With an understanding of how our environment can reconfigure our basic genetic "instructions," there is the possibility for identifying how to counter or undo these effects. Returning our genes to their earlier "settings" has the potential for altering the course of disease or a medical condition, including addiction.

THE HOST—PERSONALITY AND PSYCHOLOGICAL MAKEUP

It is important to note at the outset of this section that, in the not-too-distant past, psychological factors were seen as the single most important predictors or precursors of future dependence. The biological and/or social elements in what we now see as a threefold biopsychosocial illness received far less attention. There are probably several reasons for this. Research on what was then called alcoholism stopped during Prohibition. "No alcohol—no problem" was the short-lived attitude. Much of what we now take as fact and as always having been known was established relatively recently. Until 1953, the DTs (delerium tremens) were thought to be caused by malnutrition, not by alcohol withdrawal. It was only in 1973 that fetal alcohol syndrome was described in the scientific literature in the United States. Until 1976, it was thought that cirrhosis of the liver was due wholly to malnutrition. Molecular biology, a field that can help identify the basic mechanisms for a genetic predisposition, is a very new medical science. It wasn't that long ago that cloning sheep, much less humans, was in the realm of science fiction.

Given how little was known about the basic medical facts, it is not surprising that people looked to psychological explanations to understand the origins of alcohol dependence. Particular attention was directed to defining the nature and origins of what was presumed to be the "alcoholic personality."

Psychological Needs

We now recognize that behavior is at least partially determined by factors of which we are unaware. What are these factors? Our grade school social studies classes usually focused on food, clothing, and shelter as the three basic human needs. But human beings have emotional needs, just as real and important, that must be satisfied if they are to survive and be healthy and happy. What do we need in this realm?

> What are the emotional foods that every human being must have regardless of age? What are the basic emotional requirements that must come to every small infant, to every growing child, to every adult?
>
> In the first place, there must be affection and a lot of it. Real, down-to-earth, sincere loving. The kind that carries the conviction through

body warmth, through touch, through the good mellow ring of the voice, through the fond look that says as clearly as words, "I love you because you are you."

Closely allied with being loved should come the sure knowledge of belonging, of being wanted, the glow of knowing oneself to be a part of some bigger whole. Our town, our school, our work, our family—all bring the sound of togetherness, of being united with others, not isolated or alone.

Every human being also needs to have the nourishment of pleasure that comes through the senses. Color, balanced form and beauty to meet the eye, harmonious sounds to meet the ear. The heady enjoyment of touch and taste and smell. And finally, the realization that the pleasurable sensations of sex can be right and fine and a part of the spirit as well as the body.

Everyone must feel that he is capable of achievement. He needs to develop the ultimate conviction, strong within him, that he can do things, that he is adequate to meet life's demands. He needs also the satisfaction of knowing that he can gain from others recognition for what he does.

And most important, each and every one of us must have acceptance and understanding. We need desperately to be able to share our thoughts and feelings with some other person, or several, who really understand. . . . We yearn for the deep relief of knowing that we can be ourselves with honest freedom, secure in the knowledge that says, "This person is with me. He accepts how I feel!"[2]

If these needs are not met satisfactorily, the adult is not whole. A useful notion in assessing what has happened is to think of the unmet needs as "holes." Everybody has some holes. They vary in number, size, and pattern. And, too, some holes may prove to be more debilitating than others. What is true for all is that holes are painful. We attempt to cover up, patch over, or camouflage our holes, so that we can feel more whole, less vulnerable, and more presentable.

Early Psychological Approaches

Through the 1960s, a variety of personality theories were applied to the problem of alcohol dependence. Each represented an attempt to categorize the nature of the "holes," their origins, and the reasons that alcohol is used to cover them up. Although they were seemingly logical enough at the time, there were several major flaws in these studies. One was that the possible role of genetics and the social environment was not considered. The other flaw was that the people being studied were already alcohol dependent. The idea that an alcoholic personality might be a result of the disorder rather than an underlying cause was overlooked. One of the contributions of George Vaillant's work discussed

[2]Baruch D. *New Ways of Discipline: You and Your Child Today*. New York: McGraw-Hill, 1949.

below was that he began not with alcohol-dependent people but with individuals *before* their development of alcohol dependence. In effect, he studied large samples of people over time, beginning in late adolescence. Some of these people later developed dependence, and others did not. Thus Vaillant was able to determine what the predictors of the disease actually were.

Personality Theories Applied to Alcohol Dependence

Among the theories of personality that shaped early thinking, the first was the psychoanalytical, based on the work of Sigmund Freud. Although Freud himself never devoted attention to alcohol problems, his followers applied his theory to alcoholism. It is impossible to briefly address the whole of Freud's work. He identified stages of development, each with its particular, peculiar hurdles that a child must overcome on the way to being a healthy adult. Tripping over one of the hurdles, he felt, led to difficulties in adulthood. Emphasis was placed on *early childhood experiences*. Some of the events of childhood may be especially painful, difficult, and anxiety-producing. They may persist, unrelieved by the environment. The child seeks ways to patch over the holes. However, the existence of the hole shapes future behavior. It may grow larger, requiring more patchwork. The hole may render the child more vulnerable to future stress and lead to new holes.

There is virtually no one today who would seriously appeal to psychoanalytic theory as a significant factor in explaining alcohol dependence. But in the mid–twentieth century, this was the majority view in psychiatric circles. *Oral fixation* was one construct used to understand alcoholism. This means the holes began in earliest childhood. Observe infants and see how very pleasurable and satisfying nursing and sucking are. Almost any "dis-ease" or discomfort can be soothed this way. Individuals whose most secure life experiences were associated with this period were believed to resort to similar behaviors in times of stress. Thus, according to this theory, alcoholics are likely to be individuals who never fully matured beyond infancy. They are stuck with childlike views of the world and childlike ways of dealing with it. They are easily frustrated, impatient, demanding, wanting what they want when they want it. They have little trust that people can help meet their needs. They are anxious and feel very vulnerable to the world. According to this theory, nursing a drink seems an appropriate way of handling discomforts. Alcohol is doubly attractive because it works quickly: bottled magic.

Other personality theorists focused on different characteristics. Adler latched onto the *feelings of dependency*. He saw the roots of alcoholism as being planted in the first five years of life and tied to feelings of inferiority and pessimism. If these feelings continue into adulthood, as problems arise and create anxiety, the person may seek a sense of feeling superior rather than really working to overcome difficulties. So, theoretically, drinking as a solution is a sensible approach.

Normal Drunks

About the cause & cure of drunkenness doctors know little. But recently many of them have swung around to the theory that every drunkard is a spineless neurotic, driven to drink by some psychic gnawing. Last week this theory got a bucket of cold water thrown right in its face. [The authors of a study published] in the New England Journal of Medicine *. . . denied that there is any such thing as an "alcoholic personality." Anyone, they said, "can become an alcoholic if he drinks long enough and heavily enough." The doctors had followed like hawks the zigzag progress of 124 drunkards . . . "A more variegated collection of personalities would be difficult to assemble: some were sociable, some seclusive, some stubborn, some easily influenced . . . , ad infinitum; the only trait these people seemed to have in common was addiction to the excessive use of alcohol." Why they drank, the doctors found it impossible to discover.*

Time Magazine, November 27, 1939

In 1960 William and Joan McCord published *Origins of Alcoholism.* Their studies used extensive data collected on 255 boys throughout their childhoods and into adolescence. Their findings provided no support for the then-current psychological explanations. Rather, their work highlighted the complexity of social and psychological interactions.

Current Thinking

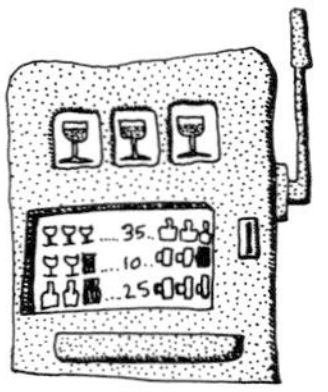

Psychologists and others no longer try to explain alcohol dependence exclusively on the basis of individual personality. However, they recognize that individual factors can and do play a role. The issue now is to better understand how individuals, given their particular genetic and physical makeup, as well as personality traits, interact with their environment. The field of psychology is especially sensitive to the different contributing factors from these domains. In an earlier edition of this book, this was referred to as "the slot machine approach." To become alcohol dependent requires having three cherries come up on the slot machine. An individual may be born with one cherry, thanks to his or her genetic makeup. The culture in which the individual is raised may provide a second, or a sociological, cherry. And the person's psychological makeup may confer a third cherry. Or there may be some variation: say, two-thirds genetic and one-third psychological. But one cherry is not an accurate predictor of who develops alcohol dependence.

Learning Theory

Learning is recognized as a major factor in molding our actions. Behavior is a result of learning, which is motivated by an individual's attempt to minimize unpleasantness and maximize pleasure. What is pleasant is a very individual thing. A child might misbehave and be punished, but the punishment, for that child, might be a reward in that it is more pleasant than being ignored. What is pleasant or rewarding is very much a factor of the individual and his or her unique environment.

When we apply learning theory to alcohol dependence, we take the view that drinking has a reward system. Alcohol or its effects are sufficiently reinforcing to cause the individual to continue drinking. We most easily learn behavior that has immediate, positive results. The warm glow and feeling of well-being associated with the first sips are more reinforcing than the negative morning-after hangover. According to this theory, anyone could become alcohol dependent if the drinking were sufficiently reinforced.

The work of Vernon Johnson, discussed in detail in Chapter 7, gave considerable emphasis to the importance of learning in explaining drinking. He noted that those who use alcohol have learned from their first drink that alcohol is exceedingly trustworthy: it works every time and it does "good things." This learning is highly successful, being sufficient to set up a lifetime relationship with alcohol. The relationship may alter gradually over time, finally becoming a destructive one, but the original positive reinforcement keeps the person seeking the "good old days" and minimizing the destructive elements. Seen in this light, alcohol-dependent people are not so distant from people who remain in what are now unsatisfactory marriages, jobs, or living situations out of habit or some hope that the original zest will return. Of course, after alcohol dependence is established, continued use isn't primarily prompted by recollections of the good old days. Learning has clearly established that a drink will relieve the considerable discomfort of emerging withdrawal.

I pray thee let me and my fellow have
A haire of the dog that bit us last night.
—JOHN HEYWOOD (C. 1500)

Rational Addiction

The rather new approach called rational addiction draws upon the field of behavioral economics. Economists see the choices we make as consumers as rational, guided by our wish to secure the greatest possible happiness from our expenditures. (Economists use the word "utility" rather than happiness.) In making decisions, we balance out an array of pros and cons. We consider our options and are guided by past experiences and future expectations. On a usual day, most of this is largely unconscious; it simply happens. If I want a candy bar, the odds are fairly good I'll go with a Hershey bar every time. I don't give it a lot of thought. With a major purchase this process is likely to be far more deliberate and can require a bit of time. Indeed, time is one of the things that we spend to make what we hope to be the right choice. If it's a new car, we may talk to friends, check reviews on the internet, visit different dealerships, compare prices. The final choice will not be governed by the sticker price alone; other things are of value to us. For some, it may be the particular manufacturer, whether the car is U.S.- or foreign-made, its color, the warranty period, gas mileage, the costs of options we really want, the ease of servicing, or later trade-in value. Each of us values these various factors differently: "as long as it's red" versus "as long as it starts." Some of the features may have an immediate value, such as the sound system, and others, such as trade-in value, will matter only in the future.

The negative consequences of addiction seem so obvious that at first glance addictions seem to be very irrational behavior. Not so, say the economists. There are simply a few quirks. For one, the payoff, the pleasure, or need for drug use at any particular moment is clearly linked to past use. With other decisions, this is not a factor. How much I enjoy my Hershey bar today can't feasibly be predicted by how many I've had in the past. In addition, for drugs, over time, *more* consumption is required to yield the pleasure that earlier came from a smaller amount. If you like to go to the movies, you don't have to go to a double feature now because you used to go to a single show. Addictive substance behaviors are different. It is a commodity for which past use does predict its value (importance) later on.

Another important characteristic is that active drug users are not future oriented: they need it *now*. To use the economic term, they discount the future costs associated with the decision to use. With drug use there is nothing equivalent to figuring out what a car's future trade-in value is likely to be. The greater the present value of using, which those in the substance abuse field might describe as craving, the more likely the person is to be short-sighted about future costs and negative effects.

The framework of economics, with its array of mathematical formulas, is used to describe not only the addictive process but also some elements of treatment. The models suggest that people will change when the long-term benefits are clearly seen as greater than the short-term costs of forgoing use. Indeed an element of treatment is to assist clients to foresee the future and to recognize the links between use and negative consequences. To use a phrase heard in AA, "Think through the drink." Rational addiction models also have been used to explain other aspects of addictive behavior, such as binge drinking and why going cold turkey may be more successful than efforts to cut down.

When you stop drinking, you have to deal with this marvelous personality that started you drinking in the first place.
—Jimmy Breslin

Expectancies

How do beliefs about alcohol—that is, our expectations—determine our response? What are the sources of information that give rise to our beliefs, and how do these change? What is the relative influence of peers versus family? How does the relative weight of these shift as children move from preadolescence through young adulthood? The research suggests that expectancies of alcohol's effects are important in drinking behavior. There are multiple sources of these beliefs. Some come from the larger cultural landscape, including everything from alcohol advertising to the depiction of alcohol use in TV and movies. Then too there is the culture of the family, how we see alcohol being used, the kinds of occasions in which alcohol is used, the kinds of behavior that occur in the presence of drinking, and the related attitudes.

Research suggests, too, that learning about alcohol occurs in very subtle ways and from a very early age. For example, it has been demonstrated that even in the first year of life infants respond to the smell of alcohol. Infants whose parents drink more heavily mouth an alcohol-beverage-scented toy more frequently than do infants with little or no exposure to alcohol. Something similar happens between the ages of three and a half and six years, but with an added twist. Children whose parents drink—in this instance, beer—either like or dislike the odor of beer, depending on how the parents use alcohol. To the extent parental drinking is escapist—that is, linked to withdrawing from people or creating emotional distance—the children are more likely to describe the odor of beer as unpleasant.

If the headache would only precede the intoxication, alcoholism would be a virtue.
—Samuel Butler (1835–1902)

Our expectations of alcohol's effects have an impact in multiple spheres. If we think that drinking and intoxication lead to aggression, the odds go up that we are more likely to find ourselves in a fight. If we believe that drinking makes us less shy and socially more outgoing, indeed we become so. Beyond affecting our behavior *when* drinking, expectancies influence the decision *to* drink.

Temperament

The field of psychology has been examining the issue of temperament, which is similar to but different from personality. Temperament is not thought to be merely or purely the product of life experiences or parenting styles. Rather, temperament represents an innate predisposition that influences one's ways of tackling the world. People seem to have an innate tendency to be risk takers or to avoid risk taking, to welcome novelty or to like things to be more predictable. Whether one is shy or outgoing, adventuresome or cautious, in part seems to be a biological given. Also there seem to be predispositions toward different cognitive styles. These have some bearing on how we tackle problem solving, as well as the degree to which we consider future consequences of actions.

A thousand cups of wine do not suffice when true friends meet, but half a sentence is too much when there is no meeting of the minds.
CHINESE PROVERB

The following traits and behavior patterns have been identified as risk factors for future alcohol or other drug problems. Some of these are seemingly interrelated. It is important to consider each of the following traits as existing on a continuum rather than as being present or absent:

- *Cognitive structure.* Those who dislike ambiguity and desire to make decisions based on definite knowledge are at reduced risk.
- *Harm avoidance.* Those who dislike exciting activities, especially involving potential physical dangers, are at reduced risk.
- *Impulsivity.* Those who are more willing to act on the spur of the moment, to speak their minds freely, or to not hide their emotions are at higher risk.
- *Playfulness.* Those who describe themselves as liking to do things just for fun or who spend substantial time in games, sports, and social activity are at higher risk.
- *Disinhibition/sensation seeking.* Those who are extroverts, who like to take both social and even physical risks just for the sake of having the experience, and who like spontaneous activities are at higher risk.
- *Stressful life events.* The presence of painful, stressful experiences increases the risk of future substance use problems. Such events include the divorce of parents and other serious life disruptions such as a parent's loss of a job, a serious illness, a death in the family, domestic violence, or physical or sexual abuse.

Such traits are considered lifelong predispositions. While seen as predispositions, nonetheless they are modified by experience, learning, and life circumstances. For example, liking novelty at age 63 probably looks far different than it did when the same person was 17 years old; the same with impulsivity.

In addition, some psychiatric disorders are recognized as being correlated with substance abuse problems in adulthood. These include conduct disorders, antisocial personality disorders, and attention-deficit/hyperactivity disorder. (See Chapter 12 for further discussion.) If or how these disorders might contribute to substance abuse problems is not clear, but what is evident is that they represent risk factors, meaning they signal a greater likelihood of a later substance abuse problem.

The other side of the coin from risk factors is protective factors. It is important to be alert not only to things that might signal a potential problem but also to those that reduce the likelihood of its occurrence. What traits and life experiences shield someone from developing alcohol problems and alcoholism? If one were to boil them all down, it might be said that basic psychological needs have been met and in some abundance. In brief, those who have positive social bonds to family, to community, to school, or to a religious community are less likely to develop problems later.

Alcohol is the anesthesia by which we endure the operation of life.
—GEORGE BERNARD SHAW

THE ENVIRONMENT—SOCIOLOGICAL FACTORS

Cultural Differences

Statistically the odds of becoming alcohol dependent have in the past varied significantly from country to country. This is not a matter of genetic differences. The genetic differences within racial and ethnic groups are greater than the differences between groups. Alcohol consumption varies widely from country to country.

We're drinking my friend
To the end of a brief episode.
Make it one for my baby
And one more for the road.
—JOHNNY MERCER
"One for My Baby"

The differences are evident in terms of drinking patterns, amount consumed, and the most common beverages. As was noted in Chapter 2, the proportion of abstainers varies widely from country to country. Other differences, as reported in the *Global Status Report on Alcohol 2004* (the most recent report), are outlined in Table 5.1. Annual consumption is in liters of absolute alcohol.

Cultural Orientation

Whether someone drinks at all depends as much on culture as it does on individual characteristics. However, differences between cultures are becoming less marked. Social media, Coca-Cola, the rise in international travel, the youth culture and pop music, the formation of the European Union, the film industry, and the rise of multinational corporations transcend national boundaries. However, historically the differences in rates of alcohol dependence from culture to culture were substantial enough to provoke study and research. Just as genetic and psychological approaches fall short of fully explaining the phenomenon of dependence, so do cultural differences. But a review of past studies is useful in considering the ways in which broad cultural attitudes seemingly contribute to high rates of problematic alcohol use or, conversely, is useful in identifying those attitudes that promote moderate use.

TABLE 5.1 International Comparisons—Top 10 Charts

Annual Alcohol Consumption (liters)

19.5	Uganda
17.5	Luxembourg
16.2	Czech Republic
14.2	Ireland
13.9	Moldova
13.6	France
13.4	Réunion
13.0	Bermuda
13.0	Germany
12.7	Croatia

Beer, Adult per capita Consumption (liters)

9.4	Czech Republic
9.2	Ireland
7.5	Swaziland
7.3	Germany
6.4	Austria
6.2	Luxembourg
6.1	Uganda
6.0	Denmark
6.0	United Kingdom
6.0	Belgium

Adult Population with Alcohol Dependence (%)

12.2%	Poland
11.2	Brazil
10.6	Peru
9.3	Canada
7.7	United States
7.3	Iran
7.0	Costa Rica
7.0	Belgium
5.5	Netherlands
5.0	Uruguay

Heavy Episodic Drinkers Adult Males (%)

52.0%	Nigeria
49.1	Finland
46.9	Mexico
46.0	Uganda
42.7	Iceland
42.1	Germany
38.3	Japan
36.6	Netherlands
32.6	Belgium
28.8	Czech Republic

Annual Unrecorded Consumption (liters)

12.0	Moldova
11.0	Mauritius
10.7	Uganda
9.0	Zimbabwe
8.0	Ukraine
7.2	Slovakia
7.0	South Korea
5.2	Seychelles
5.0	Kenya
5.0	Estonia

Wine, Adult per Capita Consumption (liters)

9.4	Luxembourg
8.4	France
7.1	Portugal
7.0	Italy
6.4	Croatia
6.2	Switzerland
5.6	Argentina
5.1	Spain
5.0	Bermuda
4.8	Greece

Mortality Alcohol Use Disorders per 100,000

44.7	Kazakhstan
36.6	Russia
29.1	Belarus
25.7	Estonia
19.5	El Salvador
19.0	Turkmenistan
8.2	Latvia
6.9	Denmark
5.8	Mexico
5.2	Luxembourg

Heavy Episodic Drinking Youth, Under 20 (%)

31.0%	Ireland
31.0	Poland
30.0	United Kingdom
27.5	Hungary
22.0	Malta
18.0	Finland
17.0	Sweden
17.0	Iceland
15.3	Canada
15.0	Norway

Spirits, Adult per Capita Consumption (liters)

11.0	Moldova
8.7	Réunion
7.6	Russia
7.3	St. Lucia
7.2	Dominica
7.1	Thailand
7.1	Bahamas
6.6	Latvia
6.5	Haiti
6.3	Belarus

Note: Annual per capita consumption is reported in liters of pure alcohol. The adult population refers to those age 15 and older.

Note: The 2011 *Global Status Report on Alcohol* uses the same consumption data.

Source: World Health Organization. *WHO Global Status Report on Alcohol 2008*. Geneva, Switzerland, 2009.

Culture includes the unwritten rules and beliefs by which a group of people live. Social customs set the ground rules for behavior. These rules are learned from earliest childhood and are followed later, often without a thought. Many times such social customs account for the things we do "just because . . ." The specific expectations for behavior differ from nation to nation and between separate groups within a country. Differences can be tied to religion, gender, age, and social class. The ground rules apply to drinking and other drug use as much as to other customs. Cultures vary in attitudes toward substance use, as they differ in the sports they like or what they eat for breakfast.

The Innkeeper loves the drunkard, but not for a son-in-law.
-Yiddish Proverb

Attitudes Toward Drinking

Virtually all societies have alcohol. At the same time, there are some dramatic differences among societies in terms of attitudes, drinking patterns, and the kinds of problems associated with alcohol use. Several distinctive drinking patterns and related attitudes toward alcohol have been identified. The orientation that predominates in a culture or a cultural subgroup was, and in certain cases still is, thought to be influential in determining that group's rate of alcohol dependence. One such attitude toward drinking is *total abstinence,* as is seen among Muslims and Mormons. With drinking forbidden, the chances of alcohol dependence are almost nil. As would be expected, these groups as a whole have very low rates of alcoholism. However, there is an interesting twist, as we'll see later, about what happens when members leave their group.

Another cultural attitude toward alcohol promotes *ritual use.* Drinking is primarily connected to religious practice, ceremonies, and special occasions. Any heavy drinking in other contexts is frowned on. When drinking is tied to social occasions, with the emphasis on social solidarity and camaraderie, it is termed *convivial use.* Finally, there is *utilitarian use,* in which the society allows people to drink for their own personal reasons, to meet their own needs—for example, to relax, to forget, or to chase a hangover. Rates of alcohol dependence are highest where utilitarian use is dominant.

Insights from Historical Differences

As noted, differences among nations are growing less marked. Nonetheless, a look at some of the differences between the traditional French and Italian drinking habits that persisted through World War II and the 1950s shows that cultural attitudes toward the use of alcohol can influence the rate of alcohol dependence. France and Italy are the top two wine-producing nations in the world. Both earn a substantial part of their revenue from the production and distribution of wine, yet in the past the incidence of alcohol dependence in Italy was less than one-fifth that of France.

Traditionally in France there were no controls on excessive drinking. Indeed, there was no such thing as excessive drinking. Wine was publicly advertised as good for the health—credited with promoting gaiety, optimism, and self-assurance. It was seen as a useful or an indispensable part of daily life. Drinking in France was a matter of social obligation; a refusal to drink was met with ridicule, suspicion, and contempt. It was not uncommon for the French to have a little wine with breakfast, to drink small amounts all morning, to have half a bottle with lunch, to sip all afternoon, to have another half bottle with dinner, and to nip until bedtime, consuming 2 liters or more a day. People did get drunk. On this schedule, drunkenness would not always show up in drunken behavior. The body, however, was never entirely free of alcohol. Even people who never showed open drunkenness could have withdrawal symptoms and even DTs when they abstained. The habit, and the social atmosphere that permitted it, seemed to be facilitating factors in the high rate of alcoholism in France.

During the same period, Italy, which had the second-highest wine consumption in the world, consumed only half the amount that was consumed in France. Italy had a low rate of alcohol dependence on a world scale. The average Italian didn't drink all day, but only with noon and evening meals. One liter a day was the accepted amount, and anything over that was considered excessive. There was no social pressure for drinking, as in France. As was commented, "In France, drinking is a must. In Italy it is a matter of choice." Drunkenness, even mild intoxication, was considered a terrible thing, unacceptable even on holidays or festive occasions.

While the attitudes in different cultures have changed over the years, some factors that affect the rates of alcohol dependence still seem to be found in certain groups. Low rates of dependence are found in cultures in which the children are gradually introduced to alcohol in diluted, small amounts on special occasions and within a strong, well-integrated family group. Parents who drink a small or moderate amount with meals and who are consistent in their behavior and attitudes set a healthy example. There is strong disapproval of intoxication. It is not socially acceptable, stylish, funny, or tolerated. A positive acceptance of moderate, nondisruptive drinking and a well-established consensus on when, where, and how to drink are evident. Drinking is not viewed as a sign of adulthood or, for men, virility; and abstinence is socially acceptable. It is no more rude to say no to alcohol than to a soda. Alcohol is viewed as an ordinary thing. No moral importance is attached to drinking or not drinking; it is neither a virtue nor a sin. In addition, alcohol is not seen as the primary focus for an activity; it accompanies rather than dominates or controls.

High rates of alcohol dependence tend to be associated with the reverse of the patterns just outlined. Wherever there has been little agreement on how to drink and how not to drink, rates of alcohol dependence go up. In the absence of clear, widely agreed-upon rules, whether one is behaving or misbehaving is uncertain. Ambivalence, confusion, and guilt easily can be associated with drinking. Those feelings further compound the problem. Individuals who move from one culture to another are especially vulnerable. Their guidelines may be conflicting, and they are caught without standards to follow. For this reason, individuals who belong to groups that promote abstinence similarly run a very high risk of alcoholism if they do drink. For example, Mormons as a group have a low rate of alcoholism, but those raised as Mormons who do drink have a much higher rate.

Cultures in Flux

A related but little discussed phenomenon involves the changes in alcohol use taking place in developing countries. Cultural stress and social change are especially striking in these societies. Nowhere in the world are the changes around alcohol use potentially more disruptive or occurring more rapidly.

A 2009 report of the World Bank indicated that globally 1.4 billion people subsist on less than $1.50 (U.S.) per day. In sub-Saharan Africa, 50% live in poverty; in South Asia, 40%; and in Latin America, 8%. The social disparities between developing and developed countries are growing. Although there are considerable differences between developing societies, there are several common features. Typically an elite class governs the country, with the bulk of the population poor and living in slums and shantytowns or eking out a livelihood in the countryside. Rapid urbanization has led to megacities: urban areas with concentrated poverty, uncontrolled sprawl, congestion, and pollution. Nonetheless, even with the migration to cities, except for Latin America, the bulk of people in developing countries continue to live in rural areas.

Accompanying social change are changes in identities for individuals, families, and communities. With migration, the traditional networks of mutual obligation and traditional customs are strained. Traditional roles defined by gender, kinship, and age are brought into question. Traditional drinking patterns too are changing. These changes are the subject of a major report, *Alcohol in the Developing Societies: A Public Health Approach,* undertaken by the Finnish Foundation for Alcohol Studies and sponsored by the World Health Organization. The following are some of the significant findings:

- Most developing societies have a tradition of alcohol production that extends back in time to before the modern era. Although there is enormous variety in customs, for the most part cultures associate drinking with sociability, with the effects on mood and state of mind probably being the most valued aspects of drinking.
- Traditional beverages typically have had a lower alcohol content than Western beverages.
- In general, adults in developing countries are more likely to abstain from drinking than are those in developed countries. Women often are non-drinkers outside of Western societies.

- In virtually all traditional cultures, with economic development alcohol ceases being a cottage industry, or a home-produced or communally produced product. It becomes a commodity. Alcohol is sold, rather than distributed through trade or as a gift.
- Industrially produced beers replace those made in the community, especially in Africa. Commercial beers gain market share on the basis of prestige and promotion, even though they are more expensive. A few examples: In the early 1970s, Carlsberg had 5% of the beer market in Malaysia; by the late 1990s it had grown to 65%. European-style malt beverages represented 9% of South Africa's market in 1970; by 1996 the share had grown to 45%. During the same period, the traditional sorghum beer fell from 50% to 20%.
- Multinational corporations are gaining an increasing share of the beer market. Although industrial production is possibly safer, no research has verified this. Breweries are being built by the multinationals in developing countries. Large-scale industrial breweries result in employment losses, especially among women, for whom cottage-produced beer was a major source of employment. For governments a major attraction of industrial-produced alcohol is the greater ease of taxing. A major problem associated with industrial-style Western production is the increase in consumption that accompanies advertising and promotion.
- Many traditional societies have a drinking pattern that includes episodes of intoxication. However, these tend to be tied to community-wide special occasions that occur infrequently, have understood rules, and might be viewed as sanctioned time-out. So for the most part the intoxication neither disrupts nor causes significant problems for the individual or the community. An illustration from Zimbabwe:

    Zimbabwean women by tradition brewed a cloudy or opaque beer made from sorghum or maize for ceremonies, spirit-medium celebrations, or the culmination of community efforts like planting and harvesting. Brewing took more than a week, and when it was ready, it had to be drunk promptly, or it would sour to the point of being undrinkable.

    During a "beer-drink," other tasks were set aside. Drinking to intoxication, but without complete loss of self-control, was a customary pleasure. The community suffered little harm from it, because it happened during a time regulated by tradition, insulated from work and other responsibilities. Made from sorghum, and averaging 3% alcohol, the beer also had some nutritional value.
- Specific, socially defined drinking styles tend to persist even when the circumstances change. The old style is transferred into the new context, which may lead to problems. If intoxication is part of the traditional, festive, or ceremonial use patterns, it may accompany the increased frequency of drinking that comes with development—and begin to resemble binge drinking.

Now is the time for drinking
[nunc est bibendum],
now is the time to make the
earth shake with dancing.
—Horace
Ode on the death of Cleopatra

Beyond describing the changes taking place in alcohol use, the report identifies a variety of steps that can be taken in the arena of health and social policy, at the local, regional, national, and international levels.[3]

Drinking Styles and Alcohol Problems

Beyond affecting the rates of alcohol dependence, the culture's attitudes, norms, and drinking patterns predict the occurrence of negative consequences arising from alcohol use. The cultural features predictive of problems include:

- Solitary drinking
- Overpermissive norms of drinking
- Lack of specific drinking norms
- Tolerance of drunkenness
- Adverse social behavior tolerated when drinking
- Utilitarian use of alcohol to reduce tension with anxiety
- Lack of ritualized and/or ceremonial use of alcohol
- Alcohol use apart from family and social functions with close friends
- Alcohol use separated from overall eating patterns
- Lack of child socialization into drinking patterns
- Drinking with strangers, which increases violence
- Drinking pursued as recreation
- Drinking concentrated in young males
- A cultural milieu that stresses individualism, self-reliance, and high achievement

Influence of Cultural Subgroups

Beyond the influence of broad-based cultural factors, researchers have been investigating the relative influence of cultural subgroups, such as family or peers, as well as the characteristics of the immediate drinking situation. Not surprisingly, much of this research has focused on adolescents and the factors that promote or protect against alcohol use and abuse. Some of these studies have resulted in some interesting findings. However, although considerable research is being conducted, each study is fairly circumscribed and specific. This body of research has yet to be integrated into a theoretical approach to the influences of the smaller social systems in which we live.

For example, among the research findings of interest, in a group of people drinking, the heaviest drinker sets the pace for the others. How much an individual drinks on a particular occasion is likely to be influenced by the amount consumed by others in the group. Another

---

[3]Room R, Jernigan D, Carlini-Marlott B, Gureje O, Makela K, Marshall M, et al. *Alcohol and the Developing World: A Public Health Perspective*. Hakapaino, Finland: Finnish Foundation for Alcohol Studies, 2002.

finding is that adolescent alcohol use increases with perceived access to alcohol and the perceived absence of adult supervision. If one were to extrapolate from the broad cultural norms, one might reasonably expect that when alcohol use is introduced in the home, this is a protective factor. However, some research has not supported that assumption. To the contrary, adolescents who are introduced to alcohol in the home are more likely than other adolescents to use alcohol in unsupervised settings. The researchers note that further study is required to examine whether later unsupervised use is an across-the-board phenomenon or is associated with different ways in which alcohol use is introduced. Having a glass of wine with a family meal may be quite different from a father and daughter each having a beer while watching a televised football game.

Legal Sanctions and Approaches

Our focus thus far has been on the unwritten rules that govern drinking behavior and that influence the rates of alcohol problems and alcohol dependence. How about the rules incorporated into law that govern use and availability? The evidence shows that these can play a significant role. Think back to this nation's experience of Prohibition. On one level, Prohibition can only be described as a fiasco. It did little to abolish problems associated with alcohol use, and it is credited with introducing other social problems, which resulted from bootlegging and the illegal market for alcohol. The conventional wisdom has been that Prohibition did have its successes. Usually it is pointed out that a decline in alcohol consumption was matched by a reduction in the prevalence of alcoholism and in deaths from cirrhosis. A closer look at the records from that era shows a more complicated picture. Both alcohol consumption and alcohol-related deaths began to decline *prior* to Prohibition, during World War I.

Imagine the rate of arrests for violation of alcohol laws during Prohibition had met the rate of arrests in 2005 as part of the "war on drugs." Rather than 482,191 arrests during the 13 years of Prohibition, the number would have been about 8.8 million.

Short of prohibition, there are significant ways society can influence the use of alcohol. The common denominator involves laws that limit access to alcohol. A major factor influencing access is price. As the price of alcoholic beverages increases, people drink less. The group that is most responsive to price changes is moderate drinkers, as opposed to light or heavy drinkers. Presumably, light drinkers use alcohol so infrequently that it is not a significant part of their household budget. Also, for them drinking tends to be tied to special occasions, such as an anniversary dinner, a retirement party, or a family reunion. For example, if you drink only once a month, even a doubling of the price isn't going to have a big impact on your pocketbook. However, for the moderate drinker, as the price of alcohol increases, there are occasions when a soda will do just as well as a cocktail or a cup of coffee will substitute for a beer. Even heavy drinkers, who tend to give up almost anything before sacrificing the alcohol, are not wholly indifferent to price.

The number of deaths from alcohol poisoning quadrupled during Prohibition. Moonshine was being produced by an army of amateurs and often resulted in products that could harm or kill. Their products were also likely to contain dangerous adulterants, a government requirement for industrial alcohol. Will Rogers remarked that "governments used to murder by the bullet only. Now it's by the quart."

—Mark Thornton

Alcohol Prohibition Was a Failure, 1991

A significant relationship has been found between the rate of cirrhosis and the level of liquor taxes. The level of taxation has been found to have a small but significant impact on rates of violent crime. As consumption declines, the rates of rape, assault, and robbery go down.

Although taxation can be a potent means of influencing alcohol use, and although there is a growing concern about the problems associated with alcohol, since the early 1950s, the tax rate on alcohol has been declining. In 1954, the average tax—the total of federal, state, and local taxes—was about half of the cost of the alcohol, before taxes were added. By the early 1980s, that tax rate had been halved. In 2000, allowing for inflation, the average tax was only one-third of what it was in the 1950s. By way of contrast, in Sweden taxes historically were imposed according to alcohol content. The tax on vodka was 90% of the retail price. One of the concerns in Sweden and other Scandinavian countries about joining the European Economic Union was that they would no longer be able to set taxes on alcohol independently and keep the price high by taxing imports of alcohol produced from other member countries.

The Last Straw

New Hampshire's budget woes have not yet set the masses marching in the streets. Warnings that our school children will be deprived have not done it. Warnings that a student's costs for attending the University of New Hampshire will rise have not done it. Warnings that there will be less treatment for the mentally ill have not done it. Warnings that there will be reduced counseling services for the troubled have not done it. Warnings that there will not be enough manpower to ensure pure water supplies have not done it. Warnings that law enforcement officials may not be able to hold down the crime rate have not done it. But now you better batten down the hatches and keep your riot shields handy. This week there was a headline that said, "LIQUOR STORES THREATENED BY BUDGET." That'll do it.

Editorial, *The Valley News*, Lebanon NH, September1977, after the New Hampshire legislature and governor failed to adopt a budget for the state

Beyond tax policy, there are other legal approaches to dealing with alcohol issues. One way is to restrict access by restricting sales hours for package stores and corner convenience stores. One example is Alaska's local option laws. Concerned about the high rate of death and injury resulting from alcohol use in native villages, the state allows individual native villages to set their own laws. These cover the sale, importation, and possession of alcohol. Rates of injury, homicide, and suicide have dropped markedly in response to the limitations on access. The same approach has been used in inner-city neighborhoods. Community groups have made efforts to reduce the number of alcohol outlets. Research has demonstrated that, as the availability of alcohol is reduced, there is a corresponding reduction in hospitalizations for alcohol-related problems.

Another legal measure that can have an impact on alcohol use is regulation of advertising. In an interesting effort to reduce advertising the late Senator Robert Byrd of West Virginia introduced an amendment into the U.S. Senate that would have ended the alcohol industry's ability to use advertising expenses as tax deductions. In Byrd's words, "This is not the introduction of a 'sin tax,' but rather an end to a 'sin subsidy' that has left American taxpayers subsidizing alcohol advertising and picking up the tab for the high costs imposed on society by alcohol consumption."

The party line of the alcohol beverage industry is that advertising does not influence whether people drink. Rather, the industry claims, advertising influences the selection of a particular beverage or brand. To use advertising jargon, the goal of advertising is to increase market share; however, research suggests that this is not quite the case. As advertising increases, so does the level of consumption. One question in public policy is how to restrict advertising. A complete ban may simply lead to other kinds of promotions. Counter-advertising, which has been suggested, raises interesting policy questions. The federal government committed $1 billion for a five-year media blitz that continued through 2002. This campaign was orchestrated by the "Partnership for a Drug-Free America." Other major partners were the alcohol and tobacco industries. Interestingly, this campaign, in focusing on illicit drugs, ignored the drugs of choice among American teens—alcohol and nicotine. We need to ask whether this oversight sends an unintended and unfortunate message—drinking and smoking are not as big a deal as illegal drugs. Of course, this $1 billion was only a fraction of the advertising and promotion budget of the alcohol and tobacco industries during the same period.

With all of the attention directed to the "war on drugs," many in the alcohol and public health fields are appalled by the lack of attention alcohol is receives. This is despite the fact that problems associated with alcohol dramatically overshadow those associated with illicit drug use. There are those, too, who remember the public's response to the counterculture of the 1960s, when psychoactive drug use and experimentation were accepted by a large segment of the adolescent and young adult population. Alcohol was then viewed as far more benign than other drugs. The refrain of parents when confronted with an adolescent's drinking was purportedly a relieved, "Well, at least he isn't on drugs." As a means of reminding everyone that alcohol is a drug, the federal Center for Substance Abuse Prevention (CSAP) adopted the terminology of "alcohol and other drug use," rather than the phrase "alcohol and substance abuse." That was later changed to "alcohol, tobacco, and other drug use," or the acronym ATOD.

Barrow, in northern Alaska with 4,000 residents, over half of whom are Inuit, has a high rate of alcohol-related problems. Over a several year period, a series of local votes were held to decide whether to ban the importation and possession of alcoholic beverages.

The first alcohol ban was passed in November 1994, repealed a year later, but re-imposed six months later. Changes in the availability of alcohol have had an immediate impact on health care utilization. The alcohol-related outpatient visits to the hospital fell from 90 per month before the first ban to 15 during the first ban. When the ban was repealed the rate rose to 60 per month, and fell again to 17 per month after the ban was re-imposed. Admissions to the local detoxification facility similarly fell dramatically during the two bans. While the number of women seeking help for violence at a women's shelter did not appear to be changed during the bans, there was a decrease in its severity.

—R. Room, D. Jernigan, et al.

Alcohol and the Developing World: A Public Health Perspective, p. 200. Hakapaino, Finland: Finnish Foundation for Alcohol Studies, 2002

Cross-Cultural Comparisons

Policy analysts often raise questions about what lessons might be learned from the experience of other countries with different laws and drinking practices. Many such queries deal with the impact of the legal drinking age. The implication is that the answer will offer guidance regarding steps that we might take in the United States. But we aren't that lucky. The issue is just not that simple. The drinking age, in this example, is embedded in a context of cultural attitudes about what represents appropriate and inappropriate use. In addition, it is only one of many laws that influence drinking, such as limits set on the numbers and locations of alcohol outlets, the taxes that thereby influence price, or the laws that govern drinking and driving.

Legal Age to Purchase

In Europe the legal age to purchase alcoholic beverages is lower than in the United States—typically between ages 16 and 18. In addition, in many countries there is not a single legal drinking age. It can vary by the setting, such as stores versus restaurants; by the type of beverages; and by the alcohol content. Table 5.2 lists the legal drinking ages in various countries.

Oglala Sioux Vote to End Century Old Alcohol Ban

By a vote of 1,843 to 1,678, the Oglala Sioux of Pine Ridge Reservation voted to end prohibition. Those supporting this say it will provide the opportunity to regulate use and earn money from sales. Those opposed fear the continuation and exacerbation of very serious alcohol problems. The community is one of the poorest in the country, with an unemployment rate estimated to be over 80% and alcohol related to crime, domestic violence, and health problems.

New York Times, August 14, 2013

TABLE 5.2 Legal Ages for Purchase of Alcohol

Country	Age for Purchase
Austria	Age for drinking in public varies by state
	Age 18, spirits (9 states)
	Age 16, wine and beer (8 states)
	Age 15 (other states)
Belgium	Age 16, beer and wine
	Age 18, spirits
Denmark	Age 16, stores, alcohol 1.2–16.5%
	Age 18, over 16.5%
Finland	Age 20, spirits (over 22% alcohol)
	Age 18, less than 22% alcohol
	Age 18, bars, clubs, and restaurants
France	Age 18
Germany	Age 14, may drink in public if with legal guardian
	Age 16, beer and wine
	Age 18, spirits
Greece	None
India	Vary by state
	Illegal in five states and one union territory
	Age 18–25, other 29 states and territory
Ireland	Age 18
Italy	Age 16
Kuwait	Illegal
Luxembourg	Age 16
Netherlands	Age 16, wine and beer*
	Age 18, spirits
Norway	Age 18, wine and beer
	Age 20, spirits
Portugal	Age 16
Saudi Arabia	Illegal
Spain	Age 16 for most areas
	Age 18 in the Basque region
Sweden	No age for light beer, 2.35 alcohol content
	Age 18, bars and restaurants**
	Age 20 in state-run liquor stores
United Kingdom	Age 16 with meals in pubs and restaurants
	Age 18 for other purchase

*Changing to age 18 in 2014.

**Lower age in bars as bartenders accountable for how intoxicated a guest becomes. Many clubs elect to set a higher age limit for service, between 20–23.

Source: International Center on Alcohol Policies. <www.icap.org/table/minimumagelimitsworldwide>
Note: The International Center on Alcohol Policies is a not-for-profit organization funded largely by the alcohol beverage industry.

Even when we know the legal age for purchase in a particular country, we need to be cautious regarding quick comparisons. Having a legal age for purchase on the books doesn't mean that it is enforced with the same rigor as in the United States. Although it is hard for Americans to appreciate this, legal drinking age simply isn't as important elsewhere as it is in the United States. The differences in language indicate this. In the United States we refer to the "legal drinking age"; in Europe the reference is to the "legal age for purchase."

Other countries are a bit befuddled at times by the extent to which we in the United States are so caught up with drinking age. While our mind-set may be a mystery to them, the reverse is equally true. The following is a good example. A study was conducted in Switzerland on adolescents' ability to purchase alcoholic beverages in bars and restaurants. In four out of five attempts, 13- and 15-year-old boys were able to purchase beer or pastis, an aniseed-flavored apéritif. In Switzerland the minimum age to purchase beer is 16 and for pastis 18. Researchers who were observing these transactions noted that "the time needed to refuse orders appeared to be a big factor in making these sales." This seemed to them a reasonable explanation. This demonstrates how much culture influences how we understand the "facts." In the United States, there would be few researchers and even fewer state liquor control board investigators who would consider "being busy" an acceptable reason not to card people. There was another part of the paper that was telling for the purpose of this discussion. Follow-up interviews with the bar and tavern owners and personnel found that only 17% knew the correct minimum legal ages for purchasing and consuming alcoholic beverages. For those of us who live in a country where seemingly every teen, every parent, and every bartender knows the legal drinking age, the more casual, from our point of view, attitude of the Swiss is difficult to imagine.

Food without drink is like a wound without a plaster.
—Brull

Drinking and Driving

Any perceived casual attitude of the people in European countries regarding age for purchase is offset by very strict laws in other areas. The most dramatic difference is around drinking and driving. In most European countries, a BAC of 0.05 is the cut-off for driving while intoxicated; penalties tend to be more harsh than in the United States. Take Sweden, for example. In 1990, Sweden lowered its level for impaired driving from 0.05 to 0.02. (This is the same level as is being promoted in the United States for those under age 21, a level referred to as "zero tolerance"—no alcohol use if driving.) The penalties for drinking and driving in Sweden are linked to the BAC. Lesser offenses are for BACs of between 0.02 and 0.10; more serious offenses are for BACs above 0.10. Lesser offenses lead to fines and license suspensions lasting anywhere from 6 months to 1 year. The driver also has to see a physician and have a liver enzyme test, which provides some indication of a history of heavy use. A physician visit and laboratory tests are required when a driver applies for license restoration. Restoration of the license is conditional, with further medical evaluations required in 6 and 12 months. Any evidence of heavy drinking results in either a continued revocation of driving privileges or re-revocation. For more serious offenses, a BAC above 0.10, there are prison terms as well as fines in about half of all cases. (Prior to 1990, prison terms were virtually routine for all serious offenses. The changes in the law were made in part to reduce prison costs.) For serious offenders, regaining one's driving license is likely to be accompanied by a number of restrictions, as well as the required medical evaluation. Driving may be limited to essential purposes, such as transportation to work, or may be allowed only on weekdays, or no driving may be allowed after 9 P.M.

Do these laws have an impact? In Sweden, alcohol is implicated in 4.8% of all driving fatalities, a rate about one-seventh that of the United States. With a population of 9 million in 2008, that represents under 40 alcohol traffic fatalities. But here, too, there are other differences. For young Swedes, beer is the most popular alcoholic beverage, as is true in the United States. But it is estimated that 60% of the beer is consumed as part of meals, rather than at parties, or outings, or, to use the American phrase, when "going out drinking."

There are a few natural occasions when it is possible to gain some insights into the impact of a particular legal approach. These occur at a time when there is an important shift in public policy or social circumstances. Here are some examples:

Policy Change	Next Year's Alcohol Consumption	Change in Indicators of Alcohol Problems
Denmark, 1917		
Huge increase in taxes on spirits, some increase in beer taxes	−76%	Cases of DTs down 93% Chronic alcoholism deaths down 83%
Sweden, 1955		
Abolition of *motbok* (alcohol rationing)	+25%	Cases of DTs up 438%
Finland, 1969		
Beer sold in grocery stores	+46%	Death from alcohol causes up 58%
Russia, 1985–1988		
Multipronged effort to reduce availability	−34%	Deaths from alcohol causes down 54% (estimated 1.5 million lives saved)
Finland, 2004		
Taxes lowered 33% on entry into European Union	+12%	Deaths from alcohol causes increased 16% for men and 31% for women

In the United States, such an opportunity to determine the impact of legal practices was provided by the change in drinking age. Thus we can compare the differences in drinking rates for various age groups as well as the differences in the level of associated problems, such as DWI, before and after the law change.

Yes, there was less drinking and there were fewer accidents when the legal age was raised. Even here, other factors are at work. For example, changes in laws are generally accompanied by publicity, stricter enforcement, and more visible law enforcement. As a consequence, there is less inclination to think that one might "get away with it."

The most dramatic and recent examples of the impact of legal changes on drinking practices and associated problems are from the former Soviet Union and Soviet-bloc countries during the 1980s and 1990s. For example, in the early 1980s, when martial law was established in Poland, vodka was rationed, leading to a decline in drinking and alcohol problems. Not many years later, between 1988 and 1991, the import taxes were abolished and millions of liters of very cheap alcohol were imported in what was known in Poland as "the schnapps-gate affair." Consumption quickly matched earlier levels.

In the Soviet Union in the mid-1980s, Gorbachev, the premier, implemented a far-ranging anti-alcohol campaign. Almost overnight, breweries were converted into manufacturing plants for fruit juices. One innovation was the introduction of replaceable caps for vodka bottles. Previous to that, fifths of vodka produced for domestic consumption had only a foil cover, which was peeled off. Why would one need a cap that could be replaced on a bottle? Typically, a fifth of vodka would be consumed at one sitting. With this array of reforms, there was a marked decline in drinking and its related problems. Between 1985 and 1988, there was a 34% decline in consumption, and deaths from alcohol-specific causes decreased by 54%.

The decline in consumption was short-lived. By the 1991 breakup of the Soviet Union, alcohol production, both legal and through black-market/private initiatives, and consumption levels had returned to their earlier levels. Several years later, due to an overproduction of alcohol, there was a new development—vodka was being sold in paper cups from kiosks on the street. Over the almost quarter century since the dissolution of the Soviet Union, the pattern of heavy drinking has continued, and there has been a steady deterioration in many areas of health. Life expectancy rates continue to decline, having reached their lowest level in over 40 years. In addition to alcohol-related illness, poisoning is quite common, as are deaths from injury and accidents. The rates for both homicide and suicide have skyrocketed. Add to all of this a rapidly rising opiate problem and an AIDS rate that may soon approximate the highest rates in Africa. The net result: the Russian population is shrinking by 1 million people annually.

An examination of the Soviet-Russian anti-alcohol initiatives demonstrates the potential for unintended and unanticipated consequences. When alcohol availability was limited by Gorbachev, there was a sudden shortage of sugar, presumably arising from the home production of distilled spirits. This is certainly consistent with the American experiment with Prohibition. But there were other reforms with unforeseen consequences. One strategy to reduce the consumption of vodka—the most popular drink—was to introduce wines and other beverages with a lower alcohol content. Vodka had never been a woman's drink. With the introduction of other alcoholic beverages, drinking among women rose markedly. Along with that, there was a corresponding sharp rise in fetal alcohol syndrome (FAS). Women had tended not to drink vodka and certainly not in the traditional Russian drinking style. The common drinking pattern in all of Eastern Europe, including Russia and Finland, is very heavy drinking at one sitting. We would term it "binge drinking." There it has no special name; it is simply "drinking." As women not only increased consumption but also adopted the standard drinking patterns, the rate of FAS rose in response. The risks to the fetus increase with the number of incidents of heavy drinking. So even with the same level of total consumption, more moderate drinking on more occasions poses less danger to the fetus than fewer drinking occasions but with greater intake per occasion.

Cultural Influences on Recovery

A classic essay, "The Cybernetics of 'Self': A Theory of Alcoholism," does not address the causes of alcohol dependence per se but suggests an interesting hypothesis on the potential impact of cultural orientation on recovery. It provides an insight into the cultural reasons that abandoning alcohol is so difficult for the alcohol dependent.

The essay's author, Gregory Bateson, pointed out that Western and Eastern cultures differ significantly in the way they view the world. Western societies focus on the individual. The tendency of Eastern cultures is to consider the individual in terms of the group or in terms of one's relationships. To point out this difference, consider how you might respond to the question "Who is that?" The Western way to answer is to respond with the person's name, "That's Eric Jones." The Eastern response might be "That's my neighbor's oldest son." The latter answer highlights the relationship among several persons.

One of the results of Westerners' zeroing in on the individual is an inflation of the sense of "I." We think of ourselves as wholly separable and independent. Also, we may not recognize our relationships to other persons and things and the effects of our interactions. According to Bateson, this can lead to problems. One example he cites is our relationship to the physical environment. If nothing else, the ecology movement has taught us that the old rallying cry of "man against nature" does not make sense. We cannot beat nature. We win—that is, we survive—only if we allow nature to win some rounds too.

How does this fit in with alcohol? The same kind of thinking is evident. The individual who drinks expects, and is expected, to be the master of alcohol. If problems develop, the drinker can count on hearing "Get your act together." He or she is supposed to fight the alcohol and win. There's a challenge. Who can stand losing to a "thing"? So the person tries various tactics to gain the upper hand. Even if he or she quits drinking for a while, the competition is on: the person versus it. To prove who's in charge, sooner or later the drinker will have "just one." If disaster doesn't strike then, the challenge continues to be to have "just one more." Sooner or later, the pattern of heavy drinking is reinstated.

Bateson asserted that successful recovery requires a change of worldview by the person in trouble with alcohol. The Western tendency to see the self (the I) as separate and distinct from, and often in combat with, alcohol (or anything else) has to be abandoned. The alcoholic must learn the paradox of winning through losing, the limitations of the I and its interdependence with the rest of the world. He continues with examples of the numerous ways in which AA fosters just this change of orientation.

Views in the Twenty-First Century

In terms of social policy, in the United States, we cannot expect to have all of the approaches described earlier implemented as one piece of legislation. American society tackles policy concerns in a more incremental fashion. A variety of steps have been taken that reflect efforts to moderate drinking patterns.

In the United States, for the most part, the laws regulating alcohol use are set by the states. This includes defining by law what constitutes intoxication, as well as setting the legal drinking age. States vary, as well, on when, where, and what a citizen may drink within their borders. And some states even vary from county to county—in Texas, for example. Laws range from dry, to beer only, to anything at all but only in private clubs, to sitting down but not walking with drink in hand, ad infinitum. States also provide a role for communities in establishing local ordinances, such as those governing the location, number, and hours of operation of alcohol retail outlets and bars.

The differences between states have significantly narrowed in response to the federal government's use of financial incentives, as well as changes in public perceptions. The uniform increase of the drinking age to 21 years, enacted in 1984, was championed by many in hopes that it would be an effective measure to reduce alcohol-related highway fatalities among young people.

Raising the legal drinking age was resisted on several grounds. Some cited the fact that the age of majority is 18 years. College

administrators, despite their recognition of problem drinking on campus, were concerned about living with a law that was so out of sync with the behavior of their students. (Indeed, in 2008 college presidents began revisiting the issue.)

Ultimately the states' changes in drinking age laws were in no small part prompted by a federal incentive—the tying of federal highway funds to a state's enactment of a 21-year-old drinking age. States were similarly encouraged to lower the standard for legal intoxication to a BAC of 0.08. Beyond this, states have begun to enact zero tolerance laws. For those under age 21, these laws establish a very low BAC, from 0.0 or 0.02, as the level for defining driving under the influence. In addition, all states have established BAC limits for operating motor boats, and some have extended these to other recreational vehicles such as snowmobiles. States, too, with the help of federal funding, have become far more involved in monitoring the ability of those who are under age to purchase alcohol and cigarettes. The failure to ask for proof of legal age and the sale of alcohol and tobacco to minors results in fines and, for alcohol outlets, suspension of licenses.

Driving fatalities attributable to alcohol continue to decline and have been more than cut in half from the high in 1977. The efforts of community- and state-level organizations—such as MADD (Mothers Against Drunk Driving) and its derivative, SADD (Students Against Destructive Decisions, originally Students Against Driving Drunk)—continue. In addition, community-level coalitions have emerged, sparked by federal and state funding of prevention programs. Lobbying for stricter penalties for drinking and driving offenses has continued. The concept of the designated driver has taken hold. Advertising campaigns to combat drinking and driving are now commonplace, at least at holiday times.

The legal system has both spurred and reflected changes in society. One influence has been the issue of legal liability and the suits that can be filed for compensation when death or injury occurs as a result of drinking. There long have been Dram Shop laws, which hold a tavern owner or barkeeper liable for serving an obviously intoxicated customer. Until relatively recently these were rarely invoked, but this is no longer the case. In addition, liability has been extended to hosts and to those who might allow an intoxicated person to use his or her car. The issue of liability, particularly in light of higher legal drinking ages, has prompted college campuses to pay attention to issues of alcohol use. Similarly, parents and other adults are being held accountable for serving alcohol to minors at private parties.

Concern about liability has touched the workplace as well. Companies no longer host parties where the alcohol flows freely, particularly on company time. If drinking takes place at work-sponsored activities, during the time for which an employee is being paid, any alcohol-impaired employee injured on the way home is a candidate for workers' compensation. In addition, the company can anticipate a lawsuit. Other changes in business practices have resulted from a small change in the Internal Revenue Code. The three-martini lunch went by the boards when the IRS no longer allowed companies to write off the purchase of alcohol as a legitimate business expense. This is a good example of how social change occurs. Small changes, such as alteration of the tax code, affect behavior, which in turn modifies perceptions or allows alternative views to be expressed. The three-martini lunch not only does not qualify as a business expense; it no longer is viewed as a requisite for doing business and, in most quarters, is considered inappropriate.

As changes have been prompted by governmental action, they have been reinforced and mirrored by the actions of private groups who also have the capacity to influence patterns of alcohol use. For example, in professional and collegiate sports, drunken fans were long seen as an inevitable part of the game. At professional sports events, drinking in the stands is spurred by beer sales at the concession stand, not an insignificant source of revenue for professional teams. In recent years, professional franchises have made efforts to sharply curtail drinking. In some instances drinking has been entirely banned in stadiums. In both professional and college stadiums there are now blocks of family seats, where no alcohol consumption is allowed. In addition, advertising at sports events is now being called into question. The National Collegiate Athletic Association (NCAA) has also limited advertising for championship games.

My Two-year-old heard a "Just Say no" ad and now That's all he Says.

Despite the considerable changes in laws and public policy, our contradictory and ambiguous views toward alcohol remain embodied in our liquor laws. Regardless of concern about adolescent use, the law implies that on that magical 21st birthday, individuals suddenly know how to handle alcohol appropriately. As the rhetoric of "just say no" is applied to alcohol, as it has been in federally funded campus prevention efforts and the growing prevention efforts among teens, it skirts the issue of alcohol's legal status for those 21 and over. There's no mention of when or under what circumstances it is OK to "say yes," nor recognition of what constitutes saying yes "safely." This is all too evident in the growing craze of 21 shots for 21st birthday celebrations, sometimes chronicled with a shotbook.

An approach well established in other countries has barely taken hold in the United States. This is the concept of *harm reduction.* From this perspective, the issue is less about whether individuals use or do not use alcohol or other drugs than it is about reducing problems associated with use. With respect to intravenous drug use, for example, the emphasis is on taking steps to reduce needle sharing and other activities that increase the risk of AIDS. In terms of alcohol, examples of harm reduction are efforts to promote designated drivers and efforts to teach teens to recognize alcohol poisonings. In the view of those involved in harm reduction, such efforts should not be seen as condoning IV drug use or as condoning adolescent drinking. What such policies try to reflect is the reality that risky behavior does occur. And in light of that reality, a harm reduction perspective maintains that it is possible and important to reduce associated risks, even as one simultaneously tries to curb the behavior. The absence of discussion of harm reduction in the United States is not simply an accident of history. In the Reagan era, NIDA (National Institute on Drug Abuse) issued a "nomenclature memorandum" with a column of terms that were henceforth forbidden in NIDA proposals, reports, and publications derived from NIDA-funded research. There was also a list of "approved" terms. For example, the phrase "illicit drug use" was forbidden; the approved term was "illicit drug abuse." In the mid-1990s the U.S. State Department asked agencies to avoid use of the phrase "harm reduction" as it was purported to be a code for legalization. (See Chapter 14 for more detail.)

Interestingly, technologies are available that could be viewed as harm reduction at a societal level, rather than as reduction of individual harm. For example, interlock devices can be installed on the cars of those arrested for DWI to prevent the car from being driven. Clearly, these do nothing to alter the individual's drinking pattern, but they do protect the public safety. Another technology available involves skin patches that can detect the presence of alcohol or other drugs. That isn't all. They can be wired to a small device, similar to a pager, that can electronically transmit a signal to a police station, for example. This provides the potential for identifying anyone convicted of DWI who takes a drink. Although these technologies are available and relatively inexpensive, they are little used. The reason is unclear.

As a society, we ideally want alcohol without the associated problems. As individuals, what inconveniences and costs are we willing to assume? Will we accept further steps to limit access to alcohol? Would we, for example, accept a ban on package sales after 10 P.M. on the assumption that folks who want to buy alcohol at that hour don't need it? Or how willing is each of us to intervene if confronted by a possible use that presents a threat to public safety? If we are driving and witness an erratic driver, how likely are we to put a call in to the police?

Recent surveys show far more support for controls on alcohol use than our current laws suggest. More than 80% of the general public support restrictions on alcohol use in public places, such as parks, beaches, concert venues, and college campuses. Eighty-two percent support increased alcohol taxes, provided the funds are used for treatment or prevention programs. Over 60% support alcohol advertising and promotion restrictions, such as banning billboard advertising, banning promotion at sporting events, and banning liquor and beer advertising on television. The climate is ripe for initiating changes in alcohol policy.

REFERENCES AND FURTHER READINGS

Several of these references may appear dated. However, those included are original primary sources—that is, the articles in which the ideas or findings set forth were first introduced in the scientific literature.

Alexander B. *The Globalization of Addiction: A Study in Poverty of the Spirit.* New York: Oxford University Press, 2011. (488 pp.)

Anderson P, Moller L, Galea G. *Alcohol in the European Union. Consumption, Harm and Policy Approaches*. Copenhagen: World Health Organization, 2012. (672 refs.) Available online: www.euro.who.int.

Bales R. Cultural differences in rates of alcoholism. *Quarterly Journal of Studies on Alcohol* 6:489–499, 1946.

Bassett JF, Dabbs JM Jr. Eye color predicts alcohol use in two archival samples. *Personality and Individual Differences* 31(4):535–539, 2001. (12 refs.)

Bateson G. The cybernetics of "self": A theory of alcoholism. *Psychiatry* 34:1–18, 1971.

Berman M, Hull T, May P. Alcohol control and injury death in Alaska native communities: Wet, damp and dry under Alaska's local option law. *Journal of Studies on Alcohol* 61(2):311–319, 2000. (24 refs.)

Blum K, Braverman ER, Holder JM, Lubar JF, Monastra VJ, Miller D, et al. Reward deficiency syndrome: A biogenetic model for the diagnosis and treatment of impulsive, addictive and compulsive behaviors. *Journal of Psychoactive Drugs* 32(Supplement):1–112 (entire issue), 2000. (636 refs.)

Bowers BJ. Applications of transgenic and knockout mice in alcohol research. *Alcohol Research & Health* 24(3):175–184, 2000. (38 refs.)

Dick DM, Agrawal A. The genetics of alcohol and other drug dependence. *Alcohol Research & Health* 31(2):111–118, 2008. (71 refs.)

Duncan AE, Scherrer J, Fu Q, Bucholz KK, Heath AC, True WR, et al. Exposure to paternal alcoholism does not predict development of alcohol-use disorders in offspring: Evidence from an offspring-of-twins study. *Journal of Studies on Alcohol* 67(5):649–656, 2006. (44 refs.)

Eberstadt N. Drunken nation: Russia's depopulation bomb. *World Affairs* 171(4):51–62, 2009.

Edenberg HJ. The genetics of alcohol metabolism—Role of alcohol dehydrogenase and aldehyde dehydrogenase variants. *Alcohol Research & Health* 30(1):5–13, 2007. (45 refs.)

Finn PR, Justus A. Physiological responses in sons of alcoholics. *Alcohol Health and Research World* 21(3):227–231, 1997. (15 refs.)

Foroud T, Phillips TJ. Overview: Assessing the genetic risk for alcohol use disorders. *Alcohol Research: Current Reviews* 34(3):266–273, 2012. (24 refs.) This issue is devoted to the genetics of alcoholism. Available online: http://pubs.niaaa.nih.gov/publications/arcr343/toc34_3.htm.

Gilbertson R, Prather R, Nixon SJ. The role of selected factors in the development and consequences of alcohol dependence (review). *Alcohol Research & Health* 31(4):389–399, 2008. (110 refs.)

Goodwin DW. Is alcoholism hereditary? *Archives of General Psychiatry* 25:545–549, 1971.

Gruber J, Koszegi B. Is addiction "rational"? Theory and evidence. *Quarterly Journal of Economics* 116(4):1261–1303, 2001. (40 refs.)

Grucza RA, Cloninger CR, Bucholz KK, Constantino JN, Schuckit MA, Dick DM, et al. Novelty seeking as a moderator of familial risk for alcohol dependence. *Alcoholism: Clinical and Experimental Research* 30(7):1176–1183, 2006. (34 refs.)

Holder HD, Giesbrecht N, Horverak O, Nordlund S, Norstrom Olsson O, et al. Potential consequences from possible changes to Nordic retail alcohol monopolies resulting from European Union membership. *Addiction* 90(12):1603–1618, 1996. (44 refs.)

Ling WB, Chikirtzhs T. Revealing the link between license outlets and violence: Counting the venues versus measuring alcohol availability. *Drug and Alcohol Review* 30(5, special issue): 524–535, 2011. (30 refs.)

Mayfield RD, Harris RA, Schuckit MA. Genetic factors influencing alcohol dependence (review). *British Journal of Pharmacology* 154(2):275–287, 2008. (144 refs.)

McCord W, McCord J. Some current theories of alcoholism: A longitudinal evaluation. *Quarterly Journal of Studies on Alcohol* 20:727–749, 1959.

Mennella JA, Garcia PL. Children's hedonic response to the smell of alcohol: Effects of parental drinking habits. *Alcoholism: Clinical and Experimental Research* 24(8):1167–1171, 2000. (28 refs.)

Mulder RT. Alcoholism and personality. *Australian and New Zealand Journal of Psychiatry* 36(1):44–51, 2002.

Nemtsov AV. Alcohol-related human losses in Russia in the 1980s and 1990s. *Addiction* 97(11):1413–1425, 2002. (42 refs.)

Noble EP. The D-2 receptor gene: A review of association studies in alcoholism and phenotypes. *Alcohol* 16(1):33–45, 1998. (119 refs.)

Peck G. *The Prohibition Hangover: Alcohol in America from Demon Rum to Cult Cabernet*. Brunswick, NJ: Rutgers University Press, 2009. (336 pp.)

Pittman DJ, White HR, eds. *Society, Culture, and Drinking Patterns Reexamined.* New Brunswick, NJ: Rutgers Center of Alcohol Studies, 1991.

Quickfall J, el-Guebaly N. Genetics and alcoholism: How close are we to potential clinical applications? (review). *Canadian Journal of Psychiatry* 51(7):461–467, 2006. (79 refs.)

Rietschel M, Treutlein J. The genetics of alcohol dependence. *Annals of the New York Academy of Science* 1282(1):39–70, 2013. (246 refs.)

Romley JA, Cohen D, Ringel J, Sturm R. Alcohol and environmental justice: The density of liquor stores and bars in urban neighborhoods in the United States. *Journal of Studies on Alcohol and Drugs* 68(1):48–55, 2007. (37 refs.)

Room R. Alcohol policy effectiveness. In: *Strategic Task Force on Alcohol, May 2002.* Dublin, Ireland: Department of Health and Children, 2002.

Room R, Jernigan D, Carlini-Marlatt B, Gureje O, Makela K, Marshall M, et al. *Alcohol in the Developing Societies: A Public Health Approach. Volume 46.* Helsinki Finland: Finnish Foundation for Alcohol Studies, 2002. (535 refs.)

Stickley A, Razvodovsky Y, Mckee M. Alcohol mortality in Russia: A historical perspective. *Public Health* 123(1):20–26, 2009. (50 refs.)

Vaillant G. *The Natural History of Alcoholism, Revisited.* Cambridge, MA: Harvard University Press, 1995.

Wagenaar AC, Harwood EM, Toomey TL, Denk CE, Zander KM. Public opinion on alcohol policies in the United States: Results from a national survey. *Journal of Public Policy* 21(3):303–327, 2000. (47 refs.)

Wand G. The influence of stress on the transition from drug use to addiction (review). *Alcohol Research & Health* 31(2):119–136, 2008. (113 refs.)

Zagler AS. Sisterhood, one shot at a time: Scrapbooks commemorate 21st birthday drinking binges. Associated Press, February 24, 2010.

Medical Complications

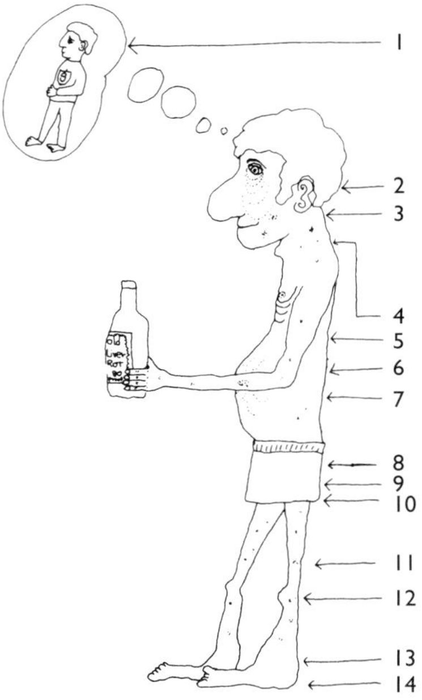

1. Distorted self-image
2. Bulbous enlarged nose
3. Sallow or jaundiced skin with dilated capillaries, spider angiomas, scabbing, crusting papules, pustules
4. Hoarse voice
5. Increased perspiration
6. Fiery red palms
7. Protruding abdomen
8. Pubic hair thinned or lost
9. Shrunken testicles
10. Hemorrhoids
11. Thin
12. Multiple bruises
13. Swollen ankles
14. Unsteady walk with broad-based gait

Alcohol use disorders are one of the most common chronic diseases in the United States. The prevalence is 9% in the population at large. Untreated, its natural history is a predictable, gradually progressive downhill course. The observable early symptoms and manifestations of the primary disease, alcohol dependence, are largely behavioral and non-physical. Later in its course, it causes a broad spectrum of secondary medical morbidities and complications involving numerous organ systems. These are associated with a host of physical signs and symptoms. These medical problems have a markedly negative impact on the overall quality of life. In fact, studies have shown that those with long-standing alcohol disorders have a worse quality of life than that reported by a variety of cancer patients.

It is important to emphasize the distinction between the primary disease of alcohol dependence and its later secondary medical complications. Alcohol dependence is one of the most highly treatable of all chronic illnesses. If recognized and treated early—before major medical complications have occurred—it may be entirely arrested, without any significant long-term continuing problems. Successfully treated individuals can function quite normally. Their only long-term limitation is that they cannot use alcohol. Its complications, on the other hand, may be progressive, irreversible, and have a fatal outcome if the underlying alcohol disorder goes untreated.

This chapter focuses on the later secondary medical complications of chronic alcohol use. Because virtually every organ system is affected, an acquaintance with the medical complications of chronic heavy alcohol use constitutes familiarity with an exceedingly broad array of medical disorders. In the past, in view of the many and exceedingly diverse multisystem manifestations of both tuberculosis and syphilis, it was often said that "to know TB or syphilis is to know medicine." The same could be said of alcohol dependence—to know alcohol dependence and its secondary complications is to know a great deal about medicine.

There is this to be said in favor of drinking that it takes the drunkard first out of society, then out of the world.
—Ralph Waldo Emerson, 1866

This chapter touches briefly, in a systems-oriented fashion, on many of the major medical problems related to long-term alcohol use and abuse. First, however, let us take a look at a composite picture of a person manifesting the visible signs of chronic heavy drinking.

VISIBLE SIGNS AND SYMPTOMS OF CHRONIC HEAVY DRINKING

Statistically, the typical alcohol-dependent person is male; thus, we will use "he" in our examples. However, females who are chronic heavy drinkers can and do show virtually all the same signs and symptoms, except those involving the reproductive organs. Indeed, among women medical complications may appear sooner and be more severe earlier in the drinking career. Bearing in mind that any given alcohol-dependent person may have many or only a few of these visible manifestations, let us examine a hypothetical chronic drinker who has most of them.

He is typically a thin, but occasionally somewhat bloated-appearing, middle-aged individual. He may appear anxious and/or depressed. Hyperpigmented, sallow, or jaundiced skin accentuates his wasted, chronically fatigued, and weakened overall appearance. He walks haltingly and unsteadily with a broad-based gait *(ataxia).* Multiple bruises are evident. He perspires heavily. His voice is hoarse and croaking, punctuated by occasional hiccups, and he carries an odor of alcohol on his breath. His dental problems are obvious. There are teeth missing, others have caries. There is serious periodontal disease and halitosis (bad breath).

His abdomen protrudes, and on closer examination it reveals the *caput medusae*—a prominent superficial abdominal vein pattern that looks like the snakes in Medusa's hair in Greek mythology. There is marked *edema,* or ankle swelling, and he has hemorrhoids. His breasts may be enlarged; his testicles may be shrunken; and his chest, axillary, and/or pubic hair may be entirely lost or thinned. Close inspection of the face reveals dilated capillaries and acne-like lesions. His nose is enlarged and bulbous, a condition called *rhinophyma.* The skin on his extremities has scabbing and crusting secondary to generalized itching. On the upper half of his body he has "spider angiomas." These are small red skin lesions that blanch with light pressure applied to their centers and spread into a spidery pattern with release of pressure. His palms may be a fiery red (liver palms). He may have "paper money" skin, so called because abnormally dilated capillaries, appearing much like the tiny, red-colored fibers in a new dollar bill, are distinctly visible. In colder climates, there may be evidence of repeated frostbite. The fingernails are likely to be affected. They may have either transverse, white-colored bands *(Muehrcke's lines)* or transverse furrows *(Beau's lines),* or they may be totally opaque without half-moons showing at the base of the nail. He may have difficulty fully extending the third, fourth, and fifth fingers on either or both hands because of a flexion deformity called *Dupuytren's contracture.* A swelling of the parotid glands in the cheeks, giving him the appearance of having the mumps, is known as "chipmunk fascies." Finally, a close look at the whites of his eyes may reveal small blood vessels with a corkscrew shape and a yellowish jaundiced appearance.

There are more old drunkards than old physicians.
—RABELAIS

With this as a picture of what is externally visible, let us look inside the body at the underlying diseased organ systems that account for these visible changes.

GASTROINTESTINAL SYSTEM

Alcohol affects the gastrointestinal (GI) system in a variety of ways. This system is the route by which alcohol enters the body and is absorbed. It is where the first steps of metabolism take place. Moderate amounts of alcohol can disturb the normal functioning of this system. Chronic heavy use of alcohol often raises havoc. Alcohol can have both direct and indirect effects. Direct effects are changes that occur in response to the presence of alcohol. Indirect effects occur as a consequence of the initial, direct effects.

Many a man keeps on drinking till he hasn't a coat to either his back or stomach.
—GEORGE PRENTICE

Irritation, Bleeding, and Malabsorption

Both acute and chronic use of alcohol stimulates the stomach lining's secretion of hydrochloric acid and irritates the lining of the gut in general. It also inhibits the muscular contractions, called peristalsis, that move food into and through the intestines and may interfere with the absorption of nutrients and vitamins. In combination, these effects often cause a generalized irritation of the mucous membranes lining the gut, especially in the stomach. Chronic heavy drinkers often complain of frequent belching, loss of appetite, alternating diarrhea and constipation, morning nausea, and vomiting. Some of these symptoms may be due to slowed gastric emptying, which occurs more frequently with wine or beer than with liquor.

Pouring to achieve a large "head" on the beer enhances the bouquet and allows less carbonation to reach the stomach.

Alcohol-induced irritation is not found throughout the entire GI system; more often it is localized to particular portions. For instance, if the esophagus is irritated, *esophagitis* results—experienced as mid-chest pain and pain when swallowing. Acute and chronic stomach irritation by alcohol results in *gastritis,* which involves inflammation, abdominal pain, and maybe even bleeding. Chronic alcohol use can certainly aggravate, if not cause, *ulcers* of the stomach or duodenum (the first section of the small intestine). *Bleeding* can occur at any of the irritated sites. This represents a potentially serious medical problem. Bleeding from the GI tract can be either slow or massive. Either way, it is serious. Frequently, in heavy drinkers the blood clots less rapidly, so the body's built-in defenses to stop bleeding are weakened. Surgery may even be required to stop the bleeding. Although alcohol may aggravate ulcers through direct irritant effects, it may also have a counterbalancing beneficial effect as it kills *Heliobacter pylori,* the stomach bacterium that plays an important role in causing ulcers.

There are additional causes of GI bleeding. The irritation of the stomach lining, not unexpectedly, upsets the stomach. With that can come prolonged nausea, violent vomiting, and retching. This may be so severe as to cause mechanical tears in the esophageal lining and bring on massive bleeding. Another cause of massive and often fatal upper GI bleeding is ruptured, dilated veins along the esophagus (esophageal varices). The distention and dilation of these veins occurs as a result of chronic liver disease and cirrhosis.

Chronic heavy alcohol use increases the severity of periodontal disease and thus contributes to tooth loss. Heavy alcohol use facilitates the development of *gastroesophageal reflux disease* (GERD) and chronic *esophagitis.* This is due to relaxation of the sphincter in the lower part of the esophagus, the muscle that normally prevents the contents of the stomach from moving back into the esophagus, and reduced motility in the esophagus. Chronic irritation of the esophagus by a combination of long-standing heavy alcohol consumption, especially liquor (distilled beverages), along with cigarette smoking, significantly increases the risk for esophageal cancer. The result of chronic, excessive use of alcohol on small intestinal function can lead to abnormal absorption of a variety of foods, vitamins, and other nutrients. No specific diseases of the large intestine are caused by alcohol use; however, diarrhea frequently occurs because absorption of sodium and water is inhibited due to alcohol's effects on the gut. Hemorrhoids, a by-product of liver disease and cirrhosis, which can cause lower GI bleeding, also are more common.

Pancreatitis

Alcohol is frequently the culprit in acute inflammation of the pancreas. This is known as acute pancreatitis. The pancreas is a gland tucked away behind the stomach and small intestine. It makes digestive juices, which are needed to break down starches, fats, and proteins. These juices are secreted into the duodenum through the pancreatic duct, in response to alcohol as well as other foodstuffs. The pancreatic secretions are alkaline and thus are important in neutralizing the acid contents of the stomach, thereby helping protect the intestinal lining. The pancreas also houses the islets of Langerhans, which secrete the hormone insulin, needed to regulate sugar levels in the blood.

Currently there are two major theories as to how alcohol causes *acute pancreatitis.* The first, which is less favored, suggests that the pancreatic duct opening into the duodenum, the first part of the small intestine, can become swollen if the small intestine is irritated by alcohol. As the pancreatic duct swells, pancreatic digestive juices cannot pass through it freely; they are obstructed or "stopped up." In addition, it has been suggested that bile from the bile duct, which opens into the pancreatic duct, may "back up" into the pancreatic duct and enter the pancreas itself. The pancreas then becomes inflamed. Because the bile and digestive juices cannot freely escape, in effect, autodigestion of the pancreas occurs.

The second theory holds that some of the excess fats in the bloodstream caused by excessive drinking are deposited in the pancreas. These fats are then digested by pancreatic enzymes, whose usual task is breaking down dietary fats. In turn, the products of this process, free fatty acids, cause cell injury in the pancreas, which results in further release of fat-digesting enzymes, thus creating a vicious cycle.

A drunkard is like a whiskey bottle, all neck and belly and no head.
—AUSTIN O'MALLEY

The symptoms of acute pancreatitis include nausea, vomiting, diarrhea, and severe upper abdominal pain radiating through to the back. Chronic inflammation of the pancreas can lead to calcifications, which are visible on abdominal X-rays. This is chronic pancreatitis, a relapsing illness that occurs in long-term heavy drinkers who are genetically predisposed to developing it. *Chronic pancreatitis* is now believed to result from the cumulative effects of repeated acute illness episodes. These repeated incidents of acute illness lead to the destruction of cells and subsequent scarring, which cause the digestive and hormonal abnormalities associated with the chronic form of the illness. Recent research shows that certain pancreatic cells contain alcohol dehydrogenase and aldehyde dehydrogenase and thus are capable of metabolizing alcohol. The by-products produced may have direct toxic effects on pancreatic cells. Diabetes can result from decreased capacity of the pancreas to produce and release insulin as a result of chronic cell damage involving the islets of Langerhans.

Pancreatic cancer is more common in those with alcohol dependence than in those without an alcohol use disorder.

Gallbladder Disease

Moderate alcohol use decreases the risk of developing gallstones and gallbladder disease.

Liver Disease

The liver is a fascinating organ. Recall that it is the liver enzyme alcohol dehydrogenase (ADH) that begins the process of breaking down alcohol. The liver is responsible for a host of other tasks. It breaks down nutrients, toxins, and medications. It manufactures essential blood components, including clotting factors. It stores certain vitamins, such as B-12, which is essential for red blood cells. It helps regulate blood sugar (glucose) levels, a critical task because glucose is the only food the brain can use. Liver disease occurs because alcohol disturbs the metabolic machinery of the liver. Metabolizing alcohol is always a very high-priority function of the liver. Therefore, whenever alcohol is present, the liver is "distracted" from attending to normal and necessary functions. For the heavy drinker, this can be a good part of the time.

As you may know, liver disease is one of the physical illnesses most commonly associated with a long-term heavy drinking. Three major forms of liver disease are associated with heavy alcohol use: acute fatty liver, alcoholic hepatitis, and alcoholic cirrhosis. *Acute fatty liver* may develop in anyone who has been drinking heavily, even for relatively brief periods of time. Fatty liver gets its name from the deposits of fat that build up in normal liver cells. This occurs because of a decrease in the breakdown of fatty acids and an increase in the manufacture of fats by the liver. The latter is a result of the "distracting" metabolic effects of alcohol on the liver (see Chapter 3). Acute fatty liver occurs whenever 30% to 50% or more of someone's dietary calories are in the form of alcohol. This is true even if the diet is otherwise adequate. Acute fatty liver is a reversible condition if alcohol use is stopped.

Alcoholic hepatitis is a more serious form of liver disease, and it often follows a severe or prolonged bout of heavy drinking. (Alcoholic hepatitis is not related to infectious hepatitis [hepatitis A], serum hepatitis [hepatitis B], or non-A, non-B hepatitis, known as hepatitis C.) Although commonly seen in the company of alcohol dependence, alcoholic hepatitis, like acute fatty liver, may occur in other situations as well. In hepatitis, there is actual inflammation of the liver and variable damage to liver cells. One also may find associated evidence of acute fatty liver changes. Frequently liver metabolism is seriously disturbed. Jaundice is a usual sign of hepatitis. Jaundice is a yellowish cast to the skin and whites of the eyes. The yellow color comes from the pigment found in bile, a digestive juice made by the liver. The bile is being handled improperly in the liver, and therefore excessive amounts circulate in the bloodstream and are deposited in the skin and eyes. Other symptoms of alcoholic hepatitis may include weakness; itching or welts, which are a variety of hives; fatigue; loss of appetite; nausea and vomiting; low-grade fever; weight loss; increasing ascites (fluid collecting in the abdomen); dark urine; and light stools.

In some patients, alcohol-induced hepatitis is completely reversible with abstinence from alcohol. In others, alcoholic hepatitis may be fatal or go on to become a smoldering, chronic form of liver disease. Among patients with alcoholic hepatitis who stop drinking, only one in five will go on to develop *alcoholic cirrhosis.* Of those who continue to drink, 50% to 80% develop cirrhosis. For many, alcoholic hepatitis is clearly a forerunner of alcoholic cirrhosis, but it is thought that alcoholic cirrhosis can also develop without the prior occurrence of alcoholic hepatitis. Alcohol consumption is the second most common cause of cirrhosis, with hepatitis C being the most common.

The liver has a remarkable ability to heal itself and regenerate, but there are limits. *Cirrhosis* is a condition in which there is widespread, permanent destruction of liver cells. These cells are replaced by nonfunctioning scar tissue. In fact, the word "cirrhosis" simply means scarring. There are many types and causes of cirrhosis. However, in the United States, long-term heavy alcohol use is the cause in the majority (80%) of cases. About 1 in 10 long-term heavy drinkers eventually develops alcoholic cirrhosis. Given the nature of the disease, it is accompanied by very serious and often relatively irreversible metabolic and physiological abnormalities, which is very bad news. In fact, more than half of the patients who continue to drink after a diagnosis of alcoholic cirrhosis has been made are dead within five years.

In alcoholic cirrhosis, the liver is simply unable to perform its work properly. Toxic substances, normally removed by the liver, accumulate and circulate in the bloodstream, creating problems elsewhere in the body. This is particularly true of the brain. The liver normally processes the majority of the blood from the intestinal tract as it returns to the heart. The cirrhotic liver, a mass of scar tissue, is unable to handle the usual blood flow. The blood, unable to move through the portal vein (the normal route from the blood vessels around the intestines to the liver), is forced to seek alternative return routes to the heart. This leads to pressure and "backup" in these alternative vessels. This condition is called portal hypertension. It is this pressure that causes the veins in the esophagus, which are part of this alternative return route, to become enlarged, producing esophageal varices and inviting hemorrhaging. The same back pressure accounts for the hemorrhoids and *caput medusae* previously discussed.

Another phenomenon associated with cirrhosis is ascites. As a result of back pressure, the extracellular fluid in the tissues of the liver "weeps" directly from the liver into the abdominal cavity. This fluid would normally be taken up and transported back to the heart by the hepatic veins and lymph system. Large amounts of fluid can collect and distend the abdomen; a woman with ascites, for example, can look very pregnant. If you were to gently tap the side of a person with ascites, you would see a wave-like motion in response, as the ascitic fluid sloshes around.

Another result of alcoholic liver disease is diminished ability of the liver to store glycogen, the body's usual storage form of sugar. There is also less ability to produce glucose from other nutrients, such as proteins. This can lead to low blood sugar levels (see Chapter 3). This is an important fact when it comes to treating diabetes because insulin also lowers the blood sugar. Another situation in which this is important is in treating coma in anyone with a significant alcohol disorder. Insufficient amounts of blood sugar may cause coma, essentially because the brain does not have enough of its usual fuel supply to function normally. Intravenous glucose may be necessary to prevent irreversible brain damage in these patients. On the other hand, alcohol and alcoholic liver damage may lead to states of diabetes-like, higher-than-normal blood glucose

levels. This occurs in large part because of both the effects of liver disease and the effects of alcohol on the hormones that regulate glucose.

Hepatic encephalopathy, or coma, can be one result of cirrhosis. In this case, the damage comes from toxins circulating in the bloodstream. In essence, the brain is poisoned by these toxins. Its ability to function is seriously impaired, leading to progressive neurological and behavioral changes and eventually coma. Cancer of the liver can be a complication of long-standing cirrhosis. Thirty percent of liver cancers are due to excessive alcohol use. Another source of bad news is that as many as 50% of those with cirrhosis also have pancreatitis. These persons have two serious medical conditions. Still other complications may include GI bleeding, salt and water retention, and kidney failure. The main elements of the treatment for cirrhosis are abstinence from alcohol, multivitamins, a nutritionally balanced diet, and bed rest. Even with such treatment, however, the prognosis for cirrhosis is not good, and many of the complications just described may occur.

The different forms of alcohol-related liver disease result from specific alcohol-induced changes in liver cells. Unfortunately, there is no neat and consistent relationship between a specific liver abnormality and the particular constellation of symptoms that develops. Although laboratory tests indicate liver damage, they cannot pinpoint the specific kind of alcohol-related liver disease. Therefore, some authorities believe that a liver biopsy, which involves direct examination of a liver tissue sample, is essential to evaluate the situation properly and fully.

Until the early 1970s, the liver damage common in alcoholism was not recognized to be a direct result of the alcohol. Rather, it was believed that the damage was caused by poor nutrition. It has since become clear that alcohol itself plays the major, direct role. Even in the presence of adequate nutrition, liver damage can occur when excessive amounts of alcohol are consumed.

In addition, in recent years it has been established that heavy alcohol consumption increases oxidative stress. This can lead to a worsening of hepatic fibrosis in individuals who already have hepatitis C.

Gastrointestinal Cancers

Chronic heavy alcohol use, especially in the presence of co-occurring tobacco use, facilitates the development of cancers throughout the gastrointestinal system—the pharynx, esophagus, stomach, colon, and liver. However, it appears that wine is less of a carcinogen than other forms of alcoholic beverages.

☐ HEMATOLOGICAL SYSTEM

The blood, known as the hematological system, is the body's major internal transportation system. Blood carries oxygen to tissues. It takes up waste products from cell metabolism and carts them off to the lungs and kidneys for removal. It carries nutrients, minerals, and hormones to the cells. The blood also protects the body through the anti-infection agents it carries. Although the blood is a fluid, it also contains "formed elements" (solid components). These formed elements include red blood cells, white blood cells, and platelets. They are all suspended in the serum, the liquid part of the blood. Each of the formed elements of the blood is profoundly affected by alcohol abuse. Whenever there is a disturbance of these essential blood components, problems arise.

Red Blood Cells

The most common problem involving the red blood cells is anemia—too few red blood cells. Anemia is a general term, like "fever." It simply means insufficient function or number of red blood cells. Logically one can imagine this coming about in a number of ways. Too few red blood cells can be manufactured if there is a shortage of nutrients to produce them or if toxins interfere with their production. Even if they are produced in adequate amounts, they can be defective. Or they can be lost—for example, through bleeding. Or they actually can be destroyed by a process called hemolysis. Alcohol contributes to anemia in each of these ways.

How does alcohol abuse relate to the first situation, inadequate production? The most likely culprit is inadequate nutrition. Red blood cells cannot be manufactured if the bone marrow does not have the necessary ingredients to do so. Iron is a key ingredient. Alcohol, or some of its metabolic products, such as acetaldehyde, are thought to interfere with the bone marrow's ability to use iron in making hemoglobin, the essential, oxygen-carrying part of the blood. Even if there is enough iron in the system, it "just passes on by." On the other hand, poor diet, common among those who are alcohol dependent, may mean insufficient iron intake and thus too little iron in the system. Chronic GI bleeding may also result from chronic alcohol abuse. If so, the iron in the red blood cells is lost and not available for normal recycling. This type of anemia is called *iron deficiency anemia.* Another variety, *sideroblastic anemia,* is also related to nutritional deficiencies. This comes from too little pyridoxal phosphate (a substance that facilitates the production of vitamin B-6-related cofactor). This substance is also needed by the bone marrow cells to produce hemoglobin.

These two varieties of anemia account for the inadequate production of red blood cells. Another variety, *megaloblastic anemia,* is also related to nutritional deficiencies. There may be too little folate or Vitamin B-12. This happens because folate and B-12 are not in the diet in sufficient quantities and/or the small intestine is unable to absorb them properly because of other problems due to chronic alcohol abuse. What results, then, is defective red blood cell production. Without folic acid

or B-12, red blood cells cannot mature. They are released from the bone marrow in primitive, less functional forms that are larger than normal.

Chronic loss of blood from the gut—GI bleeding—can lead to anemia. The bone marrow simply cannot make enough new cells to keep up with those that have been lost. The body normally destroys and "recycles" components of old red blood cells through a process called *hemolysis*. The abnormally rapid hemolysis that may occur with chronic heavy alcohol use can shorten the life span of red cells by up to 50%. One cause of abnormal hemolysis is hypersplenism, which results from chronic liver disease—the spleen, enlarged and not working properly, destroys perfectly good red blood cells as well as the old, worn-out ones. Toxic factors in the blood serum are also thought to be responsible for three other varieties of accelerated hemolysis. *Stomatocytosis* is a transient, relatively benign form of anemia related to binge drinking but unrelated to severe alcoholic liver disease. *Spur cell anemia,* on the other hand, is associated with severe, often end-stage, chronic alcoholic liver disease. The name comes from the shape of the red cell, which, when seen under the microscope, has jagged protrusions. *Zieve's syndrome* is the simultaneous occurrence, in an alcoholic patient, of jaundice, transient hemolytic anemia, elevated cholesterol levels, and acute fatty liver disease without enlargement of the spleen.

In France, other changes in red blood cells have been reported in those who drink at least two to three quarts of wine each day. These are changes typically seen with lead poisoning. (Lead, even in low concentrations, can mean trouble.) Excessive intake of wine in France is thought to be a significant source of dietary lead. In the United States, there are periodic reports of lead poisoning connected with alcohol use, but the circumstances are different. The beverage has not been wine but moonshine. In these cases, old car radiators were being used in the distilling process.

White Blood Cells

White blood cells are one of the body's main defenses against infection. The chronic use of alcohol affects white cells. It contributes to increased susceptibility to and frequency of severe infections, especially of the respiratory tract, in those with alcohol dependence. Alcohol has a direct toxic effect on white blood cell reserves. This leads to a reduced number of two types of white cells that fight infection—granulocytes and T lymphocytes (T-cells). *Chemotaxis,* or white cell mobilization, is diminished by alcohol. In other words, although the white cells' ability to kill the bacteria is not affected, they have difficulty reaching the site of infection in adequate numbers. Alcohol also interferes with white cell adherence to bacteria, which is one of the body's defensive inflammatory reactions. As a result, under the influence of alcohol, white cells may have a diminished ability to ingest bacteria.

Platelets

Those with a serious alcohol disorder are frequently subject to bleeding disorders. Bleeding can occur in the GI tract, the nose, the gums, and many other places. That is why heavy drinkers bruise easily. This is largely explained by the effect of alcohol on decreasing the number of platelets. Platelets are a major component of the body's clotting system and act as a patch on a leak. Alcohol has a direct, toxic effect on the bone marrow's production of platelets. Thus, one out of every four chronic heavy drinkers will have abnormally low platelet counts. Within one to three days of stopping drinking, the count will begin to rise. Recall that severe liver disease can cause hypersplenism. This can cause abnormally rapid destruction of platelets, as well as red blood cells, thereby contributing to the low platelet counts often seen in those with an alcohol disorder.

Clotting Factors and DIC

When the liver's metabolic processes are disrupted by the effects of chronic alcohol use, there is often a decrease in the production of some of the necessary clotting factors. Thirteen to 15 such substances are needed to make a normal blood clot. Of these, five are liver-produced. Hence, liver disease may contribute to bleeding problems due to lowered levels of clotting factors.

Severe liver damage can also contribute to the occurrence of *disseminated intravascular coagulation* (DIC). This is a life-threatening state of diffuse, abnormally accelerated coagulation. This coagulation consumes large quantities of clotting factors, as well as platelets, and leads to dangerously lowered levels of both, which in turn can result in excessive and uncontrolled bleeding and death.

Immune System

The immune system may be altered by chronic, heavy drinking. The body has two immune systems. One includes immune factors circulating freely in the blood system, such as antibodies, complement, and immunoglobulins. The other is associated with antibodies attached to individual cells. Changes in both systems can occur with chronic alcohol use. The ability of serum (the unformed elements of the blood) to kill gram-negative bacteria is impaired by alcohol. This may be related to the diseased liver's lowered ability to produce complement, an important agent in the body's inflammatory response. Many immune and defensive responses depend on adequate levels of complement.

Although not clearly established, the effects of alcohol on certain kinds of lymphocytes (B-cells) may lead to decreased production of circulating antibodies, which normally fight bacterial infections. In addition, alcohol has been shown to decrease the numbers of the other major type of lymphocytes (T-cells), which mediate cellular immunity. Moreover, alcohol inhibits their responsiveness to stimuli that ordinarily activate their functioning. These factors are believed to be major contributors to increased susceptibility to infections in heavy, long-term drinkers. Immune suppression may also be secondary to malnutrition and chronic liver damage.

Research has suggested that alcohol-induced changes in other types of white cells, together with changes in the cell-based immune system, may lead to an increased production of certain types of fibrous tissues, which are characteristic of cirrhosis. A current question is whether the scar tissue in cirrhosis is at least in part due to the white cell changes and alterations in immune response that are induced by chronic alcohol use. Similar questions are being raised in relation to the identified anti-inflammatory cardioprotective effects of moderate alcohol use (discussed below).

Excessive alcohol use has also been found to be associated with increased severity of the clinical course of HIV/AIDS patients.

Even though the hematological complications of chronic heavy alcohol use are many and potentially quite serious, in general they are totally reversible with abstinence. But the liver disease that caused some of them may be so severe as to preclude this. The speed with which these complications improve is often dependent on improvement in the underlying liver disease. Reversal can be enhanced in many instances by administering essential vitamins and minerals that are deficient, such as folate, pyridoxine, and iron, in addition to restoring a fully adequate diet. Still, cessation of alcohol is the most important factor.

☐ CARDIOVASCULAR SYSTEM

A specific form of heart muscle disease is thought to result from long-term heavy alcohol use. Known in the past as alcoholic cardiomyopathy, it is now referred to as *alcoholic heart muscle disease* (AHMD). This occurs in a clinically apparent form in 2% of those with alcohol dependence. However, it is estimated that 80% have similar, though less severe and therefore subclinical, forms of alcohol-related heart muscle abnormalities. When clinically apparent, AHMD is a severe condition characterized by low-output heart failure (meaning the heart doesn't pump the volume of blood needed to meet the body's demands), as well as shortness of breath with the least exertion, and dramatic enlargement of the heart. This is due to weakness in the pumping action of the heart muscle. Most commonly, AHMD occurs in middle-aged men who have been drinking heavily for 10 or more years. It often responds well to discontinuing alcohol, plus long-term bed rest. As some have noted, "Abstinence makes the heart grow stronger." Other standard medical treatments for congestive heart failure may be helpful as adjuncts in the treatment of AHMD.

Another form of alcoholic heart disease, high-output congestive heart failure, is known as *beriberi heart disease*. High-output heart failure is a form of secondary heart failure. It occurs when an otherwise normal heart fails because it can't keep up with the abnormally high metabolic needs of the body. For reasons that are unclear, it results from a deficiency of vitamin B-1, thiamine. It may respond dramatically to correction of the thiamine deficiency and replacement of thiamine in the diet.

Finally, a rather unusual and specific type of severe cardiac disease occurred in the past among drinkers of a particular type of Canadian beer. It was caused not by alcohol per se but by the noxious effects of small amounts of cobalt. The cobalt had been added to the beer to maintain its "head." These cases occurred in the mid- to late 1960s and had a mortality rate of 50% to 60%. Fortunately, the cause was identified, and this cobalt-induced heart disease no longer occurs. An earlier similar epidemic of congestive heart failure due to arsenic-contaminated beer occurred around the turn of the twentieth century in England. These examples demonstrate the potential problems of additives.

A variety of abnormalities in cardiac rhythm have been associated with alcohol. In fact, nearly the entire spectrum of such abnormalities may be caused by acute and chronic alcohol intake. Speeding up of the normal heartbeats is called *sinus tachycardia,* which may be associated with subjective palpitations. This is thought to occur because of the effects of alcohol and its metabolite, acetaldehyde, in releasing norepinephrine. The sinus node is the normal pacemaker of the heart. Its rate of firing can be speeded up by increasing the amount of circulating epinephrine and norepinephrine. Abnormal beating of the heart, or *arrhythmias,* may affect either the upper (atrial) or lower (ventricular) portions of the heart. The upper chambers of the heart are like the primers for the lower parts, which are the pumps. Thus, ventricular rhythm irregularities that interfere with the heart's pumping action tend to be more serious. *Atrial fibrillation* and *atrial flutter* occur in the atrial heart muscles and produce ineffective atrial beats, which diminish the pumping efficiency of the ventricular beats that follow. Atrial fibrillation can be a significant risk factor for strokes.

There are some sluggish men who are improved by drinking; as there are fruits that are not good until they are rotten.
—Samuel Johnson

Another alcohol-induced rhythm disturbance involving the upper part of the heart is *paroxysmal atrial tachycardia.* This involves a different and more rapid than usual kind of heartbeat. There are also abnormal heartbeats involving the lower part of the heart. These can be dangerous. If these irregular heartbeats occur in a particular pattern, which may be induced by alcohol, they can cause sudden death. In fact, studies have shown an increased incidence of sudden death among alcohol dependent persons. Alcohol also causes an increase in the frequency of *premature ventricular contractions.* These, along with atrial flutter and fibrillation, are the most common alcohol-induced arrhythmias. Atrial fibrillation has also been reported to occur after heavy drinking episodes; it does not appear to be associated with long-term moderate use. Alcohol is also a known trigger for Brugada syndrome, a genetic cardiac condition which can cause ventricular arrhythmias and sudden death.

Let us have wine and women, mirth and laughter. Sermons and soda water the day after.
—Lord Byron

Seasonal alcohol-induced, arrhythmia-related syndromes have been reported. They go by the name *holiday heart syndrome.* As you might expect from the name, such arrhythmias occur after heavy alcohol intake, usually around holidays, and may also occur on Mondays after heavy weekend drinking. The syndrome involves palpitations and arrhythmias, the most common of which is transient atrial fibrillation, but no evidence of cardiomyopathy or congestive heart failure. The signs and symptoms generally clear completely after a few days of abstinence.

Even in moderate amounts, alcohol exacerbates certain abnormalities of blood fats (specifically *Type IV hyperlipoproteinemia*), but not in normal persons who don't have this condition. In such patients, alcohol elevates fat levels of a particular kind believed to increase the rate of development of arteriosclerosis (hardening of the arteries). As a result, the coronary arteries become increasingly narrowed and may eventually become blocked, leading to premature heart attacks. Even small amounts of alcohol can significantly affect this disorder in individuals at risk.

Alcohol is well known for causing dilation of superficial skin blood vessels and capillaries. It does not seem to have a similar effect on the coronary arteries. Therefore, despite its use in treating angina in the past, alcohol is not currently considered helpful. In fact, current research indicates that, in persons with angina, alcohol decreases exercise tolerance. In conjunction with vigorous physical activity, alcohol use by persons with angina may be especially dangerous.

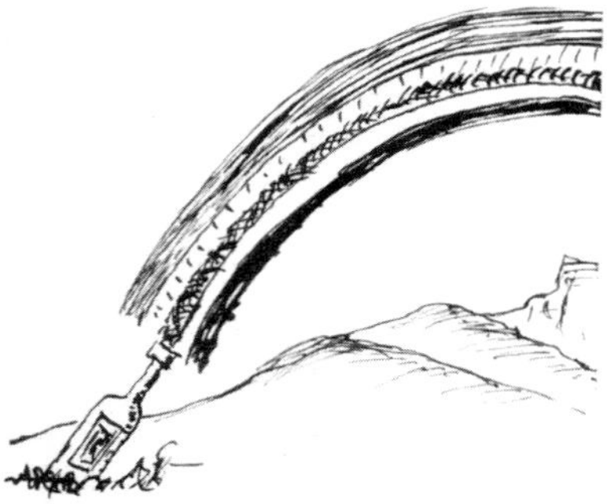

Research findings suggest that moderate amounts of alcohol may provide a protective effect against the development of arteriosclerotic coronary artery disease. The research indicates that the equivalent of one drink per day may have roughly the same effect on serum cholesterol as the average lipid-lowering diet or regular vigorous exercise. The cardioprotective effect of alcohol appears to be greatest when alcohol is taken in the form of red wine, although white wine too may be helpful. Moderate alcohol intake is known to increase levels of HDL cholesterol and decrease levels of LDL cholesterol. Higher and lower levels of these substances, respectively, are associated with lower risks of heart attacks, so moderate daily use of alcohol may be desirable from the heart's point of view.

In addition to its effects on cholesterol metabolism, alcohol itself, in moderate amounts, and the antioxidants present in wine may have an anti-inflammatory effect in the endothelial cells that line the coronary arteries. These cells are involved in the development of the plaques that play a key role in causing the blockage of vessels that results in heart attacks. Studies have shown that this reduced tendency of platelets and other cells to adhere to the endothelial cells occurs because of changes within the endothelial cells themselves that promote this adherence. While this cardioprotective effect occurs with moderate use of alcohol, higher doses of alcohol cause inflammation, which promotes adherence and therefore makes heart attacks more likely.

Wine is bottled poetry.
—Robert Louis Stevenson

Research has shown a definite link between heavy drinking and hypertension. Heavy drinkers have elevated systolic and diastolic blood pressures. This is true even when weight, age, serum cholesterol level, and smoking are controlled. Although this relationship seems well established, the specific role alcohol plays in the development of atherosclerosis (the process by which hardening of the arteries occurs) is much less clear, especially in view of the multiple factors that cause atherosclerosis. The potential importance of alcohol in causing strokes has been recognized, probably as a result of alcohol's effects on blood pressure (see the section Nervous System later in this chapter). It is well established that the cessation of heavy alcohol use reduces both systolic and diastolic blood pressures.

GENITOURINARY SYSTEM

Urinary Tract

Almost uniquely, the kidneys are not negatively affected by alcohol to any great extent. What happens in the kidneys generally is the result of disordered function elsewhere in the body. For example, alcohol promotes the production of urine through its ability to inhibit the production and output of *antidiuretic hormone* (ADH) by the hypothalamic-pituitary region of the brain. Normally blood goes to the kidneys for filtering, and water and wastes are separated from the blood and then excreted through the bladder. Usually during this process, ADH causes water to be reabsorbed by the kidneys to maintain the body's fluid balance. When this hormone's levels are suppressed, the kidneys' capacity to reabsorb water is diminished, so water is eliminated from the body. Alcohol inhibits this hormone's production when the blood alcohol level is rising. This is so after consuming as little as two ounces of pure alcohol. When the blood alcohol level is steady or falling, there is no such effect. In fact, the opposite may be true; excess body water may be retained. Alcohol can also lead to acute urinary retention and the recurrence and exacerbation of urinary tract infections and/or prostatitis. This is due to alcohol's ability to cause spasm and congestion in diseased prostate glands, as well as in the tissues surrounding previously existing urethral strictures, a narrowing of the tube that carries urine from the bladder.

It has recently been found that patients with alcoholic cirrhosis occasionally have abnormalities involving the glomeruli, the filtration units in the kidneys. The glomeruli are tiny structures at the extreme "upstream end" of the kidney's major functional unit, the nephron. They act somewhat as sieves, filtering excess fluid and wastes from the blood, while retaining the red and white blood cells, platelets, serum proteins, and other elements that are to be returned to the general circulation. Two main types of glomerular abnormalities are related to alcohol use. The first, a benign type of *glomerulosclerosis,* is the more common and rarely causes significant problems. The second, *cirrhotic glomerulonephritis,* fortunately far less common, interferes with the filtration process and the elimination of metabolic wastes produced by the kidney. Cirrhosis may cause other troubles as well. It can cause retention of sodium, which may play a significant role in the ascites and edema seen with cirrhosis, the abnormal handling of other substances, and an inability to excrete excess water normally. The complex causes of all these functional renal abnormalities are not fully understood and are very likely caused by a number of pathological factors in combination.

A nearly always fatal but fortunately uncommon consequence of chronic heavy alcohol use is *hepatorenal syndrome.* This is thought to be caused by a toxic serum factor or factors produced by severe alcoholic liver disease. These factors cause shifts in kidney blood flow and impede effective filtration of the blood by the kidneys. Unless the underlying liver disease is reversed, irreversible kidney failure can occur. Interestingly, there appears to be nothing intrinsically wrong with the kidneys themselves. They can be transplanted into patients without underlying liver disease and will perform normally. Likewise, liver transplantation in such patients will restore normal kidney function. Thus, the kidney failure is thought to be due to some circulating toxic factor or factors presumably resulting from the associated liver disease.

Reproductive System and Pregnancy

Chronic heavy alcohol use adversely affects the reproductive system in both men and women. In women there may be decreased fertility and skipped menstrual periods; in men diminished libido, impotence, and occasionally sterility may result. In addition to its many other functions, the liver plays an important role in the balance of sex hormones, so when liver function is impaired, an imbalance of sex hormones results. This can play havoc with normal reproductive functions in both men and women.

Both male and female sex hormones are normally present in both sexes, only in different proportions. Increased levels of female hormones in alcohol-dependent men, caused by decreased liver metabolism of these hormones, can lead to "feminization" of features. Breasts can enlarge, testicles can shrink, and a loss or thinning of body hair can occur. Sex-hormone alterations in males can also result from alcohol's direct inhibitory action on the testes, decreasing the production of testosterone, the main male sex hormone. Chronic heavy intake of alcohol may speed up the liver's metabolism of testosterone, thereby further decreasing its levels. Testosterone levels may also be lowered in other ways, such as by alcohol's direct inhibiting effect on the brain centers involved in the production and release of luteinizing hormone (LH), which normally stimulates the production and release of testosterone by the testicles. When alcohol diminishes LH levels, the net effect is decreased circulatory testosterone levels. This brain-mediated inhibitory effect of alcohol is a direct effect and independent of any liver or nutritional factors.

Sex-hormone alterations in women are not as well understood. In part, this is because the female reproductive system, located within the body, is less accessible to study and research. However, it is also because the effects of the use of alcohol by women as a distinct area of inquiry is a fairly recent development. Nonetheless, there is some evidence that alcohol, paralleling its effects on men, may have direct toxic effects on the ovaries and the pituitary gland. In addition, as with men, indirect endocrine effects due to liver disease may play a role. Women with abnormal liver metabolism may have increased testosterone levels, causing a loss of female sexual characteristics, thus interfering with normal sexual functioning. These effects play an important role in the menstrual and fertility changes in women who are chronic heavy drinkers.

Wine prepares the heart for love, unless you take too much.
—Ovid

Finally, although sexual interests and pursuits may be heightened by alcohol's relaxation of inhibitions, the ability to perform sexually can be impaired. For example, in men there may be either relative or absolute impotency, despite alcohol-fueled increased desire. Centuries ago, Shakespeare (*Macbeth,* Act II, Scene 1) described these paradoxical effects of alcohol:

MACDUFF: What three things does drink especially provoke?
PORTER: Merry sir, nose-painting, sleep, and urine. Lechery, sir, it provokes, and unprovokes; it provokes the desire, but it takes away the performance.

Abstinence from alcohol, improvement in liver disease, and an adequate diet will significantly improve, though often not reverse completely, the alcohol-induced changes in sexual and reproductive functions. Some males who are testosterone deficient may benefit from testosterone replacement therapy.

Fetal Alcohol Syndrome and Fetal Alcohol Effects

Since the 1970s, considerable attention has been directed toward the effects of chronic alcohol use during pregnancy. It was in 1971 that a researcher first reported his observations of infants born to alcohol-dependent mothers. The constellation of features observed has since been termed *fetal alcohol syndrome* (FAS), which has an incidence of 1 to 2 cases per 1,000 live births in the United States. Alcohol can pass through the placenta to affect the developing fetus and interfere with normal prenatal development. At birth, infants with FAS are smaller than normal, in both weight and length. The head size is smaller, probably as a result of arrested brain growth. These infants also have a "dysmorphic facial appearance"—that is, they appear "different," although the differences are not easily described. The features include an overall small head, flat cheeks, small eyes, and a thin upper lip. At birth these infants are jittery and tremulous. Whether this jitteriness is the result of nervous system impairment from the long-term exposure to alcohol and/or mini-withdrawal is unclear. There have been reports of newborn infants having the odor of alcohol on their breath. Cardiac problems and intellectual disabilities are associated with FAS in almost half of

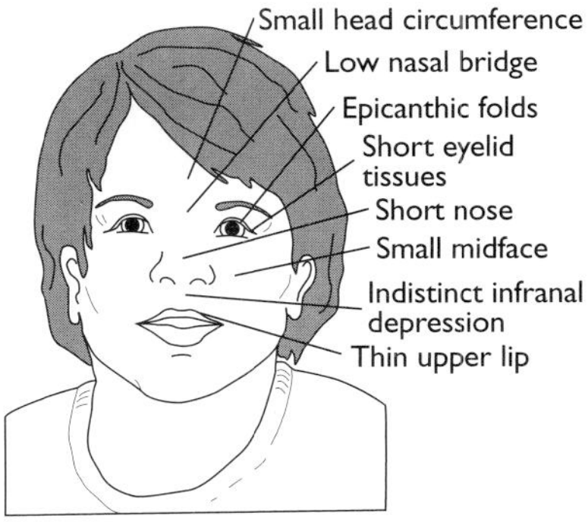

the cases (46%). FAS, in combination with fetal alcohol effects (FAE), has been established as a leading cause of intellectual and developmental disabilities in the United States—and the most preventable one. (See Chapter 8 for further discussion of the effects of maternal drinking on children.)

It is now well established that a mother does not have to be alcohol-dependent to expose her unborn baby to the harmful effects of alcohol during pregnancy. Nor do alcohol's effects on the fetus have to occur as full-blown fetal alcohol syndrome. They can occur with variable degrees of severity. When less severe, they are referred to as *fetal alcohol effects* (FAE). The full range of problems resulting from prenatal alcohol exposure is referred to as *fetal alcohol spectrum disorders*.

Perhaps even more worrisome than the classic FAS are the potential adverse effects on unborn babies of any pregnant woman drinking more than one drink (½ ounce of pure alcohol) on even a single occasion. Drinking more than one drink per day invites increased risk of abnormalities. As the amount of alcohol consumed on any given day rises, the risk of congenital abnormalities increases as well. The following figures are not a numerical average but, rather, refer to the amount of alcohol consumed on any single day by a pregnant woman:

Less than 1 drink	Very little risk
Two drinks	Threshold for risk
Two to 4 drinks	10% risk for abnormalities
Ten drinks	50% risk for abnormalities
More than 10 drinks	75% risk for abnormalities

Clearly, FAE is not restricted to the children of women who are alcohol dependent. Not unexpectedly, given similar findings with other drugs, the teratogenic effects of alcohol are greater in the first three months of pregnancy than they are in the fourth through ninth months. Based on this information, in the summer of 1977 the NIAAA issued a health warning advising expectant mothers not to have more than two drinks a day. In 1981 a much stronger warning was issued. The U.S. surgeon general (the nation's highest public health official) advised that women wishing to become pregnant, as well as women who are pregnant, consume no alcohol. More recent research confirms that this recommendation was well advised.

Heredity. *There are on record many instances of inebriety in children conceived soon after marriage (when the parents drank wine), although children born to the parents later in life (when the parents were abstinent) were temperate. If the parent is intoxicated at the time of conception, the child is likely to be a victim to insanity, inebriety and idiocy. Mothers who indulge in intoxicants freely before the birth and during the lactation of their children impart to them impulses toward inebriety.*
—Walter W. Spooner

The Cyclopedia of Intemperance and Prohibition, 1891

Current research suggests that there are both dose-related and threshold effects. "Dose-related" means that, the more alcohol consumed, the greater the likelihood of damage to the unborn child. "Threshold" refers to a particular level when the effects of drinking "kick in." Amounts below the threshold seemingly have no impact, but when drinking exceeds the threshold amount, there is a risk of alcohol-induced problems. Current research suggests that the threshold is around one drink per day during the second trimester. Drinking one to two drinks per day, for a total of 1 ounce of alcohol per day, doubles the risk of spontaneous abortions during the second trimester. Also, the age of the mother may play a role. One study found that, even with the same levels and patterns of drinking, older mothers, those over age 30, were two to five times more likely to have children with functional impairment than were mothers under age 30.

The basis for alcohol's role in fetal alcohol syndrome and fetal alcohol effects (FAS/FAE) is becoming more clear. It now appears that the presence of alcohol—even in fairly small amounts—alters neurotransmission (specifically the GABA and glutamate neurotransmitters), which suppresses and disrupts nerve cell activity. This effect interferes with the timing and sequence of normal fetal nerve development, with large numbers of neural cells receiving signals, literally, to commit suicide through a process known as *apoptosis*. Millions of brain cells are lost through this process. This is believed to be responsible for the reduced brain size and permanent neurobehavioral disturbance that are the central features of FAS.

How alcohol interferes with normal prenatal growth is not fully understood. Research with animals suggests that alcohol crosses the placenta freely and diffuses throughout fetal tissues in much the same fashion as it does in adult tissues. As a toxin, alcohol seems to disrupt the normal growth sequence; the developing fetus cannot later "make up" for these disruptions. In fact, research has shown that parental alcohol exposure causes persistent, long-term growth impairment, which has been shown to be present in 10-year-old children. The particular abnormalities seen are directly related to the critical developments that were occurring when alcohol was present.

Preliminary research suggests, too, that the alcohol level of some of the fetal tissues may be higher than that of the mother. If this is the case, the reason has not been clearly identified. Because alcohol can pass freely through the placenta to the fetus, one would predict that the alcohol should be able to exit just as easily. Therefore, both mother and fetus would be expected to have equivalent blood alcohol levels. Case reports of women who drank alcohol during labor, and in whom blood alcohol level studies were done, indicate that the newborn baby's blood alcohol and tissue alcohol levels do not drop as fast as the mother's. The reason, presumably, is that the infant has an immature liver. Newborns do not have the fully developed enzyme systems (such as alcohol dehydrogenase) necessary to metabolize and eliminate alcohol as rapidly as their mothers do. Thus, for a given maternal blood alcohol level, the fetus may have a higher blood and tissue alcohol concentration for a longer period of time.

During the years since FAS and FAE were first recognized, researchers have followed affected individuals into adolescence and young adulthood. The nature and extent of impairments found to be associated with FAS and FAE can only be characterized as devastating. Intellectual disabilities is a common part of the picture. In one large group of FAS and FAE individuals, it was found that their average IQs were 68 and 73, respectively. (Typically an IQ of 100 is considered average.)

In the study group, the range of IQs extended from 20 (severely disabled) to 105 (within the normal range). No FAS patient had an IQ of 90 or greater at follow-up. Thus, there is considerable variation, and it is impossible to predict the severity of intellectual deficits that may be present in individual cases.

What is evident is that individuals with FAE as well as FAS are at very high risk for diminished intellectual and adaptive functioning. In the study just noted, the average chronological age was 16.5 years, but in terms of general functioning and ability to get along in the world, the general level of functioning was estimated to be equivalent to normal children of 7.5 years of age. This study found that 95% of the children had been in special education classes at some point during their school experience. Impulsiveness, lack of social inhibition, and social naïveté are often problems as well. Attention-deficit/hyperactivity disorder (ADHD) is one of the more common behavioral deficits found in children with FAS. Unfortunately, compared to other children, children with FAS/FAE are generally less responsive to treatment with stimulant medications.

People with FAS often behave in ways that cause them problems because their behavior is inappropriate and potentially dangerous, or it invites being exploited by others. Inappropriate sexual behavior is common. Behavior that as children or preteens may have been seen by others as being very "friendly," involving touching and being physically close to others, becomes socially less acceptable as they grow older. Among adolescents and in adulthood, such behavior can result in social problems and legal encounters. A recently recognized problem is the presence of FAS/FAE among persons in the criminal justice system.

Most significantly, there is no improvement with age—in IQ, achievement, or ability to cope with everyday tasks. Within one large study of adults with FAS, only 5% lived alone and none were fully self-sufficient. The special needs of children with FAS/FAE persist through life. This means that protective services and special structures are necessary for these children throughout their lives. Clinical research has been directed to identifying what kinds of supportive services within schools and the community, as well as behavioral therapies, can best assist these children as they enter school and move into adulthood.

RESPIRATORY SYSTEM

Alcohol affects normal breathing. Low to moderate doses of alcohol increase the respiratory rate; presumably this is due to the direct effect of alcohol on the respiration center in the brain. In larger anesthetic and/or toxic doses, the respiration rate is decreased. This latter effect may contribute to respiratory insufficiency in persons with chronic obstructive pulmonary disease who drink heavily, or it may cause death in cases of acute alcohol poisoning.

In the past, it was thought that for the most part alcohol spared the lungs as far as direct harmful effects were concerned. This is apparently not the case. In recent years such effects have been recognized and investigated. Alcohol can interfere with a variety of important pulmonary defenses at the cellular level, both mechanical and metabolic. These impaired defenses can contribute importantly to chronic air flow obstruction and possibly produce bronchospasm in some individuals. The direct effects of alcohol on the lungs may have significant consequences for individuals with emphysema, chronic obstructive pulmonary disease, chronic bronchitis, and asthma. With the high association of smoking and heavy drinking, lung cancer is more common among those with alcohol dependence. Clinical research in recent years has established that chronic heavy alcohol use is a clear risk factor for the development of the acute lung injury and respiratory distress syndromes. Both are associated with high levels of morbidity and mortality. Possible factors explaining this relationship include frequency of pulmonary infections, trauma, and aspiration, as well as disruption of a number of normal cellular processes that protect the lungs.

Normal cilia pushing dust out bronchial tree

drunk cilia with hangovers

There also are a number of noxious effects of alcohol that can affect the lungs in an indirect fashion. The combination of stuporousness, or unconsciousness, and vomiting as a result of excessive alcohol use can lead to aspiration of mouth and nasal secretions or gastric contents. This can lead to bacterial infections and/or aspiration pneumonia. Because of alcohol-induced diminished defenses against infection, pulmonary infections, especially with pneumococci and gram-negative bacteria, occur more frequently and severely in those with a history of heavy alcohol use than in others. Also because of diminished defenses against infection, there is a higher incidence of tuberculosis. Thus, any heavy drinker with a newly positive skin test for tuberculosis should be considered for treatment to prevent possible active tuberculosis.

ENDOCRINE SYSTEM

The endocrine system is composed of the glands of the body and their secretions, the hormones. Hormones can be thought of as chemical messengers, released by the glands into the bloodstream. They are vital in regulating countless bodily processes. There is a very complex and involved interaction between hormonal activity and body functioning.

Although there are many glands in the body, the pituitary gland, located in the brain, can be thought of as the master gland. Many of its hormonal secretions are involved in regulating the other glands. This is through what is called the *hypothalamic-pituitary-adrenal (HPA)* axis.

Alcohol can affect the endocrine system in three major ways. First, alcohol can alter the function of the pituitary gland. If this happens,

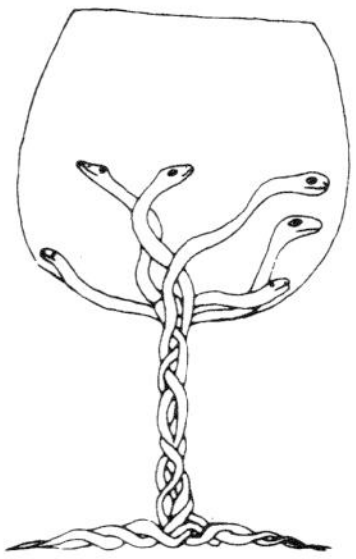

the other glands are unable to function properly because they are not receiving the proper "hormonal instructions." It is believed that chronic heavy alcohol use may lead to premature aging through alcohol's chronic activation of the HPA axis. Second, alcohol can affect other glands directly. Despite other glands' receiving the correct instructions from the pituitary, alcohol can impede their ability to respond appropriately. Third, interference with normal endocrine function can result from alcohol-induced liver damage. One of the functions of the liver is to metabolize hormones, thereby removing them from the system. Liver disease diminishes this capacity, and hormonal imbalances can result.

As previously described, the level of testosterone, the male sex hormone, is lowered by alcohol in a number of ways. First, it is lowered by the direct action of alcohol on the testes and, second, through alcohol's inhibitory action on the pituitary gland and its subsequent failure to secrete LH, the hormone that stimulates the testes' secretion of testosterone. Another factor is that the liver's clearance of testosterone may be decreased. This may lead to abnormal function in females. Finally, malnutrition, which frequently occurs in those with a serious alcohol disorder, may inhibit the function of the hypothalamic-pituitary-adrenal axis at all levels.

Serious liver disease reduces the liver's ability to break down another of the pituitary's hormones, melanocyte-stimulating hormone (MSH). This may result in increased levels of MSH, which leads to a deepening of skin pigmentation and frequently a "dirty tan" skin color. With increased levels of other hormones that stimulate the activity of other cells, the question arises whether such increased hormone levels have a potential role in the development of various cancers.

The adrenal glands are also affected by alcohol. The adrenal glands produce several hormones and thus serve multiple functions. One function known to all of us comes from the release of adrenaline (epinephrine) when we are frightened or fearful. This charge of adrenaline, with its associated rapid heartbeat and sweating, causes the fight-or-flight response. Heavy intake of or withdrawal from alcohol prompts increased release of catecholamines, such as epinephrine, by the adrenals. This may be partly responsible for the rapid heartbeat and hypertension that occur during withdrawal. Another adrenal hormone, aldosterone, which plays a major role in regulating the body's salt and water levels, increases both with heavy use of alcohol and during alcohol withdrawal. Increased aldosterone levels often lead to significant and potentially serious salt and water imbalances, visible clinically as swelling (edema). Increased aldosterone levels are frequently seen in patients with cirrhosis and ascites. This is thought to be, in part, the cause of the peripheral edema that is also seen with this condition. In some individuals the adrenals secrete excess cortisol. The excess cortisol causes a condition clinically indistinguishable from a condition known as *Cushing's disease,* except that it clears rapidly with abstinence from alcohol.

Animal research is raising several interesting questions about alcohol's effects on the endocrine system. In animals, heavy alcohol intake increases the levels of norepinephrine in the heart. This raises the question of whether increased levels of norepinephrine might contribute to the development of alcoholic heart muscle disease.

Carbohydrate metabolism, which is regulated by the hormone insulin, can be affected by chronic alcohol intake. Heavy drinking may lead to abnormally high levels of glucose similar to those seen in diabetics. This condition is referred to as *hyperglycemia.* Usually all that is needed to correct this is abstinence from alcohol and an improved, well-balanced diet. Long-term excessive alcohol intake as well as short-term heavy drinking binges can, on the other hand, lead to low blood sugar levels, known as *hypoglycemia.* This abnormality has two endocrine system–related causes. First, because of poor diet and liver dysfunction, the liver has less glycogen, the body's stored form of glucose that is usually available for conversion into circulating glucose. Second, the liver is less able to convert proteins and amino acids into glucose. Hypoglycemia can cause coma and, if severe and prolonged, can result in irreversible brain damage. This is a medical emergency and must be treated as rapidly as possible with glucose administration.

Recent studies have shown that moderate alcohol intake is associated with a reduced incidence of diabetes and diabetes-related coronary artery disease. However, the reverse seems to be true of chronic, heavy drinking.

The increased NADH to NAD^+ ratio (see Chapter 3) is a major factor in causing two dangerous forms of metabolic acidosis frequently associated with chronic heavy drinking. The first is known as *alcoholic ketoacidosis,* which occurs when the altered cofactor ratio leads to the production not of carbon dioxide and water, as alcohol is metabolized, but of ketones, which are organic acids. This disorder may be fatal. The second form, called *lactic acidosis,* also occurs because of the altered ratio of NADH to NAD^+. In this case, there is an increased production of lactate. Both types of acidosis are dangerous and must be treated with intravenous fluids and sodium bicarbonate.

Cancer

Research is being conducted to explore whether alcohol's effect on the endocrine system contributes to the development of different types of cancer. Heavy drinkers are known to have a higher incidence of skin, thyroid, laryngeal, oral, head and neck, esophageal, stomach, liver, lung, colon, prostate, and breast cancers. Recall that the pituitary gland is the body's master control gland. It influences the activity of various other glandular tissues through the hormones it secretes. Alcohol inhibits the breakdown of pituitary MSH. It may also play a role in the release of hormones that promote thyroid activity and milk production by the breast.

These three hormones have one thing in common: they affect their target tissues—the skin, thyroid gland, and breast—by causing these tissues to increase their metabolic activity. So, the pieces may be falling into place. Cancer, simply put, occurs when there is uncontrolled or abnormal cellular metabolic activity and growth and inadequate immune defenses, which normally would eliminate cancerous cells that develop. It is possible that alcohol's presence over long periods of time produces so many hormonal messages to the skin, thyroid, and breast tissues that, in certain at-risk patients, in some as yet undetermined fashion, malignant cells are produced at these sites.

Recent research has established that acetaldehyde, a carcinogen and mutagenic product of alcohol metabolism, is probably responsible for the increased incidence of cancer with heavy drinking. Because alcohol may impair the function of the body's protective immune surveillance system, malignant cells are not eliminated by the body. In fact, recent research suggests that alcohol plays an important role, not only in carcinogenesis but also in the promotion of cell invasion into healthy tissue.

☐ SKIN

Chronic alcohol use affects the skin both directly and indirectly. Its most pronounced direct effect is dilation of the vessels of the skin. A variety of pathological effects on other systems are reflected by the appearance of the skin. For example, a chronic flushed appearance, itching, jaundice, thinning of the skin, acne, changes in hair distribution, the presence of spider angiomas, a grayish cast to the skin, and fingernail changes all may reflect significant liver dysfunction. Bruising, paleness, and skin infections may reflect major abnormalities in the hematological and immune systems.

Skin changes may also suggest the presence of nutritional deficiencies in alcoholism. These include vitamin B deficiency, especially of niacin, which causes pellagra, and vitamin C and zinc deficiencies. Skin manifestations often reflect the chaotic life situations of many with well established alcohol disorders. There may be evidence of accidents, such as bruises, abrasions, lacerations, and multiple old scars. In colder climates there may be evidence of frostbite. Nicotine stains as well as cigarette burns may be present. Heavy and chronic alcohol use, among other causes, precipitates or aggravates a skin condition known as *rosacea* in predisposed persons. This condition includes flushing and inflammation, especially of the nose and middle portion of the face. Particularly striking is the excessive growth of the subcutaneous tissue of the nose, a condition called *rhinophyma* or "rum nose." Another skin condition associated with chronic alcoholism and alcoholic liver disease is *porphyria cutanea tarda.* This includes increased pigmentation, hair growth, and blistering in sun-exposed areas. It has been thought by some that there may be a causal link between other important skin diseases, such as psoriasis, eczema, and scleroderma, and heavy alcohol use. Others feel that it is more likely that these conditions are simply much harder to manage and therefore seem to be more severe in chronic heavy drinkers because of their concurrent multiple medical problems, nutritional inadequacy, and generally poor treatment compliance.

SKELETAL SYSTEM

Chronic alcohol use affects the skeletal system in several significant ways. First, at least four types of arthritis are linked to heavy alcohol use. *Gouty arthritis* results from increased uric acid levels, which can occur in two ways. One is as a result of the increased levels of organic acids that accompany the altered ratio of NADH to NAD^+. In this instance the kidneys try unsuccessfully to secrete both uric acid and these other organic acids, so excess amounts of uric acid accumulate. The other cause of gouty arthritis, called *saturnine gout,* results from consuming lead-contaminated moonshine. The lead can damage the kidneys, which leads to increased uric acid levels. In both cases, abstinence and specific treatment for gouty arthritis may prove beneficial.

Arthritis occurs, too, in conjunction with alcoholic pancreatitis. This is believed to be caused by the direct or indirect damage to joints by the enzymes that are circulating in the bloodstream as a result of damage to the pancreas. *Degenerative arthritis,* also known as "old age" arthritis or osteoarthritis, occurs more frequently with chronic heavy alcohol use. This probably comes from the higher frequency of falls, injuries, and bone fractures. *Septic arthritis* (acute infection in a joint space) also is seen more frequently in those who drink heavily. This is probably a result of several factors in combination. *Osteoarthritis* is more common and involves roughened joint surfaces, where blood-borne infectious agents may be more likely to settle. Long term heavy drinkers are likely to have a higher incidence of blood-borne bacterial infections for a number of reasons, including more frequent infections of all types, more frequent injuries, and less attention to personal hygiene. Again, in the wake of long-term heavy drinking, defenses against such infections are diminished. Interestingly, alcohol use/abuse does not appear to have either positive or negative effects on autoimmune disorders.

It's the world's first high calcium wine. It helps prevent osteoporosis so if you get drunk and fall, you're less likely to break your hip.

Osteoporosis, a generalized thinning or demineralization of the bones most typically occurring in the elderly, is accelerated by heavy alcohol use. This condition can lead to a 25% decrease in bone mass, which in turn can frequently lead to fractures. Fractures of the hip (especially the neck of the femur), the wrist, the upper arm bone (humerus), and the vertebral bodies in the spinal column are the most common. Rib fractures are also common in heavy drinkers, but they are probably caused by an increased frequency of falls and trauma rather than as a result of intrinsic changes in the rib bones. Many factors contribute to the occurrence of osteoporosis. They include alcohol-induced loss of calcium and/or magnesium due to excess excretion by the kidneys, decreased absorption of calcium and/or vitamin D by the small intestine with a diminished capacity for absorption, and the demineralizing effects of excessive adrenal corticosteroid hormones, due to the stimulating effects of alcohol on the adrenal glands. Recent research has highlighted malnutrition as a major cause of the bone thinning seen among those with heavy excessive alcohol use.

Aseptic necrosis, a form of bone death, especially of the head of the femur, caused by inadequate blood supply, is another condition especially frequent in alcohol-dependent men. In fact, as many as 50% of all people with this condition (of whom two-thirds are men) have a history of heavy alcohol use. Deformity of the hip joint often results from this and can lead to severe arthritis, which can be disabling and may eventually require total hip joint replacement. The cause is unknown but is postulated to be related to fat deposits, which are thought to be caused by pancreatitis or alcohol-induced abnormalities in the liver's metabolism of fats (see Chapter 3). These fatty deposits are believed to lodge in the small arterial vessels supplying the femoral head and cut off blood flow, resulting in bone death.

I don't care about water. I want a martini.

NERVOUS SYSTEM

The central nervous system (CNS) is perhaps the most profoundly affected of all the major organ systems by the effects of acute and chronic alcohol use. Over time, with sufficient quantities of alcohol, the CNS becomes adapted to its presence. This adaptation is what addictive states are all about. Drinking a quart of liquor daily for as little as one week can create a state of physical dependence.

Dependence, Tolerance, Craving, and Withdrawal

"Physical dependence" is defined by the presence of tolerance with increasing intake of alcohol and withdrawal with its cessation. "Tolerance" refers to physiological changes that occur as a result of repeated exposure to alcohol. Tolerance represents the nervous system's efforts to adapt and function more or less normally despite the presence of alcohol. These changes include alterations in how the body handles alcohol (metabolic tolerance) as well as changes in alcohol's effects on the nervous system (functional or behavioral tolerance). After repeated exposures, there is both an increased rate of metabolism of alcohol and a decrease in behavioral impairment at a particular blood alcohol level. Consequently, the person requires increasing amounts of alcohol to get the effects previously produced by lower doses and to ward off withdrawal symptoms.

Once physical dependence has been established, characteristic symptoms appear when consumption is curtailed. These symptoms constitute the so-called *abstinence,* or *withdrawal, syndrome.* One sure way to terminate an abstinence syndrome is to administer more of the addictive drug. The withdrawal symptoms for any drug are generally the reverse of the effects induced by the drug itself. Alcohol belongs to the depressant class of drugs. Therefore, the alcohol abstinence syndrome is characterized by symptoms that are indicative of an activated state. The hangover, a kind of mini-withdrawal, testifies to this. The well-known symptoms of withdrawal—jumpiness, edginess, irritability, and hyperactivity—are exactly the opposite of those resulting from alcohol's depressant effects.

A drunken night makes a cloudy morning.
—Sir William Cornwallis

Individuals who have regularly used large quantities of alcohol—that is, they have developed tolerance to that amount—will have withdrawal symptoms whenever there is a relative absence of alcohol. Although an individual may still be drinking, withdrawal symptoms will appear if the amount consumed is less than usual and therefore the blood alcohol level is lowered. The symptoms include intention tremors (tremors occurring when the person is trying to do something), which are rapid and coarse and involve the head, tongue, and limbs. These are the basis for the morning shakes in a heavy drinker whose last drink was the night before.

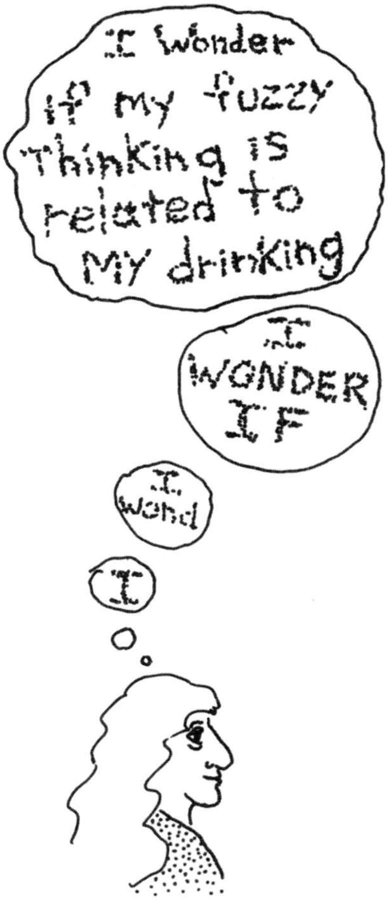

If the chronic heavy drinker does not consume more alcohol, he or she is likely to develop more serious symptoms of withdrawal. These are thought to represent a kind of rebound effect. In the absence of alcohol and its chronic suppressant effects, certain regions of the brain become overactive. The severity of the symptoms of withdrawal can vary widely, depending on the length of time of heavy drinking and the amount of alcohol consumed during that period, plus individual metabolic differences among people. The symptoms of withdrawal include tremulousness, fever, tachycardia, hypertension, agitation, seizures, and hallucinations. These will be discussed in detail later in this chapter.

Craving is also associated with addiction and results from changes in the central nervous system. With alcohol, craving is that deep desire, that virtually irresistible impulse, that strong "need" to have a drink. When it strikes, it is difficult to ignore it. Craving is different from withdrawal, although the state of abstinence may trigger it. In fact, multiple factors may be triggers—the situation, a song on the radio played at a favorite bar, certain foods, particular friends, or one's mood. These urges arise from physical changes in the brain, particularly changes in certain neurotransmitter systems. Importantly, a number of medications have been introduced into clinical practice in recent years that reduce craving and help people to decrease their use of alcohol. These drugs include naltrexone (Revia), acamprosate (Campral), nalmefene, ondansetron, and topiramate (Topamax). This represents a major step forward in the treatment of alcohol dependence.

Alcohol Idiosyncratic Intoxication

Aside from withdrawal symptoms, other important CNS disorders are related to alcohol use. A relatively unusual manifestation is a condition previously called pathological intoxication. (In later editions of the DSM it was termed "alcohol idiosyncratic intoxication" and was afterwards relegated to a category of manifestations that don't fit elsewhere, "alcohol disorders not otherwise specified.") Some susceptible persons, for reasons unknown, have a dramatic change of personality when they drink even small amounts of alcohol. It is a transient, delirium-like state with a very rapid onset. The individual becomes confused and disoriented; may have visual hallucinations; and may be very aggressive, anxious, impulsive, and enraged. In this state the person may carry out senseless, violent acts against others or him- or herself. The state can last for only a few minutes or for several hours; then the person lapses into a profound sleep and has amnesia for the episode. If interviewed later, the person might be very docile, not at all the raging mad person present during the episode. Most likely the person would report, "I don't know what happened; I just went bonkers" and would be remorseful about the harm caused during the episode. It is unclear whether there is a relationship between this syndrome and other organic impulse disorders. However, some experts believe it to be a seizure-like state triggered by alcohol.

Alcohol is a known trigger for both cluster headaches as well as migraine headaches.

Alcohol is a good preservative for everything but brains.
—ANONYMOUS

Organic Brain Disease

Newer brain imaging techniques have shown that chronic alcohol use can be accompanied by reductions in volume of both white and gray matter in the brain. Brain imaging has also shown that chronic alcohol use can also cause disruptions of white matter tracts, the bundles of axons that connect different parts of the brain. These changes have been shown to be at least partially reversible with the discontinuation of alcohol use.

Chronic heavy alcohol use can lead to varying degrees of dementia, or organic brain disease. The particular type of brain disease, its name and associated impairment, is determined by the portion of the brain involved. *Wernicke's syndrome* and *Korsakoff's psychosis* are two such syndromes closely tied to alcoholism. Sometimes they are discussed as two separate disorders; other times people lump them together as the Wernicke-Korsakoff syndrome. Both are caused by nutritional deficiencies, especially thiamine, vitamin B-1, in combination with whatever direct toxic effects alcohol has on nerve cells in the brain. Chronic heavy drinking is associated with decreased dietary intake of thiamine and decreased absorption from the small intestine, as well as diminished utilization of the available thiamine. In addition, recent evidence suggests that a genetic factor in the form of an inherited lack of an enzyme (transketolase) may play an important role in the development of Wernicke-Korsakoff syndrome in susceptible people.

The difference between these syndromes in terms of pathology is that Wernicke's syndrome involves injury to the midbrain, cerebellum, and areas near the third and fourth ventricles of the brain. Korsakoff's psychosis results from damage to areas of the brain important to memory and executive functions and is often associated with damage to peripheral nerve tissue as well. Prognostically Wernicke's syndrome has a brighter picture. When recognized and treated early, it often responds very rapidly to thiamine therapy. Korsakoff's psychosis is much slower to respond to treatment and is less likely to improve significantly. Patients with Korsakoff's psychosis often eventually require nursing home or custodial care.

Clinically a person with Wernicke's syndrome is apt to be confused, delirious, and apprehensive. There is a characteristic neurological dysfunction called *nystagmus* (abnormal, rapid lateral eye movements) as well as the possibility of paralysis of eye muscles that control particular eye movements, known as *gaze paralysis.* Nystagmus and other eye abnormalities are among the first symptoms to appear and, following treatment, the first to disappear. Difficulty with walking (ataxia) and balance are also typical of Wernicke's syndrome. This can lead to unsteadiness and gait disturbances. Both are caused by peripheral nerve damage in conjunction with cerebellar damage.

Korsakoff's psychosis presents a somewhat different picture. There is severe memory loss and confabulation. *Confabulation*—that is, making up tales, talking fluently without regard to facts—is the hallmark. It occurs in an individual who is otherwise alert, responsive, and able to attend to and comprehend the written and spoken word. Thus, the memory impairment is greatly out of proportion to other cognitive dysfunctions. Because of the severe damage to areas of the brain crucial to memory, the person simply cannot process and store new information. In order to fill in the memory gaps, he or she makes up stories. These are not deliberate lies: trickery would require more memory and intent than someone with Korsakoff's psychosis could muster. For example, were you to ask someone with this disorder if he or she had met you before, the response might be a long, involved story about the last time you had been together. It would be pure fantasy, having no basis in reality. This is the phenomenon of confabulation. Memory for things that happened both recently and long ago is variably but usually severely impaired. Things simply are not able to be stored for recall, and the person cannot remember events even five minutes after they occur. With Korsakoff's psychosis, ataxia may also be present. Ataxia causes a characteristic awkward manner of walking, with feet spread apart to prevent falls. Korsakoff's psychosis and Wernicke's syndrome can both have sudden, rapid onset. Frequently Korsakoff's psychosis follows a bout of delirium tremens (the DTs).

Cerebral atrophy (generalized loss of brain tissue), or "brain shrinkage," often occurs with chronic heavy alcohol use. Research has shown that these basic changes are due in large part to the direct toxic effects of alcohol, which particularly seem to affect the frontal and prefrontal areas of the brain. Most often this is seen in people in their 50s and 60s. Another name for this disorder is *alcoholic dementia* or, in current parlance, *alcohol-induced persisting dementia* (AIPD). Some combination of factors common in alcohol dependence is thought to cause the condition—such as malnutrition and the accompanying vitamin deficiencies, long-term exposure to the direct toxic effects of alcohol,

or a history of previous head traumas. Interesting recent research has shown that for some with AIPD, a drug called Rivastigmine, used with Alzheimer's patients, may be beneficial. As distinct from Alzheimer's, which has a progressive deterioration, individuals with AIPD may be stabilized with abstinence from alcohol.

Treatment of organic brain disease typically includes administration of thiamine and a well-balanced diet. Discontinuing alcohol is imperative. Treatment is more successful in reversing the signs and symptoms of Wernicke's syndrome. Only about 20% of persons with Korsakoff's psychosis recover completely. The recovery process is slow, often taking as long as 6 to 12 months. The mortality rate of the combined disorder is approximately 15%. The dementia associated with cerebral atrophy is irreversible. However, with abstinence and adequate nutrition it may not progress further.

Alcoholic cerebellar degeneration is a late complication of chronic heavy alcohol use in combination with nutritional deficiencies. It is more likely to occur in men, typically after 10 to 20 or more years of heavy drinking. Patients gradually develop a slow, broad-based, lurching gait, as if they were about to fall over. This results from the fact that the cerebellum, the area of the brain that is damaged, is the part of the brain that coordinates complex motor activity, such as walking. There is no associated cognitive dysfunction because the portions of the brain governing such activities are not usually affected, but signs of peripheral neuropathy and malnutrition may be present.

Alcohol is a prominent causal factor in the occurrence of cerebellum cognitive affective disorder, which is characterized by executive dysfunctions, disinhibitions, inappropriate behaviors, language abnormalities, mood and sometimes psychotic disorders, and spatial problems.

Two forms of organic brain dysfunction are a direct result of severe alcoholic liver disease. These are acute and chronic *hepatic* or *portosystemic-encephalopathy* (PSE). They are caused by the diseased liver's diminished ability to prevent naturally occurring toxic substances from getting into the general body circulation. (These toxins include ammonia and glutamine, which are normally confined to the blood vessels flowing from the small intestines into the liver, where they are usually completely metabolized.) This wreaks havoc with the central nervous system. In both the acute and chronic forms of PSE, there may be severe cognitive and memory disturbances; anxiety and depressive symptoms; sleep disturbances; changes in levels of consciousness, with the extreme being the *hepatic coma,* which can be fatal; a flapping-like movement disorder called *asterixis;* and a foul, musty odor to the breath. In the acute form, which is much less common, there is no evidence of the chronic liver disease that is almost always present in the chronic form. Along with abstinence from alcohol to allow the liver to recover as much normal function as possible, aggressive, multipronged medical management must be instituted. The goal of treatment is to reduce the body's production of toxic nitrogen-containing substances.

A particularly severe variant of chronic PSE is known as chronic *hepatocerebral disease.* This is a complication of long-standing liver disease, in which the brain has been harmed by toxins chronically circulating in the bloodstream. As a result, the brain has areas of cell death and a proliferation of scar-like CNS cells. Mirroring these, there is a corresponding loss of brain function, with dementia, ataxia, speech impairment (dysarthria), and sometimes bizarre movements. Scarred or damaged brain tissue cannot be repaired, so any such losses are permanent. Patients with this condition often require chronic nursing care facilities.

Two other organic brain diseases, which are quite uncommon but serious when they occur, are also related to alcohol abuse and nutritional deficiencies. First, *central pontine myelinolysis* involves a part of the brain stem known as the pons. This disease can vary in intensity from very mild to fatal over a two- to three-week period. The pons controls respiration, among other things. As the degeneration of the pons progresses, coma and finally death occur from respiratory failure. Second, *Marchiafava-Bignami disease,* also exceedingly uncommon, involves the nerve tracts connecting the frontal areas on both sides of the brain. Their degeneration leads to diminished language and motor skills, confusion, gait disorders, incontinence, seizures, dementia, hallucinations, and frequently death.

Nerve and Muscle Tissue Damage

Nerve cells in other parts of the body can be damaged by chronic heavy alcohol use. The most common disturbance is *alcoholic polyneuropathy,* resulting from nutritional deficiencies. This disorder has a gradual onset, progresses slowly, and can vary in severity. Recovery is often slow and generally incomplete, taking weeks to months after the discontinuation of alcohol ingestion and the administration of appropriate vitamins. Most commonly the distal nerves (those farthest from the body trunk) are affected first. The damage to these nerves seems to be caused primarily by nutritional deficiencies, though direct toxic effects of alcohol may be involved. Typically someone with polyneuropathy has a painful, burning feeling in the soles of the feet. Yet there is an absence of normal touch and position. Because there is sensory impairment, the individual doesn't have the necessary feedback to the brain to tell him or her how the body is positioned in space. This loss of position sense may lead to an unsteady, slapping style of walking because the person is uncertain where the feet and legs are in relation to the ground.

Muscle damage occurs in 40% to 60% of all chronic heavy drinkers. It often occurs in tandem with alcohol-caused nerve damage. Therefore, muscle tissue is usually wasted in the same areas that are affected by nerve damage. Other forms of muscle damage and degeneration have been reported even in the absence of neuropathy. One form involves acute muscle pain, swelling, weakness, and the destruction of muscle tissue in the aftermath of acute binges and is referred to as *acute alcoholic*

myopathy. Another form seen in chronic heavy drinkers is *chronic alcoholic myopathy,* which involves weakness, decreased muscle mass, muscle cramps, and muscle pain in the proximal muscles (those nearer the body trunk). This type of alcohol-induced muscle disease is believed to be due to long-term exposure to large amounts of alcohol and its effects on cell membranes. Improvement in muscle weakness occurs with decreased alcohol consumption.

Yet another type of muscle damage may result when a person is intoxicated, passes out, and lies unconscious in the same position for a long period. With the constant pressure of body weight on the same muscles, pressure necrosis can result, leading to muscle degeneration. Like any other acute myopathies, abnormally large amounts of certain muscle proteins (myoglobins) are released into the bloodstream. If these muscle protein levels become high enough, kidney failure can occur. Potassium is also a product of such muscle tissue breakdown. An increase in the level of potassium in the blood can disturb mineral balance throughout the body. For reasons that are currently unclear, heavy drinkers are known to be very prone to muscle cramps.

Finally, a condition known as *alcohol-tobacco amblyopia* (diminished vision) is another nervous system disorder. As the name implies, it is associated with chronic, excessive drinking and smoking. It is characterized by the slow onset of blurred, dim vision with pain behind the eyes. There is difficulty reading, intolerance of bright light, and loss of central color vision. Although blind spots can occur, total blindness is uncommon. The cause is thought to be a vitamin deficiency coupled with the direct neurotoxic effects of alcohol. Treatment includes B-complex vitamins plus abstinence, which are usually effective in reversing the eye symptoms. Typically recovery is slow and unfortunately often only partial.

Subdural Hematomas

An indirect result of chronic alcoholism is the increased frequency of *subdural hematomas.* These can be the result of falling down and striking the head, being assaulted, or being in an auto accident, all of which are more likely to occur if the individual is intoxicated. Any such injury to the head can cause tearing of the vessels of the brain lining, the dura, with bleeding resulting. The skull is a rigid box, so any bleeding inside this closed space exerts pressure on the brain. This type of bleeding can be very serious, even life-threatening, and often goes unrecognized. The signs and symptoms vary widely, although fluctuating states of consciousness (that is, drifting in and out of consciousness) are often associated with this. Treatment involves surgical removal of the blood clot.

Miscellaneous CNS Disturbances

With chronic heavy drinking, other neurological conditions occur with increased frequency. These include *bacterial meningitis, seizures following head trauma,* and *concussive syndromes. Strokes* (cerebrovascular accidents) and *brain* and *subarachnoid hemorrhages* seem to occur with increased frequency during acute alcohol intoxication. They are more common as well with chronic heavy use. These are thought to be due to the hypertensive effect of alcohol and may be aggravated by alcohol's interfering with the normal clotting mechanisms. Recent research has shown that chronic heavy drinking is associated with abnormal central olfactory processing, thus altering the sense of taste and of smell. Its severity appears to be related to the duration of drinking and may contribute to the apparent lack of interest in food that is seen in many heavy drinkers. Also, as mentioned earlier, alcohol is a known trigger for both cluster headaches and migraine headaches.

NEUROPSYCHOLOGICAL IMPAIRMENT

Personality changes have long been regarded as a prominent feature of chronic alcohol use. Historically this was chalked up to serious underlying psychological problems. Then the emphasis shifted to viewing the "alcoholic personality" as an adaptive behavior style that the person develops to rationalize his or her alcohol problems and to justify the continuation of drinking. Over the past several decades, neuropsychological research, using formal psychometric testing, has uncovered specific impairments associated with alcohol abuse.

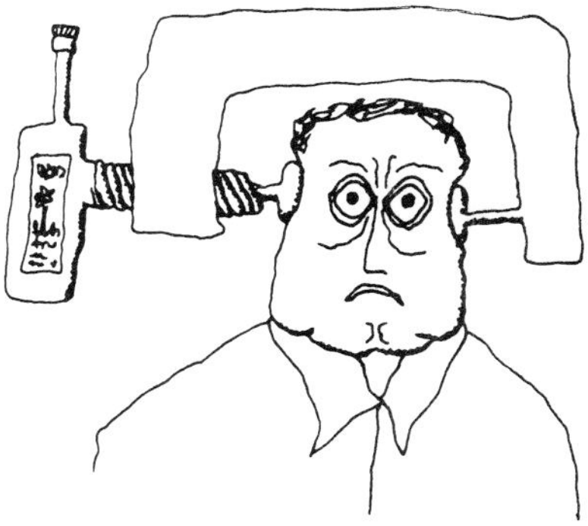

Overall intellectual deterioration is generally not seen until very late in the course of alcohol dependence. Even with a history of chronic heavy drinking, the IQ, especially verbal IQ, remains relatively intact and in the normal range. Nonetheless, other specific deficits frequently occur, including diminished ability to solve problems, to perform complex psychomotor tasks, and to use abstract concepts, as well as memory impairment. The drinking history is the major factor determining the severity of these impairments. How much alcohol has been consumed and for how long are the critical questions to be asked. Recent research suggests that genetic susceptibility may be involved. (This is suspected to involve the apolipoprotein [apo E] allele, an established risk factor for dementia.) Neurological deficits tend to improve with abstinence. The first two to three weeks of abstinence bring the most dramatic improvement. After that, further improvement occurs gradually over the next 6 to 12 months. It is important to realize that improvement, although substantial, is not necessarily complete.

The areas of the brain that seem to be the most affected are the frontal lobes and the right hemisphere—hence, the frequent presence of executive dysfunction, the so-called dysexecutive syndrome, and nonverbal functional impairments. This may also help explain the profound personality changes associated with chronic alcohol use. In fact, some of the behaviors accompanying dependence, such as an inability to abstain and loss of control, may in part be a result of organic brain dysfunction. Most of the impairments in functioning are subtle and not readily apparent to the casual observer. In fact, many of the subjects in clinical studies documenting neuropsychological impairment appeared "normal." They were often described with terms such as "young, intelligent, and looking much like any other citizen." That should alert us to the possibility that such alcohol-related brain damage and associated neuropsychological impairment may be more widespread than previously thought.

Of course, memory difficulties are a prominent feature of many alcohol-related CNS disorders. This implies adverse effects on regions of the brain involved with normal memory. In the past it was believed that no new nerve cells could be produced in adulthood. We now know that this is not the case. Neural stem cells give rise to new neurons throughout life. This process is called neurogenesis. Experimental data indicate that high doses of alcohol can disrupt neurogenesis in a number of ways. Some of these may well, in part, account for the damaging effects alcohol can have on the brain.

MISCELLANEOUS EFFECTS

Chronic alcohol use is related to a variety of other signs, symptoms, and conditions that do not fit neatly into a discussion of any particular organ system.

Hodgkin's disease is a form of lymphatic cancer that, although certainly very serious, is becoming more and more treatable. Many persons with Hodgkin's disease who drink may experience pain in the lymph nodes that are affected by the disease. Alcohol abuse may also be associated with *Dercum's disease,* which is characterized by symmetrical and painful deposits of fat around the body and limbs. This is often seen in association with liver disease, diabetes, elevated serum lipids, peripheral neuropathy, and consumption of large amounts of alcohol. Painless parotid gland enlargement, which looks very much like mumps and is called "chipmunk fascies," may be seen in as many as 25% of patients with cirrhosis.

An interesting property of alcohol is its ability to dramatically alleviate tremor in persons with *familial tremor*. As suggested by the name, this condition runs in families. It may occur in relatively young persons, although it is more common in the elderly. The cause is unknown. To account for the heavier than expected drinking seen in many patients with this condition, it has been hypothesized that they might be self-medicating their tremor by drinking, thereby inviting the eventual development of dependence. Fortunately, other drugs are as effective as, or more effective than, alcohol for this condition and are much safer. Alcohol is also very potent in relieving symptoms of social anxiety/phobia, a highly disabling psychiatric disorder. Interestingly individuals with *chronic fatigue syndrome* (CFS) find that drinking causes a number of adverse effects, such as increased tiredness, as well as nausea, hangovers, and insomnia. The impact of alcohol is evident to these individuals and sufficiently unpleasant so that in a sample of CFS patients, two-thirds reduced the amount of alcohol use and one-third stopped drinking completely.

Chronic heavy alcohol use is associated with a variety of metabolic disorders, including the following:

- *Hyperuricemia* (elevated uric acid levels in the blood), causing a number of medical complications (see the section Skeletal System)
- *Diminished potassium levels* (hypokalemia), caused by excess mineral-regulating hormone (aldosterone), associated with cirrhosis and ascites; this may cause dangerous cardiac rhythm problems
- *Decreased magnesium levels* in the blood, probably from alcohol's enhancement of the kidneys' excretion of magnesium, along with decreased oral intake of and increased loss of magnesium through the GI system
- *Metabolic acidosis,* an increase of hydrogen ion concentration in the blood, resulting from altered liver metabolism
- *Decreased levels of calcium and phosphate,* possibly due to increased neural excretion of calcium, decreased vitamin D levels, or lowered intestinal absorption of calcium, which in turn may contribute to alcohol-induced osteoporosis
- *Increased postoperative complications,* more common among heavy drinkers than moderate drinkers (at a three times greater rate). These include postoperative infections, cardiopulmonary problems, and excessive bleeding, and they are presumed to be due to a combination of depressed immune function, alcohol-related cardiac problems, and compromised clotting factors. It has been found that one month of abstinence before surgery significantly reduces the number of post-op complications. Acute alcohol withdrawal including delirium tremens may occur during the immediate postoperative period in persons who were not known to be heavy drinkers prior to the surgery.

Thus far, this chapter has focused upon the many medical complications frequently associated with chronic heavy drinking. It is important, however, to realize that health problems can arise from any alcohol use. They are not restricted to those evidencing a long-standing alcohol problem. Increasingly, alcohol use is being considered a risk factor for the development of a variety of common illnesses. The earlier general notion that alcohol poses a health hazard "only if you really drink a lot" is going by the wayside.

SLEEP AND SLEEP DISTURBANCES

Many people say they can't sleep unless they have a drink or two before bedtime "to relax." Actually, alcohol interferes with sound sleep. To understand this, consider how people sleep, how alcohol affects normal sleep, and what can be done for clients who cannot sleep after they have stopped drinking.

There are four stages of sleep that occur in a fairly predictable sequence throughout the night. Before we can fall asleep, we need to relax. This is a fairly individualized affair that leads to a person's becoming drowsy, when the brain begins to emit alpha waves, as shown on an EEG. Next comes the transition period, a time when one is half asleep and half awake. This is called stage 1. You may feel awake, but you are not really attending to what's going on in the environment. Brief dream fragments or images may occur at this time. Stage 1 sleep lasts anywhere from 2 to 10 minutes in normal sleepers; but for those alcohol dependent but not abstinent, this stage can last all night. Finally, there comes the real thing—sleep. The average, non-dreaming sleep is called stage 2. It is a medium-deep and restful sleep, and the first episode of it lasts about 20 to 45 minutes. About 50% to 60% of sleep in an evening is stage 2.

Life is something that happens when you can't get to sleep.
—Fran Lebowitz

Gradually sleep deepens, becoming the soundest sleep of the night—delta sleep. The amount of delta sleep varies by age, ranging from possibly several hours in children to little or none in older persons. Delta sleep occurs primarily in the early part of the night and rarely after the first three hours of sleep. After delta sleep, there is a return to stage 2 sleep for a while. Then, about 60 to 90 minutes after falling asleep, there is REM sleep (rapid eye movement), when dreaming occurs. If there were an EEG at this time, the brain waves would resemble the pattern when waking. The eyes move rapidly under closed eyelids, but the body is completely relaxed (in fact, it's paralyzed, except for the diaphragm and respiratory muscles). There is alternating non-dreaming (stage 2) and dreaming (REM) sleep which continues throughout the night. Dreams occur about every 90 minutes. As the night goes on, non-dreaming sleep becomes shorter, and dreaming (REM) sleep becomes longer. During dreaming, part of the brain is awake but part is not. For example, the long-range memory part of the brain does not function during dreaming. So, to remember a dream, we have to wake up from it and think about the dream immediately. Someone who claims never to dream is probably a reasonably sound sleeper, with few awakenings. That person probably also jumps right out of bed on waking and therefore forgets the dreams.

Sleep seems to be good for both body and mind. Stage 2, and especially delta sleep, is thought to be mainly body-recovery sleep. Dreaming sleep, on the other hand, has something to do with psychological recovery.

Sleep Disturbances

Why do we need sleep? Take it away and see what happens! Despite what most of us think, an occasional sleepless night is not all that devastating. Although we might feel awful and irritable, total loss of sleep for one or two nights has surprisingly little effect on normal performance and functioning. Two exceptions are very boring tasks, such as watching radar blips or driving long distances, and very creative tasks, such as writing an essay. These are affected by even one night of very little sleep. On the other hand, for most jobs of average interest and difficulty, if one really tries to do so, we draw on our reserves and rally to the task even after two to four totally sleepless nights.

Three brain systems regulate sleep: the awake or arousal system (known as the reticular activating system), the sleep system, and the REM (dreaming) system. There is a continual "struggle" among these, each one trying to dominate the others. Insomnia is usually based on either an overly active waking system or a weak sleeping system. Each of these systems has a different anatomical location in the brain with different neurotransmitters. It is alcohol's impact on neurotransmitters that underlies alcohol's impact on sleep.

Stress, as well as stimulants, such as coffee or amphetamines, strengthens the waking system; sleeping pills will help the sleeping system. Of importance, after just a few days or weeks, the brain chemistry compensates for the chemically induced imbalance, and these agents become ineffective. Significantly, after just one month on sleeping pills, an insomniac's sleep will be as poor as ever. Continued use may cause poor sleep. Furthermore, when a sleeping pill is withdrawn, sleep will become extremely poor for a few days or weeks because the brain's chemical balance is now disturbed in the opposite direction. So some people stay on sleeping pills for decades, even though the pills do not really help them because of this "rebound insomnia." Abrupt withdrawal from some sleeping pills can be dangerous and can even cause seizures.

Practically all sleeping pills, contrary to advertising, suppress dream sleep. Upon ceasing the use of these medications, dreaming sleep increases in proportion to its former suppression. It then can occupy from 40% to 50% of the night. Dreaming sleep, too, takes 10 days or so to return to normal. During these days there is very little time for deep sleep because dreaming takes up most of the night. So someone will feel exhausted in the morning because there was very little time for body recovery. It is all right to take a sleeping pill on rare occasions—say, before an important interview or after three to four nights of very poor sleep. However, it rarely makes any sense to take sleeping pills regularly for more than a few days.

Insomnia

Insomnia can be based on either an overly active waking system or a weak sleeping system. On rare occasions insomnia can have an organic or genetic basis. Some people have a defective sleep system from birth; however, most insomnias are based on psychological factors. Any stress, depression, or tension will naturally arouse the waking system. When this is the case, the cure obviously involves helping the person deal with the psychological stress.

Surprisingly, poor sleep is often little more than a bad habit! Say you went through a stressful life situation a few years back and, quite naturally, couldn't sleep for a few nights because of it. Being very tired during the day after a few bad nights, you needed sleep more and more. So you tried harder and harder to get to sleep, but the harder you tried, the less you could fall asleep. Soon a vicious cycle developed. Everything surrounding sleep became emotionally charged with immense frustration, and the frustration alone kept you awake.

How can this cycle be broken? The treatment is simple and effective, provided you stick with it. The first step is to recognize you are misusing the bed by lying in it awake and frustrated. The specific rules for treatment are as follows:

1. Whenever you can't fall asleep relatively quickly, get up, because you are misusing the bed. You can do your "frustrating" somewhere else, but not in the bedroom.
2. As soon as you are tired enough and think you might fall asleep quickly, go to bed. If you can't fall asleep quickly, get up again. This step is to be repeated as often as necessary, until you fall asleep quickly.
3. No matter how little sleep you get on a given night, you have to get up in the morning at the usual time.
4. No daytime naps!

If you stick to this regimen for a few weeks, your body will again become used to falling asleep quickly. Therapists trained in this type of behavioral treatment may be of considerable help and support.

Shortening the time spent in bed is crucial to many with insomnia. Because they haven't slept during the night, many insomniacs stay in bed for half the morning. They want to catch a few daytime naps, or they feel too tired and sick to get up after not sleeping. Pretty soon they lie in bed routinely for 12, 14, even 20 hours. They sleep their days away while complaining of insomnia. It is important that one maintain a regular day/night rhythm, with at least 14 to 16 hours out of bed, even if the nights are marred by insomnia. In some individuals, undiagnosed medical disorders or physical disturbances during sleep may give rise to insomnia.

Alcohol's Effects on Sleep

How does alcohol affect sleep? Many find that a nightcap can help turn down an overly active waking system. No question, some people fall asleep faster with a drink. However, alcohol depresses REM (dreaming) sleep and causes more awakenings later at night. So the individual may awaken many times throughout the night, which results in a lack of recovery during sleep (i.e., fully refreshing sleep). These effects are one of the features of chronic heavy drinkers, even on non-drinking days. In addition, the pressure to dream becomes stronger the longer it is suppressed. It is thought that after a period of heavy drinking, there is a tremendous recovery need for dreaming. It has been hypothesized that the DTs and the hallucinations of alcohol withdrawal may be a pressure to dream (lack of REM).

Another sleep problem of major concern is that of sleep apnea, a relatively common breathing disturbance in which a person's air passages become obstructed during sleep. It is especially common in older individuals and those who are overweight. Alcohol, by causing edema in the upper respiratory passages, can markedly worsen sleep apnea and put the affected individual at serious risk for medical complications that can be life-threatening. Often, loud snoring is an indicator of this problem.

What happens to sleep when an alcohol-dependent person ceases alcohol use? First, there is the rebound of dreaming. Increased dreaming can last up to 10 days before subsiding. Often there are nightmares because dreaming is so intense. The sleep fragmentation lasts longer. A loss of delta sleep can go on for as long as two years after drinking ceases. Even in sobriety, those with alcohol dependence, as a group, still have more sleep disturbances than others. The reasons are unknown. It could be due to chronic damage to the nervous system during binges, as has been seen in animal studies, or it could be that some were poor sleepers to start with. Of note, insomnia is associated with a higher rate of relapse following treatment. In any case, it appears that the longer someone refrains from drinking, the more sleep will improve.

BLACKOUTS AND MEMORY

Having covered a multitude of physical disorders associated with alcohol abuse, it would seem that there is nothing left to go wrong! However, there remains one more phenomenon associated with alcohol use that is highly distinctive: the blackout. Contrary to what the name may imply, it does not mean passing out or losing consciousness. Nor does it mean psychological blocking out of events, or repression.

Description

A blackout is an amnesia-like period, which is often associated with heavy drinking. "Gray-outs" are similar episodes of partial amnesia associated with heavy alcohol intake. Someone who is or has been drinking may appear to be perfectly normal. He or she seems to function quite normally with the task at hand, yet later the person has no memory of what transpired. A better term might be "blank out." The blank spaces in the memory may be total or partial. A person who has been drinking and who experiences a "blank out" will not be able to recall how the party ended, how he got home, how she landed the 747, how he did open-heart surgery, or how the important decisions at a business lunch were made. As can be imagined, this spotty memory can cause severe distress and anxiety, to say nothing of being dangerous in certain circumstances.

Alcohol's Effects on Memory

What causes blackouts? The exact mechanisms are not fully understood, but apparently, during a blackout, recent memory function is severely and selectively impaired by alcohol, while virtually all other spheres of mental functioning—cognition, behavior, remote memory, and brain function—remain relatively intact. Up to one-third of all alcohol-dependent people report never having had a blackout. Others have blackouts frequently. Then there are others who experience them only occasionally. Recent research indicates that blackouts occur in non-dependent individuals who have drunk more heavily than they usually do and to the point of intoxication. However, blackouts have usually been associated with fairly advanced alcohol dependence and thus are thought to be generally dose-dependent and dose-related. As a general rule, the greater the severity of dependence (the heavier the drinking and the greater the number of years over which it has occurred), the more likely the occurrence of blackouts. There is also a positive relationship between the occurrence of blackouts and the extent and duration of alcohol consumption during any given drinking episode. Several other factors also correlate with the occurrence of blackouts: poor diet, high tolerance, a previous head injury, and the tendency to gulp drinks.

Current research findings on blackouts differ in significant respects from the frequently quoted early alcohol research, done in the 1950s by E. M. Jellinek, which was described in Chapter 4. In considering the progression of alcoholism, Jellinek focused on blackouts as being an early manifestation of the disease or as a warning sign for those at risk for developing it. He felt that blackouts had a high degree of specificity in predicting eventual alcoholism. Thinking has now changed. Studies done more recently have found that 30% to 40% of young to middle-aged, light to moderate (social) drinkers have had at least one alcohol-induced blackout. Typically it occurs on one of the few occasions when they are truly inebriated. In fact, among these individuals, blackouts seem to be most frequent among those who generally are light drinkers.

Possible Causes

How are the disparities between the old and new research findings reconciled? One possibility is that individuals vary in their susceptibility to blackouts. Accordingly, those people who experience the blackout-producing effect of alcohol may find loss of memory for events so frightening or unpleasant that they are strongly motivated to drink only in moderation in the future. Others, possibly with a genetic predisposition to alcoholism, may have a naturally high tolerance for blackouts. Consequently they do not experience blackouts until relatively late in their drinking careers, after an alcohol disorder has been established. In effect, the absence of blackouts earlier in their drinking career, may have deprived them of an important physiological and behavioral warning signal.

Despite the still limited research, it is evident that in some people alcohol selectively interferes with the mechanisms of memory, a complex process that in general is not yet fully understood. We can recall and report what happened to us five minutes ago. Similarly, many events of yesterday or a week ago can be recalled. In many cases, our memories can extend back many years—indeed, decades. Psychological and neuropsychological research has identified different types of memory, categorizing them into immediate, short-term (recent), and long-term memory. All these types of memory involve the brain's capacity to receive, process, and store information.

According to one popular theory of memory function, the brain has at least two kinds of "filing systems" for information. Immediate memory is stored electrochemically for very short periods. Long-term memory involves a biochemical storage system that is relatively stable over long periods. Short-term, or recent, memory is a way station somewhere between these two that is thought to involve the process of converting electrochemical brain activity into stable changes in neuronal cells involving proteins at the molecular level. It is hypothesized that this is the point at which alcohol exerts its influence to impair memory function. It is suspected that this occurs because alcohol interferes with the metabolic production of proteins by certain neuronal cells. This in turn inhibits the brain's ability to move short-term memories into longer-term storage.

Of all vices, drinking is the most incompatible with greatness.
—SIR WALTER SCOTT

Although alcohol interferes with the conversion process, it does not seem to interfere directly with the electrochemical basis of immediate memory (memory for the events occurring during the blackout itself) or for events from before the blackout (those already stored in long-term memory as stable protein macromolecules). This could account for the seemingly normal appearance and function of the person in a blackout, even with respect to relatively complicated tasks.

The amnesia that occurs during a blackout is typically one of two types. It may be sudden in onset, complete, and permanent, or it can lack a definite onset and be something that the person is unaware of until he or she is reminded of or spontaneously recalls the forgotten event. In the latter instance, recall is usually dim and incomplete. Interestingly, in such cases recall may be enhanced by the use of alcohol. This facilitation of recall by alcohol is thought to reflect the phenomenon of state-dependent learning, in which whatever has been learned is best recalled when the person is in the same state or condition that existed at the time of the original learning.

We were to do more business after dinner; but after dinner is after dinner—an old saying and a true, 'much drinking, little thinking.'
—JONATHAN SWIFT, 1768

Interestingly, there has been discussion of blackouts being used as a defense in criminal proceedings. Although a novel approach, it appears that there is no evidence to support the contention that a blackout alters judgment or behavior at the time of its occurrence. The only deficiency appears to be in later recalling what occurred during the blackout. Of course, having no memory of an event would make it difficult to prepare a case or to decide from one's own knowledge whether to plead guilty or innocent. It is hoped that more will be learned about blackouts.

Research, however, is difficult because it depends almost entirely on anecdotal self-report. Thus far, no one has found a predictable way to produce blackouts experimentally. Nor can one know for sure when a spontaneous blackout is occurring. Consequently, to date it has not been possible to use any of the new, highly sophisticated, non-invasive, neurodiagnostic imaging techniques that might shed light on the neurophysiological basis of blackouts.

WITHDRAWAL SYNDROMES

The physiological basis of withdrawal is hypothesized to be related to alcohol's depressant effects on the CNS. With regular heavy use of alcohol, the activity of the CNS is chronically depressed. With abstinence, this chronic depressant effect is removed. There follows a period of rebound hyperactivity. An area of the CNS particularly affected is the reticular activating system, which modulates or regulates the general level of CNS arousal and activity. The duration of the withdrawal syndrome is determined by the time required for this rebound over-activity to be played out and a normal baseline level of neurophysiological functioning to be reestablished. Studies of CNS activity with EEGs during heavy drinking, abstinence, and withdrawal support this. Interestingly, volumetric MRI studies have shown that during withdrawal the white matter volume in the brain increases by as much as 20%.

Not everyone physically dependent on alcohol who stops drinking has the same symptoms. In part, the severity of the withdrawal state is a function of how long someone has been drinking and how much. Another big factor is the drinker's physical health plus his or her unique physiological characteristics. Therefore, accurately predicting the difficulties with withdrawal is impossible. Despite the phrase "abstinence syndrome," withdrawal can occur even while someone continues to drink. The key factor is a relative lowering of the blood alcohol level. Thus, relative abstinence is the condition that triggers withdrawal. This phenomenon often prompts having a morning drink; he or she is treating withdrawal symptoms.

Four major withdrawal syndromes have been described in conjunction with alcohol. These include a state of *hyperarousal, alcoholic hallucinosis, convulsive seizures,* and *delirium tremens* (DTs). Although they can be distinguished for the purpose of discussion, clinically the distinctions are not so neat. In reality, these syndromes often blend together.

Hyperarousal

The earliest and most common sign of acute alcohol withdrawal is a generalized state of *hyperarousal.* This can include anxiety, irritability, insomnia, loss of appetite, rapid heartbeat (tachycardia), and tremulousness (the "shakes"). Avoiding this state often is what motivates alcohol-dependent people to have a morning or midday drink. Recall that, with increasing tolerance, increasing amounts of an addictive drug are necessary to ward off withdrawal symptoms, and only a relatively lowered blood alcohol concentration (BAC) is necessary to induce withdrawal. The person who is used to drinking heavily in the evenings will eventually feel shaky the next morning. The BAC will have fallen from the level of the night before. A drink, by raising the BAC, will take this discomfort and edginess away. With time, further boosts of booze during the course of the day may be necessary to maintain a BAC sufficient to prevent the shakes. As tends to be the case with all addicting drugs, users will consume progressively increasing amounts, not for their positive effects but as a means of dealing with withdrawal symptoms.

If the physically dependent person abstains completely, there will be a marked increase in symptoms. The appearance will be one of stimulation. The person will startle easily, feel irritable, and in general be revved up in a very unpleasant way. He or she will have a fast pulse, increased temperature, elevated blood pressure, sweating, dilated pupils, a flushed face, and trouble sleeping. Usually these symptoms subside over two or three days. The shakes will disappear, and the vital signs will return to normal. However, feeling awful, being irritable, and having difficulty sleeping can persist for two to three weeks or even longer. Although the judicious use of medication, primarily the benzodiazepines in the past but now including clonidine, gabapentin, and baclofen, may make the withdrawal process more tolerable by lessening the severity of symptoms. This acute withdrawal syndrome by itself often does not require medical treatment. But it is important that the person not be left alone and be carefully observed for the occurrence of seizures or signs of incipient DTs. When the acute stage passes, the probability of developing DTs is greatly lowered. However, if the acute symptoms do not resolve or if they worsen, the person should be evaluated by a physician because such symptoms may indicate that the progression to DTs is likely.

Alcoholic Hallucinosis

A second syndrome of alcohol withdrawal, known as alcoholic hallucinosis, occurs in about 25% of those withdrawing from alcohol. It is usually seen early, within the first 24 hours of withdrawal. It includes true hallucinations, both auditory and visual. It also includes illusions, the misperception or misinterpretation of real environmental stimuli. However, the individual with hallucinosis is oriented to person, place, and time. Very bad nightmares often accompany this withdrawal syndrome. It is believed that the nightmares are due to REM rebound following the release from alcohol's long suppression of dreaming sleep. This rebound effect usually clears by the end of the first week of withdrawal. In a small number of cases, however, a chronic and persistent form of the syndrome may develop and continue for weeks to months. Acute alcoholic hallucinosis is not dangerous in itself and does not require specific medical treatment. It is important, however, to recognize it as a relatively common withdrawal phenomenon and not to be misled into thinking the hallucinations are indicative of an underlying primary psychiatric disorder.

The chronic form of alcoholic hallucinosis accompanying alcohol withdrawal is often thought of as a separate syndrome. It is characterized primarily by persistent, frightening auditory hallucinations. Usually the hallucinations have a distinctly paranoid flavor and are of voices familiar to the patient, often of relatives or acquaintances. In the early stages they are threatening or demeaning, or they arouse guilt. Because they are true hallucinations, the person believes they are real and acts on them as if they were. This can lead to the person's harming him- or herself or others. When the hallucinations persist over time, they become less frightening and may be tolerated with greater equanimity. Some patients with chronic hallucinosis develop a schizophrenia-like condition and require treatment with antipsychotic medications. However, in most instances alcoholic hallucinosis does not indicate an underlying psychiatric problem but simply represents the CNS's response to the acute absence of alcohol. Appropriate treatment entails observing someone in an environment in which he or she will be safe, plus the possible use of mild sedation. Alcoholic hallucinosis, unless very severe, probably should not be treated with antipsychotic medications during the first two to four days of withdrawal. During that period there is an increased risk for seizures, and such drugs can lower the seizure threshold.

Convulsive Seizures

This third withdrawal syndrome, convulsive seizures, sometimes referred to as "rum fits," can occur in association with acute alcohol withdrawal. These seizures are almost always generalized, grand mal, major motor seizures, in which the eyes roll back in the head; the body muscles contract, relax, and extend rhythmically and violently; and there is loss of consciousness. In fact, these seizures are so common that the occurrence of any other type of seizure should raise concern about causes other than simply alcohol withdrawal. After the seizure, which typically lasts a minute or two, the person may be stuporous and groggy for as long as six to eight hours. Although very frightening to watch, convulsive seizures in and of themselves are not usually dangerous. Any treatment during a seizure is limited to protecting the person's airway and to preventing injury from the seizure-induced muscle activity.

A serious complication of an isolated seizure is the development of *status epilepticus,* in which seizures follow one another with virtually no intervening seizure-free periods. Usually only one or two seizures occur with acute alcohol withdrawal. Status epilepticus is very uncommon with alcohol withdrawal. If present, it suggests causes other than the alcohol withdrawal. The only long-term treatment of alcohol withdrawal seizures is to prevent them through abstinence. Unless a person in withdrawal has a history of seizures, anticonvulsant drugs are not routinely prescribed. If they are used for seizures clearly attributable to acute alcohol withdrawal, they should be discontinued before discharge, because further seizures would not be expected after withdrawal. It is critical, though, to rule out any other possible cause of the seizures and not merely to assume that alcohol withdrawal is responsible. Infections, electrolyte disturbances, and falls with associated head trauma or subdural hematoma, which can accompany heavy drinking, can be causes. Seizures are most likely to occur between 12 and 48 hours after stopping alcohol use, but they can occur up to one week after the last drink. Alcohol withdrawal seizures indicate a moderate to severe withdrawal problem. Up to one-third of persons who have withdrawal seizures go on to develop DTs.

Withdrawal seizures are also thought to be caused by rebound CNS hyperexcitability. Alcohol has an anticonvulsant effect acutely in that it raises the seizure threshold. With abstinence, however, the seizure threshold is correspondingly lowered. (This has been postulated as the basis for the increased seizures in epileptics who drink, because these seizures tend to occur the morning after, when the blood alcohol level has fallen.)

Delirium Tremens. *Delirium tremens, or mania a potu, is a nervous disorder caused by the habitual use of alcoholic stimulants, and in regard to its pathological tendency may be defined as nature's ultimate protest against the continuance of the alcohol vice. The first remonstrance comes in the form of nausea, languor and sick headache—symptoms familiar in the experience of every incipient toper. Loss of appetite and general disinclination to active exercise are the penalties of intemperance in its more advanced stages of development, and those injunctions remaining unheeded, nature's ultimatum is expressed in the incomparable distress of nervous delirium.*

—Walter W. Spooner

The Cyclopedia of Intemperance and Prohibition, 1891

Delirium Tremens

Also known as the DTs, delirium tremens is the most serious form of alcohol withdrawal. In the past, mortality rates as high as 15% to 20% were reported. Untreated, as many as one of every five persons who developed DTs died. Even with modern treatment, there is a 1% to 2% mortality rate. The name indicates the two major components of this withdrawal state, and either of these components can predominate. "Delirium" refers to hallucinations, confusion, and disorientation. "Tremens" refers to heightened autonomic nervous activity, marked tremulousness and agitation, fast pulse, elevated blood pressure, and fever. Someone who eventually develops the DTs initially has all the symptoms of early withdrawal. However, instead of clearing by the second or third day, the symptoms continue and, in fact, get worse. In addition to increased shakiness, profuse sweating, fast pulse, hypertension, and fever, there are mounting periods of confusion and anxiety attacks. In full-blown DTs, there are delusions and hallucinations, generally visual and tactile. The terrifying nature of the hallucinations and delusions is captured by the slang phrase for DTs, "the horrors." Seeing bugs on the walls and feeling insects crawling all over one's body naturally heighten the anxiety and emotional responses. In this physical and emotional state of agitation and heightened arousal, infections, respiratory problems, fluid loss, and physical exhaustion can create further difficulties. These complications contribute substantially to the mortality rate. The acute phase of DTs can last from one day to one week. In 15% of cases it is over in 25 hours; in 80%, within three days. The person will then often fall into a profound sleep and, on awakening, feel better, though still weak. Usually he or she will have little memory of what happened.

Don't worry, mr. white; we'll give you some pills to make the bugs disappear.

Since there is no specific cure for DTs, treatment is aimed at providing supportive medical care while it runs its course. Vital signs are monitored closely to spot any developing problems. Efforts are made to reduce the agitation, conserve energy, and prevent exhaustion. This involves administering sedatives. Despite arguments to the contrary, there is no specific single regimen that is clearly superior. Amounts and type of medications are determined by the patient's physical condition. One of the concerns is liver function. The liver, possibly damaged by alcohol, is the organ needed to metabolize virtually any drug given. If the liver is not up to the task, drugs are not as speedily removed from the body, a situation that can lead to further problems. The benzodiazepines (Ativan, Librium, Valium, Serax) are often the first choices in drugs. They have been shown to be as effective as other agents, have a wider margin of safety and less toxicity than some of the alternative drugs, and also contribute a significant anticonvulsant effect. The specific benzodiazepine chosen depends on a number of pharmacological considerations and the adequacy of the individual's liver function. As symptoms abate, the dose is decreased gradually over time to avoid cumulative unwanted sedation.

Paraldehyde, an old, time-tested, and effective agent, has become less popular. Paraldehyde is metabolized by the liver and consequently must be used with care when significant liver disease is present. It also must be carefully stored in sealed brown bottles to prevent its breakdown into acetaldehyde. Last, it imparts an objectionable odor to the breath that is unavoidable because it is extensively excreted by the lungs. The typical major tranquilizers, or antipsychotic agents, are also somewhat less desirable. Although they may have sedative and tranquilizing properties, they also lower the seizure threshold, which is already a problem with alcohol withdrawal. This latter drawback is less of a problem with the newer atypical antipsychotic agents, which may be helpful. Whatever medication is used, the purpose is to diminish the severity of the acute symptoms accompanying the DTs, not to introduce long-term drug treatment for the alcoholism.

Although predictions cannot be made about who will go into DTs, those who fit the following description are the most likely candidates. A daily drinker who has consumed over a fifth a day or more for at least a week prior to abstinence and who has been a heavy drinker for 10 years or more is statistically very susceptible. The occurrence of withdrawal seizures, or the persistence and worsening rather than improving over time of the acute early withdrawal symptoms, should indicate that the DTs are more likely to occur. If in a prior period of acute abstinence the person had convulsions, extreme agitation, marked confusion, disorientation, or DTs, he or she is also more likely to have them again. Another ominous sign is recent abuse of other sedatives, especially barbiturates, which also have serious withdrawal syndromes much like those seen with alcohol. Abuse of multiple drugs complicates withdrawal management. If there is evidence of physical dependence on more than one drug, generally simultaneous withdrawal will not be attempted. Sequential withdrawal is the preferred approach.

Late Withdrawal Phenomenon

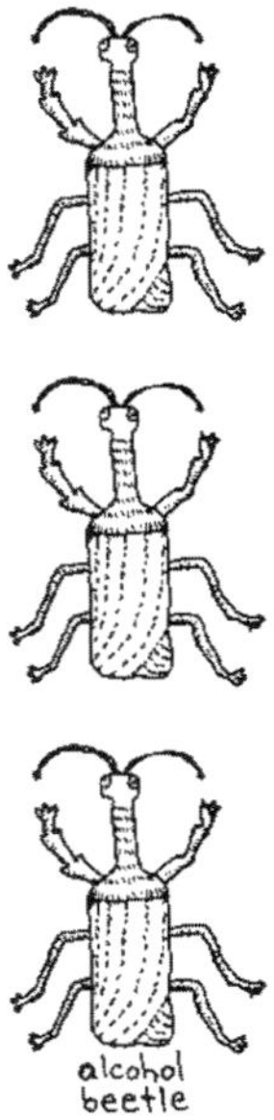

The so-called late withdrawal phenomenon is a less than tidy concept. It refers to withdrawal-like symptoms that occur after the period normally associated with withdrawal. Two different situations are covered by this phrase. Sometimes the phrase is used when there is an unexpected reemergence of withdrawal symptoms. While not common, this situation is more likely to occur in instances of dependence on several drugs. Thus, different withdrawal syndromes may be occurring simultaneously, each of which has a different timetable. If high doses of benzodiazepines are used to treat the symptoms of acute alcohol withdrawal, and these are abruptly discontinued, there may be a reemergence of withdrawal symptoms. So this may be a sedative-hypnotic withdrawal syndrome caused by discontinuing the benzodiazepines and may not be a delayed alcohol withdrawal. It can be treated by reintroducing the benzodiazepines and then discontinuing them more gradually.

Another way the phrase is used is in reference to a protracted abstinence syndrome—characterized by persistence over a variable but prolonged period (several weeks to months) of symptoms suggestive of the acute stages of alcohol withdrawal. These can include variable cognitive and memory disturbances, anxiety and irritability, insomnia, tremulousness, depressive symptoms, and an intense desire to drink. Neither the basis for this syndrome nor the frequency of its occurrence is known. The suspicion is that comorbid psychiatric conditions may play a role. Quite possibly these are symptoms of depression, or anxiety disorders, or panic disorders that previously had been masked by the alcohol. Unfortunately, alcohol provides prompt relief for this often intensely uncomfortable state.

Some Cautions

Typically those who experience withdrawal symptoms certainly don't intend to! Withdrawal occurs in a physically dependent person whenever a drug is reduced or terminated, so circumstances may play their part and catch some people unaware. Dependent individuals who enter hospitals for surgery, thereby having to curtail their usual consumption, may, to their surgeon's (and even their own) amazement, develop acute withdrawal symptoms. Another circumstance is family vacations. When the secretly drinking homemaker who has been denying a problem intends to just "sweat it out," grit her teeth, and get along without her usual alcohol intake, she can wind up with more than she bargained for.

By definition, any clinician working with alcohol-dependent persons works with people who do want to loosen their grip. Giving up alcohol can be tough on the body as well as the emotions. In making any clinical assessment of an alcohol problem, the therapist has to be concerned about the possibility of physical dependence and the likelihood of withdrawal. In all cases, medical evaluation is essential. Withdrawal needs to be medically supervised and carefully monitored. Not every withdrawing patient requires hospitalization. In fact, the vast majority of patients—up to 90% in some studies—who do not have serious medical complications can be safely and effectively withdrawn from alcohol on an outpatient basis.

Overall treatment planning has to include arrangements for care during the process of physical withdrawal. No person should be alone and unattended. Family members need to know what to be alert for, so that the necessary medical treatment can be sought when and if indicated. If there is any significant likelihood of serious withdrawal, the rule of thumb is that hospitalization is needed. Virtually everyone with a significant physical dependence on alcohol has stopped drinking for a day or so at some point. So he or she has a sense of what happened then. Any person with a history of previous difficulty during withdrawal is at increased risk in the future. Even when there is no history of difficulty during withdrawal, if current symptoms are worse, one should seek medical treatment immediately. At every step along the way, it is imperative that alcohol-dependent persons receive lots of TLC. They need repeated reassurance and support. They need their questions answered and all procedures explained. Anything that can be done to reduce anxiety and fear is vitally important. Surprisingly such support may help clients through alcohol withdrawal without the use of sedative-hypnotic medications.

REFERENCES AND FURTHER READINGS

Bates ME, Bowden SC, Barry D. Neurocognitive impairment associated with alcohol use disorders: Implications for treatment (review). *Experimental and Clinical Psychopharmacology* 10(3):193–212, 2002. (200 refs.)

Beatty WW, Tivis R, Stott HD, Nixon SJ, Parsons OA. Neuropsychological deficits in sober alcoholics: Influences of chronicity and recent alcohol consumption. *Alcoholism: Clinical and Experimental Research* 24(2):149–154, 2000. (29 refs.)

Beckman YY, Seckin M, Mnavgat AI. Headaches related to psychoactive substance use. *Clinical Neurology and Neurosurgery* 114(7):990–999, 2012. (31 refs.)

Bujanda L. The effects of alcohol consumption upon the gastrointestinal tract (review). *American Journal of Gastroenterology* 95(12):3374–3382, 2000. (84 refs.)

Carlson RW, Kumar NN, Wong-Mckinstry E, Ayyagari S, Puri N, Jackson FK, et al. Alcohol withdrawal syndrome. *Critical Care Clinics* 28(4):549+, 2012. (273 refs.)

Chen H, Yi H-y. Trends in alcohol-related morbidity among short-stay community hospital discharges, United States, 1979–2006. *Surveillance Report No. 84*. Bethesda MD: National Institute on Alcohol Abuse and Alcoholism, 2008. (12 refs.)

Chikritzhs TN, Jonas HA, Stockwell TR, Heale PF, Dietze PM. Mortality and life-years lost due to alcohol: A comparison of acute and chronic causes. *Medical Journal of Australia* 174(6):281–284, 2001. (15 refs.)

Clapp P, Bhave SV, Hoffman PL. How adaptation of the brain to alcohol leads to dependence: A pharmacological perspective (review). *Alcohol Research & Health* 31(4):310–339, 2008. (263 refs.)

Collins MA, Neafsey EJ, Mukamal KJ, Gray MO, Parks DA, Das DK, et al. Alcohol in moderation, cardioprotection, and neuroprotection: Epidemiological considerations and mechanistic studies (review). *Alcoholism: Clinical and Experimental Research* 33(2):206–219, 2009. (120 refs.)

Diaz LE, Montero A, Gonzalez-Gross M, Vallejo AI, Romeo J, Marcos A. Influence of alcohol consumption on immunological status: A review. *European Journal of Clinical Nutrition* 56(Supplement):S50–S53, 2002. (16 refs.)

Duka T, Trick L, Nikolaou K, Gray MA, Kempton MJ, Williams H, et al. Unique brain areas associated with abstinence control are damaged in multiple detoxified alcoholics. *Biological Psychiatry* 70(6):545–552, 2011. (47 refs.)

Fetal alcohol syndrome disorders. *Alcohol Research & Health* 34(1):entire issue, 2011.

Griffiths HJ, Parantainen H, Olson P. Alcohol and bone disorders. *Alcohol Health and Research World* 17(4):299–304, 1993. (18 refs.)

Halsted CH. Nutrition and alcoholic liver disease (review). *Seminars in Liver Disease* 24(3):289–304, 2004. (137 refs.)

Kershaw CD, Guidot DM. Alcoholic lung disease. *Alcohol Research & Health* 31(1):66–75, 2008. (74 refs.)

Kosten TR, O'Connor PG. Management of drug and alcohol withdrawal (review). *New England Journal of Medicine* 348(18):1786–1795, 2003. (67 refs.)

Levitsky J, Mailliard ME. Diagnosis and therapy of alcoholic liver disease (review). *Seminars in Liver Disease* 24(3):233–247, 2004. (173 refs.)

Lovinger DM. Communication networks in the brain neurons, receptors, neurotransmitters, and alcohol (review). *Alcohol Research & Health* 31(3):196–214, 2008. (141 refs.)

McKeon A, Frye MA, Delanty N. The alcohol withdrawal syndrome (review). *Journal of Neurology, Neurosurgery and Psychiatry* 79(8):854–862, 2008. (122 refs.)

Mukamal KJ, Rimm EB. Alcohol consumption: Risks and benefits. *Current Atherosclerosis Reports* 10(6):536–543, 2008. (75 refs.)

Neafsey EJ, Collins MA. Moderate alcohol consumption and cognitive risk. (review). *Neuropsychiatric Disease and Treatment* 7:465–484, 2011. (204 refs.)

Noel X, Campanella S, Pelc I, Verbanck P. Acute and chronic effects of alcohol: Some insights from cognitive sciences. *Acta Clinica Belgica* 65(Supplement 1):68–74, 2010. (38 refs.)

Nordstrom-Klee B, Delaney-Black V, Covington C, Ager J, Sokol R. Growth from birth onwards of children prenatally exposed to drugs: A literature review. *Neurotoxicology and Teratology* 24(4):481–488, 2002. (47 refs.)

Oscar-Berman M, Marinkovic K. Alcoholism and the brain: An overview. *Alcohol Research & Health* 27(2):125–133, 2003. (28 refs.)

Pietrzykowski AZ, Treistman SN. The molecular basis of tolerance. *Alcohol Research & Health* 31(4):298–309, 2008. (101 refs.)

Ross S, Peselow E. The neurobiology of addictive disorders (review). *Clinical Neuropharmacology* 32(5):269–276, 2009. (58 refs.)

Standridge JB, Zylstra RG, Adams SM. Alcohol consumption: An overview of benefits and risks (review). *Southern Medical Journal* 97(7):664–672, 2004. (73 refs.)

Streissguth A. Offspring effects of prenatal alcohol exposure from birth to 25 years: The Seattle Prospective Longitudinal Study. *Journal of Clinical Psychology in Medical Settings* 14(2):81–101, 2007. (72 refs.)

Sullivan EV, Harris A, Pfefferbaum A. Alcohol's effects on brain and behavior. *Alcohol Research & Health* 33(1–2):127–143, 2010. (136 refs.)

Szabo G, Mandrekar P. A recent perspective on alcohol, immunity, and host defense (review). *Alcoholism: Clinical and Experimental Research* 33(2):220–232, 2009. (161 refs.)

Szabo G, Mandrekar P. Focus on: Alcohol and the liver. *Alcohol Research & Health* 33(1–2):87–96, 2010. (79 refs.)

White AM. What happened? Alcohol memory blackouts, and the brain. *Alcohol Research & Health* 27(2):186–196, 2003. (80 refs.)

Yang AL, Vadhavkar S, Singh G, Omary B. Epidemiology of alcohol-related liver and pancreatic disease in the United States. *Archives of Internal Medicine* 168(6):649–656, 2008. (28 refs.)

The Behavior of Dependence

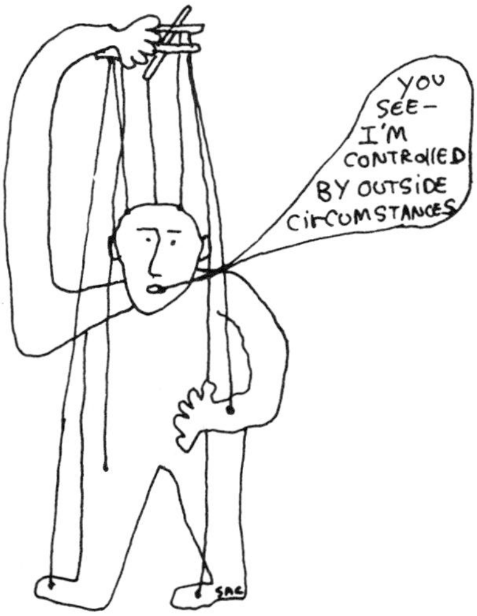

There are some striking similarities in the behavioral "look" of those with serious alcohol disorders.[1] This is true whether the person is male or female, age 17 or 57. From these similarities a general profile can be drawn. Although the profile won't fit everyone, it will cause signal bells to ring when seen by someone familiar with substance use disorders. Indeed, it was this pattern of similarities among those with alcohol dependence that in part prompted the futile pursuit for "the alcoholic personality."

☐ A BEHAVIORAL COMPOSITE

Those with serious alcohol disorders create confusion for those around them. Communications are rife with contradictions: "Come closer; understand." "Don't you dare question me!" The moods and behaviors can be very volatile: jubilant and expansive, then secretive, angry, suspicious. Laughing or crying—tense, worried, and confused, she quickly changes to a relaxed, "Everything's fine." Anxious over unpaid bills one day, the alcohol-troubled person is financially irresponsible the next. He

[1]The DSM-5 with new terminology was published while this text was being updated. For the author, the new terms sounded both odd and awkward. Over time certainly some synonyms will arise. It's hard to imagine that anyone will comment on "the alcohol use disorder (mild) clients that I see . . ." In attempting to incorporate the new diagnostic terminology in this text, "alcohol use disorders" is used to encompass the range of alcohol use problems that warrant medical attention and recognition. At some points, the phrase a "serious alcohol use disorder" or a "significant alcohol use disorder" is used as a substitute for "alcohol dependence." However, there are times when abuse or dependence continue to be used in this edition, not simply as a matter of familiarity, but to convey information. It will take a bit of time for us to understand what is being "said" when we speak of a mild, or a moderate, or a severe alcohol use disorder.

buys expensive toys for the kids while the rent goes unpaid. She may be easygoing or fight like a caged tiger over a "slight." He tells unnecessary lies, and more often than not they come to light.

A considerable amount of time is spent justifying and explaining why she does things. She is constantly minimizing any unpleasant consequences of drinking. He is hard to keep on track. There is always a list of complaints about any number of people, places, and things. She considers herself the victim of fate and of a large number of people who "have it in for her." He has thousands of reasons why he really needs and deserves a drink. She is exuberant over a minor success, only to decline rapidly into "I'm a failure because of . . ." He is elusive and is almost never where he says he'll be when he says he'll be there. She is absolutely rigid about her schedule, especially her drinking times.

Woe unto them that rise up early in the morning, that they may follow strong drink.
Isaiah 5:11

The mood swings are phenomenal. The circular thinking never quite makes sense to others. The denial can cause a lot of exasperation. Now and then the drinker even wonders if he or she might have a psychiatric problem. Those around the drinker also wonder if that is where the difficulty lies. She is a perfectionist at some times and a slob at others. Though occasionally cooperative, he's often a stone wall. Her life is full of broken commitments, promises, and dates, which she often doesn't remember making.

Most of all, the behavior denotes guilt. Extreme defensiveness accompanies alcohol dependence. This seems to be one of the key behaviors that is picked up on early and is seen, but not understood, by others: "What's up with Andy? He's so touchy!" Sometimes behavior that can only be described as that of a drunken slob is obvious. But often the really heavy drinking is secretive and carefully hidden.

It would be easier to pin down the problem if the behaviors occurred only with a drink in hand. This is rarely the case. The behaviors are sometimes more pronounced when the individual has stopped drinking or is working very hard at controlling the drinking. The confusion, anger, frustration, and depression are omnipresent until a radical change occurs in the relationship with alcohol.

HOW, IF NOT WHY?

The profile you have just read is a description of the behavior that accompanies alcohol and, for that matter, other drug dependence. This behavior is part of the disease syndrome, which develops slowly. The many changes in personality occur gradually, making them less discernible to the individual and to those around her; so the slow, insidious personality change is almost immune to recognition as it occurs. In addition, the disturbed behavior is interspersed with behavior that seems entirely normal and appropriate. This, too, is confusing.

This kind of behavior is an issue not only for family members, friends, or colleagues at work. It also represents a problem for those in the helping professions, be they social workers, physicians, clergy, or counselors. The behavior of those with a serious alcohol use disorder does not invite a warm response from others. For the most part such behavior is exactly what we try to avoid. It is irritating, distasteful, annoying, and, at the least, poor manners. These are *not* the patients who instinctively invite their helpers to go the extra mile. These clients can leave those trying to help them feeling frustrated, unappreciated, and questioning whether the energy they are expending is worth the effort.

Wine in excess keeps neither secrets nor promises.
—CERVANTES

Those in the helping professions may recognize that such responses to clients or patients are inappropriate—not how one is supposed to feel or wants to feel. But that doesn't make things OK. Lecturing oneself, gritting one's teeth, or forcing a smile just doesn't do it. Ultimately, to be able to work with alcohol-dependent clients requires a framework to make sense of this behavior. This framework has to provide a way of seeing this behavior as normal for one with alcohol dependence, as symptomatic of the condition. An important part of treatment is communicating this insight to patients. They often find themselves as confused as others. Their behavior not only creates confusion for others but also induces guilt and shame in themselves.

Despite the fact that a host of physical problems has long been known to accompany long-term heavy drinking, medical researchers are only now identifying the physiological basis for the behaviors seen (see Chapter 6). Even though our understanding of these biological factors is incomplete, there is a useful model for viewing the transformation that occurs. Vernon Johnson's classic book *I'll Quit Tomorrow* provided such a model to explain the personality and accompanying behavioral changes that mark alcohol dependence. Johnson in effect described what emerging dependence looks like from the inside out and so provided a basis for empathy among potential helpers.

What is said when drunk has been thought out beforehand.
-Flemish Proverb

The model, introduced in the 1970s, represented a *paradigm shift* in the alcohol field. This phrase refers to the adoption of a new way of thinking that makes previous views feel out of date or wrong. (Interestingly, this model is wholly consistent with learning theory which is the underpinning of many current treatment approaches.) The conventional wisdom at that time was that alcoholics (then the commonly used term) could not be successfully treated until they "hit bottom." It was as if those in the treatment community sat around, waiting for people to request treatment. Indeed, some of the policies then in place now seem punitive and virtually malpractice by the standards of the twenty-first century. For example, an inpatient program, then the norm, would require that someone not drink for the 24 hours prior to admission. This was supposed to demonstrate motivation and a *real* desire for treatment. That this might be almost impossible or dangerous seemed not to be taken into account.

What is the progression in Johnson's framework? Alcohol dependence requires the use of alcohol—an obvious fact. Another obvious fact is that, for whatever reasons, drinking becomes an important activity in the life of the problem drinker. The individual develops a relationship with alcohol. The relationship, with all that word implies, is as real and important a bond as the bond with friends, a partner, or the long-time family pet. Accordingly, energy is expended to maintain the relationship. The bond may be thought of as a love affair. Long after the good times, the pleasure, and the thrill are gone, all kinds of mental gymnastics are used to maintain the myth that it's still great.

How does this progression occur? The first step is quite simple. It applies to all who use alcohol. The individual destined for later trouble is seemingly no different from anyone else in the beginning. The "seemingly" is important. Even though some differences are now known, such as the fact that some drinkers handle alcohol "too well"—able to drink more with fewer effects and this is a risk factor for a serious alcohol problem—this is not something that the drinker or anyone around him can recognize.

For anyone who uses alcohol, the first important experience is *learning the mood swing.* This learning has a physiological basis. Alcohol's acute effect is to make us feel good. At any time, our moods could be plotted on a graph representing a continuum. One end represents pain, and the other end represents euphoria. Before drinking, if our mood falls in the middle or normal range, the effect of the drink is to shift our mood toward the euphoric end. When the effects of the alcohol wear off, we're back where we started.

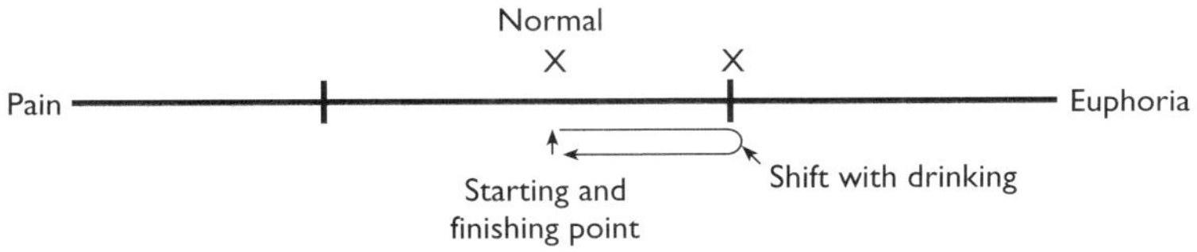

Learning the Mood Swing

Anyone who drinks learns this pharmacological effect of alcohol. Equally important, individuals learn that it happens consistently. Alcohol is a drug that can be depended on. Reflect on the discussion of alcohol's acute effects in Chapter 3; you'll recall that a number of things make this learning potent. You do not have to wait very long to experience what alcohol does. The effects of the drug can be felt almost immediately. For the new drinker, who has not acquired any tolerance to alcohol's effects, the change can be dramatic.

The physiological effects are usually considered the primary payoff for drug use. But other factors are at work. Consider nicotine. The first-time smoker does not find smoking pleasant, experiencing dizziness, feelings of nausea, and an unpleasant taste. One would have a hard time explaining continued smoking on the basis of the initial physiological effects. Rather, the positive feeling state that initially accompanies smoking is what smoking *means* to the person, not what the nicotine does. The attraction may be that smoking is considered to be sophisticated, or that close friends smoke, or that it denotes independence from parental or social norms. In the beginning, smoking occurs despite the immediate physical experience. However, the nicotine that accompanies the smoke quickly plays a role in perpetuating use. The same can be true with alcohol. The novice drinker may not like the taste. But there can be a social as well as a drug-induced payoff.

The second stage in the developmental process is termed *seeking the mood swing.* This happens after someone learns that alcohol can be counted on to enhance or improve mood. Now drinking can have a particular purpose. Anyone who drinks occasionally does so to make things better. Whatever the occasion—an especially hard day at work, a family gathering, a promotion, or recovery from a trying day of hassling kids—the expectation is that alcohol will do something nice. In essence the person has a contract with alcohol. True to its promise, alcohol keeps its side of the bargain. Furthermore, by altering the dose, the person can control the degree of mood change. Again there are no problems. Nothing up to this point suggests that alcohol use can be anything but pleasurable.

No man ever repented that he arose from the table sober, healthful, and with his wits about him.
—Jeremy Taylor
The Marriage Ring, 1653

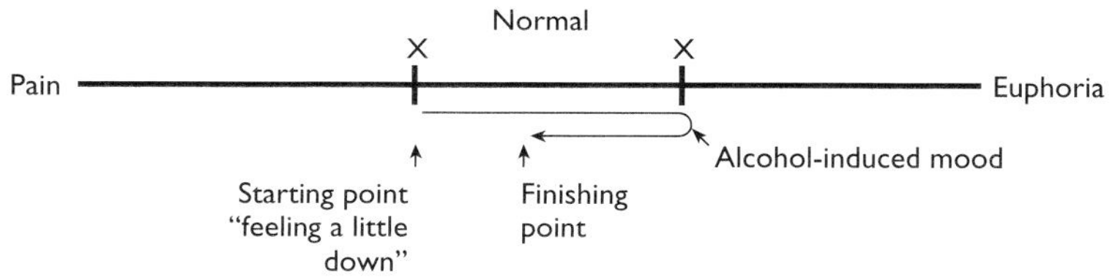

Seeking the Mood Swing

Somewhere along the line, predictably, most people who use alcohol will have a negative drinking experience. This may happen early in a drinking career. The unpleasant event can be the discomfort of a hangover or it can be the sensation of closing one's eyes and feeling the world spin. However, it need not be the physical aftermath of intoxication. Instead it can be the behavior that transpired. What occurred when drinking can make a person squirm at its recollection. At any rate, most people are quite clear that alcohol was the significant factor. They tell themselves, "No way, never again," and that's that. Possibly described as sadder but wiser as a result of what has happened, they alter their pattern of use in the future. That in turn markedly reduces the likelihood of future problems. While there may still be the occasional one drink too many, it is not the usual pattern.

For a minority of drinkers, this scenario will have a different outcome. These are the people for whom alcohol use becomes an emerging problem. In Johnson's schema, these people have crossed a thin, invisible line that separates the second and third stages.[2] The third phase is *harmful use*. Suddenly alcohol use has a boomerang effect. Whereas drinking alcohol previously had only a beneficial, positive effect, there are now negative consequences. Sketched out on the pain-euphoria continuum, initially the mood changes in the desired direction and achieves the drinker's purpose. But then something new occurs: the mood swing leaves the person feeling less comfortable than before the drinking occasion.

Who hath woe?
Who hath sorrow?
Who hath contentions?
Who hath babbling?
Who hath wounds without cause?
Who hath redness of eyes?

They that tarry long at the wine.
Proverbs 28:31–32

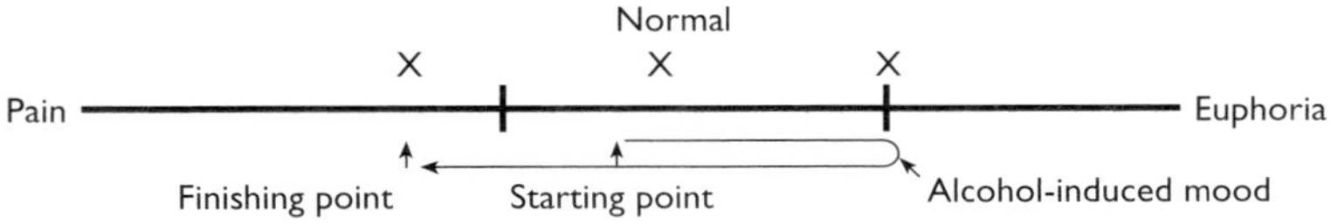

Harmful Use

Reaching the stage of harmful use has important consequences. At this point, to continue drinking in the same fashion is going to exact emotional costs. For whatever reasons, unwilling to abandon the use of alcohol as a means of altering their moods, some people are willing to pay the price and accept whatever the negative consequences may be. This decision to accept the consequences isn't a conscious one. Emotionally, drinkers remain loyal to their relationship with the drug, alcohol. It is here that denial enters the picture. There is also a revamping of priorities, which is needed to maintain the relationship with alcohol, to allow the relationship to go unexamined.

The most significant costs are psychological. Drinking and the drug-induced behavior and its consequences are inconsistent with the individual's fundamental values and self-image. To deal with this contradiction, continued use requires the individual to make personality adjustments. The normal psychological devices are used to distort reality just enough to explain away the costs. These psychological defenses are the same ones each of us uses virtually daily to some degree. If you're walking down the street, say hello to a friend, and get no response, your feelings are momentarily hurt. Almost automatically, you tell yourself, "She must not have seen or heard me." So you shut off the hurt feelings with an explanation that may or may not be true. You pick an explanation that allows you to turn off the unpleasant feelings the situation has evoked. Another time, if you're ill-tempered, a complete grouch, and behaving

One of the disadvantages of wine is that it makes a man mistake words for thoughts.
—Samuel Johnson

[2]This "thin line" is likely to be defined by biological factors that place some people at increased risk for developing an alcohol problem

in a fashion that you don't really like, you become uncomfortable with yourself. In such circumstances, you could say, "Yep, I sure am being a real pain in the neck to anyone near me." It's also possible the internal conversation will come out: "I've not been myself. The pressure of work must have gotten to me." In this way, we all attempt to control our discomfort and maintain psychic harmony. In doing so, we often overlook the obvious and adjust our experience just enough to take off the painful, rough emotional edges.

The person with a budding alcohol problem uses these kinds of defenses to maintain harmony and equilibrium in the relationship with his or her drug of choice. One way to accomplish this and explain away the costs is to *suppress emotions.* As negative emotions arise, the individual strives to keep them at bay: "I just won't think about it." So the guy who made a fool of himself at last night's party tries to ignore the whole thing: "Hey, these things happen sometimes. There's no sense in worrying about it." However, pretending emotions aren't there doesn't make them disappear. They simply crop up somewhere else. Because suppression doesn't work totally, other psychological devices need to be used. *Rationalization* is a common device—seizing an explanation that inevitably stays clear of alcohol itself: "I really got hammered last night but . . ." or "I wouldn't have been smashed if Dylan hadn't been pushing the drinks." In this latter example, *projection* is at work as well. The reason for whatever occurred and the accompanying emotional discomfort was that the drinks were stiff and it's Dylan's fault. No responsibility is accepted by the drinker or blame laid on alcohol.

A number of rationalizations are so frequently used that they might almost qualify as warning signals of alcohol dependence. For example: "I can't be alcoholic because I *never* drink in the morning." "*I'm* too young, too old, too smart, etc." "I can quit *whenever* I want to." "*Everyone* I know drinks the same way I do." "I *only* drink beer." "I drink only wine spritzers." "I never miss work." Casual drinkers do not consider such explanations necessary.

Several factors allow such distortions to go unchallenged. One is attributable to the action of the drug. Alcohol warps perceptions. The only firsthand memory anyone will have of a drinking event is the one that was laid down in a drugged state. So if someone under a haze of alcohol perceives herself as being clever and witty, sobering up in the morning is not going to be sufficient to make her realize that she was loud, coarse, and vulgar. Johnson refers to this "rosy memory" as *euphoric recall.* Until the advent of greater public awareness of alcohol problems, it was unlikely that other people would take it upon themselves to let the drinker know what really transpired.

There might not be any problems if these distortions were only occasional, but they aren't. And what proves to be even more destructive is that with continued, heavy drinking, the discrepancy becomes greater and greater between what the individual expects to happen and what does happen. Proportionately, the need for further distortion to explain this discrepancy grows.

Drinking is supposed to improve the mood, but as dependence emerges, more and more frequently the opposite proves to be the case. To illustrate this on the mood continuum, after a drinking occasion the drinker is emotionally more uncomfortable than before the drinking. As alcohol's effects wear off, he finds himself being dropped off further down toward the pain end of the spectrum. The result of alcohol use is not an enhanced but a diminished sense of well-being.

A vicious cycle is developing. The psychological mechanisms used to minimize the discomfort simultaneously prevent a recognition of what is really happening. None of the defenses, even in combination, are completely foolproof. At times, individuals feel remorse about their behavior. At those times it doesn't matter where the blame lies—on someone else, on themselves, on alcohol—drinkers regret what's happening, so a negative self-image develops.

For the most part, the drinker truly believes the reality created by his or her projections and rationalizations. Understandably, this begins to erode relationships with others. There are continual hassles over whose version of an event is accurate. This introduces additional tensions, and problems arise with friends, family, and coworkers. Self-esteem shrinks. The load of negative feelings expands. Ironically there is more and more reliance on the old relationship with alcohol. Drinking is deliberately structured into life patterns. Drinking is anticipated. The possibilities of drinking may well determine which invitations are accepted, where business meetings are held, and other activities. Gradually more and more leisure time is orchestrated to include drinking.

The stage is set for the last developmental phase in the emergence of clear-cut physiological dependence. The individual now *drinks to feel normal.* This is often wholly unappreciated by those for whom drinking is not a problem. Others assume, erroneously, that the alcohol-dependent person is drinking to feel good and have fun. By this point the idea of drinking to feel euphoric has long since gone. Alcohol has become essential, just to achieve a normal feeling state.

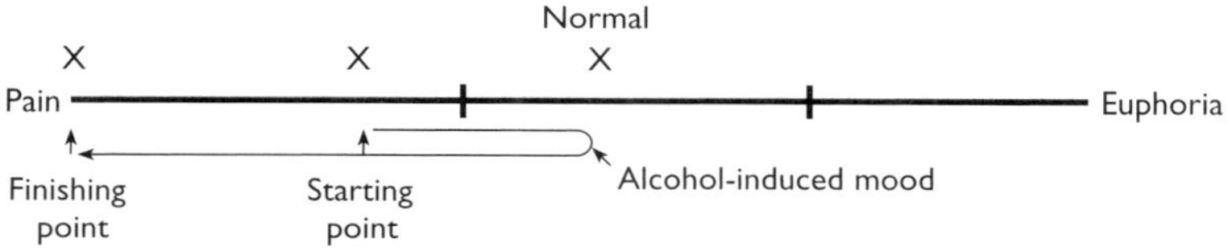

Drinking to Feel Normal

Boundless intemperance
In nature is a tyranny; it hath been
Th'untimely emptying of the happy throne
And fall of many kings.
—William Shakespeare
Macbeth

The single most important way in which alcohol may be essential to normalize function is to ward off withdrawal symptoms for the drinker who has become physically dependent. In addition, alcohol may assist normal functioning in other ways. Psychologists have documented the phenomenon of "state-dependent learning." Things learned in a particular context are most readily recalled under similar circumstances. Thus, things learned when sober are best recalled later in a sober state. Similarly, information learned while drinking is also more available for recall later when the person is again (or still) consuming alcohol. So the heavy drinker may have a repertoire of behavior, coping mechanisms, social skills, and even information that, if acquired during drinking, is less accessible when sober. In fact, drinking may be necessary to tap a reservoir of knowledge. This fact explains the scene from a classic film—*Days of Wine and Roses*—in which there is a desperate search for the liquor stashes that were hidden when drinking.

Memory distortions are not uncommon at this point. Blackouts may mean the absence of memory for some events. Repression is a psychological mechanism that also blocks out memory. Further havoc continues to be raised by "euphoric recall." The memories are only of the good times and the sense of relief associated with drinking. The problems and difficulties seemingly don't penetrate consciousness.

DETERIORATING FUNCTIONING

Because of the transformation of thinking, distorted view of reality, and ebbing self-esteem, the alcohol-dependent person's functioning deteriorates. Each of us is expected to fulfill various roles in life. For each slot in which we find ourselves, there is an accompanying set of expectations about appropriate behavior. Some of the typical roles are parent, spouse or partner, employee, citizen, or friend. Others may be more transient, such as scout leader, committee chair, patient, Rotary Club member, soccer coach, volunteer, tennis partner, or Sunday school teacher. No matter what the role, with alcohol or other drug dependence, performance usually suffers. There are expectations that others have of us in a particular role. The alcohol-dependent individual does not reliably meet them. Behavior is inconsistent. The individual is undependable—sometimes doing what is expected and doing it beautifully; the next time, it's "no show" followed by the flimsiest excuse. To add insult to injury, he or she gets furious at others for being disappointed, for being annoyed, or for not understanding.

Wine makes a man better pleased with himself;
I do not say that it makes him more pleasing to others.
—Samuel Johnson

Unreliable behavior has a profound impact on the people around the alcohol- or other drug-dependent person. Since these people have the normal insecurities of all humans, they think it might or must be their fault. Unwittingly they accept the rationalizations and projections. Some feel confused and left out. They sense and fear the loss of an important relationship, one that has been nourishing to them. In turn, their own behavior can become distorted. Now, in addition to whatever problems are directly attributable to alcohol or drug use, interpersonal relationships are impaired. This fuels the tension.

FAMILY AND FRIENDS

Focus for a moment on family, close relationships, and friends. If we apply behavioral learning terms, we would say that the alcohol-dependent person has people in his or her life on a variable interval reinforcement schedule. There they are, busily trying to accommodate. They feel that, somehow, if they behave differently, do the "right thing," the alcohol-dependent person will respond. One time they're harsh; the next time they try an understanding approach. Then another time they might try to ignore the situation. But nothing works. The dependent person does not respond in any predictable way to others' behavior. If he happens to be a "good boy" or she's been a "perfect lady" on occasion, it really has no connection to what the family or close friends have or have not done. The others, in fact, are accommodating themselves to the alcohol-dependent individual. Never sure why some times go better, they persist in trying—and trying some more. Meanwhile, the inconsistency and unpredictability remain.

Eventually families or partners, as well as close friends, give up and try to live around the situation. Family members may alternate between ignoring the drinker or feeling that they are being driven crazy. As well, whether out of love and loyalty, or the hope that maybe a change is just around the corner, or the fear that it isn't, their behavior may protect the person from the consequences of the drinking. Johnson introduced the term "enabling behavior" to describe this dynamic. Now enabling is a part of everyone's vocabulary, heard in our everyday conversations or those of TV and radio talk show hosts and their guests. The term "enabler" almost always has negative connotations. He or she is denigrated as stupid, a patsy, uninformed, self-centered, and harming others as a result of these character defects. Only rarely is there a sense of empathy, an appreciation of the pain and sense of hopelessness that may evoke this behavior, or the recognition that often it is an act of desperation. (See Chapter 8 for a discussion of the impact on the family.)

In a marriage or intimate relationship, if one partner has a major substance use problem, the other gradually assumes the accustomed functions of the impaired partner. Even though she may be the regular cook in the household, he will have contingency plans for supper in case it isn't ready that night. If he is the one who usually helps the kids with homework or attends their sports events, she may consider herself on call to fill in. In case he is up to it, fine; if not, a ready excuse is hauled out and she fills in. Such interactions can lead to resentments in everyone. The person carrying the load feels burdened; the drinker feels deprived and ashamed.

In the presence of a significant alcohol disorder, sexual problems in intimate relationships are likely. Sexual functioning is not merely a physical activity; it also has strong psychological components. How someone feels about him- or herself and a partner is bound to show up in bed. Any alcohol use can disturb physiological capacity for sex. Shakespeare said it most succinctly: alcohol "provokes the desire but takes away the performance." In the male, alcohol interferes with erection—once referred to as "brewer's droop."

The psychological realm has as strong an impact. Satisfying sexual relationships require an emotional relationship, a bond of love and affection. In a relationship with alcohol as the third member, neither partner is able to trust that bond; there are doubts on both sides. Problems arise in many ways. Intoxication invites revulsion and rejection. Any qualities of love have, for the moment, been washed away by the alcohol. Sexual intimacy can become a weapon too. One of the partners can try the tactic of emotional blackmail used in the ancient Greek play *Lysistrata:* refusing sex unless the other partner changes his or her behavior. On the other hand, both partners can approach intercourse as the magic panacea. If they can still make love, they can minimize the importance of everything else lacking in the relationship.

In the earlier stages of an alcohol problem, friends, especially close ones, will offer the same kind of excuses for the individual that family members do. But as time goes on, and problems mount as behavior deteriorates, friendships disappear in inverse relationship to their closeness. With a full-blown alcohol disorder there may be "drinking buddies" but few true friends. The reasons are fairly obvious. Casual acquaintances are unlikely to be interested in becoming friends after a few examples of erratic behavior. It's simply not worth it. Close friends who have begun to see a problem emerging may well try to help by talking to the drinker. In the early stages of an alcohol problem, this may well be effective in prompting treatment. However, defenses grow in proportion to the magnitude of the alcohol problem. In the later stages, the alcohol-dependent person may tell friends to mind their business, thus immobilizing them. The relationship with the bottle takes precedence over all others.

The exceptions only highlight the problem. One type of friend who may remain a companion is one who drinks in the same fashion and can be counted on to share the six-packs on the way home from work or to enjoy hitting the bars on the weekend. Another kind of friend will remain in loose touch, ready to lend a hand when needed. This person, possibly in recovery or who has had earlier experience with an alcohol-troubled person, knows the friendship cannot be maintained or profitably cultivated while the drinking continues. Nonetheless, he or she will often stay in touch, poised to be of assistance and support, should the drinker show evidence of wishing to face the problem and stop. On the other hand, when faced with an alcohol problem in someone close to them, recovering individuals—and treatment professionals, for that matter—often don't have an edge on anyone else. They, too, can be overwhelmed by the chaos that can ripple out from an alcohol-dependent person. They may also show denial, wanting the problem to be "anything but."

☐ WORK

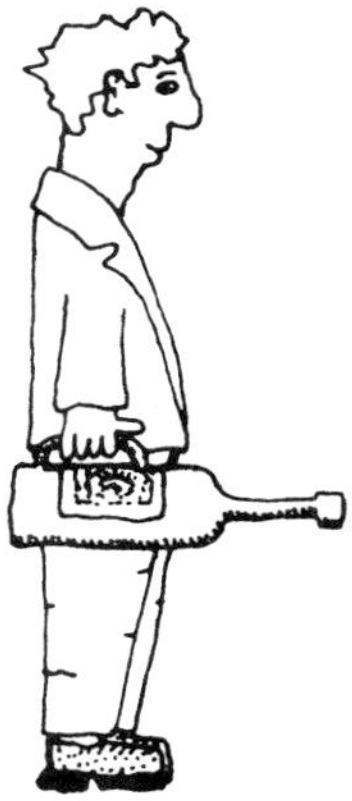

Often, although alcohol- or drug-dependent people are deeply mired in deteriorating social and family relationships and suffering physical problems, they still may be able to function at work. The work arena seems to be the last part of the drinker's life to be affected. The job is often the status symbol for both the alcohol-dependent employee and the partner. With more families counting on two paychecks, maintaining the income of both members is necessary. He or she might think or say, "There's nothing wrong with me. I'm still bringing in a good paycheck!" The spouse is likely to make excuses to the drinker's supervisor to protect the family livelihood.

Intervention at the workplace is, of course, possible at even the earliest signs. Much effort is being made to alert employers to the early signs of alcohol and other drug use problems and to acquaint them with rehabilitation possibilities. The employer is in a unique position to effect treatment at a relatively early stage. A recommendation that someone seek professional assistance or treatment may well be a precipitating factor in a recovery. The fact that the employer sees the problem and is willing to acknowledge it can go far in breaking down the facade that "everything's okay." Keeping a job may be sufficient motivation for an employee to face the problem. (Employee assistance programs, known as EAPs, and their impact on earlier intervention and treatment, are described further in Chapter 11.)

Those in serious trouble with alcohol generally believe that their public cover-up is successful, and the behavior of those around them often does little to challenge this misconception. Deteriorating functioning is covered up by other workers. Absences with the "flu" are ignored, and a gradual decline in their work is put down to "problems at home" or another such excuse. Most people, finding that it is not easy to confront someone with a drinking problem, wait until ignoring it is no longer possible. Over 20 years ago a study found that persons other than family members had noticed drinking problems on an average of seven years before the impaired person first sought help. Vaillant's work confirmed this too. Although four or more significant alcohol-related problems were virtually sufficient to guarantee a diagnosis of alcohol dependence, Vaillant found that it wasn't, in fact, until 11 separate such incidents had occurred that people entered treatment.

OTHER DRUGS OF ABUSE

Reality is a crutch for those who can't cope with drugs.
–Lily Tomlin

How might other drug use alter the scenario sketched here? Much of this model would seem to be applicable to drugs other than alcohol. However, a drug's illicit status may introduce a bit more complexity. Johnson's schema was created to describe the progression of alcohol use. The first two stages Johnson sketched out are seen as applying to anyone who uses alcohol: that is, first learning what alcohol does and then in the second stage seeking its effects. Nothing happens during the first two stages to suggest that possibly drinking isn't such a great idea.

Central to this formulation is the fact that alcohol use in the United States is widely accepted. Unlike a Muslim country in which any drinking is frowned upon, if not illegal, and any drinking that occurs is far more private, in American culture drinking is not hidden. Nonproblematic drinking is essentially a public behavior. On any run-of-the-mill day, alcohol is part of what we see around us. It is so common that it often doesn't even register. For example, we are not shocked when the evening news includes a video clip of our president toasting a foreign dignitary at a formal state dinner. The number and variety of beer logos on baseball caps we pass as we walk down the street barely register. In America, seeking the mood swing is perfectly OK in a multitude of situations.

That's not the case when it comes to illicit drugs. From virtually the start of any illicit drug use, the user can't be so casual. The significant exception would be marijuana use. According to Johnson's formulation, the equation is straightforward—the drinker compares how he or she feels before and on the heels of drinking. As long as the positives outweigh any negatives, there is no reason to think any further about alcohol use.

The illicit drug user has to consider the trade-off of the anticipated pleasures in the light of possible problems. It is unlikely that this will be particularly conscious. No one sits down with paper and pencil and makes a list of the pros and cons. But in effect such a mental calculation is being made. For example, we might factor in the ease of getting a drug, the likelihood of getting caught, what is required to lower that risk, and what the consequences would be. The decision to use on any particular occasion will be determined by how this personal cost-benefit analysis turns out. So, before seeking the mood swing, the possible user is answering the question, "Is the mood swing worth it?" The relative weight will determine the behavior. One can imagine any number of things that would cause people to weigh the same factors differently, leading to opposite responses to the question "Is drug use now worth it?" This kind of process is what behavioral economists are pointing to when discussing rational addiction, which attempts to explain behavior that seems to be totally opposed to the usual way of making decisions. (See Chapter 5.)

The hallmark of *harmful use* is when drinking continues despite the fact that the drinker's mood state is less positive after than it was before drinking. Recall, this is the point at which Johnson says psychological devices are required to distort reality, at least enough to explain away the costs. A variety of psychological mechanisms are available.

With illicit drug use these psychological defenses have to be used earlier in the game. Before the state of harmful use, at the point of *seeking the mood swing,* illicit drug users have to justify to themselves *any* use. The list of potential explanations is almost limitless: "It's no big deal" or "I'm not hurting anyone" to "It's nobody else's business" or "The laws are totally stupid." For the discussion here, the issue isn't whether these arguments are or are not valid. For this discussion, the significant factor is simply that they are required at all.

I hate to advocate drugs, alcohol, violence, or insanity to anyone, but they've always worked for me.
—Hunter S. Thompson

The question this raises is whether the need for mental gymnastics—something not required to allow or justify seeking the mood swing with drinking—has a ripple effect down the line. If a user repeatedly answers "Yes" to the question of "Is use worth it?" what does it take to begin responding "No"? If there haven't been any particular negative consequences from the user's perspective, does the "Yes" come easier? Learning theory would suggest so. Also, drug effects must be factored in. The more a user *really* likes a drug's effects, the more serious the negative consequences need to be to tip the balance.

Beyond any possible modifications to the Johnson schema, with illicit drug use there are other factors worth noting. Regular use of illicit drugs entails time and effort merely to assure a reliable supply. There isn't the option of dashing out quickly to the nearest convenience store and picking up a bag of heroin along with the half gallon of milk for the kids. There isn't the equivalent of the neighborhood bar, where you can stop on the way home from work to order up a line of cocaine instead of a beer. Depending on who your friends are, you can't count on going to a wine and cheese event and finding joints rolled up, attractively displayed next to the veggies and dip. Illicit drug use entails hustling. Part of the hustle is the unending series of choices that include not-so-good options. Do you take the kids along when you go out to score, thinking "After all, they'll probably just fall asleep in the car"? Or do you leave them alone at home, thinking "After all, it's their bedtime, and they hardly ever wake up at night, and I wouldn't be gone *that* long"?

If God wanted us high, He would have given us wings.
—Arsenio Hall

Alcohol-dependent persons may find themselves going with a cheap wine instead of the expensive bottle of an imported vintage. But there's no question it's ethanol. With many illicit drugs, who knows? Depending on the substance, contaminants or substitutions are always potential problems.

Another factor in illicit drug use is the greater likelihood of encounters with the law and higher rates of crime. Some have pointed out that ironically the growth in arrests for drug possession may be attributed to the fact that the rate of serious crime has been dropping. A criminal justice system overwhelmed by investigations of assaults and serious property crimes isn't going to make the kid in a park smoking a joint a top priority.

Adolescent Substance Use

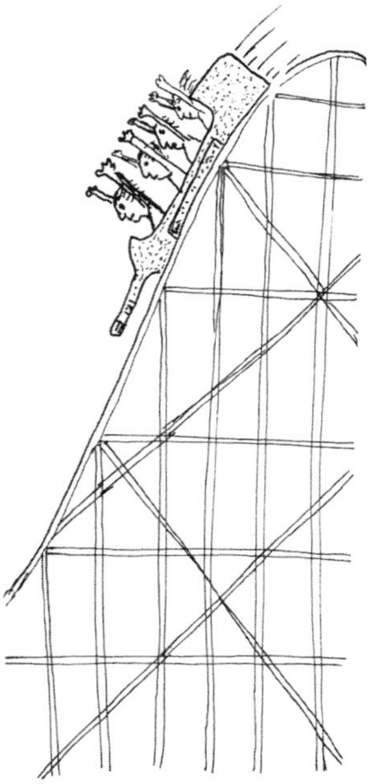

Adolescent substance use is addressed in detail in Chapter 11, so the comments here are limited. In the face of a child's alcohol or drug use, a parent's behavior can look a lot like what is described here for family members generally. Under the best of circumstances, adolescents' behavior can be fairly erratic. With the usual ups and downs, how do you know if or which parts of the roller-coaster ride can be attributed to drug use or drinking?

Parents don't always *really* want to know. What are they going to do? And the kids generally have any number of reasons to keep substance use hidden. Even if use is suspected, parents may be quite happy and relieved to hear their child claim it isn't so. And teens can be very imaginative. One good tactic adolescents use to counter suspicion is doing a few things to demonstrate how mature, responsible, and thoughtful they are—even if it's only hanging up the backpack rather than leaving it in the middle of the floor. If a parent brings up a concern about possible alcohol or drugs, adolescents are capable of performances that would warrant Academy Awards. They can act hurt, outraged, insulted, and incredulous, as if the parent's mere thought that they'd be doing drugs has to rank up there as about *the* most stupid thing the parent has *ever* done. And the merry-go-round continues.

A FINAL THOUGHT

Often alcohol- or drug-impaired persons have no idea how obvious their difficulties are to so many other people. When they are finally confronted by events, it can be a great shock to find out how much of the behavior they thought was hidden was, in fact, observed. The rationalization and denial systems can convince the alcohol-impaired person that no one on the job or in the community knows about the drinking problem.

The behavior that accompanies a serious substance use disorder causes pain and confusion for all—the individuals affected and those around them. Unfortunately, most of the family's and friends' efforts to alter the situation don't work. Regardless of goodwill, alcohol dependence rarely responds to the more common maneuvers of concerned friends or family. Altering these destructive patterns may require involvement of a substance abuse clinician: someone who is knowledgeable about the dynamics of addiction and its effects on others, is up-to-date on treatment approaches, and has the clinical skills of a disinterested, but not an uninterested, professional.

REFERENCES AND FURTHER READINGS

This chapter aims to convey what dependence feels like for the individual with the disease and for those whose lives are closely touched by it. Tackling the scientific writings, with their reports of controlled studies, tables of data, and reams of footnotes, is unlikely to be a useful avenue for further exploration. Instead, it is suggested you turn to literature. An autobiography of someone with alcohol or other drug dependence can provide insight into and understanding of the behavior and feelings that characterize the disease. Consider the plays of Eugene O'Neill. *Long Day's Journey into Night* powerfully captures the family beset by addiction.

Identify a recovering individual with whom you can just talk. Don't consider this a formal interview; consider it a conversation initiated by an interested person who wants to know what another's life is like. Take as a guide the conversation you might have with a close friend who has returned from a long-anticipated trip of a lifetime. Through your questioning and listening, by asking that person to "relive" the trip, you become a companion on the adventure.

Attend an open meeting of AA or NA or another self-help group. As members tell their "stories," as they speak about "what it was like, what happened, and what things are like now," the behavior and the emotional life of alcohol and drug dependence are powerfully conveyed.

Johnson V. *I'll Quit Tomorrow,* rev. ed. New York: Harper & Row, 1983.

Lange O. *The Trip to Echo Spring: On Writers and Alcohol.* London: Picador, 2013.

Schuckit MA, Smith TL, Anthenelli R, et al. Clinical course of alcoholism in 636 male inpatients. *American Journal of Psychiatry* 150(5):786–792, 1993.

Vaillant G. *The Natural History of Alcoholism, Revisited.* Cambridge, MA: Harvard University Press, 1995.

Effects of Alcohol Problems on the Family

In the early 1980s, a review of two books purporting to be comprehensive works on alcohol dependence noted the scanty attention paid to the impact of alcohol on the family. The reviewer plaintively asked, "Why is so much written about the effects of alcoholism upon a patient's liver enzymes and so little written about the effects of parental alcoholism on the children?" Fortunately, that question no longer has the same ring of truth to it.

One of the major developments in the alcohol field during the 1980s was the vastly increased attention to the plight of the family. For the first time, engaging families in treatment became the norm. In addition, there were efforts to reach out to family members, even if the alcohol-dependent person was not in treatment. As part of the attention to the family, alcohol dependence began to be described as a "family illness."[1]

There is no way family members can escape or ignore the alcohol-troubled member. In a Gallup poll conducted in 2000, 35% of the respondents said that at some point alcohol had been a cause of trouble in their families. In 2012, an estimated 7.5 million children under

[1]Some believe it may be time to retire the phrase "family illness" as a virtual synonym for alcohol dependence. Alcohol dependence is not the only chronic disease with a significant impact on family members. Might HIV/AIDs, diabetes, kidney failure requiring dialysis, or Alzheimer's qualify for this label? The objection to this characterization speaks as well to a larger question—a concern that as a society we pathologize any number of conditions, slap a label on something, consider it an illness, and relegate the affected individual to the ranks of the "sick."

age 18 were living with a parent with a serious alcohol problem. Nationwide that's 10.5% of all children under age 18. Picture kids on the playground. One of every 10 will be returning home to a parent with a significant alcohol problem. "Significant" means meeting the formal criteria for a diagnosis of substance abuse or dependence. The majority (80%) live in two-parent families. Almost all the rest live with a single mom (15%).

However, these estimates provide only a partial picture. Neither tobacco nor prescription drug abuse, nor illicit drug use is included. Equally important, there are children these statistics make invisible. An additional 4.5 million kids are *not* living with either parent. How might alcohol or other drug use have contributed to that situation? Certainly living in a home with a parental alcohol or drug problem can't be minimized. However, some of those children living outside of the parental home—in many real and painful ways—continue to live with parental substance use.

Don't do drugs because if you do drugs you'll go to prison, and drugs are really expensive in prison.
—John Hardwick

The majority of the impairments symptomatic of alcohol dependence or abuse are behavioral. So in the day-to-day interactions of family life, the family members are confronted by an array of behaviors that, although they result from an alcohol problem, may initially appear to have little connection to the drinking. Over time, the family can become functionally impaired in response to the turmoil that comes with an alcohol-dependent member in its midst.

Since the reviewer's lament, the issues of the family have gained the attention of both the treatment and research communities. However, there is always a lag between the time an issue gains the attention of researchers and the point at which the research is conducted, the data analyzed, the results published, the findings translated into practice, and the findings then rippling out into the treatment community. In the meantime, clinicians are forced to do the best they can, drawing on their clinical observations and using the information that is available. Inevitably, the theories and approaches that bubble up in such transitional periods will later be recognized as a combination of fact and fiction. As research findings become available, the challenge is to refine our practice to incorporate the new knowledge, and, as required, lay aside earlier formulations. This is easier said than done.

Get no kick from champagne,
Mere alcohol doesn't thrill me at all,
So tell me why should it be true
that I get a kick out of you?
—Cole Porter
I Get a Kick Out of You, 1934

It is important to recognize that there is far more variety in family life today than there was a generation or two ago. Families in the twenty-first century come in many forms. They include traditional families—statistically described as husband, wife, 2.2 children, and a dog—as well as single-parent families, unmarried couples, same-sex couples, and blended families, which include children from prior marriages or relationships. Variations on the traditional theme inevitably introduce new twists for families. Although there may be common issues, there may be differences posed by the particular family structure.

THE FAMILY'S RESPONSE

As a Process

The earliest attention to alcohol and the family can be traced to a classic monograph, published in 1954, by Joan Jackson, *Alcoholism and the Family*. It endeavored to describe the stages that occur as a family comes to grips with alcoholism. Her work paralleled that of E. M. Jellinek, who only eight years before had studied members of AA to identify the stages of alcoholism (see Chapter 4). Jackson conducted her work by attending meetings and speaking with members of a group known as the AA Auxiliary. Later, the Auxiliary became what we know as Al-Anon Family Groups. Given the era in which her research was conducted, the stages she identified are based on the family in which the husband and father was the alcohol-dependent member and a time when what was termed alcoholism was considered a disease of middle age, taking hold between the ages of 35 and 50. The six stages Jackson sketched out are described in the following sections in the order in which, in her sample, they typically unfold. The importance of Jackson's work is the groundwork it laid, providing a framework for thinking about the family, a framework we now take for granted.

Denial

Occasional episodes of excessive drinking at first are explained away by both partners. Early in the emergence of dependence, drinking because of tiredness, worry, nervousness, or a bad day is not unbelievable. The assumption is that the episode is an isolated instance and therefore no problem. If the couple is part of a group in which heavy drinking is acceptable, this provides a handy cover for developing dependency. A cocktail before dinner easily becomes two or three, and wine with the meal and brandy afterward also pass without much notice.

Attempts to Eliminate the Problem

In this stage, the drinker's partner recognizes that the drinking is not normal and tries to pressure him or her to quit, to be more careful, or to cut down: "If you would only pull yourself together," "If you would only use a little willpower," or "If you really love me, you won't do this anymore." Simultaneously, the partner tries to hide the problem from outsiders and keep up a good front. At the same time, the alcoholic spouse probably sneaks drinks or drinks outside the home, in an attempt to hide the amount he or she is drinking. Children in the family may start having problems in response to the family stress.

Historically the danger for families at this point was that they might enter some general counseling—whether with clergy, a psychologist, or a social worker—that failed to address the problem drinking head-on. In such cases, couples or individual therapy easily became a part of the denial. It could be a way for the affected person to continue drinking and for both partners to pretend to be doing something about it. Helping professionals are far more knowledgeable about substance use disorders today, so the chances of alcohol problems going undetected or unacknowledged are less likely.

Disorganization and Chaos

The family equilibrium has now broken down. The drinker's spouse can no longer pretend everything is OK and spends most of the time going from crisis to crisis. Financial troubles are common. Under a great deal of stress, possibly questioning her own emotional health, the spouse may seek outside help. In general, women are more likely than men to use outside assistance. Too often, spouses may seek help from friends who know no more than they do about what to do. Similarly, they may seek out a member of the clergy who has no training in dealing with alcohol problems. Or they may turn to the family physician, who in the past may have prescribed some "nerve" pills when confronted by their distraught condition. If at this stage the non-dependent partner seeks assistance from substance abuse professionals and/or becomes involved with Al-Anon, the process will probably take a different course altogether.

Reorganization in Spite of the Problem

The spouse's coping abilities have been strengthened. He or she gradually assumes the larger share of responsibility for the family unit. This may mean getting a job or taking over the finances. The major focus of energy is no longer directed toward getting the affected partner to shape up. Instead, the spouse takes charge. The spouse fosters family life, despite the alcohol dependence. It has since been recognized that the degree to which a stable family life can be established and maintained, even if the chronic drinker remains in the home, can have important implications for the welfare of children in the family. Children fare far better in families in which the family rituals are maintained, whether these are celebrations, such as Christmas or birthdays, regular family meal times, family vacations, or any of the other things, large or small, that "we always do."

Efforts to Escape

Separation or divorce may be attempted. If the family unit remains intact, the family continues living around the alcohol-dependent member.

Family Reorganization

In the case of separation, family reorganization occurs without the affected partner and parent. If the alcohol-dependent partner achieves sobriety, a reconciliation may take place. Either path will require both partners to realign roles and make new adjustments.

Further Thoughts

Jackson's formulations are focused on the family in which the husband is alcohol-dependent. But marriage outcomes differ, depending on which partner has the alcohol problem. Among those with alcohol dependence, the female alcohol-dependent member is much more likely to be divorced than is her male counterpart. In the past, those trying to account for this difference speculated that women who marry someone with alcohol dependence have unconscious, neurotic needs to be married to weak, inadequate males. The implication was that, because of this need, they stay married and get psychological strokes for doing so. That view no longer has much credence. Given economic realities, it is not unexpected that the nondependent wife stays in her marriage longer than the nondependent husband. She may feel a need for the husband's financial support to maintain the family. Indeed, following a divorce, the economic situation for the majority of women and their children declines. On the other side, men in general are less likely to seek outside help for any kind of problem—no matter what. Therefore, the husband of a problem drinker may see no alternative to divorce to save himself, as well as the children.

Although Jackson's model provides a useful general framework for considering the situation of a family and its efforts to cope, do not expect all families to experience these stages in a textbook fashion. Some families might get bogged down in different stages. Some never move beyond denial. Some may seem trapped in an endless cycle of chaos and crisis. And some go through a painful succession of attempts to escape from the situation, then reconciliations, followed by later attempts again to escape. Within the alcohol field the focus is upon identifying the factors that have an impact upon families and what explains the differences between families. There is a wide array of questions. Does a spouse's or partner's involvement in treatment have an impact? Yes. Are there differences based on racial and ethnic differences? Yes. African Americans and Hispanics have a broader support system, be it an extended family or church groups, which serves to buttress the family. Does it matter when the alcohol problem emerges? Yes. For marriages in which the husband is alcohol-dependent, evidence suggests that the wives most able to help themselves and their families are those who were married before their husbands became problem drinkers. What is the impact of a parental alcohol problem on children's substance use? There are a number of factors, but genetic endowment is the single most significant one.

As a Disruption in the Family System

A common dimension of virtually all current approaches to the family with an alcohol-dependent or drug-dependent member is viewing the family as a system. This is a very common perspective within the larger field of family therapy. Central to this is the belief that changes in any part of the system (any family member) affect all of the others. The other members, in response, also make changes in an attempt to maintain the family equilibrium. The metaphor that captures this close interdependence is that of a circus family specializing in a high-wire balancing act. All members of the act climb up to the top of the tent. In turn, they step out onto the thin wire to begin an intricate set of maneuvers to build a human pyramid high above the audience. Timing and balance are critical; the mutual interdependence is obvious. Each is sensitive to even the tiniest movement of the others. All of the family members in the troupe continually adjust and readjust their balance, which is necessary to maintain the routine. If only one fails to do the expected, the entire routine fails.

In essence, families with an impaired member function in a very similar fashion. The behavior that accompanies a major alcohol problem begins to invade the family routine. Everyone attempts to compensate, with the goal of restoring equilibrium in the family. Most families make precarious, and usually unhealthy, adjustments to the presence of drinking. They expend energy to maintain the status quo. The family's behavior is designed to avoid doing anything that might further upset the delicate balance that prevails, which to their minds would prompt further deterioration of the family's situation. Ironically, once a family has adjusted to a problem, significant re-adjustments would be required if the impaired member were to seek treatment.

The kinds of accommodations that families make vary widely. At one extreme, the drinking member is almost like a boarder in the family's household. The family isolates the alcohol-dependent member. They expect little. They give little. In this way, they maintain some stability and continuity for themselves. At the other extreme, all of family life is alcohol centered, responding to the crisis of the moment. In addition, families can vacillate between patterns of accommodating the impaired member and isolating the individual, depending on whether he or she is drinking or on the wagon.

Home is the place where,
when you have to go there,
They have to take you in.
—Robert Frost
"The Death of a Hired Man," 1914

Research has identified three approaches family members commonly use in living with alcohol dependence: (1) keeping out of the way of the drinker and managing one's own life; (2) caregiving, counseling, and controlling; and (3) resigning and maintaining a facade. While all are used at various times, there may be a "usual approach," and the approach most commonly chosen differs by gender and between spouse and children. Most commonly the spouse is involved with caregiving, counseling, and controlling. Children of problem drinkers, on the other hand, are more likely to opt for keeping out of the way of the drinker and managing their own lives. Men are more likely than women to adopt resignation, whereas women are likely to selectively keep out of the way while also engaged in caregiving.

Escalating Equilibrium

No family member has ever caused alcohol dependence in another, despite what the dependent member may claim. However, family members can, despite their best intentions, take actions that in hindsight can be seen as allowing drinking or drug use to continue. As discussed in Chapter 7, Vernon Johnson recognized this phenomenon and termed it "enabling." From a family systems perspective, what has been termed "enabling" is seen as "escalating equilibrium." If family members' behavior spares the alcoholic from experiencing the negative consequences of drinking, most likely the family members absorb the pain themselves. Commonly the family member may describe his or her behavior as necessary because "I care," "These things happen," "I just can't take any more," "I'm afraid of what will happen to me (to the children) if I don't," "Someone has to assume some responsibility," and on and on. As often as not, these efforts to cope with the drinking are distasteful or feel wrong, evoking twinges of guilt, anger, despair, frustration, and shame. In effect the behavior of one member reinforces and maintains the behavior of the other, while also raising the costs and emotional consequences for both. So the alcohol-impaired member's acts create stress and increase the family's anxiety level. This in turn may provoke more drinking by the alcoholic to relieve his or her own anxiety; this raises the family's anxiety even higher, and family members react by simply doing more of what they were already doing. The pattern escalates on both sides until a crisis occurs. The family is no better able to cope with the problem in its midst than is the impaired member; thus, involvement in treatment is essential.

Johnson certainly appreciated that such escalating behavior in the family was far more than a bad habit. For the family to change its behavior was to open itself to stress, pain, and discomfort, all at the very point when its members think they can't take any more. Johnson emphasized working with the family—providing support, education, and family counseling—either to provide care for them or as an essential prelude to engaging with the alcohol-troubled person.

Since being introduced, the term "enabling" has moved far beyond the substance abuse field. It is heard in general conversation, heard on a TV talk show, or overheard in the cell phone conversation of a person next to you on the bus. Rather than being a simple descriptor, the term has taken on a negative connotation. Enabling has become an accusation. As frequently used, enabling suggests that the family member is incredibly stupid or is acting without the troubled person's best interests at heart. The pain and stress that prompts enabling largely goes unrecognized.

Along with enabling, the term *co-dependency* was introduced in the same era. If alcoholism (then the commonly used term) was a family illness, was not the next logical step to provide a name for the "disease" experienced by family members? Within the substance abuse community, there was never a single consistent definition for co-dependency or co-dependent. In some instances, these were used as a label—a shorthand means to refer to problems of family members. At the other end of the spectrum were those who viewed co-dependency as a distinct psychiatric condition warranting inclusion in the American Psychiatric Association's *Diagnostic and Statistical Manual*.

At the time there were articles in various medical journals about this recently recognized syndrome. Subsequent research has not supported the notion of family members' sharing a set of symptoms that represent a discrete psychiatric entity. However, this formulation had taken on a life of its own. It was popularized within the self-help communities. Further spreading the word was a book *Co-dependent No More,* which topped the *New York Times* best-seller list for nearly a year. As authors of an academic text on substance abuse noted, "The co-dependence movement has developed a huge self-help following and created multimillion-dollar markets in both the publishing and treatment industries. Co-dependence has been described both as a national epidemic affecting 96% of the population and as 'the chic neurosis of our time . . .'"

CHILDREN IN THE FAMILY

The child living with a parent in need of alcohol or other substance abuse treatment deserves special attention. In an atmosphere of conflict, tension, and uncertainty, a child's need for warmth, security, and even physical care may be inadequately met. In a family in which adult roles are inconsistently and inadequately filled, children lack good models to form their own identities. It is more likely that such children will have a harder time than will their peers as they enter into relationships outside the home, at school, or with playmates. A troubled child may be the signal of an alcohol problem in a family.

Without question, growing up with an alcohol-dependent parent is far from ideal. At the same time, the experiences of children in these families vary greatly. There are different patterns of drinking and different behaviors associated with drinking. Children are various ages, as are their parents, when the drinking problem becomes apparent. Furthermore, there are differences in the coping styles of the non-alcohol-dependent parent, which can moderate the impact of the drinking on family life.

All these factors influence how a parent's drinking affects the child. The specific problems of particular children will vary. Furthermore, a child's own natural resilience may be buttressed by the nurturing of extended family, scout leaders, coaches, teachers and neighbors, or parents of friends. Thus, a child's experience may be less impoverished than it might appear. In addition, many of the problems encountered are not exclusive to the home with an alcohol-troubled parent. Research shows that many of the characteristics attributed to children with an alcohol-troubled parent are true of those in families that are dealing with significant stress.

Nonetheless, in thinking of children, it is hard not to think in terms of the dramatic, and the kind of situation that may be encountered. Take five minutes to imagine what life might be like for a child with a parent who is alcohol-dependent:

- *As a preschooler.* What is it like to lie in bed, listening to your parents fight? Or to have Daddy disappear for periods of time unexpectedly? Or to be spanked really hard and sent away from dinner just because your milk spilled? Or to have a succession of sitters because Mommy works two jobs? Or to get lots of attention one moment and be in the way the next instant?
- *As an elementary school child.* What is it like when Mom forgets to give you lunch money? Or to wait and wait after soccer practice for a ride, long after the other kids have been picked up? Or for Dad to cancel out on the scout hike because he is sick? Or to not be allowed to bring friends home to play? Or to have your friends' mothers not let them ride in your car? Or to be scared to tell Mom you need a white shirt to be a pilgrim in the class Thanksgiving play?
- *As an early adolescent.* What is it like if you can't participate in school functions because you must get home to care for your younger brothers and sisters? Or if the money you made mowing lawns is missing from your room? Or if Dad's name is regularly featured in the court column? Or if Mother asks you to telephone her boss because she has a black eye from falling down? Or if there's no one from your family to go to the athletic awards banquet?
- *As an older adolescent.* What do you imagine awaits you after high school? Do you really want to enlist in the service or do you just want to get away? Or what if Dad doesn't fill out the college financial aid forms on time? Or what if Mom borrows your car and crumples the fender while trying to park?

In considering the impact of such behaviors, it is helpful to consider the normal developmental tasks that confront children of different ages and consider how these may be impeded by a parental alcohol problem. Those who have studied the process of emotional development see very early childhood as the period of life in which the major emotional tasks center on developing a sense of security and an ability to trust the environment. This is the time that children should learn that they are able to interact with others to have basic needs met. For the children of alcohol-dependent parents, these basic needs may not be reliably met. For preadolescent children, a major emotional task is developing a sense of autonomy and an ability to use rules to cope with life events. For adolescents, the emotional tasks center on separating from the family and developing the ability to function independently in the world.

Prenatal Influences

The problems may have begun before birth. As discussed in Chapter 6, maternal alcohol use can influence fetal development. At its most extreme, this is expressed as fetal alcohol syndrome. In addition to the direct impact of the drug, behaviors associated with heavy drinking may affect fetal development. Physical trauma, including falls, malnutrition, or abnormalities of glucose metabolism are not uncommon. Any of these can have an impact on a developing baby.

The emotional state of the expectant mother is presumed to influence fetal development. It certainly has an influence on the course of labor and delivery. The emotional state of the alcohol-dependent expectant mother might differ dramatically from that of a normal, healthy, nondrinking expectant mother and may be a source of problems. An alcohol-troubled expectant father may exert some indirect prenatal influences. If he is abusive or provides little emotional and financial support, this can cause anxiety in the mother.

Children in the Home

Another crucial time in any infant's life comes shortly after delivery. The very early interactions between mother and infant are important influences in the mother-child relationship. A new mother needs emotional and physical support to help her deal with the presence of the baby in her life. At a minimum, the baby requires food, warmth, physical comfort, and consistency of response from the mother. In the case of a family with an active alcohol-dependent member, one cannot automatically assume that everything is going smoothly.

Hello. 911? From a child driven by her intoxicated mother

The state police report investigating a 911 call from a 13-year-old, who said she was frightened by her mother's wildly erratic driving, winding in out of traffic, and also speaking incoherently. When the police responded, they found the car parked alongside the interstate. The mother failed a field sobriety test. Her BAC was 0.18, more than twice the legal limit.

—Gabriel Falcon

CNN, July 2010

It cannot be emphasized too strongly how much remains unknown about the impact of alcohol problems on children. The earliest efforts to understand the impact on children were not based on unbiased scientific research. Much of what has been attributed to children who have grown up in a home with alcohol dependence originated in self-help groups of adults who grew up in alcohol-troubled homes. Or the information came from children of parents who have sought treatment for alcohol dependence. Although their wounds are real, one must ask how far one can safely generalize from their experiences. They may represent a minority of children in alcohol-troubled families. They may be speaking primarily for an earlier generation—when alcohol treatment was less common, when family treatment was almost unheard of, and when alcohol dependence was more of a stigma. It must be remembered that being a child in an alcohol-troubled family does not confer an automatic sentence of lifelong problems. Some children's problems may be quite apparent and obvious. Yet given the potential for a chaotic environment in the family, it is actually striking how well children cope with the presence of alcohol dependence.

Early Approaches: Children's Coping Styles

Again back in the 1980s, drawing on a family systems approach to the alcohol-troubled family, clinicians working in the field postulated several distinctive coping styles that children adopt in response to the family's problems.

Roles Two different models of children's responses to a parental alcohol problem have been suggested. One formulation outlined three roles that children may adopt. One role was seen as being the *responsible one*. This role was seen as usually falling to the only child or the oldest child, especially the oldest daughter. This child was viewed as assuming major responsibility, not only for him- or herself but also for younger brothers and sisters—taking over chores and keeping track of what needs to be done. In general, this child compensates as much as possible for the instability and inconsistency introduced by the parental alcohol problem. A second coping response was that of the *adjuster*. This child didn't take on the responsibilities of managing. Instead, the child was seen as following directions and being accommodating to whatever came along. This child was remarkable for how much he or she could take in stride. The third proposed style was the *placater*. This role involved managing not the physical affairs of the family, as the responsible one does, but the emotional affairs. This child was attuned to being concerned and sensitive to others. Placating may have included being sympathetic to one parent and alternately to the other parent, always trying to soothe ruffled feathers.

It was further hypothesized that the roles adopted in childhood could become a lifelong coping strategy. For example, the responsible one probably would be a good student, Mommy's little helper, and got praise for both. However, as a coping style, what works well in childhood can be detrimental for an adult. Thus, the responsible one might become an adult who always needs to be on top of things, in control, destined to experience the stress of attempting to be a lifetime super-achiever. The flexible one (the adjuster) may be so tentative, so unable to trust as to be unable to make the long-term commitments that are required to succeed in a career or intimate adult personal relationships, such as that of spouse or parent. Likely as not, the adjuster adults, so attuned to accommodating others, allow themselves to be manipulated. An ever present option for the adult adjuster would be to marry someone with a problem, such as alcohol dependence, which allows continuation of the adjuster role. The adult placaters are seen as continually caring for others, often at the price of being unaware of their own needs or being unable to meet them. This can lead to large measures of guilt and anger, neither of which a placater can handle easily.

A different but similar typology of the roles that children might adopt includes the *family hero,* the *lost child,* the family *mascot,* and the *scapegoat.* The first three have much in common with the three styles just discussed: the responsible one, the adapter, and the placater. Most of these coping styles would not elicit external attention or invite intervention. The exception is the scapegoat, who is the one supposedly most likely to be in trouble in school or with the authorities. This is the one who, usually acting angry and deviant, may be the only child clearly seen as having a problem. If the child is a teenager, the trouble may take the form of drug or alcohol abuse. (This is discussed in the section on adolescents in Chapter 11.) Potentially it is through the attention focused on this child by outsiders or the family that the family alcohol problem may first surface. Of course, initially the family will see the child as the central problem. And the scapegoat's behavior takes the focus off the parental alcohol problem. Having a common problem to tackle may help keep a fragile family intact. Often the family creates the myth that the drinking is the parent's coping response to the child's behavior. Alternately, the child may be held responsible for aggravating the parent's drinking.

Current Views While the preceding frameworks were once widely used, they have not fared well over time. Clinical research to verify these behavior patterns has generally been unsuccessful. At best these descriptions of children's coping can only be used as metaphors, as a way of outlining the kinds of adjustments children *might* make. No counselor should assume that children in a family will fit into one of the roles and then try to figure out which one gets which label.

Adult Children

Another aspect of the attention directed to the issues of the family was the emergence in the mid-1980s of adult children of alcoholics (ACoA) as a group seen to warrant special attention. Based on clinical observations and anecdotal reports, a set of characteristics was identified as purportedly common to adult children of problem drinkers. These characteristics included fear of losing control, fear of feelings, fear of conflict, an overdeveloped sense of responsibility, feelings of guilt when standing up for oneself, an inability to relax or to have fun, harsh self-criticism, the tendency to live in a world of denial, difficulties with intimate relationships, adopting the victim stance, the tendency to be more comfortable with chaos than with security, the tendency to confuse love and pity, the tendency under pressure to assume a black-and-white perspective, a backlog of delayed grief, a tendency to react rather than to act, and an ability to survive. The source of these traits was seen as lying in the dynamics of the alcohol-troubled family and as sparked by the behavior of an alcohol-dependent parent.

Because attention and help for alcohol dependence was then such a recent phenomenon, that era's adult children had been reared in homes where the parental alcohol problem received no treatment and they, as children, received no help. Whether the affected parent died from the disease, left the home, or recovered, those adult children saw themselves as experiencing difficulties that grew out of these earlier experiences.

Unique Versus Broader Issue?

Some research initially supported the notion of a distinctive set of traits shared by adult children. But these early studies were flawed. They studied those who were involved in treatment or in self-help groups. In any kind of psychological research, there is the possibility that individuals involved in treatment are not representative of those who don't feel a need to seek help. Subsequent research following more stringent designs has not supported the notion of a distinct set of personality traits for these adults. The current thinking is that the problems they may experience are not unique to the family with problem drinking. In fact, they also are found among adults who have grown up in families with considerable stress and serious problems, such as mental illness or domestic violence. Even here, not everyone who has grown up in families with such problems has these traits.

If there is no scientific support for these childhood roles, or for the set of symptoms ascribed to adult children, why have they not faded from discussion? Note how the ascribed characteristics are dependent on a lot of "coulds," "mights," and "tends to." In effect, a logical sequence is postulated that "could" be true. But there is more to it. An article titled "Psychological Characteristics of Children of Alcoholics," authored by Ken Sher, in a 1997 issue of NIAAA's *Alcohol Health and Research World,* addressed this question. Sher reported that it was long recognized that people are likely to accept a personality description as valid merely because it is "so vague, double-headed, socially desirable, or widely occurring in the general population that it is difficult to refute." These types of descriptions are termed "Barnum" statements in honor of noted showman P. T. Barnum, whose recipe for a successful circus was "making sure there's a little something for everyone."

Sher points out how many of the descriptors of children of alcoholics have all of the features of classic Barnum statements—for example:

Barnum Characteristic	Statement
Vague	Children of alcoholics have difficulty in determining what normal is.
Double-header	Children of alcoholics are either super-responsible or super-irresponsible.
Socially desirable traits	Children of alcoholics are sensitive to others' needs.
Common in general population	Children of alcoholics are uncomfortable when they are the center of attention.

Indeed, two researchers tested the idea that many of the traits attributed to children of alcoholics are such Barnum statements. They administered a supposed personality inventory that people were told would generate a "profile" for them, based on their individual responses. The profile actually presented, which was identical for all individuals, consisted of generalizations drawn from the literature on adult children of alcoholics. How did people respond to "their" profiles? All of the subjects rated the adult child of alcoholics profile as highly descriptive of themselves! This was equally true of those from non-alcohol-troubled or nonproblem families as it was of children with an alcohol-dependent parent. In addition, people saw these descriptions as particular to themselves and more accurate for them than for people in general.

Someone has used another analogy for this phenomenon, making a comparison to astrology horoscopes. Most of the statements that are given are the kind of things that a large number of people can identify with. After all, if they applied only to a handful of people, who would read them? So you read "You often are not as tidy as you would like to be" or "You like to have your accomplishments recognized but hate to be the center of attention." These statements work because they sound familiar to all of us.

A Clinical Dilemma

In sum, it cannot be assumed that all children who grew up or are now growing up in an alcohol-troubled home share a single set of personality characteristics. Nor can it be assumed that all problems encountered in adult life can be attributed to being a child of a problem drinker. Nonetheless, the adult-children-of-alcoholics framework may well be useful to those suffering from problems, of whatever origins, who need to find some way out of an impasse and to make needed changes. The popular acceptance of an idea that is without scientific support represents a dilemma for clinicians. "Adult children," "enabling," and "co-dependency" have clearly hit a responsive chord in the general population. Are these Barnum constructs? For those in the substance abuse field, the terms may serve to remind us of the pain that families experience in response to problems in their midst, the sense of impotence these can evoke, and their felt need for assistance in making changes. However, when such terms crop up in discussions with clients, it is important to draw on their utility as a *metaphor,* without implying or acting as if these are proven scientific concepts. No one would dispute the effects of alcohol dependence on family members or the fact that these family members are statistically more likely to encounter many problems and in greater numbers than their counterparts in the general population. However, to award labels indiscriminately and to imply that dysfunction is inevitable is a great disservice. There is a danger as well that the strengths of families and family members are overlooked when one assumes pathology.

Current Themes

With the attention directed to describing common roles for children in the alcohol-troubled family, or the expectation that problems persist into adulthood, something important was overlooked: that is, that children are not inevitably destined to problems in later life.

Resiliency

Resiliency refers to the capacity to cope with difficult situations. An important piece of research conducted by Emmy Werner examined whether children of alcohol-troubled families are inevitably destined to

problems in later life, though it did not get the attention it deserved. It compared the offspring of alcohol-dependent persons who had and those who had not developed serious coping problems by age 18. The study examined the characteristics of the children and the caregiving environment in which they were raised. Those studied were members of a multiracial cohort of approximately 700 children born in 1955 on the Hawaiian island of Kauai. Follow-up studies were conducted at ages 1, 2, 10, and 18. Of this entire group, approximately 14% had either a mother or father who was alcohol-dependent.

Children of alcoholics who had not developed serious coping problems by age 18 were distinguished from those who had, in terms of their personal characteristics and their early environment. Those without serious problems had a belief in taking care of themselves, an orientation toward achievement, a positive self-concept, and an internal locus of control (meaning that their behavior was prompted more by their own feelings and beliefs than as a response to others). In terms of the environment, in the first two years of life they received a high level of attention from the primary caregiver and experienced fewer stressful events that disrupted the family unit. Werner found it was not the presence or absence of parental alcohol dependence per se that predicted difficulties for children but, rather, the interaction of the child and the environment. Werner also identified some differences depending on the sex of the alcohol-dependent parent and the child. Sons had higher rates of psychosocial problems in childhood and adolescence than did daughters. Also, the children of alcohol-dependent mothers had higher rates of problems in childhood and adolescence than did offspring of alcohol-dependent fathers.

Risk and Protective Factors

After subsequent studies, the view now is to think in terms of risk and protective factors. *Risk factors* are those things that are associated with the emergence of an alcohol or other substance use problem. *Protective factors* are those things that seem to shield or reduce the chance of a problem. These factors can reside in the individual or the environment. In addition, it is necessary to consider *mediating variables.* These are the circumstances or conditions that influence the impact a risk or protective factor may have. By analogy, an MP3 player may be turned on, but the mediating variable is the volume control; its setting determines what comes through. For example, stress may be a risk factor for alcohol problems; however, also important are the individual's coping skills. With good coping skills and the person's belief that he or she can do something to alter the situation, heavy drinking is less likely.

Extended family members are often an underappreciated source of support for children. A study conducted in Scotland focused upon their role in protecting children from the negative effects of drug use. The extended family often provides both psychological support and practical assistance. This ranges from providing meals, to faithfully attending school functions, to providing child care, to taking the children into their homes. These relationships, while providing a buffer for children, may also widen the net of those caught up in living around and with drug dependence. Extended family may at times feel overwhelmed by the responsibility and obligations to the child. They may feel besieged by feelings of anxiety, worry, anger, and disappointment over the parent's drug problem and its impact. There is the potential that the arrangements may break down and leave the already vulnerable children exposed to further ruptured relationships and instability.

Genetic Vulnerability

The single most important way in which the child of an alcohol-dependent parent is vulnerable to problems is in terms of genetic endowment. These children are at four times greater risk for development of dependence than are those without an alcohol-dependent parent. Research has suggested that gender also can be a significant factor influencing later life problems. Sons of an alcohol-dependent parent are more likely to suffer from attention-deficit/hyperactivity disorder than are children of parents without alcohol dependence. Daughters are more likely than their brothers to encounter eating disorders or depression in later life.

Not only are children of a parent with alcohol dependence themselves at greater risk of alcohol dependence, but the unfolding of an alcohol use disorder is likely to be *telescoped*. That means moving from the point of first using alcohol to the point when signs of an alcohol problem appear takes less time than for those who have an alcohol-dependent parent. Twenty-five percent of those with an alcohol-dependent parent experienced the onset of a disorder within four years of beginning to drink; in the absence of a parental problem, it was seven years before 25% of the group showed signs of an alcohol use problem. In trying to figure out what might explain this, researchers considered a number of factors. One was whether there is a co-occurring psychiatric disorder, either depression or antisocial personality disorder. Indeed, this is associated with a more rapid appearance of an alcohol disorder. However, whether the parent is or is not actively drinking had no effect. It was found, too, that telescoping was present in respect to drug use disorders, measuring from first use of alcohol to the appearance of drug dependence. All of this suggests that genetic factors play a significant role in compressing the period between first alcohol use and the appearance of symptoms.

With one exception, compared to alcohol dependence, far less is known about genetic vulnerability in respect to other drug problems. The exception is nicotine. There is a clear genetic component for the development of nicotine dependence. In addition, a separate genetic component seems to influence the severity of withdrawal symptoms. This in turn affects the relative difficulty in smoking cessation.

The Role of Stress

The research on families touched by alcohol and other substance abuse is growing. It has become clear that families are not affected by alcohol dependence in the same way. The other insight is that the alcohol-troubled family is not unique. At the core, the problem is not the drinking, per se; it's living with chronic stress that exacts the toll. Thus, focusing on the alcohol-troubled family has had the effect of bringing to the fore the variety of stressors that can take a toll on family members. It doesn't matter whether it is the result of alcohol or other substance use, serious mental illness, domestic violence, or family disruptions due to job loss—or for military families, another deployment to a combat area.

Research has demonstrated that significant stress in childhood can have long-term effects, including premature mortality. Researchers examined multiple sources of stress experienced by children, including verbal, physical, or sexual abuse; mental illness, incarceration, or substance abuse in a household member; as well as a battered mother or parental separation and divorces. No single childhood source of stress was associated with higher death rates. However, the presence of six or more adverse events in childhood was. On average, those with a high number of adverse situations in childhood died a decade earlier than their age mates.

Among the issues now being studied are the factors that are associated with differing levels of family dysfunction. Researchers recognize that some families *are* able to function successfully, despite the presence of an alcohol problem. An exploratory study looked at families from both the United States and Canada, in which at least one parent had problems with alcohol. What was not associated with resilience is as interesting as the things that are. For example, neither socioeconomic status, nor the use of professional help, nor the perceived levels of neighbors' helpfulness were associated with resilience. It was the nature of family interactions, including the level of family cohesion, flexibility in filling family roles, the quality of communication, and family beliefs that were predictive. These were associated with the quality of parenting that was used as a key measure of a family's functioning.

Nonetheless, it would be an error to assume, based on these findings, that seeking professional advice is unhelpful. It is quite likely that resilient families felt no need for professional help. Evidence from other studies indicates that treatment of parents does have a positive impact on children in the family. Using standard measures of children's functioning, children whose parents had parenting training as part of behavioral couples therapy had fewer problems than the children whose parents had only couples therapy, or children whose parents received only individual counseling.

There is attention, too, to factors that reduce the likelihood of substance use problems among children. Frequently cited protective factors include social support, maintenance of family rituals, connections with

parents are role models, so are older children in the family. When it comes to nicotine, the smoking or nonsmoking of older siblings has as great an impact as does the smoking status of parents. The protective value of nonsmoking parents can be offset by an older sister or brother who smokes. Parents have a greater influence during early adolescence; in later adolescence siblings have the greater influence for other children in the family.

Casualties of the War on Drugs

No country in the world has a higher proportion of its citizens behind bars than does the United States. In the United States 1 out of every 100 people is incarcerated. At the state and local levels over half of those incarcerated have an alcohol disorder. Involvement with the criminal justice system is more likely with drug use than with alcohol. As noted in Chapter 2, the prison population is burgeoning in response to the war on drugs. People of color and the poor are disproportionately incarcerated. In a substantial number of cases, this is for simple possession or low-level involvement in the drug trade. An article titled "Counting the Drug War's Female Casualties" begins with a haunting illustration. It cites the case of a woman who, though having had only a minor involvement in her boyfriend's drug transactions, was sentenced to 34 years in federal prison.

A judge may have virtually no discretion in sentencing, under many state drug laws. This goes back to the Rockefeller Laws passed in New York in 1973. The laws enacted set the penalty for *selling* two or more ounces of heroin, morphine, cocaine, or cannabis *or possessing* four or more ounces of the same substances, to a minimum sentence of 15 years to life in prison, and a maximum sentence of 25 years to life in prison. The marijuana part was repealed five years later. It wasn't until 2009 that these laws were revised to remove the mandatory minimum sentences. This allowed judges to sentence individuals to treatment or set shorter sentences.

Commonly the family as a whole is affected. The impact on family was poignantly brought to my attention in a casual conversation with a friend on the use of computers in the schools. The friend teaches in a midwestern inner-city middle school. In that school, which website is most frequently accessed? It is the state's criminal justice system's site! With a parent who is incarcerated, that is where children turn for basic information about addresses or information on visiting days and visiting hours.

The removal of a parent from the home has deep cross-generational impacts for the family. A drug arrest can make the family ineligible for student financial aid, can lead to evictions and thereby increase the odds for homelessness, and can exclude the family from public housing for life, all due to the conduct of a single family member. When drug use places someone in the criminal justice system, it is not uncommon that women and children are pressed more deeply into poverty, in turn creating greater public health problems, more desperation, and arguably more

Nelson Rockefeller, RIP

Nelson was characteristically tough and imperial in the way he tackled the problem of drug abuse. His approach was draconian: long jail sentences for heroin pushers and addicts. The Rockefeller program, which of course proved finally to be a fiasco, was the epitome of the belief in treating a social or medical problem with jail and the billy club.

– An unsigned obituary for Nelson Rockefeller published in *Inquiry Magazine,* March 5, 1979 crime. Although more prisons and jails are providing treatment programs for inmates with alcohol and drug problems, these remain far too few and too often are provided too late in the criminal justice process.

Families in Their Communities

In considering the impact of substance use on the family, we need to appreciate that families too are touched by their environments. Families live in communities, in neighborhoods. The nature of that community makes a difference. With alcohol, the concentration of outlets for sales makes a difference in the levels of drinking and crime. The poorest communities have the highest concentration of alcohol sales outlets. Communities also vary on the levels of public drug use, access to drugs, acceptance of drug use, and presence of drug-related crime. An economically depressed community may present special risk factors, but economically advantaged communities are hardly immune; neither are rural communities. In all communities, there are programs that enhance protective factors and assist family members, be they recreational programs, church and religious groups, or youth and neighborhood organizations.

Secondhand Drug Use

Even the Family Dog Isn't Spared: Marijuana Toxicosis in Dogs

Marijuana (Cannabis sativa) *is a commonly used recreational drug among humans; animals may be exposed following ingestion or accidental inhalation of smoke. From January 1998 to January 2002, 213 incidences were recorded of dogs that developed clinical signs following oral exposure to marijuana, with 99% having neurologic signs, and 30% exhibiting gastrointestinal signs. The marijuana ingested ranged from 1/2 to 90 g. The lowest dose at which signs occurred was 84.7 mg/kg and the highest reported dose was 26.8 g/kg. Onset of signs ranged from 5 min to 96 h with most signs occurring within 1 to 3 h after ingestion. The signs lasted from 30 min to 96 h. All animals made full recoveries.*

Janczyk, P, Donaldson CW, et al. Two hundred and thirteen cases of marijuana toxicoses in dogs. *Veterinary and Human Toxicology*, 2004

As noted previously, the problems resulting from alcohol are due to the behavior of the family member with alcohol abuse or dependence. However, when it comes to drugs that are ingested by smoking, particularly cocaine and nicotine, or are cooked up in the family kitchen, such as methamphetamine, the drug itself is a problem. When a smoker smokes, everyone in the area smokes as well. This is referred to as *passive smoking, environmental smoking,* or *secondhand smoke,* terms that are essentially synonymous.

Methamphetamine is a different case. Commonly it is manufactured in people's homes. In this instance, the problem is not just the fumes at the time of manufacture. Equally significant is the residue that coats walls, ceilings, and every nook and cranny. There are stories of people buying a home that, totally unknown to them, had been a meth kitchen. Soon the new family will find itself with a variety of problems, including nausea, dizziness, eye and skin irritation, and headaches. In addition, a family may find itself faced with a bill as high as $50,000 to have the home decontaminated.

Of the many drugs of abuse, whether licit or illicit, nicotine has the greatest impact on other family members. At the least, smoking has an impact on the family's economic situation. For the person with a one-pack-a-day habit at $8.77 per pack—the going price in a Vermont small-town general store—that represents more than $3,100 a year literally going up in smoke.

Exposure to nicotine can occur before birth. When smoking, the pregnant woman is sharing the nicotine with the developing fetus.

Equally important, nicotine is transferred to the fetus by a nonsmoking woman's exposure to secondhand smoke. The pregnant woman is simply the vehicle for delivering others' nicotine to the unborn child. There is a four times greater risk for overall smaller size at birth among in-utero nicotine-exposed infants. The level of prenatal nicotine exposure is proportional to the level of smoking by the mother plus her exposure to environmental smoke. Smoking during pregnancy is also associated with higher levels of lead in the blood of newborns, with a 15% increase for each 10 cigarettes smoked. A careful research study suggests that a quarter of behavior problems seen at age five, especially aggression, can be attributed to prenatal nicotine exposure during early pregnancy. The hypothesis is that exposure to nicotine alters fetal brain development. Preliminary work suggests that paternal smoking even *prior* to conception may have negative consequences. One study indicates that the equivalent of five pack-years[2] of smoking prior to pregnancy is linked to a higher rate of childhood cancer.

Children exposed to secondhand smoke have an increased incidence of sudden infant death syndrome; higher rates of asthma, and more asthma attacks requiring medical intervention or hospitalization; and higher rates of coughs, pneumonia, bronchitis, middle ear infections, and tonsillectomies. Children with diabetes also have more complications if exposed to secondhand smoke. And each year children die in home fires caused by careless smoking. Parents significantly under-report exposure to secondhand smoke, and the only reliable measure is through laboratory tests of the child.

Media campaigns, in concert with schools and pediatricians and family physicians, are aimed at smoking cessation among parents. If smoking cessation doesn't succeed, the goal is to at least have the home and car be smoke-free zones. The success of such initiatives to restrict smoking varies, depending on how many other adults in the household or coworkers smoke, whether there are children in the home, the level of the smoker's dependence, plus the level of recognition by the smoker of the dangers of secondhand smoke. Although useful and to be encouraged, these bans are not 100% effective.

The impact of secondhand smoke continues throughout life. While acute respiratory problems are seen in children, chronic respiratory problems are more common among adults. For example, while smokers are at the greatest risk for lung cancer, nonsmokers too are at risk. One study of women with lung cancer found that among those who had never smoked, there was nonetheless an average of 27 years of exposure from a smoking spouse, an average of 19 years of exposure from parents, and 15 years of exposure from coworkers.

---

[2] Pack-years is used as a measure of exposure to nicotine. One pack-year is equivalent to smoking a pack per day for a year. A half pack per day for two years equals one pack-year.

The clear evidence that secondhand smoke has a major negative impact on others' health was a major factor in bans on smoking in the workplace. For nonsmoking adults, historically the workplace presented twice the risk of nicotine exposure that the home did. One of the first occupational groups to lobby for a ban on smoking in the workplace was airline flight attendants. Another group of employees at high risk were those who work in what one researcher calls the five Bs—bars, bowling alleys, billiard halls, betting establishments, and bingo parlors. These settings were found to have nicotine levels from 2.5 to 18.5 times higher than offices or homes.

The public health impact of environmental smoke has prompted changes in perceptions and public policy. The law has been used in a variety of ways to reduce harms associated with tobacco, These include mandating warning labels on nicotine products, plus smoking bans in the workplace and more recently in public places. The newest target for initiating smoking bans is multi-family dwellings, be it subsidized public housing or posh condos. Recently several colleges have initiated public smoking bans on campus. Family courts also incorporate research findings on environmental smoking. As one jurist noted, "A family court that does not issue court orders restraining persons from smoking in the presence of children under the court's care fails those children whom the law has entrusted to its care." He continued that it is both appropriate and necessary to consider exposure to smoking as a factor in awarding child custody or determining visitation.

REFERENCES AND FURTHER READINGS

Agrawal A, Lynskey MT. Are there genetic influences on addiction? Evidence from family, adoption and twin studies (review). *Addiction* 103(7):1069–1081, 2008. (122 refs.)

Alcohol Health and Research World. Special issue on children of alcoholics 21(3):entire issue, 1997.

Avenevoli S, Merikangas KR. Familial influences on adolescent smoking (review). *Addiction* 98 (Supplement):1–20, 2003. (152 refs.)

Barnard M. Between a rock and a hard place: The role of relatives in protecting children from the effects of parental drug problems. *Child & Family Social Work* 8(4):291–299, 2003.

Barrett AE, Turner J. Family structure and substance use problems in adolescence and early adulthood: Examining explanations for the relationship. *Addiction* 101(1):109–120, 2006. (63 refs.)

Beidler RJ. Adult children of alcoholics: Is it really a separate field of study? *Drugs and Society* 3(3/4):133–141, 1989.

Berends L, Ferris J, Laslett AM. A problematic drinker in the family: Variations in the level of negative impact experienced by sex, relationship and living status. *Addiction Research & Theory* 20(4):300–306, 2012. (25 refs.)

Dishion TJ, Nelson SE, Bullock BM. Premature adolescent autonomy: Parent disengagement and deviant peer process in the amplification of problem behaviour. *Journal of Adolescence* 27(5):515–530, 2004. (39 refs.)

Eiden RD, Leonard KE, Hoyle RH, Chavez F. A transactional model of parent-infant interactions in alcoholic families. *Psychology of Addictive Behaviors* 18(4):350–361, 2004. (66 refs.)

Fuller JA, Warner RM. Family stressors as predictors of codependency. *Genetic, Social, and General Psychology Monographs* 126(1):5–22, 2000. (41 refs.)

George WH, La Marr J, Barrett K, McKinnon T. Alcoholic parentage, self-labeling, and endorsement of ACOA-codependent traits. *Psychology of Addictive Behaviors* 13(1):39–48, 1999. (50 refs.)

Gordon JR, Barrett K. The codependency movement: Issues of context and differentiation. In: Baer JS, Marlatt GA, McMahon RJ, eds. *Addictive Behaviors Across the Life Span: Prevention, Treatment, and Policy Issues.* Newbury Park, CA: Sage Publications, 1993. pp. 307–339. (85 refs.)

Harrington CM, Metzler AE. Are adult children of dysfunctional families with alcoholism different from adult children of dysfunctional families without alcoholism? A look at committed, intimate relationships. *Journal of Counseling Psychology* 44(1):102–107, 1997.

Haugland BSM. Recurrent disruptions of rituals and routines in families with paternal alcohol abuse. *Family Relations* 54(2):225–241, 2005. (47 refs.)

Hudson CR, Kirby KC, Firely ML, Festinger DS, Marlowe DB. Social adjustment of family members and significant others (FSOs) of drug users. *Journal of Substance Abuse Treatment* 23(3):171–181, 2003. (48 refs.)

Hunt ME. A comparison of family of origin factors between children of alcoholics and children of non-alcoholics in a longitudinal panel. *American Journal of Drug and Alcohol Abuse* 23(4):597–613, 1997. (43 refs.)

Hussong AM, Bauer D, Chassin L. Telescoped trajectories from alcohol initiation to disorder in children of alcoholic parents. *Journal of Abnormal Psychology* 117(1):63–78, 2008. (58 refs.)

Jackson JK. The adjustment of the family to the crisis of alcoholism. *Quarterly Journal of Studies on Alcohol* 15(4):562–586, 1954.

Johnson V. *I'll Quit Tomorrow*, rev. ed. New York: Harper & Row, 1980.

Kreek MJ, Nielsen DA, LaForge KS. Genes associated with addiction: Alcoholism, opiate, and cocaine addiction (review). *Neuromolecular Medicine* 5(1):85–108, 2004. (172 refs.)

Lam WK, Fals-Stewart W, Kelley ML. Effects of parent skills training with behavioral couples therapy for alcoholism on children: A randomized clinical pilot trial. *Addictive Behaviors* 33(8):1076–1080, 2008. (18 refs.)

Melchert TP. Clarifying the effects of parental substance abuse, child sexual abuse, and parental caregiving on adult adjustment. *Professional Psychology: Research and Practice* 31(1):64–69, 2000. (39 refs.)

Menees MM, Segrin C. The specificity of disrupted processes in families of adult children of alcoholics. *Alcohol and Alcoholism* 35(4):361–367, 2000. (46 refs.)

Moe J, Johnson JL, Wade W. Resilience in children of substance users: In their own words. *Substance Use & Misuse* 42(2/3):381–398, 2007. (81 refs.)

Room R, Matzger H, Weisner C. Sources of informal pressure on problematic drinkers to cut down or seek treatment. *Journal of Substance Use* 9(6):280–295, 2004. (43 refs.)

Saatcioglu O, Erim R, Cakmak D. Role of family in alcohol and substance abuse (review). *Psychiatry and Clinical Neurosciences* 60(2):125–132, 2006. (48 refs.)

Scherrer JF, Xian H, Pan H, Pergadia M, Madden PA, Grant JD, et al. Parent, sibling and peer influences on smoking initiation, regular smoking and nicotine dependence. Results from a genetically informative design. *Addictive Behaviors* 37(3): 240–247, 2012. (42 refs.)

Sher KJ. Psychological characteristics of children of alcoholics. *Alcohol Health and Research World* 21(3):247–254, 1997. (48 refs.).

Substance Abuse and Mental Health Administration. *Data Spotlight. More than 7 Million Children Live with a Parent with Alcohol Problems*. Bethesda MD: SAMHSA, February 16, 2012. (3 refs.)

Templeton L,Velleman R, Russell C. Psychological interventions with families of alcohol misusers: A systematic review (review). *Addiction Research & Theory* 18(6):616–648, 2010. (140 refs.)

Vink JM, Willemsen G, Engels RCME, Boomsma DI. Smoking status of parents, siblings and friends: Predictors of regular smoking? Findings from a longitudinal twin-family study. *Twin Research* 6(3):209–217, 2003. (38 refs.)

Walker JP, Lee RE. Uncovering strengths of children of alcoholic parents (review). *Contemporary Family Therapy* 20(4):521–538, 1998.

Wells K. Substance abuse and child maltreatment. *Pediatric Clinics of North America* 56(2):345+, 2009. (70 refs.)

Werner EE. Resilient offspring of alcoholics: A longitudinal study from birth to age 18. *Journal of Studies on Alcohol* 47(1):34–40, 1986.

Woititz J. *Adult Children of Alcoholics*. Hollywood, FL: Health Communications, 1983.

Xian H, Scherrer JF, Madden PAF, Lyons MJ, Tsuang M, True WR, et al. The heritability of failed smoking cessation and nicotine withdrawal in twins who smoked and attempted to quit. *Nicotine & Tobacco Research* 5(2):245–254, 2003. (49 refs.)

Evaluation and Treatment Overview

When some people become aware of alcohol or other drug problems, they may ask, "What treatment is available?" Or the question might be more personal, "How can I help?" Before it's possible to answer these questions, it's necessary to consider how people recover and what treatment or intervention is about.

At this juncture in earlier editions of this book, the focus was almost exclusively on alcohol dependence. After making a principled plea for early intervention, backing that up with the reminder that this approach is indicated for any chronic disease process, then acknowledging that early intervention represented an ideal, which was infrequently reflected in actual practice, the book launched into the treatment of alcohol dependence. There was virtually no mention of evaluation, diagnostic assessment, or treatment approaches to problems associated with alcohol use. Indeed, 20 years ago many substance abuse clinicians had very little need for or opportunity to use those skills. The diagnosis of dependence, for all practical purposes, had occurred before a client even arrived in the clinician's office. Very few individuals came into contact with a substance abuse treatment facility by mistake. Back then, the chief practical use for informing substance abuse professionals of diagnostic criteria was to enable them to educate other human service professionals, thereby facilitating identification and referrals of those whose problems were going undetected. This information was also helpful in providing client education. Similarly, the major role of the substance use history was in developing treatment plans, rather than in being a prerequisite for diagnosis.

In days past, those who later would be awarded a diagnosis of alcohol abuse, were then treated as if they were in the early stages of dependence. Their life situations often were reminiscent of the typical alcohol-dependent client's circumstances 10 to 20 years before treatment. Remember, an average of 7 years elapses between the time the disease is clearly present to the point where the individual enters treatment. That fact was used to "sell" the diagnosis and attempt to have the client accept it, hopefully with gratitude! Treatment professionals obviously recognized that these individuals were different from the usual alcohol-dependent client. They recognized that providing full-blown treatment for dependence might be a bit excessive. However, it was viewed as the prudent, cautious approach. Initiating treatment seemed preferable to the alternative, which would be allowing the condition to go unaddressed—and presumably progress. The two choices were then perceived as either loss of drinking "privileges" or potential loss of life. Equally important was the fact that, back then, the clinician could offer the problem drinker no other treatment options.

Treating all alcohol problems as emerging dependence and therefore offering the usual treatment for dependence to all caused clients to balk or bolt. It also set up barriers in dealing with other professionals. Such an approach can convey the impression of substance abuse clinicians functioning not as therapists, but as technicians, always ready to apply their treatment formula indiscriminately.

The situation today is dramatically different. Clinicians now see far more diverse groups of clients, than was true earlier. A referral may have followed on the heels of a drinking incident. There are those who need an evaluation for restoration of a driver's license. There are those referred by an employer. There will be self-referrals of those who are concerned about a family member, or their own alcohol use. Similarly, treatment personnel are called on more and more by other helping professionals—school counselors, social workers, physicians, and clergy—to provide consultation.

With clients now reflecting the spectrum of substance use problems, there is increasing demand on therapists to provide a thoughtful assessment and to match clients to appropriate treatment. Assessment, evaluation, and diagnostic skills have become more central in this era of managed care. It has been a long time since insurance companies, state regulatory agencies, HMOs, or—for that matter—clients, their families, or employers unquestioningly accepted 28 days of residential treatment, once the accepted standard of care.

As mentioned earlier, the fifth edition of the APA's *Diagnostic and Statistical Manual* sets forth a new way of thinking about alcohol use disorders (see pages 101–104). They are seen as occurring along a continuum from mild to severe. This does not mean a return to considering every alcohol problem as "early dependence" and warranting identical treatment.

What defines effective treatment will be tied to the degree of severity. This suggests that the road someone is traveling on is as important as his or her location at a particular moment. By analogy, imagine yourself on I-89, one of Vermont's two interstates, which goes east-west. You get on the highway within sight of the Connecticut River, which

As muse or creative companion, alcohol can be devastating. In memoriam to some of those who did battle with this two-faced spirit:

John Barrymore
Truman Capote
Tennessee Williams
John Berryman
John Cheever
U. S. Grant
Amy Winehouse
Willem de Kooning
O. Henry (William Sydney Porter)
Eugene O'Neill
F. Scott Fitzgerald
Jack London
Ernest Hemingway
Dylan Thomas
Isadora Duncan
Sinclair Lewis
Billie Holiday
Judy Garland
Robert Benchley
Jack Kerouac
Edgar Allen Poe
Jackson Pollock
W. C. Fields
Cory Monteith
Henri de Toulouse-Lautrec
Janis Joplin
Joseph McCarthy
Baudelaire
Robert Lowell
Jimi Hendrix
Michael Jackson
Jim Morrison
Charles Coltrane
Alexander the Great
Ray Charles
Whitney Houston

constitutes the border between Vermont and New Hampshire. You head west for a scenic drive. There are 12 exits before you get to the City of Burlington on the other side of the state. Obviously, getting on the interstate doesn't mean you are destined to land in Burlington. However, if you do nothing, that is exactly where you end up. If you aren't paying attention, maybe you miss the exit you thought you'd take. But you tell yourself, "ah, there's plenty of time." Or maybe, so taken by the scenery, you decide to go a little bit farther and get off later. The longer you drive, the fewer exits there are left to take. Before you know it, the terrain is no longer farms and forests: there are signs of more people, more homes, some shopping malls; if not Burlington, it is just down the road.

A PERSPECTIVE ON TREATMENT

It may have been far simpler when the major and exclusive concern for the clinician was alcohol dependence. Knowing how to treat the person sitting in the office was rarely a difficulty. The real challenge and major frustration was in getting those who needed care across the threshold. As the clinical concerns broaden to encompass a range of substance use problems, life becomes more complicated for the clinician. The information in this chapter is intended to provide a framework and offer orientation. Specific treatment approaches are described in Chapter 10.

If treatment programs are oriented primarily toward treating dependence, ironically that orientation serves as a set of blinders preventing recognition of other kinds of substance use problems. This is reminiscent of the old adage, "If the only tool you have is a hammer, every problem tends to look like a nail." In thinking about alcohol dependence, we have tended to think of a progression, moving from alcohol use, to alcohol problems, to alcohol abuse, to alcohol dependence. In such a framework, severity depends on where the client falls on the continuum. This thinking contains some pitfalls. The necessity for action or intervention is often tied to the perception of severity. Thus, the person with the alcohol problem may be seen as being in less danger. This is not necessarily the case. Serious consequences can arise along the spectrum of alcohol problems. They are not reserved only for those with dependence.

PROBLEMS OF USE

Alcohol problems are not restricted to those who meet the diagnostic criteria for a formal alcohol use disorder. Nor are they restricted to alcohol use at intoxicating levels. For example, the danger of alcohol use by the individual who is depressed is not dependence—it is suicidal thoughts being "loosened" by the person's impaired state and diminished capacity. Therefore, those who are in treatment for depression should be counseled to abstain from alcohol.

Adolescents provide some of the most dramatic examples of the dangers of alcohol use. For teenagers, the primary danger of alcohol use isn't dependence, although it certainly does occur. The leading causes of death in this age group are accidents, suicide, and homicide, all of which are clearly linked to alcohol use. Sadly, the problem among adolescents is that they may not live long enough to develop a serious alcohol use disorder. Beyond the common list of problems, whether school performance, unwanted pregnancy, or legal problems, alcohol use may also have more subtle dangers for adolescents, such as impeding emotional and social maturation.

Any drinker is at some risk for alcohol problems. Alcohol is a potent pharmacological agent. Negative consequences can follow on the heels of a single drinking episode. These would represent problems of acute use. Negative consequences can arise from a pattern of heavy use. This represents a chronic problem. Evaluation and assessment needs to consider both possibilities.

What is a "safe" dose of alcohol or a low-risk pattern of alcohol use? This varies from individual to individual. What is judicious use varies for a single individual throughout the life span. For the pregnant woman, no alcohol is the safest alternative. Alcohol use is a health issue in the broadest sense. Treatment professionals are unlikely to see an individual until a problem becomes evident. Therefore, much of the burden of prevention and identification of individuals at risk falls to those outside the substance abuse sphere.

Chronic Disease Framework

The model for managing chronic disease is useful. When clinicians consider the spectrum of substance use problems, this model offers an approach that ensures that acute problems are effectively addressed. At the same time, it ensures that a serious alcohol problem will not develop unnoticed. All acute problems are seen as requiring attention in their own right, as well as being a potential warning of a possible long-term problem. The following example may help demonstrate this approach.

Of all the gin joints in all the towns in all the world, she walks into mine.

Rick, while drowning his sorrows
Casablanca

In the general medical management of any chronic disease, among the most significant actions are those taken before the clear onset of the full-blown disease process. Consider heart disease. A young man comes to his physician's office. He is overweight, both smokes and drinks, consumes a cholesterol-laden diet, never exercises, and has a family history of males who die before the age of 50 of coronary disease. From his physician's perspective, he is a walking time bomb. To feel comfortable intervening, the physician does not have to be convinced that this individual will be true to his genes. It is sufficient to know that statistically this individual is at risk.

Even if this patient is wholly asymptomatic, the physician will feel perfectly comfortable urging rather drastic changes to reduce risk. These changes for our hypothetical young man are equivalent to the changes associated with abstinence. If the physician were really on top of the situation, she would refer this client to a nutritionist, banish the salt shaker, tell him to cut down on the fats, load him down with pamphlets, and discuss options for exercise, whether joining a gym, finding a walking buddy, or lifting weights. Through continuing contacts, the physician will monitor compliance and provide encouragement and support. This model is the optimal approach to the management of alcohol problems. In this framework, with respect to alcohol problems, the most relevant question is no longer "Is this person alcohol dependent?" The central question instead becomes "If this person continues with the current alcohol use pattern, is he or she at risk for becoming alcohol dependent or developing other alcohol-related problems?"

Using the framework of chronic disease, many of the questions that once plagued caregivers are circumvented. In this discussion, the assumption is that alcohol dependence is a condition like heart disease. As a chronic condition it has well-demonstrated warning signs. It develops slowly, over time. For this reason, it would probably be impossible to pinpoint an exact time when someone "turns" alcohol dependent. No one wakes up in the morning having come down with a case of alcohol dependence overnight. Remember, the time when it is most critical to act is before an emerging problem is firmly established, when the individual is in that "gray" area. Thus it is useful to think in terms of whether someone is at risk for developing a significant problem. If so, then intervention is appropriate.

Such an approach makes it clear that any alcohol problem is sufficiently serious to warrant continuing attention. An alcohol problem shouldn't be assumed to be "fixed" by a single encounter with a clinician or participation in an alcohol education class. An ongoing relationship is appropriately established to monitor the client's status. Over time, the clinician needs the opportunity to assess efforts to moderate risks and alter dangerous drinking patterns. If these efforts prove to be unsuccessful, then further intervention is required. In many instances the clinician quite likely will not be a substance abuse professional, but a family doctor, or mental health worker.

Consider the changes that have occurred over the past 30 years regarding tobacco use. Questions about smoking are now a standard part of any medical history. Probably very few smokers are unaware that smoking may cause or aggravate medical problems. A smoker who sees a physician expects to be asked questions about smoking and awaits the associated comments that smoking is ill-advised. Beyond that there is the increasing likelihood that a referral will be made to a smoking cessation program. In addition, the attitudes of the general public have changed. People no longer silently put up with secondhand smoke. Concerned family members and friends of smokers express their concerns directly to the smoker. The regulation of smoking in public places is the norm. Restaurants, at the least, must provide non-smoking accommodations, but more and more are smoke-free. Beyond protecting non-smokers, these regulations certainly cramp a smoker's style and prompt him or her to consider the inconvenience as well as the problems that result from smoking. We may well be on the brink of a similar revolution with alcohol use.

Today alcohol is more commonly viewed as a drug. Drunkenness is far less tolerated than it was in the past. Intoxication is becoming less socially acceptable in more and more circles and circumstances. The exception may be Facebook postings. The possibility that an intoxicated person puts others in jeopardy is an issue of public concern. Reinforcing this awareness is the general public's heightened interest in a variety of efforts to promote health—diet, exercise, and other self-care measures. This has provided a moderating influence on alcohol use. So along with less red meat, less fast foods, running, personal trainers, and sunscreen, there's more bottled water and less alcohol. Coupled with all these changes are improvements in the professional training of physicians, clergy, nurses, social workers, and teachers about alcohol and alcohol problems.

If it is a small sacrifice to discontinue the use of wine, do it for the sake of others: if it is a great sacrifice, do it for your own sake.
—S. J. May

At the same time, we still have a way to go. In the abstract, a person can be well informed about alcohol or other drug problems, but when they pop up in real life, it can be a different matter. All too often, along with the realization that there is a possible alcohol problem comes a lot of hand-wringing and waiting. The family, friends, physician, and clergy—all those involved—can be immobilized. They often wait until the possible problem has progressed to the point where it is unequivocally and unquestionably the real thing.

Clinical Implications

Within a chronic disease framework responsibility for care doesn't fall solely to the substance abuse treatment community. Indeed the important early interventions can *only* be conducted by others. Within the medical community primary care providers are in a unique position to identify problems and intervene. However, to do so requires a simple, easy to administer screening test *and* guidelines for appropriate interventions for different scores. A screening instrument called the **A**lcohol **U**se **D**isorders **I**dentification **T**est, usually referred to as the AUDIT, fills both needs. It was developed by a special committee convened by the World Health Organization (WHO). The alcohol treatment community realized that, for some patients, brief advice or brief counseling was quite effective in addressing emerging alcohol problems. In fact, such *brief interventions* could be as successful as formal treatment. Their being disseminated as part of the AUDIT defined them as "real treatment" and gave them greater visibility.

There isn't a single, standard format for brief interventions, sometimes referred to as brief treatment. Some may consist of a single, five-minute session of advice, while others may consist of a single, hour-long session. Brief interventions are used in a variety of settings, from a doctor's office to the emergency room; used with a variety of populations, from pregnant women to those in the military; as well as used with other drug problems, particularly tobacco. Successful interventions share common features. Unfortunately, as these interventions are implemented largely outside of the formal alcohol treatment system, alcohol program staff may not be very familiar with these approaches. Even if understandable, this lack of familiarity really isn't acceptable. It would be comparable to oncologists, those who treat cancer, being unfamiliar with prevention or screening—the essential steps for avoiding dramatic, invasive treatment later. Brief interventions are discussed in more detail later in the chapter.

SCREENING AND EVALUATION

Screening efforts for any health care problem can be undertaken at various levels. They can be applied routinely to everyone, or they can be targeted, administered only to those in higher-risk groups. Broad-based screening efforts, meaning routine use of a screening tool in a range of settings, is desirable when the condition is common. Otherwise, checking everyone makes no sense. But to justify doing so, it is also important that a condition be treatable. The common cold may warrant routine screening on the basis of its being commonplace. But inasmuch as very little can be done to alter its course, and serious long-term consequences are rare, screening would be a waste of time. It is also necessary that screening efforts be practical—that the available tools be both inexpensive and easily administered. Finally, the instrument used has to be "well tuned." It needs to cast a sufficiently broad net so as not to miss many people, but at the same time it needs not to falsely include too many people who don't have the condition. Using these criteria, screening for alcohol problems is clearly warranted. The condition is common and treatable. A failure to treat carries serious consequences, and screening can be done easily and inexpensively in any setting.

Laboratory Tests

Presently there is no laboratory test that is recommended for screening. All of the screening tests described in the following section are based on interviews. There has been considerable exploration of laboratory tests that might be able to identify heavy drinkers. Until the 1990s, the most sensitive laboratory test was the GGT (gamma-glutamyl transferase), and it missed up to two-thirds of excessive drinkers or those who were alcohol dependent. At best, laboratory measures then were only able to detect the presence of medical complications that resulted from heavy drinking.

Since the 1990s several other markers have been identified. CDT (carbohydrate-deficient transferrin) holds promise for clinical use. Transferrin, produced by the liver, is a protein that is responsible for transporting iron in the blood. It is very sensitive to the amount of alcohol consumed.

Having the equivalent of four beers a day causes increased levels of CDT, so it is sensitive to actual drinking rather than to liver disease that results from the drinking. However, some questions remain to be answered to fully understand the lab results. What is the effect of age? Are there male–female differences? What other medical conditions might be associated with increased levels of CDT? (Seemingly there are very, very few.) What is the best way to measure CDT, by the absolute amount or as a percentage of the total transferrin in the blood sample? Also, is the reliability for detecting heavy drinking improved if the CDT value is combined with the results of other common lab tests? Because it measures recent drinking levels, it has potential for use in aftercare and detection of relapse.

Two more recently identified markers are similarly sensitive to recent alcohol consumption. One is based on changes in a product of serotonin metabolism (5-*hydroxytriptamine*) which is produced in the presence of alcohol. The other is a product of alcohol metabolism, *ethyl glucuronide*. The amount produced in the process of alcohol metabolism is very, very modest. Its significance is that it remains in the body for up to 80 hours after drinking. That makes it a useful tool in special situations, such as screening prior to surgery or in court cases. Costing $60–$75, this test appears to be 100% specific and many times more sensitive than tests detecting alcohol in the urine.

I like whiskey. I always did, and that is why I never drink it.
—General Robert E. Lee

It is unlikely that any of these laboratory measures will replace interview formats for broad-based screening. No laboratory test can be as inexpensive as asking several questions.

Screening Instruments

A number of screening tests are effective in identifying those with a high likelihood of having an alcohol problem. As their name indicates, they are screening instruments, not diagnostic instruments. Screening instruments do not provide sufficient information to allow formulation of a firm diagnosis or creation of a treatment plan, although there are other standardized instruments to assist with that. Screening tests, if routinely administered, are able to help identify those for whom a closer examination is appropriate. In this instance the goal is to identify those whose alcohol or other drug use warrants closer scrutiny. These screening tests are basic tools for any human service worker's repertoire. Screening for alcohol problems, tobacco use, and other drug problems should be routine in any counseling or health care setting.

These tests may have less immediate utility in a setting that deals exclusively with alcohol and/or other drug problems. Something has already occurred to suggest a problem exists. Otherwise, the client would not be sitting in a clinician's office. However, familiarity with these tools is important on several counts. Referrals to alcohol treatment services may include a report with the results of screening tests. Also, training other professionals may well be a part of the substance abuse clinician's work. This is core information to be passed on to other helping professionals.

The major screening tests are described in the following sections. First, a word to those who are suspicious of screening instruments and their ability to detect a problem, especially given that prominent symptoms of what was termed alcohol dependence include minimizing, denial, repression, plus distortions of memory and perception. The process of developing such instruments is to compare the results obtained by the test with the results of an assessment by a trained substance abuse clinician. The purpose of a screening instrument is, after all, to approximate the judgment that would be made by professionals were they to undertake a systematic evaluation. Indeed, for the instruments described here, those who answer the indicated number of questions positively are those who the clinicians would agree had the syndrome (dependence or abuse) that the instruments are designed to detect.

If you remain leery, reflect on the description of the behavior that is symptomatic of alcohol dependence in Chapter 7. The client's candor, or absence of distortion, is possibly not so unexpected. What the alcohol-troubled client often strongly disagrees with is not the facts, but their interpretation. Thus, the alcohol-dependent individual might very readily acknowledge that a family member has expressed concern about drinking but would be likely to dispute whether the concern is justified. The client may well provide the interviewer with a very lengthy and unsolicited rebuttal of the family's concern and offer justifications for the drinking.

Please note that the instruments described next are widely used. They were developed when the formal diagnostic terms were dependence and abuse. That does not make them irrelevant now. Their importance lies in their ability to identify those whose drinking presents a potentially life-threatening problem, for whom further evaluation and assessment is imperative. In this instance, the name we use for that "problem" really doesn't matter.

CAGE

Since its introduction in 1970, the CAGE, developed by Ewing and Rouse, has become recognized as one of the most efficient and effective screening devices for alcohol dependence, analogous to a severe alcohol use disorder. The CAGE is both easy to administer and less intimidating than some other screening instruments. It consists of the following four questions:

"Have you ever felt you should	**C**ut down on your drinking?"
"Have people	**A**nnoyed you by criticizing your drinking?"
"Have you ever felt bad or	**G**uilty about your drinking?"
"Have you ever had an	**E**ye-opener first thing in the morning to steady nerves or get rid of a hangover?"

Scoring: Four positive responses are diagnostic for alcohol dependence. Scoring 2 or 3 should create a high index of suspicion of the presence of alcohol dependence.

The CAGE is not intended to screen for other alcohol problems. So scoring 1 or 2 affirmative answers does not indicate alcohol abuse, or a moderate or mild alcohol use disorder.

For those concerned about being overly inclusive and thus falsely identifying as possibly alcohol dependent those who are not, the CAGE holds little danger. It is very reliable in providing a way of initially sorting those who may be alcohol dependent from those who most likely are not. Of those with a CAGE score of 1, only 20% are not dependent. As the number of positive responses increases, the individuals without alcohol problems who would be incorrectly labeled drops markedly. Only 11% of those who score 2 are, in fact, not dependent. For 3 positive responses, the proportion of non-dependent individuals drops to 1%; for 4 affirmative responses, the percentage is 0.

Michigan Alcohol Screening Test (MAST)

The MAST is one of the most widely used screening tools. The original MAST, first published in 1971 by Selzer and associates, was a 25-item yes or no questionnaire. It was designed for use either within a structured interview or for self-administration. The questions touch on medical, interpersonal, and legal problems resulting from alcohol use. Since its introduction, the reliability and validity of the MAST have been established in multiple populations. Several variations have since been developed. The Brief MAST uses 10 of the MAST items. The Short MAST (SMAST) was specifically created to be self-administered and uses 13 items found to be as effective as the entire MAST for screening. For three questions (1, 4, and 6) a negative response receives points. The questions and their scoring follow:

(1.) Do you feel you are a normal drinker? (No = 2 points)
2. Have you ever awakened the morning after some drinking the night before and found that you could not remember part of the evening before? (2 points)
3. Does your spouse (or parents) ever worry or complain about your drinking? (1 point)
4. Can you stop drinking without a struggle after one or two drinks? (No = 2 points)
5. Do you ever feel bad about your drinking? (1 point)
(6.) Do friends or relatives think you are a normal drinker? (No = 2 points)
7. Do you ever try to limit your drinking to certain times of the day or to certain places? (1 point)
8. Are you always able to stop drinking when you want to? (No = 2 points)
(9.) Have you ever attended a meeting of Alcoholics Anonymous (AA)? (5 points)
10. Have you gotten into fights when drinking? (1 point)
11. Has drinking ever created problems with you and your spouse? (2 points)

12. Has your spouse (or other family member) ever gone to anyone for help about your drinking? (2 points)

(13.) Have you ever lost friends or girlfriends/boyfriends because of your drinking? (2 points)

(14.) Have you ever gotten into trouble at work because of drinking? (2 points)

15. Have you ever lost a job because of drinking? (2 points)

(16.) Have you ever neglected your obligations, your family, or your work for two or more days in a row because you were drinking? (2 points)

17. Do you ever drink before noon? (1 point)

18. Have you ever been told you have liver trouble? Cirrhosis? (2 points)

(19.) Have you ever had delirium tremens (DTs), severe shaking, after heavy drinking? (2 points)

(20.) Have you ever gone to anyone for help about your drinking? (5 points)

(21.) Have you ever been in a hospital because of your drinking? (5 points)

22. Have you ever been a patient in a psychiatric hospital or on a psychiatric ward of a general hospital where drinking was part of the problem? (2 points)

23. Have you ever been seen at a psychiatric or mental health clinic, or gone to a doctor, social worker, or clergyman for help with an emotional problem in which drinking has played a part? (2 points)

24. Have you ever been arrested, even for a few hours, because of drunk behavior? (2 points)

(25.) Have you ever been arrested for drunk driving or driving after drinking? (2 points)

Scoring: A score of 5 or more points indicates alcohol dependence. Four points is suggestive of alcohol dependence.

There are multiple versions of the MAST. The Brief MAST consists of 10 questions—those with question number in parentheses. There is the Short Mast (SMAST)—including the 13 items with the question number underlined. Finally, there is the MAST-G, developed for use with the elderly. A hint, G=Geriatric. (See pages 444–445).

The CAGE and MAST have several limitations. One is that they look at lifetime problems. Typically the wording is, "Have you ever . . . ?" Thus, someone in middle age who hasn't had a problem for a decade could still come out with a positive score. Presumably, a few follow-up questions could pick this up rather quickly. Although a potential nuisance, this is hardly an insurmountable problem. Furthermore, knowing there is a past history of alcohol problems is important. A more serious concern is how effective these instruments are in identifying alcohol problems among women and members of racial/ethnic minority groups. Almost universally these tests were developed using white, middle-aged males. As a general rule, these tests have performed less well with women. This is a particular issue in obstetric settings, where alcohol use is a special concern and the need to intervene is so important. That is the reason for the creation of the following instrument.

TWEAK

This five-item scale was initially developed to meet the need for a sensitive, easy-to-administer screening test for pregnant women. It draws on existing tools, with the researchers eliminating or rewording questions that didn't seem to work as well with women, while retaining those that did. While designed for women, it has since been examined for use in other populations as well. TWEAK is an acronym that stands for **T**olerance, **W**orry about drinking, **E**ye-opener, **A**mnesia (blackouts), and **K/Cut** down. The positive responses are scored. The questions and scoring are as follows:

1A. How many drinks does it take before you begin to feel the first effect of alcohol? (**T**olerance) [3 or more drinks = 2 points]

or

1B. How many drinks does it take before the alcohol makes you fall asleep or pass out? Or, if you never pass out, what is the largest number of drinks that you have? (**T**olerance) [5 or more drinks = 2 points]

2. Have your friends or relatives **W**orried about your drinking in the past year? [1 point]
3. Do you sometimes take a drink in the morning, when you first get up? (**E**ye-opener) [1 point]
4. Are there times when you drink and afterwards can't remember what you said or did? (**A**mnesia) [1 point]
5. Do you sometimes feel the need to cut down on your drinking? (**K** or **C**, **C**ut down) [1 point]

Scoring: A score of 3 or more is considered positive for dependence for either version.

Alcohol Use Disorders Identification Test (AUDIT)

The AUDIT was developed through the efforts of the World Health Organization (WHO). The goal was to create a screening tool that would meet several criteria. First, it had to identify those with high-risk alcohol use, whose drinking warranted closer examination, not simply people who were alcohol dependent. Second, the screening instrument needed to be effective in different cultures, in both developing and developed countries. Third, it had to be suitable for use by an array of health care workers. The project was initiated in 1982 with the active collaboration of alcohol specialists in many countries. The AUDIT consists of 10 questions, listed below. It has been tested in a variety of populations. At this time, it is the most widely accepted screening instrument. Literally hundreds of studies have examined its use with people of different nationalities and of different age groups, and it has been translated into multiple languages. The questions and scoring follow:

1. How often do you have a drink containing alcohol?
   - Never = 0 points
   - Monthly or less = 1 point
   - 2–4 times a month = 2 points
   - 2–3 times a week = 3 points
   - 4 or more times a week = 4 points

2. How many drinks containing alcohol do you have on a typical day when you are drinking?
   - 1 or 2 drinks = 0 points
   - 3 or 4 drinks = 1 point
   - 5 or 6 drinks = 2 points
   - 7 to 9 drinks = 3 points
   - 10 or more drinks = 4 points

3. How often do you have six or more drinks on one occasion?
   - Never = 0 points
   - Monthly = 2 points
   - Weekly = 3 points
   - Daily or almost daily = 4 points

4. How often during the last year have you found that you were not able to stop drinking once you had started?
   - Never = 0 points
   - Less than monthly = 1 point
   - Monthly = 2 points
   - Weekly = 3 points
   - Daily or almost daily = 4 points

5. How often during the last year have you failed to do what was normally expected from you because of drinking?
   - Never = 0 points
   - Less than monthly = 1 point
   - Monthly = 2 points
   - Weekly = 3 points
   - Daily or almost daily = 4 points

6. How often during the last year have you needed a first drink in the morning to get yourself going after a heavy drinking session?
   - Never = 0 points
   - Less than monthly = 1 point
   - Monthly = 2 points
   - Weekly = 3 points
   - Daily or almost daily = 4 points

7. How often during the last year have you had a feeling of guilt or remorse after drinking?
   Never = 0 points
   Less than monthly = 1 point
   Monthly = 2 points
   Weekly = 3 points
   Daily or almost daily = 4 points
8. How often during the last year have you been unable to remember what happened the night before because you had been drinking?
   Never = 0 points
   Less than monthly = 1 point
   Monthly = 2 points
   Weekly = 3 points
   Daily or almost daily = 4 points
9. Have you or someone else been injured as a result of your drinking?
   Never = 0 points
   Yes, but not in the last year = 2 points
   Yes, during the last year = 4 points
10. Has a relative or friend, or a doctor or other health worker, been concerned about your drinking or suggested you cut down?
    Never = 0 points
    Yes, but not in the last year = 2 points
    Yes, during the last year = 4 points

Scores and Corresponding Interventions The points awarded for each question range from 0 to 4. The total scores range from 0 to 40. The WHO originally organized the scores into four zones, each with a suggested clinical response. It is emphasized that clinical judgment is required and must be factored in, especially when the client's score is not consistent with other evidence. Ideally the primary care provider is equipped to deal with patients falling into Zone III. However, some clinicians will be more inclined to effect a referral to a substance abuse treatment agency or a clinician with specific substance abuse expertise.

Zone I	0–7 points	Alcohol education
Zone II	8–15 points	Simple advice
Zone III	16–19 points	Simple advice plus brief counseling and continued monitoring
Zone IV	20–40 points	Referral to specialist for diagnostic evaluation and treatment

Note. As the AUDIT has been more widely used, the subtle differences between the interventions recommended for Zones II and III has been simplified, and simply described as a "brief intervention." The following elements are seen as components of a brief intervention: presenting the screening results to the patient; providing medical advice; soliciting the patient's commitment; identifying the goal, whether reduced drinking or abstinence; and giving advice and encouragement.

Structure of AUDIT The test is organized into three domains. The first three questions focus on hazardous alcohol use. Questions 4 through 6 focus on the symptoms of dependence. The last four questions focus on harm resulting from alcohol use.

AUDIT-C Just as there are multiple versions of the MAST, there have also been efforts to determine if there are subsets of AUDIT questions that could perform as well as the full test. The AUDIT-C version of the AUDIT has been the most widely studied and is being used more frequently. It uses the first three AUDIT questions. The "C" refers to consumption. The *AUDIT-C* has been examined in a number of different settings, such as primary care and emergency services, as well as with special populations—adolescents and women. In all these cases, it has performed as well as the full AUDIT in identifying harmful use, a category used in the classification schema of the WHO.

1. How often do you have a drink containing alcohol?
   Never = 0 points
   Monthly or less = 1 point
   2–4 times a month = 2 points
   2–3 times a week = 3 points
   4 or more times a week = 4 points

2. How many standard drinks containing alcohol do you have on a typical day?
   1 or 2 drinks = 0 points
   3 or 4 drinks = 1 point
   5 or 6 drinks = 2 points
   7 to 9 drinks = 3 points
   10 or more drinks = 4 points

3. How often do you have six or more drinks on one occasion?
   Never = 0 points
   Monthly = 2 points
   Weekly = 3 points
   Daily or almost daily = 4 points

Scoring: The original cutoff score indicating harmful use was 4 points for men and 3 or more for women. This has been revised to 5 or 6 points for men and 4 for women.

CRAFFT

The CRAFFT is a screening tool developed for use with adolescents. It draws on adult instruments, but the questions have been rephrased to incorporate situations suited to teens. It consists of six questions:

1. Have you ever ridden in a **C**ar driven by someone (including yourself) who was high or had been using alcohol or drugs?
2. Do you ever use alcohol or drugs to **R**elax, feel better about yourself, or fit in?
3. Do you ever use alcohol or drugs while you are by yourself? (**A**lone)

4. Do you ever **F**orget things you did while using alcohol or drugs?
5. Do your **F**amily or **F**riends ever tell you that you should cut down on your drinking or drug use?
6. Have you ever gotten into **T**rouble while you were using alcohol or drugs?

Scoring: Two or more positive responses suggest the need for further evaluation.

Interpreting Scores

The goal of any screening test is to separate people into two groups: one for those with the characteristic of interest and one for those without it. Ideally no one would be misclassified. However, the practical question is how to reduce the number of people who are misassigned. Individuals who don't have a condition, but are incorrectly identified as having it, are known as *false positives*. Those who have the condition and are falsely said not to have it are *false negatives*. This is a concern for any screening test, whether cancer screening or screening for alcohol problems. The practical challenge is to select the best possible cutoff point, the one that reduces the number of errors. In selecting a particular score, the questions being considered are, "What are the costs of missing people who have a condition?" versus "What are the costs of including people who don't have the problem?" Putting this in everyday terms, would it be less of a problem to miss 5 people who have the condition, than to include 40 people who do not?

If you drink, don't drive.
Don't even putt.
—DEAN MARTIN

Web-Based Screening

The discussion in this chapter considers screening and treatment within the context of the treatment system. However, there is a parallel universe, not as readily visible. With the internet intertwined with virtually every sphere of life, and a generation that has grown up with electronic media, it should be no surprise that the internet is becoming a force in screening and assessment. A variety of websites have assessment instruments, provide feedback about harmful alcohol use based on the responses, and compare the individual's drinking pattern to that of the larger population. The Centre for Addiction and Mental Health (Canada) has one of the oldest sites with the opportunity for self-assessment, *Personalized Alcohol Feedback* <http://notes.camh.net/efeed.nsf/newform>. Feedback is provided after the individual completes a 20-item questionnaire, which includes demographic data, along with the number of drinks consumed each day during a typical week. The personalized feedback includes a comparison of the person's drinking to the population at large for either Canada or the United States, as well as the risk for alcohol-related problems. In addition, there is an estimate of the amount of money spent annually, and even how much time the person spends intoxicated.

I feel bad for people who don't drink. When they wake up in the morning, that's as good as they're going to feel all day."
—FRANK SINATRA

In 2009, the NIAAA mounted *Rethinking Drinking* <http://rethinkingdrinking.niaaa.nih.gov/> an online version of a pamphlet by the same name. It is not a counterpart to the Canadian site just described. In comparison to the Canadian site, it is not singularly focused on

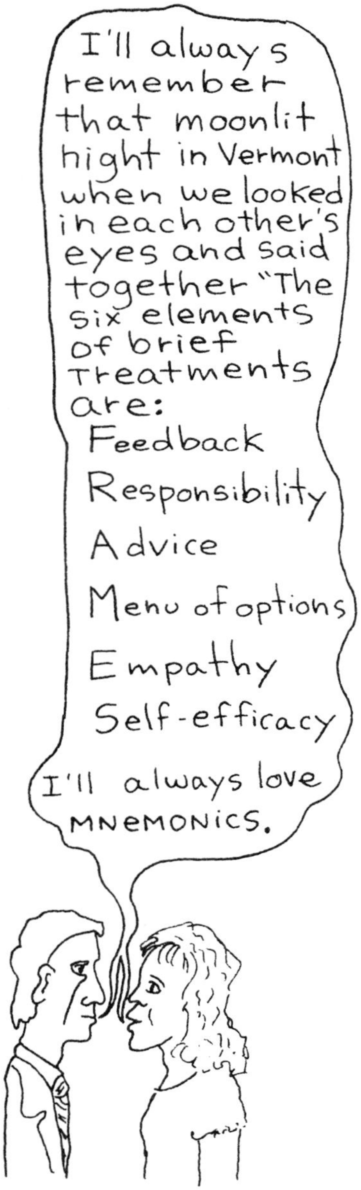

self-assessment. It is cluttered, not a good characteristic for a population that may be easily distracted. There are a host of links to sites dealing with problems beyond alcohol, including other drug use and mental health problems. It does not include a recognized assessment instrument, and the feedback and comments are superficial. Primarily it consists of basic educational materials, such as the risks that can accompany drinking, along with general tips for cutting down. It does not allow the individual to compare his or her drinking patterns to the general population, whether in terms of quantity or frequency of drinking.

In addition to websites that post self-assessment materials, there are several that go farther. In essence, they provide brief interventions to help people make changes in their drinking. The best known is the *Drinker's Check-up* <http://drinkerscheckup.com>. The *Drinker's Check-up* (see Chapter 10 for a description) is organized in several sections: following the self-assessment section are options provided for next steps the individual wishes to take.

Beyond sites directed to the general population, others are directed to special groups such as college students, adolescents, and the military. In terms of who uses internet sites, some characteristics are rather predictable—such as being computer literate, being younger, and being better educated. Those who use these sites tend to have less severe alcohol problems than those who enter traditional treatment. The use of the internet will keep expanding. Traditional treatment programs are now exploring how to incorporate e-based services into their services (see pages 342–344).

Brief Interventions

Consistently, brief interventions have been shown to reduce drinking as well as the most risky drinking patterns. Such interventions have an impact, too, on the use of health care services. Michael Fleming and colleagues explored their use in community-based primary care practices. Over the study period, more than 17,000 patients were routinely screened to identify problem drinking. From this group, about 700 patients with patterns of harmful use were selected to participate in the study. Half received a brief treatment that entailed two 10- to 15-minute counseling sessions. These were provided by the doctor, using a "script," and involved advice, education, and a contract detailing what the patient would do. Twelve months later the results were significant. The amount of alcohol consumed had been reduced; the number of days on which people drank five or more drinks (binge drinking) declined. Also there was a decline in the days of heavy drinking. Furthermore, those who received the intervention had fewer emergency room visits, fewer motor vehicle accidents, and less use of health care services.

The effectiveness of brief interventions has been seen with prescription drug use as well. For example, one study examined efforts to reduce the use of benzodiazepines (drugs such as Valium and Librium) among patients who were taking more than was medically indicated. All the intervention entailed was the physician's sending a letter instructing the patient to cut down, advising on how to do this gradually, and suggesting that perhaps in time use could be stopped. Six months later, the group as a whole had reduced this prescription drug use by a third. One out of five had ceased use entirely. All of this was the result of a single letter!

Common Elements In reviewing articles on brief treatments that have been described in the scientific literature, William Miller identified six features that appear to be common to all. These elements can be remembered by the acronym FRAMES: **F**eedback, **R**esponsibility, **A**dvice, a **M**enu of options presented to the patient, **E**mpathy, and **S**elf-efficacy.

- ***F**eedback about patients' personal risk.* Typically health professionals delivering brief intervention give feedback on the risky aspects associated with the patient's drinking. This includes current health problems aggravated by drinking or those caused by drinking, as well as other life problems that appear to be related to alcohol use. Another form of useful feedback is to describe how an individual's drinking stacks up against that of the statistically average person. (See a sample of such a feedback form in Chapter 10.)
- *Responsibility of the patient.* Research consistently shows that people are more likely to make changes if they feel their own behavior can make a difference. Therefore brief interventions generally emphasize the patient's role and responsibility for making decisions. For example, a doctor or nurse may tell patients, "No one can make you change or make you decide to change. What you do about your drinking is up to you."
- ***A**dvice to change.* Health professionals can give explicit advice to reduce or stop drinking. This can be done in the same way that they would give advice to a diabetic about diet or would give specific advice about exercise.
- ***M**enu of ways to reduce drinking.* Consistent with the idea that responsibility lies with the patient, individuals can be offered a variety of ways they can change their drinking. This can include identifying and reducing high-risk situations or finding other ways to cope with stressful situations. Professionals can offer patient education and self-help manuals.
- ***E**mpathetic counseling style.* A warm, reflective, and understanding style of delivering brief intervention is more effective than an aggressive, confrontational, or coercive style. In comparing these styles, one study found that there was a 77% reduction in drinking when an empathetic style was used, as opposed to only 5% when a confrontational approach was used.
- ***S**elf-efficacy or optimism of the patient.* Self-efficacy is the individual's belief that he or she can do things that will make a difference. In studies of treatment generally, patients who don't feel powerless do better, so efforts in brief treatment are directed to empowering patients and helping them feel optimistic about their ability to make changes.

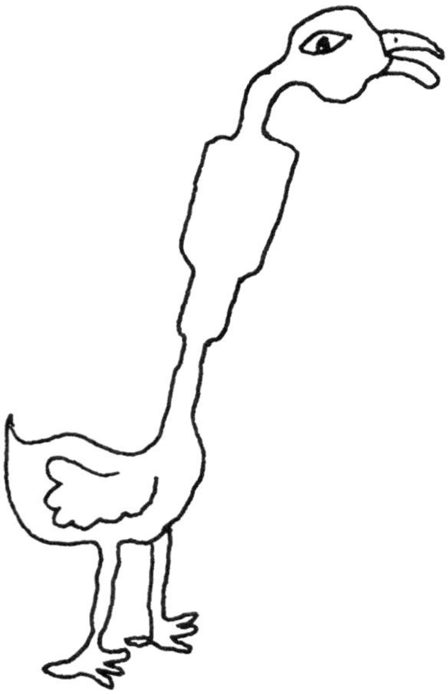

What Makes a Difference In considering what makes brief treatments work, there is an interesting insight from a research effort that was never conducted. Prior to the emergence of brief, office-based interventions, Michael Fleming, M.D., then a member of a primary care practice, wanted to study the use of a Johnson-style intervention utilizing family members to move people into treatment. (The details of these techniques are described in Chapter 10.) In brief, the family intervention, led by an alcohol professional, uses a family meeting in which family members identify specific behaviors they consider evidence of an alcohol problem and express their concern for the person. For the intended study, a group of physicians were trained to conduct such interventions. However, they never got to do it! In each instance, when the physician brought up the need for treatment, the patient agreed, and no such family meeting was required. Seemingly the physician's authority and manner of expressing concern for the patient were all that was needed. When a physician is involved, the nature of the physician's role is significant. Doctors are generally seen as acting on a patient's behalf, as having specialized knowledge, and as being objective. Although people may be suspicious of a spouse's motives, that isn't usually their response to their doctors. Even if people don't always follow a doctor's advice, at least they will listen!

Other clues come from what is called either "spontaneous remission" or "change without treatment." The first term is borrowed from the general medical field. It refers to the fact that sometimes, without treatment, patients recover for reasons that are not understood. In reference to alcohol problems, this refers to those with serious alcohol problems and alcohol dependence who stop drinking on their own. Those who have studied this phenomenon are always careful to point out that the remissions were virtually never spontaneous nor are they true remissions. Typically something happened that sparked these people to make changes. When questioned about what had prompted them to stop drinking, several factors were commonly mentioned: illness or accident (33%); extraordinary events, such as humiliation, a suicide attempt, or pregnancy (29%); religious or conversion experience (26%); alcohol-caused financial problems (22%); intervention by immediate family (18%); alcohol-related death or illness of a friend (14%); education about alcoholism (12%); and alcohol-related legal problems (8%). Change without treatment is discussed later in this chapter (see pages 283–284).

☐ WHEN SCREENING IS POSITIVE

When screening is positive, several things should be done. One is to share the results of the test and discuss them with the client. Is the individual surprised? Has the person or others close to him or her ever been concerned? Another task is to take an alcohol-drug history for use in evaluation and treatment planning. An immediate priority is to identify any medical issues related to drinking. In the discussion that follows, the type of information that is needed is described along with the kinds of questions that can elicit this. Many agencies have a standard protocol for collecting this information. A standardized format assures that the relevant information the agency considers important is gathered routinely, and the agency can count on this basic data being available for all patients.

Identifying Situations Requiring Medical Attention

Counselors should not attempt to deliver medical care, but there are situations in which being informed about medical issues is important. When screening is positive, medical information is part of the additional information required. Counselors need to evaluate withdrawal risks and to be aware of situations when medical attention is indicated. Every counselor needs to have someone to turn to as a medical backup. Generally speaking, current medical status and medical history are always important factors to determine. Because delirium tremens can be fatal in up to 25% of cases, it is crucial to determine the risk by getting a good history from the client, especially history of seizures or psychotic symptoms during withdrawal.

General Health Status

Some general questions about health status that should be asked include the following:

- Have you been seeing a doctor recently or thought that you should have seen one?
- When was the last time you were seen by a physician?
- Have you ever been hospitalized and, if so, for what?
- Do you have a history of accidents or injuries, or have you been in any fights that required medical attention? Did any of these occur when you were drinking or using drugs?

Assessing Withdrawal Risk

For clients who are drinking or using other drugs, or who have recently stopped, there is the potential for withdrawal. To assess withdrawal risks, the following information should be secured for any patient for whom there has been a decrease in regular use or a recent cessation of use:

- *Past week drinking*. Try to elicit specific details and quantifiable amounts. When the amount is essentially unknown to the individual, make efforts to infer levels of use. The following questions are the kind that will be necessary: "How often do you go to the liquor store? Go to the bar?" "How much do you purchase?" "How long does this last?" For prescription drug abuse, the questions to ask are, "How do you get these drugs?" If by prescription, "Does more than one doctor prescribe these for you?"

For illicit drugs, the key aspects are, "How often do you use cocaine or crack or (fill in the blank)? Daily? Weekends? Describe use on a usual day. What's your source?"

- *Level of tolerance.* "What is the amount of alcohol/drug you require to feel its effects?"
- *Time elapsed since last consuming alcohol and the current physical status.* This information provides a valuable means of assessing tolerance. It indicates the symptoms of withdrawal present with a declining blood level. In response to this, what objective signs are there of the presence of withdrawal? Tremulousness? Agitation? Sweating? Confusion? Hypervigilance? Rapid pulse?
- *Prior experience of either decreasing or stopping drinking.* Prior clinical status during withdrawal is significant, especially when prior withdrawal was problematic. This is not to be limited to formal detoxification. Many individuals have had periods of relative or absolute abstinence dictated by circumstances such as a deliberate effort to curtail or limit use, or being in a situation that disrupts the usual drinking pattern, or being faced with a situation in which there is no choice, such as being hospitalized.
- *Current or past medical problems, allergies.*

Other Drug Use While the questions above are directed to alcohol, similar questions are appropriate for other drug use. When it comes to drugs other than alcohol, regardless of training, clinicians will never be as knowledgeable as some of their clients regarding various drug actions and the desired effects. Don't even bother trying to pretend you are informed, when you are not. Sometimes clients refer to drugs by their street names, which you may not recognize, or talk about drug effects using street slang. Ask the client to define these terms. Ask what a drug does for him or her; ask how it is administered, the duration of the effects, and what it feels like as the effects wear off. There may be some disbelief about your naïveté, but generally clients will appreciate that you bothered to ask and were sufficiently well informed to ask the right questions.

Indications for Immediate Medical Evaluation

Many medical emergencies will be clearly recognizable. In these situations, use emergency transportation, police, or rescue squads. This is especially important if the client needs life support. This is evidenced by shallow, uneven breathing; rapid pulse; or fluctuating levels of consciousness. Another emergency situation occurs when there is a threat of danger to others or harm to self. When an individual is transported for emergency care, inform the emergency department of the patient's imminent arrival. Any information that can be provided to emergency staff is helpful, including current status, names of family or friends who may be with the patient and can provide information, diagnostic impressions, and relevant medical history.

The following indications for immediate medical evaluation may not appear to be life-threatening; however, prompt medical attention should be arranged because without an adequate evaluation, serious problems could occur:

- Recent substance intake at levels that risk developing toxicity, poisoning, or organ damage even if the patient is asymptomatic
- Ingestion of unknown quantities and substances
- Hallucinations, marked paranoia
- Confusion or delirium
- Severe agitation; unsuccessful efforts to quiet the patient
- Severe tremors
- Tachycardia (heart rate 110 per minute)
- Fever (38.0°C)
- History or evidence of trauma, especially head trauma
- Patient in semiconscious state; able to be aroused briefly but falls asleep when stimulus is removed

For individuals who have recently stopped drinking or have reduced their consumption significantly or intend to, the following suggest a significant risk for serious withdrawal:

- Consuming more than the equivalent of 12 drinks per day for more than 2 weeks
- History of a difficult withdrawal
- Seizures or history of seizures
- Dependence on multiple substances

There are also situations that, while not medical emergencies, still warrant a medical checkup. These include all clients with heavy, extended alcohol or other drug use who have not had a recent medical exam, anyone reporting a history of bleeding, and those who have a history of chronic medical illness, such as high blood pressure, who are not under a doctor's care.

Making a Referral

Having identified a significant problem with alcohol or another drug, the clinician who isn't primarily a substance abuse professional is faced with referring the client to a specialized program. This may be either for further evaluation or for treatment. Drawing on motivational interviewing, the following are key: removing barriers, practical as well as attitudinal; giving clear direction; actively helping; providing feedback; and reinforcing and supporting the client's efforts.

To make this concrete, keep several things in mind. First, you cannot enthusiastically recommend the unfamiliar. Therefore, you need to know about various facilities, their programs, and their personnel. Second, in making any referral, there's always a danger of clients falling through the cracks. Therefore, you need to be actively involved in the referral. Don't just give an agency name and phone number, with instructions to the client to "call when you get a chance." You make the appointment with a specific individual, at a specific time. With this active helping, the likelihood of the individual's following through virtually doubles, jumping from under 40% if the client is given only a phone number and told to call to over 80% when the counselor sets up the appointment. Inform the family or significant others of the actions being taken and why. Third, if you've had an ongoing relationship with the client, a referral may feel like abandonment. If appropriate, continue the contact and let the client know that you are both in this together. In some instances an agency may require that the prospective client contact them. Be sensitive to what can be done to help the client follow through.

In large measure the ability to effect a successful referral lies in conveying a sense of concern and hope. It also depends on assisting the client to see the difficulties in a new light. In discussing a referral, appreciate that someone can absorb only so much information at one time. Consider for a moment the woman whose physician discovers a lump in her breast. The physician's next step is making a referral to an oncologist. This is not the time to discuss the relative merits of radical mastectomy and/or chemotherapy in terms of five-year survival. Nor is it the time to talk of side effects from chemotherapy. This is all too much to absorb and not relevant for her taking the next step. The important messages to convey initially are (1) the situation is serious enough to warrant further investigation, (2) the patient is being referred to someone who can be trusted, and (3) both of you are in this together. The same concern is what one attempts to convey when making a referral for substance abuse problems.

There is no medicine like hope, no incentive so great, and no tonic so powerful as expectation of something better tomorrow.
—Orison Swett Marden

Finally, it is important to convey information to any clinician or program to which a client is being referred. This requires a client's permission. Imagine yourself as the person getting a referral, what information would you find helpful. Appreciate too that a client may have a case of cold feet when he or she is about to see someone new. This may lead a client to skimp on or leave out information that another clinician would find both important and helpful.

Engaging the Patient

Over the years attention has been directed at identifying factors that foster a client's commitment to treatment as well as the factors that have the opposite effect. In light of this, interest has turned to using clinical approaches specifically designed to engage the client in the treatment process as well as foster the client's commitment to make changes.

Clinical Style

It may seem so obvious as not to warrant mention, but the manner in which a clinician interacts with a client matters. William Miller and colleagues described clinical approaches that they determined were important in working with substance abuse clients. In combination these are the essence of "motivational interviewing." This approach was set forth in an era when confrontational approaches were common. At that time there was talk of "the need to break down denial" or "have the client accept the label of alcoholic or addict" or acknowledge "powerlessness." Although admittedly a caricature, this could be seen as "bludgeoning someone into sobriety."

The gods are just, and of our pleasant vices
Make instruments to plague us.
—William Shakespeare

Motivational Interviewing

Five basic principles underpin motivational interviewing:

- *Expressing empathy*. Showing respect for the client is critical. Related to this is the appreciation that a counselor doesn't "change others," that clients change themselves, and the recognition that the goal is "listening rather than telling."
- *Developing discrepancies*. This involves helping the client to recognize there is a discrepancy between his or her current situation and what is desired.
- *Avoiding arguments*. Becoming aware of discrepancies may lead clients to feel under attack, even if the "attack" is internal, the product of their remorse, guilt, and attempts to explain away their circumstances. As Miller points out, it's important to not engage in argument. It is important to appreciate that the significant arguments made are not those set forth by the counselor, but the ones the client makes for him- or herself. And that involves looking at pros and cons.
- *Rolling with resistance*. This is defined less as what the clinician does than as what he or she does not do. What is not done includes arguing, disagreeing, warning of negative consequences, trying to persuade, analyzing "reasons" for resistance, using sarcasm, or appealing to professional credentials and authority. Instead the counselor reflects back what the client is saying, as well as sometimes reframing, which invites the client to see things in a new light.
- *Supporting self-efficacy*. This includes helping the client to recognize strengths, the role of choice, and the ability to make changes.

In effect all of this is directed to identifying clinical approaches that are more likely to engage the client, rather than have a client heading for the door. (Note: A number of training materials are available for motivational interviewing.)

Stages of Change Model

For too long, the tendency has been to lay the blame for treatment failure on the client's shoulder. The individual was "in denial," wasn't ready to change, was unmotivated, hadn't "hit bottom." Motivated clients were perceived as having good outcomes; conversely, treatment failures were often chalked up to a client's lack of motivation. In the 1990s, James Prochaska, a psychologist, focused on the concept of motivation and set forth a different view. The original work focused on smoking cessation, but has since been applied to the broader area of substance abuse. This is known as the *stages of change* model.

In this view, motivation is no longer seen as a characteristic of the client, something that is either absent or present. Rather, motivation is viewed as a dynamic process, which unfolds in discrete stages that are considered to be common in anyone making significant life changes. In addition, specific clinical interventions are described as suitable or to be avoided, depending on where the client is in the change process. The five stages of change outlined by Prochaska are as follows:

1. *Pre-contemplation.* This is the point when an individual is not even considering change. There is no perceived need for it. Instead, someone else, such as a family member, physician, clergy, or coworker, recognizes the problem. In this stage, the important clinical task is to help individuals gain awareness of the dangers involved in their present behaviors.
2. *Contemplation.* Now the individual is more ambivalent, both favoring and resisting change. As change is considered, the person perceives both pluses and minuses. In this stage, if confronted with arguments on one side, the client's likely response is to defend the opposite side. So it is helpful for the clinician to address the negative effects of alcohol use, the features the client considers pluses, and the potential benefits of change. It is not uncommon for those with alcohol problems to find themselves in situations where there is a lot at stake. There is the person arrested for DWI at risk of losing driving privileges. There is the woman who risks the loss of her children due to neglect. There is the nurse who is threatened with the loss of her license.

Several studies show that people are far more likely to make changes to avoid losing something than to make changes in response to losses. How does this finding fit into this view of motivation? The prospect of loss gets the individual's attention. When weighing the negative factors associated with not doing anything, against the benefits associated with making changes, the deck is stacked in favor of the latter. Thus the balance is in favor of making changes. The person is poised to move from the stage of contemplation to the next stage. But if the loss has already occurred, and there is no longer anything to be gained by making changes, the individual is likely to move from contemplation back to pre-contemplation.

3. *Determination.* In this stage there is less ambivalence. The client often "sounds" different and can acknowledge a situation warranting change. Efforts are actively being made to consider alternatives. For the patient at this stage, rapid, immediate intervention is important. If too much time passes, the individual reverts to the stage of contemplation. Thus a potential opportunity for change has been lost. In this stage the client needs the professional's assistance in selecting an optimal strategy for making changes, plus lots of support for the resolve to follow through.
4. *Action.* At this point the client is engaged in implementing a plan, which may be formal treatment. So the clinical task is providing assistance and direction as the client carries out the plan.
5. *Maintenance.* When significant changes in behavior have been made, then maintenance of the change is what becomes important. Maintenance of change is seen as being sustained by continuing action. Interestingly, the process of making change is, in and of itself, reinforcing. It encourages the desire to make other needed changes and demonstrates that change is possible.

If relapse occurs, it is necessary to once again go through the stage of initiating change, starting with contemplation.

Clinical Responses

Different clinical approaches were identified as either helpful or to be avoided in working with clients at specific stages of change. These are outlined below.

Stages of Change	Clinician Efforts to Promote Motivation
Pre-contemplation	Raise doubts.
	Prompt the client to consider the risks and problems with the current situation.
Contemplation	Here the client is ambivalent; try to tip the balance.
	Have the client consider the benefits of change and the risks of the situation continuing as is.
Determination	Focus on specific actions the individual can take.
Action	Facilitate the steps outlined above.
Maintenance	Identify factors that may prompt a relapse and develop strategies to counter this.

Stages of Change: Some Second Thoughts

Since first set forth in the 1990s, the stages of change model has been widely disseminated and described as revolutionizing clinical care. However, a number of questions are being raised, and on a number of counts. For one, there is at best scant evidence that clients do better when clinicians match their clinical approach to the client's "stage." It is said to ignore a commonly recognized phenomenon—that individuals often change seemingly quite suddenly. If you recall the research on

"spontaneous remission," frequently individuals cited a particular life event, such as illness, as the impetus for change. As a theory, it is found lacking because a number of features are quite arbitrary. For example, in reference to smoking, a smoker is said to be in the preparatory stage if the smoker plans to quit within the next 30 days (31 days doesn't count) and had a quit attempt in the past year that lasted at least 24 hours.

The stages of change model also is seen as relying primarily on conscious planning. Critics observe that real life often doesn't work that way. One study of smoking cessation focused on patients seen by their general practitioners. Over half reported people quitting smoking, with no prior planning. Indeed, some individuals in the study didn't even finish their current pack of cigarettes. With the focus on conscious decision making, the stages of change model overlooks factors known to underpin behavior associated with addiction, particularly craving and the presence of cues that trigger use. The model also ignores the fact that in many instances people don't "need to be moved along." To the contrary, they may welcome the opportunity to try a new treatment. An example cited was the response to new medications to assist in smoking cessation.

The stages of change model may suffer the same fate as Jellinek's proposed stages in the emergence of what was known as alcoholism. Commonly, things do *not* unfold in the uniform fashion posed. As one critic noted, the stages of change model may be more of a "security blanket" for clinicians, as it meets the clinician's need for structure and gives the appearance of scientific rigor. At the same time, it is a disservice to clients when clinicians opt for "moving clients along" using weak interventions while ignoring the reality that situational factors may be a major force for change.

Substance Use History

When to Ask

It takes practice to take a reliable alcohol-drug history. It also takes recognition of timing and a good look at what is in front of you. It may seem redundant to say, but an intoxicated or withdrawing client cannot provide accurate information. You wouldn't expect accurate information from someone going under or coming out of anesthesia. Unfortunately, some of the forms designed to be filled out at intake show little recognition of this fact. Use your common sense. Try to ask the questions you need to at a time when the person is at least relatively comfortable, both emotionally and physically. Ask them matter-of-factly. Remember that your own drinking pattern is no yardstick for others. For example, when someone responds to the question "How much do you usually drink on a typical occasion?" with "About 4 or 5 drinks or so," don't stare, open-mouthed.

What to Ask

The information needed about alcohol consumption includes what the client drinks, quantity, frequency, when, where, and whether it causes, or has ever caused, a problem in any area of life, including physical problems. These questions can be phrased in different ways. A more informal approach may be better than simply sitting there, filling out a form and asking each question in order. An issue that is too often excluded is the question of what the drinking does for the client. Questions such as "How do you feel when you drink?" "What does alcohol do for you?" and "When do you most often want a drink?" can supply a lot of information.

How to Ask

If the questions are asked conversationally along with other questions regarding general health, social aspects, and other use of prescribed drugs or medications, most people will answer them. The less threatened you are by the process, the more comfortable the individual being questioned will be.

Following questions about alcohol use, queries should be directed to other drug use. You could ask a question such as "Have you used drugs other than those required for medical reasons?" If the answer is positive, the follow-up questions would be what substances, under what circumstances, with what kinds of accompanying problems, and whether there is concern by either the individual or others.

Recording the Data

Alcohol use should be adequately described in the client's chart so that changes in drinking patterns can be detected over time. If there is no evidence of alcohol being a problem, that, too, should be noted. Notes in the chart should include sufficient objective detail to provide meaningful data to other clinicians. Avoid one-word descriptions, such as "socially" or "occasionally." If the agency does not have a prescribed format, the following should be included for all clients: drinking pattern, problems related to alcohol use, expression of concern by family or friends, the MAST or CAGE score, and the presence or absence of other drug use. If an agency uses a computerized, electronic record system, the format will identify the information that needs to be included.

Additional information may be desired for the counselor's own records. The worksheet on pages 262–263 is one means of summarizing the data elicited and assembling a list of the behaviors and symptoms relevant for each of the diagnostic criteria. It may look overwhelming, but it's really not that bad. Start on the left side, and check each of the behaviors or symptoms that is reported. That completed, go to the right side, and determine which criteria have positive responses. Then simply count the check marks in the right column.

DSM-5 Diagnostic Worksheet

Client Name ____________________

Possible Symptoms			Diagnostic Criteria	Yes	No
1. ___ not typical "social drinker" ___ drinks more than intended	___ when out, plans easily modified ___ has a few more than others	___ has greater quantity than in the past ___ other________________	1. Drinking more or longer periods than intended	____	____
2. ___ told should cut down ___ believes should cut down	___ guilty about use ___ has periods of abstinence	___ periods of cutting back are stressful ___ other________________	2. Persistent desire or failed efforts to cut down	____	____
3. ___ buys alcohol at odd hours ___ likes having alcohol in home ___ hangovers common	___ pre-partying ___ welcomes hard drinking occasions	___ binge drinking ___ other________________	3. Considerable time spent in obtaining, using, or recovering from drinking	____	____
4. ___ *really* wants a drink ___ imagines how good a drink would feel	___ unable to turn off desire for a drink ___ anxiety at thought of *not* getting a drink	___ other________________	4. Craving	____	____
5. ___ misses school/work ___ arrives late ___ child care neglected	___ drinks at work or school ___ intoxicated at home ___ misses important family celebrations	___ reputation as a 'no show' ___ other________________	5. Failure to meet major role obligations: family, work, social responsibilities	____	____
6. ___ friends/family show concern ___ alcohol-related arrests ___ ultimatums about drinking	___ blackouts cause problems ___ workplace comments on drinking	___ fights/arguments when drinking ___ other________________	6. Use despite recurring social or inter-personal problems caused by drinking	____	____
7. ___ friends lost ___ less involved in casual athletic activities (e.g., shooting hoops) ___ quits team sports	___ drops or reduces involvement in civic, church, or community activities ___ doesn't attend work-related social events ___ drops out of school or college	___ doesn't take advantage of job-related training ___ misses kids' school activities ___ other________________	7. Important social, occupational, recreational activities given up or cut back because of drinking	____	____

Possible Symptoms			Diagnostic Criteria	Yes	No
8. ___ drinking and driving ___ activities requiring attention and judgment to avoid injury	___ care of children ___ going to bars or clubs known for fights ___ ignoring local wisdom about unsafe places	___ use of power tools or heavy equipment ___ other________	8. Recurrent use in situations when drinking is hazardous	___	___
9. ___ told by MD to cut down ___ sleep problems ___ feels stressed	___ feels shame or embarrassment ___ more episodes of anger	___ doesn't follow through on plans ___ other________	9. Drinking despite knowledge of physical or psychological problem caused or exacerbated by alcohol.	___	___
10. ___ consumes up to a case of beer, a bottle of wine, a fifth of liquor	___ need to drink more to "feel high" ___ 4+ drinks per sitting, little effect	___ other________	10. Tolerance. More alcohol to be intoxicated or usual amount less effect	___	___
11. ___ drinks before work ___ night sweats	___ headaches ___ shakes	___ drinks or uses drugs to self-medicate	11. Withdrawal or use of alcohol or medication to avoid withdrawal	___	___
			Total Yes ___ A. ***Level of Alcohol Use Disorder*** (only check 1) Score 0–1 None ___ Score 2–3 ***Mild*** ___ Score 4–5 ***Moderate*** ___ Score 6+ ***Severe*** ___ B. ***Physiological Dependence*** Yes ___ No ___		

Evaluation in a Substance Abuse Treatment Setting

For those working in a designated substance abuse program, the situation is a bit different. For one, there will be an established protocol for the intake and initial assessment. The comments here provide broad guidelines and things to consider. A client may be referred by an agency or another professional, or may be a self-referral. Because of the alcohol/substance abuse treatment designation, in broad terms the reason a client is there has been established. This doesn't mean that it is easier for the client to discuss alcohol and other drug use, or the problems that have accompanied use. Data collection is important, but equally important is establishing a relationship with the client. Remember the maxim, "Ask about the person not just about his or her drinking or other drug use."

Another point to consider is that you do not always have to get all the history immediately. If a client comes to a treatment facility smelling of alcohol, clearly uncomfortable, and somewhat shaky, you need to know immediately how much alcohol has been consumed, over what period, and when the last drink was taken. You also need to know about other physical problems, and what happened on other occasions when drinking was stopped. These questions are necessary to determine whether the client needs immediate attention from a physician. If the client is not in crisis, the evaluation may occur over several outpatient visits.

Initial Interview

The initial interview is intended to get a general picture. As a result of the initial interview, the alcohol clinician will want to be able to answer the following questions:

1. What is the problem the client sees?
2. What does the client want?
3. What brings the client for help now?
4. What is going on in the individual's life—that is, what are the facts of the family situation, social problems, medical problems, alcohol use (how much, for how long), and other drug use?
5. Is there a medical or psychiatric emergency?
6. What are the recommendations at this point?

Certainly, much other information could be elicited. But the answers to the foregoing questions are essential for making decisions about how to proceed. Counseling is an art, not a science. No series of rules can be mechanically followed. However, one guideline is warranted for the initial interview; it is especially apt in situations in which someone is first reaching out for help. *Don't let the interview end without adopting a definite plan for the next step.* Why? People with alcohol or other problems are ambivalent. They approach and back off from help. The concrete plan adopted at the close of the interview may be very simple, nothing more than agreeing to meet a couple more times, so that you can get a better idea of what's going on. Set a definite time. Leaving future meetings up in the air is like waving good-bye.

Even though they are talking to someone with the title of substance abuse therapist, clients who appear on an agency's doorstep aren't looking for the clinician to do his or her "treatment routine" on them. Possibly what they really want is a clean bill of health. Or they may want to figure out why their drinking isn't "working" anymore. The only thing that may be clear is the presence of drinking. Clients are often unaware of its relationship to the problems in their life. As clients paint a picture of what is going on in their lives, the therapist will certainly see things a client is missing or ignoring.

Counselor's view of client's world

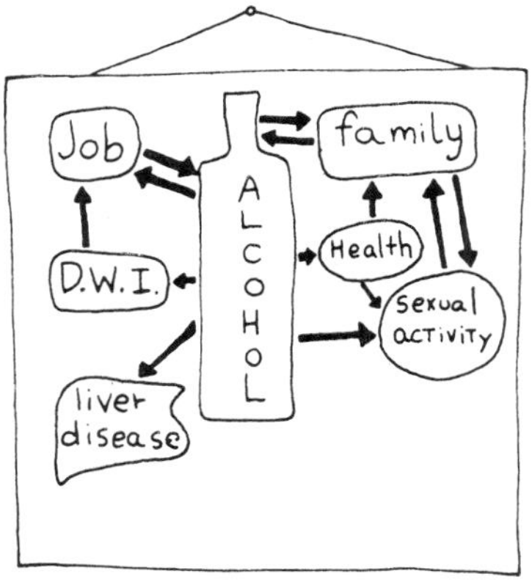

Client's view of world

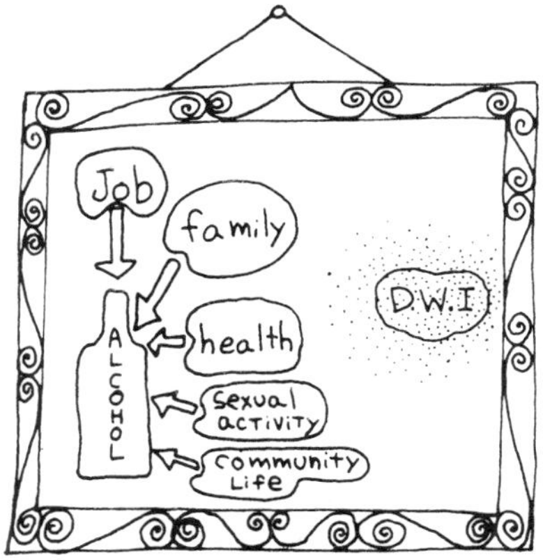

You can see, for example, that the client appears to be alcohol dependent. In your opinion, the client may unquestionably need some intensive treatment. However, at the moment, the client isn't able to use the treatment. To begin, it is necessary to make a few critical connections—that is, get the arrows pointed in the right direction.

Standardized Assessment Tools

The substance abuse field is increasingly using standardized instruments to promote treatment planning as well as to provide a yardstick for measuring treatment effectiveness. The most widely used tool for both of these purposes is the *Addiction Severity Index* (ASI). It was first introduced in the early 1980s and has been widely adopted. The ASI is a semi-structured interview that collects data from seven functional areas: medical, employment, legal, alcohol, other drug use, family-social functioning, and psychological status. For each of these areas there is a score, indicating the severity of the problems in that area. Everyone in the substance use field should acquire skill in using the Addiction Severity Index. Training programs to introduce the ASI to clinicians have been developed, some including videotape vignettes that help you learn to use the index smoothly.

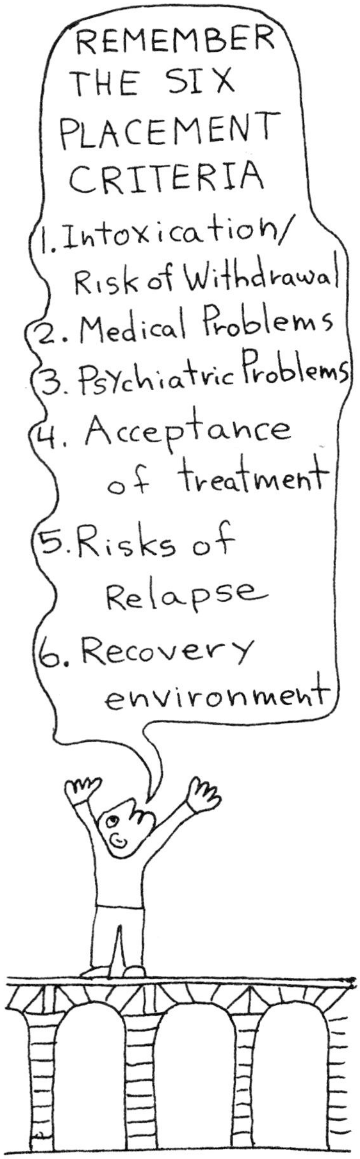
REMEMBER THE SIX PLACEMENT CRITERIA
1. Intoxication/ Risk of Withdrawal
2. Medical Problems
3. Psychiatric Problems
4. Acceptance of treatment
5. Risks of Relapse
6. Recovery environment

Family Involvement

Participation of family in the evaluation is very desirable and becoming the norm. This is so vital that it's hard to imagine why family involvement was not always the case. In some instances family members are the more reliable historians. In any case their perspective on the problem is essential. By including family members, the clinician can assess first-hand their needs and their ability to provide support, as well as engage them as partners in treatment.

Treatment Planning and Treatment Settings

An evaluation may take several sessions. In essence, the goal of the evaluation is to understand the client's situation and, based on that, to develop a plan that will offer the client the optimal chance of acquiring the skills and resources needed to maintain abstinence. The treatment plan may use many of the treatment techniques discussed in Chapter 10.

Criteria for Selecting Treatment Services

What is the appropriate treatment setting? One wants to avoid either under-treatment or over-treatment. The American Society of Addiction Medicine (ASAM) has developed *patient placement criteria* to guide decisions about the appropriate treatment setting. Six factors—or, using ASAM terminology, "dimensions"—have been identified as germane to determining the type of care required. (Note: These criteria are for adults. There is a different set for adolescents.) These dimensions are outlined in the following list, along with some of the key questions to consider to assess each:

- *Dimension 1: Acute intoxication and/or likelihood of withdrawal syndromes.* Is the patient currently intoxicated? Does the level of intoxication represent a potentially life-threatening situation? Is there evidence of physical dependence? Is withdrawal likely? If so, are there factors that may complicate detoxification, such as the presence of other medical problems or a history of serious withdrawal? If withdrawal could be accomplished without medical supervision, are family or friends available to provide support and identify any emerging problems were any to arise?
- *Dimension 2: Biomedical conditions and complications.* Are there any serious medical problems that may complicate treatment or chronic conditions that need to be monitored?
- *Dimension 3: Emotional-behavioral conditions.* Are there apparent psychiatric issues? Are they an expected part of the addictive disorder, or do they appear to be a separate disorder?
- *Dimension 4: Acceptance of need for treatment.* Does the patient recognize the need for treatment? Is the patient indicating a desire for treatment versus resisting treatment? Is the patient feeling pressured or coerced to enter treatment? To what extent is entry into treatment

prompted by internal motivation, and to what degree is it the result of external pressures?

- *Dimension 5: Relapse or likelihood of continued use.* What are the apparent immediate risks if the patient does not enter treatment at this time? What are the longer-term risks associated with continuing to drink or use drugs? What kind of skills and supports does the patient have to stop alcohol or drug use and to maintain abstinence?
- *Dimension 6: Recovery environment.* This refers to the client's social situation. What kind of family and social supports are present? What is the client's employment status, educational status, and financial situation? What community resources are needed and available—vocational counseling, social service agencies, and so on? Is the client confronted by a situation in which family members' or friends' drug or alcohol use would invite continued use or threaten participation in treatment?

Taking into account the results of the assessments of these domains, five levels of patient care have been identified. These specify the kind of care required given the client's status. These levels of care are as follows:

- *Level 0.5: Early intervention.* This level of care was not included in the first version of the guidelines but was added when the criteria were revised. So as not to introduce confusion by renumbering the existing levels, this was made 0.5 (one-half), to place it before Level I.
- *Level I: Outpatient services*
- *Level II: Intensive outpatient and partial hospitalization services*
- *Level III: Inpatient/residential services*
- *Level IV: Medically managed intensive inpatient services*

To help clinicians incorporate the data, ASAM has devised a table, in the form of a grid. For each type or level of care, the relevant factors are reviewed for each domain. In some instances, a single dimension is *the* deciding factor in specifying what kind of care should be provided. For example, if there is apt to be serious withdrawal in a medically ill patient, medically managed intensive inpatient care is indicated. In that circumstance, other domains, such as the recovery environment or degree of family support, are irrelevant. These come into play after the medical status is stabilized. They will then be considered to determine whether the client is discharged to outpatient care or to a residential program. Not only do the criteria state what kind of care is required given the patient's status in each of the six areas, but they also indicate when discharge from a particular level of care is appropriate.

Treatment Planning for Those Previously Treated

A few comments are warranted with respect to treatment planning for the client who was in treatment previously. The clinician needs to consider

prior treatment. What was the treatment? Did the client have a period of stable sobriety? If so, what contributed to its maintenance? To what do the family and the client attribute the resumption of drinking or drug use? These perceptions may be either insightful or way off base. However, they are important beliefs that will need to be either supported or challenged. If a stable sobriety or abstinence was never achieved, what are their hypotheses as to what went wrong? Is there evidence to suggest a psychiatric disorder that has gone undiagnosed? Is there multiple drug use? In light of what is known about matching patients to particular treatments, is a particular treatment approach indicated? Also, is this individual a good candidate for drug therapies?

The client who has been through treatment a number of times and has not achieved abstinence is often termed a "treatment failure." This is unfortunate. This categorization fails to recognize that relapse is not uncommon. This is obviously a very loaded label for the client and the family (if they are still in the client's life), as well as the treatment staff. It is never possible to predict when treatment will be successful. Nonetheless, simply one more exposure to the same treatment is possibly not the best clinical decision. The comparison might be made to someone with an infection that does not respond to a particular drug. Simply increasing the dose probably won't work. One of the things treatment repeaters do have going for them is a knowledge of what doesn't work. To the extent possible, the client should be actively engaged in treatment planning and committing to it—for example, agreeing ahead of time to attend a self-help group, entering a halfway house after inpatient care, and continuing in aftercare. A sense of self-efficacy is an important factor too. This refers to the individual's belief in his or her ability to effect change. Efforts to help clients focus on what they have learned and how this can be useful are important.

Another difficulty commonly encountered with these clients is that they show up in the midst of a serious crisis—for example, a medical illness requiring hospitalization, family turmoil, or legal problems. This can lead to a situation in which the person, willing to comply (or at least not to resist), in essence finds him- or herself entered into a program. Although one may need to respond to the crisis, it is imperative to engage the client as soon as possible in planning treatment after the crisis is stabilized.

If someone comes to an agency with a history of multiple unsuccessful treatment attempts in that agency's program, the question needs to be asked whether a referral to another facility might be indicated. It is important this not be done as "punishment." Instead, it should be a clinical decision based on the possibility that entry into treatment elsewhere may increase the odds in favor of a different outcome. Also, re-entry into the same program may invoke a sense of failure in both client and staff.

TREATMENT OF ALCOHOL INCIDENTS AND ALCOHOL USE DISORDERS

An intelligent man is sometimes forced to be drunk to spend time with his fools.
—ERNEST HEMINGWAY

Within the professional community there has been reasonable consensus about the core elements in the treatment of alcohol dependence. However, there are no universally accepted standards of care for the treatment of other types of alcohol problems. The guidelines provided here can serve as a reasonable approach until such time as there is greater consensus within the alcohol treatment community about treatment goals along the spectrum of alcohol use disorders.

Harm Reduction

Harm reduction efforts have long been suspect in the United States. Harm reduction, having first appeared in the drug abuse field—and including such things as needle exchange—created discomfort among some clinicians. A common complaint about harm reduction efforts has been that they promote a "double standard" or send a "mixed message." These objections are particularly strident when a harm reduction approach is considered for illicit drugs. However, as clinicians become better acquainted with harm reduction techniques, it is increasingly recognized that such concerns are off base.

I read a great article on harm reduction and I've seriously revised my goals. I'm going to cut down from 3 6-packs a day to 2½, from 3 DUIs per year to 2, from 5 blackouts per year to 3, and if I try to kill myself I'll take 50 Tylenol instead of 100.

In a nutshell, what is harm reduction? The late Alan Marlatt, a psychologist at the University of Washington, was one of the first substance abuse clinicians in the United States to espouse harm reduction as a clinical tool. He described it as *compassionate pragmatism*. Harm reduction recognizes the reality that people do and will use alcohol and other drugs. It also acknowledges the autonomy of clients, that treatment goals and approaches can't be jammed down clients' throats. It also appreciates that a client's goals may evolve and change. The person who may bolt from a program that "demands" abstinence may, in time, adopt that goal if gently helped to assess the pros and cons of treatment goals. Harm reduction does not reduce a client to a set of symptoms, straight from a medical textbook, without any unique personal characteristics of interest. In medicine, too, discussing patients as if they were equivalent to their symptoms is less common. To refer to a patient as "the liver in Room 201" will raise eyebrows and cause others to cringe.

Also of significance, as Marlatt pointed out, is that more than 22 million people in the United States have a diagnosis of substance abuse or dependence. Of these only 10% are involved in treatment. He also observed that substance users may avoid seeking help altogether because they do not have lifelong abstinence as a goal. Yet that is the orientation and only treatment goal for 75% of drug and alcohol treatment programs in the United States. Equally important, for the person on the street, abstinence is presumed to be the essence of treatment. Here are the essentials of harm reduction therapy:[1]

- Understanding substance use problems in the context of the whole person in her social environment. This includes seeing individuals as having a unique blend of strengths, needs, and rough spots.
- Rejecting negative labels and stereotypes. Common beliefs are that "alcoholics" or "addicts" are weak, manipulative, criminals, exploitative, lazy, and liars. In addition it is assumed that abuse and dependence are inevitably progressive, permanent, and eventually fatal. While clearly true sometimes, this isn't always the case.
- Engaging clients in treatment is the primary goal. This includes accepting clients' understanding of their problem as the starting point.
- Starting where the patient is, as reflected by the person's motivation, goals, strengths, values, and social situation.
- Not requiring abstinence as a precondition for treatment before really getting to know the individual.
- Developing a therapeutic relationship. This includes collaborating in negotiating goals, strategies, and treatments. The therapist is not "the expert" who goes around issuing decrees.
- Identifying and using the client's strengths to foster change.
- Recognizing that substance use falls on a continuum of harmful consequences. Use can range from relatively safe to imminently life-threatening.
- Redefining success. If abstinence is a goal, having 4 drinks a day is a failure. But if the client was downing 10 drinks a day in the recent past, this is an improvement.

One of the first newspaper reports of an arrest for DWI

Boston, Mass, Oct 27, 1908. A sentence of six months imprisonment for reckless driving of an automobile was imposed today. [the driver] appealed and furnished bail. He claimed in his defense that he had eaten poisoned food while on his way from Providence to Worchester in his machine, and after taking a drink of liquor did not know what happened, until his automobile smashed into a tree yesterday morning. He was also fined $100 for intoxication.

New York Times, 1908

Alcohol Incidents

Alcohol incidents are present when negative consequences result from an individual's drinking—whether an injury, a DWI, or a fight leading to police involvement. However, a clinical evaluation indicates no pattern of recurring problems to indicate abuse or dependence.

The "Thou Shall Nots"

Don't presume that the incident has been enough to teach someone a lesson and guarantee that there will be no future difficulties. It's easy to assume that the embarrassment, guilt, discomfort, or anxiety that resulted was sufficient. It may even seem almost cruel to discuss it further. Others may mistakenly think that the polite, kind thing to do is "just not mention it." Peers of younger people, who may be those most likely to experience an alcohol-related problem, may treat the incident

[1]Drawn from Tatarsky A, Marlatt GA. State of the art in harm reduction psychotherapy: An emerging treatment for substance misuse. *Journal of Clinical Psychology* 662(2):117–122, 2010. (9 refs.)

as a joke. What is required? All those who may have contact—be they emergency room personnel, school counselors, the police, or the family—need to acknowledge the role of alcohol in what occurred. The actual or potential seriousness needs to be made clear. But this doesn't mean delivering lectures, shaming the person, or wagging a finger. If you recall the progression of alcohol problems in the framework set forth by Johnson (described in Chapter 7), the absence of feedback by others in the face of alcohol-related incidents, in part, is what allows a chronic alcohol problem to blossom. A second such incident may be a clear tip-off that a problem is emerging. One DWI "might" just happen, but a second ought to sound a warning signal that the person is continuing in a destructive pattern, despite prior negative consequences.

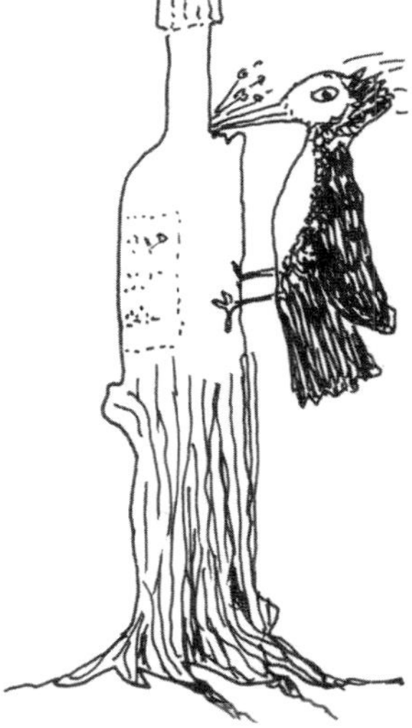

Patient Education

In the face of an incident involving alcohol, basic education is essential. This should not be cursory and superficial, but detailed and personalized. Alcohol has to be explained as a drug to the individual in light of what has occurred. What does BAC mean? How is it that alcohol can induce poor choices? What happens when someone chugs drinks? What are the mechanisms for alcohol-drug interactions? Appreciate that there is a big difference between saying "You should . . ." rather than "If you . . . , it may be more likely that . . ."

The underlying message is, if people are going to use the drug alcohol, they need to be fully informed about it. Don't assume that people, however bright and sophisticated, are sufficiently knowledgeable about alcohol and its actions to figure out what the risks are. Thus, the evaluation should include an inventory of drinking practices, a review of settings in which drinking takes place, behaviors associated with drinking, and family history of alcohol problems or medical conditions that may be adversely influenced by alcohol use. The question to be answered is this: "Are there circumstances that are likely to place the individual at risk?" If so, specific steps should be discussed to address these. What might a person do when faced with the prospect of being a passenger in a car with an intoxicated driver? For the person who takes allergy medications, what are the implications for drinking?

Help the person identify potential problems and think through—ahead of time—what might be done. One finding from the substance abuse prevention research is pertinent. One of the techniques in reducing teenage drug use is literally to have the kids practice how to say no. Adequate information alone isn't enough, nor are exhortations to "just say NO." They need some practice doing it. What is required are tips for applying this knowledge. This is very important, too, in the event that future problems with alcohol use occur. If a problem is handled in the fashion being suggested, later it could be safely assumed that the individual, from that point on, was reasonably informed.

Follow-Up

It is important that an alcohol incident not be treated as a secret. Encourage the client to share the information with family members and close friends. They need to know what's going on in order to be supportive. In an ideal world at least one follow-up visit might be scheduled just to check in with the person, but it is more likely that this will not happen. With a population that spends hours a day updating Facebook, tweeting, texting, using a smartphone, typing on a laptop, and longing for the newest iPad, can it be long before electronic media are used to check in? Actually this has begun. (See Chapter 10.) Because the family physician often is an untapped ally, it can be helpful if the doctor is informed of this event. This does require the client's permission. When a person is at risk for developing an alcohol use disorder, the signs and symptoms that signal a need for further evaluation should be understood by all.

Alcohol is a very necessary article. . . . It makes life bearable to millions of people who could not endure their existence if they were quite sober. It enables Parliament to do things at eleven at night that no sane person would do at eleven in the morning.
—George Bernard Shaw

Cautions on the Use of E-mail Having suggested that a patient's physician be posted on a client's status, a few words about the use of e-mail are warranted. While things are changing, many people tend to be rather casual about using e-mail in clinical settings. That includes the sender and the intended recipient. A colleague when away may have all his or her work e-mail forwarded to a personal account. This invites a number of possible problems. Other family members may use the same account. A g-mail account isn't really an appropriate way to handle confidential, medical information. Also there is the temptation to cc the world: the family doctor, a specialist who's treated the patient, or the clinician who referred the patient. Why not—it's so easy? In addition, it may make you feel that you are being very thorough. But because it's easy doesn't make it a good idea. Ask yourself, do each of them need the level of detail that is included? This is all the more true if you've no idea of the level of protection in place to maintain confidentiality of client information. Always double check that the recipient is the person intended. Directories that include John Smith, John B Smith, Jon Smith as well as a few others invite errors. The notice often found at the end of an e-mail, "If you are not the intended recipient, please . . ." really doesn't do it. Find out what guidelines are in place at the agency where you work.

Alcohol Use Disorders

Unlike an alcohol incident, which is an acute problem, a diagnosis of an alcohol use disorder implies chronicity. Alcohol abuse and alcohol dependence are no longer formal diagnoses, but nonetheless continue to influence our thinking. In this section these terms continue to be used. In large part this is because we still await results of research based on the *DSM-5*. In the *DSM-IV*, alcohol abuse was defined as a pattern of use that is physically hazardous, that interferes with the ability to fill major obligations—at home, work, or school—or that causes major problems with other people. There too was the sense that without intervention dependence could be "just around the corner."

Particular attention has been paid to the presence or absence of physical dependence or loss of control, these being seen as hallmarks of dependence. The issue tended to be viewed as a matter of "is" or "isn't" versus "is becoming." Interestingly, for a substantial portion of clients who use alcohol in a risky fashion, it is not easy to determine whether there is a loss of control because these folks have never made an effort to control their alcohol use! They are often in social situations where almost anything goes. Even if physical dependence is not present, for some, moderating alcohol use may still represent a monumental feat. Consider the college student who is in a heavy-drinking fraternity. Changing drinking patterns will require changes in the student's circle of friends, daily routine, and choices of recreational activities. To achieve this magnitude of change will require that the client be engaged in more than a supportive chat.

Intervening requires that the individual be engaged in a formal treatment effort, involving education, individual counseling, and possibly participation in a group with others in the same situation. Monitoring efforts to moderate alcohol use and avoid future problems is imperative. Through this process, a number of people will be able to moderate their drinking and the associated problems will fade. On the other hand, for some it will become clear that drinking in a non-problematic manner is not possible. For them abstinence and treatment for a serious alcohol use disorder are indicated.

There are two things that will be believed of any man whosoever, and one of them is that he has taken to drink.
—Booth Tarkington

Alcohol Use Disorder, Severe

Treatment of dependence, essentially synonymous with a severe alcohol use disorder, is nothing more (or less) than the interventions designed to short-circuit the disease process and provide an introduction to and support for living alcohol-free. Alcohol dependence is among the leading causes of death in the United States. It needn't be. In comparison with other chronic medical conditions, it is significantly more treatable. Virtually any alcohol-troubled person who seeks assistance and is engaged in rehabilitation efforts has the potential to lead a happy, productive life. The same may not be true for those with cancer, heart disease, or emphysema. The realization that alcohol disorders are treatable has become more widespread. The public efforts of prominent individuals who are recovering have contributed to this acceptance. Both professional treatment programs and AA are discovering that clients today are often younger and in the early or middle stages of the disease when they seek help. It is imperative for the helping professions to keep firmly in mind the hope that surrounds treatment.

Just as people initially become involved with alcohol for a variety of reasons, so is there similar variety in what prompts treatment. For every person who wends his or her way into a serious problem, there is also an exit route. Exiting may be more easily accomplished with professional help. The role of the professional is to serve as a guide, to share knowledge of the terrain, to be a support as the dependent client regains footing, and to provide encouragement. The therapist cannot make the trip for the client, but can only be a companion.

In this discussion, abstinence is presumed to be a central part of recovery from a serious alcohol disorder. Vaillant, when questioned about an alcohol-dependent person's ability to resume social drinking, called on an interesting analogy. He posed the situation of a motorist who decides to remove the spare tire from the trunk of his car. The disastrous consequences of that action may not strike the next day, or the next week, or even within the month, but, most likely, sooner or later . . . In addition, the seriousness of the consequences cannot be predicted. The disaster may be only a flat tire as the car sits in the driveway, or it may be a blowout on a busy freeway during rush hour. It may represent an inconvenience, or it may entail serious consequences. Sooo . . . why get rid of the spare?

Abstinence as a requisite for recovery is viewed as having a solid physiological basis. Tolerance, once established, remains, even in the absence of further alcohol use. Were someone who has been abstinent for a considerable period to resume drinking, the person would very quickly be capable of drinking amounts consistent with the highest levels previously consumed. Drinking isn't resumed with a physiologically clean slate. It may have taken a drinking career of 10 or more years for the alcohol-dependent person to reach consumption levels of a fifth a day. However, with tolerance established, even after a decade of sobriety, literally within days it is possible to be back to the same level. The rapid reinstatement of tolerance is recognized in medical circles as one of the hallmark signs of dependence, or what was formerly described as addiction. For those clients who ask, "Is total abstinence really necessary?" one stock response is "Your body will always remember it has developed dependence, even if you forget."

It is not I who become addicted, it is my body.
—Jean Cocteau

A major study conducted by NIAAA, discussed in more detail later, followed people who met the criteria for alcohol dependence in the past year but did not enter treatment. These people were contacted a year later to ascertain their status. Some had adopted abstinence and some had resumed non-problematic drinking, without meeting any of the criteria for dependence. So to say that ceasing drinking is the only possible response is not universally true. Of course, there is virtually no information on how likely this is for any particular person. But those who entered treatment had more serious symptoms, as well as greater likelihood of using other drugs and having a co-occurring psychiatric problem.

This too is where Valliant's question comes in. Given the nature and frequency of problems that someone has encountered, and the efforts in the past to avoid these, does the client want to set him- or herself up for more? However, if someone isn't convinced, or is unwilling to accept the evidence, what are the options? Seemingly the individual doesn't have much to lose by trying abstinence. Indeed, the attempt can provide the client with some useful information. However, the client may be unconvinced, in effect needing just one more chance. The reality is that you can't prevent someone from trying another approach. So the question is, How can this be used therapeutically? One way is to discuss the "what ifs?" In effect, what constitutes scoring an F on this test? And what will the client do then?

Obstacles to Treatment

If alcohol dependence is so highly treatable, what has been going wrong? Why aren't more people receiving help? The obstacles require examination. Historically, one big handicap has been society's attitude toward alcohol and its use. To describe someone as alcohol dependent feels more like an accusation than a diagnosis. Despite all the public information and education, the notion still remains that talking about someone's drinking is in bad taste, a taboo. It seems too private, none of anyone's business. Drinking is not a topic on which we can assume anyone would welcome another's observations. Finally, many people still view heavy drinking as a moral issue for which willpower is the presumed solution. The person with the alcohol problem believes that as firmly as anyone else and expends considerable energy on trying not to drink so much.

One difficulty is the confusion introduced by the very nature of the symptoms. One common characteristic of alcohol-dependent behavior is the extreme variation, the lack of consistency—sometimes good mood, sometimes foul mood, sometimes hammered, sometimes sober. This inconsistency prompts a host of explanations. Further, this inconsistency allows the individual, family, and friends to hope things will get better if left alone. It permits them to delay seeking assistance. It almost seems to be human nature to want—and wait for—things to improve on their own. Consider for a moment a simple toothache. If the toothache comes and goes, you probably will delay a trip to the dentist. After all, maybe it was something hot you ate. Maybe it was caused by something cold. On the other hand, if the pain is constant, if it is clearly getting worse, if you can remember wicked toothaches in the past, you'll probably call immediately for an emergency appointment with your dentist. The total time you are actually in pain in the latter case may be much less than what you would have put up with in the former example, but you are spurred into action because it doesn't appear that it will improve by itself.

Another obstacle can be the lack of treatment resources or lack of access. This is particularly true for women, adolescents, those living in rural areas, and those living in disadvantaged neighborhoods. Although the reform in health care opens a range of new possibilities, the final verdict isn't in with respect to substance use treatment. At this time, residential care is largely limited to detoxification. However, the length of time patients are in detox may be insufficient to help them understand the need for ongoing treatment and get them engaged in the process of rehabilitation. Often the patient, even though physically present, may be little able to absorb information or engage in much reflective thought, given the disturbances in cognitive function that are part of withdrawal.

Factors in Successful Treatment

Having alluded to failure and some sense of what to avoid, let us proceed to success. The likelihood of success is greatly enhanced if treatment is tailored to the characteristics of the condition being treated. The following factors, always present, should guide both the planning and process of treatment.

Dysfunctional Life Patterns The individual's life has been centered on alcohol or other drugs. If this is not immediately evident, it is because the client has done a better-than-average job of disguising the fact. Thus, the clinician cannot expect a repertoire of healthy behaviors to come automatically. Treatment will help the individual build new behaviors, as well as rediscover behaviors from the past to replace the warped alcohol-induced responses. This at times is what makes intensive treatment, whether inpatient or outpatient, desirable. Besides cutting down the number of easy drinking opportunities, it provides some room to make a new, fresh beginning.

Do you really Think I drink like a fish?

Alcohol or Other Drugs as a Constant Companion Alcohol or other drugs are used to anticipate, get through, and then get over stressful times. These individuals, to their knowledge, do not have effective tools for handling problems. In planning treatment, the clinician should be alert to what may be stressful for a particular client and provide supports. In the process, the therapist can tap skills the client can turn to instead of the bottle or the drug of choice.

Psychological Wounds Any drug, including alcohol, can be both a best friend and a worst enemy. The prospect of life without the drug seems either impossible or so unattractive as not to be worthwhile. The dependent individual feels lost, fragile, vulnerable, and fearful. No matter how well the client appears or how much strength or potential the clinician can see, the client by and large is unable to get beyond those feelings of impotence, nakedness, and nothingness. The therapist cannot lose sight of this.

Physical Dysfunctions Chronic alcohol or other drug use often takes its toll on the body. Even if spared the more obvious physical illnesses, other subtle disturbances of physical functioning are often present. For example, even after ceasing heavy chronic drinking, sleep disturbance can last up to two years. Similarly, a thought impairment sometimes occurs on cessation of drinking. In the initial stage of recovery, difficulty in maintaining attention is commonplace. There will be a diminution of adaptive abilities. During treatment, education about the drug alcohol and its effects can help allay fears. Although what the client is experiencing may be abnormal for that individual, it's not uncommon for the person who is newly abstinent. Reminding clients of this and helping them see that improvement will come with more drug-free time is helpful.

Deterioration in Family Function As described in Chapter 8, the family needs as much help as the family member who is the identified patient. Better outcomes result when the family is engaged in the treatment process, including services that specifically address their needs and are parallel to the addicted member's treatment.

Common Treatment Issues

During treatment, there are issues that come to the fore with some regularity. Some of these initially may seem trivial, such as concerns about organizing one's time. However, for the client these are important. Other tasks may appear to be major undertakings, such as attending to significant interpersonal relationships. Here are some matters that clinicians should anticipate.

Skills of Daily Living One of the tasks in early recovery is to re-master the skills of daily life. It is impossible to overemphasize the energy often required for those newly sober to attend to basic everyday tasks. They look well, feel well, and sound well—but they really aren't there yet. It is almost inconceivable to therapists (or anyone else for that matter) that a person who seems reasonably intelligent, looks fairly healthy, and is over 21 can have problems deciding when to get up in the morning or what to do after getting up! "Should I go to the grocery store before or after my appointment with the dentist?"

Clients may find themselves eager to play catch-up, taking care of all those things that were too long neglected, and then find themselves feeling wholly overwhelmed and immobilized at the prospect. For these reasons, newcomers to twelve-step programs find the slogans "Keep it simple" and "First things first" so helpful. Accordingly, one of the initial tasks of clinicians is to provide simple structure.

Acknowledging Accomplishments Along with providing structure, another clinical task is assisting clients to recognize their accomplishments and to acknowledge the positive steps they are taking. If clients are preoccupied with the things they *ought* to do, they will too easily overlook or discount what they *are* doing.

Adjusting Memories Those in recovery may find their memories require re-examination and a bit of adjustment. Memories laid down in a drugged state often differ significantly from others' recollections. A client remembers her husband as overly critical, on her back about a "few little drinks." You, as the clinician, might remind her that on the occasion in question, she was picked up for driving while impaired with a blood alcohol content of well over 0.10—clearly not just a few drinks. It may not be out of order to point out the possibility that having misperceived the amount she was drinking, she may also have misperceived her husband's behavior, and that sober observations may prove more valid.

Emotional Extremes Those in early recovery may find themselves beset by emotional extremes. These extremes have been compared to the rocks and whirlpools that must be avoided in the recovery voyage. The following extremes may be encountered:

- *Denial versus anxiety*. One of the most prominent features of alcohol dependence is denial. When faced with a massive rejection of reality, the tendency of clinicians new to alcohol treatment is to want to force these clients to face up to the facts and to do it right now. The trouble with this approach is that self-knowledge is often bought at the price of anxiety, and anxiety is a drinking trigger. What to do? Provide lots of support to counteract the initial anxiety caused by the acceptance of the reality of the drinking itself. Then, gradually, keep supporting the small increments in awareness that occur in the sober experience.

  There is a temptation to take denial personally, to think the client is "lying." Remind yourself that the person has adopted this defense as protection against the massive pain that would accompany facing the cold, hard facts. Its function is to deceive the self, not others. It is difficult, but very necessary, to remember that the denial of some particular issue is serving a useful purpose at the time, keeping overwhelming pain and anxiety at bay until more strength is available. A question is whether the denial is still necessary or whether it has become counterproductive, blocking further progress.

I'm trying to learn not to take denial personally.

- *Guilt versus blame*. The presence of denial, the function of which is to protect against emotional pain, is evidence that the behavior is not congruent with the individual's core values and internal image. (The phrase used in psychotherapy for this phenomenon is "ego-dystonic"—that is, being out of harmony with one's real self.) Thus, where there is denial, the issues of guilt and its fraternal twin, self-blame, cannot be far behind. It is clearly desirable to mitigate the degree of both. It is simultaneously necessary to avoid the pitfalls of their opposites, rejecting social values and blaming others. Although excessive guilt leads to the guilt-drinking spiral, some degree of conscience and a sense of responsibility are necessary to function in society. The therapist needs to be clear on this issue. The clinician must be able to point out unnecessary burdensome guilt yet allow honest guilt to be expressed. Dealing with both kinds of guilt appropriately is essential. On the blame issue, help is needed in accepting personal responsibility where necessary. Often it can be helpful to point out that the nature of the condition itself, rather than the individual or others, may be the cause of some of the difficulties, while gently reminding a client that he or she is responsible for what happens now.

- *Compliance versus rebellion.* Two other unhealthy extremes may be seen, particularly early in treatment: compliance and rebellion. In either case, strong confrontation is not a good strategy to choose. It seems simply to produce more of either. The compliant client becomes a model client; the rebellious one says "Aha! I was right. You are all against me," and then drinks. Moderation is again the key. The aim is to help clients acknowledge the presence of their alcohol problem and accept the facts of their situation.
- *Repression versus being awash with feelings.* Emotions, and what to do about them, are another challenge to be faced. Newly sober persons are likely to repress their feelings entirely. They do this to counteract their all-too-uncontrolled expression during the drinking. Respect for this need to repress the emotions should prevail in the initial stages of recovery. But the eventual goal is to assist the client to recognize these emotions and deal with them appropriately. Clients need to learn (or relearn) that feelings need not be repressed altogether or, conversely, wildly acted out. Instead, acknowledging them can lead to better solutions.

These are by no means the only examples of extremes for which the therapist needs to be alert. The therapist needs to be wary when dealing with any extreme behavior or reaction to avoid having the client plunge into its opposite. Some of these problems are continuing ones and may require different tactics at different points in recovery.

Relationships: Dependence and Intimacy Many articles and, indeed, whole books have been written about emotional dependency and alcohol problems. Historically, the alcohol-dependent individual was depicted as an emotionally needy and psychologically dependent person who had resolved conflicts inappropriately by using alcohol. This is a variant of the mistake mentioned earlier, of confusing the symptoms of alcohol dependence with the individual's personality before its onset. Anyone working with alcohol-troubled people is bound to hear this remark at some point: "Sending someone to AA just creates another dependency." The implication is that you are simply moving the dependency from the bottle to AA and ducking the "real" issue. That the dependency shifts from alcohol to AA or to a clinician or to a treatment program for the newcomer is certainly true. This should be viewed as a plus. After all, people in early recovery don't have a wealth of recent useful experience to fall back on.

It is crucial to address issues of dependency throughout treatment. A physician who was one of the pioneers in the alcohol field summed up the whole of treatment as "the task of helping people to become dependent upon people rather than booze." Be alert during treatment of the client's characteristic all-or-none approach. There is the vacillation between stubborn independence and indiscriminate dependence.

During the early months of recovery, the individual may need to poll everyone he or she has ever known to make a decision on some seemingly inconsequential matter. However, when a major decision comes along, no advice is solicited. As individuals discover their need for others, this can lead to discomfort and confusion. On one hand, there is the potentially mistaken notion that turning to others is evidence of weakness, and a voice within says, "I should be able to do this myself." On the other hand, having little recent history of good judgment and little reason to trust one's own capacities—and feeling there may not be much margin for error—there is a tendency to turn to others for almost everything.

One of the long-term tasks of recovery is not only to recognize the need for dependence but also to become more discriminating in handling it. While not explicit, the basic questions a client will be addressing in this process are "Whom should I be dependent on? Whom can I be dependent on? For what? At what cost? For what gain?"

Closely tied to the issue of dependency is that of intimacy. Intimacy is the capacity for closeness, for allowing oneself to be vulnerable to another. One of the tasks in early recovery is becoming reacquainted with oneself while growing emotionally. To be rediscovering oneself while also establishing relationships with others is not an insignificant undertaking. Here, too, left to their own devices, those in early recovery seem to have an uncanny capacity for finding persons with whom they forge destructive relationships. There are always those around who would rescue them and be willing to assume the role of their perpetual caretakers.

Single persons or those in unhappy marriages may find themselves suddenly involved in an affair or an extramarital relationship. There is a reawakening of a host of long dormant feelings. In this sense, it may be like the bloom and intensity of adolescence. A romantic involvement may follow very naturally. Unfortunately, it can lead to disaster if followed with abandon. A counselor needs to be alert to this general possibility, as well as the possibility of being the object of the crush.

One of the features of AA that contributes to recovery is that AA provides a community in which the traditions of the fellowship provide safeguards and limits for all its members as the issues of dependency and intimacy in relationships get sorted out. It is also a setting in which one discovers that people are all interdependent to some degree.

"Why Do I Drink?" This is the recurrent theme of many who enter treatment. Generally it is of little value to focus on this question, even when it seems most pressing to the client. It takes the client off the hook. It looks to the past and to external causes. The more important question addresses the present moment: "What can be done now?"

If there is a time to deal with the "whys," it comes later. Don't misunderstand. Even later, long hours spent studying what went wrong, way back, are rarely helpful. On the other hand, the "whens" can be very instructive. The question *"When do I want a drink?"* points out the areas in which work can be done to prevent relapse. Typically some clues can be discerned from current daily-life events, those occasions when taking a drink is most tempting. Examining such situations can provide clients with a wealth of practical information about themselves for their immediate use and can allow them to develop strategies to address these situations in other ways. Dealing with the present is of vital importance. Newly recovering individuals, who have spent their recent lives in a drugged state, have had less experience than most of us in doing this. The tendency is to analyze the distant past or worry about the future. The only part of life that any of us can hope to handle effectively is the present.

Relapse

Any individual with a chronic condition is subject to relapse. For those with alcohol dependence, relapse means the resumption of drinking. Why does this occur? The reasons are numerous. For the newly sober person, it may boil down to a gross underestimation of the seriousness and severity of the disease—a failure to really come to grips with the difficulty of dealing with it single-handedly. Hence, while perhaps going through the motions of treatment, there may be a lingering notion that although others in recovery may need to do this or that, somehow he or she is exempt. This may show up in very simple ways, such as the failure to address the little things that are likely to make drinking easier than not drinking: "Hell, I've always ridden home in the bar car; after 20 years that's where my friends are." "What would people say if . . . ?" "There's a lot going on in my life; getting to the couples group simply isn't possible on a regular basis." If families and close friends are not well informed about treatment and are not willing to make adjustments, they can unwittingly support and even invite this dangerous behavior.

It is important for clinicians to recognize that a break in sobriety is part of the natural history of alcohol dependence. It is not inevitable, but neither is it rare. What is critical is the response to it. One of the dangers for recovering individuals with more substantial sobriety is their considering alcohol dependence to be a closed chapter. This is the origin of the preference for the adjective "recovering" rather than "recovered." The use of "recovering" serves as a reminder that one is not cured of alcohol dependence.

When considering the treatment of addiction, Mark Twain's comment on stopping smoking—"I've done it many times"—contains a useful insight. The more difficult task for clients is not necessarily stopping the drinking or substance use but maintaining abstinence. In the past the temptation for treatment professionals, when confronted by a client's relapse, was simply to add more and more components to the original treatment regimen, as if engaged in a search for the missing ingredient. The popular view now is that the maintenance of sobriety entails

The crucial question Mr. Jones is whether we are dealing with a lapse, a prelapse, a relapse, or a collapse.

different tasks for the client than those necessary for ceasing initial use and that one can teach skills that will enhance a client's ability to maintain sobriety. Relapse prevention has become a formal part of many treatment centers' standard programs (see Chapter 10).

It is recommended that how a drinking episode is to be handled, were it to occur, be discussed and incorporated into the continuing treatment plan. After all, relapse occurs. It is far better for the client, family, and clinician to openly discuss how it will be handled beforehand. In the midst of the crisis of relapse, neither the family nor the client can do their most creative and clear-headed problem solving. Also, having gotten this taboo subject out in the open, it may be easier for all to attend to the work at hand, rather than worry about "what if." Any plan for responding to a relapse should be very explicit and concrete; for example, the family will contact the therapist and the client will agree to do A, B, and C.

"Relapse" has been used to refer to any drinking. However, it is important to recognize that, while any drinking is a source of concern, there can be significant differences between drinking episodes. Some drinking may be better described as a "break in sobriety," but not relapse in the sense that the individual resumes drinking as if the period of sobriety had never occurred.

Seasoned clinicians often say that the most dangerous thing for a recovering person is a "successful drink." By this, they refer to the recovering individual who has a drink, does not mention it to anyone, and suffers no apparent ill effects. It wasn't such a big deal. A couple of evenings later it isn't a big deal either. Almost inevitably, if this continues, the individual is drinking regularly, is drinking more, and is on the threshold of being reunited with all the problems and consequences of alcohol dependence. The danger, of course, is that the longer the drinking continues the less able the individual is to recognize the need for help or to reach out for it. Someone who had a difficult withdrawal in the past may be terrified of the prospect of stopping again. It may be wise for the counselor to make an agreement with the client that if he or she has a drink—or a near encounter—this has to be discussed.

With some substantial sobriety, re-entering treatment after a relapse may be especially difficult. Among a host of other feelings there is embarrassment, remorse, guilt, and a sense of letting others down. Recognition that alcohol dependence is a chronic disease and that it can involve relapses may ease this. However, refrain from giving the impression that relapse is inevitable. Following a relapse, it is necessary to look closely at what led up to it, what facilitated its occurrence. The client can gain some valuable information about what is critical to maintaining his or her sobriety. This is another reason it is so important to deal with a relapse openly.

Therapists must also be sensitive to the issues that a relapse may evoke in the family. For the moment, the family may be thrown back into functioning just as it did during the old days of active drinking. The old emotions of hurt, anger, righteous indignation, and the attitude of "to hell with it all" may spring up as strongly as before. This is true even if—or especially if—the family's functioning has vastly changed and improved. All of that progress suddenly evaporates. There also may be the old embarrassment, guilt, and wish to pretend it isn't so.

In this discussion, the emphasis has been on the role of the clinician in dealing with relapse, as well as the presence of a formal relapse prevention component within treatment programs, to provide skills to reduce the likelihood of relapse. Some clients have multiple treatment episodes before achieving a stable sobriety. For these individuals, more is required. Recognizing this, one program began providing post-discharge "recovery management checkups." The checkups included an assessment of the client's status, motivational enhancement, and possible resumption of formal treatment, rather than awaiting further deterioration. Two years later, those who received the recovery management checkups were functioning better than those who had not received this service. Indeed, this is consistent with the way chronic diseases are generally handled. Those with hypertension or diabetes see their physicians on a regular basis, and if things are found to be going well, everyone is pleased.

Treatment Outcome

Does treatment work? This is a common question. There are several ways of examining it. One is to compare those who receive treatment to those who do not. Another approach is to see how people's lives change following treatment.

Treatment Versus No Treatment Our usual assumption is that, in the absence of treatment, people will at best continue to have problems or get worse. Is this in fact the case? While clinicians providing treatment need to consider how their patients fare, it is also important to look at the larger picture. A national survey conducted by the NIAAA makes this possible. The survey, based on personal interviews of a sample of Americans 18 and over, generated a wealth of data. Rather than just looking at those who entered treatment, it looked at people who had a diagnosis of alcohol dependence at least a year or more previously. The following questions were then considered: What proportion entered treatment? What kind of treatment? Were there factors that seem to differentiate between those who did or didn't enter treatment? Also, what were the outcomes, with or without treatment?

The first thing of note is that for all those defined as alcohol dependent, based on *DSM-IV* criteria, only a small fraction, around 10%, had ever received any treatment. For those who received treatment, the majority (about two-thirds) participated in both formal treatment and a twelve-step program. Formal treatment included everything from inpatient care to clergy counseling to private physicians to alcohol rehab programs to psychiatric hospitals. Of the remaining one-third who reported having had treatment, 20% had only formal treatment and a little over 10% used only a twelve-step program.

Recovery was defined as the absence of any of the diagnostic criteria during the past year. Abstinence was not a requirement, but those drinking in a high-risk fashion were automatically excluded from the category of recovery. Of those who had received treatment, 46% were in recovery. Among those who had not been in treatment, the number was 33%. Over half (51%) of those who received formal treatment and were involved in self-help were in recovery. The rate of recovery for formal treatment without self-help was much lower (28%). Those who had been in treatment were more likely to report abstinence recovery (29% vs. 7%). Non-abstinence recovery was more common among those who had not received formal treatment.

What were the differences between those who sought treatment and those who did not? Those who received treatment were much more likely to have a history of smoking and other drug use, to have a psychiatric disorder, or to have a close relative who was alcohol dependent. Those who received treatment tended as well to be older, to have been married, to have been divorced, and to have experienced more symptoms of dependence. In addition, those who entered treatment generally consumed twice as much alcohol at the point of their heaviest drinking, 14 versus 7 drinks per day. Clearly those who entered treatment had more serious problems.

For those who entered treatment, the onset of dependence most commonly occurred between the ages of 16 and 25. Given the relatively early age when symptoms of dependence first appear, the question arises as to whether those who enter treatment are on a "fast track" to dependence. The others, even though having symptoms of dependence, were able to moderate the destructive drinking patterns later, as they graduated from college, began jobs, or assumed other responsibilities and found themselves in an environment in which heavy drinking was far less common and acceptable.

Outcomes with Treatment It would be an error to use the above data to make the case that treatment isn't important or necessary. If you are one who considers the odds before you gamble, the best bet for being in recovery is entry into treatment and participation in AA. These people are almost twice as likely to be in recovery as those who do neither. Abstinence-based recovery is four times more common among those who have received treatment. To point out the obvious, encountering problems with alcohol is more likely if you are drinking than if you are not.

The treatment outcomes just described are consistent with those reported by other studies, including those with longer periods of follow-up. Typically, in the vicinity of half of all those treated establish stable recovery. For particular populations and in certain circumstances, even higher rates of abstinence are the rule. For example, there are those who are pushed into treatment and have to participate actively in aftercare to retain their jobs or professional licenses. This includes those in the military, physicians, nurses, and pilots. In these situations, up to 80% are abstinent at one year.

A review published in 2001 investigated the impact of treatment, examining the results from seven large programs drawn from multiple sites. These included outpatient and inpatient programs, programs with a broad spectrum of clients. The study found that a year after entering treatment, 1 in 4 clients had been continuously abstinent. In addition, 1 in 10 were using alcohol moderately and without problems. For the remaining individuals (about two-thirds) alcohol consumption had decreased by 87%, and alcohol problems also decreased by 60%. This data does not tell the number who were abstinent at one year, just those abstinent for the entire year. So someone who had a brief lapse in the beginning of treatment isn't included in this figure, despite the fact that most clinicians would consider the individual to be doing well. Also these figures describe the result of a *single* treatment episode.

In considering these results, the authors make several important points. First, they suggest a comparison to other chronic illnesses. If, one-year later, 98% were alive, of whom one-third were totally symptom-free, and the remaining people improved by an average of 57%–87%, everyone would be thrilled! Frequently, success is measured by a single variable, drinking or not drinking. The authors argue that other factors need to be taken into account. For example, finding a lower rate of problems has a social benefit in addition to any benefits to the individual.

Factors Influencing Treatment Outcome It has long been recognized that among the most significant factors influencing treatment outcome are client characteristics pre-treatment. Those who are still employed, those whose family is intact, those who have social supports—these are the people who do better.

And, yes, the clinician plays a role in determining the effectiveness of treatment. A variety of studies have looked at client outcome in terms of clinician characteristics. Of interest is whether there are differences in rates of clients dropping out of treatment and in rates of abstinence at follow-up. A variety of clinician characteristics have been examined. There are the obvious ones, such as age, education, gender, race and ethnicity, and personal experience with alcohol or other drug abuse. Also examined is how clinicians interact with clients. This includes clinicians' emotional responses to clients, the therapeutic alliance—the bond between client and therapist—personality traits, beliefs about substance use disorders, and, if there is a specified treatment format, how well the clinician sticks to the prescribed protocol, sometimes called "manualized therapies."

Among all of the factors studied, which do *not* predict a client's outcome? It may be surprising, but neither the therapist's age, gender, professional training, nor recovery status are associated with how clients fare. Factors that are related to client outcomes included the following:

- *Clients' evaluation of their counselor's competence.* These evaluations are based on the client's ratings of his or her clinician's helpfulness, self-confidence, knowledge, and organizational skills.

- *Clinicians' emotional responses.* By listening to tapes of therapy sessions, clinicians can be rated by their level of anxiety, anger, and positive or negative connections with patients. As anticipated, the clinicians with the most positive interactions had better outcomes.
- *Adherence to standardized approaches.* Differences between individual therapists fade when they follow procedures set forth in manualized therapies. This suggests that if counselors are trained to use standard approaches and follow these, there is less likelihood that there will be differences in patients' progress depending on the particular counselor they have. But there is an important exception. A recent study found that the best outcomes were found when two conditions were met. First, there was a strong therapeutic alliance. Second, the therapists were *only* moderately compliant with the manualized approach. It did not define what "moderate" compliance meant. The suspicion is that these clinicians relied on their clinical judgment and drew on the manualized approach in a thoughtful, deliberate fashion, rather than blindly following the script, when it didn't seem quite the thing to do.
- *Clinicians' interpersonal style.* Empathy is a factor that has been regularly reported as influencing a client's response to treatment. Among one group of clinicians studied, the least effective therapist in an alcohol program had a 25% rate of successful outcomes. The most effective clinician had a 100% rate. The major factor explaining the difference in outcome was the therapists' degree of empathy. Along with empathy, other related factors identified as important are being genuine, being respectful, and being concrete. Patients of clinicians with a supportive style do better than those whose therapist uses a confrontational approach.
- *Therapeutic alliance.* The therapeutic alliance, the sense of connection between client and therapist, is increasingly recognized as possibly the most important factor in treatment. The client and therapists' ratings to a significant degree predict treatment outcome. This includes retention in treatment as well as the outcome. Importantly, the quality of the therapeutic alliance seemingly can counter the client characteristics that typically don't bode well, such as a lower level of motivation or self-efficacy (the sense that one is capable to effect change). In the presence of a strong therapeutic alliance, treatment outcome is equivalent to those who entered treatment with higher levels of motivation or higher levels of self-efficacy.
- *Length of contact and duration of treatment.* Continuing contact over longer periods of time is associated with better outcomes. These extended contacts may be no more than periodic brief visits or even periodic telephone contacts, but they make a difference. Although alcohol dependence is typically described as a chronic condition, oddly most of the treatment provided fits the model for treating acute illnesses. In an acute illness model, it's get sick, go to the

doctor (or a substance abuse treatment center), receive care, get better, and go on your way. For chronic conditions such as diabetes or hypertension, regular medical appointments for the patient to check in and see how things are going is the rule. As required, adjustments are then made in the treatment regimen. In the absence of such ongoing monitoring, it is all too likely that patients would be seen only at the point of a medical crisis that may require hospitalization. The whole point of ongoing, routine contacts is to avoid these serious events. With substance use problems, lapses in sobriety are part of the terrain. If there is continuing routine contact, it is likely that a number of relapses can be prevented or appropriate interventions can be provided much earlier to stabilize the situation.

Iatrogenic Effects In thinking about the impact of treatment, typically we consider two possibilities. One is that the treatment is effective and that a patient's functioning improves. The other is that the treatment has not had the desired result and that a patient's situation is essentially unchanged. A third possibility is little considered or discussed. It is that as the result of treatment, a client's situation actually deteriorates. The patient is worse off. "Iatrogenic" means "harm that is caused by the treatment itself." This is certainly something that happens in other areas of medicine.

A review of treatment outcome studies suggests that between 10% and 15% of clients are worse off after treatment than before. This is in the vicinity of negative outcomes reported for psychotherapy and counseling. In endeavoring to access the causes, two different types of factors were considered. Some are rooted in *client characteristics* that seem to make them more vulnerable to deterioration, and others flow from program characteristics. Patient factors include the presence of psychiatric illness or co-occurring substance use disorders. Other characteristics are being younger, unmarried, moving more frequently, being unemployed, and lacking a close friend, as well as having poor or antagonistic relationships with family and running with a crowd in which alcohol and drug use is accepted, all of which suggest fewer ties and connections to others and being socially isolated.

Program Factors The nature of the treatment program itself has been examined to see if this is associated in any way with clients' deteriorating status during treatment. Several things stand out. One is engaging clients in ways that are likely to have a high emotional charge, such as the use of confrontation and criticism. An example would be a group session when the counselor says, "Amy, how about sharing with the group what it was like to be raped at the bar where you used to hang out?" A second is a very informal style, with the absence of regular routines, accompanied by a failure to monitor how clients are doing. This is apt to be particularly difficult for those with co-occurring psychiatric illness. A third is when programs inadvertently model the very behavior that they are trying to change. This is most commonly discussed in terms of adolescent therapy groups. Peers can provide far more reinforcement than the leaders ever can. Any adult leader who thinks that his or her influence can counter a group of kids who, through their laughter, cheers, hoots, and howls, encourage one another's escapades, had better think again! The final factor associated with client deterioration is the absence of a professional clinical style, marked by a lack of empathy and respect, and treating clients as incompetent, morally flawed, and having little chance of recovery.

What this boils down to is that to enter treatment is to take a risk. If the circumstances leave the client feeling he or she is without support after trying the only thing left to do, and it isn't working, then what other outcome can be expected? This points out the importance of being aware of a client's particular vulnerabilities and endeavoring to provide care that addresses them. In addition, it is critical that treatment programs systematically review their efforts and not automatically consider treatment failure to be a client's fault.

With this information as a backdrop, Chapter 10 turns to various treatment approaches, from individual counseling to group work to family counseling and self-help.

REFERENCES AND FURTHER READINGS

Screening and Assessment

Aalto M, Alho H, Halme JT, Seppa K. AUDIT and its abbreviated versions in detecting heavy and binge drinking in a general population survey. *Drug and Alcohol Dependence* 103(1/2):25–29, 2009. (23 refs.)

Allen JP, Litten RZ, Fertig JB, Babor T. A review of research on the Alcohol Use Disorders Identification Test (AUDIT). *Alcoholism: Clinical and Experimental Research* 21(4):613–619, 1997.
Note: There are many articles on the use of the AUDIT—in different countries, in different clinical settings, and among different ethnic groups and age groups—as well as alternative versions based on subsets of the questions.

Allen JP, Wilson VB, eds. *Assessing Alcohol Problems. A Guide for Clinicians and Researchers,* 2nd ed. Bethesda, MD: NIAAA, 2003.

Babor TF, Higgins-Biddle JV, Saunder JB, Monteiro MG. *The Alcohol Use Disorders Identification Test. Guidelines for Use in Primary Care. Second Edition.* Geneva, Switzerland: World Health Organization, Department of Mental Health and Substance Dependence, 2001. (44 pages.) Publication number: WHO/MSB/01.6a
Note: This also provides guidance on discussion of the different interventions and addresses consideration on program implementation.

Bien TH, Miller WR, Tonigan JS. Brief interventions for alcohol problems: A review. *Addiction* 88(3):315–336, 1993. (94 refs.)
Note: This is a classic paper that continues to be one of the best descriptions of brief interventions, the range of their use, treatment outcome, and central features.

Bradley KA, DeBenedetti AF, Volk RJ, Williams EC, Frank D, Kivlahan DR. AUDIT-C as a brief screen for alcohol misuse in primary care. *Alcoholism: Clinical and Experimental Research* 31(7):1208–1217, 2007. (50 refs.)

Das SK, Dhanya L, Vasudevan DM. Biomarkers of alcoholism: An updated review (review). *Scandinavian Journal of Clinical & Laboratory Investigation* 68(2):81–92, 2008. (141 refs.)

Ewing JA. Detecting alcoholism, the CAGE questionnaire. *Journal of the American Medical Association* 252(14):1905–1907, 1984.

Koski-Jannes A, Cunningham J, Tolonen K. Self-assessment of drinking on the Internet, 6- and 12-month follow-ups. *Alcohol and Alcoholism* 44(3):301–305, 2009. (26 refs.)

Neumann T, Gentilello LM, Neuner B, Weiss-Gerlach E, Schurmann H, Schroder T, et al. Screening trauma patients with the Alcohol Use Disorders Identification Test and biomarkers of alcohol use. *Alcoholism: Clinical and Experimental Research* 33(6):970–976, 2009. (37 refs.)

Palmer RB. A review of the use of ethyl glucuronide as a marker for ethanol consumption in forensic and clinical medicine. *Seminars in Diagnostic Pathology* 26(1):18–27, 2009. (68 refs.)

Saitz R, Larson MJ, LaBelle C, Richardson J, Samet JH. The case for chronic disease management for addiction. *Journal of Addiction Medicine* 2(2):55–65, 2008. (170 refs.)

Saunders JB, Aasland OG, Babor TF, de la Fuente JR, Grant M. Development of the Alcohol Use Disorders Identification Test (AUDIT): WHO Collaborative Project on Early Detection of Persons with Harmful Alcohol Consumption. II *Addiction* 88(6):791–804, 1993. (53 refs.)

Schwan R, Albuisson E, Malet L, Loiseaux MN, Reynaud M, Schellenberg F, et al. The use of biological laboratory markers in the diagnosis of alcohol misuse: An evidence-based approach. *Drug and Alcohol Dependence* 74(3):272–279, 2004. (412 refs.)

Selzer M. The Michigan Alcoholism Screening Test: The quest for a new diagnostic instrument. *American Journal of Psychiatry* 127(12):1653–1658, 1971.

Skinner HA. The Drug Abuse Screening Test. *Addictive Behavior* 7(4):363–371, 1982.

Motivation

Britt E, Blampied NM, Hudson SM. Motivational interviewing: A review. *Australian Psychologist* 38(3):193–201, 2003. (103 refs.)

Carroll KM, Ball SA, Nich C, Martino S, Frankforter TL, Farentinos C, et al. Motivational interviewing to improve treatment engagement and outcome in individuals seeking treatment for substance abuse: A multisite effectiveness study. *Drug and Alcohol Dependence* 81(3):301–312, 2006. (49 refs.)

Ilgen MA, McKellar J, Moos R, Finney JW. Therapeutic alliance and the relationship between motivation and treatment outcomes in patients with alcohol use disorder. *Journal of Substance Abuse Treatment* 31(2):157–162, 2006. (25 refs.)

Miller WR. *Enhancing Motivation for Change in Substance Abuse Treatment. Treatment Improvement Protocol (TIP) Series 35.* Rockville, MD: Center for Substance Abuse Treatment, 1999. (285 refs.)

Shen Q, McLellan AT, Merrill J. Client's perceived need for treatment and its impact on outcome. *Substance Abuse* 21(3):179–192, 2000. (64 refs.)

Clinical Care

Barry KL. *Brief Interventions and Brief Therapies for Substance Abuse. Treatment Improvement Protocol (TIP) Series 34.* Rockville, MD: Center for Substance Abuse Treatment, 1999. (540 refs.)

Dawson DA, Grant BF, Stinson FS, Chou PS, Huang B, Ruan WJ. Recovery from *DSM–IV* alcohol dependence: United States, 2001–2002. *Addiction* 100(3):281–292, 2005. (45 refs.)

Dawson DA, Grant BF, Stinson FS, Chou PS. Maturing out of alcohol dependence: The impact of transitional life events. *Journal of Studies on Alcohol* 67(2):195–203, 2006. (45 refs.)

Dennis M, Scott CK, Tuck R. An experimental evaluation of recovery management checkups (RMC) for people with chronic substance use disorders (review). *Evaluation and Program Planning* 26(3):339–352, 2003. (105 refs.)

Fleming M, Manwell LB. Brief intervention in primary care settings: A primary treatment method for at-risk, problem, and dependent drinkers. *Alcohol Research & Health* 23(2): 128-137, 1999. (28 refs.)

Maisto SA, Saitz R. Alcohol use disorders: Screening and diagnosis. *American Journal on Addictions* 12(Special):s12–s25, 2003. (71 refs.)

Marlatt GA, Witkiewitz K. Update on harm-reduction policy and intervention research. *Annual Review of Clinical Psychology* 6:591–606, 2010, (88 refs.)

McKay JR, Hiller-Sturmhofel S. Treating alcoholism as a chronic disease: Approaches to long-term continuing care. *Alcohol Research & Health* 33(4):356+, 2011. (79 refs.)

McLellan AT, McKay JR, Forman R, Cacciola J, Kemp J. Reconsidering the evaluation of addiction treatment: From retrospective follow-up to concurrent recovery monitoring (review). *Addiction* 100(4):447–458, 2005. (74 refs.)

Miller WR, Rose GS. Toward a theory of motivational interviewing. *American Psychologist* 64(6):527–537, 2009. (93 refs.)

Miller WR, Walters ST, Bennett ME. How effective is alcoholism treatment in the United States? *Journal of Studies on Alcohol* 62(2):211–220, 2000. (41 refs.)

Moos RH, Moos BS. Rates and predictors of relapse after natural and treated remission from alcohol use disorders. *Addiction* 101(2):212–222, 2006. (58 refs.)

National Institute on Alcohol Abuse and Alcoholism. *Helping Patients with Alcohol Problems: A Health Practitioner's Guide (revised).* Bethesda MD: National Institute on Alcohol Abuse and Alcoholism, 2005. (25 refs.)

O'Connor PG, Schottenfeld RS. Patients with alcohol problems (review). *New England Journal of Medicine* 338(9):592–602, 1998. (112 refs.)

Rhule DM. Take care to do no harm: Harmful interventions for youth problem behavior. *Professional Psychology: Research and Practice* 36(6):618–625, 2005. (45 refs.)

Smedslund G, Berg RC, Hammerstrom KT, Steiro A, Leiknes KA, Dahl HM, et al. Motivational interviewing for substance abuse (review). *Cochrane Database of Systematic Reviews* 5: CD008063, 2011. (292 refs.)

Witkiewitz K, Marlatt G. Relapse prevention for alcohol and drug problems: That was Zen, this is Tao (review). *American Psychologist* 59(4):224–235, 2004. (138 refs.)

to divine the darkest, deepest secrets of the client's mind. We can't help thinking the therapist must have a T-shirt with a big letter "S" underneath the button-down collar. The media do an excellent job of teaching us that things are not always as they seem, yet in real life they often—indeed, usually—are.

Observation

Each day we process vast amounts of information without much thought. Our behavior is almost automatic. Without a clock, we still can make a reasonable estimate of the time. When shopping, we can distinguish the clerk from fellow customers. Sometimes, though, we can't find a person who seems to be the clerk. Consider the clues you use in separating the clerk from the customer. One is dress. Another clue is behavior. The clerks stand behind counters and cash registers, the customers in front. Customers stroll about, casually looking at merchandise; clerks arrange displays. Another clue might be the person's companions. Clerks are usually alone, not hauling their children or browsing with a friend. This is essentially the *good guys wear white hats* principle. Although we have all had some experience with guessing incorrectly, it rarely happens. Before a word of conversation is spoken, our observations provide us with some basic data to guide our interactions.

Presumably you are convinced everyone has observational skills. The only difference between the clinician and others is that the therapist will cultivate this capacity, listen carefully, and attend to how something is said and not merely to what is said. The counselor will ask him- or herself "What is the client's mood? Is the mood appropriate to what is being said? What kinds of shifts take place during the session? What non-verbal clues, or signs, suggest how a client feels?" In a counseling session, from time to time, momentarily tune out the words and take a good look. What do you "see"? Reverse that. Turn off the picture, what do you hear?

One important thing to note is that the questions you ask yourself (or the client) are not "why" questions. They are "what" and "how" questions that attempt to determine what is going on. Strangely enough, in substance abuse treatment, successful outcomes can occur without ever tackling a "why." Ignoring what or how issues may well mean you'll never even get into the ball park.

So what is the importance of observation? It provides data for making hypotheses. A question continually before the therapist is "What's going on with this person?" What you see provides clues. You do not pretend to be a mind reader. Despite occasional lapses, you do not equate observations, or hunches, with ultimate truth. Observation, coupled with a knowledge of alcohol and drugs and their impact on people, suggest where attention might be focused. For example, a client whose coloring is poor and who has a distended abdomen and a number of bruises will alert the counselor to the possibility of serious medical problems. The client may try to explain this

all away by "just having tripped over the phone cord," but the therapist is unlikely to be persuaded.

You do your work by observing, listening, and asking the client (and yourself) questions to gain a picture of the client's situation. The image of a picture being sketched and painted is quite apt to capture the therapeutic process. The space below is the canvas.

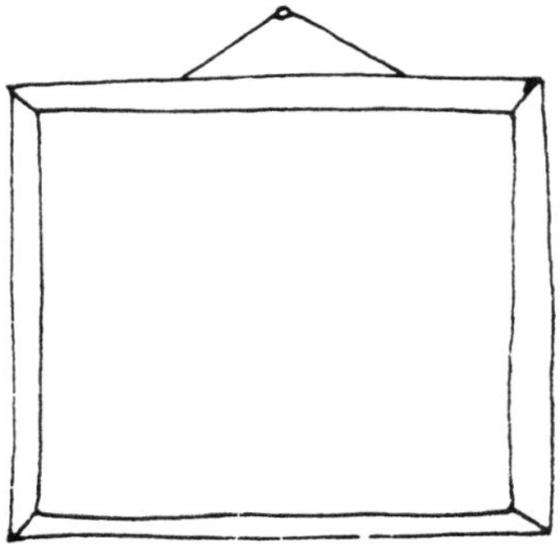

The total area includes everything transpiring in the individual's life. As the client speaks with the therapist, this space is filled in. Now the therapist is getting a picture of the client's situation. Not only do you have the "facts" as the client sees them, but also you can see the accompanying mood and feelings, and thus get a sense of what the world and picture feel like for the client. As this happens, the space gets filled in and begins to look like this:

You have a notion of the various areas that make up the client's life: family, physical health, work, economic situation, community life, and the person's self-image. You also are aware of how substance use may affect these areas. As necessary, you will guide the conversation to ensure that you have a total picture of the client's life. You are aware that if the client is having a problem, it means that the pieces are not fitting together in a way that feels comfortable. Maybe some parts have very rough edges. Maybe one part is exerting undue influence on the others. You must attempt to see the relationship and interaction between the parts.

Feedback

A common feature of a significant alcohol use disorder is a warped perception of reality. The ability of the therapist to provide accurate feedback to the client, giving specific descriptions of behavior and of what the client is doing, can be valuable. The client has lost the ability for self-assessment. It is quite likely that any feedback from family members or friends has been warped as well as laced with threats. In the counseling session, it may go like this: "Well, you say things are going fine. Yet as I look at you, I see you fidgeting in your chair, your voice is quivering, and your eyes are cast down toward the floor. For me, that doesn't go along with someone who's feeling fine." Period. The therapist simply reports the observations. There is no deep interpretation. There is no attempt to ferret out unconscious dynamics. The client is not labeled a "liar." The therapist's willingness and ability to simply describe what is observed is a potent therapeutic tool.

Feedback can also include information that allows clients to see how their drinking compares to that of others (see the Sample Feedback Sheet on page 294).

Education

Clients also need information about alcohol as a drug, about other drugs, and about the process of addiction. Provide facts See Table 10.1. A variety of pamphlets are available from state alcohol agencies, medical societies, the federal alcohol and drug institutes, insurance companies,

TABLE 10.1 Alcohol Consumption Norms, U.S. Adults

Drinks per Week	Cumulative % Men	Women	Total	Drinks per Week	Cumulative % Men	Women	Total
0	29%	41%	35%	9	73%	90%	82%
1	46	68	58	10	75	91	83
2	54	77	66	15	80	94	87
3	57	78	68	20	86	96	91
4	61	82	71	30	92	98	95
5	67	86	77	40	94	99	96
6	68	87	78	50	97	99	98
7	70	89	80	60	97	99	98
8	71	89	81	100	99	99.9	99

Source: Adapted from Roberts LJ, McCrady BS. *Alcohol Problems in Intimate Relationships: Identification and Intervention*. Bethesda, MD: National Institute on Alcohol Abuse and Alcoholism, 2003.

Standard Drink Equivalents

Beer (5% alcohol)
12-oz. can = 1 standard drink
16-oz. can = 1.3
22-oz. can = 2

Malt Beer (7% alcohol)
12-oz. bottle = 1.5 standard drinks
16-oz. bottle = 2
22-oz. bottle = 2.5

Wine (12% alcohol)
'usual' bottle (25 oz.) = 5 standard drinks

Liquor (80 proof/40% alcohol)
shot (1.5 oz.) = 1 standard drink
pint (16 oz.) = 11
fifth (25 oz.) = 17

Note: A standard drink contains 14 grams of pure alcohol, about 1.2 tablespoons

Sample Feedback Sheet

1. Based on the information I obtained during the assessment, I calculated the number of standard drinks you consumed each day and have summarized three important indicators of your drinking:

   Total number of standard drinks per week __________

   Average number of standard drinks per drinking day __________

   Highest consumption in a day __________

2. When we look at everyone who drinks in the United States, you have been drinking more than approximately __________ percent of the population of women/men in the country.

3. I also estimated your highest and average blood alcohol level (BAL) in the past month. Your BAL is based on how many standard drinks you consume, the length of time over which you drink that much, whether you are a man or a woman, and how much you weigh. So,

   Your average peak BAL in an average week was __________

   Your estimated average BAL in an average week was __________

   This is a measure of how intoxicated you typically become. Throughout the United States the legal intoxication limit is 0.08.

4. You have experienced negative consequences from drinking. Here are some of the most important:

   ____________________ ____________________

   ____________________ ____________________

   ____________________ ____________________

   ____________________ ____________________

   ____________________ ____________________

   ____________________ ____________________

Source: Roberts LJ, McCrady BS. *Alcohol Problems in Intimate Relationships: Identification and Intervention*. Bethesda, MD: National Institute on Alcohol Abuse and Alcoholism, 2003.

and self-help groups. People like to understand what is happening to them. This is becoming increasingly apparent in all areas of medicine. Some institutions have hired professional staff as patient educators. Patient education sessions on diabetes, heart disease, cancer, and care of newborns are commonplace.

Education about alcohol and other drug problems is important for two reasons. Information is a necessary tool to displace old ideas and form new ones. Information also is necessary to help a client handle feelings of guilt and low self-esteem. The chances are pretty good that the client's behavior has looked downright crazy—and not just to others. The fact that he or she has been denying a problem confirms this. There is no need to deny something unless it is so painful and so inconsistent with a person's values that it cannot be tolerated.

Learning the facts can be a big relief. Suddenly, things make a bit more sense. In part, successful recovery is related to a client's understanding of an alcohol use disorder as a medical condition. The individual is relieved of the need to hash around in the past to uncover causes, to figure out what went wrong. There is no need to dwell on the pattern of harmful, senseless behavior; it becomes merely a symptom, one that the individual isn't doomed to re-experience if efforts are made to maintain sobriety and to live drug-free.

Self-Disclosure

At this juncture it seems appropriate to add some cautionary words about the technique of *self-disclosure.* If seen as a counseling technique, it requires the same thoughtful evaluation of its usefulness as does any other counseling tool. It is important to recognize that self-disclosure is not limited to sharing information about one's own problems with alcohol. Self-disclosure in counseling or therapy refers not only to sharing the facts of one's life but can also include speaking of one's feelings and values. This approach is in contrast to the style of the early psychoanalysts, who never revealed personal information nor in any way presented themselves as individuals to clients. Counselors are self-disclosing when they express empathy or when they note that the client's concerns are those with which other clients have also struggled.

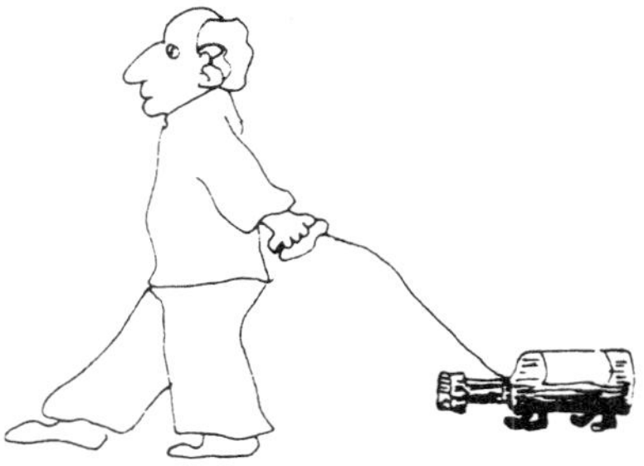

Self-disclosure has special meaning in the alcohol and substance abuse field. The clinician may be in recovery and may be involved in AA, where self-disclosure is encouraged. But professional counseling is a different story. In the early stages of the client's treatment or in the assessment process, it may seem natural to allay some of the client's nervousness or resistance with the news that a clinician, too, has "been there," knows how he or she feels, and furthermore can testify to the possibility of a successful recovery. What seems natural may, however, be totally inappropriate as well as counter-therapeutic. It is just as likely that the client may become suspicious and wonder whether you are guilty of seeing substance use problems everywhere. Therapists need to remember that their professionalism is important to the client. That professionalism is reassuring. The patient in an intensive cardiac care unit is interested in the physician's medical assessment, what the recommended next steps are, and the possible outcome. The patient is not interested in hearing the physician's personal story of her own heart attack.

This is not to imply that self-disclosure should never be used or that it is ineffective. But the technique too often is used as a matter of course without proper thought given to the possible ramifications.

When is self-disclosure therapeutic? There may be times when the client is overwhelmed by a sense of worthlessness, isolation, and pervasive hopelessness. In such circumstances, self-disclosure may be useful. It may provide a desperately needed human connection, helping relieve feelings of utter despair, and may spark just a glimmer of hope and a recognition that maybe, just maybe, things can be different. In a group setting, the goal would be to have other group members reach out. The general rule is that self-disclosure is *not* the rule, but the exception.

Possible Mis-steps

The therapist expects the client to assume responsibility for his or her actions. You do not accept clients' views of themselves as either pawns of fate or helpless victims. An ironic twist is present. You make it clear that you see the client as an individual who is accountable for making choices. Simultaneously you are aware that those dependent on alcohol, when drinking, abdicate control to a drug. A client's assuming personal responsibility is important in dealing with the mundane everyday life events. The therapist needs to be alert to not taking on tasks that clients can do for themselves.

Those with alcohol dependence are sometimes described as being manipulative or as being con artists. These kinds of descriptions may capture how *others* interpret the client's behavior, whether family or friends. But if that is how the counselor feels, there is a big problem. These are angry terms, and being angry is not a helpful stance. Clients may be representing the reality as they experience it. Equally important, they are far more interested in deceiving themselves than in deceiving you. You flatter yourself if you take it personally. To the extent clients deliberately misrepresent events, it's not unlike young children whistling in the dark to chase away monsters. And, yes, this can be magical thinking too. Just as a woman hopes a lump in her breast is benign, so, too, the problem drinker wants to find a way to make the craziness of his or her life go away while avoiding the label "alcohol-dependent" and what it implies.

I've heard him renounce wine a hundred times a day, but then it has been between as many glasses.
—Douglas Jerrold

Faced with a resistant client, some clinicians may try, although perhaps not consciously, to seduce the client into treatment. Possibly aware of prior treatment failures and sensitive to the alcohol-dependent client's distrust, apprehension, and isolation from others, these counselors are *very* understanding; they avoid anything that might cause the individual discomfort. They may try all manner of things—expressing compassion and understanding to win the client over. But no therapeutic relationship, no matter how good, can ever compete with the alcohol-dependent person's primary relationship—the one with alcohol. The therapist cannot be available on demand, on call 24 hours a day, or be guaranteed to make the person feel better, dissolve fears, and wash away concerns. If the counselor isn't aware of this, the client certainly is.

Problem Identification and Problem Solving

In therapy, problem identification and problem solving constitute a recurring process. No matter what the problem, two kinds of forces are at work: some factors help perpetuate the problem; other factors encourage change. These can be sketched out in a diagram. Suppose the problem is "I don't like my job." The line going across represents the current situation. The arrow pointing upward stands for the factors that ease or lighten the problem. The arrow pointing downward represents the factors aggravating the problem.

If the individual's goal is to be more confident at work, this can happen in several ways. The positive forces can be strengthened or others added, or attempts can be made to diminish the negative ones. A similar sketch might be made for drinking. This kind of chart can help you decide what factors might be tackled to disturb the present equilibrium.

Left to his or her own devices, the client could avoid discomfort for years. The clinician's prompting such discomfort to surface may be the most helpful thing that can be done. The fact that the client is sitting in front of you indicates that something has jiggled the equilibrium. This is significant. Take advantage of it. Jiggle the equilibrium further. In the illustration above, taking away the family denial or coworker cover-up would blow the whole act.

The Therapeutic Relationship

Whole volumes have been written on the nature and components of the therapeutic relationship. This book cannot even begin to summarize what has been set forth. Some of the attributes of the helping relationship were alluded to at the beginning of Chapter 9. The therapist is a guide. The therapist cannot do the work and can only bring the client's attention to work that needs to be done. The therapist may provide some "how to" suggestions but will proportionally provide more support as the client does the actual work.

You're Just doing this because you get paid for it.
You're right. But is that any reason for you to disregard what I have to say?

One important thing to keep in mind is that whatever the unique nature of the client–counselor relationship, it is *not* a friendship. It is not based on liking one another. Although it may initially sound demeaning, in fact, the therapist is most effective with clients when the relationship *is* just part of the job. The value of the therapist to the client is paradoxically that the counselor is *not* a friend; the therapist does not need to exact anything from the client. Indeed, if that sneaks into the equation, then the potential value of the therapist is accordingly diminished. Beyond being someone with a knowledge of alcohol and drugs and their effects, the therapist is someone who can be trusted to be candid and open and who strives for objectivity. He or she can be counted on to say what needs to be said and trusted to hear the difficult things a client says without scolding or judging.

With the client–counselor relationship outside the realm of friendship, several potentially difficult situations for the clinician are more easily avoided. Some predictably difficult situations nonetheless will still arise when the client becomes angry, threatens to drop out of counseling, claims you are taking someone else's side, or insists that you don't care or understand. It's very tempting and so easy to experience such situations as personally (and undeservedly) directed toward you. So first take a deep breath. Second, remind yourself it isn't you who's being attacked. This is not an occasion for either reminding the client of "everything you've done" for him or her, or just how experienced you are, even if the client doesn't appreciate it. As quietly and calmly as possible, discuss what's going on, which includes acknowledging the feelings the client is experiencing. Resist trying to make the patient feel better or talk him or her out of those feelings. Expression of negative emotion should be anticipated. Indeed, if it never occurs, it may mean that the therapist is sending signals that it is not permitted. Allowing negative feelings to be expressed doesn't mean being a sponge for everything, or not setting limits, or not stating a different perspective if you have one. One of the most important lessons the client may need to learn during treatment is that negative emotions can be expressed and the world doesn't fall apart.

The other side of the "emotions coin" can present a different trap. It is difficult not to respond to "You are so wonderful," "You are the only person who really understands," or "You are the only person I can say this to." Beyond the danger of inflating the therapist's ego, there is the danger for the client that all the power is invested in the therapist. In the process of treatment, it is important that the client experience, and take credit for, the therapeutic work that is being done. So, for example, in responding to "You are the only person who really understands," a gentle reminder of the client's share of the work is appropriate.

Evidence-based Treatment

Increasingly, agencies are drawing on treatment approaches that have been studied to demonstrate their effectiveness. These are thus termed "evidence-based." Each approach has a manual setting forth guidelines for conducting the treatment (and so are also called "manual-guided"). To replicate the research results in the larger treatment community requires that clinicians follow the treatment in the format found to be effective. This is commonly referred to as fidelity. If a therapy includes group discussions with set themes, it isn't OK to substitute your favorite topic. This would be a bit like your doctor, instead of prescribing a drug widely accepted for your medical condition, substituting a drug that is the same shape, the same size, and the same color, ignoring the differences that lie within. Both training and supervision are important in adopting a manual-guided approach.

In the alcohol field, the first manual-guided therapies emerged from an NIAAA research program, Project MATCH, which studied the effectiveness of different treatment approaches. The manuals represent a tool box, everything that you would need, from specifying the number of sessions and the focus and goals for each, down to the finest details such as how much time to spend on a particular activity within an hour-long session. The specific treatment approaches examined in Project MATCH are discussed later in the chapter.

Case Management and Administrative Tasks

An inevitable and necessary part of a therapist's work is administrative—writing notes in charts, contacting agencies or counselors for previous records, dictating discharge summaries, and contacting the referring party or others to whom a client will be referred. This is often perceived as a pain in the neck and the portion of one's job most likely to get short shrift. However, attending to these details is an important part of good clinical care. Treatment is rarely a solo act, but instead is a team effort. How effectively the team functions often depends on the clinical personnel who orchestrate and coordinate the various efforts.

The client's chart or medical record is an important vehicle for communicating information. This is especially true in a residential facility, with multiple staff working different shifts. There are often questions as to what should and shouldn't go in a chart. Although the concern for confidentiality should not be minimized, you should realize that it can be a red herring. In thinking about what to include in the chart, ask yourself, "What do others need to know to respond therapeutically?" Rarely does this have anything to do with "deep, dark secrets." More often it has to do with the everyday nuts and bolts—worrying over a date for discharge, preoccupation with an upcoming court appearance, or a strained family meeting. The chart is not the place for verbatim accounts of individual sessions. But notation of any general themes, plus any modification of treatment plans, is needed. It also falls to the client's primary therapist to make presentations at team meetings. On such occasions preliminary thought helps. What information do you wish to convey? Do you have special questions you'd like to pose to others?

Beyond orchestrating the activities of an agency treatment team, it falls to the case manager to be a liaison, and often an advocate, with external groups, such as employers, vocational counselors, social service workers, or the courts. Many clients have considerable need for these supportive services. In such situations, you must *always* have the client's permission before acting. Also, it is important not to do for clients what they can do for themselves. Generally, it is more therapeutic to be encouraging, to help the client think through what needs to be done, rather than doing it yourself in the interest of efficiency. This can be very time-consuming, but this work should never be dismissed as less important than other aspects of treatment.

GROUP WORK

Being part of a group can promote some powerful therapeutic work. Some consider group therapy as an essential part of any treatment. One researcher noted that "in the group setting, the 'cost' of character traits is illuminated." A pioneer in group therapy, Irving Yalom, in commenting on groups for alcohol problems, observed that there is power in groups—"the power to counter prevailing pressures to drink, to provide support, to offer role models, and to harness the power of peer pressure."

Group as Therapy

Membership in a group can provide individuals with important information about themselves. Each of us has characteristics and traits that are visible to others but that are unknown to us, as illustrated by the following diagram, which is called a Johari Window.

	Unknown to Self	Known to Self
Known to Others	• reactions of others • mannerisms	• age • height • gender
Unknown to Others	• unconscious	• feelings • family history

Through the group process, the size of the area "unknown" to the individual becomes smaller.

In a group setting, an individual's character traits can be illuminated for the individual. This news isn't always welcome. What the individual sees, or realizes others can see, may create discomfort. It can evoke shame and guilt. In the past, such feelings have been drowned in alcohol, so surviving these feelings without drinking can in itself be a powerful experience. In a group, where the members feel safe, new behaviors can be explored. Historically the phrase *tiger land* was used by alcohol-dependent persons to describe the world. That's a fairly telling phrase. Through group treatment, ideally the client will re-experience the world differently. The whole thing need not be a jungle—other people can be a source of safety and strength.

Another bonus from a group experience is derived from individuals' opportunities to become reacquainted with themselves—not their drinking selves, but the selves who have been submerged by the drinking. A group provides its members with a chance to learn who they are, their capabilities, and their impact on and importance to others. Interacting candidly and openly provides an opportunity to adjust and correct their mental picture of themselves. They get feedback. Group treatment of those in a similar situation reduces the sense of isolation. Those with active alcohol dependence tend to view themselves very negatively and have an overwhelming sense of shame over their behavior. Coming together with others proves that one is not uniquely awful.

When you ask one friend to dine,
Give him your best wine!
When you ask two,
The second best will do!
—LONGFELLOW

Mere confession is not therapeutic, however. Something else must happen for healing to occur. Just as absolution occurs in the context of a church, in a group that functions therapeutically the members act as priests to one another. Members hear one another's confession and say, in essence, "You are forgiven; go and sin no more." That is to say, group members can see one another apart from the behavior that accompanies the drinking. They can also often see a potential that is unknown to the individual. This is readily verified in our own lives. Solutions to other people's problems are so obvious, but not so solutions to our own. Members of the group can see that people need not be destined to continue their old behaviors. Old "sins" need not be repeated. Thus, members instill hope in one another.

Interestingly enough, one often finds that people are more gentle with others than they are with themselves. In this regard, the group experience has a beneficial boomerang effect. In the process of being kind to and understanding of others, the members are in turn forced to accord themselves similar treatment.

Groups for Aversion Therapy

In the former Soviet Union, aversion therapy using disulfiram was far and away the most widely used treatment for alcohol dependence. Furthermore, treatment was conducted in a group setting, with up to 50 patients. An exchange program of those in the addiction field gratefully missed seeing the actual treatment. However, we were shown where the treatment takes place. Cots, each with a starched white sheet, were perfectly aligned in five rows. Beside each cot were two items. One was an empty glass, awaiting the vodka; the other was an empty gallon pail, which each patient was responsible for emptying into a vat as he exited the room.

The ways in which a group experience takes place can vary widely. Group therapy comes in many styles and can occur in many contexts. Being a resident in a halfway house puts one in a group, just as does participation in outpatient group therapy. Group therapy means the use of any group experience to promote change in the members. Under the direction of a skilled leader, the power of the group process is harnessed for therapeutic purposes.

Types of Groups

In contemplating group work for those with alcohol or other drug problems, the leader needs to consider several basic issues. What is the purpose of the group? What are the goals for the individual members? Where will the group meet? How often? What will the rules be? The first question is the key; the purpose of the group must be clear in the leader's mind. There are many possible legitimate purposes. Experience shows that not all can be met simultaneously. It is far better to have different types of groups available, with members participating in several, than to lump everything into one group and accomplish nothing. Among the most common types of groups are psychoeducational, support, problem-solving, and activity groups.

Psychoeducational Groups These are among the most common type of group experience within alcohol treatment programs. Typically these groups are organized around a lecture, film, or presentation by a specialist in the substance abuse field, followed by a group discussion. Topics may include alcohol's effects on the body, symptoms of addiction, and the role of drinking in generating problems with others. In the discussion, members are encouraged to explore their own personal experience to identify the way the information presented applies personally to them. There is a complex relationship among knowledge, feelings, and behavior. Facts and information do not stop serious problematic drinking, but they can be important in breaking down denial, which protects the drinking or drug use. Information provides an invaluable framework for understanding what has happened and what treatment is about. In a psychoeducational group, clients acquire some cognitive tools to participate more successfully in their own treatment.

Sunday night I go to a parent support group Monday night I have my NA meeting Tuesday night is my Overeaters Anonymous meeting Wednesday night is my children of alcoholics group Thursday there's a single mother's support group Friday is my emotions anonymous group And Saturday nights I stay home and watch television. I love Saturday nights.

Support Groups A primary purpose of these groups is to promote self-awareness. The group function is to support abstinence and to identify the characteristic ways in which people sabotage themselves. In these groups, the emphasis is on the here and now. The participants are expected to deal with feelings as well as facts. The goal is not for members to achieve an intellectual understanding of why things have occurred or are occurring. Rather, the goal is to have members discover how they feel and learn how feelings are translated into behavior. Then they can choose how they would prefer to behave and try it on for size.

Problem-Solving Groups These groups tackle specific problems or stressful areas in the group members' lives. Discussion, role play, or a combination may be used. For example, how to say no to an offer to have a beer, how to handle an upcoming job interview, or how to get through the upcoming holidays can be an appropriate subject. The goals are to develop an awareness of potential stressful situations, to identify the old, habitual response patterns, to recognize how these patterns have created problems, and then to try new behaviors. These sessions provide practice for more effective coping behaviors.

That is a treacherous friend against whom you must always be on your guard. Such a friend is wine.
—C. N. Bovee

Activity Groups These groups are least likely to resemble the stereotype of group therapy. In these groups an activity or a project is undertaken, such as planning for a picnic. The emphasis is on more than the apparent task. The task is also a sample of real life. It provides an arena for the clients to identify areas of strength and weakness in interpersonal relationships. Here, too, is a safe place to practice new behaviors.

Group Functions

No matter what the nature of the group, a number of functions will have to be performed. For any group to work effectively, there are essential tasks, regardless of the goal. Initially the leader may have to be primarily responsible for filling these roles, in effect providing the members with a model. The key functions include:

- *Initiating:* suggesting ideas for the group to consider, getting the ball rolling
- *Elaborating or clarifying:* clearing up confusion, giving examples, expanding on the contributions of group members
- *Summarizing:* pulling together loose ends, restating ideas
- *Facilitating:* encouraging others' participation by asking questions, showing interest
- *Expressing group feelings:* recognizing moods and relationships within the group
- *Giving feedback:* sharing responses to what is happening in the group
- *Seeking feedback:* asking for others' responses about what you, a member, are doing

As time goes on, the leader teaches the group members to share the responsibility for these functions. These represent skills, too, that have application to a variety of interactions and settings.

Different types of group therapy can be useful at different times during recovery. During the course of a residential stay or intensive outpatient treatment, a client might well attend a psychoeducational group, a relapse prevention group, and a couples group. In addition, the person could attend outside self-help meetings. In this example, the client would be participating in four types of groups. On discharge the person may return for a weekly group and with a spouse continue in a couples group. None of these group experiences is intended to substitute for self-help groups. The most effective treatment plans will prescribe self-help plus substance abuse–related group therapy. Being treated for diabetes clearly wouldn't exclude one from AA or group therapy. They have different purposes. So, too, self-help involvement (AA) doesn't preclude formal group therapy. These groups have different purposes and are neither in conflict with one another nor substitutes for one another.

I would never belong to a group that would accept someone like me as a member.
—GROUCHO MARX

WORKING WITH FAMILIES

Historically, and for too long, family members of those being treated for alcohol problems were shortchanged. In the past, if a family member contacted a treatment agency about an alcohol problem in the family, what was likely to happen? He or she may have been told to have the troubled person call on his or her own behalf or may have heard a sympathetic "Yes, it's awful" and be told to call Al-Anon. It was unusual that family members were invited to come in as clients in their own right. If the alcohol-troubled person was seeking help, the family may have been called in by a clinician to provide background information and was then subsequently ignored. Any further attention family members received came only if a problem arose or if the counselor believed

In every dispute between parent and child, both cannot be right, but they may be, and usually are, both wrong. It is this situation which gives family life its peculiar hysterical charm.
—ISAAC ROSENFELD

family members weren't being supportive. Treatment efforts did not routinely address problems the family faced and their own, independent need for treatment. Although this may still occur, very few in the field would claim that the approach is adequate. By definition, treatment that ignores the family has come to be seen as second-rate care. Although larger treatment programs now have staff whose specialty is family work, every clinician needs to have some basic understanding of the issues that confront families, of whatever composition, and needs to develop basic skills for working with family members.

Too often, any family that doesn't match the traditional mold is invisible. The importance of the extended family as a support system can go unrecognized. The special problems of single mothers, the difficulties that confront blended families, or tension in intergenerational households can be overlooked. The poet Robert Frost defined "home" as the place where, "when you have to go there, they have to take you in." Calling on this definition, "family" includes all those in the "home." This is the model to keep in mind.

Clinicians may find that more of their clients are, in fact, family members. The most important thing the clinician needs to keep in mind is that the client being treated is the person in the office—in this case, the family member. The big temptation is to try treating the alcohol-dependent family member in absentia. This may be a family member's wish, too, but the immediate task is assisting family to recognize the impact the drinking has upon them.

Family Members Touched by Another's Alcohol Use

Domestic Violence

In any initial contact with a family member, one topic needs to be addressed: the presence or fear of domestic violence. This is emphasized in a guide for marriage and family therapists published by the NIAAA. It points out that violence is more common when alcohol and other drug use, particularly stimulants, is present. An immediate priority is ensuring the safety of family members. Attention needs to be paid to specific aggressive behaviors, such as throwing objects, grabbing a family member roughly, slapping, pushing, hitting, or threatening harm, as well as the presence of guns or weapons in the home. If violence is present, steps to ensure the safety of the family are essential. Work with family members may be needed to convey the fact that violence is *not* normal. A related problem is controlling behavior, such as demanding to know where a spouse is going, with whom, and exactly what time a partner will return. If none of these behaviors has actually happened, does either partner worry that it's just a matter of time? Beyond the harms from an incident of violence are other less appreciated consequences. A woman who has been a victim of domestic violence has a five times greater risk of social problems or depression, a two times greater risk of lacerations, and a three times greater risk of being diagnosed with a sexually transmitted disease.

Although the assumption may be that women are the victims and men are the perpetrators, the actual picture is a bit more complicated. Women, too, are perpetrators of domestic violence. Also of note is that substance abuse by *either* party increases the risk of domestic violence. It may be natural to think in terms of the perpetrator and the victim, commonly the spouse or partner, but there are other victims—children in the family or household.

In the substance abuse field two approaches are widely used and have been successful in addressing domestic violence: Community Reinforcement and Family Training, known as CRAFT, and Behavioral Couples Therapy, discussed below. Research consistently shows that these techniques lead to reduced drinking and greater satisfaction with the marriage (or other relationship). Of significance here is that they are more successful than individual therapy in reducing domestic violence.

What does the family system need? One important need is for education about the nature of alcohol and other drugs in the picture and the problems that evolve with chronic heavy use and dependence, as well as the impact on the family. Family members also need to sort out their feelings and realistically come to grips with the true dimensions of the problem and the toll being exacted from them. Accompanying all this is the need to examine their options, given what is facing them. Most important, the family members require support to live their own lives despite the alcohol problem in their midst. Paradoxically, when family members pay attention to themselves, the actual chances of short-circuiting the process of addiction are enhanced.

Those with dependence do not display identical symptoms or have the same degree of chronicity and level of impairment; the same is true of family members. In the assessment process, many of the same questions the therapist asks in dealing with the individual should be considered. What has caused the family member to seek help now? What is the family's understanding of the problem? What supports do family members have? What is the economic, social, and family situation like? What coping devices do they use? What are their fears? What do they want from the clinician? Where the clinician goes in working with the family will depend on the answers to these questions. Treatment plans for family members might include individual counseling, support groups, and services from other community agencies.

In this discussion, "families" and "family members" are used interchangeably. Contact with a helping person is made by an individual, not a group. This individual may be speaking on the family's behalf, but not always. Efforts to include the other members of the family may have been unsuccessful. The family member making the contact may be experiencing a sense of isolation, feeling that he or she is carrying the burden alone and that no one else in the family cares. Sometimes the family member reaching out may fear that other family members will disapprove of his or her spilling the beans. With support from the counselor, the individual family member may later elect to involve other members.

Family Interventions

The initial focus has to be working with the family members on their problems. Nonetheless, the indisputable fact is that the dependence is the central problem and the family would like to see the alcohol-dependent member receive help. It is important to recognize that, ineffective as their efforts may have been, much of a family's energy has gone into "helping." As a result of education and assistance sorting out their own situation, family members become better equipped to act effectively in relation to the alcohol-dependent person.

All happy families are alike; each unhappy family is unhappy in its own way.
—Leo Tolstoy

In the early 1970s, the alcohol field believed that treatment could not be successful unless the alcohol-dependent individual hit bottom and requested help. Then a new clinical technique came along—the intervention. It was introduced by the Johnson Institute in Minneapolis to work with family and significant others to help move the alcohol-dependent member into treatment. This intervention technique and its supporting rationale were first described in *I'll Quit Tomorrow*.

The introduction of the intervention dramatically changed the treatment field. It forced clinicians and the recovering community—all concerned about those with alcohol dependence—to rethink some of the earlier assumptions about what was necessary for successful outcomes. Family and clinicians no longer had to sit around helplessly, waiting and praying for some magic insight to prompt the request for help. Whether described as "raising the bottom," "early intervention," or "confrontation," clinicians gained a therapeutic tool that could help move troubled people into care.

With the introduction of the intervention technique, it become apparent, too, that successful treatment can occur in a number of situations in which the initial entry into treatment might be considered "coercive." Among the programs with the best treatment outcomes are those in which the stakes are quite clear, such as employee assistance programs (EPAs), programs conducted by the military, court-mandated treatment, or treatment offered to professionals where there is close monitoring post-treatment, such as occurs with airline pilots, physicians, and nurses. In such instances, even though the individual may not be highly motivated to enter treatment, entry into care is clearly preferable to the alternative. Recall the earlier diagram depicting forces promoting or opposing change. External circumstances often play a role in sparking change. With hindsight it is now apparent that the early treatment field did not appreciate how common ambivalence is.

A dysfunctional family is any family with more than one person in it.
—Mary Karr

The Johnson-Style Intervention

The Johnson intervention involves a meeting of family, and possibly other concerned persons, and the affected individual, conducted under the direction of a trained clinician. Each family member, after one or more preparatory sessions, in turn, reading from a prepared list, presents a specific incident related to drinking that has caused concern. Each person also expresses the hope that the affected individual will enter treatment. The term "intervention" is sometimes used to describe something different than what Johnson had in mind. In these instances it might be best described as an aggressive, even hostile form of "tough love," with the emphasis on the tough, not the love. The term is associated with boot camp–style drug programs, or Synanon therapeutic communities. As originally used, "confrontation" did *not* equal attack. Confrontation essentially means a face-to-face meeting. The way Johnson saw it, the person with alcohol dependence truly does not see the situation as others do, hence the need for others to convey their sense of the reality. Johnson also realized that, for the alcohol-dependent person to hear anything, family members needed to speak with genuine concern for his or her welfare. To use the language of motivation and stages of change, the intervention can be seen as moving someone from pre-contemplation to determination. By force-feeding the painful facts, the intervention process cuts a wedge in the denial and can be viewed as precipitating a crisis.

It should be clear that conducting an intervention is not something one does on the spur of the moment. It is not something to be done impromptu, just because the family is together. Nor is it something you describe to the family and suggest they do on their own, after supper some evening.

The effectiveness of an intervention depends on the participants' ability to convey a genuine concern and describe incidents that have caused concern in an objective, straightforward manner. The participants also need to discuss what treatment options are to be presented and the actions they will take if the person does not seek help. Is the grown daughter ready to say she will not be comfortable allowing Mom to babysit for the grandchildren anymore? Are the parents ready to make continuation of college tuition payments contingent on their son's entering treatment? A successful intervention also requires that the therapist be supportive to all present, equally, and deflect the affected member's anxiety and fears, which may surface as anger. As might be surmised, family members may require several sessions to sort through and lay aside their anger and pain in order to experience the concern they hope to convey.

Other Interventions to Promote Treatment

The formal Johnson-style intervention described above is less common today. However, other approaches have been developed to promote entry into treatment. An interesting modification of the Johnson-style intervention is a manual-guided approach known as *ARISE,* which stands for **A R**elational **I**ntervention **S**equence for **E**ngagement. Although having some features in common with the Johnson approach, there are some significant differences. For one, the ARISE approach begins at the point a family member first contacts an agency. It uses both telephone contacts and meetings with family members and includes a modified Johnson-type intervention. ARISE uses a stepped approach and begins with the least demanding option. However, the therapist does not act as the "facilitator" in a family meeting. Rather, the therapist acts as a consultant and coach to the concerned family members, who then meet with the alcohol-drug-involved member.

SAC
I drink
when I have
occasion, and
sometimes
when I have
no occasion.
-Cervantes

The *Community Reinforcement and Family Training* (CRAFT) approach was developed as a brief therapy for the family member who lives with a treatment-resistant partner. This includes assisting the concerned family member to encourage sobriety by reinforcing abstinence, while also allowing the drinking member to experience the negative consequences that result from drinking. Whatever protective actions were being used become a no-no. The partners' communications are a main target. The focus in working with the concerned family member is on being brief rather than rambling, being positive rather than critical, and being specific and clear rather than wandering all over the place. Additionally, a goal in working with family members is to help them to label their feelings, to express understanding for the other's perspective, to accept partial responsibility when appropriate, and to extend offers to help. The CRAFT approach is sensitive to the presence or risk of domestic violence and provides actions that can be taken to defuse any escalating arguments or conflicts. The family member also agrees to participate in the drinking partner's treatment if the partner agrees to enter treatment.

Family Involvement in Alcohol Treatment

Everyone thinks of changing the world, but no one thinks of changing himself.
—Leo Tolstoy

By whatever process and at whatever point individuals enter formal treatment, involvement of the family is critical. The family should be included as early as possible. During the course of treatment the clinician will be working with the family on a number of occasions. Early on there may be a family meeting to help gather information that will help in guiding treatment. Later there may be formal family therapy sessions, as well as meetings to discuss aftercare or a particular family concern.

Initial Contacts

Family involvement is far from being elective or a nice touch; it is vital to securing an adequate database for treatment planning as well as laying the groundwork for the treatment that lies ahead. If alcohol dependence is clearly evident—having progressed to the stage at which it could be diagnosed by the parking lot attendant—the family may be the only reliable source of even the most basic information. In addition, the client's judgment may be so severely impaired that others need to make key decisions about care.

A family meeting is virtually a routine part of the admission process. At this time, the clinician will seek the family members' views of what is happening. In initial contacts with the family, the clinician doesn't go into a family therapy routine. It is data-collecting time. For a newly involved clinician, the task is to understand how the family sees and deals with the substance abuse in its midst. In meetings with multiple family members, be prepared to provide the structure and lay the ground rules. For example, explain that people often see things differently and that you want to know from each of those present what has been going on. If need be, reassure them that everyone gets equal time, but there will be no interruptions by other family members.

During the individual's treatment, the family may become involved in regularly scheduled family counseling sessions or participate in a special group for family members or couples, in addition to possible self-help efforts. Some residential treatment programs are beginning to hold family weekends. In these programs the families of patients are in residence and participate in a specially structured program of education, group discussion, and family counseling.

Many substance abuse clinicians find themselves with clients referred from other sources. In these instances, the individual and his or her family are new patients. Even the best crafted letter of referral or prior telephone contact only imparts basic information. This information needs to be supplemented by working with the patient and family to develop treatment plans. Even more important, although a medical record or chart can be used to pass a client from one clinician to another, therapists cannot pass along or be the recipient of another's therapeutic relationship. Each clinician needs to establish this for him- or herself.

General Guidelines

The following are some general suggestions for working with families, whatever the reason for the family meeting. It is also helpful to remind yourself that you are the most objective person present. Therefore, it is up to you to attend to and guide the process. Keep the following guidelines in mind:

- *Concentrate on the interaction, not on the content.* Don't become the referee in a family digression.
- *Teach family members how to check things out.* People tend to guess at other people's meanings and motivations. They then respond as though the guesses were accurate. This causes all kinds of confusion and misunderstandings and can lead to mutual recriminations. Put a stop to these mind-reading games and point out what is going on.

- *Be alert to scapegoating.* A common human tendency is to lay blame on someone else. This is true whatever the problem. The family with an alcohol-dependent person tends to blame the drinker for all the family's troubles. Other family members thereby can neatly avoid any responsibility for their own actions. Help them see this as a no-no.
- *Stress acceptance of each person's right to his or her own feelings.* Any good therapy stresses this. One reason is that good feelings get blocked by unexpressed bad feelings. One of the tasks of a therapist is to bring out the family's strengths. The focus has been on the problems for so long that the family has lost sight of the good points.
- *Be alert to avoidance transactions.* Avoidance transactions include such things as digressing to Christmas three years ago in the midst of a heated discussion of Dad's drinking. Point this out to the family and get them back on track. In a similar vein, "speak the unspeakable" to bring out in the open the obvious, but unmentioned, facts.
- *Guide the family into problem-solving techniques as options.* Make functional and dysfunctional patterns clear to the family. Help them begin to use the healthy techniques in therapy, with an eye to teaching the family to use the techniques on their own.

Couples and Family Therapies

Beyond the general tips for working with families just given, there are also a number of evidence-based[1] family therapies. Several are described here.

Behavioral Couples Therapy Designed for married couples or partners who've been living together for at least a year, Behavioral Couples Therapy was initially developed as an alternative to family therapies derived from a "family disease" model. It assumes that the couple's, as well as the family's, interactions reinforce drinking. Accordingly, the effort is to break the cycle of behaviors that provide positive reinforcement for drinking while building alternative behaviors that support abstinence. It focuses on identifying discrete behaviors that can be altered. Behavioral Couples Therapy can be used by itself as the central treatment approach or in conjunction with other treatment options. Typically it includes 15 to 20 sessions over a five- to six-month period. It has been adapted for use in a group setting, which generally involves three or four couples.

There are several exclusion criteria. One is the presence of domestic violence that has required medical attention in the past year. Another is that both parties are not committed to maintaining the relationship. The final one is the presence of serious cognitive impairments or psychiatric disorders that would make it difficult to process new information or

[1]Evidence-based treatments are discussed in more detail later (see pages 333–334). Basically these are treatments known to be effective, based on carefully designed clinical research studies.

practice new skills. When both partners have an alcohol or drug problem, especially if they think that their "best" times together are when they are both drinking or using, the situation is especially challenging.

Behavioral Couples Therapy includes a "recovery contract" with features that both partners agree to, with designated ways of reinforcing them. This is coupled with homework and behavioral assignments designed to increase positive feelings as well as improve communications and support. The recovery contract also includes the stipulation that both partners agree not to discuss past drinking or drug use or possible future use. Such discussions are to be saved for the therapy session. Prescription of medications to help achieve and maintain abstinence is included in the contract.

Community Reinforcement and Family Training (CRAFT) Although CRAFT has been discussed as a therapy to promote entry into treatment, and to address domestic violence, it is used in couples therapy as well. In these instances there are from 6 to 10 sessions, with sufficient intervals in between to allow practicing new skills. Being sensitive to the presence or risk of domestic violence, it emphasizes actions that can be taken to defuse any escalating arguments or conflicts.

Multi-dimensional Family Therapy This is a comprehensive family therapy for outpatient or partial hospitalization (day treatment) programs for substance-abusing adolescents, as well as adolescents with co-occurring substance use and psychiatric problems. It involves individual sessions with the teen, sessions just for the parents, as well as sessions for the family unit—the adolescent, parents and siblings, and other family members. There are specific assessment and treatment modules. For the adolescents the therapy is conducted in 12 to 16 weekly sessions or twice-weekly sessions of between an hour and an hour and a half. The goal is to provide more effective coping and problem-solving skills. In work with parents, attention is directed to defining family roles, establishing boundaries, enhancing parenting skills, establishing parental authority, and structuring family routines. There is also an interest in the parents' general functioning, beyond the parenting role. Also considered are the relationships with external groups such as the school.

A family is a unit composed not only of children but of men, women, an occasional animal, and the common cold.
—Ogden Nash

Family Support Network This outpatient treatment program for adolescents, originally a therapy incorporated into the Cannabis Youth Treatment Program, is directed to parents and the substance-using teen. For the adolescent there are 2 individual motivational enhancement sessions, followed by a series of 10 group therapy sessions, with the goal of imparting skills for refusing cannabis, problem solving, coping with cravings, building a better social network, managing depression, planning for emergencies, getting involved in activities unrelated to prior drug use, developing anger awareness and management, and coping with relapse. The family component is directed to

I began drinking alcohol at the age of thirteen and gave it up in my fifty-sixth year; it was like going straight from puberty to a midlife crisis.
—George Montgomery

establishing a support system for parents, encouraging family communication, and enhancing parenting skills. The family component includes six every-other-week multiple education meetings, covering topics such as adolescent development and the recovery process. Staffing requires a parent educator, a family therapist, a case manager, and a mental health therapist.

Family Issues

There are some reasonably predictable concerns among family members. Equally important are issues that the counselor recognizes as potentially problematic, thus warranting attention.

Problems Prompted by Entering Treatment

The client's entry into treatment may create immediate problems for a family. The spouse may be concerned about even more unpaid bills, problems of child care, loss of a job, or fears of yet more broken promises. In the face of these immediate concerns, the possibility of long-range benefits may offer little consolation. Attention must be paid to helping the family deal with the details of everyday living. Just as the alcohol-troubled individual in early treatment requires a lot of structure and guidance, so does the family.

Another issue for the family is to develop realistic expectations for treatment. On the one hand, they may think everything will be rosy, that their troubles are over. On the other hand, they may be exceedingly pessimistic. Commonly they will bounce back and forth between these two extremes. In addition, family members at some point will need to have the affected member "really hear," at an emotional level, what it has been like for them. If there has been an intervention, it stressed objective, factual recounting of events and sympathy for the affected member. Although a presentation of the family's emotional reality is not appropriate initially, it must take place at some point.

If the family is to be reintegrated into a functioning unit, it is going to require that both "sides" gain some appreciation of what things have been like for the other. How this occurs will vary. Within a series of family sessions there may be a session specifically devoted to feelings, led by a skilled family therapist. These can be highly charged, "tell-it-like-it-is" cathartic sessions. To conduct such a meeting successfully requires considerable skill on the therapist's part, as well as a structure that provides a lot of support for all family members. For the individual, the pain, remorse, and shame of his or her drinking or drug use can be devastating. For the family, witnessing the remorse and shame can, in turn, invoke guilt and remorse in themselves. These responses must be addressed; a session cannot be stopped with the participants left in those emotional states. More commonly this material will be dealt with over time, in smaller doses. The important thing to remember is that this is an essential task. If family issues are not addressed, the family is left with a closet full of secrets that will haunt them, come between them, and interfere with their regaining a healthy new balance.[2]

Pregnancy

You may recall some of the particular family problems that relate to pregnancy and the presence of young children in the family. A few specific words should be said about the issue of pregnancy. Contraceptive counseling is important. Pregnancy is not a cure for alcohol problems in either partner. In a couple in which one or both partners are actively drinking, they should be advised to make provisions for the prevention of pregnancy until abstinence is well established. It is important to remember that birth control methods adequate for a sober couple may be inadequate when alcohol is present. Methods that require planning or delay of gratification are likely to fail. Rhythm, foam, diaphragms, and prophylactics are not wise choices if one partner is drinking. A woman who is actively drinking is not advised to use the pill. So the alternatives are few. In the event of an unwanted pregnancy, the possibilities of placement or abortion are difficult options that may need to be considered. At the moment, no amniotic fluid assay test exists that can establish the presence of fetal alcohol syndrome.

Should pregnancy occur and a decision be made to have the baby, intensive intervention is ever so important. If the expectant mother is drinking heavily, every effort should be made to initiate treatment. Even if abstinence is not achieved, a reduction in drinking is important. Regular prenatal care is also important. If alcohol is present, counseling and support for both parents is essential to help them handle the stresses that accompany any pregnancy. If the prospective father is alcohol-dependent, it is important to provide additional supports for the mother.

Pregnancy is a stress for any couple or family system. Contraceptive counseling should be considered for persons in early recovery. At that point, the family unit is busy coping with sobriety and establishing a solid recovery.

Children in the Family

A few words on behalf of older children in the family are in order. In many cases, children's problems are related to their parents' stress. Children may easily become weapons in parental battles. With alcohol or other drug dependence, children may think their behavior is causing the problem. A child needs to be told that this is not the case. In instances when the clinician knows that physical or significant emotional abuse has occurred, child welfare authorities must be notified. In working with the family, the clinician may bring additional parenting figures into the

Brothers and sisters should never be in the same family.
—CHARLES M. SCHULZ

[2]For the person involved in AA, dealing with the effects of drinking on the family may be part of taking an inventory (Step 4) and making amends (Step 8), discussed later in this chapter.

picture. Going to a nursery school or day care center may help the child from a chaotic home.

It cannot be over-emphasized that children must not be forgotten or left out of treatment. Sometimes parents consider a child too young to understand or feel that their children need to be protected. This can easily lead to the child feeling even more isolated, vulnerable, and frightened. Children in family sessions tend to define an appropriate level of participation for themselves. Sometimes the presence of children is problematic for adults, not because they won't understand but because of their uncanny ability to see things exactly as they are. For example, without self-consciousness, the child may say what the rest are only hinting at. Or the child may ask the most provocative questions. Along the same line, while a parent is actively drinking or using, the inevitable concerns and questions of the child must be addressed. Children may not need all the details, but the pretense effected by adults that everything is OK is destructive.

It is also critically important to address children's concerns when the parent or caregiver has a serious medical problem, such as HIV/AIDS or hepatitis C, that may require hospital stays and that has a poor prognosis. Often information is withheld from the children in the interest of preventing worry. What is going on does not escape them. The big questions for them are, "What will become of me?" and "Who will take care of me?" Making arrangements for children may be very hard for a sick parent; discussing them with a child can be even harder. Research suggests that the absence of this information and the uncertainty are far more troubling than the facts, including an open discussion of plans for custody.

When initially involving the family, consider the children's needs in building a treatment plan. Many child welfare agencies and mental health centers conduct group sessions for children around issues of concern to children, such as a death in the family, divorce, or substance abuse problems. Usually these groups are set up for children of roughly the same age and run for a set period, such as six weeks. The goal is to provide basic information, support, and the chance to express feelings the child is uncomfortable with or cannot bring up at home. The subliminal message of such groups is that the parents' problems are not the child's fault, and talking about it is OK. In family sessions, you can make the message clear too. You can provide time for children to ask questions and provide them with pamphlets that may be helpful.

Occasionally a child may seem to be doing well. The child may reject efforts by others to be involved in discussion groups or treatment efforts. If the parent who is alcohol-dependent is actively drinking, the child's resistance may be part of the child's way of coping. Seeing a therapist may be perceived by the child as taking sides, or it may force the child to look at things he or she is trying to pretend are not there.

Resistance to joining family meetings during early sobriety also may surface for many of the same reasons. Listen to the child's objections for clues to his or her concerns. Do not to let a child's assertion that "everything is fine" pass without some additional questioning.

On the other hand, beware of embarking on a witch hunt to ferret out the unspoken problems of children. Children cannot be expected to function as adults. Although they can be amazingly insightful at times, don't presume that those who do not voice "the unspeakable" are therefore hiding something. It is important to appreciate the defenses that children have. Defenses are never to be viewed as good or bad but as fostering or impeding functioning. Children's defenses may be quite important for them. In dealing with children, if you have any questions or are concerned you are in danger of getting in over your head, seek advice from a child therapist.

Recovery and the Family

A common mistake when working with the family is to assume that, once the drinking stops, things will get better, yet with abstinence the family again faces a crisis and time of transition. Such crises can lead to growth and positive changes, but not automatically or inevitably. For the family who has lived with alcohol, there has been a long period of storing up anger and of mistrust and miscommunication. This may have been the children's only experience of family life. At times, children who previously were well behaved may begin acting out when a parent becomes sober. Children may feel that earlier their parent loved alcohol more than them and that now their parent loves AA more. The parent may have stopped drinking, but in the children's eyes they're still in second place.

Recovering families have a number of tasks to accomplish before they return to healthy functioning. They must strengthen generational boundaries. They must resume age- and sex-appropriate roles in the family. They must learn to communicate in direct and forthright ways with one another. They must learn to trust one another. And finally they must learn to express both anger and love appropriately. It might be expected, if one considers the family as a unit, that there are stages or patterns of a family's recovery. This has not yet been adequately studied. No one has developed a "valley chart" that plots family disintegration and recovery.

It has long been a part of the folk wisdom that the alcohol-dependent individual's psychological and emotional growth ceases when the heavy drinking begins. So with sobriety, the individual is going to have to face some issues that the drinking once prevented attending to. In respect to the family system, what may be the equivalent of this Rip Van Winkle experience? Imagine a family in which the father is the alcohol-dependent individual, whose heavy drinking occurred during his children's adolescence and whose recovery begins just as the children are entering adulthood. If he was basically "out of it" during their teenage years, they grew up as best they could, with little fathering from him. When he "comes to," they are no longer children. In effect, he was deprived of an important chunk of family life. There may be regrets. There may be unrealistic expectations on the father's part about his present relationship with his children. There may be inappropriate attempts by him to regain the missing time. Depending on the situation, his therapist may need to help him grieve, to help him recognize that his expectations are not in keeping with his children's adult status. Then the task is to help him find other outlets to experience a parenting role as well as re-establish and enjoy appropriate contacts with his children.

Separation or Divorce

It is hard for anyone who is dissatisfied not to blame some one else, and especially the person nearest of all to him, for the ground of his dissatisfaction.
—Leo Tolstoy

George Vaillant, in examining the course of recovery in men, found that in recovery men "often acquired a new love object." Among several other factors, one that frequently differentiated those who recovered from those who did not was having found someone to love and be loved by. This "someone" generally had not been part of his life during the period before treatment. This cannot be used as evidence that family treatment is not warranted because there has been too much water over the dam, too much pain, and too much guilt. The men in Vaillant's study were those who were treated before the time in which family involvement in treatment was commonplace. So who knows what the outcome would have been had attention been directed to family members as well. Early intervention was not the rule then. His sample consisted of men with long-established cases of dependence. However, it does remind us of an important fact. Not all families will come through alcohol treatment intact. Divorce is common in our society. Even if alcohol-troubled individuals had a divorce rate similar to those without alcohol problems, it would still mean a substantial number of divorces during or following treatment. Therefore, for some families, the work of family counseling will be to achieve a separation with the least pain possible and in the least destructive manner for both partners and their children.

For those who enter treatment divorced or estranged from their families, the task during the early treatment phase will be to help them make it without family support. Their family members may have come to the conclusion long ago that cutting off contact was necessary for their own welfare. Even if contacted at the point of treatment, they may refuse to have anything to do with the client and his or her treatment. However, with many months or years of sobriety, the issue of broken family ties may emerge. Recovering individuals may desire a restoration of family contacts and have the emotional and personal stability to attempt it, be it with parents, siblings, or their own children. If the client remains in follow-up treatment at this point, the clinician ought to be alert to his or her attempts to reconcile with the family. If the individual is successful, it will still involve stress; very likely many old wounds will be opened. If the attempt is unsuccessful, the therapist will be able to provide support and help the person adjust to the reality of those unfulfilled hopes.

After some success, when things seem to be going better, there may be some resistance to continuing therapy. In some instances, the family fears a setback and wants to stop while they're ahead. Simply point this out. They can try for something better or terminate. In other instances, the family, simply put, may need some time out, an opportunity to consolidate the work that has been done. In either case, leave the door open. Whatever the reasons for termination, the family may return in the future if it hits rough spots.

Self-Help for Families

Long before alcohol dependence was widely accepted as a medical concern, much less one that also affects family members, the wives of the early members of AA recognized disturbances in their own behavior. They also encountered problems living with their spouses, whether sober or still drinking. They saw that a structured program based on self-knowledge, reparation of wrongs, and growth in a supportive group helped promote an individual's recovery, and asked, "Why shouldn't there be a similar program for spouses and other family members?" In its earliest days, what became Al-Anon was known instead as the AA Auxiliary. Al-Anon was officially formed and became a separate program in its own right in the mid-1950s.

Al-Anon

The basic premise of Al-Anon is that the only person anyone can change or control is oneself. Members are encouraged to explore and adopt patterns of living that can nourish them, regardless of the actions of the alcohol-dependent individual in their lives. As does AA, Al-Anon conducts a triennial survey of its membership. The last survey, conducted in 2012, provides a snapshot of Al-Anon membership. In the United States members are predominantly white (91%), female (86%), and over the age of 35 (95%). The average age is 56. The majority live in cities and are married. The average length of affiliation is 12 years. Close to half (46%) credit a professional for the referral to Al-Anon. About three-quarters were receiving some kind of treatment prior to involvement; in addition, 42% sought professional help after joining Al-Anon. In both instances, this was judged to be important or very important to them.

Using the twelve steps of AA as a starting point, the program also incorporated the AA slogans and meeting formats. The major difference is that Al-Anon members' powerlessness is over others' alcohol use, rather than over their own alcohol use. Effort is directed at gaining an understanding of their habitual responses to situations that are dysfunctional and evoke pain and at substituting behaviors that will promote health and well-being. They are encouraged to accept responsibility for themselves by abandoning their focus on the alcohol-dependent family member as "the problem." Instead, they can see by shared example the effectiveness of changing themselves, of "detaching with love" from the drinker.

Many people have found support and hope in the Al-Anon program. Although no promises are made that this will have an impact on a still-drinking family member, there are examples of such an outcome. At the very least, when others stop the behaviors that tend to perpetuate the drinking, not only will their own lives be better, but the odds are this will also have an impact on the drinking member.

Alateen

Alateen is an outgrowth of Al-Anon set up for teenagers with an alcohol-dependent parent. Their issues are different from those of adult family members, especially the partner. Accordingly, they need a group specifically to deal with their problems. Under the sponsorship of an adult Al-Anon or AA member, they are taught to deal with their problems in much the same manner as in the other programs.

Even with current widespread information about alcohol dependence, families still feel stigmatized. Most of them feel completely alone. It is such a hush-hush issue that those in its clutches think they are unique in their suffering. The statistics about the percentage of the population with alcohol problems provides no solace. It is very painful to have a problem about which you are afraid to talk because of the shame of being different. One of the greatest benefits of both Al-Anon and Alateen is the lessening of this shame and isolation. Hard as it may be to attend the first meeting, once there, people find many others who share their problems and pain. This can begin a therapeutic process.

Although Al-Anon and Alateen can be of tremendous assistance to the family, the clinician needs to point out what Al-Anon and Alateen are *not* designed to do. Frequently confusion is introduced because all family treatment efforts may be erroneously referred to as "Al-Anon." Al-Anon is a self-help group. It is not a professional therapeutic program whose members are trained family therapists, any more than AA members are professional clinicians. However, Al-Anon participation can nicely complement other family treatment efforts.

SELF-HELP

Mention the phrase "self-help" and odds are that Alcoholics Anonymous will come to mind. It is the oldest and best known of self-help programs and is the model for other twelve-step efforts, whether Gamblers Anonymous, Overeaters Anonymous, or Narcotics Anonymous. A number of other self-help programs not based on the twelve-step model have also emerged.

Alcoholics Anonymous

As a prelude to this discussion of AA, there are several underlying assumptions to be made explicit. One is that experience is the best teacher. If you want to learn about AA, this text will be relatively unhelpful, compared with attending some AA meetings and watching and talking with people in the process of recovery actively using the AA program. Another assumption is that AA works for a variety of people and for this very reason deserves attention.

Whether used alone or in tandem with professional treatment, Alcoholics Anonymous generally is associated with better treatment outcomes. The exact whys and hows of its workings are not of paramount importance, but a clinician needs some understanding of it to genuinely recommend it. Presenting AA to a client with such statements as "AA worked for me; it's the only way," or conversely, "I've done all I can for you; you might as well try AA," are unlikely to be received with enthusiasm.

History

Alcoholics Anonymous began in 1935 in Akron, Ohio, with the meeting of two alcoholics. About a year before the meeting, one of them, "Bill W.," had had a spiritual experience that was the major precipitating event in his becoming abstinent. Then, on a business trip to Akron after about a year of sobriety, he was overtaken by a strong desire to drink. He hit on the idea of seeking out and talking with another suffering alcoholic as an alternative to taking that first drink. He made contact with some people who led him to "Dr. Bob," and the whole thing began with their first meeting. The story of AA's origins and early history is told in the book *AA Comes of Age.* The idea of alcoholics helping each other spread slowly in geometric fashion until 1939. At that point, a group of about a hundred sober members realized they had something to offer the thus far "hopeless alcoholics." They wrote and published *Alcoholics Anonymous,* known as the "Big Book." It was a report of what they had done to get sober and what kept them sober. The past tense is used almost entirely in the Big Book. In writing this, the group saw their task as presenting their experiences in a framework that could be useful to others who might try it for themselves. This story is also covered in *AA Comes of Age.* However, it was in 1941 that AA was thrust into the public eye, as the result of an article published in a widely read national magazine, *The Saturday Evening Post.*[3] The article was entitled "Freed Slaves of Drink, Now They Free Others." In the year following publication, membership

Not Your Usual Dinner Party

Last week one of the best-known teetotalers in the U.S., John D. Rockefeller, had 60 people to dinner. No cocktails were served, for several of Mr. Rockefeller's guests were members of "Alcoholics Anonymous," a widespread, publicity-shy group of one-time guzzlers who have cured themselves. . . . Aware of his interest in liquor control, some of the group wrote to John D. Rockefeller two years ago—asking not for money but for advice. Mr. Rockefeller asked a representative to look into their doings, grew so interested that he helped to publish a book, Alcoholics Anonymous.

Alcoholics Anonymous, *Time,* February 19, 1940

[3]Reading the article by Jack Alexander is worth your while. It offers a firsthand view of alcohol problems in that era and what it was like for the early members of AA (*Saturday Evening Post,* March 1, 1941).

quadrupled, growing from 2,000 members to 8,000. In 2012, there were an estimated 2.1 million AA members worldwide, and AA is present in over 170 countries.

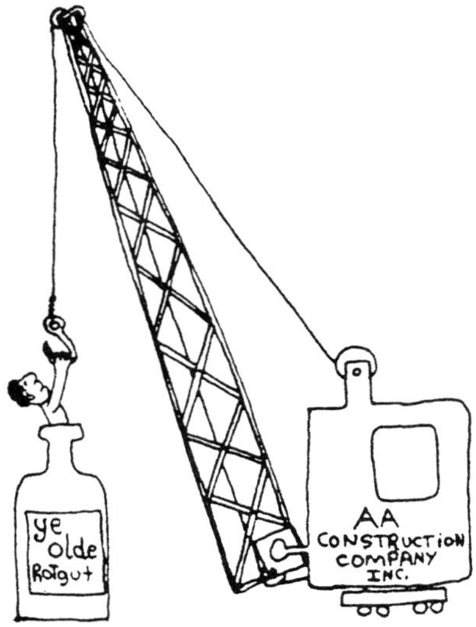

Goals

Alcoholics Anonymous stresses abstinence and contends that nothing can really happen until "the cork is in the bottle." So the primary goal is becoming sober and maintaining sobriety. Beyond that there is wide variation in the goals of individual members: simple abstinence to adopting a whole new way of life are the ends of the continuum. Typically personal goals, too, will change over time. AA includes those with drug as well as alcohol problems. For those entering AA at a younger age, drug use of some kind often accompanies alcohol dependence. References to alcohol in the following sections do not exclude the use of other substances.

In AA the words "sober" and "dry" denote quite different states. A dry person is simply not drinking at the moment. Sobriety means a more basic, all-pervasive change in the person. Sobriety does not come as quickly as dryness and requires a desire for, and an attempt to work toward, a contented, productive life without use of alcohol. The twelve steps provide a framework for achieving this.

A piece of advice a newcomer to AA receives is the importance of getting a sponsor. A sponsor is a person with substantial sobriety with whom the newcomer feels comfortable. "Comfortable" does not primarily mean being of similar backgrounds, social class, ethnicity, or any of those things, although it is suggested that a sponsor be of the same sex. It refers to someone the newcomer respects and therefore can speak with and, most important, listen to and hear. The role of the sponsor is to be a mentor and a guide and to assist the newcomer in working the program. "Working the program" refers to efforts to use the twelve steps in making life changes. Much of this occurs outside of formal meetings. The sponsor is someone who will keep an eye out for the newcomer, leading him or her through difficult times and helping out in situations that are better dealt with outside the context of meetings. A sponsor helps the newcomer focus on the basic principles and not get sidetracked by extraneous, secondary issues. The sponsor is one of the most valuable resources a newcomer can have.

The Twelve Steps

The twelve steps function as the therapeutic framework of AA. They were not devised by a group of social scientists, nor are they derived from a theoretical view of alcohol dependence. Rather, the twelve steps of AA grew out of the practical experience of the earliest members, based on what they had done to gain sobriety. Hence, the past tense is used. It's "we did _______," not "you should_______." The steps require action. AA involvement is not a passive process.

The twelve steps of AA, as experienced by its sober members, offer hope for a life that is not dominated by alcohol, a life that otherwise would be unimaginable.

Step 1. "We admitted we were powerless over alcohol—that our lives had become unmanageable."
In this step, the individual acknowledges the true culprit, alcohol, and the scope of the problem, the whole life.

Step 2. "Came to believe that a Power greater than ourselves could restore us to sanity."
This step recognizes the insanity of the drinking behavior and allows for the gradual reliance on an external agent, something beyond oneself (be it God, another spiritual concept, the AA group) to aid an about-face.

Step 3. "Made a decision to turn our will and our lives over to the care of God as we understood Him."
This enables the person to let go of the previous life preserver, the bottle, and accept an outside influence to provide direction. It has now become clear that, as a life preserver, the bottle was a dud, but free floating cannot go on forever either. The search outside the self for direction has now begun.

Step 4. "Made a searching and fearless moral inventory of ourselves."
This step provokes a close look at the basic errors in perceiving the world and at behaviors that were part of the drinking debacle. This is the step that begins the process of teaching alcohol-dependent people about their own responsibility during the drinking days. This step also includes space for the positive attributes that can be enhanced in the sober state. An inventory is, after all, a balance sheet.

Step 5. "Admitted to God, to ourselves, and to another human being the exact nature of our wrongs."
The fifth step provides a method of cleaning the slate, admitting just how painful and destructive it all was, and getting the guilt-provoking behavior out in the open instead of destructively bottled up.

Step 6. "Were entirely ready to have God remove all these defects of character."

Step 7. "Humbly asked Him to remove our shortcomings."
Steps 6 and 7 continue the "mopping-up" process. Step 6 makes the individual aware of his or her tendency to cling to old behaviors, even unhealthy ones. Step 7 takes care of the fear of repeated errors, again instilling hope that personality change is possible. (Remember, at this stage in the process, the recently sober person is likely to be very short on self-esteem.)

Step 8. "Made a list of all persons we had harmed and became willing to make amends to them all."

Step 9. "Made direct amends to such people wherever possible, except when to do so would injure them or others."

Steps 8 and 9 are a clear guide to sorting out actual injury done to others and deciding how best to deal with it. They serve other purposes too. First, they force the person to confront the habit of blaming others for life's difficulties. To make an amend—that is, to attempt to atone for a wrong committed—does not require the forgiveness of the receiver. The recovering person's part is to make the effort to apologize, pay back money, or do whatever is necessary to try to balance the scales. These steps clearly relate to the importance of acknowledging and owning up to events that have occurred. The "except when to do so would injure them or others" is also very important.

Step 10. "Continued to take personal inventory and when we were wrong promptly admitted it."

Step 11. "Sought through prayer and meditation to improve our conscious contact with God as we understood Him, praying only for knowledge of His will for us and the power to carry that out."

Step 12. "Having had a spiritual awakening as a result of these Steps, we tried to carry this message to alcoholics and to practice these principles in all our affairs."

Step 10, along with Steps 11 and 12, promotes the maintenance of sobriety and the continuation of the process of change that has begun. Step 10 ensures that the alcohol-dependent person need not slip back from the hard-won gains. Diligence in focusing on one's own behavior and not making excuses keeps the record straight. The 11th step fosters continued spiritual development. The 12th points the way to sharing the process with others. This is one of the vital keys Bill W. discovered to maintain his sobriety. It also implies that a continued practice of the new principles is vital to the sober life.

You may hear reference to "two steppers." This is used to describe the individuals in AA who enter AA, announce they are alcoholics, dry out, and set out to rescue others. However, it is often said in AA that "you can't give away what you don't have." This refers to a quality of sobriety that comes after some long and serious effort, applying all the twelve steps to one's life. It is interesting to note that "carrying the message" is not mentioned until Step 12. Once that point is reached, however, it is important that the member reach out to others—repaying a debt, so to speak—and in the process experience feelings of usefulness again.

No AA member who is serious about the program and sober for some time would ever imply that the steps are a one-shot deal. They are an ongoing process, which evolves over time—a great deal of it—into ever widening applications. When approached with serious intent, the steps enable a great change in the individual. That they are effective is testified to not only by great numbers of recovering persons in the fellowship but also by their adoption as a basis for such organizations as Overeaters Anonymous, Narcotics Anonymous, and Gamblers

Anonymous. These other fellowships simply substitute their own addiction for the word "alcohol" in Step 1.

A therapist, counselor, or friend should be alert to the balance required in this process of working the program. The newcomer who wants to tackle all twelve steps the first week should be counseled with one of AA's slogans: "Easy does it." The member hopelessly anguished by Step 4, for instance, could be advised that perfection is not the goal and a stab at it the first time through is quite sufficient. The agnostic having difficulty with "the God bit" can be told about using the group or anything else suitable for the time being as the external agent to rely on. After all, the spiritual awakening doesn't turn up until Step 12 either.

The Twelve Traditions

AA has very little structure as an organization. It describes itself as a fellowship and functions around the twelve steps and twelve traditions. The twelve traditions cover the organization as a whole, setting forth the purpose and principles of conduct. For example, AA does not affiliate with other groups or lend its name to any endeavor. In addition, AA should not be organized and should remain forever non-professional. Individual AA groups are autonomous and decline outside contributions. Care is taken not to obscure or lose sight of the organization's purpose. The individual groups function in accord with these principles. Their focus is on sobriety, anonymity, and individual application of the program, which includes meetings, attempts to work the twelve steps, and service to other alcoholics.

I'm afraid, Mr. Jones, that you've misunderstood things. We're supposed to turn things over to our "higher power," not our "hired power," and your accountant can't take your inventory for you!

Anonymity is of particular importance. Alcoholics Anonymous's 12th tradition reads as follows: "Anonymity is the spiritual foundation of all our traditions, ever reminding us to place principles before personalities." This concept evolved out of the growth pains of the organization. Early members admitted candidly that fear of exposure of their problem was their original motivation for remaining anonymous: the need "to hide from public distrust and contempt." However, the principle of anonymity, which was introduced into the fellowship on the basis of fear, soon demonstrated its value on a totally different level. The same process tends to occur for most individual members of AA. At first, the promise of anonymity is viewed as a safeguard against exposure. The stigma attached to alcohol problems has not yet disappeared. Added to this are the individual's feelings of guilt, sense of failure, and low self-esteem. It is vital to maintain the promise of anonymity to encourage fearful newcomers to try out the program while assuring them of complete confidentiality. As individuals gain sobriety, fear gives way to the deeper understanding revealed in the practice. To be simply Joe or Mary, one alcoholic troubled among many, has a therapeutic value.

In practice, anonymity takes the form of the use of first names only during the meetings, not identifying oneself through the media as a member of AA, and being careful not to reveal anyone else's attendance at meetings. Some meetings end with the reminder, "Who you see here and what is said here stays here." It is important that this principle of anonymity be respected for AA to be able to continue its mission to assist others.

Meetings Plus

There are open meetings—open to any spouses, friends, interested parties, and so on—and closed meetings, for those who identify themselves as alcohol-dependent. Both types can be speaker or discussion meetings. Speaker meetings have one to three speakers, who tell what it was like drinking (for the purpose of allowing newcomers to identify), what happened to change this, and what their sober life is now like. In a discussion meeting, the leader may or may not tell his or her story briefly (or "qualify," in AA jargon). The focus is a discussion of a particular step, topic, or problem with alcohol, with the leader taking the role of facilitator.

Attendance at meetings is not all there is to AA. The AA meeting is like a patient's visit to a doctor's office. The office visit doesn't constitute the whole of therapy. It is a good start, but how closely the patient follows the advice and recommendations and acts on what is prescribed makes the difference. Sitting in the doctor's office doesn't do it. The person who is seriously trying to use AA as a means of achieving sobriety will be doing a lot more than attending meetings. Those successful in AA will spend time talking to and being with other, more experienced members. Part of this time will be spent getting practical tips on how to maintain sobriety. Time and effort go into learning and substituting other behaviors for the all-pervasive drinking behavior.

Alcoholics Anonymous contacts are a valuable resource for relaxation. It is a place a newly recovering person will feel accepted. It is also a space in which the drinking possibilities are greatly minimized. A new member of AA may spend a couple of hours a day phoning, having coffee with, or being in the com[illegible] other AA members. Although it is strongly recommended tha[illegible]bers seek sponsors, newcomers will be in touch with a larger c[illegible]ple. Frequent contact with AA members is encouraged, not on[illegible]n useful information but also to make it easier for the new m[illegible]reach out in times of stress, when picking up a drink would b[illegible]nd instinctive. For an AA newcomer, contacting a fellow AA [illegible]hen a crunch time comes often makes the difference between [illegible]d relapse.

Slogans

Slowly the new member's life is being [illegible]tured around not drinking, and usually the slogans are the basis for this: "One day at a time," "Easy does it," "Keep it simple," "Live and let live," and "Let go and let God" are just a few. Although they can sound trite and somewhat corny, remember the description of the confused, guilt-ridden, anxious product of alcohol dependence. Anyone in such a condition can greatly benefit from a simple, organized, easily understood schedule of priorities. A kind of behavior modification is taking place so that changes may begin. Some new members feel so overwhelmed by the idea of a day without a drink that their sponsor as well as others will help them literally plan every step of the first few weeks. They keep in close hourly touch with older members. Phone calls at any hour of the day or night are encouraged as a way to relieve anxiety.

View of Recovery

One thing assumed in AA is that recovery is a serious, lifelong venture. Safety does not exist, and some kind of long-term support is necessary. Everyone has a selective memory. For those with alcohol dependence, the danger is that, after periods of dryness, only the *relief* of drinking is recalled, not the consequences. A reminder of reality seems to be necessary. Any person with long-term sobriety will be able to tell about the sudden desire to drink popping up out of nowhere. Those who do not succumb are grateful to some aspect of their AA life in getting through. No one knows exactly why these moments occur, but one thing is certain: they are personally frightening and upsetting. They can reduce the reasonably well-adjusted recovering person to a state similar to that of very early sobriety. The feelings can be compared to the feelings after a particularly vivid nightmare. Whatever the reason for the phenomenon, these unexpected urges to drink do spring up. This is one reason continued participation in AA is suggested. Another is the emphasis (somewhat underplayed from time to time) on a continued growth in sobriety. Certainly, groups will rally around newcomers and help them learn the basics. In discussion meetings with a group of veterans, however, the focus will be on personal growth within the context of the twelve steps. Alcoholics Anonymous may advertise itself as a "simple program for complicated people," but an understanding of it is far from a simple matter. Its simplicity is deceptive and on the order of "Love thy neighbor as thyself"—a simple goal, yet mastering it could easily take a lifetime.

Referral

Simply telling someone to go to AA probably won't work. On the other hand, it is noteworthy how many people do refer themselves to AA. In most areas of the country, AA has an answering service, listed in the phone book under AA. Daily AA gets calls from those who want to know where a meeting will be held that day or how to speak to a member. Hopefully a clinician will do more than hand over the phone book in making a referral. Alcoholics Anonymous is a self-help group. What AA can do and offer is by far best explained and demonstrated by its members. The clinician can assist by making arrangements for a client to speak to a member of AA or can arrange for the client to be taken to a meeting. Many helping professionals, whether dealing exclusively with addiction or not, have compiled a list of AA members who have agreed to be available. Even if the clinician is an AA member, a separate AA contact is advisable. It is less confusing to the client if AA is seen as distinct from, although compatible with, other therapy. The therapist need not defend, proselytize, or try to sell AA. Alcoholics Anonymous speaks eloquently for itself. You do your part well when you work with clients to open them up to attend, listen with an open mind, and stay long enough to make their own assessments.

A standard part of many treatment programs is an introduction and orientation to AA or other twelve-step programs. This seems very important because treatment programs are an ever growing source of referrals. Many residential treatment programs or intensive outpatient programs include AA or NA meetings that are held at the facility. In addition they may make arrangements to transport clients to outside meetings. It is not unusual for presentations on AA to be included in an educational series. Some programs encourage—indeed, some push—clients to work on Steps 1 through 5 while they are actively involved in treatment. The hope is that this will give clients added insight into AA and increase the chances of their continuing involvement.

As a growing source of referrals to AA, treatment programs are challenged in several respects. Although wishing to be supportive of AA, treatment programs need to respect the boundaries between AA and treatment. One challenge to treatment programs is to help clients distinguish between formal treatment and AA. Nowhere may this be more important than in terms of aftercare. It must be pointed out that attending a treatment program's alumni group is not the same as going to AA. Nor for that matter is a chat with a sponsor a substitute for an aftercare session. Conversely, having a therapist should not be allowed to be seen as a substitute for having an AA sponsor. Other challenges for programs include not appropriating AA through overly lengthy intellectual presentations on the nature of AA. Similarly, treatment programs should not use the language of AA and its slogans to mislead clients into thinking such discussions and their treatment are the same as AA involvement. There is a danger of clients' becoming pseudo-sophisticates with respect to AA. They can use the jargon properly, can make reference to the slogans and the steps, but have very limited firsthand experience of the AA fellowship.

Twelve-Step Facilitation Counseling

A manual-guided therapy to promote involvement in Alcoholics Anonymous, known as *twelve-step facilitation therapy*, has been developed. It consists of 12 to 15 one-hour individual sessions. The therapist actively encourages clients to attend meetings, get a sponsor, examine the first steps, and read AA material as well as learn to use AA resources in times of crisis. The manual outlines the material for each of the sessions and presents strategies for handling common clinical problems.

While twelve-step facilitation therapy was initially designed for individual counseling, there have been subsequent adaptations for its use in a group format and for use with drug problems other than alcohol. For those with drug abuse, the major change recommended is increasing contacts during the first three weeks to at least twice-weekly sessions. With the use of twelve-step facilitation, it is recommended that the initial focus be on establishing sobriety and delaying treatment of other related problems. The exceptions are the presence of major psychiatric conditions such as debilitating depression.

The emergence of twelve-step facilitation therapy clearly suggests that AA involvement is seen as a positive factor in recovery. However, despite its being a mainstay of alcohol treatment for a long time, until quite recently, research on AA was limited. This has changed. A growing body of research supports the clinical wisdom that involvement in AA has a positive impact. The positive impact for individuals also has a ripple effect in the larger community. Research in Canada found that where there are higher levels of involvement in AA, there are lower suicide and homicide rates in the general population, as well as a lower level of liver cirrhosis.

Resistance

Some clients and their families may be resistant to AA. A therapist often finds they may agree to anything, as long as it isn't AA. This resistance probably has a number of sources. It may be based on erroneous information and myths about AA. For some it is embarrassment, plain and simple. The client may have been notorious at the neighborhood bar, appeared regularly in the newspaper for drinking and driving offenses, or almost single-handedly kept the neighborhood general store solvent with beer purchases. But heaven forbid the individual should be seen entering a building where an AA meeting is held.

Sometimes clients will have had some limited prior exposure to AA, which they use as the basis for their objections. In these instances don't be surprised if they recount that their best drinking buddies have had similarly negative experiences and agree with them that AA doesn't work. For clinicians it helps to keep in mind that generally it matters little whether people *like* any other prescribed treatments as long as the treatment produces positive results. No one likes braces or casts on broken limbs or hospital stays for any reason, but they are accepted as necessary to produce a desired result. It is the results that are important. Of course, twelve-step facilitation therapy is useful in working around clients' resistance.

Professional resistance toward AA is certainly less than it once was, but it has not wholly disappeared. Some professionals in the general helping professions are uncomfortable in routinely expecting their clients to use AA. At times one gets the sense that AA is not considered a "real" treatment or that it is considered less sophisticated. Another point of possible professional resistance is their taking client objections too seriously. With alcohol problems being addressed at earlier points, there may be a tendency too for helping professionals outside of the substance abuse field to consider that AA involvement is only for those whose disease has been long-standing. In other words, some people's alcohol dependence isn't seen as bad enough to warrant prescribing AA. Finally, professionals sometimes have mistakenly gotten the impression that AA, as an organization, holds AA to be incompatible with other therapies. This is not true. Nothing in the AA program supports this premise. Certainly, an occasional client will give this impression, in which case as a therapist you can help clear up this misconception. As you'll see below, a significant percentage of AA members are involved in other treatment.

Membership

Since 1968, the General Service Office of AA has conducted a triennial survey of its members. The most recent survey, conducted in 2011, provides a profile of the membership. Ages run the gamut, from those in their teens to those in their 80s.

The 2011 survey shows the average age is 49, two-thirds of members are male, and one-third are females. The following is the breakdown by other demographic characteristics:

Age		**Marital Status**		**Racial and Ethnic Groups**	
under 21	2%	Married	36%	White	87%
21–30	11	Single	34	Black	5
31–40	15	Divorced	22	Hispanic	4
41–50	24	Other	8	Native American	2
51–60	27			Asian & other	2
over 61	21				

What are the paths to AA? Of those surveyed in 2011, about 32% of members reported being introduced to AA through treatment programs, about 25% mentioned a family member, 14% mentioned a counseling agency or health care provider, and 12% mentioned a court order. Before going to AA, 63% of members received some type of treatment or counseling, and 75% of those members said it played an important part in directing them to AA. After coming to AA, 63% of members were involved in some type of treatment or counseling, and 82% of those said it was important to recovery. Consistent with results in prior surveys, about 75% report that their doctors know they are in AA.

In terms of length of sobriety, 48% of members have been sober over five years, 24% have been sober between one and five years, and 27% represent newcomers, those sober less than one year. The average length of sobriety is more than eight years.

There has been a gradual increase in the average age of AA members in the United States and Canada. At the point of the first survey in

1968, the average age was 46 years. It then dropped to a low of 41 years in 1989. In the quarter century since, each membership survey shows a year or two rise in the average age. It was 49 years in 2011. The data available don't show whether this is due to fewer younger persons joining, or an increase in longevity, or both. Interestingly, in the many articles on AA, there have been no comments about younger people finding themselves in meeting rooms filled with gray-haired old folks. To the contrary, the response of younger members tends to be both appreciative and surprised by members' acceptance of them and the support they provide. In such an atmosphere, age may well be incidental.

In closing, you are urged to attend a variety of AA meetings. So much has been written about AA that people assume they know what it's about without firsthand knowledge. Just as you would visit treatment programs or community agencies to see personally what they are about, so, too, go to an AA meeting.

A number of other self-help groups have sprung up, some modeled after AA. Collectively they are referred to as twelve-step programs. In brief, they have adopted the twelve steps of AA and simply substitute the name of another substance or another condition for alcohol. These include Narcotics Anonymous, Cocaine Anonymous, Nicotine Anonymous, Overeaters Anonymous, and Gamblers Anonymous. Drawing from a community newspaper's listing of meeting times for self-help programs, there is also Depression Anonymous, Phobics Anonymous, Food Addicts in Recovery Anonymous, as well as Co-Dependents Anonymous.

Research Insights

As a self-help group the only "research" AA conducts is its triennial survey, which defines the composition of the Fellowship and provides data on people's length of affiliation, level of attendance, path into AA, and the like. Until recently there was essentially no research involving Alcoholics Anonymous beyond this basic data. The situation has since changed, sparked in part by large research efforts such as Project MATCH. The following is a snapshot of the research findings.

Treatment Outcome The most basic criteria used to evaluate treatment outcome is drinking behavior. Is the person abstinent, and if not, what was the period of abstinence after treatment? If the person is drinking, there are questions about drinking patterns in terms of the frequency of drinking and consumption levels. In addition, there may be questions about employment status, family relationships, and the like. All of the studies involve follow-up, some with follow-up for 16 years post-treatment.

Project MATCH found that involvement in AA was associated with better outcomes. Plus, those who received twelve-step facilitation therapy were more likely to become affiliated with AA. In addition, it was associated with better results than other therapies, unless there was a co-occurring psychiatric illness. Research since Project MATCH has confirmed these findings. Often AA involvement is thought of as aftercare. Longer formal treatment during the first year is associated with better outcomes than are found for those with a lesser level of involvement in treatment. However, to extend formal aftercare treatment beyond the first year does not have any additional benefits. In contrast, longer periods of AA involvement do have a positive impact. For previously untreated people, those with continued AA involvement had better 16-year outcomes. During long-term follow-up studies, the level of attendance at year 1 predicted status one year later. At the point of follow-up, continuous AA participation is associated with the lowest levels of alcohol use, whereas non-attendance is associated with the highest levels of alcohol use, even when controlling for the length of formal treatment and the severity of dependence.

AA affiliation is not only associated with better outcomes in terms of drinking, but better outcomes are seen in other domains as well. Extended affiliation is associated with personality change; namely, less impulsivity and fewer legal problems even 16 years after formal treatment. Reports of improved family relations are also a product of participation in AA.

Predictors of Treatment Outcome A number of factors have been identified as related to more successful outcomes for those participating in AA. One might be considered the "dose" of AA that the client chooses, meaning the number of meetings and the length of participation over time. In addition, participation, rather than mere attendance, makes a difference. The timing of AA involvement with respect to the entry into treatment has an impact as well. Those who became involved with AA early in treatment have better long-term outcomes than those who delay involvement. On the other side, those who are involved in AA first and then enter treatment have poorer outcomes.

Among the interesting findings is that the benefits of AA attendance are greatest for persons with the highest number of risk factors for relapse. One study found that the association of attendance with abstinence was greatest among members who were younger, white, less-educated, unstably employed, less religious, and having fewer interpersonal skills, for whom AA is a lifeline in multiple ways. Another possibly unexpected finding is that Alcoholics Anonymous affiliation may be most helpful for those people who initially had little intention of becoming involved.

Against diseases the strongest fence is the defensive virtue, abstinence.
–Robert Herrick

Active Therapeutic Elements A number of articles have tried to define the "something" that is therapeutic about AA. One point frequently cited is the presence of a social network that is not supportive of drinking. This is particularly important for those whose prior social circle was built around drinking. One author suggested AA should be given special consideration for such clients irrespective of the therapy they will receive. Other factors suggested as therapeutic include the presence of positive role models; new social norms; being involved with rewarding pleasant activity other than drinking; and enhanced self-efficacy and coping skills. It has been suggested that helping others has benefits as well.

Some Tentative Conclusions An annual meeting of the Research Society on Alcoholism devoted several sessions to research reports on Alcoholics Anonymous. At the concluding session, a panel of other researchers summarized what they considered the key points. Their seven conclusions are that (a) AA cannot be ignored in treatment outcomes; (b) it is possible to facilitate AA attendance; (c) treatment is the time to promote AA attendance; (d) attendance is not equivalent to involvement; (e) AA participation predicts better outcomes; (f) continuous abstinence is the outcome most likely to be affected by AA; (g) the abstinence message of AA does not seem to be deleterious.

Non-Twelve-Step Programs

In the alcohol field, other self-help groups have emerged as alternatives to AA. These programs explicitly reject the twelve-step approach and several basic tenets of AA, particularly the emphasis on spirituality, the notion of disease, and views of the individual as powerless, as set forth in the first step of AA. In exchange, these alternatives emphasize a capacity for change and the ability to make choices. (In some instances, these differences might be viewed as a discussion of whether the glass is half empty or half full.) These alternative self-help programs include Women for Sobriety, Rational Recovery, Secular Organizations for Sobriety, SMART Recovery (**S**elf **M**anagement **A**nd **R**ecovery **T**raining), and Moderation Management.

Self-Help Group Websites

Alcoholics Anonymous
www.AA.org/

Moderation Management
www.moderation.org/

Rational Recovery
http://rational.org/

SMART Recovery
www.smartrecovery.org/

Women for Sobriety
www.womenforsobriety.org/

Women for Sobriety

Founded in 1976, Women for Sobriety is one of the first self-help groups established as an alternative to AA. Its founding coincided with the emergence of the women's movement, and it was established at a time when women were in a distinct minority in AA. Women for Sobriety emphasizes the need and ability to make choices. Rather than the twelve steps, it is based on 13 principles, listed below, seen as encouraging personal and emotional growth and thus providing the foundation of the "New Life Program."

1. *I have a life-threatening problem that once had me.*
   I now take charge of my life. I accept the responsibility.
2. *Negative thoughts destroy only myself.*
   My first conscious act must be to remove negativity from my life.
3. *Happiness is a habit I will develop.*
   Happiness is created, not waited for.
4. *Problems bother me only to the degree I permit them to.*
   I now better understand my problems and do not permit problems to overwhelm me.
5. *I am what I think.*
   I am a capable, competent, caring, compassionate woman.
6. *Life can be ordinary or it can be great.*
   Greatness is mine by a conscious effort.

7. *Love can change the course of my world.*
   Caring becomes all important.
8. *The fundamental object of life is emotional and spiritual growth.*
   Daily I put my life into a proper order, knowing which are the priorities.
9. *The past is gone forever.*
   No longer will I be victimized by the past; I am a new person.
10. *All love given returns.*
    I will learn to know that others love me.
11. *Enthusiasm is my daily exercise.*
    I treasure all moments of my new life.
12. *I am a competent woman and have much to give life.*
    This is what I am and I shall know it always.
13. *I am responsible for myself and for my actions.*
    I am in charge of my mind, my thoughts, and my life.

Rational Recovery

Wine is a mocker, drink a brawler, and whoever is led astray by it is not wise.
PROVERBS 20:1

Founded in 1985, Rational Recovery identifies itself as an alternative to those who are turned off by AA. While AA members refer to one of AA's key publications as the Big Book, Rational Recovery has dubbed its publication *The Little Book.* Rational Recovery repudiates the concept of powerlessness. In contrast, it emphasizes the perspective that individuals are capable of making the choice not to drink and can take charge of their lives. Rational Recovery advocates the use of a technique it refers to as *addictive voice recognition technique* (AVRT) to help people recognize the automatic thoughts that support continued drinking. These automatic thoughts are described as the voice of "the beast," the metaphor used to describe the part of the self that seeks instant pleasure without regard for the consequences.

Moderation Management

Eat not to fullness, drink not to elevation.
—BENJAMIN FRANKLIN

Founded in 1994, Moderation Management (MM) differs from the other self-help groups in that abstinence is not a requisite goal. It is not intended for those with alcohol dependence, but for problem drinkers who have experienced mild to moderate alcohol-related problems. A survey of those who have contacted the national toll-free number for MM shows that the typical caller is female, under age 40, has never been in any formal treatment program, and is not open to entering formal treatment. Also, the typical caller is better educated and economically more advantaged than those who participate in traditional twelve-step programs.

Moderation Management makes explicit the kinds of behaviors that are consistent with moderate drinking. Equally important it defines situations and circumstances that are incompatible with moderate alcohol use. The latter are generally referred to as limits. Both are a prominent part of MM literature and are set forth below.

A Moderate Drinker:

- considers an occasional drink to be a small, though enjoyable, part of life.
- has hobbies, interests, and other ways to relax and enjoy life that do not involve alcohol.
- usually has friends who are moderate drinkers or non-drinkers.
- generally has something to eat before, during, or soon after drinking.
- usually does not drink for longer than an hour or two on any particular occasion.
- usually does not drink faster than 1 drink per half-hour.
- usually does not exceed the 0.055% BAC moderate drinking limit.
- feels comfortable with his or her use of alcohol (never drinks secretly and does not spend a lot of time thinking about drinking or planning to drink).

The MM Limits:

- Strictly obey local laws regarding drinking and driving.
- Do not drink in situations that would endanger yourself or others.
- Do not drink every day. MM suggests that you abstain from drinking alcohol at least 3 or 4 days per week.
- Women who drink more than 3 drinks on any day, and more than 9 drinks per week, may be drinking at harmful levels. (See Note below which defines a "standard" drink.)
- Men who drink more than 4 drinks on any day, and more than 14 drinks per week, may be drinking at harmful levels.

Note: A standard drink is one 12-oz beer (5% alcohol), one 5-oz glass of wine (12% alcohol), or 1 oz of 80-proof liquor (40% alcohol).

No one can quibble with the fact that the MM guidelines are consistent with low-risk drinking. But what is going on with people who need a self-help group to do what most drinkers do automatically? If a client is involved in MM, this suggests that monitoring or follow-up is warranted. Consider making a contract with that client about what actions will be taken if the client is not following the MM guidelines. An inability to stick with the guidelines is significant. The literature of Moderation Management notes that about 30% of its members move on to join an abstinence-based group, such as AA. Thus, for some it is a route to abstinence.

Any clinician whose client reports having used MM in the past should take careful note of that fact. It shows that there were serious concerns about drinking and significant efforts to control drinking in the past. If he or she is now in the office of a substance abuse counselor, this

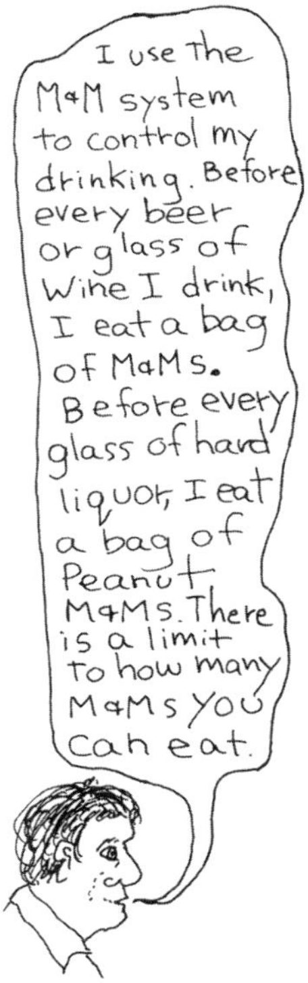
I use the M&M system to control my drinking. Before every beer or glass of wine I drink, I eat a bag of M&Ms. Before every glass of hard liquor, I eat a bag of Peanut M&Ms. There is a limit to how many M&Ms you can eat.

suggests that efforts at moderation have not been successful and points to a diagnosis of dependence.[4]

Which Self-Help Approach?

For the clinician, deciding whether to refer a client to a traditional self-help group, such as AA or NA, versus Rational Recovery or Women for Sobriety, may not be the big issue it might appear at first glance. Setting aside whatever biases the clinician may have, there are several practical matters. Which groups are present in the client's community? AA is available almost everywhere, while other groups may not be. On the other hand, if a client tries AA and even after a reasonable exposure vigorously resists and is having problems making a connection, then a referral to an alternative program is warranted. Whatever the biases of the counselor, if it works, it works. Remember, what is important is the destination, not necessarily the route.

PSYCHOSOCIAL THERAPIES

There are many psychosocial treatment approaches. Were you to wonder which particular treatment would be best for a particular individual, you would not be alone. A number of large studies have been conducted to examine this very question.

Thinking About Different Therapies

Equas quamvis adequatus enchiridion legere cogi non potest.
—NOTICE ON WALL OF COMPUTER PROGRAMMER
[You can lead a horse to water but you can't make him read a manual.]

In discussions of virtually any treatment approach, a number of terms are bandied about, in some cases used interchangeably and possibly incorrectly. These include "manual-guided," "evidence-based," and "best practices." *Manual-guided,* as described earlier in this chapter, refers to efforts to train clinicians to use a treatment that has been found to be successful; part of the training is use of a manual that sketches out the important elements in considerable detail. If you are interested in a new technique, you can't expect to scan the manual before a session, take a few notes, and then give it your best shot. Almost universally, becoming skilled in a new treatment requires structured training, which includes explanation of the assumptions that underpin the therapy, a discussion of the relevant research, a review of the materials, opportunities

[4]In 2000, the group's founder was arrested for an accident that occurred while she was driving with a BAC of 0.26. She was headed the wrong way on an interstate and crashed into another car, killing two people. Newspaper accounts noted that she had had an alcohol problem since high school and had been in treatment multiple times. She was immediately admitted to an alcohol treatment program. She pleaded guilty to the charge and issued a statement about ceasing involvement in MM and joining a twelve-step program. This episode certainly cannot be seen as a basis for dismissing the efforts of MM. However, it does demonstrate the importance of routinely monitoring alcohol consumption, for example, by a primary care physician, for anyone with a history of problematic drinking.

to view seasoned clinicians in action, as well as role playing in small groups to practice the therapy. Such training may extend over several days. Beyond the initial training, there is also clinical supervision as the therapist begins to use the technique.

Evidence-based refers to treatment techniques that have been studied to determine their effectiveness. "Studied" isn't simply a matter of polling clinicians to find out who used a particular approach and inquiring whether the clinician thought "it worked." Studied means systematic research. This includes attention to how the therapy was delivered to assure that clinicians were following the approach. It also involves following up with patients over time. The follow-up interviews inquire about a client's functioning in multiple domains, not just with alcohol or drugs.

In respect to alcohol use, it isn't simply a matter of abstinence versus drinking. If the client is drinking, further questions must be asked. How long was the period of abstinence before resuming alcohol use? What is the pattern of drinking in terms of frequency and amount? Are there alcohol-related problems? Even this isn't the whole of it. If a client is doing better after treatment than before, the question becomes, "How effective is this treatment compared to other treatments?"

Every evidence-based treatment entails a standardized protocol and thus is also manual-guided therapy. On the other hand, some approaches that are described as manual-guided may *not* be evidence-based. For example, an agency may want to introduce something new, and as part of introducing this to staff, may compile a set of guidelines. However, although there is a manual to guide the effort, systematic research to determine the effectiveness of the new treatment approach has not been conducted, so it doesn't qualify as evidence-based.

The meaning of *best practices,* another term frequently heard, is a bit of a puzzle. Sometimes best practices is used as if it were a synonym for evidence-based. But it's not always clear how the technique being discussed came to be defined as the "best" or "one of the best"—or who defined it as such. There usually isn't any mention of what is "second best" or the point of comparison for this "best practice." A NIDA publication on drug abuse counseling seems to confirm that "best practices" is not a very exact term. The monograph was intended to present "various counseling approaches used in some of the best known and most respected treatment programs in the United States." Best practices in this instance is defined by familiarity, widespread acceptance, and prestige, with the underlying, but unconfirmed, assumption that this must be equivalent to being "the best." So be cautious in assuming you know what "best practice(s)" means. It may be less than you think!

More attention is being paid to the principles that underlie a particular therapy. A number of therapies are based on learning principles, with attention to how behavior is learned, what maintains a behavior, and what is involved to effect change. These are commonly termed behavioral

Treatment Techniques Used Frequently or Often in U.S.

Substance abuse counseling	*96%*
Relapse prevention	*87*
Cognitive-behavioral	*66*
12-step facilitation	*56*
Motivational interviewing	*55*
Anger management	*39*
Brief intervention	*25*
Contingency management	*27*
Trauma-related counseling	*21*
Relational/emotive therapy	*18*
Matrix Model	*17*
Community-reinforcement	*5*

Source: Office of Applied Studies *The N-SSATS Report: Services Provided by Substance Abuse Treatment Facilities in the U.S.* (Septermber 10, 2010) SAMHSA

therapy. Recall the discussion in Chapter 7 of the Johnson model to explain the acquisition of drinking behavior and the emergence of problematic use. That explanation was based on learning principles. People learn what alcohol can do (learning the mood swing); next, people learn that alcohol is very dependable and has a positive outcome from the drinker's perspective (seeking the mood swing). Thus the drinking is reinforced, the behavior continues, and becomes more ingrained—so much so that it continues, even when there are negative consequences (drinking despite problems). Or imagine the chain of thoughts that can follow from the thought of a drink. The person pictures the cold beer, imagines pulling the tab, tasting the first sip, and then the sense of relaxation that follows.

The basic assumption underlying behavioral approaches is that if a behavior can be learned, it can also be unlearned, or changed. To oversimplify, this can happen in one of two ways. One way is to introduce a new and competing behavior in place of the old, unwanted behavior. If the new behavior is reinforced, associated with positive events, it tends to be repeated. In effect, the old behavior is "squeezed out." The other approach involves negative reinforcement, so the behavior occurs less and less frequently due to the negative associations. With enough negative reinforcements, the behavior disappears.

In contrast to behavioral approaches, other therapies might be broadly defined as supportive-expressive therapies. Here the emphasis is less "task driven" and based more on efforts to assist clients in understanding the reasons for drug use as well as the obstacles to making changes.

Therapies Used in Substance Abuse Treatment

Treatment programs are rarely based on any single approach. Most treatment programs include a variety of modalities. SAHMSA, the federal agency that includes NIAA and NIDA, maintains a database of evidence-based practices for alcohol-drug abuse as well as mental health problems, visit <www.nrepp.samhsa.gov>. A number of these are described below, but first a brief historical note.

Aversion Therapy

Behavioral therapy rose to prominence in the early 1950s. Aversion therapy was the first effort to explicitly use learning principles in alcohol treatment. The rationale was that linking unpleasant experiences with the unwanted behavior, drinking, would extinguish the behavior. The important part is the *immediate* link to the act of drinking. Obviously, for those with alcohol dependence, drinking is coupled with negative events; after all, that is what defines it as a problem. However, the negative consequences aren't felt immediately, but down the line, whether it's hours or days later, or further down the road. The most immediate experience is positive—a feeling of relief, the anticipation of worries or problems being washed away.

This early behavioral approach now seems rather primitive to us. In some instances electric shock was administered. A variant involved the drug disulfiram (Antabuse). If someone who has been taking disulfiram consumes alcohol, this causes nausea, vomiting, and a host of other unpleasant things. As part of aversion therapy, people who had been on disulfiram were given alcohol to drink. This was repeated until it was felt that the drinking was so thoroughly associated with discomfort that the person would be unlikely to continue drinking alcohol. Although short-term success was ensured, those results were not maintained over the long haul.

Aversion therapy is rarely used today. There are, however, still a handful of specialized treatment programs that are based on aversion therapy. An internet search brings them to the fore. A big part of the pitch is that these programs are less intrusive in someone's life, require a shorter period of treatment, and don't entail continuing follow-up or becoming involved in self-help programs. Rather than Antabuse, either emetine or ipecac is used. For over a hundred years, through the early 1990s, families kept ipecac in the family medicine cabinet to treat cases of accidental poisoning. Both ipecac and emetine are derived from a plant root, and they induce vomiting, so unlike disulfiram, their action is not based on an alcohol-drug interaction.

Behavioral Coping Skills Therapy

One of three approaches used in NIAAA's Project MATCH, Behavioral Coping Skills Therapy, is based on the principles of learning theory and views alcohol-dependent drinking as functionally related to major problems in a person's life. The protocol calls for a total of 12 sessions. Seven of these are core components and focus on drinking. These address topics such as dealing with cravings, managing thoughts of drinking, drink refusal skills, and responding to an emergency. The four other sessions are "electives," with the particular topics selected from a menu of 14 options. A number of these address broader social skills, ranging from how to start a conversation, receiving criticism, becoming aware of anger, and enhancing social supports to a meeting with family or partner to increasing pleasant activities. For each session there are a variety of handouts to record events during the following week and a variety of exercises used in the session, including role play.

Motivational Enhancement Therapy

Also used in Project MATCH, Motivational Enhancement Therapy is a behavioral approach that combines assessment and feedback, and draws upon the principles of motivational interviewing (see page 257). Generally this involves a maximum of four sessions. It is particularly well suited to patients who are resistant and angry as they enter treatment.

Twelve-Step Facilitation Therapy

The third treatment included within Project MATCH, Twelve-Step Facilitation Therapy (TSF), was described earlier as part of the discussion of Alcoholics Anonymous (see pages 326–329). As its name suggests, the objective is to promote involvement in a twelve-step program. In Project MATCH this was AA. This technique addresses resistance to involvement in a twelve-step program; explores some of the key tools within the program, such as the twelve steps; and prompts connections with recovering persons.

Relapse Prevention

Relapse prevention is a behavioral approach, similar to Behavioral Coping Skills Therapy, and is increasingly a standard component of substance abuse treatment programs. Alan Marlatt and colleagues from the University of Washington were among the first to incorporate specific activities during treatment that would reduce the likelihood of relapse. A variety of relapse prevention curricula have been developed. These consist of defining the content and approaches to use in a series of counseling sessions. This approach can include homework assignments, worksheets, skills training, role play, interactive videotapes, and lifestyle interventions, such as exercise, stress management, and relaxation techniques. The common elements include the following:

- *Identifying high-risk relapse situations and developing strategies to deal with them.* Beyond providing people with essential skills, such efforts also increase the sense of competency. When they have been provided with a set of tools, clients aren't left feeling vulnerable with nothing to do but "keep a stiff upper lip" when problematic situations arise. In this, as well as all of the following instances, the effort is not for the counselor to identify the high-risk situation but for the client to do so.
- *Seeing relapse as a process, not as an event.* Relapse doesn't just come out of the blue. Often a series of things, a chain of events, precedes a relapse, be it experiencing stress or negative feelings or finding oneself (or placing oneself) in a vulnerable situation, such as going to a favorite old haunt, "just for the music." From this perspective, any number of steps can be taken to avoid the accumulation of things that lead to relapse.
- *Dealing with drug and alcohol cues and cravings.* Cues are the little things that can trigger cravings. There are many possible cues, or reminders. Clients need to identify their own special package of things that set the ball rolling. It may be a morning cup of coffee for those hooked on cigarettes. It may be a particular setting or social situation, such as the Friday night after-work stop at a tavern with coworkers. In some instances people can avoid the situations that trigger the cravings. In other instances they may think through where the triggering event leads and create a new competing and negative association.
- *Facing social pressures.* Social pressures include situations in which clients might believe that not drinking or using will make them feel conspicuous or out of place. These situations might include being offered a drink—or outright comments from others. Such offers generally are not

motivated by someone out "to get" the client but may be quite innocent. When a waiter hands out the wine list, or asks whether anyone wants something to drink prior to ordering dinner, he does not know that a customer is a non-drinker or someone trying to be.

- *Creating and nurturing a supportive social network.* Clients need to be able to recognize the supports that are available to them—including families, friends, and self-help programs—and, in turn, to consider ways to use them.
- *Developing skills to handle negative emotional states.* One common trigger for a drink is, simply put, "feeling bad." A variety of very different clinical techniques may be used, depending on the nature of the bad feeling, to avoid such states. For someone who is very passive, never stating his or her views, assertiveness training may be useful. Or if the demon is frustration, finding alternative means of handling the emotion is required.
- *Correcting errors in thinking.* Cognitive distortions—that is, automatic ways of thinking that don't really mesh with reality—can be a problem. For example, some people see disaster around every corner, and some jump to conclusions. Efforts to correct these erroneous assumptions are sometimes termed "cognitive therapy." Essentially this is a form of behavioral therapy that considers thoughts as internal tapes we carry about and listen to without reflection. A variety of exercises have been devised to identify these internal voices, to examine the errors, and to draft new scripts to replace those old ones.
- *Developing a healthy and balanced lifestyle.* Much of the emphasis needs to be on balance. Working hard and accumulating stresses need to be balanced by relaxation, time-outs, and activities undertaken for no better reason than that they are enjoyable. It is also important to consider the role of exercise in providing a sense of well-being.

Contingency Management

Introduced initially in drug treatment programs, Contingency Management is becoming more widely used in a variety of settings. Goals are set with clients or are set by the program and agreed to by clients; there are rewards for meeting these goals. In drug programs, for example, rewards might be earned for clean urine at drug testing. The rewards may also increase with increased length of time being drug-free, so the longer someone stays clean, the greater the reward. Clients can earn either money or vouchers that can be redeemed at local stores. There is a considerable body of research indicating the success of this approach. It is based on learning theory and the fact that behavior followed by a reward is more likely to be repeated.

Medical Management

The Medical Management approach was designed for use by a physician, a non–substance abuse specialist. It was included within Project

Combine, a federal research effort to compare the effectiveness of different medications in combination with psychosocial interventions (see page 359). It involves nine sessions. In this model, the physician reviews the alcohol diagnosis and the negative consequences of drinking, which provide the basis for a recommendation of abstinence. The physician meets regularly with the patient, reviews his or her status, evaluates the use of medication and compliance in taking it, and provides support and encouragement to attend self-help groups. This version of "medical management" is more intensive than what is usually provided in most health care settings. In the Combine study, this was supposedly the "weaker" of the two behavioral interventions. However, as one author noted, this may have been a gross underestimation of the potential role of the physician. The importance of medical management is clear if you remember that the overwhelming majority of those with a substance use problem do not enter formal treatment or become involved in self-help.

Targeted Therapies

A number of therapies have been developed, not for general use, but for use in particular circumstances. For the sake of convenience, these have been organized here into three categories: those adapted for particular populations, those intended for substance abuse and co-occurring psychiatric disorders, and those developed for those abusing a specific drug.

Special Populations

There are a number of therapies intended for particular groups. For example, *BASICS (***B**rief **A**lcohol **S**creening and **I**ntervention for **C**ollege **S**tudents) is a brief harm reduction initiative to reduce high-risk drinking among college students. It was developed by the University of Washington's Addictive Behaviors Research Group. It includes two sessions and involves assessment, personalized feedback, and homework assignments. It has been offered in a variety of campus settings, from health services to residence halls. Another example is Multisystemic Therapy, intended for juvenile offenders with substance abuse or dependence who also have a history of violent behavior.

Co-occurring Psychiatric Disorders

A number of special therapies have been developed for those with a substance use problem and a co-occurring psychiatric disorder. These therapies are not intended as a substitute for treatment of the co-occurring disorder. The following are two examples:

- *Relaxation therapy.* This technique has long been used to assist patients with *anxiety disorders*. In recovery the client is likely to face a multitude of problems. One of these may be a high level of anxiety. It can be temporary, the initial discomfort with the non-drinking life, or more chronic if a client is the "nervous" type. Whether temporary or chronic, it is an uncomfortable state, and the client has a very low tolerance for it. Those dependent on alcohol, for example, have become accustomed to using alcohol for the quick, if temporary, relief of anxiety. What is later remembered (and longed for) is the almost instant relief of a large swig of booze. When alcohol or drugs are no longer an option, the recovering individual faces the problem of how to deal with anxiety. Many simply "sweat it out"; others relapse.

Relaxation therapy is based on the fact that if the body and breathing are relaxed, it is impossible to feel anxious. The mind rejects the paradox of a relaxed body and a tense mind. Often, the therapist guides a client through a progressive tensing and relaxing of the various body parts. The relaxation can start with the toes and work up or with the scalp and work down, with directions given in a modulated, soft voice. When the client is quite relaxed, the therapist suggests that a soothing picture be held in the mind. The client is provided with a CD of the process to take home, with instructions on its use, as an aid in learning relaxation. With practice, the relaxed state is achieved more easily and quickly. In some cases, the client may finally learn to relax totally with just the thought of the "picture." Once thoroughly learned, the relaxation response can be substituted for anxiety at will.

- *Seeking Safety.* This therapeutic approach was initially directed to women with PTSD (post-traumatic stress disorder) who had experienced physical and/or sexual abuse. It has since been adapted for use with men and women in the criminal justice system. As designed, it includes 25 sessions of cognitive behavioral therapy and addresses both alcohol dependence and PTSD simultaneously. It is delivered in a group format and includes safety as well as coping skills. It's website <www.seekingsafety.org> provides a description of the approach, provides the relevant literature, and notes training opportunities.

There are also targeted treatments for other co-occurring disorders, such as social phobia and depression. Depression is a particular concern, given the high rate of suicide among those who abuse alcohol and other drugs.

Other Drug Problems

Three major federally supported research efforts were developed for treatment of cocaine, marijuana use among adolescents, and amphetamines. The *National Collaborative Cocaine Treatment Study* included four different treatment approaches. Two of these involved cognitive behavioral therapy and the Community Reinforcement Approach described earlier. Other approaches included supportive-expressive therapy as well as

A family is a unit composed not only of children but of men, women, an occasional animal, and the common cold.
—Ogden Nash

individual and group counseling in a variety of formats. The *Cannabis Youth Treatment Project* included a variety of therapies for adolescents with marijuana problems, their parents, and the family unit. The other is the *Methamphetamine Treatment Program*, sponsored by the Center for Substance Abuse Treatment. It is an outpatient treatment initiative to examine different psychosocial treatments. Of note is one unique intervention. There is a special format for the first session after any episode of alcohol or drug use when abstinence is the treatment goal. The goal is to reframe the experience, not as evidence of failure, but to promote learning about what prompted use and alternative coping strategies.

☐ OTHER APPROACHES

New Media

Texting . . . Twitter . . . Facebook . . . e-mail . . . blogs . . . discussion groups . . . chat rooms—electronic communications are a part of everyday life. A number of online sites have become available to help people assess the presence of an alcohol problem or to identify high-risk drinking. More recently, formal treatment programs have begun to use electronic media as well.

This field is so new that there are a variety of terms being used, whether it's "web-based treatment" or "e-therapies" or "online counseling." Which particular term is used seems rather random, and quite often two people can be speaking about the exact same thing, even though they give it different labels.

Brief Interventions

Beyond the web-based self-assessment tools described earlier, the internet is also a vehicle for brief motivational interventions. The best known is the *Drinker's Check-up*, designed for use with at-risk drinkers and alcohol-dependent individuals who are ambivalent about changing their drinking. It is organized in a step-wise fashion. The assessment component includes a questionnaire regarding drinking patterns and problems. Based on these responses, there is personalized feedback comparing the individual's drinking to the general population, providing information on the severity of a problem as well as the accompanying risks. Next is the decision-making component, which offers three alternatives. One is for those who are *not ready* or interested in making a change. A second option is for those who are *unsure,* with the opportunity to complete an exercise that can set forth the pluses and minuses. The third option presents the individual who is *ready to make changes* with the opportunity to develop a plan, part of which includes looking at the pros and cons regarding abstinence or efforts to moderate alcohol use. If the latter is the avenue selected, further information is provided, including a definition, the indications and contraindication of that option, and an assessment that provides information on the likelihood of achieving that goal.

The Drinker's Check-up was compared to other sites that provided only alcohol information (these other sites were considered the non-intervention group). Those who completed the Drinker's Check-up were more than three times as likely to reduce alcohol consumption to what is a non-problematic pattern. Compared to those who used the alcohol information only, on average those using the Drinker's Check-up consumed 12 fewer drinks per week. Overall, there was also a decline in alcohol-related problems, more days of abstinence, and fewer drinks per day. Interestingly, almost all change occurred within the first three months; after that further changes were modest. A similar site reported that a quarter of those who used it indicated they were very interested in entering some form of traditional treatment. One of the outcomes of using web-based interventions may be to increase acceptance of treatment.

e-Therapy

The use of new media is also wending its way into formal treatment programs. For example, one program texts clients three times a day to remind them to take medication. Another texts clients daily to have them check in and report how things are going. There are reports of online support groups incorporating behavioral therapies, such as relapse prevention exercises. Even individual counseling is being offered via web-based video-conferencing. These approaches have not been widely studied, but the initial reports have generally been positive. Web-based counseling had equivalent or better "attendance" and reductions in substance use equivalent to those of clients seen on site. Surely more is on the horizon. These approaches are especially suited to younger people. After all, most people under 30 grew up as their household's information technologist. The challenge is likely not for potential clients but for agency and program directors, who are generally far less familiar with new media and don't appreciate the range of possibilities or how widely accepted they are.

The number of web-based intervention programs is growing exponentially. They are being used in an increasing number of ways. In some instances they are the alternative to standard, face-to-face treatment. In others they are a component within an established treatment program. They have been used in smoking cessation treatment and treatment of other drug use disorders, including marijuana and cocaine dependence. There are e-based versions of standard interventions, such as contingency management and cognitive behavioral therapy. In some instances web-based interventions are used by physicians, such as primary care providers, to complement brief interventions or by emergency services as follow-up on the heels of an alcohol/drug-related encounter.

These interventions are far too new to make any kind of definitive statements about their effectiveness. Nonetheless, there are several points of general consensus. Web-based interventions are used by people who would not seek treatment otherwise. Consistently e-therapies/web interventions have a positive impact. In some instances they have led to better outcomes than are found with "treatment as usual," whether at 3 months or at 12 months. There have been clear differences between those seen in face-to-face counseling and those who use e-therapies—in terms of age, gender, education, work situation, previous alcohol treatment—but, the differences are shrinking. The best guess is that as these become better known, the "traditional" clients are more likely to try them. Web-based therapies can be offered at far less cost, as well as having the potential for reaching a larger segment of the population, in terms of geography as well as demographic characteristics. One of the interesting questions in studying web-based treatments has been, "How do you measure the intensity and duration of treatment?" By the time spent online? By the number of times someone signs on? Or, when applicable, by the number of "exercises" completed? Notice, it is "exercises"; there is a real effort to avoid the word "assignments"! For now the completion of exercises and number of logins are the most frequently used measures.

Use by Self-Help Programs

The web is also used by self-help programs. Beyond the expected uses—posting general information, lists of meetings, and literature—some have begun to conduct meetings online. At this point, there is little information on how these new forums are used, by whom, and in what situations or how effective they are. But they are proliferating.[5]

Spiritual Counseling

Possibly at the opposite end of the spectrum from technological approaches is the matter of spiritual counseling. Those with alcohol problems may have a need for pastoring, "shepherding," or spiritual counseling, as do other members of the population. In fact, their needs in this area may be especially acute.

Crisply defining what is encompassed by spiritual issues is not easy; it's easier to say what it is not. "Spiritual" does not mean organized religions and churches. Religions can be thought of as organized groups

[5]This use of technology isn't totally new. In the early days of AA, when meetings were less available and people had to travel long distances, it was not uncommon for people to record meetings, using old-fashioned reel-to-reel tape recorders, then circulate the tapes among members. For those on merchant ships or in the Navy or living in isolated spots, these tapes were the only way to "attend" AA meetings.

and institutions that have arisen to meet spiritual needs. The spiritual concern is more basic than religion. That civilizations have developed religions throughout history can be evidence of a spiritual dimension.

Over the past several decades there has been a renewed interest in spiritual concerns in America. Whether transcendental meditation, the teaching of Eastern gurus, fundamentalism, mysticism, television evangelism, or the more traditional Judeo-Christian Western religions, Buddhist traditions, or Islamic traditions, people have been flocking to them. People are attempting to follow these teachings and precepts in the hope of filling a void in their lives. Many express the belief that the "bottom line" may not be adequately calculated in terms of status, education, career, or material wealth. The culturally defined evidence of achievement and success can leave someone feeling that something is missing. This "something" is thought by many to be of a spiritual nature. This missing piece has been described as a "God-shaped hole."

There is considerable diversity in religious affiliation in the United States, marked by regional differences, differences by age, and differences by racial and ethnic groups. Over the past decade there has been an increase in those who describe themselves as unaffiliated with a religious tradition, as well as an increase among persons who changed their religious affiliation. Church attendance historically has been lowest among adolescents and young adults. With maturity and some life experiences, a portion of adult development entails a reexamination of values, priorities in life, and redefinitions of what is important. An offhand comment seems to capture this well: "No one on a death bed ever expressed regret that he or she hadn't spent more time on work."

Alcohol Dependence as a Spiritual Search

How do spiritual concerns fit in with alcohol use and alcohol dependence? First, it is worth reflecting on the fact that a word commonly used for alcohol is "spirits." This is surely no accident. Indeed, consider how alcohol is used. Often it is in the hope it will provide that missing something or at least turn off a gnawing ache. From bottled spirits, a drinker may seek a solution to life's problems, a release from pain, an escape from circumstances. For a while it may do the job, but eventually it fails. To use spiritual language, you can even think of alcohol dependence as a pilgrimage that dead-ends. Alcohol can be thought of as a false god or, to paraphrase the New Testament, as not being "living water."

If this is the case and alcohol use has been prompted in part by spiritual thirst, the thirst remains even though drinking ceases. Part of the recovery process must be aimed at quenching the thirst. Alcoholics Anonymous has recognized this. It speaks of alcoholism as a threefold disease with physical, mental, and spiritual components. Part of the AA program is intended to help members by focusing on their spiritual needs. It is also important to remember that AA makes a clear distinction between spiritual growth and religion.

Working with Clergy

How can the clergy be of assistance? Ideally clergy are society's designated experts on spiritual matters. Notice the word "ideally." The realities of religious institutions may have forced some to be fund-raisers, social directors, community consciences, almost everything but spiritual mentors, yet there are those who do, and maybe many more who long to, act as spiritual counselors and advisers. One way the clergy may be of potential assistance is to help those in early recovery deal with sin[6] and feelings of guilt, worthlessness, and hopelessness. Many Americans with alcohol dependence, along with the public at large, are walking around as adults with virtually the same notions of the Judeo-Christian God they had as five-year-olds. God has a white beard, sits on a throne on a cloud, checks up on everything we do, keeps a ledger of our behavior, and punishes us if we aren't "good." This is certainly a caricature but possibly not that far from how some feel, if they really think about it.

The sway of alcohol over mankind is unquestionably due to its power to stimulate the mystical faculties of human nature, usually crushed to earth by the cold facts and dry criticisms of the sober hour. Sobriety diminishes, discriminates, and says no; drunkenness expands, unites, and says yes.
—William James
The Varieties of Religious Experience, 1902

Those just getting sober feel remorseful, guilt-ridden, worthless, endowed with a host of negative qualities, and devoid of good. In their minds, they certainly do not fit the picture of someone God would like to befriend. On the contrary, they probably believe that, if God isn't punishing them, He ought to be. So these persons may need some assistance in updating their concept of God. There's a good chance some of their ideas will have to be revised. There's the idea that the church, and therefore (to them) God, is only for the "good" people. A glance at the New Testament and Christian traditions doesn't support this view, even if some parishes or congregations may act that way. Jesus of Nazareth didn't travel with the "in crowd." He was found in the company of fishermen, prostitutes, lepers, and tax collectors. Or consider the Judaic tradition as reflected in the Torah. The chosen of God were constantly whining, complaining, going astray, and breaking as much of the Law as they followed. Nonetheless, God refused to give up on them. Virtually all spiritual traditions have taken human frailty as a given. Whether a new perspective on God or a Higher Power leads to re-involvement with a church, assists in affiliation with AA, or helps lessen the burden of guilt doesn't matter. Whichever it does, it can be an important factor in recovery.

It is hard to believe in God, but it is far harder to disbelieve in Him.
—Emerson

Insights of Carl Jung

Interestingly, an eminent psychiatrist recognized the spiritual dimension of alcohol dependence and recovery back in the days when alcoholism was considered hopeless by the medical profession. The physician was

[6]The word "sin" comes from the Greek, and its meaning had nothing to do with morality or with someone being "bad." It means "to miss the mark." The word was used in archery practice. Someone stood by the target and shouted back to the archer whether or not he had hit the target or had missed the mark—that is, had "sinned"—thus allowing the archer to make corrections.

Carl Jung. A man named Roland H. had been through the treatment routine before seeking out Jung in 1931. He admired Jung greatly, saw him as the court of last resort, and remained in therapy with him for about a year. Shortly after terminating therapy, Roland lapsed back into drinking. Because of this unfortunate development, he returned to Jung. On his return, Jung told Roland his condition was hopeless as far as psychiatry and medicine of that day were concerned. Very desperate and willing to grab at any straw, Roland asked if there was any hope at all. Jung replied that there might be, provided Roland could have a spiritual or religious experience—a genuine conversion experience. Although comparatively rare, this had been known to lead to recovery. So Jung advised Roland to place himself in a religious atmosphere and hope (pray) for the best. The "best," in fact, occurred. The details of the story can be found in an exchange of letters between Bill W. and Jung, published in the AA magazine *The Grapevine.*

In recounting this story many years later, Jung observed that unrecognized spiritual needs can lead people into great difficulty and distress. He wrote that either "real religious insight or the protective wall of human community is essential to protect man from this." In talking specifically of Roland H., Jung wrote: "His craving for alcohol was the equivalent, on a low level, of the spiritual thirst of our being for wholeness, expressed in medieval language; the union with God."

Such concepts are largely foreign in contemporary American society. Take a survey of those in a few bars—be it the neighborhood tavern or a high-class hotel. How many drinkers do you expect to find who equate their use of alcohol with a search for God? Yet an objective examination of their use of alcohol may reveal otherwise. Alcohol is viewed as a magical potion, with the drinker expecting it to do the miraculous. The problem is that for a time it does, by alleviating shyness or awkwardness, or simply by turning off painful feelings. The backlash occurs later.

Every form of addiction is bad, no matter whether the narcotic be alcohol or morphine or idealism.
—Carl Jung
Memories, Dreams, and Reflections, 1962

The Clinician's Role

If convinced that attention to spiritual issues may be useful for some in treatment, what do you as a therapist do? First, cultivate some members of the clergy in your area. It seems that many communities have at least one member of the clergy who has stumbled into the alcohol field. It was often not a deliberate, intellectual decision. It may have occurred through a troubled parishioner who has gotten well or one who was drinking him- or herself to death—so that the clergy member, unable to watch the deterioration any longer, blundered through the equivalent of an intervention. The pastor may have aided a parishioner with an alcohol problem and then found more and more people with alcohol problems showing up on his or her doorstep. Or the clergy may themselves be in recovery and thus drawn into helping others. At any rate, this is the one you want. If you cannot identify such an individual, find one with whom you are comfortable talking about spiritual or religious issues. That means one with whom you don't feel silly or awkward and, equally important, who doesn't squirm in his or her seat, either, at talk of spiritual issues. Discussion of God and spiritual concerns can make people, including some clergy, as uncomfortable as does talk of drinking.

Once you find a resource person, it is an easy matter to provide your client with an opportunity to talk with that person. One way to make the contact is simply to suggest that the client sit down and talk with Joe Smith, who happens to be a Catholic priest or a rabbi or something else. It may also be worth pointing out to the client that the topic of concern is important and that the individual mentioned may be helpful in sorting it out. Set up the appointment, and let the clergy member take it from there. Some residential programs include a chaplain as a resource person. This person may simply be available to counsel clients or may take part in the formal program—for example, by providing a lecture in the educational series. What is important is that the presence and availability of this person give the message to clients that matters of the spirit are, indeed, important.

There are those for whom it may be especially important to reconnect with their spiritual and cultural roots. For example, someone can be culturally or ethnically Jewish but may not have been religiously Jewish. The intrusion of an alcohol problem may well provide the push to explore his or her spiritual heritage. Another group for whom spiritual issues may be of particular importance are Native Americans, as spiritual issues are integral to traditional culture. There are programs serving Native Americans that incorporate traditional healing ceremonies.

But What Is Spirituality?

Alcohol doesn't console, it doesn't fill up anyone's psychological gaps, all it replaces is the lack of God. It doesn't comfort man. On the contrary, it encourages him in his folly, it transports him to the supreme regions where he is master of his own destiny.
—Marguerite Duras

A review of the medical and psychological academic literature documents the burgeoning interest in spirituality. From the early 1920s through the 1970s, there were 26 papers with spirituality as a major topic. From 1981 through 2001, the total number was over 3,200. The bulk of these, especially the earliest materials, deal with addictions and substance use. While there is clearly a growing interest in spirituality, exactly what this means is unclear. In reviewing the academic publications, efforts were made to categorize a particular perspective on spirituality, a difficult task. In some cases, the emphasis was placed on what it does not mean—for example, that it is not synonymous with religious groups or formal church involvement. However, 12 conceptualizations of spirituality were identified. These different definitions and points of focus included:

- *Relatedness:* interpersonal relationships
- *Transcendence:* recognition of a transcendent dimension to life
- *Humanity:* the distinctiveness of humanity

- *Core/force/soul:* the inner "core," "force," or "soul" of a person
- *Meaning/purpose:* meaning and purpose in life
- *Authenticity/truth:* authenticity and truth
- *Values:* values, importance, and worth
- *Non-materiality:* opposition of the spiritual to the material
- *Non-religiousness:* opposition of spirituality to, or identity with, religion
- *Wholeness:* holistic wellness, wholeness, or health
- *Self-knowledge:* self-knowledge and self-actualization
- *Creativity:* creativity of the human agent

There is increasing interest in the spiritual dimension in medicine generally. This is reflected by the growing number of studies published in medical journals that examine the spiritual domain in respect to healing. It has long been recognized that those with religious affiliations or who express a belief in God often do better medically. Generally these findings are explained in terms of natural as opposed to supernatural phenomena. Possible psychological benefits associated with religion, that have been posed, include the presence of support systems, stress reduction, and the placebo effect. (The placebo effect is the benefit associated with hope or expectations, as seen in improvements that occur when people think they are taking a medication when, in fact, it is a sugar pill.) But there are those, while without a pretense of an answer, are suggesting in some instances there appears to be a "something more."

Religious societies that formerly made use of alcoholic wine in the celebration of the Lord's Supper have discovered that the use of it at the communion service has, in many instances, aroused the appetite for intoxicants in reformed persons, and thus have started them again on the declivity to ruin. Churches have likewise learned the use of alcohol as a beverage is the greatest barrier to the progress of religious truth.

J. M. Ferrington, quoted in *New York Times*, October 21, 1898. From a presentation to the New York Medical Association, provided as an example of changing cultural views.

While limited, nonetheless there is an emerging discussion of the role of spirituality in substance abuse treatment. This is evidenced by the growing number of studies on the topic being published in substance abuse journals. At this point, the challenge is to define spirituality and determine how it might be considered in thinking about important components of recovery. (In contrast to spirituality, religiosity is far easier to describe and to quantify!) Among the points most frequently mentioned as seemingly important are the sense of transcendence, the emergence of a life purpose, and a sense of renewal. To the extent the therapist might be involved, one author commented that the challenge is balance and at times abandoning the role of "expert" while learning to fill the role of the evocative facilitator.

The clinician, as an individual, may or may not consider spiritual issues personally important. What the caregiver needs is an awareness that this may have importance to a client. Current research findings indicate that an active spiritual or religious involvement reduces the risk of alcohol or other drug abuse. The risk for alcohol dependency is 60% higher among drinkers with no religious affiliation than among members of conservative Protestant denominations. Religiously involved individuals are consistently less likely to use alcohol and other drugs and, when they do so, are less likely to engage in heavy use and suffer its adverse consequences.

Spiritual Issues Versus Faith-based Initiatives

As discussed here, spirituality is seen as different from affiliation with a particular religious tradition or specific religious group. This distinction is important. Unfortunately, some of the efforts under way at the federal level are not as clear on this. There have been moves to increase public support for "faith-based programs." This includes faith-based substance abuse treatment, particularly in the correctional system. For many years, a variety of social service programs have been sponsored by religious groups. However, in most instances this does not dictate the nature of the treatment or services provided. However, when it comes to substance abuse treatment, not to mince words, a central ingredient in the programs is adoption of a particular religious view and practices, especially with a fundamentalist Christian orientation. For example, in these instances, core elements of the faith-based programs are Bible study and worship services.

Alcohol may be man's worst enemy, but the bible says love your enemy.
—Frank Sinatra

Faith-based programs have not been systematically studied. The chances are greater of finding information about them on the internet than in the research literature. Some of the claims made for them, such as 80% success rates, are unsupported. Clearly such initiatives may work for some; after all, it is clear that some people recover without any treatment. There is discomfort with the role of religious proselytizing within treatment programs, as well as some of the special handling these programs are requesting, such as being exempt from state licensing regulations.

Meditation

Meditation is frequently suggested as an aid in achieving and maintaining sobriety. It is increasingly being used in many areas of medicine. Any number of approaches are available to those wishing to try it, and many treatment centers include an introduction to one or more of these methods. Meditation classes are now widely available through hospitals, community centers, and churches. Although meditation has different results depending on the type practiced, reaching a meditative state is somewhat similar to practicing relaxation. A fairly relaxed state is necessary before meditation can begin. Some schools of meditation use techniques quite similar to relaxation methods as a lead-in to the meditation period. In yoga, physical exercises are coupled with suggested mental images as a precursor. Studies have shown that altered physiological states accompany meditation and deep relaxation. Altered breathing patterns and different brainwave patterns are examples. These changes are independent of the type of meditation practiced. The real physical response, in part, accounts for the feelings of well-being after meditation periods. Those who practice meditation find it, on the whole, a rewarding experience. Many also find in the experience some form of inspiration or spiritual help.

What is a meditation?

Perhaps a meditation is a daydream, a daydream of the soul as the beloved and God, the lover, their meeting in the tryst of prayer, their yearning for one another after parting; a daydream of their being united again.

Or perhaps a meditation is the becoming aware of the human soul of its loneliness and the anticipation of its being united with the One who transcends the All and is able to come past one's own defenses.

Or perhaps again it is a standing back with the whole of the cosmos before one's mind's eye as one's heart is being filled with the sheer joy of seeing the balances of the All and one's own self as part of it.

Or, perhaps a searching into one's own motives, values, and wishes with the light of the Torah against the background of the past.

Or perhaps . . .

Source: Siegel R, Strassfeld M, Strassfeld S. *The Jewish Catalogue*. Philadelphia: The Jewish Publication Society of America, 1973.

Activities Therapy

Activities therapy has been a mainstay of inpatient psychiatric treatment for a long time. It includes recreational and occupational therapy. To those unfamiliar with this field, the activities that are encompassed may look like "recreation" or diversionary activities, not real treatment. For the activities therapist, the event—such as a picnic, with the associated menu planning, food preparation, setup, and cleanup afterward—is of far less importance than the process of organizing the activity.

Recall that the alcohol-dependent person's repertoire of social skills has been depleted. Plus, it may have been a long time since there have been social interactions without alcohol, tasks completed, or responsibilities assumed and fulfilled. In addition, many clients have come to think of drinking not only as part of relaxation or leisure time but also as necessary to get some time out from responsibilities, to turn off tensions, or to get into some diversions. Then, too, during treatment the client can spend only so many hours a day involved in individual counseling, attending group therapy sessions, or listening to lectures and films. Activities therapy programs can be the forum in which the client has the opportunity, with support and guidance, to try out some of the new behaviors that may have been discussed elsewhere and will be necessary in sobriety. Activities therapy may be the portion of the therapeutic program that will most closely approximate real life.

A common dilemma for those in recovery is how to fill the time that they used to spend drinking. A part of the activity therapist's task will be to identify past interests or activities that can be reawakened and resumed, not only to fill time but also to provide a sense of accomplishment and belonging. The activities therapist will be sensitive to the client's limitations. The person who used to have a half-acre garden and is now going to make up for lost time by plowing up another half-acre can be cautioned to take it easy. One or two tomato plants plus a few lettuce and radish plants may be the place to start.

One of the early adaptations of activities therapy in alcohol treatment was the use of Outward Bound programs. Outward Bound grew out of training measures adopted by the British Merchant Navy in World War II. It was discovered that, among the merchant marines who were stranded at sea, those who survived were not the youngest or those who were most physically fit. Rather, it was their older, "life-seasoned" comrades. From that observation, an attempt was made to provide a training experience that incorporated physically challenging and psychologically demanding tasks that would provide these skills.

Outward Bound was introduced in the United States in 1961. Since that time, its programs have been conducted in a range of settings from rehabilitation programs for people with disabilities to training programs for corporate executives. The programs can be a day, several days, or a week in length. Typically an Outward Bound experience combines group exercises, such as a group being given the task of getting all of its members over a 10-foot wall, with individual activities, such as rock climbing. Within alcohol treatment programs, this therapy was used with individual clients, sometimes used with a family group, and was commonly used with adolescents. The staff typically included a professional alcohol clinician, as well as the Outward Bound instructors. Integral to Outward Bound is discussing and processing what transpires during each exercise. Alcoholics Anonymous adages such as "One step (day) at a time" and "Easy does it" might be the topic of a group meeting. These take on a new meaning to someone who has been involved in scaling a cliff or negotiating a ropes course 20 feet off the ground. In the course of a residential treatment program, clients might participate in one or two such sessions.

Since first introduced in alcohol treatment, there has been a proliferation of programs that have used such activities. Some of these programs are accredited by health and outdoor educational associations; others are not. This leads to a wide range of quality. A large proportion are directed at adolescents. Among the most troublesome are those sometimes referred to as "boot camps," which have little resemblance to Outward Bound programs. Rather than being one activity within a larger program, these *are* the programs. They are more likely to be punitive than supportive. Staff may have no credentials in substance abuse or human services or outdoor education. Sadly, periodically there is an account of an adolescent who has experienced serious harm or death. The circumstances might be something such as a "forced march" in the heat of the day, without being provided water or being allowed to rest in the shade.

The man that isn't jolly after drinking is just a drivelling idiot, to my thinking.
—EURIPIDES

Recreation and Fun

A common complaint from the person entering treatment is "Everyone drinks! How can I have any fun if I'm the only one who doesn't?" Despite the fact that this is often a last-gasp effort to discount the need for treatment, it does point to a problem down the line—how to have fun without alcohol or, for some, how to have fun at all. What is the clinician to say? There may be little to be said at the point the question is raised, when the more significant question is, "Is life fun now?" But it is an issue that has to be taken seriously.

In planning treatment, the issue of leisure needs to be addressed. Fun, ultimately, is not what we do but how we experience what we do. It is not an event but an experience. The word "recreation," thus, may be more apt to capture the phenomenon. It flows from the activities in life that refresh us, renew us, and offer us the sorely needed counterpoint to the hectic, busy lives we live. One person's recreation is another's work. Recreation can encompass active pursuits, such as a brisk walk or a pickup game of basketball at the school playground. Recreation can be individual, a private activity with some solitary time for reading a book or tending a garden. Recreation may be a group activity. It may be spontaneous or planned. An essential characteristic of recreation is that it is wholly engaging. When we are living in the present, we can neither worry about tomorrow nor relive yesterday.

Initial treatment, whether in a residential or an outpatient setting, is going to be highly regimented and entail a well-structured schedule. The idea is not to schedule assigned time slots in which clients are instructed to have fun. They would be at a total loss. To relax or have fun does not usually occur on command either. For those in recovery, it is a capacity that will need to be evoked and rediscovered. For many, the initial moments of relaxation may go unrecognized. They may be quite unspectacular moments. A game of cards, a conversation, or a movie—recreation can encompass anything that pushes alcohol from the foreground and turns off a preoccupation with oneself and one's plight. It is important to assist clients to recognize these moments and to not discount the enjoyment. It is more important, too, to incorporate events that up the odds of these moments occurring. During later recovery, recreation is no less an issue. At this point it may be considered as a part of the task that confronts us all. It can be put under the rubric of taking care of ourselves. Recreation is a necessary self-indulgence.

Fitness and Well-Being

Activities that center on fitness and sports are becoming a more important element in many individuals' efforts to take care of themselves. Within treatment programs, efforts to address general fitness are now more common. In residential settings, without conscious effort to have it be otherwise, the day would be filled almost exclusively with sedentary activities. The treatment of alcohol abuse can address larger issues of general health without diverting attention from the focus on alcohol. Regular exercise and good nutrition do have a significant impact on how people feel. This in turn can set in motion a positive cycle—one where change promotes further change. Feeling better and being proud of efforts that contributed to this leads to an improved sense of competence, reinforces expectations that things can improve, and opens up new possibilities for activities that are rewarding and enhance self-worth.

In keeping with a self-care orientation, many alcohol treatment programs have become "smoke free," do not allow smoking, and promote or require smoking cessation as well as abstinence from alcohol use. The case for not allowing nicotine use can be made on many grounds: (1) smoking is viewed as a health issue and medical concern, as serious as chronic alcohol use; (2) smoking is seen as a behavior that often accompanies drinking, so that if not discontinued it will be a ready cue to take a drink; (3) nicotine is viewed as a drug that is as addictive as or more addictive than alcohol or other substances; or (4) all of the above. As a practical point, the physical and emotional discomfort of withdrawal from alcohol is not compounded by the simultaneous withdrawal of nicotine. Residential programs that have initiated such policies have reported a relatively infrequent number of client complaints in respect to giving up nicotine as well.

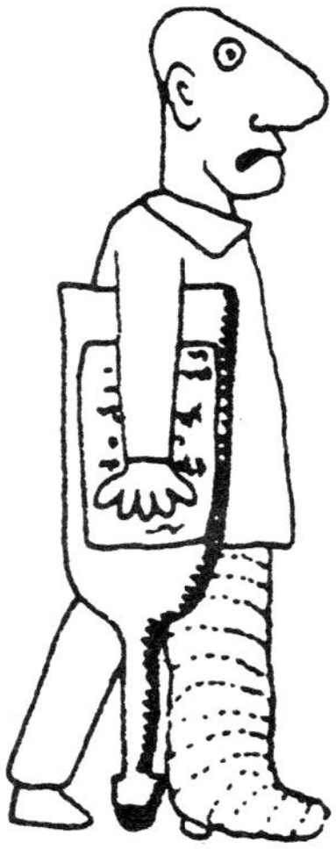

PHARMACOTHERAPY

Increasing knowledge about the biological factors that are a part of abuse and dependence has opened the doors for the development of drug therapies that may be useful in the treatment of addictive disorders. A better understanding of the changes in the central nervous system that accompany abuse and dependence has set the stage for the development of targeted pharmacological agents. The substance abuse field has seen some resistance to the use of drug therapies. The objections at the core seem essentially punitive and moralistic, though that explanation risks oversimplification. For some, pharmacological intervention is seen as offering dependent individuals an easy way out. Closely aligned with this is the notion that the use of drugs to treat addiction may be a "slippery slope"—sending a "mixed message" and suggesting that drugs can be used to solve problems or implying that sobriety or a drug-free life isn't really necessary. Some, too, have described drug therapy as a crutch. This doesn't seem out of place when one's legs are impaired. To the contrary, one might think of drug therapies as vital aids. For the alcohol-dependent person, drug therapy can buy sober time until the legs are steadier and other healthy supports are developed. The supports may be available already, but the individual has to be able to use them successfully.

Disulfiram (Antabuse)

Disulfiram has been available for 60 years. It was discovered in the late 1940s, through a series of accidents. A group of Danish scientists found that disulfiram, the drug they were testing for other purposes, led to a marked reaction when the researchers who had been working with it had a drink. Disulfiram alters the metabolism of alcohol by blocking an enzyme necessary for the breakdown of acetaldehyde, an intermediate product of alcohol metabolism. Acetaldehyde is normally present in the body in small amounts, in somewhat larger ones when alcohol is ingested, and in toxic amounts when alcohol is taken into the body after disulfiram medication. Thus, the basis for disulfiram's effects is its effect on metabolism, not its influence on the brain. In fact, sometimes the reaction that occurs with drinking is called an "acetaldehyde reaction."

This adverse physical reaction is characterized by throbbing in the head and neck, flushing, breathing difficulty, nausea, vomiting, sweating, tachycardia (rapid heartbeat), weakness, and vertigo (dizziness). The intensity of the reaction varies from person to person and varies with the amount of disulfiram present and the amount of alcohol taken in. Disulfiram is excreted slowly from the body, so the possibility of a reaction is present for four to five days after the last dose and, in some cases, longer. Because of this reaction, Antabuse has been used in the treatment of alcohol dependence. There have recently been a spate of articles suggesting that Antabuse is being under-utilized. There has also been discussion about whether a "test drink" might lead to better outcomes, since people would have a firsthand experience of what occurs with drinking. To examine this question, researchers interviewed people who in fact had consumed alcohol when taking disulfiram. Interestingly, this did *not* lead to better treatment outcomes. However it did lead to significantly earlier termination of disulfiram.

Prescription, Administration, and Use

Over the years since disulfiram's discovery, trial and error and research have led to some suggestions for its prescription, administration, and use in alcohol treatment. Disulfiram is not a cure. At best, it can postpone the drink. If the recovering client chooses to use disulfiram as an adjunct to AA, psychotherapy, group therapy, and so forth, it can be most useful in helping someone not have the impulsive drink. Because disulfiram stays in the system for such a long time, whatever caused the impulsive desire for a drink can be examined during the five-day grace period.

Anyone who wishes to use disulfiram should be allowed to do so, provided they are physically and mentally able. The client should first be thoroughly examined by a physician to determine physical status. Some conditions contraindicate disulfiram usage. There is still some debate about the need for such caution with lower doses, but only the client's physician can decide this point. In some cases, physicians consider the risks of a disulfiram reaction not as dire as continued drinking certainly would be. When disulfiram is prescribed, generally 1 tablet (0.5 gm) is given daily for five days, and half a tablet daily thereafter. During the initial five days the client is carefully monitored for side effects. Once the client is receiving the maintenance dose, the client can continue for as long as it is beneficial. There are those who suggest that administration should be supervised for at least a short time, preferably not by the spouse. Rather, supervision can be provided through a visit to an outpatient clinic or an employee health clinic. Disulfiram should be used in combination with other supportive therapies.

Alcohol, the Ultimate Additive

Someone is putting brandy in your bonbons, Grand Marnier in your breakfast jam, Kahlua in your ice cream, Scotch in your mustard and Wild Turkey in your cake.

—MARIAN BURROS

New York Times, December 20, 1986

The client taking disulfiram must be thoroughly informed of the dangers of a possible reaction. A variety of substances (such as cough syrup, wine sauces, and paint fumes) that contain some alcohol can cause a reaction. Clients taking disulfiram should be provided with a list of such substances. Carrying a card or wearing a "Med-Alert disk," stating they are taking disulfiram, may be wise. Some medications given to accident victims or in emergency situations could cause a disulfiram reaction, compounding whatever else is wrong. There is no way to tell whether an unconscious person has been taking disulfiram without such a warning.

Disulfiram can free the client from the constant battle against the bottle. When someone decides to take the pill on a given day, that person has made one choice that will postpone that drink for at least four or five days. If continuing to take it daily, that fourth or fifth day is always well out ahead. This allows time to begin acquiring or relearning behaviors other than drinking behaviors, and the habits of sobriety can take hold.

A physician addressing an annual convention of Connecticut physicians at Groton offered homespun family practitioners a few points in the treatment of drunkards, whom he calls "problem-drinkers." For the past six years he has been treating them on his Wakefield, R.I., farm. . . . "Problem-drinkers should always have something to think about and something to do." The best thing Dr. Durfee has found yet is farm life. He keeps his patients digging ditches, mending fences, clearing fields, tending bees. After six years of curing drunks, Dr. Durfee has an extraordinarily good-looking farm.

Time Magazine, June 13, 1938

Medications Containing Alcohol

Alcohol, in its many forms, was for centuries virtually the only pharmacological agent available to physicians. Beginning in the twentieth century, alcohol has had limited medicinal uses. Now, in addition to being used externally as an antiseptic (e.g., to wash the skin before giving an injection or taking a blood sample, except when this sample is being obtained to measure blood alcohol levels), its major use is as an "inert" medium or carrier for liquid medications. Alcohol is an almost universal ingredient of cough medicines and liquid cold preparations sold over the counter or by prescription. Furthermore, the percentage of alcohol in such preparations can be substantial. NyQuil, for example, contains 25% alcohol. That's 50 proof. Alcohol is also an ingredient in a variety of other kinds of commonly used liquid medications. Recovering individuals may be advised to avoid alcohol-containing preparations. For those taking disulfiram, it is imperative. Preparations for coughs and colds that do not contain alcohol are increasingly available. A pharmacist is always the most knowledgeable person to provide information on alcohol content of over-the-counter drugs and the availability of alternative preparations.

Anti-Craving Agents

While potentially triggered by events, feelings, and situations, craving has a physiological basis. The increased knowledge of brain chemistry and the various neurotransmitter systems that play a role in dependence opens a large array of possibilities for the development of drugs that can aid treatment. One drug, *naltrexone,* first used in the treatment of opiate addiction, has been found to be helpful as well in the treatment of alcohol dependence. In clinical trials it was found that those taking naltrexone reported fewer episodes of craving. In addition, they reported less of a response to alcohol and drinking smaller amounts if drinking occurred. These early reports in treatment settings were particularly encouraging because the patients taking naltrexone were the "treatment failures"—those who had been in treatment several times and had never achieved sustained sobriety. Naltrexone was approved for alcohol treatment in 1995 and is marketed as Revia.

In 2004, *acamprosate,* marketed as Camporal, was approved for use in the United States. It had been available in Europe for a number of years. Exactly how it works is unclear; unlike disulfiram, it doesn't interfere with alcohol metabolism and induce nausea. Unlike naltrexone, it doesn't appear to block the high associated with alcohol. However, it does act on one of the major neurotransmitter systems (GABA). It appears to reduce craving. Both of these drugs, like disulfiram, can be useful in opening a window of opportunity for clients, by buying time. By addressing the acute, short-term pressures, there is the chance to gain the tools needed to maintain sobriety and to make the needed long-term changes.

Both naltrexone and acamprosate are referred to as anti-craving medications, but there are differences between them. The title of a research article pointed to one difference: "Acamprosate Supports Abstinence, Naltrexone Prevents Excessive Drinking." Both have been found to help maintain abstinence. However, if/when drinking occurs, naltrexone is associated with less heavy drinking. However, acamprosate, while equally successful in maintaining abstinence, does not alter the amount consumed after the first drink.

Disulfiram, naltrexone, and acamprosate are the only medications currently approved specifically for use in treating alcohol dependence. Other drugs are being studied, ranging from anticonvulsants, to drugs used in treating psychiatric illness, to one used in treating hypertension. More should be expected. We have moved far beyond the situation that confronted the Danish laboratory staff who discovered that the beer with dinner didn't sit so well. As more is learned about the impact of alcohol on the brain and the role of neurotransmitters, there will be the potential for making educated guesses about the characteristics of a particular drug that may make it useful. Also, it needs to be appreciated that the likelihood that there will be a single wonder drug is even less likely than your chances of winning the Megabucks pot.

Alcohol dependence has been described as a heterogeneous condition. This means that while alcohol dependence looks essentially the same on the outside, a variety of biological features predispose someone to develop dependence, or play a role in how dependence emerges, or influence the degree of severity or the likelihood of accompanying medical problems. At this time our ability to distinguish between different "types" of alcohol dependence is limited—familial versus non-familial, or Type A versus Type B, early onset versus late onset. However, that will change with our increasing understanding of genetics and the way different genes influence the unfolding of alcohol dependence. The federally funded Combine Study, analogous to Project MATCH, was initiated to gain a better understanding of the effectiveness of drug therapy or placebo, in combination with behavior therapy, for different types of alcohol dependence.

TREATMENT MATCHING

With such a variety of treatment approaches, the important question becomes "What works for whom?" Is it simply a matter of taste and clinician preference? Are some treatment approaches better suited for some clients? Is it possible to match patients to treatments that represent a better fit and yield better outcomes?

Project MATCH

As the name indicates, the problem that prompted the NIAAA to launch the major, multisite research effort known as Project MATCH was identifying which treatments might be most effective with particular patients. The three treatment approaches that were examined were selected because research had shown them to be effective in treating alcohol dependence. So the natural follow-up question was, "Are there some patients who would do better using one approach over the others?" The three therapies—Twelve-Step Facilitation, Motivational Enhancement, and Cognitive-Behavioral Coping Skills—were all provided as part of outpatient treatment. However, for some patients this outpatient treatment followed an inpatient stay and thus represented aftercare.

The 1,700 clients who participated in the study were alcohol-dependent. Each client agreed to an initial assessment and then to accept assignment to one of the treatment approaches. The initial assessment took about eight hours. The goal was to measure 21 client characteristics that prior research had shown were related to treatment outcome. These included gender; drinking pattern; cognitive impairment; severity of alcohol dependence; prior AA involvement; self-efficacy (level of confidence that one can take action versus feeling immobilized); level of social functioning; presence of any psychiatric problem, and if present what type and its severity; religiosity; readiness to change; social support for abstinence; level of anger; and type of alcohol dependence. There was follow-up of patients at one year and again at three years.

With only a few exceptions, clients, whatever their characteristics, did equally well in each of the treatment approaches. Four patient characteristics were significant. Persons with the following attributes did better or worse in their assigned treatment approaches:

1. *Presence of any psychiatric problem.* For those without any prior inpatient care, and those without a co-occurring psychiatric illness, Twelve-Step Facilitation led to the best outcomes.
2. *Severity of alcohol dependence.* Those with more severe alcohol dependence who were receiving the assigned treatment (as aftercare) following inpatient care did better with Twelve-Step Facilitation.
3. *Level of anger.* Motivational Enhancement Therapy worked best for people who had high levels of anger and had not had inpatient treatment immediately prior to this therapy.

4. *Social support for abstinence.* Twelve-Step Facilitation therapy worked best for those with little family support. In effect, the members in Twelve-Step Programs became a substitute supportive family for these people. This approach was also most effective for those whose social networks involved heavy drinking or centered on drinking.

Possibly the most useful immediate result of the Project MATCH research initiative was not the findings, but the manuals that were developed. Originally used to train the clinicians participating in the study, they have since been a vehicle for disseminating these approaches throughout the treatment community.

Combine Study

The Project MATCH research described above was concerned with determining the effectiveness of three different treatment approaches. However, it is not uncommon for medical conditions to be treated with different types of therapies at the same time. Take heart disease. Although drugs may be prescribed, the optimal approach requires far more than swallowing pills. Equally important are "lifestyle changes." Those in the substance abuse field certainly appreciate that "lifestyle changes" may sound simple, but are anything but.

The Combine Study, an initiative of NIAAA, following Project MATCH, was directed at examining the effects of drug therapies—acamprosate and naltrexone, either alone or together—when combined with one of two therapies, or both. One of the therapies was *combined behavioral intervention,* which draws upon both motivational interviewing and cognitive behavioral therapy and involved four treatment sessions. The other therapeutic approach was *medical management.* Among the findings were that patients who received medical management with naltrexone, or combined behavioral intervention, or both, had the best outcomes in terms of drinking. Even if a placebo was used instead of naltrexone, the outcomes were still better than the combined behavioral intervention alone. There was support for the use of acamprosate, with or without combined behavioral intervention. If one considers that a small proportion of those with alcohol problems ever receive treatment, the positive result of naltrexone with medical management is an important outcome. It provides another venue for treatment that has the potential for reaching a substantial number of people.

Looking Ahead

Treatment matching in the not too distant future is likely to be far more sophisticated. Our ever-increasing knowledge of the biological basis of alcohol use disorders will influence the selection of treatment modalities in a given case. One of the common refrains in the substance abuse field is to refer to addiction as a *brain disease*. Indeed, in a relatively brief period, much has been learned about the role of various neurotransmitters and genetic influences. On the other hand, while almost sounding contradictory, the diagnosis of substance use disorders is still based exclusively on behavioral symptoms, not biological indicators. Similarly, research on treatment outcome finds that probably the oldest modern treatment for alcohol disorders is associated with the best outcomes—i.e., Alcoholics Anonymous. Ironically, maybe the most pressing challenge is to enhance access to treatment for substance use problems, to act as if early detection is as critical as early diagnosis of cancer, to call upon the considerable knowledge of risk and protective factors, and to have substance use disorders become a public health priority.

REFERENCES AND FURTHER READINGS

A wealth of publications for the general public and substance abuse clinician are available from the three federal agencies involved in substance abuse. These are NIAAA <www.niaaa.nih.gov/publications/>; NIDA <www.drugabuse.gov/publications>; and SAMHSA <http://store.samhsa.gov/home>. Unfortunately, there is no "one stop shopping." Of particular interest to clinicians are *Addiction Science & Clinical Practice* and *NIDA Notes* (from NIDA); *Alcohol Research: Current Reviews* (NIAAA); and selections from special series such as the "TAP (Technical Assistance Protocols) Series" and the "TIP (Treatment Improvement Protocols)" available from the SAMHSA store. Also SAMHSA includes a host of regular newsletters on trends taken from a wide, wide range of topics, from patterns of substance use trends to issues of special populations.

AA World Services. *Alcoholics Anonymous 2011 Membership Survey*. New York: AA World Services, 2012.

Abraham AJ, Ducharme LJ, Roman PM. Counselor attitudes toward pharmacotherapies for alcohol dependence. *Journal of Studies on Alcohol and Drugs* 70(4):628–635, 2009. (20 refs.)

Al-Anon Family Groups. *2012 Membership Survey Results and Longitudinal Comparisons*. Virginia Beach VA: Al-Anon Family Groups, 2013.

Alemi F, Haack MR, Nemes S, Aughburns R, Sinkule J, Neuhauser D. Therapeutic emails. *Substance Abuse Treatment, Prevention, and Policy* 2:article 7, 2007. (40 refs.)

Barth KS, Malcolm RJ. Disulfiram: An old therapeutic with new applications. *CNS & Neurological Disorders. Drug Targets* 9(1):5–12, 2010. (64 refs.)

Bickel WK, Christensen DR, Marsch LA. A review of computer-based interventions used in the assessment, treatment, and research of drug addiction (review). *Substance Use & Misuse* 46(1):4–9, 2011. (45 refs.)

Bryant-Jefferies R. *Counselling the Person Beyond the Alcohol Problem*. Abingdon, UK: Radcliffe Medical Press, 2006.

Cook CCH. Addiction and spirituality. *Addiction* 99(6):539–551, 2004. (31 refs.)

Copello AG, Velleman RD, Templeton LJ. Family interventions in the treatment of alcohol and drug problems (review). 24(4):369–385, 2005. (166 refs.)

Fals-Stewart W, Lam WKK, Kelley ML. Learning sobriety together: Behavioural couples therapy for alcoholism and drug abuse. *Journal of Family Therapy* 31(2):115–125, 2009. (27 refs.)

Fernandez AC, Begley EA, Marlatt GA. Family and peer interventions for adults: Past approaches and future directions. *Psychology of Addictive Behaviors* 20(2):207–213, 2006. (51 refs.)

Flores PJ, Georgi JM. *Substance Abuse Treatment: Group Therapy. Treatment Improvement Protocol (TIP) Series 41*. Rockville, MD: Center for Substance Abuse Treatment, 2005. (218 refs.) Available online at www.ncbi.nlm.nih.gov/books/bv.fcgi?rid=hstat5.chapter.78366.

Huebner RB, Kantor LW. Advances in alcoholism treatment. *Alcohol Research & Health* 33(4):295–299, 2011. (7 refs.)

Humphreys K. A research-based analysis of the Moderation Management controversy. *Psychiatric Services* 54(5):621–622, 2003. (10 refs.)

Humphreys K, Wing S, McCartry D, Chappel J, Gallant L, Haberl B, et al. Self-help organizations for alcohol and drug problems: Toward evidence-based practice and policy. *Journal of Substance Abuse Treatment* 26:151–158, 2004. (25 refs.)
Note: This is a consensus statement that reviews the effectiveness of self-help groups and discusses policy initiatives to promote their use.

Kaskutas LA, Turk N, Bond J, Weisner C. The role of religion, spirituality and Alcoholics Anonymous in sustained sobriety. *Alcoholism Treatment Quarterly* 21(1):1–16, 2003. (26 refs.)

Kelley M, Klostermann K, Doane AN, Mignone T, Lam WKK, Fals-Stewart W, et al. The case for examining and treating the combined effects of parental drug use and interparental violence on children in their homes. *Aggression and Violent Behavior* 15(1):76–82, 2010. (119 refs.)

Koerner BI. Secret of AA: After 75 Years, We Don't Know How It Works. *Wired.* June 23, 2010.

Kranzler HR, Gage A. Acamprosate efficacy in alcohol-dependent patients: Summary of results from three pivotal trials. *American Journal on Addictions* 17(1):70–76, 2008. (35 refs.)

Landau J, Garrett J. Invitational Intervention: The ARISE Model for engaging reluctant alcohol and other drug abusers in treatment. *Alcoholism Treatment Quarterly* 26(1/2):147–168, 2008.

Lipsky S, Caetano R. Is intimate partner violence associated with the use of alcohol treatment services? Results from the National Survey on Drug Use and Health. *Journal of Studies on Alcohol and Drugs* 69(1):30–38, 2008. (76 refs.)

Meyers RJ, Miller WR, eds. *A Community Reinforcement Approach to Addiction Treatment.* Cambridge: Cambridge University Press, 2006. (191 pp.)

Moos RH. Iatrogenic effects of psychosocial interventions for substance use disorders: Prevalence, predictors, prevention. *Addiction* 100(8):595–604, 2005. (96 refs.)

Moos RH, Moos BS. Participation in treatment and Alcoholics Anonymous: A 16-year follow-up of initially untreated individuals. *Journal of Clinical Psychology* 62(6):735–750, 2006. (51 refs.)

Moos RH, Moos BS. Paths of entry into Alcoholics Anonymous: Consequences for participation and remission. *Alcoholism: Clinical and Experimental Research* 29(10):1858–1868, 2005. (42 refs.) Note: reports of 16-year follow-up.

Mutschler J, Dirican G, Funke S, Obermann C, Grosshans M, Mann K, et al. Experienced acetaldehyde reaction does not improve treatment response in outpatients treated with supervised disulfiram (review). *Clinical Neuropharmacology* 34(4):161–165, 2011. (29 refs.)

Office of Applied Studies, Substance Abuse and Mental Health Administration. *The NSDUH Report: Participation in Self-Help Groups for Alcohol and Illicit Drug Use: 2006 and 2007* (November 13, 2008). Rockville MD: Substance Abuse and Mental Health Administration, 2009. (6 refs.)

O'Malley SS, O'Connor PG. Medications for unhealthy alcohol use. *Alcohol Research & Health* 33(4):300+, 2011. (83 refs.)

Postel MG, de Haan HA, ter Huurne ED, Becker ES, de Jong CAJ. Characteristics of problem drinkers in e-therapy versus face-to-face treatment. *American Journal of Drug and Alcohol Abuse* 37(6):537–542, 2011. (25 refs.)

Roozen HG, Blaauw E, Meyers RJ. Advances in management of alcohol use disorders and intimate partner violence: Community reinforcement and family training. *Psychiatry, Psychology and Law* 16(Supplement S):s74–s80, 2009. (50 refs.)

Rosner S, Leucht S, Lehert P, Soyka M. Acamprosate supports abstinence, naltrexone prevents excessive drinking: Evidence from a meta-analysis with unreported outcomes. *Journal of Psychopharmacology* 22(1):11–23, 2008. (78 refs.)

Ruff S, McComb JL, Coker CJ, Sprenkle DH. Behavioral couples therapy for the treatment of substance abuse: A substantive and methodological review of O'Farrell, Fals-Stewart, and colleagues' program of research. *Family Process* 49(4):439–456, 2010. (44 refs.)

Russell KC, Hendee JC, Phillips-Miller D. How wilderness therapy works: An examination of the wilderness therapy process to treat adolescents with behavioral problems and addictions. *USDA Forest Service Proceedings* RMRS-P-15 (Vol. 3): 207–217, 2000. (16 refs.)

Sacks S, Ries RK. *Substance Abuse Treatment for Persons with Co-Occurring Disorders. Treatment Improvement Protocol (TIP) 42.* Rockville MD: Center for Substance Abuse Treatment, 2005. (874 refs.)

Saladin ME, Santa Ana EJ. Controlled drinking: More than just a controversy. *Current Opinion in Psychiatry* 17(3):175–187, 2004. (96 refs.)
Note: This special issue examines different approaches to controlled drinking, from the earliest use and controversy to clinical approaches in the 21st century.

Segun M, Lesage A, Xhewky N, Guy A, et al. Suicide cases in New Brunswick from April 2002 to May 2003: The importance of better recognizing substance and mood disorder comorbidity. *Canadian Journal of Psychiatry* 51(9):581–586. (28 refs.)

Shannon L, Logan T, Cole J, Walker R. An examination of women's alcohol use and partner victimization experiences among women with protective orders. *Substance Use & Misuse* 43(8/9):1110–1128, 2008. (60 refs.)

Smith PH, Homish GG, Leonard KE, Cornelius JR. Women ending marriage to a problem drinking partner decrease their own risk for problem drinking. *Addiction* 107(8):1453–1461, 2012. (29 refs.)

Steinglass P. Systemic-motivational therapy for substance abuse disorders: An integrative model. *Journal of Family Therapy* 31(2):155–174, 2009. (45 refs.)

Stuart GL, Temple JR, Follansbee KW, Bucossi MA, Hellmuth JC, Moore TM. The role of drug use in a conceptual model of intimate partner violence in men and women arrested for domestic violence. *Psychology of Addictive Behaviors* 22(1):12–24, 2008. (62 refs.)

Taskforce of College on Problems of Drug Dependence, Stitzer ML, Owen PL, Hall SM, Rawson RA, Petry NM. Standards for drug abuse treatment providers. *Drug and Alcohol Dependence* 71(2):213–215, 2003.
Note: This policy statement was adopted in the wake of discussion of funding faith-based programs. The concern of the college is not sponsorship of treatment by religious organizations, but the need, in all settings, for evidence-based clinical approaches to ensure that quality care is provided.

Special Populations

There may be remarkable similarities between the 15-year-old alcohol abuser who also dabbles with club drugs and the 72-year-old retired schoolteacher who never drinks anything stronger than a nice white wine. But that should not blind us to the equally significant differences. In this chapter, the focus is on the distinctive characteristics of special populations, particularly adolescents, college students, the elderly, women, and those in the workplace. The groups selected for attention here are those that cut across all segments of society. Of course, no segment of the population is untouched by alcohol or other drug problems, and the chapter concludes with some suggested ways to identify the needs and issues of groups not specifically discussed in this chapter.

Much work has been done with respect to special population groups. The discussion here just begins to skim the surface. Also, space does not allow equal discussion of racial and ethnic groups or other groups with special issues, such as gays and lesbians. This textbook cannot begin to acquaint you with the characteristics and issues you may have to consider when working with clients from any particular ethnic, racial, or religious group. You are urged to speak with more experienced colleagues, as well as to turn to the ever-increasing body of literature on minorities, racial and ethnic groups, and other special populations—African Americans, Native Americans, Asian Americans, Hispanics, migrant workers, and those with disabilities. However, thinking about the special considerations of the groups that are discussed here may make you more sensitive to the characteristics of any client—that is the hope.

ADOLESCENTS

Adolescence is indeed a special period of life. It lies at the backdoor of childhood yet at the very doorstep of adulthood. At no comparable time in life do more physical and emotional changes take place in such a narrow span of time. "Adolescence" as we understand the concept is less than 150 years old. Before the mid–nineteenth century, the prevailing view was that one grew straight from childhood into adulthood. The needs of family and culture demanded earlier work and community responsibilities. Survival depended on it. With increasing industrialization, children left the factories and fields to spend more time in school, play, and idle time. Society became increasingly aware of the presence of teenagers as a group who had, and still have, fairly indefinable roles and rights. Most texts define "adolescence" as the period from 10 or 12 to 21 years of age. Physical and legal determinants would suggest otherwise. Physical changes indicative of the beginning of adolescence may begin as early as age 7 and not end until the mid-20s. Setting the voting and the draft registration age at 18 has clouded the definition.

There is no time like the old time,
when you and I were young.
—Oliver Wendell Holmes
"No Time Like the Old Time," c.1858

Physical Changes and Developmental Issues

The most striking aspect of adolescence is the rapid physical growth, which is mediated by the sex hormones. The accompanying charts indicate that the first recognizable change in the male is caused by a fat increase dictated by a small but gradual increase in estrogen. Every boy gains weight at the expense of height during these years. Some boys who will become tall and muscular men are quite chubby during these early adolescent years. The next body part to grow is the feet, then the thighs, making boys appear short-waisted and gawky at this time. Growth of these parts slows, allowing the rest of the body to catch up. Androgen influence appears later, with pigment changes in the scrotal sac, then

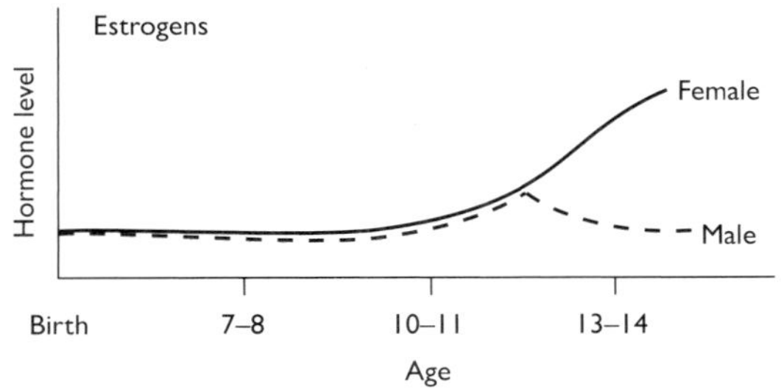

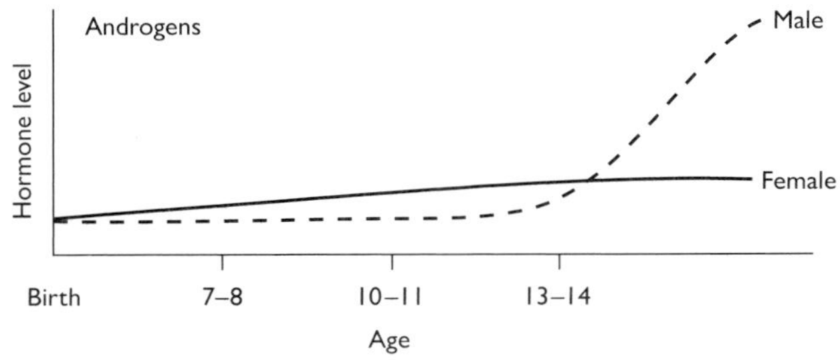

enlargement of the testes and penis, the beginning of pubic hair, and early voice changes. The first nocturnal emission, or "wet dream," may occur as early as age 10 or as late as age 15. Even so, the majority of boys remain "relatively sterile" until age 15. The major male growth spurt appears at age 14½ and is due primarily to growth in the backbone. This averages 4 to 4½ inches over an 18-month period. Some boys shoot up 8 to 10 more inches during this time. Axillary and facial hair soon follow. Facial hair may develop entirely in one year. Other boys, equally normal but with different genes, may not complete the facial- and body-hair growth until their mid- to late 20s.

A girl's first hormonal response is around age 7 or 8, with a normal vaginal discharge called leukorrhea. The feet then grow, but this is rarely as noticeable a change as in the male. A breast "button" begins about age 10 under the skin of one breast first, to be followed in weeks or months under the other breast. The breasts develop into adult breasts over a span of four to five years. Pubic hair begins approximately six months after the breast button stage. The hips widen, and the backbone gains 3 to 4 inches before she is ready for her menses. Although a critical body weight is not the only initiator, the timing is influenced by this. If other criteria are met, such as developing breasts, pubic hair, widened hips, and growth spurt, a sample of American girls will begin their menses when weighing from 100 to 105 pounds. Nutrition has a great deal to do with the menarche (first menses); girls in countries with poor nutritional standards begin their menses two to three years later. The mean age for menarche in the United States is 12. (Pilgrim girls, who suffered from many nutritional deprivations, often had menarche delayed until age 17.) A regular menstrual cycle is not established immediately. Quite commonly a girl will have anovulatory (no egg) periods for 6 to 18 months before having ovulatory periods. This change may bring an increased weight gain, breast tenderness, occasional emotional lability, and cramps at the mid-cycle. These are consequences of progesterone, a hormone secreted by the ovary at the time of ovulation. An adult pattern in ovulation will not be completed until the early 20s.

We are indeed taller than our ancestors, which can be shown from historical evidence. Clothing, doorways, and furniture were made for shorter men and women. Better nutrition is mainly responsible for the changes seen.

Until puberty, boys and girls are equal in muscle strength (if corrected for height and weight). Total body fat increases in girls by 50% from ages 12 to 18, whereas a similar decrease occurs in boys. Muscle cell size and number increase in boys; muscle cell size alone increases in girls. Internal organs, such as the heart, double in size. Blood pressure increases with demands of growth. Pulse rate decreases, and the ability to break down fatigue metabolites in muscle prepares the male, especially, for the role of hunter and runner, which was so important for survival centuries ago.

Marked fatigue, coupled with overwhelming strength, is often difficult to fully appreciate. An adolescent may wolf down several quarts of milk, a full meal or two, play many hours of active sports, and yet complain bitterly of being tired at all times. This human metabolic furnace needs the food and rest as well as the drive to have the machine function and test itself out. These bodily inconsistencies often show in mood swings and unpredictable demands for self-satisfaction and physical expression.

The rapidity of these changes tends to produce an almost physiological confusion in many adolescents. Quite commonly they become preoccupied with themselves. This can lead to an undue concern with their health. In some instances it is almost hypochondriacal. Adolescents may complain of things that to an adult appear very minor. The thing to remember is that their concern is very real and deep. Attention should be paid to their concerns. Remembering the rapid rate of physical changes that confront adolescents makes their preoccupation with their bodies understandable.

Characteristics of Adolescence

Characteristically, adolescence is an extremely healthy time of life. In general, adolescents do not die from the kinds of things that strike the rest of us, such as heart disease. The major causes of adolescent deaths are accidents, suicide, and homicide. Because of this healthiness, adults tend to assume that adolescents with problems are not really sick and thus do not give their complaints the attention they deserve. Furthermore, teens themselves may not perceive the behaviors that put their health at risk as dangerous or may be unable to articulate their concerns.

Another characteristic of adolescence is a tremendous need to conform to peers. There is the need to dress alike, wear the same hairstyle, listen to the same music, and even think alike. The perpetual concern is being different. Although the sequence of physical development is the same, there is still variation in the age of onset and the rate of development. This can be a big concern for adolescents, whether the teenager is ahead, behind, or just on the norm. Worry about being different is a particular concern for the adolescent who may want or need professional help. The adolescent will not seek help unless it is "peer acceptable." Kids also often stay away from caregivers out of fear. If they try to get help, they fear, sure enough, something really wrong will be found. This, to their minds, would officially certify them as different. They cannot tolerate that. They also fear that counselors will not respect confidentiality and will serve as parent surrogates, rather than working with the teen in a true counselor–client relationship.

Also characteristic of adolescence is wildly fluctuating behavior. It frequently alternates between periods of wild agitation and acquiescence. A flurry of even psychotic-type thinking is not uncommon. This does not mean that adolescents are psychotic for a time and then get over

it. There are just some periods when their thinking makes sense only to themselves and possibly to their friends. For example, if not selected for the play cast he may see it as a sign he will be a failure his entire life. If she is denied the use of the family car on Friday, she may overreact. With a perfectly straight face, she may accuse her parents of never letting her have the car, even as she stands there with the car keys, ready to drive off.

Adolescence is very much a time of two steps forward and one step back, with an occasional jog to one side or the other. Despite the ups and downs, it is usually a continuing, if uneven, upward trip to maturity.

An important fact is that in early adolescence girls are developmentally ahead of boys. At the onset of puberty, girls are physically about two years ahead. This makes a difference in social functioning because social development takes place in tandem with physical development. This developmental difference can cause problems in social interactions for boys and girls of the same age. Their ideas of what makes a good party or what is appropriate behavior may differ considerably. The girls may consider their male peers "total losers." The boys, aware of the girls' assessments, may be shaken up, but the girls feel dislocated too. With the uneven development of boys and girls during early adolescence, girls may be a year ahead of boys. There is a catching-up period later, but in dealing with younger adolescents, keep this disparity in mind.

Developmental Stages

Developmental psychologists often speak of stages of adolescence as a framework for thinking about this intense period of life. *Early adolescence* is seen as extending from age 10 to 14, when teens are just beginning to confront puberty and when ties with parents tend to remain strong. In this stage, adolescents tend to be cooperative both with parents and with other adults and also to have strong anti–substance use attitudes. *Middle adolescence* is seen as encompassing those age 15–17. This is when peers come center stage, with adolescents exerting greater influence in one another's life than was true earlier. This is the period when rejection and rebellion become more common. In terms of substance use, it is suggested that in this middle stage, adolescents may tend to misperceive their peers' substance use as well as the attendant potential health risks. *Late adolescence,* assigned to those ages 18–21, is seen as marking the transition to adulthood. While more self-reliant, adolescents will seek adult guidance and also have a better appreciation of the health and emotional consequences of their choices.

Youth is the season made for joys.
—Alexander Pope
An Essay on Criticism, 1711

A problem with dividing adolescence into a sequence of stages is that it suggests things are more orderly than is the case. Another way to consider the adolescent period is not in terms of calendar years, but in terms of developmental issues. Fairly clear-cut signs mark the beginning of the adolescent period. But when does adolescence end? Clearly there is more to adolescence than just physical maturation. Trying to define the end can lead to philosophical discussions of "maturity." Doesn't everyone know a 45-year-old or 65-year-old "adolescent"? There is more to assigning an end point than just considering a numerical age. One way of thinking about the adolescent period is to assign to it four developmental tasks. From this point of view, once the tasks have been reasonably accomplished, the person is launched into adulthood. These tasks are not tackled in any neat order or sequence. Emotional and social development do not follow the consistent pattern of physical development. The tasks involved are more like four interwoven themes, the dominant issues of adolescence.

Developmental Tasks

The first task of adolescence is *acceptance of the biological role.* This means acquiring some degree of comfort with one's identity as either male or female. It is an intellectual effort that has nothing to do with sexuality or experimentation with sexuality.

The second task is the *struggle to become comfortable with one's sexuality.* This does not mean struggling with the question of "how to make out." It is the more important question: "Who am I as a sexual person, and how do I get along with those to whom I am actually or potentially sexually attracted? It also includes questions of sexual orientation." Before adolescence, children are far more casual with each other. With adolescence, those days are over. Simply to walk by someone to whom one could be sexually attracted and say, "Hi," without blushing, giggling, or throwing up can be a problem. To become a person capable of sexual and emotional intimacy—able to carry on all manner of social and eventually sexual activities with another person—does not come easily. It is fraught with insecurity and considerable self-consciousness. If you force yourself to remember your own adolescence, some memories of awkwardness and uncertainty come to the fore. Thus, there is the adolescent who does not ask for a date because of the anticipated no. Being dateless is much more tolerable than hearing a no.

I know a lot of Rock Stars are in AA, but to be in AA first you have to be an alcoholic. I'll show you. It's in my business Plan.

The third task is the *choice of an occupational and social identity.* It becomes important to find an answer to "What am I going to do (be)?" As important as a specific occupational niche are the values and attributes that are seen as a part of it. Most of us have several false starts on this task. Think of the five-year-old who wants to be a fireman. He probably never will be, but he gets a lot of mileage for a while just thinking he will. It is not so different for adolescents. It's not helpful to pooh-pooh the first ideas they come up with. Nor is handing over an inheritance and saying "Go for it" recommended. They need some time to work an identity out in their heads. A fair amount of indecision, plus some "crazy" ideas, are to be expected.

The fourth task is the *struggle toward independence.* This entails major conflict. The internal push to break away from home and parents is at war with the desire to remain comfortably cared for. The conflict shows up in rebellion, because there are not many ways to feel independent when living at home, being fed, checked on, prodded, and examined by parents. Rebellion of some type is common during this period, especially among male adolescents. However, the rebellion need not be over major issues and may be relatively invisible and non-traumatic for both adolescent and parent, if the parents can avoid being drawn into power struggles.

Hide our ignorance as we will, an evening of wine soon reveals it.
—HERACLITUS, C. 500 B.C.E.

There are many roadblocks to the completion of these four basic tasks. One results from a social paradox. Adolescents are physically ready for adult roles long before our society allows them to assume those roles. Studies of other societies and cultures point this out. In some societies adolescence doesn't cover a decade or more; young people leave school, for example, at earlier ages to go to work or into apprenticeships. Our society dictates, instead, that people stay in an adolescent position for a long time: middle school, high school, college, graduate school. Another social paradox comes from the mixed messages: on the one hand, it's "Be more social; don't just hang out in your room." "Get a job," "Be grown up." On the other hand, it's "Be back by 1 A.M.," "Save the money for college," and "Don't argue with me." The confusion of "Grow up, but stay under my control" can introduce tensions. Another roadblock can be posed by alcohol and other drug use. Of all groups, adolescents are those most likely to be involved with drugs other than alcohol. In considering adolescents, it is imperative to think broadly, in terms of substance use and problems associated with use, not just in terms of alcohol and alcohol abuse or dependence.

Rebellion

Rebellion can be seen in such things as manner of dress and appearance. It is usually the opposite of what the parents' generation accepts. Little ways of testing a parent crop up, such as coming in late after being out with friends, buying something without permission, or arguing with parents over just about anything. The kids are aware of their dependence, and they don't like it. There is even some shame over being in such a position. It is important that parents recognize the rebellion and respond to it. As if following the edict of "Be friends with your kids," some well-meaning parents may accept any behavior from their kids. For example, if the kids, for the sake of rebellion, bring home some marijuana to smoke, their parents might just light up too. Often the kids will do whatever they can just to get their parents angry. They are often reminded by others of how much they look or act like their father or mother, and they don't want that. Adolescents want to be themselves. They do not want to be simply younger copies of their parents, whom they probably don't like much at the moment. Going out and drinking with their crowd, doing something weird to their hair that Mom and

Dad will hate, not cleaning their rooms, or helping the neighbors but not their parents are all fairly common ways of testing out and attempting to assert independence.

Destructive rebellion can occur when the parents either do not recognize the rebellion or do not respond to it. It can take many forms, such as running out of the house after an argument and driving off at 80 miles per hour, getting really drunk, running away, or, for girls, getting pregnant despite frequent warnings from their perhaps overly restrictive parents to avoid all sexual activities.

Alcohol and Other Drug Use

Alcohol and other drug use is common in adolescence. According to *Monitoring the Future,* the regular federal survey of adolescent alcohol and other drug use, in 2012, among 8th-graders, 30% had tried alcohol. By the 12th grade, the percentage who had ever used alcohol increased to 69%. Under half of high school seniors (42%) were current drinkers, having had a drink in the past month. Of these seniors, about 28% reported being drunk in the past month.

Drink not the third glass,
which thou can't tame
When once it is within thee.
—George Herbert
"The Church Porch," 1633

In terms of illicit drugs, 19% report having used an illicit drug by 8th grade, with that number rising to 49% for those in 12th grade (see Table 11.1). Note that drug use patterns change, and adolescents who used a drug regularly in the past may have since quit using it. The term "non-continuance" in the table refers to people who have used a drug in the past, but not in the past year.

Among adolescents, whether legal or illicit, across the board whites have the highest rate of substance use, followed by Hispanics. African Americans have the lowest rates. The differences are marked. In 2012, among high school students, the proportion of white students who smoked during the past year was two and a half times higher than the rate for African Americans. The rate of heavy drinking was over two times as high for whites (26%) as for African Americans. In the past year, among high school seniors, 27% of whites reported illicit drug use other than marijuana; the rate for Hispanics was 23%, and for African Americans, the rate was 8%, a third of the rate for whites.

Regional differences are also evident. The West had the highest rate of any illicit drug use among high school seniors in the past year (46%), with the Midwest having the lowest rate (35%). However, the opposite is the case for an illicit drug other than marijuana. The region with the lowest rate was the Northeast (5.2%), followed by the West (6.9%). The highest rates were in the South (7.8%), with the Midwest slightly behind (7.4%).

Among adolescents there are also gender differences. Across the board, males drink more frequently, drink larger quantities, and have more occasions of binge drinking. In terms of illicit drugs, on average, females use fewer types of drugs and tend to use them less frequently than their male counterparts. The differences are least for marijuana use. However, by 12th grade, males'

TABLE 11.1 Alcohol and Other Drug Use by 8th-, 10th-, and 12th-Graders, 2012

Substance	Lifetime Use (%)			Past-Year Use (%)			Past 30 Days Use (%)			Non-Continuance Use* (%)
	8th Grade	10th Grade	12th Grade	8th Grade	10th Grade	12th Grade	8th Grade	10th Grade	12th Grade	12th Grade 2008
Alcohol	29.5%	54.0%	69.4%	23.6%	48.5%	63.5%	11.0%	27.6%	41.5%	9%
Tobacco										
Cigarettes	15.5	27.7	39.5	—	—	—	4.9	10.8	17.1	20
Smokeless	8.1	15.4	17.4	—	—	—	2.8	6.4	7.9	18
Any illicit drug	18.5	36.8	49.1	13.4	30.1	39.7	7.7	18.6	25.2	—
Illicit drug use other than marijuana	8.7	14.9	24.1	5.5	10.8	17.0	2.6	5.0	8.4	—
Marijuana	15.2	33.8	45.2	11.4	28.0	36.4	6.5	17.0	22.9	20
Inhalants	11.8	9.9	7.9	6.2	4.1	2.9	2.7	1.4	0.9	—
Hallucinogens	2.8	5.2	7.5	1.6	3.5	4.8	0.6	1.2	1.6	36
Ecstasy	2.0	5.0	7.2	1.1	3.0	3.8	0.5	1.0	0.9	48
Cocaine	1.9	3.3	4.9	1.2	2.0	2.7	0.5	0.8	1.1	44
Heroin	0.8	1.1	1.1	0.5	0.6	0.6	0.2	0.4	0.3	41
With needle	0.6	0.7	0.7	0.4	0.4	0.4	0.2	0.2	0.3	—
No needle	0.5	0.8	0.8	0.3	0.4	0.4	0.1	0.2	0.2	—
Prescription drug, non-medical	—	—	21.2	—	—	14.8	—	—	7.0	—
Prescription narcotic	—	—	—	—	—	7.9	—	—	3.0	35
OxyContin	—	—	—	1.6	3.0	4.3	—	—	—	—
Vicodin	—	—	—	1.3	4.4	7.5	—	—	—	—
Amphetamines	4.5	8.9	12.0	2.9	6.5	7.9	1.3	2.8	3.3	34
Meth	1.3	1.8	1.7	1.0	1.0	1.1	0.5	0.6	0.5	38
Tranquilizers	3.0	6.3	8.5	1.8	4.3	5.3	0.8	1.7	2.1	37
Sedatives	—	—	6.9	—	—	4.5	—	—	2.0	35
Steroids	1.2	1.3	1.8	0.6	0.8	1.3	0.3	0.4	0.9	30

Source: Johnston LD, O'Malley PM, Bachman JG, Schulenberg JE. *Monitoring The Future. National Survey Results on Drug Use, 1975–2012. Volume 1. Secondary School Students.* Ann Arbor MI: Institute for Social Research, University of Michigan, 2013. Available online: www.monitoringthefuture.org.
*"Non-continuance" is defined as use at some point previously, but *not* during the past twelve months, thus it includes those just experimenting.

rates of use are between two and six times higher than females', depending on the drug. Interestingly, the differences are not as marked in the earlier grades. In speculating why, one theory is that females mature earlier and thus may be more likely at a younger age to be hanging out with older kids.

Trends Over Time: Glass Half-Empty or Half-Full?

Few people would ever try to make the case that alcohol and other drug use among adolescents is no big deal and nothing to worry about. On the other hand, if your only information comes from TV, the talk shows, or a local community organization, you'd think that things have never been worse. Looking at trends over time shows this is not the case. A 2009 report by the NIAAA reviewed underage drinking trends from 1991 through 2007. The percentage of adolescents using alcohol in 2008 was the lowest in 17 years.

After wine, out comes the truth.

Chinese proverb

Past Month Alcohol Use

	8th Grade (%)	10th Grade (%)	12th Grade (%)
1991	25%	43%	54%
2012	11	28	42
% decline	−56	−35	−29
% initiated before grade 6 (2012)	13.8	8.9	4.7

Glass Half-Empty Versus Half-Full: Use Versus Non-use

The average age of initiating drinking was 13.7 years in 1991. The average age rose to 14 years in 2007. When the level of alcohol use is in the foreground, we lose sight of the proportion who do not drink. How different would it be if the data in the right-hand columns below were discussed more frequently—namely, that over a third of high school seniors are non-drinkers and over half have not been intoxicated in the past year?

	Drinkers % of Grade	Non-drinkers % of Grade	Been Drunk % of Grade	Not Been Drunk % of Grade
8th grade	11.0%	89.0%	3.6%	96.4%
10th grade	28.0	72.0	14.5	85.5
12th grade	42.0	58.0	28.1	71.9

Illicit Drugs

Trends in illicit drug use mirror the trends for drinking. The *Monitoring the Future* survey has been conducted for 35 years. During this period, 1979 was the year with the highest rate of illicit drug use, at 54%. In 2012, the rate was 37%. However, the trend has not been steadily downward; rather, there have been ups and down, with an overall downward course.

Making sense of this is a challenge. In comparing the trends of alcohol to illicit drugs, the comparison is between 1 substance and more than 20 other drugs. Even if the total percentage of those using illicit drugs were to remain the same over a number of years, there would likely be changes in the level of use for different substances. The drug that may be popular now can be replaced by another in a rather short time. In recent years, several things stand out. Prescription drugs represent a growing proportion of illicit drug use, particularly pain medications such as OxyContin and Vicodin; stimulants, such as Ritalin and Concerta, used to treat attention deficit/hyperactivity disorder; and tranquilizers, such as Xanax and Valium.

Other drugs that have been used more frequently over the past decade are *not* psychoactive drugs. These are the performance-enhancing drugs, including those sold in a health food store rather than in a pharmacy. Creatine is one. In 2008, the annual prevalence was 3% of 8th graders, 12% of 10th graders, and 16% of high school seniors.

Attitudes and Knowledge

The *Monitoring the Future* survey asks questions about kids' notion of the risks that accompany the use of different drugs, their sense of how easy it is to get alcohol or other drugs, as well as their level of disapproval of substance use. Consistently the level of use of any drug is related to the individual's perceptions of riskiness and the level of personal disapproval. As perceptions of risk go down, use goes up. Or possibly is the opposite true: as use goes up, the perception of riskiness declines? There is no way to determine which of these is the case by looking at the survey results. Interestingly, some responses are contradictory. For example, more 12th graders disapprove of drinking one or two drinks per day than disapprove of weekend binge drinking. At the same time, almost twice as many think that weekend binge drinking is more dangerous than having one or two drinks nearly every day.

Despite widespread alcohol use, adolescents tend to be uninformed about the effects of alcohol as a drug. Particularly in middle adolescence, short on facts, they tend more than adults to rely on myths. For example, beer, the overwhelmingly favorite beverage, is thought to be less intoxicating than distilled spirits. The same thinking is evident in their attitudes toward nicotine. Teenagers seem to have bought the notion that "light" cigarettes pose fewer health hazards and are less likely to prompt addiction than regular cigarettes. Adolescents chalk up adult smoking to addiction. They attribute smoking by adolescents as efforts to "be in" or to "make a statement." Certainly this is true, but the role of dependence in explaining nicotine use among those their own age is ignored.

Adolescent Versus Parental Views Not unexpectedly, adolescents view alcohol or other drug use quite differently than do their parents. If asked about motives for adolescents' drug use, parents almost always cite things with negative connotations, such as boredom, rebellion, loneliness, or social pressure. However, when kids are questioned, the reasons they put forward tend to be positive—they use drugs or alcohol for fun, curiosity, good feelings, and relaxation. Long before adolescence, children are aware of different drugs and the varying ways in which they are used. As early as first grade, children have fairly well-formed notions of whether they will try different drugs—whether alcohol, tobacco, marijuana, or inhalants—when they get older. Sure enough, at later follow-up, the kids who voiced an intention to try drugs indeed did so.

. . . my father was the best man in the world and probably worth a hundred of me, but he didn't understand me. The town he lived in and the town I lived in were not the same."
—Bob Dylan, Chronicles, Vol. 1

Adolescents use alcohol in many different ways, some of which are a normal part of adolescent development. The "try it on" thread runs throughout adolescence. Alcohol is just one of the things to be tried. With drinking such a large part of adult society, it is natural that the adolescent struggling toward adulthood will try it. Drinking is also attractive as either rebellious or risk-taking behavior. In addition, given its pharmacological properties, alcohol can serve to anesthetize the pain of adolescents who are isolated or who are subjected to abuse by family or peers. Whatever the supposed reasons for use, problems can follow in the wake.

Associated Problems

Not unexpectedly, problems accompany adolescent drinking and drug use. To cite just a few of the statistics from the ever growing pile:

- Twenty-four percent of high school seniors report having had five or more drinks in a row in the past two weeks.
- Twenty-eight percent of high school seniors report having been drunk in the past month.
- Adolescents who begin drinking before age 15 are five times more likely to develop alcohol dependence than those who begin drinking at age 21.
- In a large study of adolescents age 14 or 15 seen in an emergency room for life-threatening injuries, 71% tested positive for alcohol or drugs.
- Alcohol use problems are associated with an average of 1.5 fewer years of education, and the high school graduation rate is 4.3% lower.
- In 2012, during the past year, 5.2% of the 16- to 17-year-olds and 13.5% of those ages 18–20 reported having driven after drinking. If drinking and driving is considered a matter of poor judgment, then the 16- to 17-year-old group has better judgment than all their elders except those 65 and older!
- In New York City the fifth major cause of emergency department visits among teens is dangerously high alcohol levels.
- In the United States, 71% of all deaths among youth and young adults 10 to 19 years old result from just four causes: motor vehicle crashes,

other unintentional injuries, homicide, and suicide. All of these are alcohol-related.
- The use of alcohol and other drugs in early adolescence increases the risk of dropping out of school, becoming pregnant or impregnating someone, becoming a teenage parent, and living independently from parents or guardians prematurely.
- Underage drinking is estimated to be responsible for 19.7% of all expenditures for alcohol.

Alcohol Use and Developmental Tasks

One way to understand the high incidence of problems with substance abuse in adolescence is in terms of the adolescent developmental tasks cited earlier. The first task described was the acceptance of one's biological role. For women, the onset of their menstrual cycle provides clear biological evidence of their transition into adulthood. For males, the transition may be more difficult to identify. But for both in contemporary America the question of how to know one is an adult is often difficult. For many adolescents, drinking serves as a rite of passage. Not only is it an adult activity, but it is also a way to be part of the crowd. Drinking can provide entry to a group of peers. Even as an adult, one is often encouraged to drink and given messages that not to drink is to be antisocial. For adolescents, with their intolerance of differences and their increased vulnerability to following along with peers' behavior, not drinking at a party where others are drinking may be even harder than for adults.

As some heads cannot carry much wine, so it would seem that I cannot bear so much society as you can. I have an immense appetite for solitude.
—Henry David Thoreau
Letter to Daniel Ricketson, 1857

The second developmental task is the struggle to become comfortable with one's sexuality. This can be threatening to many adolescents. Alcohol can be used to avoid intimacy or to seek intimacy without responsibility. It can also help them avoid dealing with concerns or confusion related to sexual orientation. "I sure missed last night—I was really tanked!" can be said by either boys or girls to disavow what happened the night before. The same is true in the sexual realm, as a means of experimenting without taking responsibility. In our society, being drunk has long provided a "way out." Often people are not held accountable for actions that occur when they are intoxicated. Thus getting drunk can often help adolescents express these increasingly powerful impulses, without really taking direct responsibility for their behavior. This can include not taking proper precautions, as the rising number of AIDS cases among this group as well as unwanted teenage pregnancies can testify.

Alcohol postpones anxiety, then multiplies it.
—Marion Cooley, 1991

The third important task mentioned is the choice of an occupational and social identity. A part of gaining an independent identity involves experimentation in all realms. Adolescents may use alcohol for help in experimenting with various roles and identities. Closely connected to this experimentation is risk taking, some of which involves physical danger. Adolescents are said to have a "sense of invulnerability."

Unfortunately, alcohol can further increase this sense of invulnerability and lead to risk taking with dangerous consequences.

Part of the task of attaining independence is learning to set limits for oneself, to develop self-control. For some adolescents, this is more difficult than for others. It is particularly difficult with activities like drinking where societal messages and advertising suggest that "having more than one" is appropriate adult behavior. In the process of learning self-control, adolescents react negatively to adults setting limits. If parents are too aggressive in forbidding alcohol use, it may backfire. Further confusing matters is the fact that adolescent development is characterized by changes in patterns of thinking. Before the ages of 12 or 13, adolescents generally adhere to concrete rules for behavior. From ages 13 to 15, adolescents are likely to question the justification of set rules. They feel that conventions are arbitrary, so rules supporting them are invalid. By the age of 16, most begin to realize that some rules are necessary.

As these adolescent developmental tasks are accomplished, the number of problem drinkers declines. Also, problems associated with drinking decline. But for a significant proportion of adolescent drinkers, the problems will persist and grow worse. For far too many, the problems associated with drinking may end in death or disability.

Risk Factors

When thinking of risk factors for substance use and abuse, it is easy to feel lost under a pile of data. One way to think of these is in terms of concentric circles. At the center are the risk factors that reside in the individual. Surrounding these individual-based factors are external factors that can be just as influential.

In terms of the *individual,* the most potent risk factor is genetic endowment. This can be a predisposition to alcohol and other substance use problems. Another risk factor is one's temperament: the tendency for risk taking, for novelty seeking, being less socially inhibited (see Chapter 4). Age at first use has been described as being associated with an increased risk for problems. However, it now appears that age of initiating regular use and the age at which heavier use appears may be more significant landmarks than first use. Appearing older than peers increases risk. Other things that increase vulnerability are rebelliousness, nonconformity, resistance to authority, alienation from the culture, feelings of failure, hopelessness, and a failure to form close relationships, along with inadequate tools for coping and low self-esteem.

Beyond genetic factors and temperament, future alcohol problems are predicted by life adversities. The risk is cumulative, increasing with the number of these events. Of note, the impact on risk is equivalent whether the adverse incident was recent or occurred much earlier. One research group identified forty-one different negative events for inclusion in a survey. These ranged from school failure to events in the home,

Cyberbullies—aka Keyboard Gangsters

Cyberbullying is a growing concern. There are similarities to the 'old fashioned' variety. The intent of both is to harass and humiliate the target, and to be deliberately harmful. But there are differences.

Cyberbullying does not occur in a physical location. Awareness is not limited to those who witness it, or those in a circle of people, who have learned of it secondhand. It takes many forms. It may involve posting of rumors, pictures (whether real or doctored), false accusations, and disclosure of an array of personal information (such as addresses and cell phone) which can make the victim more vulnerable. Social media make it easy for others to join in. It occurs 24-7. It is not limited to the school day.

The underpinnings of bullying are little understood. However there are associations with high risk behavior. (Keep in mind that associations are not causes.) Both victims and perpetrators have higher levels of alcohol and drug use, including marijuana and prescription drugs. It is associated with a higher sense of schools being unsafe. It is associated too with taking weapons to school, though not necessarily guns. Both perpetrators and victims are more likely to be males.

such as unemployment, domestic violence, parental divorce or separation, the loss of the home due to natural disaster, abuse by a caretaker, or abandonment or out-of-home placement. There were also events that occurred in the community, such as involvement in a serious accident, whether from natural disasters or driving. Violence in the community is involved with a number of negative events, such as witnessing violence, being threatened, being a victim of assault, or being chased in a situation that could lead to real harm, even if no one is caught. The final group of negative incidents involved relationships, including death of someone important, whether a parent, grandparent, sibling, child, or very good friend. The rate of negative events was higher among teens with an alcohol problem for 85% of the items surveyed.

The NIAAA has initiated a series of rigorous studies of the natural history of alcohol use disorders. Among the factors that stand out is the presence of childhood psychiatric disorders, including conduct disorder, attention-deficit/hyperactivity disorder, and major depression. A common denominator of these disorders might be a more general trait indicating psychological dysregulation, which has a significant genetic component. Also, we now recognize that the adolescent brain is still maturing and that the rate of maturation may be a factor in placing some teens at risk, as well as being a process disrupted by alcohol use.

Beyond the factors residing in the individual, there are risk factors associated with characteristics of the *family.* There is increased risk of substance use problems in those who grow up in families with less cohesiveness, where there is less of a feeling of "family-ness." Also, parenting styles can increase risk—an absence of supervision, overpermissiveness, an absence of clear disapproval of teen substance use. In addition, access to alcohol or drugs in the home increases risk. A history of childhood neglect, the death of an important person in the teen's life, or physical or sexual abuse are also risk factors. Adolescents who have lost a parent as a result of his or her drinking warrant particular support. In terms of the family's alcohol use, while parental drinking exerts an influence, it is modest compared to drinking by siblings.

Peers can be another source of risk. Risk increases if peer groups include those who use and are experimenting with alcohol as well as other drugs or who provide access to them. Typically teens' use of alcohol and other drugs mirrors that of their friends. Of course, this raises the perennial chicken and egg problem. However, there is the sense that teens who are susceptible to alcohol and drug use find one another, as opposed to recruiting their "innocent" peers. The teen years are marked by belonging to cliques: the jocks, the nerds, the cheerleaders, the preppies, the artsy types. And then there is the inevitable group known as the "druggies." Those who don't fit elsewhere may find a home here.

Certain school experiences, aside from friends, are associated with risk factors. Dropouts are at greater risk. Interestingly, attending a private school does not reduce the risk of alcohol or other drug use. But the levels of use are highest among kids who attend alternative high schools. Having a job can be a risk factor. Those who work at an outside job are more likely to use substances, and the risk increases with the number of hours worked. To what extent this is an issue of money or of increased opportunities due to associations with older persons is unknown.

Further removed from the individual level are the factors that reside in the *community*. Unsafe, chaotic communities, without social services or recreational opportunities, but possibly with a drug trade, can spawn substance abuse and are associated with higher levels of violence. Communities differ along other dimensions as well, such as access to alcohol. Then there is the larger social scene that touches everyone.

Protective Factors

Some factors that reside within the individual, the family, and the community are protective, associated with lower risks of alcohol and other drug problems. Protective factors include strong ties to family and community; involvement in church/religious groups; style of parenting that involves setting limits, supervision, and explicit expectancies around substance use; certain personality characteristics such as a sense of optimism, self-esteem, being a non–risk taker; living in a stable community without drug trade and street violence. Many protective factors are the mirror image of risk factors.

Signs of a Possible Problem

Often the temptation is to dismiss adolescent alcohol or other drug problems, considering them as just a stage, a normal feature of adolescence. On the other hand, it's possible to presume that any use of substances will destine the adolescent to dependence. This too is not the case. The following signs may signal a substance use problem, but they are not exclusively linked to substance use. If an evaluation rules out substance use, further exploration is required to address what is going on.

Family Relationships

- Less interest in school or family social activities, sports, and hobbies
- Not bringing friends home
- Failing to return home after school
- Unaccounted-for personal time
- Failing to provide specific answers to questions about activities
- Unexplained disappearance of possessions in the home
- Verbal (or physical) mistreatment of younger siblings

Relationships with Friends

- Old friends dropped
- New group of friends
- Attendance at parties where parents or adults are not present
- Strange phone calls

School Activities
- Unexplained drop in grades
- Unexplained drop in school performance
- Irregular school attendance

Health Status
- Accidents
- Frequent "flu" episodes, chronic cough, chest pains, "allergy symptoms"
- Feelings of loneliness or depression
- Inability to fight off common infections, fatigue, loss of energy
- Short-term memory impairment
- More than "the normal" adolescent mood changes, irritability, anger

Personal Issues
- Increased money or poor justification of how money was spent
- Personal priorities changed
- "Druggie" clothing and jewelry
- "Drug" memorabilia
- Preference for isolation, solitude

Indicators of a significant problem would include any covering up or lying about drug and alcohol use or activities, losing time from school because of alcohol or drug use, being hospitalized or arrested because of drinking or drug-related behavior or truancy, as well as the alcohol or drug use itself. Alcohol or drug use at school generally indicates heavy use. Be alert to these signs and symptoms in children of alcoholics, who have a genetic predisposition and a parent for whom alcohol is a loaded issue.

Natural History

One way to think about the emergence of alcohol use disorders is as a series of stages. One such perspective is sketched out in Figure 11.1. There are six stages: abstinence, experimentation, regular use, problem use, abuse, and dependence. This is only a framework or a model. Upon

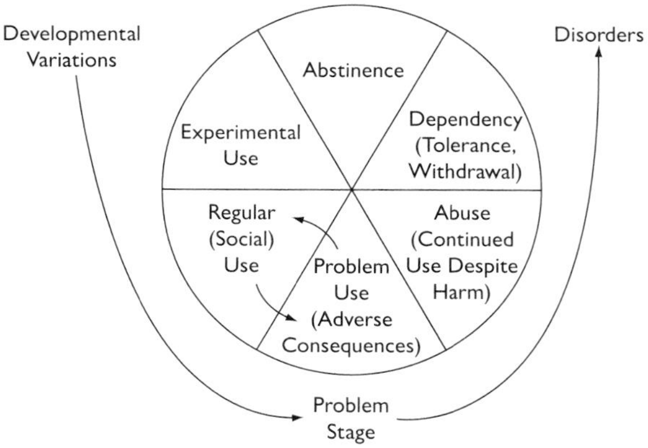

FIGURE 11.1 A developmental view of adolescent alcohol and other drug use.
Source: Knight JR, Shirer LA, Bravender TD, Farrell M, Vander Bilt J, Shaffer HJ. A new brief screen for adolescent substance abuse. *Archives of Pediatric and Adolescent Medicine* 153:591–596, 1990.

entering middle schools, teens are not given instructions on how alcohol problems are to unfold!

This model is very similar to the stages and progression that were sketched out by Vernon Johnson and discussed in detail in Chapter 7. There is one significant difference. Johnson had identified four stages: learning the mood swing, seeking the mood swing, harmful use, and drinking to feel normal. The transition between stages 2 and 3 was defined by Johnson as an "invisible line." What signaled that this line had been crossed was the continued use of alcohol despite negative consequences. Johnson's formulation was derived from reports of adults. It is not surprising that a 38-year-old who has been drinking for over two decades cannot remember the events taking place at that point of transition. However, if one could move back in time, it might be a different story.

Imagine taking a microscope to examine the space between Johnson's second and third stages, the point of the invisible line. What one would see is neither "invisible" nor a "line." Rather, one finds terrain that in essence is the equivalent of the "Problem Use" pattern found in Figure 11.1. This is the stage in which things are fluid. There is the potential for the individual to recognize problems, identify behaviors and situations that are related to problematic use, and make significant changes that reduce further risk. Alternatively, in the absence of change, there is significant probability that harmful use, including dependence, may emerge. The characteristics of each of these stages are summarized in Table 11.2.

Research Insights and Questions

The model described above is a useful paradigm that has emerged from work with adolescents. Major research is only now being conducted on adolescent alcohol use disorders. Inevitably, down the line, the results will entail rethinking how we view alcohol use disorders in adolescents. Some of the highlights and questions:

- In this research, the terminology being used is the broad category of "alcohol use disorders," which encompasses high-risk or dangerous use, as well as alcohol abuse and alcohol dependence.
- The diagnostic criteria used with adults are not a perfect fit when it comes to teens (see page 388). There is considerable variability in adolescent substance use disorders, as well as treatment outcomes. For example, some adolescents with a diagnosis of abuse seemingly use alcohol in a non-problematic fashion in later life.
- Marijuana and tobacco are often called gateway drugs. This terminology is prompted by the notion that the use of some common substances increases the risk of using other illicit drugs. An alternative view is termed the *common risk model*. In this view—which research seems to support—general factors increase the likelihood of using any

TABLE 11.2 Natural History of Substance Use Problems: Signs and Symptoms of Adolescent Substance Use

Stage	Pattern of Use	School	Peers	Family	Self
Experimentation	Occasional	← Few effects →			
Regular use (Seeking the mood swing)	Weekends; occasional weekdays	Grades may become erratic	Hanging around drug-using crowd	Some increase in family conflict; some isolation, secrecy	Changes in dress or choice of music; increased mood swings
Use Disorder—Mild (Negative consequences)	Weekends; occasional weekdays	Grades may become erratic	Hanging around drug-using crowd	Some increase in family conflict; some isolation, secrecy	Changes in dress or choice of music; increased mood swings
Use Disorder—Moderate (Preoccupation with use)	Occasional weekdays, e.g., before or after school	Decreased school performance	Avoids straight friends	Verbal and physical fights	Depression, stealing, fabrication, and misperception of events
Use Disorder—Severe (Use to feel normal or as a requisite for functioning)	Daily, instead of usual activities	May drop out or be expelled	Alienation from original friends, antisocial behavior, sexual acting out	Increased shame and conflict	Guilt, remorse, depression, anger, paranoia, physical deterioration

Source: Modified from Kinney J. *Alcohol Use and Its Medical Consequences: Alcohol Use, Abuse and Dependence.* Timonium, MD: Milner Fenwick, 1989.

alcohol or drugs. However, the particular substance used is often a matter of circumstances.

- Alcohol involvement appears to interfere with the maturation of the nervous system; the area affected is the hippocampus, a portion of the brain involved with aspects of memory and emotion. Imaging studies have shown a reduction of the volume of the hippocampus among some teens who have been drinking heavily.
- A major research interest is describing and understanding the way that innate neurological differences, which are significantly related to genetic endowment, influence the emergence of alcohol problems. Two questions are at the top of the list: "To what extent is the increased risk of dependence associated with the effect of the drug alcohol's effects on a still developing brain?" and "Is early drinking evidence of an underlying trait that is known to be associated with alcohol use problems?" If an adolescent tends to be impulsive, to be a risk taker, to be rebellious, what behavior can fit the bill better than taking up drinking? How might these factors be related to the observed phenomenon of a "telescoped" development of dependence?

Working with Adolescents

Adolescent substance abuse and dependence clearly exist and require treatment. However, the more difficult tasks are tied to earlier stages of adolescent substance use: specifically, experimentation, the emergence of a regular pattern of use, and the occurrence of problems associated with use. This is a major conundrum. Our society deems there to be no socially or legally acceptable use prior to age 21. But the reality is that slightly over a quarter of 10th graders and virtually two-thirds of high school seniors can be described as regular drinkers, having had a drink in the past month. If imploring "you really shouldn't"—whether by parents, teachers, coaches, clergy, government officials, or substance abuse counselors—were going to have had an impact, presumably we should have seen it by now! With such a substantial percentage of adolescents being regular drinkers, it is disingenuous to try to respond to those who drink as if they were particularly deviant or troubled. In fact, adolescents' acceptance of drinking by adolescents has been increasing. According to the *Monitoring the Future* survey, fewer adolescents strongly disapprove of teens' regular drinking and fewer consider regular or binge drinking a great risk.

Another reality needs to be acknowledged. The opinion of a parent or a teacher or a school nurse simply doesn't carry much weight, especially after the fact. To drink or not to drink is ultimately going to be the decision of the adolescent, even though it may not be the product of careful thought. The best others can do is to provide information that may make this as informed a decision as possible. Collectively, as adults, we can have more influence in delaying the onset of use and by taking steps to reduce high-risk drinking when teens choose to drink. However, the latter isn't possible if there is a societal atmosphere of denial and collusion not to acknowledge what is going on. Clinicians who are going to work with adolescents need to be able to respond to adolescent alcohol-drug use as a given and not presume that the task is convincing adolescent clients that drinking (drug use) is "wrong." If clinicians are unable to lay aside these judgments, then their ability to work with adolescents will be exceedingly limited.

O thou invisible spirit of wine,
if thou hast no name to be known by,
let us call thee devil.
—William Shakespeare
Othello

The clinical field has made some initial moves to respond in new ways, in exploration of a harm reduction perspective. In many respects society continues to deny that adolescent alcohol-drug use occurs, so we continue to have more questions than answers. For example:

- With respect to adolescent alcohol use, following experimentation, what does a "regular" pattern look like? "Regular" can vary from daily to only Saturday nights or to only some Saturday nights, at most once a month.
- Are there "regular" patterns that are likely to be more problematic than others? A related issue is whether there is an evolution of the "regular" pattern. Is use becoming more frequent, and does it involve greater consumption? Is it more like viewing a static picture or a kaleidoscope?

- What kinds of activities accompany drinking? Is it sitting around at someone's house, talking and listening to music, or is it driving in large groups, searching for a party?
- Have the adolescents created some safeguards for themselves, even though they may not spell them out for their parents? Such safeguards may involve a decision to sleep over at someone's house, so no one is driving if there is going to be drinking. Or is there a designated driver who drinks nothing? Among girls it may involve an agreement, when they go out with one another, that they arrive and leave together; no spontaneous and potentially ill-advised change of plans is allowed.

Are we taking drunken drivers off the road only to turn them into drunken pedestrians?
—Lawrence Harris
North Carolina State Medical Examiner, commenting on motor vehicle deaths involving pedestrians, 1986

However, if adolescents and their parents, caregivers, and other adults in their lives continue to pretend alcohol and substance use isn't happening, there is no opportunity to address and implement harm reduction measures.

Clinical Approaches

In working with adolescents, there are some general points to consider. It is wise to avoid obvious authority symbols, such as white lab coats, framed diplomas plastering the walls, and a remote clinical attitude. Adolescents probably already have some difficulty with authority figures, anyway, and they don't need you added to that list. Casual clothing in a casual setting can remove one barrier. On the other hand, having spiked hair, listening to an iPod, and sitting on a floor when clients arrive won't go down very well either. They want you to know about those things, but not be into them. An attempt to fake out adolescents will fail. They are a hard group to fool, and they place a high premium on honesty. Respect this and honestly be yourself. This means asking for a translation of their vocabulary if you are not familiar with the terms.

Empathy rather than sympathy is the goal. This is true of all therapeutic relationships. Sympathy is feeling like the other person. Empathy is knowing how the person feels but not sharing that feeling at the moment. For instance, it is simply not helpful to be depressed along with the client.

In general, three types of therapy are done with adolescents. One involves manipulation of the environment. This can include arranging for the father to spend more time with his child, getting the kid who hates Shakespeare into a different school program, or organizing a temporary placement for the child whose parents are non-supportive at the time. These can be very valuable interventions.

Standard insight therapy—psychologically oriented therapy—is not often used. Not many adolescents are ready for, or could even benefit from, this kind of therapy. The ones who can benefit from it tend to be bright, advantaged young people who seem more capable and older than their peers or than their chronological age would suggest.

The most commonly productive individual therapy is what could be termed a relational approach. This requires time for you and the adolescent to become well acquainted and for the adolescent to feel comfortable with you. You are a neutral person, available to the adolescent in a very different way than are parents or peers. For many adolescents, AA, particularly a young persons' group, can be a helpful way to be involved in relational therapy and also to have successful adult role models for sobriety. As described in Chapter 10, treatment approaches have been developed specifically for work with adolescents.

Confidentiality

The issue of confidentiality always comes up. It can be a mistake to guarantee that "nothing you say will ever leave this room." The therapist has a responsibility to others as well as the adolescent client. Given blanket protection, what happens when the kid announces he plans to rob the local deli or another says she plans to drive the family car off the road at the first opportunity? A different approach was suggested by the late Hugh MacNamee. His practice was to tell patients that though most of what they told him would be held in confidence, if they told him anything that scared him about what they might do, that would be harmful to themselves or others, he was going to blow the whistle. He made it clear he would not do so without telling them; nonetheless, he would do it. In his experience, adolescents accept this, maybe even with relief. It may help to know that someone else is going to exert some control, especially if adolescents are none too sure about their own inner controls at the moment.

In a similar vein, MacNamee suggested keeping the adolescent posted on any contacts you have with others about him or her. If a parent calls, start off the next session by informing the adolescent, "Hey, your dad called me, and he wanted . . ." If a letter needs to be written to a school, probation officer, or someone else, share what you are writing with the adolescent. The chances are fairly good his or her fantasy about what you might say is worse than anything you would actually say, no matter what the problem. Because trust is such an issue with adolescents, it is important that you be willing to say to them what you would say about them.

Although the aforementioned is a good general approach to the issue of confidentiality, you may need to be aware of other complicating factors. This refers to the legal issues of a child's right to care versus parental rights to be informed. There may be circumstances in which an adolescent has a legal right to be seen and treated without parental knowledge or consent. Both federal and state regulations address this, so it's necessary for any clinician to be aware of the specific rules and laws. In any case, it is important that the ground rules you are following are clear to the adolescent client.

Guidelines for the General Clinician

Dealing with alcohol and other drug use issues in adolescents isn't restricted to those who are in the substance abuse field. Indeed, some of the most important tasks occur long before an adolescent would arrive at the doorstep of a substance abuse treatment agency. The framework that follows is adapted from a protocol for pediatricians and can serve as a blueprint for clinicians generally.[1] There are several central tasks: broaching the topic, assessing general risk and protective factors, screening, anticipatory guidance and harm reduction, plus the process of making a referral for further assessment and treatment when a problem is identified.

Broaching the Topic

At the very outset, deal with *confidentiality*. Given the range of differences between states, the clinician needs to determine the regulations in his or her state.

A sense of *general risk and protective factors* can be gleaned by inquiring about major life domains. For example:

- *Family relationships.* Relationships with parents/step-parents and siblings.
- *School performance.* Academic performance, attendance, relationship with teachers, and personal goals.
- *Leisure activities.* "What are the things that you like to do when you're not in school?"
- *Self-esteem.* "Describe yourself. What are your strengths?"
- *Other health risk behaviors.* Smoking, sexual activity, diet.

In bringing up the topic of drugs and alcohol, the *tone of the questions* and comments is as important as their content. Introduce the topic in a non-judgmental way—for example, "I know that some kids your age use alcohol, or smoke, or use other drugs." In any setting, be it health care or a social service setting, introduce the topic of substance use in the context of concern for the patient's well-being. For example, start by saying, "I'd like to know a little bit about you and alcohol and drugs and how you feel about this, because this is something that potentially can cause problems."

The *CRAFFT* is a screening instrument for adolescents (see Chapter 9). Each positive response is awarded one point.

1. Have you ever ridden in a ***C***ar driven by someone (including yourself) who was high or had been using alcohol or drugs?
2. Do you ever use alcohol or drugs to ***R***elax, feel better about yourself, or fit in?

---

[1]Adapted from Project Cork. *Interview Guidelines for Pediatricians.* Hanover, NH: Project Cork, 2000. Used with permission.

3. Do you ever use alcohol or drugs while you are by yourself (***A***lone)?
4. Do you ever ***F***orget things you did while using alcohol or drugs?
5. Do your ***F***amily or ***F***riends ever tell you that you should cut down on your drinking or drug use?
6. Have you ever gotten into ***T***rouble while you were using alcohol or drugs?

Scoring: A score of two or more positive responses identifies those whose alcohol or drug use warrants further assessment.

The Next Steps

The CRAFFT score, in combination with other information gathered, determines the next step. And *there always needs to be a next step*. This is true whether the adolescent is or isn't using alcohol or drugs, and if using, whether there is or isn't a problem. This is definitely not a time to announce "No problem" and send the adolescent on his or her way with a pat on the back.

Anticipatory Guidance, for Those Who Have Not Used Alcohol or Other Drugs This is an important prevention strategy. Few of us think well on our feet, especially when a situation arises that we've never experienced. Anticipatory guidance with adolescents is aimed at dealing with that very situation. It attempts to determine the likelihood that the adolescent will be in a situation in which alcohol or drugs are present and how he or she can deal with the inevitable situation when it does arise.

- Assess exposure. "Have you ever been in a situation in which you were tempted to try drugs or alcohol?" "Or thought you might be pressured to?" "Has this happened to your friends?"
- Allow the adolescent to describe his or her understandings of the problems of alcohol and drug use. Correct misunderstandings. Provide factual information about alcohol and drug use.
- Reinforce positive attitudes expressed about avoiding alcohol and drug use.
- Discuss strategies for handling situations in which the opportunity for use *may arise*. Also discuss strategies for handling the situation if/when it *does arise*.[2]

Harm Reduction, for Those Who Do Use Alcohol and Other Drugs When there is a history of occasional use or experimentation, as well as more regular use, it is important to address the notion of harm reduction. This discussion can include some basic facts about a drug's effects, such as effects on judgment and motor response/reaction time. Addiction

[2] Some parents and teens have a plan in place to help the adolescent get out of an uncomfortable or dangerous situation. Today nearly every teenager has a cell phone or can borrow one. Basically, the adolescent is aware he or she can call home, and a parent will pick the teen up. Some have agreed on a "reason" the pick-up is needed so the teen doesn't have to invent a reason on the spot.

potential is another useful piece of information; the line between "experimentation" and regular and increasing use can be very fine. Tobacco is the best example. Identify situations in which use of drugs or alcohol may invite risk, such as driving or sexual behaviors. Discuss ways to avoid these high-risk situations. Special case: For some drugs—inhalants, opiates, amphetamines, street drugs—any use places a teen at risk.

The following are some of the lines you can use:

- "When someone uses alcohol or other drugs, it is important to know what these drugs do . . ."
- "From a medical perspective, drugs can cause problems in different ways. With some you can quickly become 'hooked'—for example, with cigarettes. In other cases, the dangers are the result of the drug's immediate effects, the way it changes judgment and behavior. Alcohol is a good example of that."
- "Also, being the non-drinker or one of those who is straight in a situation in which others are using or drinking may result in your being the one who is faced with having to deal with problems that arise from someone else's use." Provide some basic facts on intoxication, high BACs, unknown amounts, dangers of putting someone to bed, or letting them "sleep it off." Identify someone who could be called in an emergency.
- Keep the door open. Identify yourself as someone to whom questions can be addressed.

Further Evaluation, for an Identified Problem If an adolescent is drinking or using in a way that goes far beyond "a little experimentation" and with negative consequences, it is helpful to get further details to assess the severity.

These follow-up questions deal with the drinking pattern and consequences:

- *Drinking frequency.* "Do you drink regularly? About how often? Every day? Once or twice a week?"
- *Drinking quantity.* "How much did you drink the last time you got drunk? How much do you usually drink? Do you ever drink to pass out? How often do you get drunk?" (Risk of acute problems is related to the frequency of intoxication and activities when intoxicated.)
- *Drug use frequency.* "About how often do you use drugs? Every day? Once or twice a week?" Get specifics, such as how much.
- *Source of drugs.* "Where do you usually get these drugs? From a friend, or family member? Or from someone else? Do you buy them?"
- *Places of use.* "Where do you drink or take drugs? Parties only? With friends in cars? Home? School? By yourself at home or in school?"
- *Dependence.* "Do your social activities usually involve alcohol or drugs? What would happen if you couldn't have any alcohol or drugs?"
- *Social consequences.* "What kinds of trouble have you gotten into because of alcohol or drugs? Do your parents suspect that you drink or do drugs?"

Negotiate Follow-Up, for Identified Substance Use Problems Begin by allowing the adolescent to describe his or her understanding of his or her alcohol and drug use. "How would you describe your alcohol or drug use? Do you ever think it has become a problem for you?" Then it's your turn:

- State clearly that you believe there is a problem with substance use. Provide concrete examples of the behaviors that are of concern.
- Stress the importance of involving the parents. How parents might best be involved depends on a variety of factors. Do the parents suspect alcohol or drug use? What is the nature of the relationship between the parent or parents and the teen? Is there a history of or fear of physical abuse? What are the teen's concerns about involving parents? The clinician needs to take the lead in approaching parents. This is not handled by a call announcing that "Joe is into drugs in a big way. Maybe we could all meet two weeks from now." This is a surefire way to guarantee stress for all. Depending on the circumstances, it may be useful to identify adults in the teen's life who are viewed as supportive—a teacher, a coach, the parent of a friend, an aunt or uncle.
- Negotiate for a follow-up appointment, ideally with the parents present.
- Assume responsibility for acting as an intermediary between the patient and parents. "I can meet with you and your parents and explain this to your parents in a way that they can understand. Then we can all work together to help you."
- Solicit the patient's verbal agreement to involve parents.
- Solicit the patient's agreement to come for a follow-up appointment and schedule it.
- Be prepared with concrete suggestions for the next step.

Thou wine are the friend of the friendless, though a foe to all.
—HERMAN MELVILLE
Mardi, 1885

Wine does not intoxicate people —they do it to themselves.
Chinese proverb

Treatment

Once it has been determined that an adolescent needs "to do something" and has agreed to see someone, what options are available? Some schools have in-house substance abuse counselors. Every state has a system of substance abuse services, which includes clinicians and offices throughout the state. Many major medical centers offer substance abuse services. The agreement to "see someone" should not be considered as an agreement to enter substance abuse treatment. Indeed, for some adolescents, the next step may be some kind of counseling to better evaluate the nature of a substance use problem, as well as to assist the adolescent to recognize that these are problems that accompany substance use, essential preliminary work enabling the adolescent to become engaged in treatment. The clear exception is when the adolescent is in immediate danger to himself or others or when a substance use problem is so clear-cut that immediate involvement in treatment is required.

For some adolescents, part of the assessment may involve a thorough medical and psychiatric evaluation. Formal treatment options include outpatient, residential, or hospital-based care and can involve individual, group, and family counseling, plus self-help groups such as AA or NA (Narcotics Anonymous).

Diagnostic Criteria: Adult–Adolescent Differences

As part of the effort to prepare the fifth edition of the APA's *Diagnostic and Statistical Manual,* a major concern is whether the diagnostic criteria for adults are equally appropriate for adolescents. Indeed, a number of problems have been identified.

Consider the criterion "Drinking a larger amount than intended." It is fair to say that many adolescents have no clear intention about how much alcohol they will consume on any particular occasion. They can't even figure out until the last minute what movie they want to see. The scenario is just as likely to be "screw the movie, let's go hang out at the mall, pick up a video, and then . . ." For adolescents to have an amount in mind that they will drink when they go out is foreign to their thinking and developmental stage. Consider, too, the criterion for tolerance: "a need for increased amounts of alcohol to achieve intoxication or the desired effect." All new drinkers, by definition, are acquiring tolerance, so the ability to drink more without feeling impaired is true for the vast majority of adolescent drinkers. As a result, this criterion doesn't distinguish between adolescents with or without an alcohol use disorder. There is another difference between adolescents and adults. Compared to adults, adolescents are less likely to experience withdrawal symptoms.

Finally, another issue of concern with adolescents is the presence of *diagnostic orphans.* This refers to those who meet some criteria for either abuse or dependence, but not a sufficient number to qualify for a formal diagnosis. All told, these examples confirm the suspicion that some modification of diagnostic criteria was needed to better reflect the presentation of alcohol disorders in adolescents.

Internet Addiction

Internet addiction didn't make it into the DSM-5, as a non-substance use disorder. While a topic of growing attention, there is far from a consensus as to its basic core elements. Nor is there any clear consensus about how to measure it. One question that can't be ignored is whether this is a "diagnosis" awarded by an older generation which has virtually no understanding of how 21st century youth use the internet. Anyone who thinks of the internet as something you "log onto" is a bit out of date.

With the ever growing variety of internet environments, there are a diversity of ways in which an "internet addiction" might be manifested. Is it the sheer number of hours "online?" Is someone's mood a significant clue, something associated with depression and low self-esteem. Is it associated with anxiety, i.e. FOMO. Is it escapism into a virtual world. Is it marked by how often folks check in on Facebook, or do the number of selfies posted? As for games, given the incredible variety, is there a common denominator. Are some conducive to making social connections and others interfere. Then there is the whole matter of smart phones. Is there such a thing as too many apps. Is it being obsessed with them rather than using them.*

Consider what behaviors you automatically associate with a mention of internet addiction."

*translation. Fear of Missing Out

Alcohol-Drug Assessment

Once the issue of confidentiality has been cleared up, it is important to take a family history. Ask about alcohol or other drug problems, prescription or non-prescription. Include questions about the grandparents, uncles, aunts, brothers and sisters, cousins, as well as the parents and step-parents. Another important part of the history includes asking adolescents how they spend their time. Ask them to describe a typical day. Ask what they and their friends do on a typical Saturday night. Ask about their peer groups—peers' ages, activities, and drug and alcohol use. Ask how they are seen and described by other groups in their school, and then ask about the adolescent's own use of drugs and alcohol. Ask about parental relationships. Ask about sleep, appetite, depression, and the possibility of physical or sexual abuse. Also be able to discuss issues of sexuality and sexual orientation. It is also important to determine adolescents' risk for HIV infection.

The fact that adolescent alcohol abuse can go on for as long as six years without being diagnosed is a tribute to several factors. There is the ability of these adolescents to hide their problems, complemented by their parents' ability to avoid recognizing problems in their children. It is also a testimony to the failure of health care providers to address substance abuse and other sensitive issues, as well as the ability of school systems to ignore or expel problem children. It is not unusual for parents to be actively protecting, rescuing, and taking care of a substance-abusing adolescent without realizing that this supports and prolongs the abuse. For instance, they make good on forged checks. They hire lawyers and pay fines. They go to bat for them at school or blame school authorities for the problems.

When asking adolescents about drug and alcohol use, begin by asking about the first time they were drunk, how much they drink now, how often, if they have ever tried to stop or cut down. Ask about blackouts, legal problems, and school problems. Ask about pot, crack, cocaine, acid, stimulants, the non-medical use of prescription drugs, and whatever the current "in" drug is. Increasingly, younger adolescents are beginning their experimentation with intoxication by using inhalants that are easily available in any supermarket or drugstore. Finally, don't assume that an adolescent is providing a wholly accurate history of drug and alcohol use. Denial is a central characteristic of adolescent alcohol or drug problems.

Adolescent Treatment

Although occasionally adolescents will spontaneously request treatment, more often they come to treatment under duress. In working with them, it is important to make it clear that your task is to help them and that you are not an agent of their parents, the law, or the school system.

In dealing with adolescents, the importance of working with the family cannot be overemphasized. The parents need to deal with their child's substance abuse. And they must consider their own behaviors that may have protected, covered up, excused, or, for that matter, contributed to the problem. When it is clear that there is a significant problem and all efforts to involve the adolescent in treatment have failed, the parents may need to seek legal help. Most states allow parents to request state assistance if they feel they cannot enforce safe limits for their child. Although this is a very drastic and difficult step to take, it can be important when alcohol-abusing adolescents are acting in ways that endanger their lives. Probation can also be a way of mandating treatment for adolescents, but again this works only if the parents can stop protecting the adolescent from the consequences of his or her behavior.

Once it has been determined that an adolescent needs treatment and the adolescent has agreed to treatment, it is important to proceed in a careful way. Because medical and psychiatric complications frequently accompany adolescent substance abuse, a thorough medical and psychiatric evaluation should precede or be an early part of any treatment plan. The American Academy of Pediatrics suggests the use of the guidelines developed by the American Society of Addiction Medicine in determining the type of care required (see Chapter 9).

We only use the stocks during the first phase of treatment.

There are very good substance abuse treatment programs for adolescents. There are those, on the other hand, that might most kindly be described as non-traditional. This includes the boot camp programs, which submit kids to a military-like environment, with forced marches and endless push-ups, and which, frankly, are abusive rather than supportive and "firm." In some cases this type of treatment has resulted in deaths. Here, too, the Academy of Pediatrics has developed criteria for selecting a treatment program. The following are suggested as things to look for:

1. The program views drug and alcohol abuse as a primary disease, rather than as a symptom.
2. The program includes a comprehensive evaluation of the patient and attends itself to or makes referral for any associated medical, emotional, or behavioral problems identified in the assessment.
3. The program adheres to an abstinence philosophy. Any use is abuse. Drug use is a chronic disease, and a drug-free environment is essential. Tobacco ideally should be prohibited, or nicotine cessation should be part of the overall treatment plan for patients who smoke.
4. There is a low ratio of patients to staff. Treatment professionals are knowledgeable about substance abuse and adolescent behavior and development.
5. Professionally led support groups and self-help programs are integral parts of the program.
6. Adolescents are separate from the adult groups if both are treated at the same facility.
7. The entire family is involved in treatment. The program relates to parents and patients with compassion and concern, with the goal of reunification whenever possible.
8. Follow-up and continuing care are integral parts of the program.
9. As progress is made in the program, patients have an opportunity to continue academic and vocational education and are assisted in restructuring family, school, and social life.
10. The program administration discusses costs and financial arrangements for inpatient and outpatient care and facilitates communication with managed care organizations.
11. The program is as close to home as possible to facilitate family involvement, even though separation of the adolescent may initially be indicated.

The questions to ask are "Does the program work?" "Is the program drug free?" "Is there a strong family component?" "Is there a strong therapeutic component?" "Is there a strong educational component?" "Is the adolescent involved in treatment planning?" "Is there a peer component?" "Are there provisions for aftercare?" "What are the costs and risks of treatment, including both financial cost and time cost?" "What beliefs are instilled?" "What are the staff's credentials, including training, experience, licensure, and certification?" "Is there a full range of services, including pediatric, psychiatric, educational, psychological, and substance abuse clinicians?" "Is there involvement with AA?" "How does the program feel when one visits it?" "Is the program accredited?" "If so, by whom?"

Co-occurring Psychiatric Disorders Psychiatric problems are common among adolescents with alcohol or other drug use problems. Several studies of adolescents in treatment found that more than 80% had another psychiatric disorder. This is not to suggest that this holds true for all adolescents with substance use problems. Possibly the presence of other psychiatric disorders causes more disruptions and thus increases the likelihood of these teens entering treatment. Among female adolescents with alcohol problems, there is a greater incidence of other substance abuse disorders, as well as depression and eating disorders. There is also a higher incidence of post-traumatic stress disorder. For these girls, this often includes a history of childhood abuse. Attention-deficit/hyperactivity disorder (ADHD), more common among males, doubles the risk of alcohol or other drug dependency in adolescents and increases the likelihood of relapse following treatment.

One of the questions sometimes raised is whether a preadolescent's use of stimulant drugs for treatment of ADHD is later associated with substance abuse in adolescence. Multiple studies have found that children treated with stimulants have no heightened risk for experimentation and use, or abuse or dependence, in adolescence or adulthood. The far greater danger is a failure to treat the ADHD adequately.

There is virtually no data on the use of drug therapies for alcohol use disorders in adolescents. Disulfiram has been used with adolescents, but with some reluctance. Given adolescents' greater impulsivity, clinicians are concerned about the greater risk of drinking and the associated disulfiram reaction. The only data on the use of newer anti-craving agents, only recently on the market in the United States, come from European studies where these drugs have had longer use.

Adolescents and AA For the adolescent with an alcohol or substance abuse problem, how might AA or NA be of use? The first thought might be that the adolescent would never identify with a group of predominantly 35- to 55-year-olds. In many areas of the country, that stereotype of the AA group does not necessarily hold true; some locales have what are called "young people's groups." There the average age is the early to mid-20s. Even if there are no young people's groups in the vicinity, age need not be a barrier to an adolescent's affiliating with AA. On the contrary, several features of AA might attract and intrigue the adolescent. It is a group of adults who will definitely not preach at him or her. Furthermore, given the collective life experiences within AA, the members are not likely to be shocked, outraged, or, for that matter, impressed by any of the adolescent's behaviors. The members will generally treat the adolescent as an adult, presumably capable of making responsible choices although cognizant that to do so isn't easy for anyone. Within AA there is a ready assortment of potential surrogate parents, aunts, uncles, and grandparents. The intergenerational contact, possibly not available elsewhere to the adolescent, can be a plus. Also, AA remains sufficiently "unacceptable" so as not to be automatically written off by an adolescent wary of traditional, staid, "out-of-it" adult groups. Because being alcohol or drug dependent is still a stigmatized condition, the parents may be more uncomfortable than their children about their adolescents' AA attendance. The therapist may need to help parents with this. In making a referral, the same guidelines outlined in the section on AA apply (see Chapter 10). The adolescent is full of surprises, and a willingness to attend AA may well be one.

When I'm sober I use safe sex. When I'm drunk, every thing seems safe.

Adolescents and AIDS A growing concern is the rapid increase of AIDS among younger adults, indicating that they contracted HIV during adolescence. Any discussion of adolescents and AIDS requires thinking about the role of the other A—alcohol. Alcohol is involved in this equation for two reasons. First, there's the well-known disinhibiting effect of alcohol and the impaired judgment that is a part of that. Sexual encounters are more likely when drinking. It is less likely that condoms will be used, increasing the risk of a variety of sexually transmitted diseases, including HIV. Sexual encounters are also more likely to be casual, involving partners with little history and no ongoing relationship. With the advent of AIDS, the important message to be conveyed is that there is no longer, if there ever was, such a thing as casual sex. The stakes are high, and the costs are no longer simply psychological wounds.

The second important factor that has considerable significance in thinking about adolescents, alcohol, and AIDS goes beyond simply altered judgment. It appears that one of the effects of alcohol—in anyone, not just in those who are alcohol dependent or who drink heavily—is to interfere temporarily with the immune system. Possibly for a day or two alcohol seemingly "turns down the volume" on the body's defenses. Thus, the body's usually available means of fighting off infections and viruses are not up to par. Alcohol use allows infections to gain a foothold, although the body otherwise would have fought them off.

Adolescent treatment programs, as well as prevention efforts, need to be involved in AIDS education. Some treatment programs, in addition to including an educational component, also discuss the issue of HIV testing; several programs have adopted HIV testing routinely. Beyond the fact that it really does matter if one is or is not HIV-positive, these activities reinforce the point that HIV/AIDS is a major issue. It isn't something that can't or wouldn't touch an adolescent's life. These programs emphasize that it is the choices that adolescents make or don't make that have an impact on them.

Treatment Outcome The data on treatment outcomes remain limited. Programs treating adolescents for alcohol use disorders typically have abstinence as the treatment goal. However, the information from follow-up suggests this goal is rarely achieved for extended periods. Nonetheless, there is generally substantial improvement in functioning. In one larger study at one-year follow-up, about 20% were abstinent. Another 30% used alcohol occasionally, but had no symptoms of either abuse or dependence. Furthermore, among those drinking, but without symptoms, their psychological and social functioning seemed to more closely resemble that of the abstainers than those for whom problematic use continued.

Based on what is known of adults who report the emergence of alcohol problems in adolescence, it would be expected that any alcohol problem that becomes apparent in adolescence would be characterized as a chronic condition, with a steady downhill progressive course. Among a group of adolescents followed through their mid-20s, 55% were found to have an alcohol use disorder. Clearly the presence of a diagnosis in adolescence increased the risk of alcohol problems later. On the other hand, there was a significant portion for whom this wasn't the case.

It may go against the grain for substance abuse clinicians, and fly in the face of conventional wisdom, but quite possibly for some adolescents an alcohol use disorder may be developmentally limited. For some adolescents there may be a maturing out of a "mild" or even "moderate" alcohol disorder. If indeed this is the case, it doesn't suggest that treatment isn't required because adolescents will "grow out of it." For one, this is not the case for all adolescents. Second, it is just possible that treatment is a major factor that facilitates a maturation out of alcohol abuse. If nothing else, entering formal treatment is likely to get an adolescent's attention! It may also provide some useful time out. Buying one year of light, non-problematic drinking during adolescence is no small accomplishment. It may allow for further maturation, derail dysfunctional patterns, instill better coping skills, and remove the adolescent from a heavy-drinking peer group.

In a review of factors related to treatment outcome, several have been identified: the level of severity, the extent of family and interpersonal problems, the presence of other substance use, and the presence of co-occurring psychiatric conditions, especially antisocial behavior and major depression.

Prevention

Considerable attention and money are being directed to prevention. The Center for Substance Abuse Prevention (CSAP) has funded research initiatives as well as community projects to implement the approaches

shown to be successful. Several different approaches are used. Some are directed at the environment, that is, the larger society. These include efforts, for example, to curb underage sales. Other prevention programs are broad-based, touching all teens, such as public service ads to promote the use of designated drivers. Or programs can be targeted to special situations, such as organizing alcohol-free proms or graduation parties. Other programs directed at individuals try to reach adolescents who are at higher risk. These can include special programs for children from families with a substance use problem and efforts to identify children with behavioral risk factors, such as ADHD or conduct disorders. (See Chapter 14 for further discussions of prevention.)

One important task for anyone working with adolescents is to be aware of the potential problems that virtually every adolescent will encounter with respect to alcohol and other drugs. If adolescents are not currently into drugs or alcohol, that is the point for *anticipatory guidance,* as described earlier. Contacts with adolescents, for whatever reason, can be used. This might be the school counselor who meets with the adolescent to discuss next year's course offerings. Or it may be a physician conducting the physical examination required before participation in high school athletics.

In many communities, there are also efforts under way through parent groups and groups of adolescents to support the development of healthy peer values and norms about alcohol and other drug use. It is almost impossible to speak of adolescent alcohol or other drug use without hearing the phrase "peer pressure." This, for many, conjures up the image of someone sidling up to a kid and saying, "Want to try some beer?" or "How 'bout a joint?" The most potent form of peer pressure, however, is what adolescents *think* everyone else is doing. Teens are apt to overestimate the numbers of their peers who drink by up to 100%. Friends do have considerable influence; however, parents and other adults do as well. The expectations of adults in the community have an impact.

In thinking about prevention, one thing cries out for attention. This is preparing adolescents to deal with *alcohol or other drug emergencies.* Don't worry about sending out a mixed message. Get real. You don't withhold potentially life-saving information because kids might think it implies approval of drinking. The reality is that it likely will fall to the adolescent who isn't drinking to do what needs to be done in such circumstances. All teens need to know how to respond to a possible overdose, such as knowing the dangers of letting a really drunk kid "just sleep it off." Adolescents need to learn that when they are in the presence of drinking, they need to be their brother's—and sister's—keeper. (See Box 11.1, page 424, on responding to alcohol emergencies.)

For some adults, there is the temptation at some point to "finally" take a stand regarding adolescent drinking. Unfortunately, this often occurs after a lengthy period of vacillating behavior. And when dramatic action is taken, it may not be well thought out. For example, several years ago there was a growing awareness and concern about alcohol use in a local high school. There were the usual incidents for the age group—having unchaperoned parties with drinking, parents allowing alcohol to be served in their homes, drinking and driving, taking alcohol to school dances, and going to dances after drinking.

That year the soccer team had an outstanding season and made it to the playoffs for the state championship. A parent put a bottle of champagne on the bus. The team subsequently won. In the course of the celebrating, someone remembered the champagne. The players proceeded to pour it over one another. This led to a public uproar. In the aftermath, the team members refused to tell who got the champagne from the bus. Interestingly, the parent who provided the champagne never confessed either. As a result, the next year's team was not allowed to participate in any postseason games, regardless of its playing record. Beyond the questions of delaying punishment for such an extended period or penalizing players who may not have even been present, there was a further irony. Not only were the students following a well-established tradition witnessed at the conclusion of every professional championship series, but this incident also may have represented the most appropriate, most non-destructive use of alcohol ever displayed in the school. But this was the time to "put one's foot down." Although an extreme example, it points out the capacity to undermine one's efforts if action is taken precipitously.

Being a Community Resource

Clinicians who are seen as an expert in the area of adolescent substance abuse will find themselves being called upon to speak to community groups. If, or more realistically, when that happens, there are several basic themes you might consider incorporating into your spiel:[3]

Correct common misconceptions. For example, provide data on the actual alcohol-drug use patterns in the community. Parents underestimate alcohol use, and adolescents significantly overestimate it. An annual survey conducted by the CDC in the schools, the *Youth Behavioral Risk Survey,* available online or from a state agency, commonly the state's alcohol or drug agency or state's department of education, is a source of data. Point out that parental behaviors have more influence than do peer behaviors. The time and quality of family relationships are more important influences than the particular constellation of the family or socioeconomic status.

Convey what adolescents value. While no one wants to come off as a tyrant or nag when it comes to alcohol and drug use, being "neutral" isn't a good choice. An important predictor of an alcohol-related driving offense or accident is whether a teen's parents are neutral (rather

[3]Adapted from Project Cork. *Parents Make a Difference*. Hanover, NH: Project Cork, 2002.

than negative) about teenage drinking. Similarly, adolescents' perceptions of the *parenting style* in their homes is linked to substance use. The lowest rate of alcohol and drug use is among teens who view their parents as generally authoritative (know what they are talking about), and who see their parents as having standards and clear expectations. What is associated with greater risk of substance use is parents who are seen as having either a laid back, anything-goes style, or who play the tyrant and rely on a "Do-it-because-I-say-so" line.

Caution realism. Point out the importance of recognizing the complexity of this issue. There is no one thing that leads to, nor one single thing that prevents, substance use. Parents see alcohol and drug use as motivated by factors with negative connotations, such as boredom, rebellion, loneliness, and social pressure. Their children are more likely to cite factors that are more positive, such as curiosity, fun, and insight/experience.

Identify what parents can do. Point out that it's inevitable that at some point every teen is in a situation in which alcohol or other drugs are present. Help adolescents anticipate how they can respond gracefully, to avoid embarrassing themselves or others. Be sure your son or daughter knows how to respond to an alcohol or drug emergency. Be informed. Expect others in your child's life—pediatrician, coach, clergy—to discuss substance use. Talk to other parents. Participate in community efforts clearly directed to increasing safety, such as the alcohol-free graduation party. Make certain children and others know where you stand on drug and alcohol use.

Most important, remind parents to never forget that what they do or fail to do can be a matter of life or death.

Minority Youth

With the exception of Native Americans, minority youth use less alcohol and other drugs than do whites. Much of what has been said about the presentation and treatment of substance abuse does not capture the problems of many urban minority youth. Regardless of whether these youths are African American, Hispanic, or Native American, they are far more likely to live in substandard housing, be in families with fewer economic resources, have less access to medical care, attend substandard schools, or be school dropouts. If they live in urban areas, they are more likely than their white peers to live in areas in which drug use is prevalent and accompanied by violence in the community.

Wine is a good familiar of creature, if it be well used.
—William Shakespeare
Othello

The Homeless, Runaways, and Castaways

If there is any group of adolescents who warrant special mention, it is adolescents who are not living with family or other caring adults. These are the kids who to a large extent are invisible to most of us and struggling to just get by. Contrary to what may be expected, lack of stable housing commonly precedes alcohol and other drug problems, rather than being the result of it. Homeless adolescents often have a history of sexual abuse, trauma, physical abuse, placement in foster care, involvement with the criminal justice system, and family members with a history of alcohol or drug problems. Those on the street are at increased risk for psychiatric disorders, at rates as high as 17 times the rate for the general population for a particular disorder. They experience a high rate of violence, including physical abuse or assault. Infection is more common, be it HIV, sexually transmitted disease, hepatitis B, or hepatitis C. Criminal activity is common and a distinguishing feature of homelessness, but again does not usually precede living on the street. "Survival sex" is common, being a source of money, drugs, clothing, shelter, or food. Mortality is 11 times the expected rate, based on age and gender. While always elevated, one study reported a rate of substance abuse or dependence of 75%. Housing is provided by crisis centers, shelters, drop-in centers, or the like. Some people have a network of places that provide the opportunity for bunking somewhere for a night or two.

The bulk of the academic literature is directed to describing the population, the past history of those who are on the street, and the nature of current problems. Very few articles consider treatment services. The few that do consider treatment outcomes report short-term gains, which are not maintained due to the absence of essential supportive services.

Teens' Use of E-Cigarettes Doubles in a Year

The Centers for Disease Control report the use of teen's use to e-cigarettes has doubled in a year. Health officials worry the devices may cause more children to become addicted to tobacco products. E-cigarettes are sold in an assortment of sweet, kid-friendly flavors including 'vivid vanilla,' 'cherry crush' and chocolate, and they increasingly are marketed using themes and images long used to market regular cigarettes to kids. . . . Although e-cigarette manufacturers contend that they only market to existing smokers, often as a way to quit the habit, the new CDC statistics show the marketing is enticing children to start what could become a lifelong addiction to tobacco products. . . . While there's no hard evidence that e-cigarettes lead to smoking real cigarettes, it's likely to increase the risk of smoking. There is no upside to teens being exposed to e-cigarettes.

Morbidity and Mortality Weekly Review, September 6, 2013

Nicotine: The Elephant in the Room

Which drug has had only three passing mentions in this section? Since 1975, which substance is the one most frequently used by adolescents on a daily basis? Of those who have used a drug other than alcohol, which one has the lowest rate of discontinuation, meaning no use in the past year, despite earlier use? *Nicotine*.

Too often the issue of adolescents and nicotine is addressed only within the context of prevention. However, as the *Monitoring the Future* study shows, for a significant portion of adolescents, it's past the point of prevention. In 2012, about 17% of high school seniors were current smokers as were 5% of eighth graders.

Smoking Cessation

A significant majority of adolescent smokers, around 85%, think about quitting, and between 70% and 90% made an effort to quit during the past year. Success in quitting is tied to a number of things. As might be expected, the level of dependence, marked by the number of cigarettes smoked per day, predicts success or failure. Other factors teens mention as helping with cessation are having non-smoking friends and the nature of their schools' rules and the level of enforcement, which in combination make smoking more difficult. When teens are asked "Why do you want to quit?" the top reason offered by girls is health (65%) and among boys it's athletic performance (51%). Also mentioned are cost, social influences, setting an example for others, general appearance, plus no perceived positive reinforcement for smoking.

It is unclear to what extent adolescents are aware of the kinds of programs or approaches available to assist with smoking cessation. Or as one study found, they may tend not to think of themselves as such hard-core smokers that they need external assistance. The same modalities used with adults are being used with teens—nicotine replacement, medications, brief interventions, motivational enhancement.

Currently only a handful of smoking cessation programs are specifically tailored to adolescents. One of these is a program designed by the American Lung Association, called Not-on-Tobacco (N-O-T). It is among the more intensive initiatives, conducted over a 10-week period. Compared to brief interventions, Not-on-Tobacco has far better outcomes, especially among those with higher levels of nicotine dependence. In fact, the evidence to date suggests that brief treatments are effective only with low-dependence smokers. Another approach being explored is promoting smoking cessation in teen worksites, which has been initiated by a large supermarket chain. Each store typically has more than 40 teen employees. Dubbed SMART, it involves diverse components ranging from mailings to health education promotions, contests, games, and peer-led groups. The interactive components are organized at the worksite, out of the employee break room.

Beyond the workplace, the other obvious site to offer smoking cessation programs is in schools. Evidence to date from a statewide effort in Illinois shows that these can succeed. Obviously, the first step is getting students to attend! An important factor that predicts attendance is offering smoking cessation programs during the school day, rather than as an evening or after-school extracurricular activity. Other factors that predict participation are prior unsuccessful efforts to quit smoking and higher levels of dependence, which seemed to translate into greater motivation. Some characteristics of the school also influence student participation, such as the percentage of low-income students, which reduced participation, and levels of support for not smoking, as well as the degree of disapproval of smoking.

Although research is limited, the findings suggest some factors may enhance the outcomes for smoking cessation initiatives. One is the need to be alert to possible depression provoked by smoking cessation. For a large group of adolescent girls, concerns about weight are closely tied to smoking. For them smoking may be viewed as a means of weight control. Adolescent women who are daily smokers are four times as likely to fast, use diet pills, and purge as a way to control weight. Adolescents

E-cigarette regulation: The fight revs up

Beginning in mid-2016, advertising for e-cigarettes will be banned in the 28 nations of the European Union, as it already is for ordinary tobacco products. E-cigarettes would also be required to carry graphic health warnings and must be childproof. The amount of nicotine would be limited to 20 milligrams per milliliter, similar to ordinary cigarettes.

An earlier version of that proposal had the backing of the 28 European Union member states. But in October the Parliament, one of the three main voices in European policy, voted to keep the products regulated as tobacco, [rather than medicine], after intense lobbying from the tobacco industry and tens of thousands of "vapers," or people who smoke e-cigarettes.

The fight will probably continue as Big Tobacco and e-cigarette start-ups looks to protect their business. For example, the tobacco companies' case has previously been taken up by countries like Ukraine, Cuba and Indonesia in a challenge to Australia's rules at the World Trade Organization, arguing that the regulations constitute "technical barriers" to trade and violate the companies' intellectual property rights.

Excerpt from: Jolly D. European Parliament approves tough rules on electronic cigarettes. *New York Times.* February 14, 2014.

may prove to be a unique asset to one another. Non-smoking teens may be an untapped resource in promoting other teens' cessation efforts. Of those surveyed, fully 90% of the adolescents reported knowing someone whose smoking was a concern to them, most commonly a parent or friend. In addition, they indicated a strong willingness to provide support to help that person quit.

COLLEGE STUDENTS

College was long seen as a period of sanctioned "time out," with excess to be expected, especially around drinking. In turn the accepted societal response was to turn one's head and overlook what was going on. The attention now devoted to alcohol use on the college campus demonstrates the extent of changes that have occurred.

How society should address campus alcohol problems and other drug problems is far from clear, with alcohol being a particular concern. In 2008, over a hundred college presidents issued a statement entitled "The Amethyst Initiative." Amethyst does not refer only to a gemstone. "Amethystic" refers to a sobering agent, an agent that protects from intoxication. In that vein, the presidents were requesting that public officials review the legal age for drinking. This was prompted by the recognition that drinking is a significant problem and that college drinking obviously occurs even if illegal. The college presidents' statement suggests that, when illegal, drinking becomes more hidden, more dangerous, and thus more difficult for campus officials to address. While possibly seen as an act of frustration, this statement emphasizes the societal nature of alcohol problems and the diversity of interventions required.

As might be expected, the Amethyst Initiative sparked considerable discussion. It certainly never rallied the support required to be taken seriously as a policy initiative. Within the medical community and substance abuse fields the most vocal opponents were those involved in community public health. No one was dismissive about the dangers that accompany hidden drinking. However, the point was made that whatever the number of problems that might be averted, a significantly larger number would be encountered by reducing the legal drinking age to 18, which would put the legal drinking age into the population still in high school.

One way to deal with the problems of hidden drinking has emerged. A number of schools have introduced "medical amnesty" around drinking. This is sometimes referred to as a Good Samaritan provision. If one student seeks help for another out of concern about alcohol toxicity or overdose, neither student will face disciplinary actions for violating campus rules on alcohol or drug use.

Patterns of Alcohol and Other Drug Use

Monitoring the Future, a NIDA-sponsored national survey of college students and young adults conducted since 1979, includes information on alcohol and other drug use for college students and their non-college age mates.[4] The rates of alcohol and drug use among college students in 2011 are outlined below.

Substance	Past Year	Past Month	Substance	Past Year	Past Month
Alcohol	79.2%	67.7%	Amphetamines	11.1%	2.8%
Cigarettes	23.4	12.5	Hallucinogens	3.9	1.1
Marijuana	34.9	20.5	Cocaine	3.1	1.1
Illicit drug other than marijuana	17.1	7.8	Sedatives	2.2	0.8
			Inhalants	1.5	0.2
			Heroin	0.1	0.1
Narcotics other than heroin	5.4	2.2	Steroids	0.3	0.0

TOBACCO RESEARCH INSTITUTE
Compared with non-college peers, college students are more likely to drink heavily and less likely to smoke, so I think we should market a brandy-laced cigarette.

High school students who plan to attend college are less likely to be involved in heavy drinking than their classmates who don't plan to go to college. However, upon their hitting the college campus, the situation is reversed, and they become the heavier drinkers. Fraternity and sorority membership adds to the disparity. The higher rates of college drinking and heavy drinking are attributed to two demographic factors. First, alcohol use increases when young adults move away from their parents and begin living independently. Second, drinking declines after marriage for both men and women. Those who do not go to college are more likely to live at home or be married, both of which are associated with less drinking.

The proportion of college students who use alcohol has changed little over the past 15 years, with between 81% and 85% of students having used alcohol at some point during the year. In terms of past month drinking, in 2012, 67% of college students reported having had a drink in the past month. Among this group of drinkers, in terms of quantity, a little under half (46%) might be described as "moderate" drinkers, with no instance of binge drinking during the month. However, the majority of

[4] Data on substance use among college students are drawn from three sources: *Monitoring the Future* <www.monitoringthefuture.org>, an ongoing survey sponsored by NIDA; the most recent reports for the *Core Survey* <www.core.siuc.edu/>, funded by the U.S. Department of Education and conducted between 1995 and 2006; and the *College Alcohol Survey* <www.hsph.harvard.edu/cas/>, conducted between 1993 and 2005 funded by the Robert Wood Johnson Foundation. These three surveys provide comparable information on substance use patterns. However, each has had unique questions that made it possible to look at different aspects of substance use. Data are drawn from the *Monitoring the Future* survey, unless the *Core Survey* or the *College Alcohol Survey* is noted in the text.

past month drinkers (54%) qualify as problem drinkers, at least in terms of the quantity consumed. Of all the drinkers, 7% were "super-super binge" drinkers, reporting at least one episode of 15 or more drinks. Plus there were the 21% who had at least 10–14 drinks at least once, as well as the 25% who "merely binged" (5–9 drinks) at least once.

The *Core Study* (2005) used another method to categorize drinking patterns among college students. Three major categories were identified. There were the *infrequent drinkers,* the 17% of the students who had between 1 and 6 drinks in the past year. Then there were the *moderate drinkers,* the 42% of students whose drinking ranged between a drink per month to a drink per week. That translates to 1 to 4 drinks a month. Then there were the *frequent drinkers,* the 24% of all students who drank three or more times per week. (The remaining 17% did not fit into these categories.) In the week prior to the *Core Survey,* 36% of students had not used alcohol; 12% had had only 1 drink; 30% reported from 2 to 10 drinks; and 23% reported 10 or more. Just as is true of the general population, clearly there is no "average" college drinker.

These findings on college drinking practices were confirmed by a survey of alcohol use conducted at a New England private college. The alcohol consumption was divided into four quartiles by levels of drinking (each quartile represents 25% of the students). The lowest quartile consumed 1.5% of all alcohol, the second quartile consumed 11.5%, and the third quartile consumed 23.0%. The highest drinking quartile consumed 64%, close to two-thirds of all the alcohol. In translating that to a "typical week," 57% of students reported having from 0 to 6 drinks. At the other end of the spectrum were the 2.3% of the students who reported having had between 40 and 50.

Smoking, however, is less common among college students than those not attending college. Here, too, the differences can be traced back to high school. Among high school students, the rate of smoking a half-pack-a-day is four times higher for those not college-bound. This disparity grows during the college years, with 2.4% of college students smoking a ½ pack a day versus 11% of non-college peers. The challenge on the college campus is intervening to prevent the occasional smoker from becoming a confirmed regular smoker.

Gender Differences

The proportion of college women who drink approximates that of men. However, women drink less per occasion and drink less frequently. They are less likely to be heavy drinkers or daily drinkers. In 2011, half (43%) of college males reported an incident of binge drinking, having had five or more drinks in a row in the past two weeks; the rate for women was a quarter lower. Women are also less likely to use illicit substances. About a quarter of both male and female students are daily smokers.

Racial and Ethnic Differences

There is relatively little published data on racial differences for alcohol and drug use among college students. However, throughout high school, African Americans consistently have lower rates of substance use than Hispanics and whites. Among high school seniors, the rate of smoking for whites is two and a half times greater than that for African Americans. Heroin use is less than half the rate for whites and Hispanics. When it comes to heavy drinking, the rate for African Americans is only a third of the rate for whites, and half of the rate for Hispanics. These differences presumably continue into college. These significantly lower levels of alcohol and drug use are present from eighth grade. So the rates among seniors cannot be attributed to differing dropout rates. The traditionally African American colleges have significantly lower levels of alcohol and other drug use and a lower rate of problems associated with use. In addition, African Americans drink less than white students, wherever they are attending school.

Trends

There has been a general overall decline in licit and illicit substance use since 1980. In 2011 use of any illicit drug in the prior month was virtually half of what it had been in 1980 (21% versus 38%). Use of marijuana dropped by 37% in the same period. The changes around drinking have also been remarkable. Compared to 1980, in 2011 the rate of current drinkers was down by 18%, and the rate of daily drinking was down by almost 40%.

Interestingly, students' drinking practices did *not* change substantially following the changes in the legal drinking age that occurred in the 1980s. When the legal drinking age was raised, there was only a transient impact on college students' drinking. There was a decrease in consumption immediately after the legislation was passed, but with time the numbers of students drinking returned to the previous levels.

Binge Drinking: A Caution

Binge drinking is clearly a matter of concern, but the definition raises one significant question: What is the duration of "the drinking occasion"? If students are attending a party that goes from 9 P.M. to 2 A.M., the five drinks that define a binge represent one drink per hour. That is the rate at which alcohol is metabolized; the student partygoer could go home with essentially a zero blood alcohol level. That is a different scenario from the group that heads to a local pub and has five beers in an hour and a half.

At the turn of the century, a thematic issue of *Psychology of Addictive Behaviors* (vol. 15, no. 4) was devoted to binge drinking. Articles examined the utility of binge drinking as a marker for high-risk drinking, the advantages and disadvantages of the use of the concept, and some alternative perspectives and indicators of alcohol problems. Several articles question the use of binge drinking as an indicator for intoxication and provided results of studies that demonstrated its limitation as a measure. One study found that among those who were classified as binge drinkers, the last time they drank, based on the length of the drinking episode, weight, and gender, the majority (63%) would have had a BAC under 0.10, about half (48%) would have had a BAC under 0.08, and 30% would have had a BAC under 0.06%. Similarly, a study of college students and young adults as they were returning from bar-hopping in Tijuana found that the definition of "binge drinking" was not a good measure of the levels of actual intoxication.

A later study supports these views. Breath tests were administered to more than 800 students as they returned to their dorms one evening, between 10 P.M. and 3 A.M. Among the students whose self-reports would classify them as heavy drinkers based on consumption during the past two weeks, virtually half had a zero BAC on that evening. For males who said they had five drinks (four for women) on the evening of the breath test, the average BAC was under the legal level of intoxication (0.08). Very high BACs, of 0.15 or above, were quite rare, found in only 1.3% of the students tested. Also of significance is that students' definitions of binge drinking may be at odds with those of researchers or college health staff. For students, binge drinking does not represent the number of drinks on a drinking occasion. For them it is synonymous with rapid drinking, drinking to intoxication, and drunkenness. The general consensus is that while heavy drinking is indeed a concern, binge drinking is an inadequate measure or method to identify high-risk, problem use. Indeed, it serves to exaggerate problems related to college drinking and, as one author has noted, tends to demonize students or perpetuate a mythology that may be valued by many.

An alternative view, though not necessarily a contradictory view, has been posed in the book *Swimming with Crocodiles.* The authors point out that heavy/binge drinking is increasingly a global phenomenon that has sprung up in a relatively short time. In reflecting on this, the authors suggest "extreme drinking" as an alternative to the term "binge drinking." The authors think this better captures the different aspects of this drinking, and doesn't lose sight of the fact that the focus *is* the drinking—heavy, excessive, and unrestrained drinking. It is suggested that "extreme drinking" is comparable to other "extreme" behaviors, such as extreme sports. All of these offer a challenge, their pursuit is motivated by an expectation of pleasure, and they are, by design, not without risk to those who engage in them, others around them, and potentially society as a whole. Within this framework, it is out of place to question whether what is called binge drinking is really dangerous; to ask mundane questions about what is the "actual" BAC of students isn't in keeping with the mythology of binge drinking that has taken hold.

Problems Associated with Substance Use

Data on the magnitude and nature of problems related to alcohol and substance use on college campuses were scant for a long time. The *Core Survey* and *Campus Alcohol Survey* significantly eased the information deficit. Individually, colleges did not systematically gather such data. If the information was collected, it was generally treated as confidential and rarely published in the professional literature. Colleges are concerned about their public image. They worry that if such data were available to the press, the institution might be viewed less favorably by the public; alumni; prospective students or, more important, their parents; potential donors; and, for public institutions, the state legislature, which controls the purse strings.

- *Types of problems.* A variety of problems can result from substance use. The following is a comparison of the problems identified by students in the 2005 and the 2011 *Core Surveys.*

	% Reporting Problem		
Problem	2005	2011	Change
Had a hangover	62.8%	60.2%	< 1%
Got nauseated or vomited	53.8	51.2	↓ 5
Did something later regretted	38.1	33.6	↓12
Had a memory loss	34.3	33.8	↓ 1
Got into argument or fight	31.0	29.4	↓ 5
Missed a class	30.7	25.7	↓16
Was criticized by someone	30.3	28.0	↓ 8
Drove while under the influence	26.3	21.3	↓19
Performed poorly on a test	21.8	19.4	↓11
Was hurt or injured	15.5	15.5	—
Trouble with police or authorities	13.9	11.8	↓15
Thought may have a problem	10.4	9.3	↓11
Taken advantage of sexually	10.3	8.2	↓20
Responsible for property damage, e.g., pulled fire alarm	7.0	5.2	↓26
Tried to stop using	4.8	4.4	↓ 8
Thought of committing suicide	4.0	4.0	—
Took advantage of another sexually	3.0	2.1	↓30
Arrested for DWI	1.4	1.1	↓21
Tried to commit suicide	1.1	1.1	—

Drinking, Driving, Texting

Car and Driver conducted a small experiment to determine the impact of texting—reading and sending texts—on reaction time, compared to the impact of driving with a BAC of 0.08, the standard for being legally intoxicated.

When unimpaired and going 70 mph, it took about a half second to brake. How much further does the car travel under these conditions?
Legally drunk? add 4 feet
Read an e-mail? add 36 feet
Send a text? add 70 feet

Source: www.caranddriver.com/

- *Morbidity and mortality.* The federal government does not directly gather information on morbidity and mortality among college students. Instead, it makes estimates based on the rates of death and illness among the general population, ages 18–22. So for example, in 2005, nationally there were an estimated 1,700 alcohol-related college student deaths. However, a study conducted in 2011 by the American College Health Association (the organization of college student health centers) demonstrated that this earlier approach was flawed. This study surveyed over 150 colleges and universities, with a combined enrollment of over one million students, to inquire about the number of student deaths in the preceding year. Strikingly, across the board, college students have a much lower mortality rate than their age mates in the general population. Suicide rates were 40% lower, homicide rates were 96% lower, driving-related alcohol deaths were 60% lower, and alcohol-related deaths from other causes were 76% lower. So instead of the earlier estimate of 1,700 alcohol-related deaths, the revised estimate was 394 alcohol-related deaths. Of those, about two-thirds were vehicular accidents.

- *Academic performance.* Certainly not least, academic performance is related to alcohol consumption. An early study reported that what distinguishes the *D* or *F* student from the *A* student is that the former student drinks over twice as much per week. Although no one else has verified this ratio, or even tried to, a number of studies have found that academic performance declines with increased drinking. Heavier alcohol use is also associated with a greater likelihood of dropping out of college. Also associated with poorer academic performance are stimulant prescription drugs prescribed for ADHD (particularly Ritalin). That stimulant use is also associated with skipping more classes gives a clue as to what may be going on. It may not be that the stimulants are "causing" lower grades, but that those who have not been studying and who have fallen behind may believe that taking stimulants is the only way they'll be able to pull the whole thing off!
- *Relation of drinking frequency and alcohol problems.* Does a student's drinking pattern have any relationship to the likelihood of an alcohol-related problem? Yes. Results from the *Campus Survey* show that the more frequently students report five or more drinks per drinking occasion, the greater the likelihood of negative consequences.

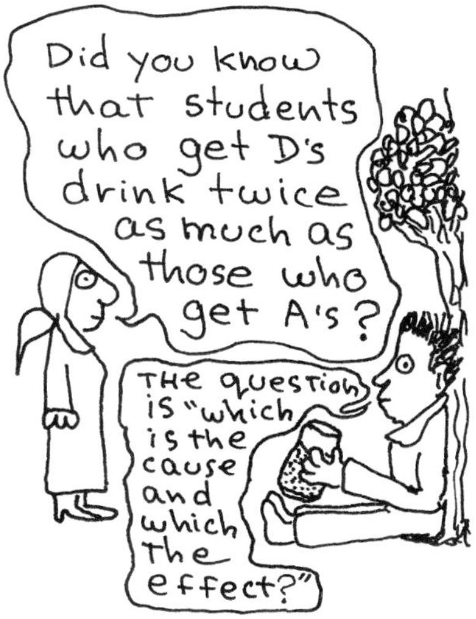

	Frequency of 5+ Drinks		
Problem	Never	Rarely	Frequently
Do something you regret	18%	22%	42%
Not use protection when you have sex	4	19	20
Damage property	2	9	20
Hurt or injured	4	11	27
Drive after drinking	19	40	57
Trouble with campus or local police	1	5	13
Five or more alcohol-related problems since the start of the school year	4	17	48

- *Drinking, violence, and victimization.* Alcohol use is recognized as contributing to campus violence and harassment. The *Core Survey* 2011 found that the consumption of alcohol or other drugs is linked as well to being a victim of violence. The percentage of all the students surveyed who reported an episode of violence or harassment is presented below, along with the proportion of that group who had been drinking or using drugs before the event.

Type of Incident	Reporting Incident	Alcohol or Drug Use before Incident
Ethnic or racial harassment	6.4%	14.2%
Threats of physical violence	8.0	43.7
Actual physical violence	4.0	54.7
Theft involving force or threat of force	1.7	33.5
Forced sexual touching or fondling	4.2	66.2
Unwanted sexual intercourse	2.7	75.6

- *Effects of problems on others.* An individual's drinking has an impact on others. Borrowing a phrase associated with smoking, "secondhand smoke," the negative consequences for others have been termed "secondhand drinking." The *Core Survey* found that the rate of binge drinking on a campus has an impact on drinking's consequences for others. In brief, the higher the campus level of binge drinking, the higher the odds that non-binge students experience the following types of episodes.

Problems Reported by Non-Binge Drinkers	Campus Binge Rate (%)		
	Low	Medium	High
Was insulted or humiliated	21%	30%	34%
Had serious argument or quarrel	13	18	20
Was pushed, hit, or assaulted	7	10	13
Had property destroyed	6	13	15
Had to care for a drunken student	31	57	54
Had studying or sleep interrupted	42	64	68
Experienced unwanted sexual advance	15	21	26

Cyberbullying on campus

Research conducted at 4 Canadian universities involving over 2,000 students has found that despite what is commonly thought, cyber-bullying is not left behind when adolescents head off for college. Over a one-year period, one in five of the university students reported having been a victim of cyberbullying. The perpetrators included university friends and acquaintances, persons unknown to them, and for a small minority of students (2–3% of cases) faculty. In most cases this was via Facebook, text messages and e-mail.

Faculty too are targets. The perpetrators include both students and colleagues. There's a widely used web-site that allows students to rate professors anonymously and post comments. This is a commonly used vehicle. The faculty report that the stakes of this cyber-harassment are significant, including ruined reputations, the loss of professional relationships, and lead to insomnia, anxiety, feelings of hopelessness, and even thoughts of suicide.

—The Canadian Press. Posted March 11, 2014.

Students at Risk

Several groups of students are at particular risk for acute problems. These are discussed below. One issue, however, touches everyone: *Ignorance*. Without accurate information to determine what represents low-risk drinking, often people use how they feel as the yardstick. Too often, by the time a drinker begins to feel intoxicated, others know that the person is indeed drunk. Plus, at this point, some of the alcohol consumed may not even have been fully absorbed, so the blood alcohol level could still be rising.

In terms of specific subgroups of students, *inexperienced drinkers* are among those with the greatest risk. Many student health services find that freshmen are most likely to be seen for overdoses and acute alcohol poisoning. In the vicinity of 15% to 20% of the typical freshman class didn't drink in high school. Most of them become drinkers during their first year of college. Problems accompany this transition from non-drinker to drinker, as well as the transition from infrequent to regular drinker. Underage drinkers, also the younger drinkers, are more likely to experience negative consequences. They have a 50% greater rate of being injured (15% vs. 10%). In addition, they have significantly higher rates of driving after drinking, doing something they later regret, having unplanned sexual activity, and damaging property.

Don't do drugs, kids. There's a time and place for everything. It's called college.
—SOUTH PARK

Fraternity and sorority members are another group at special risk for acute problems. Much of the social life of these organizations revolves around drinking. Members of Greek organizations consistently are more likely to be drinkers, as well as heavy drinkers. Drinking games are part of the Greek scene. While drinking games are thought of as the domain of male students, women take part just about as frequently. However, women are more likely to experience a negative consequence as a result. Drinking games are one way that incoming students are socialized into a problematic drinking pattern. Research into personality traits that are associated with playing drinking games reveals that being a risk taker, a sensation seeker, as well as being impulsive and less socially inhibited, is associated with drinking games. Motives for playing drinking games include fun/celebration and sexual manipulation. Drinking games are strongly related to negative consequences and instances of sexual victimization.

The *level of high school drinking* is possibly the best single predictor of alcohol problems in college. A number of years ago, a study conducted by the Health Service at the University of Pennsylvania found that the best predictor of alcohol problems during college was the frequency of drinking to intoxication reported by incoming students. Incoming freshmen who were the heaviest drinkers in their class and who had had a prior alcohol-related incident were at much higher risk for problems during college. By the end of their sophomore year, these students had more overall visits to the health center, more alcohol-related visits to the health center, and a lower grade point average.

Always do sober what you said you'd do when you were drunk. That will teach you to keep your mouth shut.
—ERNEST HEMINGWAY

Ending up in an emergency room with a physical injury is tied to the *frequency of drunkenness*. Students who get drunk at least once a week are more likely to be hurt or injured. Also, those who get drunk at least once a week are more likely to cause an injury that requires someone else to get medical care. The single question, "In a typical week, how many days do you get drunk?" identifies college students who are at increased risk of injury from their own or others' drinking.

For the general population, a number of factors are recognized as being associated with a greater risk of developing a significant alcohol problem. (See Chapter 5.) One worth particular mention is an *individual's response to alcohol*. Some people experience far less impairment than others at an equivalent blood alcohol level. This trait is most commonly found among those with a family history of alcohol problems. Living in a community where heavy drinking is accepted, and in some circumstances is applauded, raises the odds for an alcohol problem for those with this genetic vulnerability.

Student Athletes: A Special Case

According to the folk wisdom, athletes drink less than other students. The assumption has been that they have less free time, are more concerned with fitness, and are bound by training rules. Not quite. Both the *Core Survey* and the *Campus Alcohol Survey* found intercollegiate athletes are more likely to be drinkers and to be heavier drinkers than non-athletes. Those who are also fraternity members have the highest levels of heavy drinking. Every four years the NCAA (National Collegiate Athletic Association) surveys alcohol and other drug use among member schools. Its 2009 survey, the most recent available, included 1,076 schools (all of the NCAA member schools), with each school asked to survey 1–3 pre-selected teams. Over 20,000 athletes participated. Data was collected for a variety of variables: e.g., frequency of use, seasonal and off-season use, typical amount used, motives for use and motives for non-use, negative consequence associated with use, use patterns for specific sports, and demographic factors. In respect to lifetime use, more than 88% reported using alcohol, followed by marijuana (36%), cigarettes (25%), smokeless tobacco (23%), amphetamines (6%), narcotics (5%), and anabolic steroids (1%). In comparing use patterns for different sports, among men's teams, track had the lowest rate of use for all substances. The highest rate was among lacrosse players. For various sports there are significant differences in levels of use; e.g., lacrosse players were eight times more likely to use cocaine than the basketball players. While there was no discussion of possible reasons, this suggests that one factor is likely to be different ethos among different teams. Women's teams did not have such disparate levels of use by sport.

Problems Among Athletes

Athletes have a higher rate of negative consequences than the general student body. There are several exceptions. They are less likely to drive after drinking. Ironically, they are also less likely to wonder whether they have an alcohol problem. Some do acknowledge that their drinking interferes with athletic performance. A third even say that their drinking has led to a poorer performance in practice or a game. Furthermore, 11% say that occurred more than once or twice. Beyond that, 12% say their drinking caused them to be late or miss a practice or a game.

Among the common problems and the differences between athletes and the general student body are the following:

Problem	All Students (%)	Athletes (%)
Had a hangover	62.6%	66.5%
Got nauseated or vomited	53.2	53.6
Did something later regretted	38.2	45.0
Missed a class	33.1	44.5
Drove while under the influence	32.5	30.8
Had a memory loss	31.7	30.5
In an argument or fight	30.8	36.3
Criticized by someone	30.3	35.1
Performed poorly on test	23.5	34.5
Was hurt or injured	14.3	21.1
Trouble with authorities	13.7	18.0
Taken advantage of sexually	11.7	12.0
Thought drinking maybe a problem	10.7	8.2
Damaged property	8.2	10.5
Tried to stop using	5.8	6.2
Thought about suicide	4.6	4.7
Took sexual advantage	4.6	6.2
Arrested for DWI	1.5	2.8
Tried to commit suicide	1.4	2.0

I don't know what's wrong with me? I'm doing great in my courses, and I like my roommates, but I don't seem to enjoy getting drunk and throwing up.

Drinking Patterns

Since the NCAA's prior report there was a 5.6% increase in past year drinking by student athletes. When they do drink, virtually half say they have five or more drinks, qualifying as binge drinking. The intercollegiate or intramural athletes' competitive spirit isn't limited to the playing field. It extends to drinking games. Consumption in the context of drinking games accounts for greater levels of consumption than among non-athletes and, as would be expected, for higher peak blood alcohol levels. Participation in such games accounts for a significant amount of the alcohol consumed. While athletes drink more than other students, the rates are higher in the off seasons than during training and the season of competition. The alcohol–sports connection isn't limited to athletes. Campus sports fans also drink more heavily and have more alcohol-related problems than students who don't describe themselves as sports fans. When fans spill out of bars into the streets after playoff games, brawling, and burning cars, their behavior isn't fueled simply by whether their team won or lost.

Performance-Enhancing Drugs

I'm in favor of it [drug testing] as long as it's multiple choice.
—Kurt Rambis

In addition to alcohol, a unique concern for college athletes is the use of performance-enhancing drugs. In case anyone may have missed it, in larger schools, college athletics is big business. At a fair number of schools, football and basketball coaches earn more than the college's president. In one state the highest-paid state employee is not the governor. It's not the chief of the state supreme court. It's the basketball coach at the state university. College athletic programs, particularly among Division I schools, essentially serve as the minor leagues for professional sports. Beyond whatever pressure there is to win the big game, any student who has ever nourished a dream of a professional career has certainly at least thought about the potential benefits of performance-enhancing drugs. Although the data are sparse, it appears that a substantial number of college athletes have more than thought about using performance-enhancing agents. At one point a number of years ago, someone surveyed five college ice hockey teams, finding that over half of the members had used metabolic stimulants at some point in their careers. A quarter were then current users. Virtually everyone recognized that these were banned by the NCAA. Virtually everyone was aware that serious side effects were linked to use. Ephedrine, for example, is associated with insomnia, hypertension, even sudden death. Nonetheless, a third of those polled indicated they would use a banned substance if it would help them get into the National Hockey League. Whatever the risks, the possible rewards loomed larger.

Anyway, no drug, not even alcohol, causes the fundamental ills of society. If we're looking for the source of our troubles, we shouldn't test people for drugs, we should test them for stupidity, ignorance, greed and love of power.
—P. J. O'Rourke

Education, Drug Testing, Policy, and Referral

There has been much discussion of drug testing at the college level. According to its website, the NCAA introduced drug testing in 1986 at its championship events. Then four years later random drug testing was introduced as a year-round program in Divisions I and II. In addition, many schools introduced their own drug testing programs. However, this is a case where you have to read the small print. Things are not quite as comprehensive as these kinds of statements suggest. While some championship events involve annual testing, the commitment is to test each championship event once every five years.

The NCAA testing program has its critics. For one, as structured, it allows students a variety of ways to avoid compliance. The drug tests are neither random nor unannounced. Among student athletes, under a quarter have been tested by the NCAA or their school. That's not an impressive percentage. The actual drug testing is conducted by a private company founded by a former NCAA staff member. The company has a \$5.5 million dollar contract with the NCAA, as well as a number of the schools. In light of the rates of substance use reported in the NCAA's survey, oddly in over two decades the portion of positive results has never exceeded one percent. Someone involved in the Olympic game drug testing described the NCAA's efforts as being used to mislead fans. As for quality of its work, the company was characterized as "not really doing anything [I] would call drug testing."[5]

A poll of coaches and other staff associated with athletic programs brings to light other problems related to alcohol-drug use and college athletes:

- Thirty percent of schools do not have a total ban on alcohol use during recruitment of student players, most of whom are presumably underage.
- In four out of five schools, the drug-alcohol education programs provided via athletic departments to student athletes consist of one or fewer sessions per semester.
- Less than half of the schools have a drug testing program.
- Of schools with drug testing, one-third test for anabolic steroids, although 98% test for marijuana.
- Who do schools notify if someone tests positive on a drug test?

Director of Athletics	94%	School Counselor	52%
Student/Athlete	91%	Team Doctor	45%
Coach	88%	Parents	44%
Trainer	79%		

- Suspensions after a positive test. Forty-four percent of schools suspend a student from the team, after the first positive test. This rises to 71% for a second positive test, and 72% after a third positive test.
- Referral for treatment. For Division I schools, 85% of schools have procedures in place to make a referral. For Division III schools, the figure is less than two-thirds.

Perceived Benefits of Drinking

An important element in considering the consequences of campus alcohol use is often overlooked by researchers and college administrators. But students don't miss it. That is the perceived benefits associated with use. The negative consequences of drinking get all of the attention. If that were all there was to it, and for the most part, only bad or neutral outcomes were associated with drinking, isn't it likely that campus drinking patterns would look quite different? A study examined the positive consequences that college students associate with drinking. There are many. Equally important, when students weigh the intensity of negative and positive outcomes, the positive consequences are judged to be

[5] The performance-enhancing drug scandal for 2013 was not in college sports but in major league baseball. Twelve players accepted negotiated suspensions for 50 games. One player (A-Rod) while fighting the suspension, lost on appeal. He will be sitting out the entire 2014 season, of over 200 games. How were these players identified? It wasn't the League's drug testing program. It was a disgruntled employee and former client, out to get the owner of an 'anti-aging' and 'wellness' clinic, who provided the names of the players and their drug regimens to a Miami newspaper.

greater, and positive outcomes are seen as occurring far more frequently than negative fallout. Just as students can recount a negative episode and re-experience the embarrassment or guilt, so too can students recall the specific pleasures associated with a drinking event. "I had a blast dancing at the bar with friends." "I could really talk to others and express my true feelings." Among the things cited as benefits are more fun, better times with friends, less tension, and easier socializing. To draw upon learning theory, the positive responses associated with alcohol occur more frequently and are encoded in each event, reinforcing the belief that drinking leads to more fun. For the most part, this is equally true for men and women, although men do report both greater positive and negative consequences, and women may be more open than men to moderating drinking after negative consequences.

Natural History of Collegians' Alcohol Use

This is the way I look when I'm sober. That's enough to make a person drink, wouldn't you say?

Kristine, after not having a drink for two days, from the movie, *Days of Wine and Roses, 1962*

Researchers at the University of Washington have done considerable work in studying the effects of brief interventions, including the use of brief interventions among college students. Before utilizing this approach with college students, they first had to define the natural history of alcohol use and alcohol problems during the college years.

In any study of the effectiveness of a treatment or prevention activity, there are several factors to consider. First, an appropriate comparison, or control, group is needed because any treatment ought to lead to a better outcome than if nothing had been done. Hence the question, "What is the natural history for the condition?" Many surveys have found that, during college, the rate of drinking and the associated problems *do* decline. If that is so, does an intervention produce better outcomes than would have occurred anyway? If not, is there a difference in the rate at which alcohol problems resolve? Can the "natural" rate of improvement be accelerated? If so, that is a justification for the intervention. A related question is, "How long should the follow-up period be to determine if changes endure?" This question is especially important when evaluating the effects of prevention programs. It is not uncommon to find that students who have received a prevention program differ from a comparison group immediately after the program, or at a month or even after several. But by a year later, these differences may have evaporated. The same question arises in respect to treatment effectiveness. Has enough time passed so that one can be confident that any improvement is not transitory? To put it differently, has enough time passed so that, if things were going to fall apart, that would have already happened?

You'd be surprised how much fun you can have sober.
When you get the hang of it.

Joe, from the movie, *Days of Wine and Roses*

University of Washington researchers traced drinking patterns over the course of four years of college, tracking drinking frequency, quantity consumed, and negative consequences. The typical incoming student drinks more often than he or she did in high school. However, after the first year, the frequency of drinking declines. Then as an upperclassman and upon reaching that magic 21st birthday, drinking frequency increases. But what about the quantity consumed? This may come as a surprise: there is a modest increase during the first two years. However, when students are upperclassmen, the total amount of alcohol consumed declines, despite the fact that there are more drinking occasions. In effect, they drink more frequently but consume less on each drinking occasion.

While the previous paragraph described the picture for students as a whole, there was a subgroup who were clearly "not" average. They entered college with a history of problematic alcohol use. The study followed this at-risk group too. For the students to qualify as "at risk," there had to be one incident of binge drinking in the past month and a history of several negative consequences on at least three occasions in the preceding three years. What was immediately evident was that at-risk students entered college drinking more often and consuming larger amounts than the average student. Over their four years of college, their frequency of drinking remained relatively constant. At graduation they were drinking about as often as they had in high school, four years before. However, as a group, throughout the college years, there was a steady decline in the quantity they drank. These at-risk students were drinking significantly less at graduation than they did as entering freshmen. With the decline in quantity, there was a corresponding decrease in the number of alcohol-associated negative consequences. During college, the level of negative consequences was never as high as it had been in high school.

During college, the drinking patterns of at-risk students changed, with a decline in how often they drink, how much, and the number of problems that result. Nonetheless, when their pattern is compared with that of students generally, one thing still stands out. Those in the high-risk group still drank more frequently, at higher levels of consumption, and with more negative events than the student body as a whole. For the high-risk group, their lowest scores on these measures still exceeded the highest level for the general student body. So while levels of risk decline, they consistently exceed the highest risks for the average collegian.

Exceptions to the Norm

A few students follow a different path than does the "average" student or the high-risk student. For some, college is where alcohol problems first emerge. A significant minority—23%—leave college with more than a diploma. They have also developed an alcohol problem. As for those who enter college as at-risk drinkers, not all of them turn in the six-pack for a briefcase, send out a résumé, buy a suit, and live happily ever after. Half leave with drinking problems essentially at the same level as when they entered as freshmen. For 40% of these, the situation is essentially the same. But for 10% the problem has become worse.

What factors are at work to help make sense of these patterns? Several perspectives are useful. Clearly there is a *maturational process* at work. Leaving home and going off to college is a significant developmental milestone for many. This is a time when parental bonds soften, including the rules that accompany living with parents. This is a period of increased independence. Alcohol is part of the picture. There are also *expectancies* operating—the belief that alcohol is a part of relaxing, reducing stress, and being more comfortable socially, as well as the sense that drinking is part of college life, independence, and adulthood. College students typically have positive expectancies for drinking. They may also erroneously believe that the degree of enjoyment associated with alcohol is related to the amount consumed, so "If some is good, more is better."

The University of Washington researchers suggest, too, that *learning* is also taking place, especially for the rank-and-file relatively inexperienced and newer drinkers. In essence, they discover the fallacy in the perspective that more is better. As the researchers put it, students discover there is "a point of diminishing returns." There exists a point at which more alcohol does not bring more enjoyment but has the opposite effect. As one upperclassman put it, "It's no longer fun to get smashed the way we used to." This is as true for the at-risk students as for students generally. Over the course of their four college years, they drink less and with fewer negative consequences. While entering college is a developmental milestone, so is graduation. The college years are essentially a period of transition.

Wine should be taken in small doses, knowledge in large ones.

Chinese proverb

On the other hand, some students don't learn from their mistakes. This seems to be true of students with an established pattern of heavy drinking. Students who reported an array of negative consequences—ranging from vomiting, to hangovers, to regretted sexual encounters—were asked to estimate the number of drinks it might take to cause such problems. Even when they knew the number of drinks they'd had when such problems occurred, when they looked to the future, that information was ignored. Their estimates of what would be a "safe" limit to avoid such problems exceeded the amount that had in fact been associated with negative consequences.

They are not long, the weeping and the laughter,
Love and desire and hate:
I think they have no portion in us after
We pass the gate.

They are not long, the days of wine and roses:
Out of a misty dream
Our path emerges for a while, then closes
Within a dream.

—Ernest C. Dowson

"Vitae Summa Brevis" 1896

Environmental Risk Factors

Beyond the immediate campus environment, the larger community influences drinking behaviors. Interestingly, there are marked differences from school to school in rates of student drinking and driving. This isn't a random event. Schools with lower rates of drinking and driving are generally located in states and communities with more restrictions—whether bans on happy hours or bans on advertising bargain-rate specials—and greater enforcement of underage drinking laws. Another difference between colleges is the number of bars and drinking establishments that fringe the campus. The sheer density of drinking establishments surrounding the campus correlates with students' levels of heavy drinking.

Access to Alcohol

Think of "access" in the broadest sense, as legal access, physical access, and also economic access, meaning cost. Many colleges and universities find that their closest neighbors include a disproportionate number of alcohol outlets: package stores, bars, taverns, and cafés. The sheer number is not the only problem. They are doing their own version of social marketing, promoting their wares in an aggressive fashion. There are the Happy Hours, two for one specials, the pitchers of beer, and half-price drinks for women between the hours of 5 and 7. Is there a holiday that does not warrant some special attention: St. Patrick's Day, Columbus Day, Groundhog Day, Election Night? These places can afford to undercut each other in terms of price, because they make up for it in volume.

Of course, licensed establishments are not the only or even the primary source of alcohol for most students. Older students are a major supplier, followed by parties. Students report that alcohol is a bargain. In a follow-up to the *Campus Survey,* students from 10 large universities provided the cost of different kinds of activities. It appears that alcohol is the cheapest form of entertainment.

Campus Initiatives to Reduce Risk

It has long been recognized that among adolescents generally, one of the best predictors of a particular teen's drinking is the drinking pattern of his or her friends. What people think "everyone" is doing has an impact. Many adolescents have been found to have inaccurate perceptions of the drinking patterns in their schools or town. Typically they overestimate the rates of heavy drinking. It is hypothesized that this either frees or pressures adolescents to alter their drinking to approximate what they think is the norm.

Social Marketing

In the late 1980s and early 1990s, it was recognized that misperceptions of drinking norms were common as well on the college campus. Accordingly, a campus prevention approach was designed that goes by the term "social marketing," essentially an effort to educate students as to the actual drinking patterns. Commonly these involve a campus-wide media campaign—ranging from posters, to spots on the campus radio station, to articles in the campus newspaper. One of the first such programs, launched in the late 1980s at a medium-size university in the Midwest, found that the campus binge drinking rate fell markedly, with the rate of binge drinking dropping from 45% to 28% over a six-year period. Similarly, a public university in the Southwest found that its campus's rate of binge drinking declined from 43% to 31% over three years. These kinds of results certainly captured the attention of other institutions.

An evaluation of the program in the Southwest also found that along with the decline in binge drinking, there was a change in student attitudes, especially in how students characterized their own and others' alcohol use and drinking behavior. Over the course of the study, there were changes in the number of students who agreed with the following statements:

Belief	Agree	Drop in Agreement
"Most college students have 5 or more drinks when they party."	40%	↓30%
"Most students drink heavily during Spring Break."	78	↓ 8
"'Alcohol-free' events are not as much fun as an event with alcohol."	27	↓27
"I would rather go to a party that served alcohol than one that did not."	48	↓17
"Most college students are not interested in alcohol-free events."	41	↓20
"Drinking alcohol increases sexual opportunity."	52	↓15

Good wine needs no bush,
And perhaps products that
people really want need no
hard-sell or soft-sell TV push.
Why not?
Look at pot.
—OGDEN NASH

"Most Doctors Recommend or Yours for Fast Fast Fast Relief," 1972

Notice which statement generates the highest rate of agreement and a rate that changed least over time: "Most students drink heavily during Spring Break." Notice, too, how "Spring Break" is capitalized. This suggests it isn't just a time period; it is an event. Does it spark fantasies that rank right up there with the perfect New Year's Eve? Spring break is a time when students are dispersed, off campus, with no student able to know what is truly transpiring with others. If asked to assess drinking during "Spring Break," what do you base your estimate on? Likely, your imagination or postings on Facebook are your major source of information. Does anyone factor in those who don't do anything special, who hang out at home, sleep in, maybe catch up on some reading, and get bored? But then, that's "spring break" not "Spring Break!"

Limitations For social marketing to have the desired impact—whatever the setting or behavioral changes desired—certain conditions must be met. First, it's necessary that a significant number of individuals, in this instance students, have a misperception. Furthermore, in this case, the incorrect estimates need to be overestimates. Second, the misperception must involve behavior that people can't, individually, know with full certainty. Third, the individuals being targeted with a message must care about the group whose values, behaviors, and so forth are being held up as a standard, or norm. Whether one sees oneself as in or out of step with "the group" has to matter at some level for this to motivate behavioral change.

Studies have shown that some groups on campus, such as those in Greek organizations, are less susceptible to broad social marketing campaigns. This shouldn't be surprising. The group that matters most is their own fraternity or sorority, so they may care little what the general campus is doing. In addition, they *do* know what the drinking norms are in their group. So there is no discrepancy that can be exploited.

Another potential limitation was identified by the *Campus Alcohol Survey*. It found that unlike a decade earlier, most students were estimating the level of campus binge drinking quite accurately. The discrepancy described above had eroded. The majority of students at 60% of schools rated the level within 10% of the actual rate. For 31% there was an underestimate; for only 8% was there an overestimate. Thus only 8% of schools are seemingly good candidates for social marketing. Those with accurate perceptions don't need it. And for the roughly one-third who underestimate the level, there is the danger of inviting students to increase their drinking to match the true norm.

It is tempting to think of social marketing as a magic bullet. There is something else to consider. The number of students who report binge drinking is different from the number of binge drinking occasions. Possibly the total number of binge drinking episodes has as much impact on the atmosphere of a campus as does the number of students involved. Consider the following scenario. One student engages in binge drinking in 1 out of every 10 drinking occasions. Another student binges on virtually every drinking occasion. If the infrequent binge drinker is the person who changes, the impact on the total number of binge drinking episodes is far less than if it's the person who binges every time who is the one who changes.

Injunctive Versus Descriptive Norms There are different types of norms, something rarely noted in discussions of campus social norms and social marketing. Usually discussions of social norms refer to *descriptive norms;* that is, the perception of drinking behaviors that describe the drinking patterns on campus. Social norms also can be viewed from the reference point of *injunctive norms*, the "Do's and Don'ts," the sense of what is appropriate. Injunctive norms are always present, even if little discussed. How might students describe the dominant rules regarding drinking? "Someone's drinking is no one else's business, and comments by others are out of bounds." "If there's a potentially dangerous situation, others need to get involved." A number of years ago, an effort at Rutgers University drew upon the concept of injunctive norms in working with dormitory groups, one component of a larger campus-wide effort. The goal was to have dorm groups articulate the expectations they wished to establish and adopt for their own and others' drinking behavior.

Campus Policy

In considering campus drinking practices, the question arises as to whether there are any campus factors that are protective that are associated with lower levels of heavy drinking. The *Campus Survey* compared schools that had an on-campus alcohol ban for all students versus schools without such a ban. First, there wasn't a difference between the schools in terms of the students they attracted; both kinds of schools have the same proportion of heavy high school drinkers. But at the schools with an alcohol ban, there was a substantially lower rate of heavy drinking, 30% lower. Of interest is that collegians who had been heavy drinkers in high school were not more likely to be heavy drinkers in college. So for them, the college atmosphere was a moderating influence. But among the heavy-drinking college students, the rate of alcohol problems was the same, regardless of the institution's alcohol policy.

Social Capital

Another campus characteristic is associated with lower levels of binge drinking. Schools were rated by the average time per month that their students spend doing volunteer work, which was referred to as "social capital." Of note is that schools with a higher-than-average level of volunteer student effort also had a 25% lower level of binge drinking, even though the schools were similar in most other respects. It is interesting to speculate how this phenomenon might be explained. One possibility is that engaging students in the community beyond the campus's ivy-covered walls facilitates the students' maturation process. This in turn may affect the campus climate.

Impetus to Institutional Action

If you are poor, avoid wine as a costly luxury. If you are rich, shun it as a fatal indulgence. Stick to plain water.
—Herman Melville
Mardi, 1855

The earliest pressure to address alcohol and substance use problems—back in the 1970s—came from recovering alumni. Many campus alumni magazines have periodically printed first-person accounts by recovering alumni. Typically these individuals do not blame their alma maters for causing their alcohol dependence, but they claim that the campus environment provided fertile ground for its later emergence. Another factor in the 1970s that gave rise to campus initiatives was the availability of federal monies for pilot demonstration educational programs specially targeted at college students.

Certainly the attention paid to alcohol problems on college campuses is a manifestation of society's generally increasing awareness of alcohol and substance use problems. However, some factors have been unique to the campus community.

The rise in the legal drinking age highlighted the issue of institutional liability. Although the number of cases that have been litigated has been small, they have received attention. Under its "duty to care," a college is responsible for the well-being of its students. Although the institution's obligation to supervise student conduct may be limited, it cannot claim a total absence of responsibility. The institution can be deemed involved based on its sponsorship and regulation of student organizations. Another domain in which there is potential liability is in the institution's role as proprietor, with the duty to maintain safe premises. This includes handling rowdiness at football games or parties and protecting others from a student who is known to be abusive.

Other factors that have prompted college action include the NCAA's mandatory drug testing. In theory this is only one component of a larger substance use educational and prevention effort. However, testing has received the most attention and institutional resources. Also federal efforts to establish drug-free campuses have played a role. The drug-free campus legislation has made distribution of federal funds contingent on colleges' establishing programs to promote non-use among students and employees. These mandated programs are to include clearly established disciplinary actions for those who are found to be in violation of the campus policy.

Impediments to Campus Programs

Although campus efforts to address student alcohol and substance use now seem to have been around forever, that isn't the case. For example, the American College Health Association (ACHA), which has a reputation for its progressive stance toward health care issues, incorporated alcohol services into its standards for member institutions less than 15 years ago. Although they are far from uninterested, many campus administrators have little sophistication with respect to alcohol and substance use problems. As elsewhere, personal biases and impressions substitute for information and data.

Also, a number of myths continue to hold sway. One is the view that heavy drinking is "just a stage." With a diploma, a little more maturity, and some adult responsibilities, this developmental period, marked by excessive alcohol consumption, will pass. While this is generally true, there are exceptions. Plus, given the dangerous situations that can occur, a student may not survive to outgrow the problem. Considering the strong reliance on alcohol and other drug education as the basis of programs, there are those who apparently think substance use problems represent an educational deficit, with students merely uninformed about alcohol or other drugs. This ignores the fact that students arrive on campuses having already been targets of educational programs throughout grade school, middle school, and high school. This stance also overlooks the fact that changes in knowledge do not necessarily lead to changes in behavior. (While education is a common element, programs that are built primarily or solely around education have little impact.)

There are those, too, who see substance use problems as a case of bad manners, which is essentially a moral issue. Those with alcohol problems are regarded as having poor attitudes and questionable values. The goal, therefore, is to have students "shape up." Discussion of "responsible" drinking can reinforce this orientation. The obvious counterpoint to responsible drinking is irresponsible drinking. Many students may be at substantial risk but do not view themselves as being irresponsible, nor are they considered so by their peers. Students, too, can mistakenly be viewed as non-drinkers who are thrust into a drinking culture. On the contrary, the majority of students enter college with an established drinking pattern; for some, the drinking pattern upon entering college places the student at risk for problems.

Campus Initiatives

Alcohol and Drug Policy

An important component of an institution's effort is formulating an alcohol and drug policy. A policy should not read like a penal code. It should set forth a clear, direct statement of the institution's stance toward alcohol and other drug use and the steps and means it intends to use in addressing these. Consider, as a parallel, institutional statements on academic honesty. In such statements, the institution's stance is clear. The standards set for members' behavior are unambiguous. There is no effort to establish comprehensive policing efforts to ensure compliance. However, if violations of the honor code come to the administration's attention, they will be treated without hesitation as serious breaches of the ethos underpinning the community's intellectual life.

A question that commonly arises when alcohol policies are discussed is, "Can we enforce the policy?" One response is opting to go no further than creating "all the policy we think we can enforce," which often is little. Administrators seem to have thought that more limited statements would reduce liability, which is not the case. No institution can protect itself from suit in a litigious society. The institution is usually *the* deep pocket. The best protection for the institution if litigation occurs is a comprehensive student education and treatment referral program.

A comprehensive program needs to involve all sectors of the campus community. This does not mean that everyone need be a "true believer" in the same fashion. For some, public relations may be a major concern; for others, the impetus for involvement may be institutional liability; and for others it may be the record on the playing field or not jeopardizing the school's status with the NCAA by coming up with positive urine screens. For yet others, the quality of life is a major motivation, or perhaps it is the quality of academic life. For some, it is a health concern, and for others it may be personal identification with the issues of children of alcoholics or alcohol dependence. A model program can encompass all of these motives, not deeming some as more legitimate and noble than others. Ultimately, campus-wide involvement occurs when alcohol issues are recognized as intruding on each of us.

One segment of the community often overlooked when defining the need for change and formulating policy is the students. The administration formulates policy, makes the basic decisions, and then puts a draft policy to the students for some review and comment, which is often unfavorable. Those charged with planning then become bogged down in attempting to determine how to engineer students' acceptance. Students' negative responses may speak as much to their exclusion from the process as to their resistance to the policies proposed. Recent surveys have found that the majority of students do support a variety of policy initiatives.

NCAA Recommendations

> *Wine sets even a thoughtful man to singing, or sets him into softly laughing, sets him to dancing. Sometimes it tosses out a word that was better unspoken.*
> —HOMER, THE ODYSSEY

Campuses are touched by the larger culture. One area where this is clearly evident is campus athletics, particularly in Division I schools. In 1999, an invitational symposium on intercollegiate athletics was convened to consider steps to mitigate campus alcohol and other drug problems. Representatives were drawn from campuses ranging in size from Division I to Division III. The symposium participants agreed on the importance of reaffirming the educational mission as the top priority of colleges and universities. It also adopted a series of recommendations, which don't apply just to athletes but can be seen as the basis of a general campus policy. The recommendations touched on alcohol advertising and sponsorship, control measures for public events, an examination of sports recruiting practices, and finally consideration of the pros and cons of support from the beverage industry, including responsible drinking campaigns.

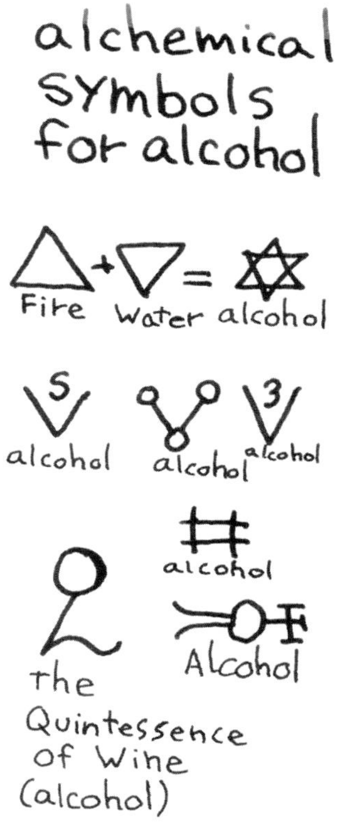

However, the NCAA appears not to have taken all of these recommendations to heart. Its approach might be better described as "Do as I say, not as I do." Its current policy guidelines allow for up to 60 seconds per hour for televised advertisements for malt beverages, beer, and wine as long as the alcohol content doesn't exceed 5%.

In 2004, with much fanfare, the NCAA issued a press release highlighting the finding of a survey it had commissioned. The press release was entitled "Unprecedented Survey Reveals 9 in 10 College Students 'Tailgate' Safely." There are several apparent contradictions. Ninety-three percent of students reported that "their behavior is responsible and safe during tailgating or pre-game parties." *But* only 80% of students think that others drink responsibly and in moderation. Of students who drink during games, it's 82%, not 93%, who report that they drink responsibly and in moderation. An even smaller proportion (79%) claim to drink in that fashion at post-game parties.

Whether a pre-game party, the game itself, or the post-game festivities, consistently at least 95% of students say they are aware of their surroundings and the people around them. Presumably, the NCAA considers this evidence that these students weren't intoxicated. But almost 50% of students report having been driven home by a designated driver, almost 25% took a cab, and 19% used public transportation to prevent drunken driving. Maybe students' drinking wasn't as responsible or as moderate as is being suggested. Among the names on the press release as a source of further information was someone from Anheuser-Busch.

Environmental Initiatives

Efforts to address campus alcohol and other drug problems are increasingly looking at broader issues that can contribute to substance use problems.

- *Assessment of social fabric of the campus.* This includes considering the nature of social life and particularly the extent to which it is tied to Greek organizations and heavy drinking. Are there any or many alternatives to Greek organizations? Or is the campus dependent on fraternities and sororities to provide social opportunities? Tied to this discussion is concern about the campus's ability to foster a community that consists of culturally and ethnically diverse groups.
- *Alcohol-free residence halls.* More and more colleges are providing students the choice of residences that are alcohol-free. Rates of drinking and negative consequences are lower among students in these dorms, and many campuses find there are more students interested in alcohol-free dorms than there are rooms available. The presence of alcohol-free dorms also makes a statement to the general community. It supports nondrinking in a visible fashion and makes it a legitimate, official choice.

- *Athletics and alumni events.* The NCAA guidelines contain initiatives that a number of campuses have instituted. There have been efforts to put an end to tailgate parties before football games, to restrict the availability of alcohol at college events of any kind, to establish and enforce restrictions against drinking in public areas of campus, and others.
- *Reducing alcohol promotions.* The beverage industry spends a significant amount of money promoting alcohol on campus. Promotional efforts directed at campuses have ranged from providing kegs of beer as prizes for campus events, such as blood drives, to distributing beer mugs or baseball caps with logos. Some students are compensated for being campus promotional representatives, distributing advertising paraphernalia, such as caps, posters, and napkins with the brewer's logo. Beer companies are major advertisers in campus newspapers and other campus publications. These activities have led to the adoption of marketing guidelines for promoting alcoholic beverages or limiting alcohol beverage promotions on campus.
- *Outreach to the local community.* Many campuses are working with local town and city governments to address alcohol-related problems, including the density of drinking establishments near campus, the enforcement of open container laws, the reduction of underage sales by liquor stores, and the serving of underage drinkers in bars, as well as efforts to keep high school students out of the fraternities. Towns that may have historically looked the other way when it came to alcohol issues are being asked to stop doing so. Collaborations between the campus and community coalitions provide a more comprehensive approach with benefits to both and a reduction in problems among both college and high school students.
- *Applications of research findings.* Gaining greater attention in the general substance abuse literature is the role of contingency management,

offering frank rewards for desired behaviors. One research group applied this to a fraternity party setting, with people having the opportunity to win a cash prize if they had a BAC below 0.05. Over a series of parties, twice as many were intoxicated at the parties at which there was no prize option than at the parties where the lottery was held. Never underestimate the attraction of winning the lottery!

Use of Electronic Media

As might well be expected, the college campus is in the forefront when it comes to the creative use of electronic media. Indeed the setting couldn't be better suited, with a population that is technically savvy, and, unlike their parents or grandparents, expects to communicate electronically. E-media are being used in a host of ways, to conduct student surveys, for education and prevention initiatives, as well as providing clinical care. A research report in the spring of 2012 described the innovative use of e-therapy to target students at high-risk due to their being far less sensitive to alcohol's effects.

The University of Tennessee initiated a campus-wide effort to reduce the rate of binge drinking and heavy drinking. The intervention was provided to all students through the campus computer network system. It involved a standardized assessment, and then feedback. The population of particular interest was those with "unsafe" drinking patterns. What were the results over a three-year period?

- The rate of binge drinking dropped by 27%.
- The rate of frequent binge drinking declined by 44%.
- The number of citations for liquor law violations among under-age drinkers decreased from 542 to 158 during the academic year.

Intervention and Treatment

Given the natural history of alcohol use, colleges are confronted by several clear problems. Occasions of intoxication are common. Along with them comes the risk of negative consequences, ranging from incidents of violence to unwanted sexual encounters to injuries. Such episodes are likely to bring a student to official attention. In addition to efforts that will reduce the campus-wide level of high-risk drinking, other interventions must be directed at particular individuals.

Alcohol Emergencies

There may not be much to recommend education as *the* major means of dealing with college alcohol issues. However, one piece of information is essential for any member of the campus community—how to recognize and respond to an alcohol emergency. This information is the alcohol-use equivalent of knowing CPR. Many schools make concerted efforts to inform students about what to do and what not to do in the case of an alcohol overdose. This information is posted alongside guidelines

BOX 11.1 Alcohol First Aid

Severe intoxication and/or alcohol poisoning can be dangerous. Here are some basic guidelines to help you size up the scene and decide how to deal with a drunken friend.

Do

1. Assist the person to be comfortable. Make sure the person is in a safe place.
2. Use a calm, strong voice; be firm.
3. Assess whether the person is in a life-threatening situation, and get help if you need it.
4. Lay the person down on his or her side with knees up to prevent choking in case of vomiting.
5. Check breathing every 10 minutes.
6. Do not leave the person alone.
7. Be sure the person doesn't swallow or breathe in vomitus.

Don't

1. Give the person cold showers.
2. Don't try to walk the person around.
3. Don't provoke a fight by arguing or laughing at someone who is drunk.
4. Don't try to counsel the person. Confront the behavior later, when he or she is sober.
5. Don't give anything to eat or drink. Coffee and food won't help, and the person may choke.
6. Don't permit the person to drive.
7. Don't give any drugs; they will not sober someone up; in combination with alcohol, they may be lethal.
8. Don't induce vomiting.

Emergency Guide

Call Safety and Security *if*

- The person cannot be aroused by shaking or shouting.
- The person's breathing is shallow, irregular, or slowed to fewer than 6–7 breaths per minute.
- The person drank alcohol in combination with any other drugs.
- The person sustained a blow to the head or any injury that caused bleeding.
- The person drank a large quantity within a short period and then collapsed.

If You Are Not Sure What to Do,
But Think That the Person Needs Help
Call for Medical Advice.

on how to contact emergency services, such as campus police or the fire department. Box 11.1 contains the information Haverford College (Pennsylvania) provides. It is found in the student handbook, and the emergency guide is posted prominently around campus, virtually as visible as fire extinguishers.

Brief Interventions

College students represent a segment of the population crying out for brief interventions. The number at risk is substantial, and the potential for making changes is significant. Every campus alcohol program needs to determine the threshold of concern with respect to individuals. Phrased another way, what is the institution prepared to overlook? The threshold for concern should be low. The best stance is probably to err on the conservative side. Whether an alcohol incident represents an isolated event or a chronic problem will never be outwardly and immediately apparent. Thus, for those who come to attention, some intervention is warranted.

One model for a brief intervention was part of the University of Washington study that tracked the natural history of drinking. Some of the incoming high-risk students were randomly assigned to a preventive intervention. They were contacted during the winter term to schedule an individualized feedback session in two weeks. These students were asked to self-monitor their drinking during the period prior to the appointment. In the discussion during the visit, based on the two-week diary and the earlier survey, the student received information about his or her drinking compared with that of others. Also covered was the student's sense of the risks and benefits of drinking, highlighting any discrepancies between current behavior and aspirations, goals, and plans. Efforts were also made to counter any myths about alcohol and its effects. At the conclusion, the student got a one-page handout of tips on reducing drinking risks.

This approach was based on a harm reduction model. There was no discussion of legal issues and being underage and no efforts to persuade the student to stop alcohol use. A manual was used to guide and structure the session. The following year, the sophomore year in college, there was a follow-up contact. This was individualized, again summarizing the person's drinking in relation to that of others. (For those at highest risk, there was also a phone call, expressing concern about the student's level of risk. Students were also offered the possibility of further follow-up contacts to see how things were going. A small minority took advantage of this.) This preventive intervention had a clear impact when these students were compared with their at-risk classmates who did not receive it. The changes set in motion persisted over the remaining three and a half years of college. This intervention can be thought of as having facilitated and sped up the "maturing out" process.

College Health Center The challenge is always how to transfer to the everyday world procedures created in the research arena. At the University of Washington, the task was devising a brief intervention that could be conducted in the health center. This meant that the original research procedures had to be streamlined dramatically and boiled down to activities that the health center clinician could do in three to five minutes.

Here is what was devised. Students going to the health center are invited to arrive 15 minutes early to take a computerized interactive assessment covering a number of health issues. If a student's responses suggest he or she is at risk for alcohol problems, the computer automatically generates additional questions. The questions and available feedback anticipate common responses. At-risk students typically express disbelief to find they are in the upper levels of consumption: "Ninety-eighth percentile?" "No way." "*Everyone* I know drinks as much or more." To counter this, a number of questions ask for estimates of the "average" college student. Students can request feedback based on the assessment and elect to make a copy available to the practitioner the student is scheduled to see. (To ensure privacy, and to deal with issues such as informed consent, the student does not provide any identifying information in the computer session.)

During the medical appointment, the doctor or nurse reviews the feedback sheet with the patient. These feedback sheets were carefully designed to get the student's attention, as well as to make it easy for the doctor or nurse to zero in on the key information. The practitioners are trained to ask themselves the following questions:

- "What is the pattern of use?"
- "What most concerns me about the student's risks?"
- "What would make it worth the student's while to moderate his or her alcohol use?"
- "What will get in the way of the student's using the information?"
- "Where will I have my biggest impact, such as teaching one skill, or emphasizing that the decision is the student's?"
- "Is the student at imminent risk, or is there significant motivation to change so that follow-up or referral is warranted?"

After considering these questions, the clinician has four basic tasks. To help staff remember what these are, the acronym and mnemonic REAP was coined. **R**eview the students' current drinking habits and risks. **E**ncourage students to reduce risks by moderating consumption. **A**dvise students on specific strategies to reduce risky drinking. **P**rovide materials, follow-up, or referral if needed. The materials include a computer-generated personalized tip sheet, as well as a moderation management handout. A month later, there is a follow-up contact.

Assessment and Treatment

The brief intervention is a preventive activity. Inevitably there will be contacts where a more serious problem is evident. There are also situations that bring someone to the health service in which alcohol is clearly implicated—accidents, injuries, alcohol poisonings, and requests for the morning-after pill. Or a student may come to the attention of college administration as the result of an alcohol-related event—a fight that involved the police, dorm damage, or arrest for a DWI. Whatever the route, an assessment is required. Whether this is something that can be undertaken by a substance abuse clinician who is part of the health service or counseling service or whether this is something that is automatically referred out will vary by campus.

If treatment is warranted, the question becomes whether this is something that the health center service staff is capable of providing or whether a referral should be made to a community agency or clinician. There is also the student's openness to treatment. The institution does have significant leverage as the student considers whether or not to seek treatment. There will be times when the institution has good reason to insist that continuation in school is dependent on entry into treatment and compliance with treatment recommendations. There are times that a medical leave may be advisable, to enter treatment elsewhere. If so, when the student returns, it will be necessary to provide follow-up, continuing supportive efforts, relapse prevention, and involvement in self-help.

Anti-smoking Efforts

Alcohol use is a major concern, but colleges are also paying attention to other drug use, particularly tobacco. Programs are aimed at preventing students from initiating tobacco use as well as helping others quit. Just as first-year students are at greatest risk of alcohol problems, they too are at greater risk for becoming smokers. Over half of college seniors who smoke began smoking when in college. Two factors recognized to be associated with smoking—depression and dieting concerns—may be most pronounced among incoming students. Also of concern is that smoking cessation during the college years is rare. In the vicinity of 85% of daily smokers and almost half of occasional smokers continued to smoke. Though colleges frequently cite nicotine as a concern, their actual efforts don't live up to the rhetoric. A survey of eight universities in North Carolina found the health services were only screening for tobacco use in two out of every three visits. In addition, staff seemed to be a bit dismissive of non-daily smokers as requiring a "serious" smoking intervention. Another study found that students were more interested in interventions to cut their alcohol use. The non-daily smokers while interested in stopping smoking don't think of themselves as requiring what they thought of as the usual smoking cessation efforts, involving medication or nicotine replacement. They were particularly interested in programs available on the web.

The American College Health Association, along with other national health organizations, has been concerned about the rise in tobacco use among college students and has recommended colleges enact a variety of measures. These include establishing smoking bans in and around all campus buildings—including student housing—and prohibiting the sale, advertisement, and promotion of tobacco products on campus. Public institutions were interviewed to assess the degree to which such measures have been adopted. Over half have smoking bans in all campus buildings and residences—which students also strongly support—68% have no tobacco sales on campus, and 32% of the schools' newspapers do not accept tobacco advertising.

Closing Thoughts

In conclusion, consider how campus efforts might be evaluated. A variety of parameters can be used to measure program impact, such as levels of dorm damage, the number of emergency visits to the local hospital emergency department, the number of cases involving alcohol or other drug use that come before the campus judiciary system, and how each of these is handled. However, there is another dimension. It does not easily lend itself to measurement but is also important. This is captured by the following vignette.

At the prodding of concerned friends, a fraternity member was seen by a substance use counselor and eventually entered treatment. This set off a wave of referrals from the student's fraternity, one of which turned out to be the current president. This student was treated as an outpatient on campus and became active in AA as part of continuing treatment. Following that year's fraternity rush, the first house meeting with the new pledge class was held. Of those present, each in turn introduced himself. In a parody of introductions at AA meetings, one of the first pledges to introduce himself, after giving his name, added "and I'm an alcoholic." This was met with tittering and laughter. Each subsequent pledge introduced himself in a similar fashion, concluding with "and I'm an alcoholic." Finally it was the president's turn. He looked around at each person and introduced himself in a quiet but forthright way: "I'm Joe, and I really am an alcoholic." There was dead silence.

Ultimately the goal is for change to permeate the community, so that everyday encounters between persons, of the sort that go unnoticed by others, will embody increased awareness and an appreciation of the problems that can accompany alcohol and other drug use. Such moments as the one in the fraternity house represent the outcome of many years' work and are among the most eloquent testimonies to a campus's efforts.

THE ELDERLY

Dishonor not the old, we shall all be numbered among them.

Apocrypha Bensira 8:6

On one of the earliest television talk shows—one that only the elderly will remember—Art Linkletter, the host, was interviewing children. The topics were a bit different than they are today. The children came up with the following answers to a question he posed: "You can't play with toys anymore. The government pays for everything. You don't go to work. You wrinkle and shrink." The question was, "What does it mean to grow old?" These responses contain many of the stereotypes our society attributes to the elderly. They also show that this negative picture develops from a very early age. There is a stigma about growing old. The notion is that for older adults there is no play or fun, no money, no usefulness, and no attractiveness.

In considering the elderly, it is important to recognize that we really are talking about ourselves. It is inevitable: we will all age; we will all become elderly. A participant at a geriatric conference reported being asked by a friend, "What can I do to keep from getting older?" The response the person received was simple: "Die now!" There is no other way to avoid aging. So, for those not yet elderly, when you think about the older person, imagine yourself years in the future, because many of the circumstances will probably be the same.

The elderly form the fastest growing segment of the population. In 2012, there were more than 43 million Americans age 65 and older, the group arbitrarily defined as the elderly, or aged, about 13.7% of the population. Increased longevity has contributed to this change, as has a declining birthrate among younger people. By 2030, this segment of the population is projected to be twice as large as it was in 2000, growing to an estimated 72 million and constituting 20% of the population.

Stresses of Aging

Despite the inevitability of aging and physical problems arising as the years pass, it has been said many times and in many ways that "you are as young as you want to be." This is possible, however, only if a person has some strengths going for him or her. The best predictor of the future—specifically, how someone will handle growing old—is how the individual has handled the previous years. Individuals who have demonstrated flexibility as they have gone through life will adapt best to the inevitable stresses that come with getting older. These are the people who will be able to feel young, regardless of the number of birthdays they have celebrated.

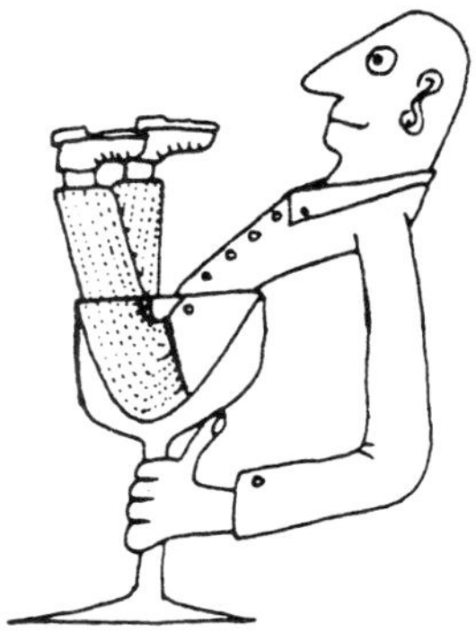

Interestingly, as people get older, they become less similar to one another and more individual. One person commented that, as people grow older, they become "more like themselves." The only thing that remains alike for the members of this group are the problems they face. There is a reason for this. In going through life, people rely most heavily on the coping styles that seem to have served them well previously. With years and years of living, individuals gradually narrow down their responses.

What looks, at first glance, like an egocentricity or eccentricity of old age is more likely a lifelong behavior that has become one of a person's exclusive methods for dealing with stress. An example illustrating this point arose in the case of an elderly surgical patient for whom psychiatric consultation was requested. This man had a constant smile. In response to any question or statement by the nurse or doctor, he smiled, which was often felt to be wholly inappropriate. The treatment staff requested help in comprehending the patient's behavior. In the process of the psychiatric consultation, it became quite understandable. Friends, neighbors, and family of the man consistently described him as "good ole Joe, who always had a friendly word and a smile for everyone, the nicest man you'd ever want to meet." Now, under the most fearful of situations, with many cognitive processes depleted, he was instinctively using his faithful, basic coping style. Very similarly, the person who goes through life with a pessimistic streak may become angry and sad in old age. People who have been fearful under stress may be timid and withdrawn in old age. On the other hand, people who have been very organized and always reliant on a definite schedule may try to handle everything by making lists in old age. What is true in each case is that the person settles into a style that was successful in earlier life.

Time is the rider that breaks youth.
—George Herbert
Jacula Prudentum, 1651

In dealing with the elderly it is important to keep in mind that the particular stresses common to this group differ somewhat from those of younger people. Stresses may arise from social factors, psychological factors, or biological problems. Iatrogenic stresses (harm caused by efforts to heal) can also occur as the helping professions serve (or inadequately serve) older people.

Social Stresses

Social stresses can be summarized under the phenomenon of the national addiction to youth. Television commercials highlight all types of products that can be used to disguise the process of aging. There is everything from hair colorings to dish detergents, which if used will make a mother's hands indistinguishable from her daughter's. Look around you. Who is being hired and who is being retired? Aging is equated with obsolescence and worthlessness. People who have been vital, contributing members of an organization suddenly find themselves with the title "honorary." It is often not an honor at all. It means these people have become figureheads; they have been replaced. The real work has been taken over by someone else—someone younger.

The process of receiving medical care and paying medical bills can in itself be a stressor for older people. Elderly people have twice as many visits to a physician, their average hospital stay is three and a half times longer than for persons under age 65, and the hospital stay costs five times more than for the under-65 age group. Insurance coverage, including Medicare, is often inadequate, especially for preventive services. The chronic illnesses older people suffer often require much time and few high-tech interventions. Historically, the American insurance system reimburses especially poorly for this type of care. Under the new Affordable Care Act, things will clearly change, but how much remains to be seen.

If you resolve to give up smoking, drinking and loving, you don't actually live longer; it just seems longer.
—Clement Freud

The real issue is one of attitude. If one examines the dynamics behind this attitude, then one can see why there has been a lack of interest as well as avoidance. Generally the medical profession and other helping people, including family and friends, are overwhelmed by the multiplicity, chronicity, and confusing nature of the disorders of aging. Caregivers often feel helpless in dealing with the elderly and harbor self-doubts about whether they can contribute in a satisfactory manner that is also personally gratifying. To put it another way, most of us like to see results, to see things happen, to believe there is a "before" and an "after" picture, in which the difference is clear. Also, it is important to feel that the part we have played, however big or small, has made a difference.

Helpers like it when someone puts out a hand and says, "Thank you." The elderly often say, "Don't bug me. I don't want help." If you consider who it is that voluntarily goes into most clinical agencies, it is not the elderly. Those who do go have usually been coerced. Helpers do not like complainers. What do the elderly say? "This hurts; that hurts. You're not nice enough. You don't come soon enough. My old doctor was much better. Do this; do that." Helpers like patients who receive maximum cures in the minimum amount of time. This certainly is not the elderly. There are more visits, for more problems, requiring more time. Helpers like patients who get well. How many of the elderly are cured? How can you take away their diabetes, their arthritis, the pain from the memory of a lost spouse? Helpers like patients who take their advice. With the elderly, helpers suggest A but patients often do B.

While understandable, these interactions only aggravate the problem. They may rub the helper's instincts the wrong way. The result is that many potential caregivers decide they do not like working with this population, and it shows. Very few clinicians volunteer to take on elderly clients. If an elderly client goes to a helping agency, the chances are good that the person who sees the client will soon decide to transfer the case to someone more "appropriate" or will refer the client to another agency. In health care, this should change with the creation of a new medical specialty, geriatrician.

First I lost my hair. Then I lost my wife. My children have all moved away. My best friends have died, my vision is going, my hearing is going, and now you want me to give up alcohol. It's all I've got left.

Another factor that gets in the way of their receiving adequate care from helping people is that the elderly may resent the helper's youth, just as the helper fears the client's age. Also, the elderly generally dislike the dependent status that goes along with being a client or patient. It is the opposite of what they want, which is to be independent and secure and to feel a sense of worth. Being in treatment implies that something is wrong with them. It also means that someone else is partially in charge and telling them how to run their lives.

Psychological Stresses

The greatest psychological stress the elderly must face is loss. In the geriatric population, losses are steady, they are predictable, and they often occur in bunches. And even if they do not, they are still numerous. What are the specific losses?

There is the loss that comes from the illnesses and deaths of family and friends. The older you get, statistically the more likely that those about you will begin to falter. So there are the obvious losses of support and companionship. Not necessarily as obvious is that the deaths of others also lead to questioning the loss of self, anticipation of one's own death. This may sometimes be the source of anxiety attacks among the elderly.

There is the loss that comes from the geographical separations of family. This begins earlier in life, as children go to school and later leave home for college or the armed services and then eventually marry. For the elderly, this may be especially difficult, because 50% of all grandparents do not have grandchildren living close by. As new generations are being born, they are not accessible to the older generation, whose lives are coming to a close.

There is the loss of money through earned income. Whether income is comprised of pensions, Social Security, or savings, the elderly usually do not have as much money as they did earlier in their lives. Dollars represent not only buying power but also have symbolic values. Money represents power, stature, value, and independence. Lack of money has obvious implications in vital areas of self-esteem.

There's a shadow hanging over me,
Oh yesterday came suddenly.
—John Lennon and Paul McCartney
"Yesterday," 1965

There are the losses that accompany retirement: loss of status, gratification, and, often most important, identity. With retirement, you lose who you have been. This refers not only to retirement from a job but also to retirement from anything—from being a mother, from being a grandmother, or from just being a person who is capable of walking around the block. Often accompanying retirement is a loss of privacy. For married couples, retirement may mean more togetherness than they have had for years. Both spouses will have to change routines and habits and be forced to accommodate the presence of the other. The expectations may also be tremendous. Retirement, in most people's fantasies, is thought to usher in the "golden years" and provide the opportunity to do the things that have been put off. This may well be a letdown.

There is also the loss of body functions and skills, which may include a loss of attractiveness. Older people may develop body odors. They lose their teeth. They are more prone to infection. For women, the skin may become dry, including the surface of the vagina, which can lead to vaginal discharges and dyspareunia (painful intercourse). For men, there is general loss of muscle tone. Everything begins to stick out where it shouldn't. As physical problems arise, this may lead to loss of skills. A carpenter who has arthritis or the tremors of Parkinson's disease will be unable to do the things that were formerly possible and rewarding.

"They smell bad, have diseases, and are lazy."
Royal Canadian Mounted Police, reporting on hippies in the late sixties. M. Martel, *Canadian Historical Review*, 2009

Responses to Stress

The elderly may try to handle stress in a number of ways. One is the widely used defense of *denial*. In response to an observation that his hand is more swollen, a client may well say, "Oh, no, it's no different than it's always been." If a close friend is in the hospital and very seriously ill, an elderly friend may dismiss the seriousness and claim it is just another of her spells: "She'll be out, perky as ever, in a day or two."

Do not go gentle into that good night,
Old age should burn and rage at
close of day;
Rage, rage against the dying of the light.
—Dylan Thomas
"Do Not Go Gentle into That Good Night," 1952

Another common way of handling loss is by *somatization*. This means bringing the emotional content out in the open, but "saying" it in terms of its being the body that hurts. This is why so many of the elderly are labeled hypochondriacal. When an old man says his knee hurts and he really cannot get up that day, what he also may be saying is that he hurts inside, emotionally. Because he may not get attention for emotional pains, having something wrong physically or "mechanically" is socially more acceptable.

Another way of handling loss is *restricting affect*. Instead of saying a loss does not exist, as with denial, the elderly may withdraw. They may become less involved, so they don't hear about the bad things happening. By being less a part of the world, they are less vulnerable.

Unfortunately, all these defenses boomerang and work against the elderly. Love, affection, and concern are expressed through words, behavior, and many non-verbal cues—a smile, a nod, a touch. After so many years of living, the elderly certainly know the signs of affection and caring as well as those of distancing and detachment. By withdrawing when they are fearful, they may see others reciprocally withdrawing; they may then be left without any source of affection, interest, or caring. This, in turn, they read as dislike, and they may feel their initial withdrawal was justified. Therefore, one of the prime treatment techniques with the elderly is to reach out to them, literally. Smile, touch them, sit close to them. Attempt to reach through the barrier they may have erected with their protective psychological defenses.

The elderly frequently are hurt by what helping people instinctively say when reaching out to the aged. Statements such as "You're lucky to be alive," "Quit worrying about things," and "Grow old gracefully" are often misinterpreted by the elderly as being told to ignore their losses, or they may interpret this as indicating that others do not want to get close to them. The response of the elderly is that they do not want to grow old gracefully; they do not want to be "easy to manage"; they want to go out with a bang and leave a mark—they want to be individuals to the last day.

How about sex and the elderly? The most prevalent myth is that they have no interest in sex. Physiologically, aging itself need not greatly affect sexual functioning. With advancing years, it takes a little longer to achieve an erection and a little more time to the point of ejaculation, orgasm is a little less intense, and a little more time is required before orgasms can be re-experienced. However, if the elderly are physically healthy, there is no reason they should not be sexually active. The biggest factors influencing sexual activity are the availability of a partner and social pressures. Among the elderly when a partner dies, the survivor may not be encouraged to date or remarry. What is considered virility at age 25 is seen as lechery after age 65. Even when both partners are alive, if they are living in an institution or in the home of their adult children, sexual activity may be frowned on or "not allowed."

Another loss is that of sensation. With aging, the senses become less acute. What this means is that the elderly are then deprived of accurate cues from their environment. This may be a big factor in the development of suspiciousness in older persons. Any paranoid elderly person should have his or her hearing and vision evaluated. The most powerful loss, the loss no elderly person is prepared to understand or accept, is the loss of thinking ability. This loss may occur imperceptibly over time. It comes from the loss of cortical brain function. Suddenly a person who has been an accountant or a schoolteacher, for example, is adding 2 + 2, and it doesn't equal 4 every time. This is embarrassing and scary. Although the person may be able to stand losing other things, to lose one's mind is the ultimate indignity.

The result of all or any of these losses is that self-respect, integrity, dignity, and self-esteem are threatened. The implication can be that usefulness is questioned and life is ebbing away. The feeling may be that "my work is over."

Biological Stresses

Approximately 5% of the elderly are institutionalized in nursing homes, convalescent centers, or similar facilities. However, about 50% have some serious *physical disability,* such as heart disease, diabetes, lung disease, or arthritis. About 25% also have a significant functional psychological problem, with depression being the most prevalent. Understandably, as life expectancy increases and we live longer, there is more vulnerability to the natural course of disease.

May you live all the days of your life.
—JONATHAN SWIFT
Polite Conversations, 1738

Depressive illness is very prevalent. It affects an estimated 6% of those 65 and older, including 25% of those with chronic disease and 50% of nursing home residents. There may be a physiological basis for this. The levels of neurotransmitters (serotonin, monoamine oxidase, and norepinephrine) associated with depression change as people age. These depressions, then, are not necessarily tied solely to situational events. However, because so many things are likely to be going on in the surrounding environment for the elderly, it is too easy to forget the potential benefits of judiciously prescribed antidepressants (with emphasis on judiciously). Malnourishment, for instance, is all too common. Nutritional deficiencies can cause several syndromes that may look like depressions. Many physical ailments, such as thyroid dysfunctions, and illnesses caused by the disease processes themselves manifest as depression.

Tears, idle tears, I know not what they mean,
Tears from the depth of some divine despair
Rise in the heart, and gather to the eyes.
In looking on the happy autumn days
And thinking of the days that are no more.
—ALFRED, LORD TENNYSON
"Tears, Idle Tears," 1847

Depression in the elderly may not be the same as depression in younger persons, with tearfulness, inability to sleep, or loss of appetite. Some of the tips for recognizing depression in elderly persons are an increased sensitivity to pain, a refusal to get out of bed when physical problems don't require bed rest, poor concentration, a marked narrowing of coping style, and an upsurge of physical complaints. Often, the poor concentration leads to absent-mindedness and inattentiveness, which are misdiagnosed as defective memory and ultimately as "senility," while the depression goes unrecognized and untreated. "Senility" is a useless clinical term. The proper term is "dementia," which means irreversible cognitive impairment. However, all cognitive impairment should be considered reversible (delirium) until proven otherwise. It should also be remembered that alcohol abuse, while sometimes creating problems itself, can, in patients with dementia, also make the confusion worse. The elderly deserve an aggressive search for potentially treatable, reversible causes of organic brain syndromes by qualified medical personnel.

Suicide has always been more common among the elderly than among younger persons, and particularly so for those 85 and older. Commonly this is attributed to the use of more lethal methods among the elderly—hanging, and firearms—as well as the presence of untreated depression. However, over the past decade, there has been a dramatic shift. In 2010, the age group 35–64 had the highest rate of suicide. For the first time, the suicide rate in the U.S. exceeded the historic high of 1933, in the Depression, when 25% of the population was unemployed.

A variety of changes associated with aging make the elderly more *vulnerable to the acute effects* of alcohol. Body water content declines and body fat content increases with age. Between the ages of 20 and 70, there is a 10% decrease in lean body mass. With a given amount of alcohol, these combined reductions lead to a higher blood alcohol level among the elderly. Furthermore, with aging there is diminished blood flow through the liver. This means that while the rate of metabolism is unaltered, the alcohol is cleared more slowly. For any given amount, the peak blood alcohol level will be 20% higher for a 60-year-old than for a 20-year-old. At age 90, the peak blood alcohol level is 50% higher. Elder persons who may have some existing impairment in cognitive functioning have even greater sensitivity to alcohol. In addition to the increased acute effects of alcohol, a variety of other physical changes make them more vulnerable to the medical consequences of use. By age 75, there is a 50% reduction in lung capacity, the kidneys work at only 45% of their earlier capacity, and heart function is reduced by 35%.

Iatrogenic Stresses

"Iatrogenic" refers to harm caused by efforts to heal. Some of the stresses on the elderly are, in fact, the product of the health care system and the insensitivities to the psychological and basic physiological changes in the elderly. All too often, medication is over-prescribed in an attempt to keep behavior controlled rather than diagnosed. Too few clinicians take into account the dramatically altered way the elderly metabolize medications, which means that fewer medicines in combination and lowered doses of drugs are frequently required. There is also a tendency by everyone concerned to ignore the fact that alcohol, too, is a toxic drug. The combination of alcohol with other medications in light of the altered metabolism for both can create serious problems. Rarely is there any thought of whether an elderly patient can afford the medicine prescribed. Also, the individual's ability to comply with directions for taking medications is over-estimated.

A poignant example of problems with medications is the case of an elderly woman who was discharged from the hospital with a number of medications. She had been admitted with severe congestive heart failure but had responded well to drug therapy for her hypertension and fluid retention. Within two weeks of returning home, her condition began deteriorating, a source of dismay to her physicians. She was suspected of purposefully causing her ailments, and a psychiatrist, who was asked to consult on the case, decided to make a home visit. The woman knew which medications to take, when, and for what conditions. However, there was one problem. As she handed the bottle of capsules to the psychiatrist, with her crippled arthritic fingers, the "diagnosis" became obvious: the child-proof cap. This is a vivid reminder of the need to consider all the available information in assessing the problems of the elderly.

Patterns of Alcohol and Other Drug Use

Substance use patterns of the elderly differ from those of other groups in the population.

Alcohol

This is your wine and cheese crowd, and nothing ever goes wrong at such events.

–New York City policeman, commenting on picnickers attending a summer Philharmonic concert in Central Park. *New York Times,* 1984

The elderly have a lower rate of alcohol use than other age groups. This is commonly attributed to the historical era in which they grew up. The proportion of lifetime abstainers (20%) is higher than among the general population. In addition, the elderly generally drink less frequently. Accordingly, the most recent *National Survey on Drug Use and Health* (2011) found that while slightly over half of those over age 65 had a drink during the past year, a smaller proportion (40%) had a drink in the past month, thereby qualifying as current drinkers. Of these current drinkers, about 8% had at least one occasion of five or more drinks, and about 20% of those had that amount on multiple occasions. With advancing years, what earlier was "social drinking" becomes excessive use due to alcohol's causing or aggravating a range of health problems or the body's simply being more sensitive to alcohol's effects on any drinking occasion. As a general rule of thumb, anything over two drinks per day or seven drinks per week is defined as excessive alcohol use.

As is true of other age groups, the prevalence of drinking varies considerably by geographic region. Similarly, men are more likely than women to be drinkers.

Little is known about the relationship of alcohol use to life stresses and changes, although there has been speculation. The advent of retirement communities has provided an interesting opportunity to examine some aspects of these questions. It appears that in these settings—which offer their residents a variety of leisure activities, such as golf, swimming, craft classes, and discussion groups—social isolation is not tied to higher levels of alcohol use. On the contrary, the heaviest drinkers (defined as drinking at least two drinks per day), who constituted 20% of those studied, were also those who were socially more active. Since entering the community, one-third of the individuals noted a change in drinking patterns, with three-fourths of those people reducing their alcohol use. The other one-fourth (8% of the total group) said their drinking had increased. One of the questions raised is whether social activity in retirement communities is tied to alcohol use and thus facilitates, or even promotes, heavier drinking by some individuals.

Beyond retirement communities, there has also been examination of the drinking patterns of those in assisted living facilities. One study, based on the observation of nursing aides working in these settings, suggests that a majority of residents (69%) are thought to use alcohol, with a third drinking daily; and for about 20%, drinking adversely affected their health, for example, due to a fall or an interaction with medication. There clearly is no consensus about alcohol policies. Some facilities ban alcohol, some allow residents to use alcohol with a physician's permission, and there are those communities that host happy hours.

Nicotine

About 66% of the elderly used tobacco at some point. About 9% currently smoke.

Over-the-Counter Preparations

For many people, use of over-the-counter medications is the first response to an illness or a medical problem. These self-prescribed preparations are used more extensively than are prescription medications. The typical American household is estimated to have an average of 17 different over-the-counter products on hand. In one study, in response to the question of how they handle everyday health problems, 35% of the elderly report they do not treat the problem, 35% report using an over-the-counter medication, 15% use prescription medications available in the home, 11% use some other home remedy, and 13% contact their doctor or dentist. If they take any action in response to a health care problem, the odds are good that they will use an over-the-counter preparation.

When chronic illness accompanies aging, there is an understandable tendency to seek preparations to ease discomfort. Elderly people are more likely than any other segment of the population to use these preparations. They take many times more over-the-counter drugs than do members of any other age group. One study of healthy elderly people identified 54% as regularly using over-the-counter drugs. Fifty percent of that group reported that they typically used analgesics, laxatives, or antacids four to six times per week. Of those who use over-the-counter drugs daily, 80% are believed to simultaneously be using prescribed drugs, alcohol, or both. Some may often use six or more preparations.

The number of over-the-counter preparations is growing. A relatively new addition to the array of over-the-counter preparations are herbal remedies and dietary supplements. One survey found that among those age 75 and older, three-quarters took at least one supplement. Of the 22 most widely used herbal remedies and dietary supplements used by the elderly, 10 have interactions with commonly prescribed medications. Many people tend to think of over-the counter products as helpful and benign. Many times people in providing their doctor a list of all the medications they take, don't include over-the-counter drugs or dietary supplements. In addition, health care professionals do not rank very high as a major source of information about over-the-counter preparations. Among the elderly, the internet along with advertising are the primary sources of information for 25% of those surveyed. Pharmacists and friends, relatives, and neighbors were tied for second place, each being the source of information for 20% of those surveyed. The label on the product itself was noted by 13%, and in virtual last place were physicians, consulted by only 14%.

Valium's half-life—the amount of time it takes for half of the drug to be removed from a person's bloodstream—in a young person is typically about 24 hours. . . . In a frail 80-year-old man, that half-life can be extended to 80 hours, and if an overweight person is taking Tagamet and drinking alcohol, the half-life of Valium is extended to a whopping 210 hours.
–L. LIPSON, M.D.,
Polypharmacy. *USC Health Magazine, 1996*

Prescription Drugs

The elderly take about a third of all prescription medication. Upward of 60% have prescribed medication. Those using five or more prescription medications increases steadily with age. Some of the drugs most commonly prescribed are also those with a high potential for adverse drug reactions.

Adverse Drug Reactions Adverse drug reactions are more common among elderly people. One major reason for this is that they use more drugs than do younger people. Because of multiple chronic illnesses, they may be under the care of more than one physician, none of whom may be fully informed about the complete range of medications the patient is taking. As drug regimens become more complex, there is a greater probability of error by the patient as well as greater potential for interactions between drugs. Concurrent use of drugs, even 10 or more hours apart, can significantly affect absorption, distribution, metabolism, and toxicity. A recent study found that about 5% of the elderly use medications that pose a risk of a major drug-drug interaction, and half of these involve non-prescription drugs.

The more drugs being used, including alcohol, the greater the potential for adverse interactions. A study of hospitalized patients found that all patients taking more than eight drugs had at least one interacting pair of drugs in that mix. A study of 75-year-olds living at home found an average of 5.6 drugs being taken. Their primary care physicians were unaware of a quarter of these. Even before factoring in any alcohol use, 15% of these patients are at risk for drug interactions. For those over age 65, the chance of visiting an emergency room due to adverse drug interactions is double that for those under age 65; the chances are five times greater that an elderly person will require hospitalization as a result of drug effects.

Back in 1991, to address the problems associated with prescription drug use among the elderly, an expert panel was convened to consider prescribing practices, especially for those in nursing homes, and to identify drugs that were considered inappropriate because of their having limited effectiveness among older people or because of the increased risk of problems resulting from use. This list is known as the Beers

Criteria. It has been updated several times, most recently in 2012. There are now a total of 53 medications included which are described as falling into one of three categories: those always to be avoided; those potentially inappropriate for individuals with particular medical problems; and those to be used with caution.[6]

Alcohol-Drug Interactions The unique physiological changes that accompany aging and affect drug distribution and metabolism contribute to the increased risk of drug-alcohol interactions. The risk of an adverse drug reaction in those 50 to 59 years old may be as much as a third greater than for those in their 40s. Above age 60 there appears to be a further two- to threefold increase. Diagnosis of adverse drug reactions may be hampered because they can resemble common illnesses in old age, such as gait disturbances and cognitive impairment.

Many commonly prescribed drugs can interact with alcohol. Such interactions can occur by several mechanisms. Some of the effects are due to changes in liver metabolism that occur with age. Remember that normal changes in liver function are compounded by the presence of alcohol. For this reason, medications ranging from common over-the-counter preparations (such as aspirin, acetaminophen, or antihistamines) to prescription drugs (such as oral anticoagulants, the oral medications used with diabetes, and pain medications) can present problems in the presence of alcohol. Other interactions occur for reasons besides diminished liver function. For example, anti-ulcer drugs, such as cimetidine, inhibit alcohol metabolism in the stomach, resulting in greater absorption of alcohol and higher blood alcohol levels per drink. Since elderly people already obtain higher blood alcohol levels per drink due to age-related changes in drug distribution, this effect is of special importance. Alcohol used at the same time as some nonsteroidal anti-inflammatory drugs may substantially increase the risk of gastrointestinal inflammation and bleeding. Then there is increased sedation, delirium, and psychomotor impairment, which can occur when alcohol is used with benzodiazepines and other drugs that affect the central nervous system. One of the most dire effects of benzodiazepines, whether used alone or in combination with alcohol, is a greatly increased risk of falls.

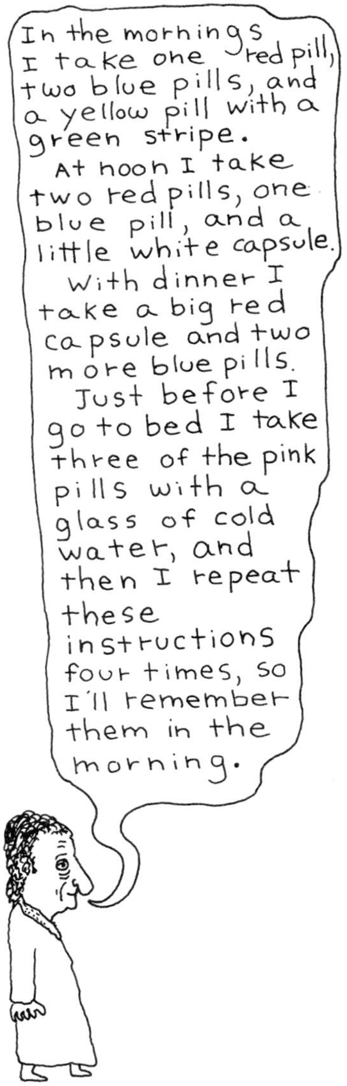

Illicit Drug Use

Illicit drug use has long been considered rare among the elderly. This is attributable to several factors. One is that rates of alcohol and drug use decline as people age. Second, those with substance use problems have increased mortality and simply die earlier. Third, the current elderly and those preceding them grew up in an era in which illicit drug use was relatively rare. However, all of this is about to change. The first of

[6] Beers Criteria available on the American Geriatrics Society <www.americangeriatrics.org/>

the baby boomers, those born after World War II who were the hippies and flower children in the 1960s, now receive a Social Security check. Though their rates of current illicit drug use are not at the levels they would have reported two or three decades ago, illicit drug use is not wholly ancient history. The following summary of illicit drug use demonstrates this.

Age Group	Illicit Drug Use: Lifetime (%) 2000	2005	2011	Past Year (%) 2000	2005	2011	Past Month (%) 2000	2005	2011
40–44	58.1%	60.9%	55.4%	10.4%	13.6%	11.7%	6.5%	8.3%	6.4%
45–49	49.9	61.6	57.3	6.9	11.9	11.2	4.8	6.7	6.7
50–54	35.5	54.6	61.9	4.5	9.1	10.9	2.4	6.0	6.7
55–59	28.6	43.4	56.0	4.2	4.9	9.5	2.3	2.4	6.0
60–64	14.4	28.2	41.9	1.8	3.4	5.9	1.5	2.1	2.7
65+	6.4	9.8	16.5	0.7	1.1	1.6	0.3	0.7	1.0

In examining these numbers, two things stand out. One is that the rate of lifetime illicit drug use is growing. In 2011, for those in their 40s and 50s, the rate of lifetime illicit drug use is virtually four times greater than that of the current over-65-year-old group. In addition, over the 11-year period, the use of illicit drugs in the 45-and-older group has mushroomed. Within the group ages 60–64, there was close to a tripling of lifetime illicit drug use between 2000 and 2011.

This development has implications for the treatment community. The National Institute on Drug Abuse has estimated that by the year 2020, the number of the elderly needing drug abuse treatment will be five times greater than at the millennium. The handwriting is on the wall. For example, in methadone maintenance programs, one-third of the patients are over age 40, and one-fourth are between the ages of 40 and 49. Looking down the line, it is estimated that by the year 2020, alcohol-drug treatment capacity will need to be quadrupled in response to the increasing rate of problems among the elderly.

Alcohol Use and Health Status

No body system is immune to the effects of alcohol (see Chapter 6). An examination of one state's Medicare claims found that those with a substance use disorder had higher rates for 14 of the 15 most common medical conditions, including cancer, diabetes, COPD/asthmas, arthritis, osteoporosis, and cardiovascular problems. But what about the effects of drinking, in the absence of a substance use disorder? Among the elderly a smaller amount of alcohol can create more medical problems. Hypertension, which is common, is more common among the elderly who drink. For those over 50, two to three drinks per day is associated with an increase in blood pressure. For those having three drinks per day, about one-half (52%) have hypertension, compared with only a third (35%) who are non-drinkers. That is a 50% higher rate. Drinking is also associated with injuries, particularly falls. Those who drink 1,000 grams (about 35 drinks) of alcohol per month have a risk of falling that is eight times that of abstainers. A large study of residents of a retirement community found that those who drank three drinks per day were three and a half times more likely to commit suicide than abstainers. Heavy drinking is also associated with decreases in bone density, which in turn contributes to the risk of injury from falls. Drinking is associated with dementia and confusion among the elderly. Also, while alcohol-related confusion improves with abstinence, this happens more slowly and is less complete than with younger people. In terms of death rates, overall mortality for women increases at levels above two drinks per day, and for men at four drinks per day. In light of all this, the current NIAAA recommendation is that both elderly men and women limit daily alcohol consumption to one drink per day.

Alcohol Problems

Not only do the patterns of substance use, including alcohol, vary among elderly people, but the associated problems and presentations do as well. In 2008, about 1% met the criteria for substance abuse and dependence, and alcohol accounts for 80% of this. There may be an additional 10% who have problems related to drinking, even if not severe enough to meet the criteria. In general, men have a much higher likelihood of being problem drinkers than do women. The prevalence decreases with increasing age, and there is considerable geographic variation in the prevalence of alcohol dependence. In medical settings, the prevalence is higher, and it appears to increase with increasing level of care. In primary care settings, 10% to 15% of elderly patients meet the diagnostic criteria for alcohol abuse or dependence, while up to 25% of hospitalized elderly people do. Recognizing alcohol problems among elderly people in medical settings can be very challenging. In the past, physicians recognized and intervened with only a small proportion of these patients. Nonetheless, studies of treatment populations consistently find that about 10% of patients entering alcohol treatment programs are age 65 and older.

Let me die in a tavern, let the wine be placed near my dying mouth, so that when the choirs of angels come, they may say "God be merciful to this drinker."
—The Archpoet
Confessions, twelfth century

Natural History of Alcohol Problems in Later Life

A unique study involving a 10-year follow-up of problem drinkers sheds light on the course of alcohol problems as people approach old age. Problem drinkers were enrolled in the study when they were between the ages of 50 and 65. They were followed up at year 4, and then at 10 years. At that time a number of comparisons were made among those whose problem had resolved, those for whom it continued, and a comparison group without a history of alcohol problems. Several interesting things stood out. Those whose drinking problem resolved were more likely to have friends who were less approving of drinking. Those whose problems resolved had fewer signs of dependence, had fewer drinking episodes, and were less likely to say they drank to forget or to get high. In addition, their problems tended to appear later in life.

The was an old woman from Ghent Who thought beer was all heaven sent But a man from Anheuser Was sadder Budweiser And said we shouldn't go where she went.

In comparing the resolved problem drinkers with "normal" controls at 10 years, in many areas they were quite similar. But of the resolved problem group, for the 75% who continued to drink, the level of drinking was higher than it was for those who had never had an alcohol problem. Those who had had a problem used more psychoactive substances and had more depressive episodes. In addition, they were more likely to report "motivated" drinking, for the purpose of getting high and forgetting problems. Only 11% of the entire group reported having had alcohol treatment. It was equally common among the resolved and the continuing problem groups, so here treatment did not promote higher rates of improvement. While clearly improved, on a variety of measures the resolved problem group was still not functioning on par with the general population. This is of interest because at 10-year follow-up, treated individuals are essentially indistinguishable from the general population.

What factors were associated with the resolution of problems? Several things stand out. At the four-year follow-up, those who later improved had more acute medical problems. Possibly this served as a wake-up call and prompted a reduction in drinking. Also, those whose alcohol problem diminished were more likely to give up other substance use, especially nicotine. Among those whose problem had resolved, abstinence was more common than non-problematic drinking. Also, there were changes in coping patterns. Those who were improved were more likely to call upon others, rather than evoking a stiff upper lip, "going-it-alone" style.

Types of Alcohol Dependence

Alcohol problems can make an appearance at any point in life. A majority of the elderly with alcohol dependence have a long-standing problem that began much earlier. For whatever reasons, one probably being good genes, they have been relatively resistant to the associated medical problems through middle age. When they reach their 60s and 70s, this is less true. They may then begin to experience deterioration of physical and cognitive functioning. From age 50 onward, an increasing proportion of those entering treatment are doing so for the first time. This is not simply a matter of delaying treatment. There are those for whom alcohol dependence only develops later in life. These two differing patterns of alcohol dependence are commonly termed "early-onset" or "late-onset." Researchers have adopted different age cutoff points to distinguish these varieties, cutoff points that fall anywhere between ages 40 and 60. Despite the differences in distinguishing the two varieties, there is general agreement that, of older people with alcohol dependence, approximately 50% began drinking heavily before age 40 and approximately two-thirds before age 60. Thus the ratio of early-onset to late-onset alcohol dependence is around 2:1. Some differences between those with early- and late-onset alcohol dependence are summarized below.

Characteristics	Early Onset	Late Onset
Separated or divorced	22%	55%
Widowed	33	9
Time spent in jail	78	55
Symptoms of organic brain disease	11	36
Serious health problem	44	91
Family history of alcohol dependence	86	40

Problems from alcohol use sometimes emerge in later life even absent changes in alcohol consumption. Because of the normal aging process, what had previously been a benign if heavy social drinking pattern for some individuals becomes problematic. Some seem to develop drinking problems as a maladaptive response to social stresses, such as retirement, loss of a spouse, grief, economic hardships, social isolation, and changes in living situations. At any age, alcohol can be used to cope with major life stresses. For some of the elderly, the stresses of aging may have been too great or may have come too fast. However, the assumption that changing life circumstances and social isolation are primarily responsible for alcohol problems in this population is largely speculative.

Wine and cheese are ageless companions, like aspirin and aches, or June and moon, or great people and noble virtues.
—M.F.K. FISHER
Wine and Cheese, 1981

Presentations

For those with early-onset alcohol abuse or dependence, the odds are greater that some of the usual social indicators of dependence are evident when reviewing the person's medical and social history. There is also a greater probability of prior treatment. However, commonly alcohol problems among older people have nonspecific presentations. The negative consequences of alcohol use that immediately come to mind as signaling a problem, such as job difficulties or family or legal problems, often don't apply. The elderly who are alcohol dependent are more likely prompted to seek care by medical complications from the drinking. Some of these problems are often mistaken for other age-related illnesses or medical conditions, such as malnutrition, falls, other accidents, depression, confusion, less attention to self-care, and unexpected reactions to prescribed medications. Medical issues that

With full-span lives having become the norm, people may need to learn how to be aged as they once had to learn how to be an adult.
—Ronald Blythe
The View in Winter

may suggest an alcohol problem include treatment that is not working for a normally treatable medical illness, including hypertension; insomnia or chronic fatigue as a result of poor sleep; diarrhea; urinary incontinence; weight loss or malnutrition; complaints of anxiety, which can be undiagnosed withdrawal; requests for tranquilizers, sedatives, or sleeping pills; or unexplained agitation, anxiety, or confusion after an operation.

Screening

The importance of taking an alcohol and other drug use history does not decline with the patient's increasing age. The commonly used MAST (Michigan Alcoholism Screening Test) has been adapted for older populations, the *MAST-G*. The questions are as follows:

1. After drinking have you ever noticed an increase in your heart rate or beating in your chest?
*2. When talking to others, do you ever underestimate how much you actually drink?
3. Does alcohol make you sleepy so that you often fall asleep in your chair?
*4. After a few drinks, have you sometimes not eaten or been able to skip a meal because you didn't feel hungry?
*5. Does having a few drinks help you decrease your shakiness or tremors?
*6. Does alcohol sometimes make it hard for you to remember parts of the day or night?
7. Do you have rules for yourself that you won't drink before a certain time of the day?
8. Have you lost interest in hobbies or activities you used to enjoy?
9. When you wake up in the morning, do you ever have trouble remembering part of the night before?
10. Does having a drink help you sleep?
11. Do you hide your alcohol bottles from family members?
12. After a social gathering, have you ever felt embarrassed because you drank too much?
13. Have you ever been concerned that drinking might be harmful to your health?
14. Do you end an evening with a night cap?
15. Did you find your drinking increased after someone close to you died?
16. In general, would you prefer to have a few drinks at home rather than go out to social events?
17. Are you drinking more now than in the past?
*18. Do you usually take a drink to relax or calm your nerves?
*19. Do you drink to take your mind off your problems?
*20. Have you ever increased your drinking after experiencing a loss in your life?

21. Do you sometimes drive when you have had too much to drink?
*22. Has a doctor or nurse ever said they were worried or concerned about your drinking?
*23. Have you ever made rules to manage your drinking?
*24. When you feel lonely, does having a drink help?

Note: The questions marked by an asterisk comprise the Short MAST-Geriatric version.

Scoring: Each positive response is scored as 1 point. For both the full and the short versions, five or more positive responses are seen as possibly indicative of an alcohol problem.

Medical and Clinical History

One goal of taking a history is to identify alcohol or other drug dependence. An additional goal assumes greater importance with increasing age—to identify medically hazardous alcohol use, including potential alcohol-drug interactions. Asking about quantity and frequency of use is therefore as important as asking about adverse consequences of drinking. Several techniques have been shown to help enhance the accuracy of self-reported quantity and frequency of drinking. Asking about each type of alcoholic beverage separately will increase the accuracy of reporting. The "time line follow-back" procedure uses a calendar and visual aids to enhance reporting of alcohol consumption. This procedure asks about drinking on each specific day of the week for as far back as the interviewer deems important. Heavy drinking determined by this method has been shown to be a good indicator of problem drinking.

Obstacles to Identification and Intervention

Many of the widely used screening instruments were based on the behavior of younger people, and with men, and do not transfer well to older people. Since many older people are retired, for instance, they do not have problems at work. Since many live alone, they are less likely to have alcohol-induced marital problems. Hence the MAST Geriatric version. However, the AUDIT is one test that has been found to be effective across all age groups.

A particular challenge is identifying problem drinking in people with cognitive impairment. Family, friends, and neighbors are important sources of information about those who are unable to give a good history themselves.

Other factors also contribute to poor recognition of alcohol problems. Classic signs of alcohol dependence may be obscure. Tolerance, manifested by requiring more alcohol to achieve the same effect, is a hallmark of alcohol dependence. Older people, who obtain higher blood alcohol levels per drink, may honestly report requiring less alcohol intake to get the same effect as before. Withdrawal, though its signs and symptoms are little different in older people, may not be recognized until late in the course. Many other possible causes of tachycardia, hypertension, delirium, and so on, that signal withdrawal will be thought of first in elderly people. Social decline is often marked by non-specific features, such as dropping out of the bridge club, which differs from the presentation in younger people.

As happens in other segments of the population, elderly people are likely to be protected by family, friends, and caregivers. These people may fail to see the problem, ignore what they suspect, or justify not intervening because no one wants to take away someone's "last pleasure." Thinking "What do they have to live for, anyway? They have been drinking all these years, they'll never stop now, and I don't want to be the one who asks them to give up the bottle" is also common. There are times that the person is dependent on some outside assistance to continue drinking. For example, a neighbor or housekeeper may ensure access to alcohol by purchasing it for the homebound person. In situations where family members or friends support problem drinking or are reluctant to intervene, it is important to point out that problem drinking is not pleasurable drinking. Such complications of heavy drinking as cognitive impairment, gait disturbances, and other physical dependencies are greatly feared by most older people. These impairments often lead to nursing home placement, which most people wish to avoid at almost any cost.

Detoxification and Treatment

Detoxification protocols need to be adjusted for elderly people. Generally, because of autonomic and cardiovascular instability, detoxification is better managed in a hospital than as an outpatient. Although the general strategy is similar for managing withdrawal in younger patients, there are several caveats. Withdrawal is likely to take longer, especially for those with cognitive impairment. The use of benzodiazepines, as a preventive measure, in the absence of withdrawal symptoms is unwise; this can provoke delirium. It is generally recommended that benzodiazepine use be delayed and that the drugs be prescribed *only* in response to specific signs and symptoms of withdrawal. Drugs with a short half-life are preferable to longer-acting agents. Usual dosage can be reduced by one-half to two-thirds. In a person also dependent on benzodiazepines, withdrawal may take considerably longer than alcohol withdrawal alone.

The use of Antabuse (disulfiram) has been suggested by some as potentially useful. Careful consideration needs to be given to the risks and potential benefits. Among the elderly, the risks may be considerable. Physically, they are more frail. Their metabolic ability to handle disulfiram is a factor. They may be less able to comply with the restrictions because of cognitive impairments. Their greater use of over-the-counter preparations increases the probability of inadvertent drug reactions. A disulfiram reaction that might be uncomfortable for someone younger may represent a medical crisis and have a lethal outcome for someone elderly. Of note, the newer anti-craving agents, naltrexone and acamprosate, not only are well tolerated but also reduce the risk of relapse.

Elderly people need the same type of rehabilitation services as younger persons—education, counseling, and involvement in self-help groups. Treatment programs typically incorporate these clients in their general programs. The prognosis is as good as it is for younger persons. Older persons are as likely as younger persons to affiliate with AA and to participate in aftercare. Also of note, they are as likely as younger persons to respond to brief interventions. In addition to a treatment program's standard regimen, the elderly require a thorough medical evaluation and potentially more extensive social service involvement at discharge to facilitate aftercare.

The earliest research on treatment outcomes from the early 1980s indicated that older persons with alcohol dependence had outcomes comparable to those of younger patients. This was interpreted as refuting the need for specially focused programs for older persons. For most clinicians, the issue of specialized versus standard programs is likely to be nothing more than an academic interest, because so few programs have been developed for this population. However, more recent studies have demonstrated that programs tailored to older people enhance outcomes by reducing treatment dropout, by increasing rates of aftercare, and by dealing with relapses if they occur so that the person is not lost to treatment.

Many of the benefits of programs designed for elderly people can be achieved within the standard programs, with some inventiveness. Referring agencies and health care providers need to be sensitive to the accommodations that can easily be made to better serve them. Matching patients with clinicians who are knowledgeable about and comfortable in treating older people within standard programs and who are able to work at a slower, gentler pace can be beneficial. Furthermore, abrasive confrontation, which is used in some programs, is not likely to be effective. Programs that emphasize that style of group work may be poor choices for a referral.

Groups are important to elderly clients in many ways. They reduce the sense of isolation, can enhance communication skills, provide a forum for problem solving, and address denial. Small group sessions or individual therapy within a general treatment program can help develop the special skills the older person may need for coping with losses, enjoying leisure time, and developing new relationships after the loss of old ones. A particular element found to be important is referred to as life review. Groups need to allow for the the elderly person's reminiscence and processing of the past. This is important for all elder persons to see their lives as a whole. For those in treatment for alcohol problems, incorporating this process in a way that does not diminish self-esteem or devalue the person's life is important. This is important not only in formal alcohol treatment but also in contacts with health care and social service professionals.

Treatment of the cognitively impaired individual is especially difficult. Often a prolonged period of enforced abstinence from alcohol will be needed in order to determine whether the person will recover sufficient cognitive function to pursue and participate in treatment. If not, a permanently supervised living situation, such as a nursing home or group home where alcohol is not available, will probably be needed.

Prevention

Your middle-aged patient of today is another clinician's elderly patient several years hence. Today's adolescent is establishing a framework for making independent decisions about self-care and health care practices. These will have a bearing on lifelong health habits. What kind of questions should any individual consider before he or she decides to take medication? What specific questions are important for the particular patient? Patients rarely consult their doctors before making such decisions. In fact, no doctor would want to be contacted on that basis. A resource available to everyone is the pharmacist. Though almost always available, the pharmacist is an underutilized resource. One of his or her jobs is patient education. Patients need instruction about the kind of questions to ask: Are there any contraindications when using this product? Is there a need for concern about interactions with other prescription medication being taken? Are there any side effects?

Working with the Elderly

Remember that they are survivors. Those who are old now have lived through hard times. For the oldest, getting through World War II and a host of social changes required strength and resiliency. Those who survived have a wealth of experience to bring to coping with the stresses of aging. Make it clear that you respect their strengths and experience and that you have high expectations for their ability to overcome their problems.

Because many elderly persons are reluctant to seek or receive help, a family member is often the person to make the initial contact. The family's views of the situation, their ideas and fears, need to be discussed. Whatever the problem, the chances are good that something can be done to improve the picture and improve functional status. It often comes as a surprise to families that there is hope for recovery. Professionals can help the family, too, as they cope with a difficult situation, such as by arranging for Meals-on-Wheels or making simple suggestions about how to make routines easier.

Tobacco, coffee, alcohol, hashish, prussic acid, strychnine, are weak dilutions; the surest poison is time.
—Ralph Waldo Emerson
Old Age, 1870

In conversation, do not stick with neutral topics, such as the weather, all of the time. Discuss topics of common interest to you both, such as gardening or baseball, as well as some controversial topic, something appealing. You can enhance self-esteem by letting the person know that not only do you want their opinions but you also want them to listen to yours.

Multiple resources may be needed to assist these clients. Many older adults with alcohol problems need to become re-involved in the world. Meaningful contacts can come from a variety of people, not just from professional helpers. The janitor in the client's apartment building, a neighbor, or a crossing guard at the street corner may all be potential allies. If the person was once active in a church group, a civic organization, or another community group but has lost contact, recommend that he or she get in touch with the organization. There is often a member who will visit or be able to assist in other ways. Many communities have senior citizen centers that offer social programs, Meals-on-Wheels, and counseling on Social Security and Medicare: they may also provide transportation.

I think I don't regret a single "excess" of my responsive youth—only in my chilled age, certain occasions and possibilities I didn't embrace.
—HENRY JAMES
Letter to Hugh Walpole, 1913

When cognitive impairment is a factor, providing cues to orient the person may be helpful. Mention dates, day of the week, and current events. Do not, however, expect a cognitively impaired person to retain such information or to learn new skills. Since remote memory is usually preserved longer than recent memory, discussing past events and interests may be socially rewarding.

If you give specific information to the client, write it down legibly. This makes it much easier for the client to comply. If family members are present, give them the directions too. In thinking about compliance and what can be done to assist the elderly in participating in treatment, take some time to think about how your agency functions. What does it involve for the person coming to see you? Are there long waits at several offices on several floors? Does it require navigating difficult stairs, elevators, and hallways in the process? Are there times of the day that make use of public transportation easier? Consider such factors, and make adjustments to make it much easier for these clients. In specific terms, make every effort to do things in as uncomplicated, convenient, non-embarrassing, and economical a fashion as possible.

Separate sympathy from empathy. Sympathy is feeling sorry in company with someone. The elderly don't want that; it makes them feel like children. Empathy means you understand or want to understand. This is what they would like.

Be aware that you may be thought of and responded to as any number of important people in your client's long life. Also, you may alternately represent a grandchild, a child, a parent, a peer, and an authority figure to them at various points in treatment, even within the same interview and at the same time.

Have integrity with the elderly. Do not try to mislead or lie to them. They are too experienced with all the con games in life. If they ask you questions, give them straight answers. This, however, does not mean being brutal in the name of honesty. For example, in speaking with a client, you might say, "Many other people I talk with have concerns about death; do you?" If the client responds, "No, I haven't thought much about it," you don't blurt out, "Well, you'd better think about it, since you have only six months to live." That is not integrity.

It is important, too, to set specific goals. Make sure that the initial ones are easily attainable. This means they can have some surefire positive experiences. With those under their belts, they are more likely to take some risks and attempt other things.

Consider making home visits. These can be the key to working with this group. It may be the only thing that will break down their resistance and help them enter treatment. Very few will seek help on their own initiative. So, if someone is not willing to come to your office, give him or her a call. Ask if you can make an appointment to see him or her at home. If the response you get is "I don't want you to come," don't quit. Your next line is "Well, if I'm ever in the area, I'd like to stop by." After your visit, you may well find the resistance has disappeared. The home visit can be vital in making an adequate assessment. Seeing the person in his or her own home, where security is at its peak, provides a much better picture of how the person is getting along, as well as the pluses and minuses of the environment. It also allows the client to be spontaneous in emotions and behavior. If you regularly make home visits, beware of making the person "stay in trouble" to see you. Don't just visit in a crisis. Instead, stop in to hear about successes. Your visits may be a high point for the person, who may not like to think of losing this contact. Make a visit the day after the client's first day on a new volunteer job, for example.

Beware of those who arrange trivial activities for older people to occupy their time. Craft classes, for instance, ought to teach usable skills, not just keep people busy. Many also have something they can teach others. For example, the carpenter who is no longer steady enough to use tools will be able to provide consultation to people who want to do some work on their homes. The elderly have a richness of life experiences and much to contribute.

It is important that the substance abuse clinician work closely with the client's physician and health care providers. There are few situations in which it is more important that everyone is singing from the same page.

WOMEN

Alcohol dependence, heavy drinking, problem drinking, and other drug use were long assumed to be problems of men. Accordingly, for a long time research on substance abuse problems among women was very limited. With respect to alcohol, a literature review indicates that only 28 English-language studies of women with alcohol dependence were published between 1928 and 1970. Another assumption has been that, when present, alcohol dependence is alcohol dependence and drug dependence is drug dependence, regardless of gender.

Despite the growing attention to women's problems, the available data are not easily synthesized. One problem results from the fact that researchers frequently study women who enter treatment. This limits what can be said about the extent, nature, and magnitude of problems among women in general. Further complicating the situation is the fact that those being studied seemingly represent all of the possible combinations of alcohol and other substance use. Subjects of research studies range from alcohol-dependent women to women with drug dependence to women with alcohol dependence who use/abuse/are dependent on other substances to female substance users who drink/drink heavily/are alcohol dependent. The extent to which these populations are distinctive or overlapping is unknown, so generalizations from any of these individual studies is difficult. In addition, some research to date has used relatively small samples and has focused on narrow topics, such as the use of day care by urban women in substance abuse treatment. While such details are very important, a multitude of detail doesn't necessarily make seeing the big picture easier. Although facts proliferate and there is more information, there is not always greater understanding.

Gender Differences

Women represent a growing percentage of drinkers, including those with alcohol problems and those with alcohol dependence.[7] For younger women in the general population, the proportion of drinkers is beginning to equal that of men. The differences between male and female drinking rates are due in part to the large number of abstainers among older women. These older women, born on the heels of Prohibition, are of an era in which women's drinking was less socially acceptable and far less prevalent. The behavior of their granddaughters is quite different.

Historically men's use exceeds women's for all types of drugs. The rates for past-year use follow. The smallest differences are for legal substances, including prescription drugs, even though used for non-medical purposes. The only drug for which women's and men's use is equivalent is stimulants.

Substance	Men	Women	Women's Use as % of Men's
Alcohol	74.9%	67.4%	90%
Tobacco	41.9	25.9	62
Cigarettes	31.3	24.2	77
Any illicit drugs	19.0	12.7	67
Marijuana	15.4	8.8	57
Cocaine	2.8	1.0	36
Crack	0.6	0.2	33
Inhalants	0.7	0.2	29
Prescription drugs	7.0	5.9	84
Pain relievers	5.5	4.1	75
Hallucinogens	2.2	1.0	45

* Includes retired, homemakers, students.

[7] In this section, unless noted otherwise, the 2012 *National Survey on Health and Drug Use*, referred to as the *National Survey*, is the source of statistics on alcohol and other drug use.

International Differences

Gender differences in substance use exist worldwide. Recall that in Chapter 2 (page 41) information was provided on per capita alcohol consumption in different countries. As was shown, the amount of alcohol consumed annually ranged from 0 liters per person in Algeria, to 8.5 liters in the United States, to 14.45 liters in Ireland, and a high of almost 20 liters in Uganda. While demonstrating the considerable variation in drinking practices, the table also depicted a constant, which may not have been immediately evident. Whatever the level of drinking within a country, the proportion of women who drink is smaller than that of men. Not only is male drinking more prevalent, it is also heavier than women's and is associated with more negative consequences. Gender differences are less marked in the more developed countries. However, that does not mean differences between genders evaporate. There are, for example, to name just a few, differences based on gender in terms of medical consequences that result from alcohol and other drug use, the nature of social problems that arise, the barriers to entering treatment, and the level of stigma associated with having a substance use problem.

Differences Among Women

A number of differences among women in alcohol use are based on demographic characteristics such as age and racial/ethnic membership.

Age

Past-year substance use also varies by age group, as is evident from the 2012 *National Survey*. Typically, those 18–25 have the highest levels of drug use. The one exception is inhalants, which are most commonly used by those under age 17.

Substance	All Women	12–17 Yrs.	18–25 Yrs.	>25 Yrs.
Alcohol	62.9%	28.6%	75.9%	64.8%
Tobacco	25.1	14.4	41.1	23.7
Nicotine	27.9	15.1	40.9	24.0
Any illicit drug	12.2	18.8	30.4	8.5
Marijuana	8.9	13.3	25.9	5.6
Cocaine	1.0	1.0	3.4	0.6
Crack	0.1	0.1	0.3	0.1
Hallucinogens	1.1	2.3	5.3	0.3
Inhalants	0.5	3.5	1.2	0.1
Prescription pain relievers*	3.8	6.5	8.6	2.8

*Non-medical use.

Racial and Ethnic Considerations

While data remain limited, the 2011 *National Survey* indicates racial and ethnic differences in women's drinking patterns. White women are more likely than either Hispanic or African American women to be drinkers and to be smokers. In terms of binge drinking, the highest rate is found among Native American and Alaska Native women (41%), followed by white women (17.5%). The lowest rate is among African American women (14.3%). In terms of heavy drinking (five or more episodes of binge drinking in the prior month) the highest rates again are found among Native American and Native Alaskan women (4.4%), again followed by white women (4.1%). In respect to tobacco, African American women have the highest rate of use (41.8%) and the lowest rate of use is among Asian Americans (8.3%). In terms of illicit drugs, where there seem to be racial or ethnic differences, these disappear when age, education, and household income are taken into account.

Sexual Orientation

With the limited attention to substance use problems of women generally, it is not surprising that there has been very little discussion directed to lesbian and bisexual women. It needs to be pointed out that the language is changing. "Sexual minorities" is replacing the drawn-out phrase "homosexuals, gays, lesbians, and bisexuals." Beyond sexism, substance use among lesbians and bisexual women has long gone unaddressed because of homophobia and the attendant societal stigma. Research is limited. Many of the published studies involve small samples, such as 45 individuals or 120 individuals. This is not the basis for making conclusions about any segment of the population as a whole.

We cannot keep turning our backs on gay and lesbian Americans. I have fought too hard and too long against discrimination based on race and color not to stand up against discrimination based on sexual orientation.
—John E Lewis

It has long been held that lesbians and bisexual women are at greater risk for substance use problems than are heterosexual women. Early estimates were that from 25% to 35% of lesbians had a serious substance use problem. This elevated level of substance use disorders was attributed in part to the "fact" that much of lesbian social life supposedly revolves around bars. Although reports continue to note an elevated risk of alcohol and substance use problems among lesbians and bisexual women, the rates don't begin to approach those cited earlier. As one writer noted, either the prior estimates were inflated, or heavy drinking and alcohol problems have declined. A recent research report from a seven-year follow-up of over 13,000 participants in the *Growing Up Today Study* suggests that the situation is more complicated. Compared to heterosexual participants, all of the sexual minorities reported an earlier age of initiating alcohol use, a factor recognized as associated with later alcohol problems. However, the greatest risk of alcohol use during adolescence was consistently found among heterosexual males and females as well as bisexual women, but not lesbian women.

The subgroup of lesbians that may be particularly vulnerable to substance use problems is adolescents. A common theme in any study or report of lesbian, gay male, and bisexual youth is the chronic stress created by the verbal and physical abuse they receive from peers and adults. This can lead to a number of problematic outcomes, ranging from difficulties at school, to running away or being ejected from home, to encounters with the law, to prostitution, to substance abuse and suicide attempts. Family rejection of adolescents as a result of sexual orientation is particularly devastating. Young adults, between the ages of 21 and 25, who reported high levels of rejection as teens had an eight times greater rate of suicide attempts, a six times greater rate of depression, and a three and a half times greater rate of illicit drug use.

Though the rates of problems may not be elevated to the degree that had been presumed, there remain unique treatment issues. Lesbian and bisexual women entering treatment confront special issues, such as when and how to reveal their sexual orientation and deal with the associated prejudices. There is a small but rich literature with respect to treatment, the issues to be confronted, the perceptions of treatment, and the treatment process, both in formal treatment and in the use of self-help groups.

The toll of AIDS in the gay community is well known. Lesbian women are also at elevated risk for HIV/AIDS if sexually active with a partner who is an intravenous drug user. Data suggest that a very high percentage of all HIV/AIDS cases (possibly upward of 90%) reported among women are those whose only partner had been a woman, a woman involved in intravenous drug use.

Natural History of Alcohol and Other Drug Problems

In what other ways do the alcohol and other drug problems of women differ from those of men? The major differences that have been described are noted in the following list.

- *Specific triggers.* More alcohol-dependent women than men can point to a specific trigger for the onset of heavy drinking. This might be a divorce, an illness, the death of a spouse, children leaving home, or some other stressful event. If a woman seeks help at such a point, both a careful alcohol use history and education about the potential risks of alcohol use are warranted. The danger of relying on alcohol or other drugs is that the crisis can take on a long-term life of its own. The challenge to those dealing with a woman in the face of life changes and crises is in providing empathy rather than sympathy. Either overtly or covertly, the danger is often to imply that, if that had happened to us, we would probably have responded in the same fashion. The current dangerous misuse of alcohol and other drugs can become lost in the forest of other problems. A history of abortion is also associated with an increased risk of substance use problems.

- *A telescoped course.* Women's alcohol dependence is often described as "telescoped." This means the disease appears later and progresses more rapidly. The period of time between the onset of heavy drinking and entry into treatment is shorter among women too. The same is apparently true of other drug use, with a shorter interval from first use to dependence.
- *Medical complications.* Women are more susceptible to medical complications than are alcohol-dependent men. For men, the presence of medical complications is tied to long-term, regular, heavy use. The several six-packs a day over time will take their toll. For women, the situation can be different. Medical complications among women appear to be more related to the frequency of heavy drinking occasions than to the amount typically consumed. Thus, very heavy drinking once or twice a week may wreak more havoc than if the same amount of alcohol were spread out over time. Women have particular susceptibility to liver disease. This may well be tied to the differences in the way men and women metabolize alcohol (see Chapter 3). Women with alcohol dependence have consumed significantly less alcohol during their drinking career than have men, perhaps 45% less, yet they still experience difficulties of a similar magnitude. Some physical measures confirm this greater vulnerability to alcohol. Differences have been found in measurements of changes in the brain associated with heavy drinking; women have a greater reduction in gray and white matter.
- *Entry into treatment.* Women with alcohol dependence tend to enter treatment earlier than men. The time between the onset of heavy drinking and a referral for treatment is likely to be shorter. This is believed to be due to higher rates of medical complications. Women, too, tend to exhaust the social supports and resources needed to continue alcohol use. Also, women have a greater number of alcohol-induced problems than do men, even when the length of drinking, the presence of psychiatric problems, and work status are taken into account. Men, however, outnumber women entering treatment by almost four to one. In terms of what prompts treatment and the perceptions of problems when entering care, women have been found to differ from men in several ways. Generally women report more depression, anxiety, powerlessness, hopelessness, and guilt than men report. This is not the result of their having more psychiatric illness but is part of the female pattern of alcohol dependence. While reporting less support for entry into treatment, women, more than men, credit pressure from others as a major factor in their seeking treatment, whether from children, other relatives, coworkers, or their physicians.

- *Violence and abuse.* Women entering treatment often have experienced recent episodes of violence. In some populations, such as women entering drug abuse treatment, the percentages reach 80%. These include episodes of child sexual and physical abuse, date rape, sexual assault, partner domestic violence, and physical assault.
- *Family issues.* If the woman is unmarried or a divorced single parent, there are not only additional emotional demands but also economic burdens. In the aftermath of divorce, almost three-quarters of women and their children are economically less well off, if not downright poverty stricken. Entry into treatment may stretch an already difficult financial situation. A concern unique to women is fear of losing custody of children. This is especially an issue for women who are involved with illicit drug use. In a marriage in which one spouse is alcohol-dependent, when it is the woman, there is a significantly greater likelihood of divorce. If the wife has alcohol dependence, the chance of divorce is nine times greater than for alcohol-dependent males. An important consequence is that the family and emotional support systems that are an asset in recovery are less likely to be present. Interestingly, whatever the woman's marital situation, it has been found that women entering treatment do not receive the solid support for that decision that men generally receive from family and friends. Women with alcohol or other drug problems are more likely than men to have a drug-dependent partner.

- *Alcohol and other drug use.* Women have higher rates of using other drugs when drinking than do men. In contrast to men, women are at greater risk for non-medical use of prescription drugs, particularly benzodiazepines and narcotic analgesics. They are prescribed mood-altering drugs much more frequently. A sample of alcohol-dependent women found that 70% had a history of having been prescribed psychoactive drugs, a rate 1.5 times greater than for alcohol-dependent men. Of the women prescribed psychoactive drugs, one-half could recall at least one occasion of having used alcohol in combination with the medication; also, one-half had been prescribed more than one category of drug. This suggests the need for obtaining a very careful drug use history, with a wary eye for multiple drug use and abuse. It also increases the possibility of overdose.
- *Workplace and vocational spheres.* In the workplace and vocational arenas, differences between men and women are evident. With respect to employment and vocational status, women with substance use problems—just like women in the general population—have fewer vocational skills and training and are less likely to be employed, to hold high-status jobs, to be self-supporting, and, if drugs are involved, to be financing their own drug use. In these circumstances, women may support their drug addiction with petty larceny, shoplifting, and

prostitution. Women with alcohol or other drug problems are more likely to be dependent on a family member or on public welfare for survival than are men.

- *Perceptions.* Women with dependence are reported to have lower expectations for their lives than men and to express more concern with survival and minimizing discomfort. More commonly, women do not see either alcohol or other drug use as their primary problem. Thus, they are inclined to express concern about the ability of a substance abuse program to assist them. This also means that it is particularly important for treatment personnel to help them make the connection between their life problems and alcohol or other drug use.
- *Personality.* Little is known about the personality factors that may predate the emergence of alcohol dependence in women. A follow-up in later life of a sample of women college students found that the factors predictive of alcohol dependence in later life were considerably different from those among men. The best predictor for alcohol dependence in women might be termed "purposeful drinking"—that is, drinking to relieve shyness, to get high, to be happy, and to get along better. Research also indicates that women who are heavy social drinkers have the expectation that drinking will relieve worries, nervousness, and tension.
- *HIV/AIDS.* A problem of growing concern is the rise of HIV infection and AIDS among women, primarily related to their own intravenous drug use or to their having a sexual partner with AIDS. Young women with alcohol and multiple substance use problems are a population at particular risk. While a 3:1 ratio of male-to-female intravenous drug users has frequently been cited, among younger women this disparity is disappearing. Women appear to have a faster transition from drug use initiation to dependence; tend to be introduced to drug use by partners; have drug-using partners, which promotes access to drugs; are more likely to engage in needle sharing; and, with the potential for prostitution, are likely to have greater ease in maintaining a steady supply of drugs. All of these factors contribute to an increased risk of HIV/AIDS infection. Beyond the risk to these women, the other issue of concern is perinatal transmission in pregnancy. A public health priority is intervention to reduce the spread of HIV/AIDS in this population.

From birth to age eighteen, a girl needs good parents. From eighteen to thirty-five she needs good looks. From thirty-five to fifty-five on, she needs good cash.
—SOPHIE TUCKER, 1953 (AT AGE 69)

- *Family relationships.* Gender-based differences are evident in women's relationships to family and spouse or partner. Women who come from families where drugs were commonly used as a primary coping strategy are themselves more likely to become addicted. Women with substance use problems have often experienced greater familial disruption than have men with such problems. In contrast to men, both alcohol- and opiate-involved women come from drug-abusing and disorganized families. Female heroin addicts are more likely than are male heroin addicts to have first been introduced to heroin by family members or others close to them. The development of dependence is linked to the family's approval of use or the absence of clear disapproval of use, in combination with easy access to the drug.

- *Emergency room care.* With respect to the drinking population, women are overly represented in emergency room visits, as indicated by data drawn from the Drug Abuse Warning Network (DAWN). It is speculated that this is due to women's greater vulnerability to overdoses at lower levels of consumption and their greater likelihood to use alcohol in combination with other drugs. With many overdoses reported as accidental, one important intervention is education about the effects of alcohol and other drugs, alone and in combination. Among women admitted to a large regional trauma center, one-third were identified as having an alcohol problem based on laboratory test results and the MAST screening instrument.
- *Suicide.* Alcohol problems in women greatly increase the risk for suicide. One study determined that alcohol-dependent women have a history of suicide attempts five times greater than that of non-alcoholic women, with 40% of the alcohol-dependent women in the study reporting a suicide attempt. Furthermore, close to 50% who make one attempt will make a future suicide attempt. Among women, youth coupled with alcohol or other drug use and abuse are a high-risk combination.

Assessment and Treatment

The TWEAK is a screening instrument developed specifically for women (see Chapter 9). While it may be obvious, in assessing drinking patterns and quantity, the result is dependent on the size of the glass. A study of women who were attending a public prenatal clinic provides a dramatic reminder of this. When women were shown glasses of different sizes and asked to select the one(s) that applied to them, the quantity of alcohol they typically consumed skyrocketed in comparison to the amount they reported. For beer, the amount reportedly consumed had to be increased by a third, and for spirits, the actual amount consumed was 300 times higher. For the high-risk women in this group, the "4 drinks" became 10 drinks.

Several treatment approaches have been developed specifically for women. *Residential treatment* programs created for women and their children, described further below, are becoming more common in many communities. Evaluation studies suggest that such settings increase retention in treatment. Also of significance is their impact on the overall family unit. There is improvement, not only in the women but also in the children. At 6- and 12-month follow-ups, children had fewer emotional and behavioral problems.

Brief intervention, particularly with women who are pregnant or of childbearing age, is a promising approach. Given the social costs as well as the consequences for the woman and her child, any effective intervention is important. Recently brief interventions were examined in the context of postpartum visits. A program called Healthy Moms was conducted in 34 obstetrical community practices. For women identified as high-risk drinkers, there was a four-session intervention. Six months later at a follow-up visit, there was a 19% decline in the number of drinking occasions and the average number of drinks per occasion, along with a 36% decrease in the number of heavy drinking days.

Within the substance abuse field, an emphasis is placed on the benefits of *integrated treatment,* which typically refers to the treatment approach for those with both a substance use disorder and a co-occurring psychiatric disorder. (See Chapter 12.) As the term suggests, this entails treating both conditions simultaneously. However, in discussion of treatment for women, "integrated treatment" may mean something else. It may refer to women who have been victims of domestic violence or it may refer to the mother whose children have become involved in the child welfare system due to negligence, neglect, or child abuse. In both of these instances, the issues are central to the woman's life and thus need to be clearly addressed and interwoven into the substance use treatment.

With the interest in substance use among pregnant women, there has been some exploration of what is involved in getting people off of the most common drugs used in combination: alcohol, nicotine, and caffeine. Typically these cluster together. Find a smoker and the odds are you also have a drinker. Those who use multiple substances are less likely to quit one than are those who use only one substance. In one case study, being a non-smoker predicted quitting alcohol. And being neither a smoker nor a drinker predicted quitting caffeine. However, if those who were into all three did manage to quit one, then they were more likely, rather than less likely, to proceed to cease other legal substance use. So for them it was seemingly an all or none approach. One of the challenges is to figure out the best treatment strategies in approaching cessation of multiple legal drugs. At this point, we don't know—is it better to do this all at a time or in sequence?

"You can't change her life, but you can change how she feels about it."

The caption next to a picture of a sad looking woman, standing behind an ironing board, as she looks off into the distance.

Advertisement directed to physicians for Librium, the first benzodiazepine (1967)

"You've come a long way baby."

The Phillip Morris ad campaign directed to women for its new cigarette Virginia Slims (1968)

"OMG give me some MommyJuice right NOW!"

"Being a mom is a constant juggling act. Whether it's playdates and homework, diapers and burp cloths, or finding that perfect balance between work and home, Moms everywhere deserve a break. So tuck your kids into bed, sit down and have a glass of MommyJuice–because you deserve it."

An ad for a new trendy wine. The owner of the wine company credits her children with providing the name. When very young, upon seing a wine glass, they would exclaim, "That's mommy's juice!"

The web marketing site (2013)

Treatment Themes

For women with dependent children, there can be a host of logistical problems. For a woman with young children, arranging treatment may be more difficult. This will likely be especially so for women who are single parents. Models of treatment to address these problems are being tried in many areas throughout the country. But in too many places the usual facilities are still the only ones available. You will need to stretch your creativity to the limit to deal with this problem. When inpatient treatment is warranted, there may be no way to allow a client the optimum advantage of an extended residential stay. There are no easy formulas, and the therapist is left to work out the best solution possible in each case.

Mothering is an aspect of self-esteem unique to women. Aside from the many logistical concerns, during the course of treatment, a woman will be dealing with broader questions related to her role as a mother. Some of the questions she may well be asking herself include the following: "Am I a good mother?" "Can I be a good mother?" "Have I hurt my children?" "Can I ever cope with my children if I don't drink or use drugs?" These may not be explicit in the therapy sessions, but they do cross her mind. The process of treatment, along with sober and straight time, will begin to provide answers. Family meetings may also be one way she gains answers to these questions and recognizes the necessary changes she can make. In those cases where child abuse is present, notification of child welfare is required. A referral to a children's agency, a family-service agency, or a mental health clinic may be important. One of the things any mother will need to learn if she is to regain her self-esteem as a mother is a sense of what the "normal" difficulties are in raising children.

Concerns about sexuality may surface. If she has had a divorce or an affair, a woman may well be wondering about her worth and attractiveness as a woman. Even if the marriage is intact, there may be sexual problems. On the one hand, the sexual relationship may have almost disappeared as the drinking progressed. On the other, it may have been years since she has had sexual intercourse without the benefit of a glass of wine or a couple of beers. Here, too, length of sobriety may well be the major therapeutic element. But couples therapy as well as sexual counseling may be needed if marital problems are not resolved. What about single women and women caught in an unsatisfactory marriage? Some find themselves "suddenly" involved in an affair or an extramarital relationship. This may have several roots. Possibly with sobriety comes a sense of being alive again, plus a new love may seem to be part of a new life. However, a mad love affair can lead to disaster, if followed with abandon. This can be equally true for men.

A word of caution to male therapists working with women is warranted. If you are the first person in many years to accept her and if you have been making attempts to raise her self-esteem, she may mistake her gratitude for a personal emotional attachment to you. Your recognition of this "error" is imperative. If you provide contacts for her with other women in recovery, she may be better able to recognize this pitfall as well.

Self-Help Participation

A referral to AA or NA is as important for women as for men. A few trips to local meetings should assure a woman that it is no longer the male stronghold it once was. In many communities, one will also find women-only groups. A common criticism of Alcoholics Anonymous and the related twelve-step programs is that they foster continuing female dependence. This, however, is not a universally accepted view. As one feminist author commented, "Those I see going into Twelve-step programs are basically trying to stay alive. They are not the people that one would see at political meetings. Without recovery they would probably be dead, and dead women don't have any politics."

Treatment Access

Access to treatment is a dimension on which men and women differ. For women there are the issues of child care and cost of treatment, because women have historically had lower wages and benefits and may be the family's sole source of financial support. Women may need more ancillary supports and services because of their status as single mothers or as victims of domestic violence or the absence of supportive people in their environment.

In light of the impediments to women's entering and remaining in treatment, programs designed specifically for women have begun to emerge. The Center for Substance Abuse Treatment (CSAT) funded demonstration projects in the mid-1990s for women and their children. These programs were unique in several respects. They were residential programs designed to involve stays of 6 or 12 months, they included not only women but also young children, and they provided a comprehensive range of services for clients and their children. In addition to the usual substance abuse treatment, the programs offered prenatal care, pediatric and medical services, mental health treatment, vocational training, parenting classes, legal services, nursery and preschool for children, transportation, and assistance with securing transitional housing.

The earliest reports of the outcomes of these programs have been very positive. One such report describes the outcomes for women with serious drug problems. Alcohol was the common ingredient, but crack cocaine, powder cocaine, heroin, methamphetamines, over-the-counter drugs, and marijuana also were used. These were women with multiple problems: unemployed (92%), few skills, little education (over half without a high school education); pregnant at admission (25%); separated/divorced/never married (82%); three or more children (54%); medical problems (60%); criminal justice system involvement at admission (50%); and children removed from the home by child protection services (47%). The mean age was 30 years old, and the mean years of substance use was over 15. At one-year follow-up, 70% of those who had stayed

six or more months had maintained complete abstinence. In addition, health status was significantly improved, and 66% were employed or in vocational training programs. Arrest rates or involvement in illegal activities was about 2%. Over 80% lived with at least one child. Only 5% lived with a drug-involved spouse or partner, compared to 44% prior to treatment.

Residential care for women and their children, ideally, is family-centered care for both. As part of the evaluation of women's residential programs there has been some exploration as well of their impacts on the children. Many of these children are at risk for future problems. There may be biological risks (such as prenatal exposure to alcohol or other drugs). In addition, they confront an array of environmental risks, including low income, low maternal education, maternal mental illness, instability in caregivers, residential instability, child abuse and neglect, little father involvement, and experiences in foster care. The presence of children in the residential setting shouldn't be seen merely as a nice touch for the mothers' benefit, but the opportunity to provide services to these children as well. In one description of such a family-based setting, it was noted that serving these children on site is more effective than trying to use community-based services. Beyond providing for better integration of services, just imagine the logistics. Ask any soccer mom what would be entailed in arranging for doctor's appointments, speech therapy, remedial reading, play groups, and school activities for potentially 15 to 20 children. In such a residential family-centered setting, women are not just getting parenting classes. There is active support for parenting, in a variety of ways from mother–child activities to support and modeling. After the period of residential care, services to children ought to be included in aftercare planning, with home visits, case management, and supportive services for children in their school or nursery school settings.

Treatment Outcome

There has been little systematic research on whether there are differences in treatment outcomes by gender. Both males and females with similar demographic characteristics, in comparable stages of their illness, are presumed to do equally well in similar treatment settings. A few recent studies do suggest that women may have more satisfactory outcomes a year post-treatment than do men. On the negative side, women's rates of entrance, retention, and completion of treatment are significantly lower than rates for men.

As in the case with men, alcohol and drug use problems are related to premature mortality. Over a 25-year follow-up period following the first admission for treatment in a Swedish women-only program, an increased rate of mortality was found, virtually two and a half times greater than for women in the general population, with the rate for the youngest women even higher, four times greater. The bulk of the these deaths occurred in the first five years after the treatment and, no surprise, alcohol-related causes predominated. This is reminiscent of George Vaillant's observation on the natural history of alcoholism: there are essentially only two outcomes—recovery or premature death.

Program Factors Results differ depending on whether treatment is women-only or mixed-gender. Among women with a co-occurring psychiatric disorder, several studies have shown better outcomes in women-only settings. Intensive case management is another program factor that has been associated with better outcomes. Women with intensive case management were more engaged in treatment. It is accompanied by more contacts with the counselor, as well as higher levels of self-help participation. Interestingly, too, it appeared to counterbalance to a significant degree factors commonly associated with poorer outcome, such as the presence of a co-occurring psychiatric disorder. An outcome measure of importance to clients is reunification with children. Women involved with programs that have a higher degree of family-related and education/employment services were twice as likely to regain custody of children.

Relapse The nature of social networks is an important predictor of relapse. The size of the social network that is supportive of abstinence and not organized around alcohol or drug use, along with the frequency of daily contacts, is an important predictor of relapse. The single greatest risk factor for relapse after drug treatment is living with a drug-involved partner. For one thing, those with drug-using partners are likely to leave treatment earlier. For another, drug-using partners not only come with their drugs, they also come with an accompanying set of problems. They are more likely to be unemployed, have less education, have legal problems, and have more health problems. They are seen as less supportive and in fact are more likely to undermine treatment by providing money for drugs.

A Special Case: Pregnancy

Women ages 18–44 are considered to be of child-bearing age. Alcohol use drops markedly during pregnancy. The recommendations that pregnant women not drink during pregnancy has gotten through. Drinking rates are 12% for pregnant women, compared to 42% for recent mothers, and 54% for non-pregnant women this age. Women who breastfeed are advised to abstain from alcohol as small amounts can be transmitted to breast milk. The age group of greatest concern is pregnant teenagers,

15–17 years old. The rate of drinking is 16%, with an average of 24 drinks in the past month, and an average of 4 drinks on each of these occasions. While fetal alcohol syndrome and fetal alcohol effects are a concern (see Chapter 6), there is also a higher incidence of other medical problems associated with maternal drinking. These include an apparent higher risk of childhood leukemia; higher rates of obesity; and higher rates of some psychiatric conditions such as attention-deficit/hyperactivity disorder, conduct disorder, and antisocial personality disorder.

When it comes to illicit drugs, 6.4% of non-pregnant and 2.8% of pregnant women report using illicit drugs. During pregnancy there is a reduction in illicit drug use, with the rate of abstaining increasing from 28% in the first trimester to 93% by the third trimester. Marijuana represents three-quarters of the illicit drug use. Among those using illicit drugs, half of the pregnant and two-thirds of the non-pregnant women also used alcohol and tobacco.

However, following delivery, there is a significant resumption of use, as shown below, and only one-third continue to refrain from illicit drug use.

	Alcohol	Binge Drinking	Marijuana	Nicotine
3rd trimester	6.2%	1.0%	1.4%	13.9%
Mothers with infant, 3 months or younger	31.9%	10.0%	3.8%	20.0%

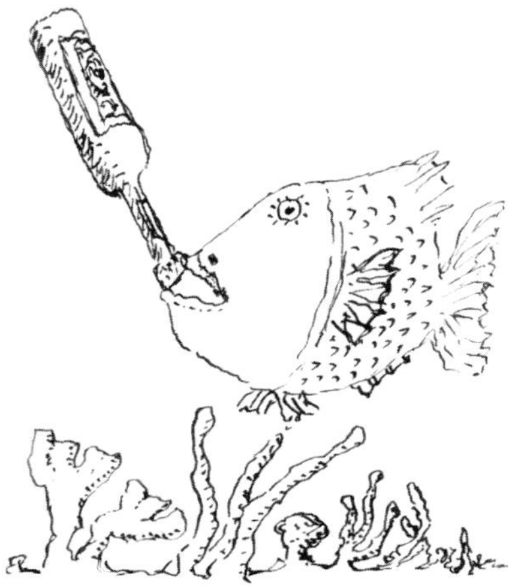

Pregnancy and childbirth are points when the potential for intervention is often greatest. Medical treatment for alcohol- and drug-dependent pregnant women must include perinatal services, pharmacotherapy, health education, and referral. Perinatal services should encompass evaluation and treatment by a perinatologist and a perinatal nurse clinician. HIV counseling and testing and nutritional counseling are important. The mother should deliver in a hospital where emergency services are readily available in case of complications. Many infants are low birth weight and need intensive care. For women who are drinking heavily, even if abstinence cannot be achieved, a reduction in drinking reduces the risks of fetal alcohol syndrome and fetal alcohol effects.

Nicotine is also a significant issue during pregnancy. The importance of smoking cessation during pregnancy has begun to receive increased attention. In part this appears to be attributable to the 1998 Master Settlement Agreement between the states and the major tobacco companies. Smoking cessation was one major initiative that resulted. New York City embarked on a comprehensive program, which ranged from smoking bans, to increasing the price of cigarettes, to promoting smoking cessation. In a review of the rates of smoking during pregnancy, over a 10-year period, one thing stands out—a 60% decline in smoking among pregnant women.

Smoking during pregnancy is associated with a long list of problems: preterm delivery, spontaneous abortion, restricted intrauterine growth, and increased risk of sudden infant death syndrome; in addition, the increased irritability that commonly occurs after delivery, along with other factors, is beginning to raise questions about neonatal nicotine withdrawal syndrome. It probably shouldn't be a surprise, but maternal smoking is linked to earlier hospital discharges following delivery.

The problems of prenatal nicotine exposure don't disappear after infancy. While the mechanisms may not be fully understood, there are a growing number of conditions now recognized as more common among those with in utero nicotine exposure. Prenatal exposure to nicotine is associated with a variety of conditions: earlier age of menopause; tendency for higher levels of cholesterol; a greater risk of nicotine dependence; a greater risk of asthma, which is independent of environmental smoking; and an increased risk of smoking. It is also a contributor to orofacial clefts. Preliminary studies have identified changes in the brains of adolescents that are associated with prenatal nicotine exposure. Just as nicotine affects neurotransmitters in the smoker, so too it has an impact on the same systems in the developing fetus. Although possibly not as dramatic as the problems associated with fetal alcohol syndrome, prenatal nicotine exposure also may have lifelong effects.

One disturbing social development is the emergence of court actions filed against pregnant women who are dependent on drugs, particularly cocaine, and alcohol to a lesser degree. Women have been charged with child abuse on the basis of administering cocaine to the fetus through the umbilical cord. Unfortunately, judges, legislators, and prosecutors, like the public in general, have obtained most of their information about drug- and alcohol-dependent pregnant and parenting women from the popular press. The coverage of the so-called crack epidemic and crack babies has been inaccurate and alarmist. Though not supported by research, the prevailing assumption is that children exposed prenatally to crack are inevitably and irremediably damaged.

The reactions to the problems of drug- and alcohol-dependent pregnant women have been largely punitive. Hundreds of women have been prosecuted on unproven theories of fetal abuse and drug delivery through the umbilical cord. These prosecutions continue, despite the fact that no appellate court in the country has upheld one. Thousands of women too have been reported under civil child neglect laws and have been investigated for being neglectful or abusive, based solely on a positive urine toxicology specimen at the birth of their child. African American women have been arrested and disproportionately reported to authorities, despite evidence that white and African American women in similar situations use illegal substances at approximately the same rate. Judges often assume, incorrectly, that drug-dependent pregnant women have access to appropriate drug treatment, to contraceptive and abortion services, and to prenatal care. Moreover, they do not view addiction as a disease or understand that relapse may be part of recovery. The public policy statements of leading medical and public health organizations opposing punitive responses have helped. The continued prosecution of pregnant women, cutbacks in services for pregnant and parenting drug users, and the continued belief among many leaders that children's physical and emotional health problems can be blamed exclusively on cocaine or other drugs suggest the need for extensive judicial and public education and organized opposition to punitive approaches to this health problem.

THE WORKPLACE

Some Basic Statistics

In 1994, the *National Survey* for the first time included questions about alcohol and other drug use in relation to work. Those surveyed were asked about work-related issues, such as missed work, whether they had been fired, workplace accidents, their occupation, size of the workplace, whether they had ever been provided with information about alcohol and other drug policies at work, the existence of an EAP (employee assistance program), the use of drug testing, and their attitudes toward testing.

The most recent data available is from the 2012 *National Survey on Drug Use and Health*. Past month use of alcohol, tobacco, marijuana, and any other illicit drug use for those 18 and older are summarized below:

	Employment Status			
	Full-time	Part-time	Unemployed	Other*
Tobacco	27.2%	23.8%	43.0%	20.8%
Alcohol	63.0	55.5	55.5	40.4
Binge Drinking	30.3	8.1	33.4	3.5
Any Illicit Drug	8.0	10.2	19.6	4.9
Marijuana	6.1	8.5	16.5	3.3
Substance Use Disorder	10.2	11.0	19.0	—

* Includes retired, homemakers, students.

Another measure of the direct impact of alcohol on the workplace is in the proportion of people in the last year who have a drink within two hours of showing up for work (1.8%) or the number who drink during the workday (7%) or who work while under the influence (1.7%) or who come to work with a bad hangover (9%). This adds up to 15% of the entire workforce, or about 19.2 million people. There are differences based on gender, race, age, marital status, occupation, and work shift.

Patterns of heavy alcohol as well as illicit drug use vary among segments of the workforce. To begin with, the rates of heavy drinking and illicit drug use are higher among part-time workers and the unemployed. Compared to women, men have twice the rate of heavy drinking and one and a half times the rate of alcohol abuse or dependence. Similarly with illicit drugs, men are twice as likely to be current users or to have reported symptoms indicating a diagnosis of abuse or dependence in the past year. Age differences are reflected in the fact that heavy drinking is twice as common among those 25 and younger compared to those 35 and older, with respective rates of 17% and 7.2%. The differences between age groups is even more striking for illicit drug use. Younger workers are over three times more likely to have used illicit drugs in the past month than older workers. Interestingly, for all age groups, the differences between any illicit drug use or heavy drinking in the past month are modest. Those who used illicit drugs or are heavy drinkers were more likely to have worked for three or more employers during the past year. They were also more likely to have voluntarily left a job. In addition, they also reported more absenteeism.

The rates of employer drug testing are rising. In 2006 it was estimated that more than 80% of larger employers have some kind of drug testing program. Beyond testing at hiring, employers may also conduct random tests as well as test upon reasonable suspicion. However, the results of workplace drug testing and the results of national surveys appear to be at odds. This was pointed out in a 2008 article by J. Michael Walsh. Over a 17-year period (1987–2004), the number of positive workplace test results decreased by two-thirds. However, during the very same period, national surveys indicated that drug use had increased by almost a third. In trying to make sense of this, the author mentions several factors. One, the majority of drug tests used involve urine samples, which invites people to submit substitute samples. Possibly more important is that the available tests vary in their ability to detect different substances. In particular, the ability to detect cocaine is very dependent on the particular testing device used. More significant, it was observed that "the ability to detect cannabis use is generally poor across all devices." Given that this is the most commonly used illicit drug, this might in part explain the discrepancy between test results and surveys of use patterns.

Over the years, studies have consistently found that substance use has a statistically significant effect on labor supply, absenteeism, and retention, and it influences a variety of performance measures. As business and industry began to recognize the costs to them of employees with alcohol problems, programs emerged to identify problems and initiate treatment. The earliest work-based programs emerging in the 1970s focused on alcohol and were sometimes called occupational alcohol programs. That term has been replaced by employee assistance programs (EAPs). Attention is no longer primarily or narrowly directed to alcohol or even substance use, but includes the array of issues that might influence job performance, whether family problems, financial problems, or mental health concerns. These programs are sometimes called enhanced EAPs. An examination of the effect of moving to an enhanced EAP model showed that the average number of women and minority cases per worksite increased by 58%, white male cases by 45%, and total EAP cases by 53%. This change in program orientation was accompanied by efforts to reach out to women and minorities.

EAPs are more common in worksites with 50 or more full-time employees as well as those with unions. More large companies have begun to self-insure rather than purchase market group health insurance. The self-insured firms are more likely to have an EAP, suggesting that it is cost-effective, as well as desired by the workforce. In 2000, the median cost per employee for EAPs was about $20.00 per person. EAPs are increasingly interested not just in addressing problems but in preventing them. As a result, they have developed employee wellness programs. These can include stress reduction courses, programs on nutrition, or exercise programs; in many places fitness centers are on site. Alcohol risk reduction is often included in these general wellness programs. Web-based educational and screening efforts are being introduced as well.

Portrait of a man who stops in a bar for 3 drinks on his way home from work every night.

Historically, drinking has been interwoven with work, in the form of the office party, the company picnic, the wine and cheese reception, the martini lunches, the "drink date" to review business, the bar car on the commuter train, the old standby gift of a bottle for a business associate, the round of drinks to celebrate the closing of a business deal, and the construction crew's stopping off for beers after work. However, meshing of drinking and business has come under fire. First, the IRS decreed that the martini part of the martini lunch is not a legitimate business expense. Then the growing interest in physical fitness took its toll. Concern about liability when alcohol is a part of company-sponsored parties came into play, although court cases addressing this go back to the mid-1970s. Nonetheless, for too long drinking in many work situations was not only accepted but also expected. Whenever alcohol use is tolerated, the potential for alcohol problems among susceptible individuals rises, more so if drinking is subtly encouraged.

Drug Use and the Workplace

With the passage of the drug-free workplace legislation in the 1980s, drug use also became a workplace concern. It was at this point that drug testing became common. The assumption was that testing would serve as a deterrent and preventive measure. If, for the sake of argument, one grants that drug testing serves as a deterrent, questions remain. For example, how many cases would need to be prevented to justify testing everyone at a cost of $40–$50 per test? In addition, drug testing typically indicates past use; does all such use have implications for workplace performance?

Some of these questions are now being answered. A study conducted in a major manufacturing company several years ago provided some interesting insights. The study was intended to answer the question, "What drug testing policy would be associated with the lowest level of medical care costs?" In that company there was random drug testing, at variable intervals and involving variable percentages of the workforce. A positive drug test was grounds for firing. It was found that random testing of under half of employees (42%) would reduce medical costs to the lowest level possible. Presumably, for that organization, a 42% testing rate was high enough to lead employees to think that there was a reasonable chance of being tested. Since one didn't have to test a higher proportion of employees to achieve the deterrent effect, the costs of any additional tests could be seen as wasted. The relationship of the rate of testing and injuries was also examined. Indeed, it was determined that by doubling the rate of testing, it would be possible to cut the rate of accidents in half. However, there was a kicker. The rate of injuries was already very, very low, under 1% per month. Cutting that percentage further was seen as having only a marginal benefit and would require testing hundreds more employees.

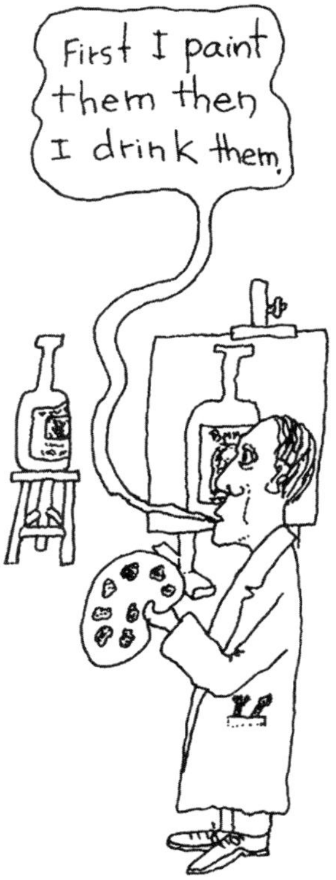

Data from the *National Survey* provide some insights into drug testing—whether pre-employment, random, or suspicion-based, testing has an impact on the likelihood and frequency of employee drug use. Indeed it does. The employees of firms that have drug testing programs have both lower levels of drug use and fewer chronic drug users. However, this raises the question of whether the drug testing itself deters use or whether those who use drugs are drawn to work settings without such testing programs.

Clearly the focus of the Drug-Free Workplace legislation was on drugs as opposed to alcohol. At the same time, these initiatives have conveyed the message that alcohol no longer enjoys the status of being "OK," while all other drugs are "bad." Substance use of whatever variety can and does interfere with performance and productivity and is therefore a legitimate business concern.

Well, Rickey's not one of them, so that's 49 percent right there.
—RICKEY HENDERSON
On reports that 50 percent of ballplayers use steroids

In a similar vein, for a long period, smoking at work was an accepted practice. This is no longer the case, and many worksites, beyond banning smoking in the workplace, offer smoking cessation programs to help employees quit. No longer being able to smoke at work has certainly raised the quit rate. There is also the phenomenon of "exiled" smoking—people taking smoking breaks—and questions are now being raised about the impact of this practice. One is, "What is the impact on performance of smokers' experiencing withdrawal?" and another is, "What is the impact on non-smokers' morale as they witness coworkers' taking authorized and unauthorized cigarette breaks?"

A partial response to the first of these questions is provided by examining the effects of withdrawal on pilots who are regular smokers. Using flight simulators, the pilots were examined after 12 hours of abstinence.

In brief, all tests showed declines in cognitive functions and higher levels of reported nervousness, tension-anxiety, fatigue, difficulty concentrating, less alertness, disorders of fine motor adjustments, prolonged reaction times, anger and irritability, drowsiness, and impaired judgment. Physiological measures showed changes in blood pressure and heart rate.

Work is the curse of the drinking class.
—Oscar Wilde

Some companies have extended the ban on indoor smoking to include the entire workplace property, a tactic known as "smoke-free grounds." This makes "just stepping outside" no longer an option. After an extended ban, the quit rate during one company's smoking cessation program was 52%. That rate far exceeds the outcomes for virtually all smoking cessation programs, for which very good outcomes are around 20%. Simply enacting a smoke-free workplace policy, even without providing a formal smoking cessation program, provokes a substantial number of people to quit smoking. The state of Minnesota, in examining different approaches to prod people statewide to quit smoking, determined that promoting smoke-free workplaces throughout the state would have a greater impact than would providing free nicotine patches.

Smoking in the workplace has also received attention in another context because of efforts to protect workers from the effects of secondhand smoke. This was a key factor in the efforts to ban smoking on airplanes, which exposed flight attendants to passive smoking. Following that the issue arose in the context of bars. A number of municipalities have enacted smoking bans in bars as well as restaurants. Research confirmed what was long suspected; ventilation systems installed in restaurants and bars are largely ineffective. As a result, in many restaurants there is no such thing as a non-smoking area. Whenever there is a single ventilating system, the air from smoking and non-smoking areas is collected by that single system and redistributed. Non-smokers who work in places without a smoking ban have 10 times the exposure to smoke, and those who work in places with designated smoking areas have 3 times the levels of secondhand smoke of those who work in smoke-free areas.

Another group of workers for whom there is concern with respect to nicotine is farm workers. Tobacco leaves can effectively act as giant nicotine patches and cause nicotine poisoning. This condition is called *green tobacco sickness.* Symptoms include weakness, headache, nausea, vomiting, dizziness, stomach cramps, breathing difficulty, abnormal temperature, diarrhea, and chills, along with fluctuations in blood pressure or heart rate and increased perspiration and salivation. Treatment includes changing clothing to reduce exposure from any nicotine on garments, showering, rest, and cessation of work and possible medication to handle the nausea and vomiting. Many of those who harvest tobacco are low-wage workers, often migrant workers, with limited access to health care, and they are often victims of exploitation. Protective clothing can potentially reduce the risk, but enforcement of regulations where these do exist is limited.

High-Risk Factors

Although a job cannot be said to cause alcohol-drug dependence or abuse, it can contribute to its development. Factors that have been recognized as job-based risk factors include the following:

- Absence of clear goals (and absence of supervision)
- Freedom to set work hours (isolation and low visibility)
- Low structural visibility (such as salespeople working away from the business place)
- Overinvestment in one's job
- Occupational obsolescence (especially common in scientific and technical fields)
- New work status
- "Required" on-the-job drinking (such as salespeople's drinking with clients)
- Reduction of social controls (occurs on college campuses and other less structured settings)
- Severe role stress
- Competitive pressure
- Presence of illegal drug users

In addition to the preceding risk factors related to the workplace, the absence of a workplace is also a significant risk factor. Extended involuntary unemployment is a predictor of heavy drinking. And this is independent of gender, age, race/ethnicity, marital status, prior heavy drinking, and present socioeconomic status. Today, this is of particular significance as the United States is experiencing the greatest recession in decades, and there is the strong likelihood that not all of the jobs lost will be coming back.

The Workplace Response

If bringing up the drinking practices and potential problems of a family member or close friend makes someone squirm, the idea of saying something to a coworker is virtually unthinkable. Almost everyone accepts a separation between work and home or professional and private life. So until the alcohol problem flows into the work world, the worker's use of alcohol is often considered no one else's business. That does not mean that no one sees a problem developing. The suspicion is that someone with even a little savvy can often spot potentially dangerous drinking practices. The office scuttlebutt or the work crew's bull sessions plus simple observation make it common knowledge who really put it away over the past weekend, who just got picked up for a DWI, or who will always be available to go for a drink after work.

Even if an employee does show some problems on the job, whether directly or indirectly related to alcohol use, coworkers may try to help out by doing extra work or at least by not blowing the whistle. Because employee assistance programs, if they are available, are based on identifying work deterioration, any attempt by coworkers to help cover up job problems makes spotting the problem all the more difficult. If a company does not have a program to help those employees with substance abuse problems, odds for a cover-up by coworkers are even greater. Another important party in this concealment strategy is predictably the spouse, who usually doesn't want to do anything to threaten the paycheck.

Historically, if an alcohol problem officially came to light, the employee usually got fired; this may still happen in many companies. In such instances, the enterprise may lose a formerly valuable and well-trained worker—statistically, a costly "solution." The current thinking is that it is cheaper for a company to identify problems earlier and to use the job as leverage to get the employee into treatment and back to work.

Workplace Interventions

Facts and experience suggest that the occupational environment is one of the most efficient and economical means for early identification and treatment of alcohol dependence and alcohol- and other drug-related problems. Early intervention increases the chances for recovery for the following reasons:

- Physical health has not deteriorated significantly.
- Financial resources are not as depleted as they would be later on.
- Emotional supports still exist in the family and community.
- Threat of job loss can be used as leverage.

The following are among the more common signs and symptoms that point to a troubled employee and thereby help identify the problem drinker or substance abuser:

- Chronic absenteeism
- Erratic behavior
- Physical signs, alcohol-induced medical problems
- Spasmodic work pace
- Lower quantity and quality of work
- Partial absences
- Avoidance of supervisors and coworkers
- On-the-job drinking or drug use
- On-the-job accidents and lost time from off-the-job accidents

Training supervisors and others to recognize these signs and symptoms is important, so that early detection can occur. Training is also critical in helping employers document, not diagnose. Where there have been broad educational efforts through information sessions, posters, pamphlets, and so forth, there has been an increase in peer- or self-referrals. Such referrals may make up the bulk of referrals to a program. The culture of the workplace has a significant impact on the use and acceptance of EAPs. While supervisory personnel are a major factor, equally important are the attitudes of close coworkers. The workplace medical clinic is also well positioned to promote screening and to conduct brief, office-based interventions. One Swedish study found that, when employees were offered an alcohol screening as part of a routine occupational health visit, 98% took advantage of the opportunity. Of those screened, 21% were found to have excessive alcohol consumption and were contacted to arrange a follow-up visit. Of those contacted by telephone, 80% went in for a follow-up visit, compared with only 17% who were sent a letter. Of equal interest is that this program also prompted persons who had not been initially screened as positive for a possible alcohol problem to call for an appointment.

Implications for Treatment

It is important that substance abuse professionals be knowledgeable about workplace programs. They can thereby better coordinate treatment efforts for the employed client.

Does the individual's employer have an EAP? If so, who is the EAP clinician? What services are offered? For any client, it is important that you be aware of any work-related problems. If so, what is the current job status? Has a disciplinary procedure been instituted, or has the employee been informally warned and referred for treatment? In addition, to avoid future conflict, learn about any union involvement. Such information can help in formulating realistic treatment plans.

It is important to be sensitive to the policies and politics of the employed client's work setting. Without this knowledge and awareness, there is the danger of violating confidentiality or conversely of not taking full advantage of the opportunity to cooperate with the employer on the client's behalf. If there is a company policy, learn about it, so that you can plan realistically and avoid treatment and work conflicts. The nature of the client's work and the potential impact of any prescribed medication must be considered. A follow-up plan must consider the working person's hours and geographical location. The flexibility and accessibility of the treatment facility can be key factors in successful rehabilitation. Evening office hours and early-morning and weekend appointments may have to be arranged, so that treatment will not interfere with the job. On the other hand, if there is an EAP with clinical personnel, this may be the most appropriate site for follow-up and continuing care, after the initial intensive treatment.

You may find that some individuals will have to be treated as outpatients even when inpatient services are more appropriate. The employee may not be able to take the time off or may not have adequate insurance coverage. Insurance plans are less likely to cover inpatient treatment; if they do, the stays will be limited. The rationale is that outpatient care is less expensive and that little or no evidence indicates that inpatient care provides better treatment outcomes. These assumptions are based on data derived from group statistics. Both ends of the spectrum are lost to the statistical average.

Many larger companies use managed health care plans. This means that there are designated providers, as in an HMO (health maintenance organization), which provide either the medical care that is needed or the required prior approval for a treatment referral, if the insurance is to cover the costs. The rationale for such arrangements is that unnecessary services will be eliminated and health care dollars will be used more wisely. Although laudable in concept, in practice this arrangement has caused concern. With respect to alcohol and substance abuse services, several problems have been identified. Some managed health care systems have developed contracts with specific treatment agencies to provide all necessary services. Payment is often based on a per capita formula, with a set reimbursement paid for a diagnostic category, rather than reimbursements being made on the basis of actual costs incurred. In effect this establishes a clear incentive to limit services. This may work for the "average" client. However, the average person in treatment is, by analogy, like the statistically average drinker described in Chapter 2, virtually non-existent. The provision of individualized treatment needed to ensure optimal care can be sacrificed to indiscriminately delivering the statistically predetermined norm.

OTHER SPECIAL POPULATIONS

An "average client" is virtually non-existent. All kinds of factors have an impact, particularly cultural factors, including race and ethnicity, in combination with age and gender. These can be important in several ways. These factors, for example, determine what kinds of behavior are viewed as evidence of a problem, to whom people turn for help and under what circumstances, and a client's comfort in using professional care. In light of this, the substance abuse field as well as other human service fields has begun to discuss issues of cultural diversity and acknowledge the unique constellation of characteristics found in segments of the population. Population subgroups are commonly termed "special populations." Being informed about cultural issues of importance to members of a segment of the population is often termed "cultural sensitivity." Special populations are not defined exclusively by racial or cultural characteristics. Life circumstances may define a special population: for example, veterans, victims of domestic violence, those with a co-occurring psychiatric illness. In respect to the magnitude of substance use problems, one special population warranting attention is prisoners.

Those in prison or jails are sometimes described as the "triply troubled," a play on the reference to dual diagnosis for those with a substance use disorder plus another mental illness and the self-help group known as Double Trouble for those with substance use disorders and psychiatric illness. About 55% of everyone incarcerated in the U.S. has a substance use disorder. Only 25% of these inmates receive treatment either when incarcerated or after release. Plus 43% have a psychiatric disorder. Among women almost half have both of these conditions, as too do a quarter of men. Upon release these problems dramatically raise the odds of being reincarcerated. Those with substance use disorders and mental illness are at an increased risk of treatment recidivism and a return to prison. Treatment programs offered within prisons have varying degrees of success. Methadone- or buprenorphine-based programs have better outcomes than do drug-free programs. The outcomes are similar to those in the general community. A therapeutic community program was introduced in one institution. The outcomes for those who participated were no better than those of prisoners who had not been in treatment. Over 60% of both groups had returned to prison within two years. By year 5, the percentage climbed to 73% and the rearrest offenses were similar for both groups. Twelve-step programs are available in many institutions, and participation is associated with better outcomes for those who continue to participate after their release.

Those with a history of problems with opiates are at significantly greater risk of a drug overdose shortly after their release. Drug substitution therapy provides a number of benefits, whether methadone or buprenorphine. Treatment outcome is comparable to the outcome for those treated in community settings. It also provides an opportunity to recruit problem opioid users into treatment, to reduce illicit opioid use and risk behaviors during their time incarcerated, and potentially to minimize overdose risks on release. For prisoners in such programs before imprisonment, the presence of a prison program offers continuity of care.

In this chapter, neither racial nor ethnic groups are discussed specifically. The U.S. census provides a number of choices for respondents to designate their race: (1) White, (2) Black or African American, (3) American Indian or Alaska Native, (4) Asian (with choices of being Asian Indian, Japanese, Vietnamese, Korean, or other), (5) Native Hawaiian and Other Pacific Islander (including Guamanian, Samoan, Filipino, or Other), or (6) some other race. In the 2000 census, for the first time people were able to select more than one race to describe themselves, and about 10% did so. Hispanic or Latino status is not considered a race—Latinos can be either white, black, or multiracial. Hispanic/Latino designates a cultural orientation and encompasses those whose heritage is tied to Spanish-speaking areas in the Americas—Mexico, the Caribbean, Central and South America. These groups are probably those who first come to mind if there is mention of race/ethnicity. However, there are countless other identifiable cultural groups, each with its distinctive characteristics that are relevant for the clinician, be it the Portuguese New England fisherman; the Amish who live in Pennsylvania, Ohio, and Indiana; or the Tibetan neighborhood in a small Midwestern city. Even within a particular group there can be considerable diversity. This can be based on geographical location, whether a client is a recent immigrant or native born, and the client's generation in the family's constellation.

A client's cultural heritage and orientation are important in the clinical arena. In working with the member of a particular special population group, recognize that one of the client's important relationships is to his or her traditional culture as well as to the larger, dominant culture. This is sometimes referred to as cultural orientation, meaning the sets of rules an individual instinctively follows. The basic question is to what extent the client identifies with a traditional ethnic group and to what extent he or she is comfortable in functioning not as a member of a particular ethnic group but as part of the American mainstream. Some of the terms used to describe these different orientations are "assimilated" (as opposed to "non-assimilated") and "bicultural." In brief, those individuals who are not assimilated think of themselves in terms of the values and rules of behavior of their group of origin. Those who are assimilated may or may not be familiar with the traditional ways; however, they are most comfortable functioning in the usual style of the dominant American culture. Those described as bicultural are able to function by the rules of either their native culture or the majority American culture.

In working with clients who are members of ethnic groups, a sense of their cultural orientation is important. Table 11.3 indicates the different areas that might be considered.

In working with clients who are members of any cultural group other than your own, it is important to become familiar with the values, practices, and ways of seeing the world that are part of that group. Often a useful place to start is by considering the nature of your biases and the source of any preconceived notions.

TABLE 11.3 Assessing Cultural Orientation

	Traditional Culture or Culture of Origin	Majority Culture
Social	• close friends from same ethnic background • leisure activities within ethnic communities	• close friends not restricted to ethnic group • leisure not primarily restricted to ethnic group within ethnic community
Language	• primarily uses native language	• not fluent in native language
Spiritual	• familiar with and participates in ethnic traditional ceremonies and celebrations	• unfamiliar with and does not participate in native festivities
Family	• defined by customs of the ethnic culture	• considers family the nuclear family unit, i.e., spouse, parents, and children

Suggesting that a referral be made to a counselor or clinician who is from the same cultural group as the client may be good advice, but it isn't always possible to do. At the very least it is important to know about the client's cultural history and traditions. In terms of alcohol problems, how are drinking problems defined? What are the behaviors that within the community would signal an alcohol problem? To whom do people tend to turn for help in time of trouble? Are there any biases against seeking professional care or getting help from an "outsider"? Are there any customs that would make getting help more difficult? Be alert to any barriers caused by language. Do not be surprised to be watched closely for signs of prejudice or disinterest. As necessary, certainly acknowledge the limits and differences of your own experience and background. Wise advice that holds here as elsewhere is that the patient is the best instructor, but it requires that you open yourself to learning.

REFERENCES AND FURTHER READINGS

Adolescents

American Academy of Pediatrics, Substance Abuse Committee. Indication for management and referral of patients involved in substance abuse. *Pediatrics* 106(1):143–146, 2000. (18 refs.)

American Journal on Addictions 15(Supplement 1):entire issue, 2006.

This special issue deals with advances in the assessment and treatment of adolescent substance use disorders.

Andrews JA, Tildesley E, Hops H, Duncan SC, Severson HH. Elementary school age children's future intentions and use of substances. *Journal of Clinical Child and Adolescent Psychology* 32(4):556–567, 2004. (44 refs.)

Bachman JG, Safron DJ, Sy SR, Schulenberg JE. Wishing to work: New perspectives on how adolescents' part-time work intensity is linked to educational disengagement, substance use, and other problem behaviours. *International Journal of Behavioral Development* 27(4):301–315, 2003. (77 refs.)

Casadio P, Fernandes C, Murray RM, Di Forti M. Cannabis use in young people: The risk for schizophrenia (review). *Neuroscience and Biobehavioral Reviews* 35(8, special issue): 1779–1787, 2011. (131 refs.)

Chun TH, Linakis JG. Interventions for adolescent alcohol use (review). *Current Opinion in Pediatrics* 24(2):38–242, 2012. (22 refs.)

D'Amico EJ, McCarthy DA. Escalation and initiation of younger adolescents' substance use: The impact of perceived peer use. *Journal of Adolescent Health* 39(4):481–487, 2006. (39 refs.)

Fisher SL, Bucholz KK, Reich W, Fox L, Kuperman S, Kramer J, et al. Teenagers are right: Parents do not know much. An analysis of adolescent-parent agreement on reports of adolescent substance use, abuse, and dependence. *Alcoholism: Clinical and Experimental Research* 30(10):1699–1710, 2006. (38 refs.)

Foltran F, Gregori D, Franchin L, Verduci E, Giovannini M. Effect of alcohol consumption in prenatal life, childhood, and adolescence on child development (review). *Nutrition Reviews* 69(11):642–659, 2011. (256 refs.)

Frese WA, Eiden K. Opioids: Nonmedical use and abuse in older children (review). *Pediatrics in Review* 32(4):e44–e52, 2011. (31 refs.)

Grimshaw GM, Stanton A. Tobacco cessation interventions for young people (review). *Cochrane Database of Systemic Reviews* 4(article no. CD003289), 2006. (110 refs.)

Gunja N. Teenage toxins: Recreational poisoning in the adolescent. *Journal of Paediatrics and Child Health* 48(7):560–566, 2012. (50 refs.)

Kaufman J, Yang BZ, Douglas-Palumberi H, Crouse-Artus M, Lipschitz D, Krystal JH, et al. Genetic and environmental predictors of early alcohol use. *Biological Psychiatry* 61(11):1228–1234, 2007. (47 refs.)

Lloyd DA, Turner RJ. Cumulative lifetime adversities and alcohol dependence in adolescence and young adulthood. *Drug and Alcohol Dependence* 93(3):217–226, 2008. (57 refs.)

Miller JW, Naimi TS, Brewer RD, Jones SE. Binge drinking and associated health risk behaviors among high school students. *Pediatrics* 119(1):76–85, 2007. (61 refs.)

Miller TR, Levy DT, Spicer RS, Taylor DM. Societal costs of underage drinking. *Journal of Studies on Alcohol* 67(4): 519–528, 2006. (91 refs.)

Nanda S, Konnur N. Adolescent drug & alcohol use in the 21st century. *Pediatric Annals* 35(3):193–199, 2006. (33 refs.) Note: Reviews risk factors and the physiological consequences associated with the drugs most commonly used by adolescents, including alcohol, nicotine, inhalants, stimulants, heroin and opiates, the club drugs (ecstasy, GHB, and ketamine), hallucinogens, and anabolic steroids, as well as drugs used by athletes. Tables provide the street names of common drugs.

Patten CA, Lopez K, Thomas JL, Offord KP, Decker PA, Pingree S, et al. Reported willingness among adolescent nonsmokers to help parents, peers, and others to stop smoking. *Preventive Medicine* 39(6):1099–1106, 2004. (46 refs.)

Perepletchikova F, Krystal JH, Kaufman J. Practitioner review. Adolescent alcohol use disorders: Assessment and treatment issues (review). *Journal of Child Psychology and Psychiatry* 49(11):1131–1154, 2008. (168 refs.)

QuickStats: Death rates for leading causes among youths aged 12–19 years—National Vital Statistics System, United States, 1999–2006. *MMWR. Morbidity and Mortality Weekly Review* 59(24):752, 2010.

Somaini L, Donnini C, Manfredini M, Raggi MA, Saracino MA, Gerra ML, et al. Adverse childhood experiences (ACEs), genetic polymorphisms and neurochemical correlates in experimentation with psychotropic drugs among adolescents (review). *Neuroscience and Biobehavioral Reviews* 35(8):1771–1778, 2011. (104 refs.)

Stone A, Becker LG, Huber AM, Catalano RF. Review of risk and protective factors of substance use and problem use in emerging adulthood (review). *Addictive Behaviors* 37(7):747–775, 2012. (196 refs.)

Sussman S. A review of Alcoholics Anonymous/Narcotics Anonymous programs for teens. *Evaluation & the Health Professions* 33(1):26–55, 2010. (84 refs.)

Sussman S, Skara S, Ames S. Substance abuse among adolescents (review). *Substance Use & Misuse* 43(12–13):1802–1828, 2008. (121 refs.)

Vardakou I, Pistos C, Spiliopoulou C. Drugs for youth via Internet and the example of mephedrone (review). *Toxicology Letters* 201(3):191–195, 2011. (31 refs.)

Vital Signs: Drinking and driving among high school students aged ≤16 years, United States, 1991–2011. *MMWR. Morbidity and Mortality Weekly Report* 61(39):796–800, 2012. (21 refs.)

Wakefield M, Flay B, Nichter M, Giovino G. Role of the media in influencing trajectories of youth smoking (review). *Addiction* 98:79–103, 2003. (204 refs.)

Wilens TE, Faraone SV, Biederman J, Gunawardene S. Does stimulant therapy of attention-deficit/hyperactivity disorder beget later substance abuse? A meta-analytic review of the literature (review). *Pediatrics* 111(1):179–185, 2003. (56 refs.)

Young AM, Glover N, Havens JR. Nonmedical use of prescription medications among adolescents in the United States: A systematic review (review). *Journal of Adolescent Health* 51(1):6–17, 2012. (48 refs.)

Yule AM, Prince JB. Adolescent substance use disorders in the school setting (review). *Child and Adolescent Psychiatric Clinics of North America* 21(1):175+, 2012. (63 refs.)

COLLEGE STUDENTS

Arria AM, O'Grady KE, Caldeira KM, Vincent KB, Wish ED. Nonmedical use of prescription stimulants and analgesics: Associations with social and academic behaviors among college students. *Journal of Drug Issues* 38(4):1045–1060, 2008. (21 refs.)

Bache M, Guldberg A. Young people who have lost a parent because of alcoholism need special attention. *Nordic Psychology* 64(1):58–71, 2012. (28 refs.)

Beirness DJ, Foss RD, Vogel-Sprott M. Drinking on campus: Self-reports and breath tests. *Journal of Studies on Alcohol* 65(5):600–604, 2004. (16 refs.)

Bents RT, Tokish JM, Goldberg L. Ephedrine, pseudoephedrine, and amphetamine prevalence in college hockey players: Most report performance-enhancing use. *Physician and Sportsmedicine* 32(9):30–34, 2004. (20 refs.)

Berg CJ, Sutfin EL, Mendel, Ahluwalia JS. Use of and interest in smoking cessation strategies among daily and nondaily college student smokers. *Journal of American College Health* 60(3):194–202, 2012. (51 refs.)

Bracken NM. *National Study of Substance Use Trends Among NCAA College Student-Athletes.* Indianapolis, IN: NCAA, January 2012. <www.ncaapublications.com/p-4266-research-substance-use-national-study-of-substance-use-trends-among-ncaa-college-student-athletes.aspx>.

Campo S, Cameron KA. Differential effects of exposure to social norms campaigns: A cause for concern. *Health Communication* 19(3):209–219, 2006. (88 refs.)

Core Institute. *Results Core Survey, 2005.* Carbondale, IL: Core Institute, Southern Illinois University, 2007. Available: www.core.siuc.edu/home.htm.

DeSimone J. Fraternity membership and drinking behavior. *Economic Inquiry* 47(2):337–350, 2009. (24 refs.)

Ernst FA, Hogan B, Vallas MA, Cook M, Fuller D. Superior self-regulatory skills in African-American college students: Evidence from alcohol and tobacco use. *Journal of Black Studies* 40(2):337–346, 2009. (36 refs.)

Johnston LD, O'Malley PM, Bachman JG, Schulenberg JE. *Monitoring the Future: National Survey Results on Drug Use, 1975–2011. Volume II College Students and Adults Ages 19–50.* Bethesda, MD: National Institute on Drug Abuse, 2012.

Mallett KA, Lee CM, Neighbors C, Larimer ME, Turrisi R. Do we learn from our mistakes? An examination of the impact of negative alcohol-related consequences on college students' drinking patterns and perceptions. *Journal of Studies on Alcohol* 67(2):269–276, 2006. (41 refs.)

Martinic M, Measham D, eds. *Swimming with Crocodiles: The Culture of Extreme Drinking*. London: Routledge, 2008.

Pedersen ER, LaBrie J. Drinking game participation among college students: Gender and ethnic implications. *Addictive Behaviors* 31(11):2105–2115, 2006. (30 refs.)

Ragsdale K, Porter JR, Mathews R, White A, Gore-Felton C, McGarvey EL. "Liquor before beer, you're in the clear": Binge drinking and other risk behaviors among fraternity/sorority members and their non-Greek peers. *Journal of Substance Use* 17(4):323–339, 2012. (39 refs.)

Ridout B, Campbell A, Ellis L. "Off your Face(book)": Alcohol in online social identity construction and its relation to problem drinking in university students. *Drug and Alcohol Review* 31(1):20–26, 2012. (40 refs.)

Schaus JF, Sole ML, McCoy TP, Mullett N, O'Brien MC. Alcohol screening and brief intervention in a college student health center: A randomized controlled trial. *Journal of Studies on Alcohol and Drugs* (Supplement 16):131–141, 2009. (48 refs.)

Schuckit MA, Kalmijn JA, Smith TL, Saunders G, Fromme K. Structuring a college alcohol prevention program on the low level of response to alcohol model: A pilot study. *Alcoholism: Clinical and Experimental Research* 36(7):1244–1252, 2012. (62 refs.)

Scott-Sheldon LAJ, Carey KB, Carey MP. Health behavior and college students: Does Greek affiliation matter? *Journal of Behavioral Medicine* 31(1):61–70, 2008. (68 refs.)

Scribner R, Mason K, Theall K, Simonsen N, Schneider SK, Towvim LG. The contextual role of alcohol outlet density in college drinking. *Journal of Studies on Alcohol and Drugs* 69(1):112–120, 2008. (29 refs.)

Singleton RA. Collegiate alcohol consumption and academic performance. *Journal of Studies on Alcohol and Drugs* 68(4): 548–555, 2007. (19 refs.)

Sutfin EL, McNamara RS, Blocker JN, Ip EH, O'Brien MC, Wolfson M. Screening and brief intervention for tobacco use by student health providers on college campuses. *Journal of American College Health* 60(1):66–73, 2012. (36 refs.)

Theall KP, DeJong W, Scribner R, Mason K, Schneider SK, Simonsen N. Social capital in the college setting: The impact of participation in campus activities on drinking and alcohol-related harms. *Journal of American College Health* 58(1): 15–23, 2009. (29 refs.)

Turner JC, Keller A. Leading causes of mortality among American college students at 4-year institutions. Paper presented to Annual Meeting American Public Health Association. Wednesday, November 2011. Washington DC: APA, 2011. <https://apha.confex.com/apha/139am/webprogram/Paper241696.html>.

Wechsler H, Nelson TF. What we have learned from the Harvard School of Public Health College Alcohol Study: Focusing attention on college student alcohol consumption and the environmental conditions that promote it. *Journal of Studies on Alcohol and Drugs* 69(4):481–490, 2008. (90 refs.)

Weitzman ER, Folkman A, Folkman KL, Wechsler H. The relationship of alcohol outlet density to heavy and frequent drinking and drinking-related problems among college students at eight universities. *Health & Place* 9:1–6, 2003. (14 refs.)

Wodarski JS, MacMaster S, Miller NK. The use of computer technology to reduce and prevent college drinking. *Social Work in Public Health* 27(3):270–282, 2012. (20 refs.)

Yusko DA, Buckman JF, White HR, Pandina RJ. Risk for excessive alcohol use and drinking-related problems in college student athletes. *Addictive Behaviors* 33(12):1546–1556, 2008. (65 refs.)

The Elderly

Blazer DG, Wu LT. Nonprescription use of pain relievers by middle-aged and elderly community-living adults: National Survey on Drug Use and Health. *Journal of the American Geriatrics Society* 57(7):1252–1257, 2009. (20 refs.)

Blow FC. *Substance Abuse Among Older Adults. Treatment Improvement Protocol*. (TIP) Series 26. Rockville, MD: Center for Substance Abuse Treatment, 1998. (418 book refs.)

Budnitz DS, Pollock DA, Weidenbach KN, Mendelsohn AB, Schroeder TJ, Annest JL. National surveillance of emergency department visits for outpatient adverse drug events. *Journal of the American Medical Association* 296(15):1858–1866, 2006.

Caputo F, Vignoli T, Leggio L, Addolorato G, Zoli G, Bernardi M. Alcohol use disorders in the elderly: A brief overview from epidemiology to treatment options (review). *Experimental Gerontology* 47(6):411–416, 2012. (41 refs.)

Castle NG, Wagner LM, Ferguson-Rome JC, Smith ML, Handler SM. Alcohol misuse and abuse reported by nurse aides in assisted living. *Research on Aging* 34(3):321–336, 2012. (31 refs.)

Center for Substance Abuse Treatment, Dupree LW, Schonfeld L, eds. *Substance Abuse Relapse Prevention for Older Adults: A Group Treatment Approach*. Rockville, MD: Center for Substance Abuse Treatment, 2005. (29 refs.)

Culberson JW, Ziska M. Prescription drug misuse/abuse in the elderly. *Geriatrics* 63(9):22+, 2008. (25 refs.)

Duncan DF, Nicholson T, White JB, Bradley DB, Bonaguro J. The baby boomer effect: Changing patterns of substance abuse among adults ages 55 and older. *Journal of Aging & Social Policy* 22(3):237–248, 2010. (28 refs.)

Han B, Gfroerer JC, Colliver JD, Penne MA. Substance use disorder among older adults in the United States in 2020. *Addiction* 104(1):88–96, 2009. (50 refs.)

Johnson-Greene D, McCaul ME, Roger P. Screening for hazardous drinking using the Michigan Alcohol Screening Test-Geriatric Version (MAST-G) in elderly persons with acute cerebrovascular accidents. *Alcoholism: Clinical and Experimental Research* 33(9):1555–1561, 2009. (28 refs.)

Lin WC, Zhang JY, Leung GY, Clark RE. Chronic physical conditions in older adults with mental illness and/or substance use disorders. *Journal of the American Geriatrics Society* 59(10):1913–1921, 2011. (30 refs.)

Moos RH, Schutte KK, Brennan PL, Moos BS. Older adults' alcohol consumption and late-life drinking problems: A 20-year perspective. *Addiction* 104(8):1293–1302, 2009. (50 refs.)

Pringle KE, Ahern FM, Heller DA, Gold CH, Brown TV. Potential for alcohol and prescription drug interactions in older people. *Journal of the American Geriatrics Society* 53(11):1930–1936, 2005. (29 refs.)

Qato DM, Alexander C, Conti RM, Johnson M, Schumm P, Lindau ST. Use of prescription and over-the-counter medications and dietary supplements among older adults in the United States. *Journal of the American Medical Association* 300(24): 2867–2878, 2008. (33 refs.)

Rochon PA, Drug prescribing for older adults. *UpToDate*. June 2013. (131 refs.) <www.uptodate.com/contents/drug-prescribing-for-older-adults>.

Satre DD, Mertens JR, Arean PA, Weisner C. Five-year alcohol and drug treatment outcomes of older adults versus middle-aged and younger adults in a managed care program. *Addiction* 99(10):1286–1297, 2004. (47 refs.)

Schutte KK, Moos RH, Brennan PL. Predictors of untreated remission from late-life drinking problems. *Journal of Studies on Alcohol* 67(3):354–362, 2006. (51 refs.)

Wetterling T, Veltrup C, John U, Driessen M. Late onset alcoholism. *European Psychiatry* 18(3):112–118, 2003. (36 refs.)

Wu LT, Blazer DG. Illicit and nonmedical drug use among older adults: A review. *Journal of Aging and Health* 23(3):481–504, 2011. (54 refs.)

WOMEN

Acierno R, Resnick HS, Flood A, Holmes M. An acute post-rape intervention to prevent substance use and abuse. *Addictive Behaviors* 28(9):1701–1715, 2003. (35 refs.)

Ashley OS, Marsden ME, Brady TM. Effectiveness of substance abuse treatment programming for women: A review (review). *American Journal of Drug and Alcohol Abuse* 29(1):19–53, 2003. (102 refs.)

Blume S, Frausto T, Guschwan M, Silverman S, Trautman R, Virzi O, et al. Position statement on the care of pregnant and newly delivered women addicts. *American Journal of Psychiatry* 158(7):1180, 2001.

Burd L, Blair J, Dropps K. Prenatal alcohol exposure, blood alcohol concentrations and alcohol elimination rates for the mother, fetus and newborn. *Journal of Perinatology* 32(9):652–659, 2012. (40 refs.)

Burns E, Gray R, Smith LA. Brief screening questionnaires to identify problem drinking during pregnancy: A systematic review (review). *Addiction* 105(4):601–614, 2010. (80 refs.)

Champion HLO, Foley KL, DuRant RH, Hensberry R, Altman D, Wolfson M. Adolescent sexual victimization, use of alcohol and other substances, and other health risk behaviors. *Journal of Adolescent Health* 35(4):321–328, 2004. (55 refs.)

Conners CA, Grant A, Crone CC, Whiteside-Mansell L. Substance abuse treatment for mothers: Treatment outcomes and the impact of length of stay. *Journal of Substance Abuse Treatment* 31(4):447–456, 2006. (45 refs.)

Corliss HL, Rosario M, Wypij D, Fisher LB, Austin SB. Sexual orientation disparities in longitudinal alcohol use patterns among adolescents: Findings from the Growing Up Today Study. *Archives of Pediatrics & Adolescent Medicine* 162(11):1071–1078, 2008. (52 refs.)

Dauber S, Neighbors C, Dasaro C, Riordan A, Morgenstern J. Impact of intensive case management on child welfare system involvement for substance-dependent parenting women on public assistance. *Children and Youth Services Review* 34(7): 1359–1366, 2012. (63 refs.)

Fleming MF, Lund MR, Wilton G, Landry M, Scheets D. The Healthy Moms study: The efficacy of brief alcohol intervention in postpartum women. *Alcoholism: Clinical and Experimental Research* 32(9):1600–1606, 2008. (28 refs.)

Gutierres SE, Van Puymbroeck C. Childhood and adult violence in the lives of women who misuse substances (review). *Aggression and Violent Behavior* 11(5):497–513, 2006. (117 refs.)

Haas AL, Peters RH. Development of substance abuse problems among drug-involved offenders: Evidence for the telescoping effect. *Journal of Substance Abuse* 12(3):241–253, 2000. (35 refs.)

Haver B, Gjestad R, Lindberg S, Franck J. Mortality risk up to 25 years after initiation of treatment among 420 Swedish women with alcohol addiction. *Addiction* 104(3):413–419, 2009. (34 refs.)

Kalmakis KA. Cycle of sexual assault and women's alcohol misuse (review). *Journal of the American Academy of Nurse Practitioners* 22(12):661–667, 2010. (40 refs.)

Kaskutas LA, Graves K. Pre-pregnancy drinking: How drink size affects risk assessment. *Addiction* 96(8):1199–1209, 2001. (26 refs.)

Li Q, Fisher WW, Peng CZ, Williams AD, Burd L. Fetal alcohol spectrum disorders: A population based study of premature mortality rates in the mothers. *Maternal and Child Health Journal* 16(6):1332–1337, 2012. (36 refs.)

Linowski SA, DiFulvio GT. Mobilizing for change: A case study of a campus and community coalition to reduce high-risk drinking. *Journal of Community Health* 37(3):685–693, 2012. (25 refs.)

Macy RJ, Goodbourn M. Promoting successful collaborations between domestic violence and substance abuse treatment service sectors: A review of the literature (review). *Trauma, Violence & Abuse* 13(4):234–251, 2012. (40 refs.)

Manwell LB, Fleming MF, Mundt MP, Stauffacher EA, Barry KL. Treatment of problem alcohol use in women of childbearing age: Results of a brief intervention trial. *Alcoholism: Clinical and Experimental Research* 24(10):1517–1524, 2000. (38 refs.)

McCabe SE, Hughes TL, Bostwick WB, West BT, Boyd CJ. Sexual orientation, substance use behaviors and substance dependence in the United States. *Addiction* 104(8):1333–1345, 2009. (65 refs.)

Office of Applied Studies, Substance Abuse and Mental Health Administration. *The NSDUH Report: Alcohol Use Among Pregnant Women and Recent Mothers: 2002 to 2007* (September 11, 2008). Rockville MD: Substance Abuse and Mental Health Administration, 2009.

Office of Applied Studies, Substance Abuse and Mental Health Administration. *The NSDUH Report: Substance Use Among Women During Pregnancy and Following Childbirth* (May 21, 2009). Rockville MD: Substance Abuse and Mental Health Administration, 2009.

Wilsnack SC, Hughes TL, Johnson TP, Bostwick WB, Szalacha LA, Benson P, et al. Drinking and drinking-related problems among heterosexual and sexual minority women. *Journal of Studies on Alcohol and Drugs* 69(1):129–139, 2008. (16 refs.)

The Workplace

Arcury TA, Quandt SA, Preisser JS, Bernert JT, Norton D, Wang J. High levels of transdermal nicotine exposure produce green tobacco sickness in Latino farmworkers. *Nicotine & Tobacco Research* 5(3):315–321, 2003. (27 refs.)

Arjomandi M, Haight T, Redberg R, Gold WM. Pulmonary function abnormalities in never-smoking flight attendants exposed to secondhand tobacco smoke in the aircraft cabin. *Journal of Occupational and Environmental Medicine* 51(6):639–646, 2009. (53 refs.)

Bush DM. The US Mandatory Guidelines for Federal Workplace Drug Testing Programs: Current status and future considerations. *Forensic Science International* 174(2–3):111–119, 2008. (10 refs.)

Cowell AJ, Bray JW, Hinde JM. The cost of screening and brief intervention in employee assistance programs. *Journal of Behavioral Health Services & Research* 39(1):55–67, 2012. (44 refs.)

Frone MR. Prevalence and distribution of alcohol use and impairment in the workplace: A US national survey. *Journal of Studies on Alcohol* 67(1):147–156, 2006. (28 refs.)

Giannakoulas G, Katramados A, Melas N, Diamantopoulos I, Chimonas E. Acute effects of nicotine withdrawal syndrome in pilots during flight. *Aviation, Space, and Environmental Medicine* 74(3):247–251, 2003. (74 refs.)

Halpern MT, Dirani R, Schmier JK. Impacts of a smoking cessation benefit among employed populations. *Journal of Occupational and Environmental Medicine* 49(1):11–21, 2007. (32 refs.)

Jacobson JM, Sacco P. Employee assistance program services for alcohol and other drug problems: Implications for increased identification and engagement in treatment. *American Journal on Addictions* 21(5):468–475, 2012. (71 refs.)

Jordan N, Grissom G, Alonzo G, Dietzen L, Sangsland S. Economic benefit of chemical dependency treatment to employers. *Journal of Substance Abuse Treatment* 34(3): 311–319, 2008. (24 refs.)

Lopez MAC, Fontaneda I, Alcantara OJG, Ritzel DO. The special severity of occupational accidents in the afternoon: "The lunch effect." *Accident Analysis and Prevention* 43(3):1104–1116, 2011. (34 refs.)

Mossakowski KN. Is the duration of poverty and unemployment a risk factor for heavy drinking? *Social Science & Medicine* 67(6):947–955, 2008. (60 refs.)

Ozminkowski RJ, Mark TL, Goetzel RZ, Blank D, Walsh JM, Cangianelli L. Relationships between urinalysis testing for substance use, medical expenditures, and the occurrence of injuries at a large manufacturing firm. *American Journal of Drug and Alcohol Abuse* 29(1):151–167, 2003. (25 refs.)

Phan HM, Yoshizuka K, Murry DJ, Perry PJ. Drug testing in the workplace (review). *Pharmacotherapy* 32(7):649–656, 2012. (20 refs.)

Siegel M, Skeer M. Exposure to secondhand smoke and excess lung cancer mortality risk among workers in the "5 B's": Bars, bowling alleys, billiard halls, betting establishments, and bingo parlours. *Tobacco Control* 12(3):333–338, 2004. (42 refs.)

Walsh JM. New technology and new initiatives in US workplace testing. *Forensic Science International* 174(2/3):120–124, 2008. (18 refs.)

Webb G, Shakeshaft A, Sanson-Fisher R, Havard A. A systematic review of work-place interventions for alcohol-related problems (review). *Addiction* 104(3):365–377, 2009. (28 refs.)

Weisner C, Lu Y, Hinman A, Monahan J, Bonnie RJ, Moore CD, et al. Substance use, symptom, and employment outcomes of persons with a workplace mandate for chemical dependency treatment. *Psychiatric Services* 60(5):646–654, 2009. (42 refs.)

Other Psychiatric Considerations

Substance use disorders are in themselves psychiatric conditions. In this chapter, the focus is on broader psychiatric issues of importance for the substance abuse clinician. These topics include suicide evaluation and prevention, the elements of the mental status examination, the major categories of co-occurring psychiatric illness, and the medications used in their treatment. The classifications for mental illness are important on several counts. First, some clients will have a separate, coexisting psychiatric illness in addition to their alcohol or drug use disorder. Second, many colleagues are from the mental health field. It is important to be comfortable with the terminology they use and issues with which they deal. Finally, alcohol or other substance use problems often mimic psychiatric conditions. Being informed about these conditions is vital when the task is determining whether the behavior being observed or reported is a symptom of a substance use problem or another psychiatric illness.

☐ SUICIDE EVALUATION AND PREVENTION

Substance use—alcohol use, in particular—and suicide go together. Recall from Chapter 1 that in a substantial number of suicide attempts the individual has been drinking, and that approximately 40% of all completed suicides are alcohol-related. The suicide rate for those with a serious alcohol disorder is 50 times that of the general population. Before we are overwhelmed by these statistics, we should consider why suicide and alcohol are connected and what we can do about this.

For practical purposes, clinicians need to consider several groups when thinking about suicide. First are the *completers,* those who take their lives and intended to. Classically, these are lonely white men over 50 years of age or lonely teenagers. They use violent means, such as a gun or hanging. Their methods are calculated and secretive.

Second are those who succeed but did not intend to. These are the *attempters.* Classically, they are white women, ages 20 to 40, often with interpersonal conflicts, who use pills. The suicide attempt is often an impulsive response. Attempters die by mistake or as a result of miscalculation. For example, they lose track of dosage, or something goes wrong with their plans for rescue. The attempter does not intend to die but hopes to elicit a response from others. Emergency room psychology, which dismisses these clients with irritation and anger, is inappropriate. Someone who is trying to gain attention by attempting suicide is in reality ill and deserves care.

Third are the *threateners.* These are individuals who use suicide as a lethal weapon: "If you leave me, I'll kill myself." They are often involved in a pathological relationship. Threateners usually do not follow through, but they are frightened and guilt-ridden. In responding to them, the therapist will attempt to challenge the threat and thereby remove the deadlock it has created.

Finally, there are those termed *parasuicidal.* These people harm themselves for the release of either tension or emotional pain. Commonly, they have a history of physical or sexual abuse or severe neglect as children. Though they may intentionally seriously injure themselves, they usually do not have suicide in mind when they do so. They differ from attempters in that their impetus is not to get the attention of others but to relieve internal emotional pain. However, there are often errors, and deaths occur.

Statistics and High-Risk Factors

The statistic to keep in mind is that suicide is the second-leading recorded cause of death in people under 18 or over 65 years of age. Sixty percent give some prior indication of their intent, thereby making suicide preventable. Typical indications include hypothetical statements such as "I have a friend who has been feeling down . . ." or "What would you think if someone said . . . ?" People planning to commit suicide may stockpile drugs or give away possessions. New behaviors can be important cues. When people begin doing things they have never done before, they may be signaling that they have suddenly decided to commit suicide and are now at peace. For example, they might start playing cards, dancing, or taking out the garbage when they have never done so before.

Certain high-risk factors should be identified. These include experiencing the recent loss of a loved one; being single, widowed, or childless; living in an urban area; and being unemployed, non-religious, or "oppressed." High-risk emotional factors include anger plus hopelessness, broken or pathological family/friend communications, and isolation in a marriage or another ongoing relationship. Verbal high-risk cues can take the form of both direct statements, "I'm going to kill myself," or indirect indications, "I won't be around to give you any more trouble." People entering and leaving a depression are especially vulnerable, as are those with chronic illnesses, such as arthritis, high blood pressure, ulcers, and malignancies.

Drunkenness is temporary suicide.
—Bertrand Russell

Recall that 40% of all suicide attempts are related to alcohol. There are several factors behind this correlation. First, the chemical nature of alcohol tends to release certain brain areas from control. Guarding mechanisms are let down. Hidden thoughts and impulses are released. (You may have witnessed incidents such as an intoxicated employee calling the boss a creep.) Second, the alcohol creates a state wherein the integrative capacity of the brain is diminished—a condition in which aspects of memory and concentration are lost. Third, alcohol initially produces a mood of relaxation and pseudo-stability. In this state, people may think things are just the way they should be. They feel cool, calm, and collected, so that suicide at this point may seem relevant and a good idea: "I'll just jump. It's the rational solution." More alcohol acts as a true depressant, with obvious potential consequences. Finally, alcohol may also bring out psychological vulnerabilities. It may place people on the edge of reality, lead to loose associations, bring out psychosis, disinhibit normal fears, and produce voices, saying, "The world is better off without you." In all these cases, alcohol acts as a catalyst, both physically and psychologically.

Clinical depression provides the most fertile grounds for suicide. Most people who simply have the blues are not suicidal. They might think, "Gee, I wish I were dead; things are going so badly," or "I don't know how I'll make it. I might just drive off the road if things don't get better." Things usually do get better, however. On the other hand, clinical depression is characterized by a consistently low mood over a period of weeks, plus weight changes, sleep problems, and other physical symptoms. Pessimism is a symptom of the illness, just as fever is a symptom of the flu. The depressant effects of alcohol can synergize with symptoms of depression, leading to suicidal conclusions: "There is no way out," or "I'm a bad person—the only way out is to kill myself."

How to Ask About Suicide

The therapist should always ask about suicide when talking with any person who is depressed. Always remember that therapists have never killed anybody by asking, although they have certainly missed the chance to help people by *not* asking. You won't instigate a suicidal attempt via a commonsense question. In fact, your clients will be relieved if you do ask them. Use your own emotional barometer to find out whether they are depressed or whether they are sad. Check yourself in an interview every so often. Block out the client for a moment and ask yourself, "How am *I* feeling right now? Am I sad, angry, scared? What am I feeling?" It's probably a pretty good barometer of how the client is feeling. Clients often say they feel great; check your own gut reactions and trust them.

Ask every client about suicide, but let rapport develop first. Don't ask intimate questions, such as "How's your sex life?" "Been hallucinating lately?" or "Feel like killing yourself?" as soon as the client walks in—he or she will probably want to kill you. Let rapport develop, and later say, "Now, we've talked about a lot of things these past 20 minutes. Have any of them ever gotten you to the point of feeling you couldn't go on any longer?" Don't leave it there; explain that you are asking about suicide. Always say the word "suicide." Do not just ask clients if they have ever thought of "throwing in the towel" or some other euphemism. They can take you quite literally and might say, "Well, no. I dried myself pretty well this morning." You have to get yourself to say "suicide." Practice. It's not so easy to come right out and say it. The first few times it bombs, something like this: "Gee, we've talked about a lot of things. Have any of them ever gotten you to the point of thinking about committing s-s-ah-s-th-?" It's almost the kind of thing you need to practice in front of a mirror: "Su-i-cide. Suicide." Another straightforward approach is to ask, "Have these things upset you enough that you've had thoughts of killing yourself?" Again, no room for misinterpretation here.

Clients may say, "Boy, you're kidding!" but it's not a hostile response. If anybody does say yes—and the client probably will tell you if he or she has been thinking about it—obtain as much information as you can. Ask, "Well, when was the last time you thought of it?" and "How about today?" Find out when the client last thought of suicide. What was the person doing when the thoughts surfaced? Ascertain the plans for committing suicide as specifically as possible. It is crucial to know how close the client is to taking action on suicidal thoughts. In cases of most serious intent, the client will probably say, "Well, not only have I been thinking of it today, but I've been cleaning my gun. It's in my car, and my car's outside." In other words, get all the data.

Responding to Suicidal Patients

Try to defuse the situation psychologically and in practical ways. For instance, offer alternatives, such as "On the other hand, what specific reasons do you have for living?" Try to get to a positive reason. Start initiating reasons to live. The more seriously depressed the client, the fewer reasons will come to mind. Remember, that is part of the illness. The client will say, "Nothing," and cry. At that point, try to reiterate things you've already been told that are reasons to live—a child, a spouse, a business. Provide the reason to live: "That child really needs you." If the client comes up with even one reason, support that enthusiastically: "You're right. . . . Yes!" Back the client up. Fill in the picture, and lead him or her into ways to stay safe. This usually means identifying how the client can remove any weapons from the home (and following up with any responsible parties at home to ensure this has happened). Also identify who the client can spend the next 24 hours with and any practical safety plan that minimizes aloneness and maximizes exposure to deterrents. Calling (or helping the client call) a close relative to ensure the client can be in a supportive environment during such times of instability is always a good practice.

It's also important to make a referral, whenever possible, to a mental health clinic or mental health specialist. As a counselor, you have a key role in identifying potential suicides. You cannot expect that you will be able to single-handedly treat and manage the situation. Request a consultation for further evaluation. Possibly the person has a clinical depression and needs medication or the supervision of an inpatient facility. In that case, call and make an appointment before the client leaves the office. In conjunction with the mental health clinic, a decision can be made about how quickly the person should be seen—immediately, later today, or tomorrow. If immediately, send the patient to the nearest emergency room to be evaluated by a mental health professional. If the client is already being seen by a therapist, contact the therapist. A therapist who is unaware of the situation will want to know and will be able to provide guidance for you, so that you are working together. Don't be afraid you are stepping on anyone's toes. Anybody contemplating suicide cannot have too many people in his or her corner.

Maybe here we can lay to rest any discomfort that arises from the philosophical debates on whether someone has a right to commit suicide. There is considerable discussion about the right to die. Looking at it realistically, anyone who thinks he or she has that right wouldn't be in your office but would have carried out the plan. Anyone who "happens" into a counselor's office, or phones, and acknowledges suicidal thoughts, directly or indirectly, is not there by chance. These individuals are seeking help in settling the internal debate over life versus death. You must come down clearly on the side of living. When depressed, a client cannot rationally make this decision. Once the depression clears, most clients are very pleased that you interfered with their suicide plans.

Hi, I'm Mr. Jones. Ms. Willow, my alcohol counselor, said I had to leave my weapons at the reception desk.

Comments on Safety

If a client has a weapon, ask that it be checked at the reception desk or elsewhere on the premises. Or have the client give you the weapon personally if necessary. If it is at home, ask that someone else take possession of it and notify you when that is done. Even if a client's mood improves during the interview—and it usually improves during the interview—never let a client who is suicidal leave your office without your double-checking the person's plans for the rest of the day. Be specific. Call home to make sure someone will be there, if that is the expectation. Give the client chores and support. Have somebody there to watch the client around the clock and to give the attention he or she needs. Set up another appointment to see the person within 48 hours. Have the client call you to check in later that day, or you can call the client. Be specific. Say, "I'd like to call you between 4 and 5," or at least "this afternoon." It is better not to give an exact time because that is often hard to meet. This kind of paternalism is needed at such a time. Fostering independence can come later. Give reinforcements: "What do you like to do? What do you have to do? Do it and let me know how it goes."

Be wary of the following situations when you are talking with clients: If the client's theme is rejection and loss, for example, be careful you don't reject the person or put him or her off. Also, take care to avoid supporting negative feelings. If you agree with the client about how bad things are—for example, the client says, "I am a worthless person. I beat my child"—you might find yourself conveying your negative feelings about this. You might communicate, "Well, you're right; that was a horrible thing to do." Don't support the punitive guilt response. Similarly, expressions of empathy can be misplaced. When clients say how miserable they feel, you may be tempted to say, "I understand how bad you feel. I often feel that way myself." You're trying to sympathize and share the misery, but clients interpret this as permission to feel the way they do. You're getting away from the reasons the client has to live and are underscoring the pessimism.

Get histories of previous suicide attempts. Anyone who has tried it once has a poor track record. A family history of suicide, other losses in childhood from divorce or illnesses, or a history of childhood sexual abuse also increases the risk. If a client either has already attempted suicide or is thinking about it, reduce that person's isolation from family and friends. Hospitalization under close supervision may be needed if supports are lacking. Remove access to guns, ropes, pills, and so on. Shake hands with the client as he or she leaves the office, and give something of yourself for the person to take along, such as a piece of paper with your name and phone number. Try to make sure the client does not have what would constitute a lethal dosage of medication.

You need to think ahead of time about special situations that might occur. If you happen to get involved in an emergency in which someone is about to shoot him- or herself, jump from a window ledge, or do something else rash, try to be calm. Keep your voice down. Don't ask philosophical questions, but ask practical questions: "What's your name?" or "Where are you from?" Try to have a non-threatening conversation. This is a grueling situation and can last for hours. Wear the person down. Do not ever be a hero. Do not rush a person with a gun. Stay alive to help the people who can be helped.

In dealing with suicide, trust your gut reactions, but, most important, don't feel that it is your fault if you are unsuccessful.

☐ MENTAL STATUS EXAMINATION

The mental status examination is a tool used by mental health professionals to guide observation and to assist the interviewer in gathering essential data about mental functioning. It consists of standard items, which are routinely covered, ensuring that nothing important is overlooked. The format also helps mental health workers record their findings in a fashion that is easily understood by their colleagues.

Three aspects of mental functioning are standard parts of a mental status examination: mood and affect, thought processes, and cognitive functioning. "Mood and affect" refer to the dominant feeling state. They are deduced from the feelings the client reports and the client's general emotional appearance. "Thought processes" zero in on how the client presents his or her ideas. Are the thoughts ordered and organized, or does the client jump all over the place? Are the sentences logical? Is the content sensible, or does it include delusions and bizarre ideas? Finally, "cognitive functioning" refers to intellectual functioning, memory, ability to concentrate, comprehension, and ability to abstract. This portion of the mental status examination involves asking specific questions about current events, definitions of words, or meanings of proverbs. The interviewer considers the individual's education, lifestyle, and occupation in making a judgment about the responses.

Becoming skilled in doing a simple mental status examination can help you spot clients with particular problems. It can also greatly facilitate your communication with mental health workers. Just telling a psychiatrist or psychiatric social worker that the person you are referring is "crazier than a bedbug" isn't very useful.

☐ MAJOR CATEGORIES OF CO-OCCURRING PSYCHIATRIC ILLNESS

Understanding the relationship between alcohol or other drug use and mood, thoughts, or behavior is one of the most challenging and essential components of anyone's work in the substance abuse field. An effort to determine the relative contributions of addictive and non-addictive psychiatric disorders to abnormal mental states is essential for several reasons. First, the prevalence of co-occurring psychiatric disorders is so great in persons with alcohol use disorders that having a co-occurring psychiatric condition is an expectation, not an exception, in treatment settings. Second, studies have shown that the risk of having a problem with alcohol use increases 10 times if a person has schizophrenia or 15 times if a person has an antisocial personality disorder. Third, alcohol dependence and withdrawal can produce symptoms that resemble many other psychiatric disorders. For this reason, psychiatry, perhaps more than any other medical discipline, must respect alcohol disorders as "the great mimicker." Fourth, the co-occurrence of a psychiatric condition with an alcohol disorder significantly worsens the clinical course and outcomes for individuals with both disorders. Because of this, it is imperative that all mental health workers screen for and assess alcohol use disorders for all people seeking mental health treatment and that all addiction staff screen for and assess co-occurring psychiatric disorders. Furthermore, if alcohol or drug use co-occurs with another psychiatric disorder, both disorders should be treated concurrently and aggressively. An integrated treatment plan is a necessity.

In this text, we have placed considerable emphasis on the fact that psychological problems are not the cause of alcohol disorders per se. However, in remembering that message, don't lose sight of the fact that an individual may have both an alcohol problem and another psychiatric condition. Whether dependence grows in the soil of some other psychiatric condition (sometimes termed "secondary" or "reactive alcoholism") or whether it co-occurs with another psychiatric problem, when present, it develops a momentum of its own. The client's ability to establish and maintain sobriety may be dependent on actively treating other psychiatric conditions as well. The clinician confronted by clients with co-occurring addictive and mental disorders faces both diagnostic and treatment challenges, and all too frequently the client faces administrative and systemic barriers.

The next eight sections cover the major classes of psychiatric illness as they relate to alcohol use disorders.

Mood Disorders

Mood and emotion are what you feel and how you show it. Mood disorders are feelings that go beyond the normal experiences of sadness or elation. About 9% of Americans suffer some form of mood disorder every year. There are two extremes—people who are manic and those who are depressed—and those who fluctuate between these two extremes, a condition termed bipolar disorder. Lesser degrees of depression over longer periods of time are called dysthymia, and a lesser degree of mania is termed hypomania.

People in a *manic episode* show characteristic behavior. Often they have grand schemes, which seem outlandish to others. Their conversation is very quick and pressured. Often they jump from topic to topic. They may watch two television shows at the same time while they look through magazines. In a conversation about the state of the union, a person in a manic episode might say, "And, yes, Texas is a very pretty state. Former President Bush was the governor of the state, and the governor of my car is out of kilter. The left tire is flat, out of air like a balloon. Suzy got a balloon at the circus where she stained her best dress with cotton candy . . ." Although there is a logical connection among these thoughts, there is an inability to concentrate on any single thought. This pattern of thinking is termed "flight of ideas." One thought is immediately crowded out by the next. Someone who is manic may also be aggressive and irritable or, alternatively, may feel very attractive, sexually irresistible, or capable of superhuman performance. This is termed "grandiosity." People in a manic episode are perpetually in high gear, have difficulty sleeping, and may have trouble concentrating. Simply being in their company might make you feel exhausted, and the stress they place on their families cannot be overstated. Auditory and visual hallucinations complicate the more extreme forms of mania. About 13% of those who enter alcohol treatment also have mania as a separate psychiatric disorder.

Depression, the other side of the mood coin and far more common, has all the opposite characteristics. Rather than being hyped up, people with depression grind to a halt. They find very little pleasure in most activities and often feel hopeless. Movements, speech, and thinking may be slowed down. Biological changes can accompany depression and are called vegetative symptoms. These include disturbances of normal sleep patterns, slowed motor activity, changes in appetite, and weight loss or gain. Of note, women are far more likely than men to present with symptoms of depression. In extremes, the person with depression stops eating, is unable to rest, experiences a complete depletion of energy, and expends available motor energy in repeated, purposeless motions, such as hand-wringing and pacing. Such depression is associated with a sense of self-reproach, irrational guilt—especially over the burden that they feel they place on others—worthlessness, hopelessness, and loss of interest in life. In full force, these phenomena may culminate in suicidal thoughts, plans, or actions. In psychological autopsies after a completed suicide, depression is found in up to 70% of the deaths. Severe depression is a life-threatening disorder. About 14% of those seeking alcohol treatment have a co-occurring major depression, and 11% have dysthymia.

Most depression and mania are believed to have a biological basis. They are also episodic disorders. Between episodes, the mood states typically return to normal. This is not to imply that one simply sits back and waits for the manic or depressive episode to pass. Just as suicide is an ever-present possibility with depression, individuals with mania may incur phenomenal life problems, which may wreak havoc for themselves as well as for their families. These conditions are highly treatable with medications (see the section Psychotropic Medications, later in this chapter). Talking therapies, particularly cognitive behavioral therapies, may be helpful in less severe conditions but are of little use when someone's perception of reality and thought processes are seriously altered.

Alcohol use and alcohol disorders are intertwined with mood disorders in several ways. Those with mood disorders are at higher risk of developing a co-occurring alcohol use disorder and should be warned of this possibility as a preventive measure. In individuals with primary depression, 20% to 30% report increased alcohol intake during their mood disturbance. Up to 40% of people with alcohol use disorders seeking treatment will have a mood disorder, the vast majority of which are not alcohol-induced and require treatment. Although most co-occurring mood disorders are not caused by drinking, alcohol consumption can cause depressive symptoms in anyone. Alcohol can produce a toxic depressive state that embraces the full range of depression's symptoms, including anorexia, insomnia, physical complaints, suicidal thoughts, and despair. Experimental studies have demonstrated that heavy drinking can induce depressive symptoms. This is true in both those with alcohol dependence and those without dependence. A temporary depression is frequently described as a feature of dependence and tends to remit with abstinence.

It is estimated that 4% to 15% of those with a serious alcohol disorder commit suicide. Conversely, of those who commit suicide, 40% have a history of an alcohol use disorder. Although suicidal behavior in general increases when under the influence, those with an alcohol problem attempt suicide far more often when drinking than those without an alcohol problem. Several factors contribute to this. An alcohol disorder may be an indicator of a suicide-prone individual; the condition itself can be considered a form of slow suicide. The loss of cognitive function resulting from alcohol abuse creates an increasing gap between personal expectations and actual performance, resulting in despair. Beyond the acute effects of the drug alcohol, chronic alcohol abuse often leads to deteriorating social relations, loss of employment, homelessness, associated trauma, and loss of health, which are factors also associated with depressed states. The multiple losses that often beset those dependent on alcohol can compound the sense of hopelessness. In assessing suicide potential among those with alcohol abuse or dependence, further risk factors to consider are the loss of a close interpersonal relationship within the previous six weeks, unemployment, serious medical illness, living alone, and suicide communications. The alcohol-dependent person with suicidal thoughts, whether inebriated or not, needs to be taken seriously.

Melancholy should be diverted by every means but drinking.
-Dr. Johnson

Because some symptoms of depression are the result of alcohol dependence—representing a secondary substance-induced depression—abstinence indirectly treats the depression symptoms. In other instances, it is likely that the depression will not lift with abstinence and alcohol treatment. At the point of entry into treatment, it may be difficult to get the information needed to distinguish initially between an independent, primary depression and depression that results from an alcohol disorder. The client may have difficulty providing an accurate chronology of events due to cognitive deficits that are a part of both the alcohol problem and the depression. The most reliable information is often provided by family and friends.

If the depressive symptoms lift with abstinence, then a clinician can be confident that the mood disturbance was secondary to the alcohol abuse. However, research suggests most depression in persons with alcohol use disorders is independent of the alcohol use. If intense, depressed symptoms persistent after several weeks of abstinence, then the clinician

should consider the possibility of a co-occurring mood disorder, and concurrent treatment for depression would be indicated.

An extended period of sobriety before making the diagnosis of depression, though preferable, may not always be possible. On occasion, the clinician may be so impressed with the severity of depressive symptoms that waiting for weeks or months cannot be justified. This is critical, because without effective integrated treatment these clients are likely to see themselves as treatment failures. For them, things have not gotten better with sobriety. Also, they may be urged by AA friends or treatment personnel simply to "work the program harder." In fact, they have been giving it their all. All treatment programs for persons abusing alcohol must include education about depression—including information on its biological basis and how medications can be useful. Discomfort may surface around the use of medications, especially because many treatment programs caution clients about the dangers of psychoactive drug use. Clients need to be reassured that the medications prescribed for depression have no addiction potential and are not associated with abuse. It is important to keep in mind that several medical conditions, for example, thyroid disease, can cause mood disorders as well.

Another association between mood disorders and alcohol use is that drinking can escalate during the period of mood disturbance. Research indicates that 20% to 60% of clients with bipolar disorder report excessive use of alcohol during the manic phase of their illness. It is unclear whether this is an effort to self-medicate their disturbing manic symptoms or whether it is a result of the poor judgment that is part of this phase of the illness. Regardless of why alcohol use increases, the consequences of the disinhibiting effects of alcohol, on top of the impaired judgment generally present, are often disastrous. The focus of therapy for bipolar clients with alcohol abuse is two-pronged. The primary disorder may require medication (lithium, other mood stabilizers, and/or antipsychotic agents) while simultaneous counseling and education are necessary to address alcohol use issues.

Many times, a reactive depression may be seen in family members. One out of three American families has direct contact with someone who has a serious alcohol problem. Family members may develop depression as their defenses are overwhelmed by the constant stress of dealing with emotional and physical abuse, economic instability, and their perceived impotence to change their loved one's behavior. Obviously, for most, a referral to Al-Anon or an alcohol treatment program is far more appropriate than a prescription for antidepressant medications.

Disorders Involving Psychosis

Psychosis is a disturbance of perception and thought processes that is frequently associated with disturbances in function. Psychotic symptoms may be associated with a variety of psychiatric disorders, including substance-related disorders, but they are often prominent in schizophrenic disorders. Schizophrenia and other psychotic disorders are a group of chronic, fluctuating disturbances that are among the most incapacitating of the mental disorders. They exact an enormous cost in human suffering and public and private resources. These disorders have a biochemical basis but are subject to environmental influences.

Schizophrenia occurs in about 1% of the general population. Schizophrenia is heterogeneous in its presentation. Those with schizophrenia may have "positive" or "negative" symptoms. Positive symptoms include hallucinations (a sensory perception with no corresponding stimulus), delusions (fixed, false beliefs), and incoherence of thought with resultant disorganized speech. Negative symptoms include shyness or withdrawal from social contacts, difficulty communicating, and a restricted emotional range, making someone appear dull and listless. Attention and cognitive disturbances are frequently present. Attempts to communicate are difficult because the person with schizophrenia may perceive reality very differently than others do. The individual with schizophrenia often misinterprets environmental stimuli. This altered perception can be very subtle or very marked. Clients with schizophrenia may make unwarranted connections between events. For example, a client may hear a car backfire, see the landlord in the hallway, and develop a concern that the landlord is "out to get me." If the client then hears imaginary voices saying, "He'll shoot first, ask questions later," the person's sense of paranoia becomes even greater. The treatment of schizophrenic disorders, as well as other psychotic disorders, includes medications (see the following section) as well as ongoing supportive counseling and other rehabilitative efforts.

Some conditions associated with alcohol abuse closely resemble psychotic disorders. One study found a history of psychotic symptoms in over 40% of those with alcohol dependence who sought treatment. One such condition that may be misdiagnosed and thus lead to the inappropriate use of antipsychotic medication is that of *alcoholic hallucinosis* (see Chapter 6). Although seen in less than 3% of those with chronic alcoholism, it is easily confused with schizophrenia. Most commonly it is part of withdrawal states, but it can also occur in an actively drinking individual. The symptoms include auditory, tactile, or visual hallucinations, and the person typically develops persecutory delusions related to these hallucinations.

FORMAL THOUGHT DISORDER

Several features help distinguish alcohol hallucinosis from schizophrenia. The client has a history of heavy alcohol use. The majority of those with this condition will have their first episode after the age of 40, while schizophrenia typically appears earlier in life, in the early to mid-20s. The client usually has no family history of schizophrenia, but there may be a family history of alcohol dependence. Unlike schizophrenia, there is little evidence of a formal thought disorder—for example, loose associations and disorganization of thinking. The content of the hallucinations is fairly simple, unlike the less understandable or bizarre hallucinations of schizophrenia. In alcohol hallucinosis, the resolution of these symptoms is usually quick, occurring over the course of one to six days. Management should include hospitalization, close observation, and some minor tranquilizers. *Wernicke-Korsakoff syndrome* (see Chapter 6) also includes psychotic symptoms. This is an irreversible organic brain syndrome resulting from chronic alcohol abuse; it is characterized by prominent memory impairment and striking personality changes.

It is estimated that an alcohol use disorder co-occurs with schizophrenia 14% to 50% of the time. In such cases, symptoms may be seen with levels of alcohol consumption that would typically not be thought of as problematic in the general population. The combination of schizophrenia and alcohol abuse often results in a rocky clinical course and a poor prognosis. Without specialized services, these individuals may have difficulty complying with any treatment plan. They frequently do not take medications as prescribed and may be unwilling or unable to follow recommendations for abstinence from alcohol. Efforts to end drinking in this population must be based on an assessment of what alcohol provides for the individual. If drinking is used to reduce anxiety around hallucinations, then increasing antipsychotic medication may be appropriate. If drinking is used to reduce uncomfortable side effects from antipsychotic medication, then a reduction in or substitution of medications may be necessary. If drinking represents an effort to achieve peer acceptance, then non-alcohol-centered social alternatives should be developed. For these clients, the need for compliance with prescribed medication cannot be overemphasized. Abstinence for some persons with schizophrenia may be indicated because even moderate drinking may, for them, be disruptive, suggesting a vulnerability to the effects of alcohol.

When schizophrenia is accompanied by alcohol abuse, patients may see the standard alcohol or drug treatment regimen as threatening. Poor treatment outcomes in traditional alcohol treatment settings are associated with the severity of psychiatric symptoms. Persons with schizophrenia tend to do poorly in group settings with lots of confrontation. But the same patients can be treated quite effectively in less threatening groups. In recent years attention has turned to matching treatment interventions to the motivational state of the patient. Engagement, persuasion, active treatment, and relapse prevention phases have been outlined to guide treatment planning and treatment goals. Incorporating motivational interviewing techniques can accelerate movement through the phases of recovery. If AA is to be used as part of the treatment plan, these clients must be thoroughly prepared for AA experiences after they have accepted the need for abstinence. The host group should be assessed in advance for receptiveness to the psychiatrically impaired. Specialized dual recovery self-help groups for this are ideal and are increasingly available in many regions. Recent reviews of integrated treatment for schizophrenia and alcohol use disorders have shown promising results in achieving stable recovery and improved functioning.

Anxiety Disorders

Anxiety disorders are relatively common and involve incapacitating nervousness, tension, apprehension, and fear. These symptoms may appear episodically and without warning, as in panic attacks. The anxiety may be a fear of particular places or situations (*agoraphobia*), or the anxiety may be a symptom of fearing a specific object, such as spiders (a simple *phobia*). For others it may take the form of unrelenting, recurrent ideas (*obsessions*) or the need to perform repetitive rituals (*compulsions*). The anxious person may experience physical symptoms, including diaphoresis (sweating), tremor, nausea, diarrhea, pallor, rapid pulse, shortness of breath, headache, or fatigue. These "panic attacks" can be very frightening. In contrast to other mental disorders, which may also be associated with a significant amount of anxiety, the anxiety disorders do not involve major disturbances in mood, thought, or judgment. Care must be taken to rule out other medical problems or medications as the cause of anxiety symptoms.

The relationship of anxiety disorders to alcohol problems remains controversial. As with mood disorders, the anxiety experienced may be independent of or may be secondary to an alcohol disorder. Most clinicians know clients who drink to control symptoms of panic or phobic disorders. This self-medication may then take on a life of its own, leading to an alcohol disorder. There is a high prevalence of anxiety disorders among those in alcohol treatment. Several studies have reported the rate of associated anxiety disorders to be in a range between 22% and 44%, with specific phobias most common, followed by generalized anxiety disorder in frequency. Investigators concede that the sequence of anxiety and drinking is highly variable among individuals.

Understanding the relationship of anxiety symptoms to the drinking behavior is essential. Abstinence alone may "cure" the anxious symptoms if they are the consequences of drinking. On the other hand, severe anxiety may increase the dually diagnosed client's vulnerability to relapse. Treatment decisions must be based on a careful history of symptoms and observation of the individual following detoxification. If a co-occurring anxiety disorder is felt to be present, an integrated treatment plan might include the use of psychotherapy, behavioral therapy, as well as medications. Participation in safe, supportive twelve-step programs may reduce the symptoms of anxiety disorders. Antidepressants, such as venlafaxine (Effexor) or sertraline (Zoloft), are very effective with certain anxiety disorders and have very little abuse potential. Benzodiazepines are often effective for the symptoms of anxiety, but because of their high abuse potential, they should be lower on the list of medication alternatives. Buspirone (BuSpar), which has no euphoric properties and has a good safety profile and few drug interactions, can be useful in treating an anxiety disorder in individuals with a physical dependence on alcohol. Cautious prescribing practices and regular monitoring of clinical progress will minimize the risk of drug abuse and maximize the chances of successful recovery.

An anxiety disorder worth particular mention is *post-traumatic stress disorder* (PTSD). It can occur when someone experiences, witnesses, or hears about a *trauma* (a life-threatening or otherwise horror-inducing event). This might be living through a natural disaster or its aftermath, such as Hurricane Katrina, or being in a war zone, whether as a soldier or a civilian, or experiencing a physical attack, such as a rape. As can well be imagined, such events have an impact. For several weeks most people who have gone through a trauma will "play it back" in their minds, have trouble sleeping, and find talking about it difficult. However, most people, about 90%, return to normal functioning within a few weeks.

For the remaining 10%, the symptoms persist. While genetics may increase vulnerability, the more significant factors are the duration of the trauma and the type of event. The longer a trauma extends, the greater the odds of developing PTSD. Likewise, traumas that are perceived as having been caused by others, such as war or rape, are more likely to lead to PTSD than are events that are seen as natural disasters, such as an earthquake. Populations at particular risk for PTSD are combat veterans, sex workers, homeless people, refugees from high-conflict zones, and victims of sexual assault.

Typically PTSD has three major elements. Individuals find themselves *re-experiencing* the episode. This can occur while asleep in the form of recurring nightmares. Or it can occur when fully awake, in a flashback, which is re-experiencing the trauma as if watching it in a film. Another feature is *avoidance*. This entails efforts to avoid thoughts or conversations or attempts to stay away from people, places, or situations that may be reminders. The final element is *hypervigilance and hyperarousal*. These terms refer to the fact that those with PTSD are perpetually on guard, constantly scanning the environment, even in familiar settings, for possible dangers. Many times, grocery stores are intolerable for people with PTSD. Leaving a cartful of groceries to flee such an environment is commonplace. Something unexpected, such as a loud noise when a door closes, can cause the person to jump or have a violent startle reaction.

By putting an individual into a constant "fight or flight" mode and always on the alert, these symptoms can be thought of as the brain's way of keeping the victim "safe" from being re-traumatized. It appears the adrenaline (norepinephrine) system is involved because medications that reduce or block this neurotransmitter's action (clonidine, prazosin, and propranolol) help reduce such symptoms, while medications that increase norepinephrine function (yohimbine) can actually trigger flashbacks.

The person with PTSD is at considerable risk for developing substance abuse because each of these painful symptoms cries out for means to quiet, to soften, to deaden, and, if only temporarily, to forget and to turn off memory of the event. In screening individuals with possible PTSD, it is crucial to be sensitive to the fact that the client will not want to talk about the nature of his or her trauma. You will get a sense of this immediately when probing. It is more helpful to get a rough idea of the nature of the trauma and the chronicity, rather than to determine exactly what happened. Make a referral to a mental health professional if PTSD is suspected, as the client can benefit tremendously from medications as well as appropriate psychotherapeutic counseling.

Personality Disorders

Everyone has a unique set of personality traits that is evident in a range of social situations. When these traits are so rigid and maladaptive that they repeatedly interfere with a person's social or occupational functioning, they constitute a personality disorder. People with these disorders have the capacity "to get under everyone's skin." Ten types of personality disorders are described in the *DSM-IV-TR*, but the three most commonly associated with alcohol problems are the antisocial, obsessive-compulsive, and borderline types.

Antisocial Personality Disorder

Those with an antisocial personality disorder are frequently in trouble, getting into fights, conning others for personal profit, committing crimes, and having problems with authority. They seemingly just "wouldn't get with the program." There appears to be a genetic predisposition for development of antisocial personality disorder. This is independent of a genetic predisposition to develop alcohol dependence. Although these two disorders are not genetically linked, those with antisocial personality disorder are at high risk for developing an alcohol disorder. Studies have found rates of alcohol dependence as high as 20% in people with antisocial personality disorder. In addition, chronic heavy alcohol consumption can lead to personality changes that closely resemble the antisocial personality. However, these behaviors may disappear following abstinence. Studies have found that from 10% to 20% of men and about 5% to 10% of women in alcohol treatment facilities meet the criteria for antisocial personality disorder. Women with alcohol use disorders are six times more likely to have an antisocial personality disorder than women without alcohol problems. For this group as a whole, the prognosis is poor. Their social problems do not disappear with abstinence. They are generally resistant to any type of intervention, lack remorse for their behavior, and frequently alienate seemingly everyone—treatment personnel, members of a self-help community, as well as family.

Obsessive-Compulsive Personality Disorder

People with obsessive-compulsive personality disorder (OCPD) are preoccupied with perfectionism and control at the expense of flexibility and efficiency. They may repeatedly check to see whether doors are locked or ovens are turned off, sometimes missing important appointments. They may scrub a wall so often that the paint is worn off in their effort to eliminate germs. Things must be perfect and their effort to achieve this state may prevent them from finishing the task. They may hoard objects and sometimes get crowded out of their own living space by magazines, books, and "collectibles." Alcohol may initially give them a break from their ritualistic behavior, but it can quickly become a disorder in itself.

Typically those with OCPD are not in the least troubled by their rigid behavior patterns. (While potentially confusing, there is a wholly separate condition with a very similar name, Obsessive Compulsive Disorder, referred to as OCD. While having some characteristics in common, one of the distinguishing features is that those with OCD are typically tormented by intrusive thoughts as well as compulsions.)

Borderline Personality Disorder

Those with borderline personality disorder may act impulsively, with multiple suicide attempts; may exhibit inappropriate emotions, whether it's intense anger or putting on a facade of affection; may have feelings of emptiness or boredom; and may have frequent mood swings. They often use alcohol in chaotic and unpredictable patterns. People with borderline personality disorder often evoke strong negative feelings from their caregivers. Among those seeking treatment for alcohol dependence, 13% to 28% will have this personality disorder. Again, it is important to try to separate out the sequence of behavioral problems and alcohol abuse in developing appropriate treatment plans. All suicidal behavior, from threats to attempts, must be taken seriously. Treatment objectives include the creation of a safe and secure relationship and environment.

Attention-Deficit/Hyperactivity Disorder

Some children are unable to remain attentive in situations where it is socially necessary to do so. This is often first recognized in the challenging environment of elementary school, but it also can be apparent in the home. In the past these conditions were termed hyperactivity or minimal brain dysfunction; they are now known as attention-deficit/hyperactivity disorder (ADHD). ADHD occurs in 3% to 5% of school-aged children, and boys are four times more likely than girls to have the condition. Children with ADHD have an increased risk of a serious alcohol disorder in adulthood. It has been hypothesized that a subgroup of those with alcohol problems began drinking to stabilize areas of the brain that are "irritable" due to damage earlier in life. For them, alcohol can be considered self-medication. Alcohol may improve performance on cognitive tasks, allow better concentration, and offer a subjective sense of stability. Such a response to alcohol would be highly reinforcing and thus increase the risk of dependence.

With adults, it is very difficult to sort out the cognitive impairment caused by alcohol from a preexisting, underlying deficit. As is true with anxiety disorders, here too prolonged abstinence is desirable prior to making a diagnosis. On the other hand, these clients may be unable to achieve and maintain sobriety.

When confronted with an individual who has been through treatment several times and has never been able to establish sobriety, take a careful childhood history. If there is evidence of difficulties in school or other problems suggesting ADHD, further evaluation and use of medication may be recommended. The medication prescribed in such cases belongs to the stimulant class; however, for such clients it has a paradoxical "calming" effect. Use of these medications in childhood does not increase the risk of substance abuse later in life. Actually, the opposite is true. The failure to adequately treat ADHD during childhood places these kids at higher risk of substance abuse as adults.

Psychiatric Disorders Due to a General Medical Condition

A psychiatric disorder is diagnosed as due to a medical condition when the symptoms, based on evidence from the history, physical examination, or laboratory findings, are judged to be the direct physiological consequence of a medical condition. The causes can vary. For example, psychiatric disorders can result from trauma to the central nervous system, from a brain tumor, from a stroke, or from a variety of infections. These impairments in brain function limit the person's ability to think and respond meaningfully to the environment. Usually there are significant changes in cognitive function. Problems with memory, an inability to concentrate, or a loss of intellectual capacity are common.

These disorders can represent permanent impairment, or they can be completely reversible. Which of these outcomes occurs depends primarily on whether there has been only temporary interference with the brain's function (such as through the ingestion of drugs or an active infection of the brain) or whether there has been permanent damage to brain tissue. A reversible disorder due to a medical condition is called *delirium.* Typically the onset of delirium is rapid, and if the cause is identified and treated, the person may return to his or her usual self within days. Another component of delirium can be visual hallucinations, especially at night, which can be particularly terrifying.

Dementia, on the other hand, generally refers to irreversible changes in cognitive function due to medical conditions. Usually these changes have a more gradual onset, with a gradual deterioration of function over the course of years. Beyond the limitations these disorders create, equally significant is how the individual perceives them. If the symptoms appear slowly, the individual may be able to compensate—that is, for the most part, appear normal—especially if in a familiar environment with no new problems to solve. However, if the symptoms appear rapidly, the person may understandably be extremely upset. As the person experiences a reduction in thinking capacity, anxiety often results and is very apparent.

In treating psychiatric disorders due to a medical condition, the goal, when possible, is to correct the underlying cause. If the medical condition is a tumor, surgery may be indicated; if it is encephalitis, antibiotics are necessary; if it is drug-induced, withdrawal of the toxic agent is necessary. If permanent impairment is associated with organic mental disorders, rehabilitation measures will be initiated to assist the person in coping with limitations.

They wanted to do a CAT scan of Harry's brain, but I warned them that Harry was allergic to cats.

Severe cognitive deficits following a long history of heavy drinking may lead to the diagnosis of *alcoholic dementia.* This type of dementia develops insidiously and typically occurs during the fifth or sixth decade. The symptoms include a deteriorating memory and often dramatic personality changes. Mood swings are common; moods can swing from anger to euphoria. This condition is related to widespread brain damage and actual shrinkage of brain tissue, which is apparent if the person has a CAT (computerized axial tomography) scan of the brain. With abstinence, there may be some recovery over the first six weeks. This too would be evident on a CAT scan. Abstinence, unfortunately, is difficult to achieve. The impairment in thinking doesn't allow the standard counseling and educational approaches to take hold. Generally some degree of dementia persists after abstinence.

The elderly are particularly susceptible to mental disturbances caused by alcohol. Metabolism slows with age, leading to higher blood levels of alcohol than were present with the same level of consumption earlier in life. Their increased use of prescribed medication also increases the likelihood of a medication–alcohol interaction, often leading to episodes of confusion. In a study of elderly patients seen in an emergency room, confusion was virtually three times more common for those with an alcohol problem. Older people have a heightened sensitivity to all psychoactive compounds, including alcohol, leading to greater cognitive changes when drinking. As demographic changes in the United States result in a higher percentage of older people, practitioners will be increasingly challenged to identify alcohol-related cognitive deficits and not simply chalk them up to aging. An alcohol-related diagnosis is often missed in this population because older adults tend to be protected by their friends and family. They may not meet strict *DSM-5* criteria for a formal diagnosis, but they still may be drinking pathologically.

Drug Problems in Combination with Alcohol Disorders

Alcohol abuse among those who are primarily abusing other licit and illicit substances is frequently overlooked. In one study, 70% to 77% of clients entering treatment for benzodiazepine (anti-anxiety agents) abuse also met the criteria for alcohol abuse; of opioid-addicted persons in treatment, 20% to 35% were found to have alcohol-related problems. The danger in such instances is that an alcohol problem is treated lightly: no alcohol assessment is conducted nor alcohol treatment provided. The cocaine abuser who routinely uses alcohol to offset the stimulant's effects may not be aware of a developing alcohol dependence. The alternative is equally true. For anyone with an alcohol problem, look for other drug use problems. The rate of other drug abuse or dependence in treatment samples of those with alcohol problems ranges from 12% to 43%.

Behavioral Addictions

As noted earlier, the concept of addiction is being applied to behaviors that do not involve alcohol or other use. Among the first were, eating disorders and pathological gambling. Some people refuse food intake because they believe they are too fat, although the scales say differently (*anorexia nervosa*). Others stuff themselves and purge by vomiting or abusing laxatives over and over (*bulimia*). Each of these behaviors has an addictive quality: anorexia nervosa is an addiction to food avoidance, while bulimia is an addiction to food binges. Anorexia and bulimia occur primarily in females. Social influences, such as how one should look, are important contributors to the development of these disorders. Case reports of associations between eating disorders and alcohol abuse are increasing as recognition of each illness improves. A striking phenomenon is the frequency of referral for alcohol treatment of individuals who had eating disorders in earlier years. Among those with anorexia, there appears to be a higher incidence of a family history of alcohol problems, which also increases the risk of developing this dependency. Although prospective studies are needed, the potential risk of alcohol problems among those with eating disorders should be recognized.

Gambling is another example of an impulse control disorder that can disrupt personal, family, and vocational goals. Those with a gambling addiction speak of the arousal they seek in much the same way those with an alcohol problem describe drinking. They are preoccupied with planning the next gambling venture, they continue to gamble despite efforts to cut back, and they may become restless or irritable when attempting to stop. When not gambling, they may be "workaholics" or workers who require a deadline to motivate action. Treatments

The Homeless

On a single night in January 2012

- *There were 633,782 homeless people in the United States.*
- *Two-thirds were single individuals. One-third were families.*
- *Sixty-one percent were in shelters, 39% were on "the street."*
- *Five states—California, New York, Florida, Texas, and Georgia accounted for nearly half of the nation's total homeless population.*
- *In 10 states over half of the homeless population are unsheltered.*
- *Veterans represented 13% of the homeless.*

During the prior year

- *Homeless individuals were predominantly male, three-quarters were over age 30, and over two-thirds had a disability.*
- *There was a 9% increase in "doubled-up" households.*
- *The number of homeless children-rose by 2%.*
- *Of those in shelters, 63% were single individuals, 10% were 2 people, 11% were 3 people, and 16% were 4 or more.*
- *The proportion of homeless families increased 30% since 2007.*
- *Of those entering an emergency shelter, 39% were already homeless; 12% came from an institution or a setting such as a motel; the remaining 42% had been staying with family or friends.*
- *The adults in homeless families are overwhelmingly women (80%), and most are under-age 30, with a very low rate of disability. Over half of children in homeless families are under-age 6.*

Office of Community Planning and Development. *The 2012 Annual Homeless Assessment Report to Congress, Vol. I & II.* Washington DC: Department of Housing and Urban Development, November 2012. <www.onecpd.info/resources/documents/2011AHAR_FinalReport.pdf>

for eating disorders and gambling are complex. The growth of Overeaters Anonymous and Gamblers Anonymous groups in America speaks to the growing recognition of these addictive behaviors.

There are a number of other conditions as described in Chapter 4 referred to as behavioral addictions. These were not designated as psychiatric disorders by the American Psychiatric Association in the *DSM-5*. Nonetheless there is growing attention being paid to these conditions and exploration of appropriate interventions.

Clinical Considerations

Because of the high prevalence of co-occurring psychiatric conditions, all clients should be screened for co-occurring disorders. Screening determines the likelihood of a co-occurring mental disorder and thus indicates who needs an in-depth assessment. Such screening should be brief and occur soon after the client presents for services. The Mental Health Screening Form III is a practical tool that covers most of the disorders discussed in this chapter. (This is available at no charge <www.idph.state.ia.us/bh/common/pdf/substance_abuse/integrated_services/jackson_mentalhealth_screeningtool.pdf.>. When screens are positive for a possible co-occurring psychiatric condition, substance abuse treatment personnel should either conduct a thorough assessment or consider consultation from a psychiatrist or mental health worker. When a co-occurring condition is diagnosed, it as well as the alcohol disorder are considered primary. Treating both conditions simultaneously is necessary and requires an integrated treatment plan. The treatment of psychiatric illness must be coordinated carefully with rehabilitation efforts. Under any circumstances, extra support and education are essential. Effective programs recognize that recovery tends to occur over months or years and that long-term, community-based strategies are required. The client needs to appreciate that he or she is being treated for two very different conditions. For long-term success, control of both is very important. Helping the client integrate information from both treatment perspectives requires thoughtful treatment planning and follow-up.

Homelessness, Alcohol Use, and Chronic Mental Illness

Although homelessness is not an illness, it represents a point at which chronic mental illness intersects with alcohol problems. Alcohol dependence is one pathway toward homelessness. On the other hand, homelessness can be a condition that precedes increased alcohol abuse. Either way, alcohol-related problems within the homeless population are enormous. On any given night, more than three-quarter million people in the United States are without adequate shelter, and about two-fifths of these people have an alcohol problem. Certainly the "skid row bum," whose repeated detox and jail stints leave lasting impressions on health care providers, remains inextricably linked with homelessness in the popular consciousness. Historically the "chronic public inebriate" frequently ended up on the streets. Increasingly, these individuals are being swept into the criminal justice system through cycles of arrest, release without adequate treatment and support, and re-arrest. Homeless persons with alcohol dependence have unique service and housing needs, requiring creative responses.

The homeless alcohol abuser has been shown to be multiply disadvantaged, with higher rates of physical, mental, and social problems than the non-alcohol-abusing homeless person. Most homeless alcohol abusers are male, white, and elderly. Many have troubled marital and family histories and poor employment records, and many are transient and socially isolated. They are frequently incarcerated for petty crimes and often are victims of violent attacks. The majority of alcohol-abusing homeless persons have an additional psychiatric diagnosis. Homeless alcohol abusers are at high risk for neurological impairment, heart disease and hypertension, chronic lung disease, liver disease, and trauma. These clinical features complicate engagement, intervention, and recovery.

Successful treatment of a serious alcohol disorder requires a social and physical environment where sobriety is positively supported. These are hardly the conditions encountered when living on the street. Therefore, the needs of the homeless go beyond offering substance abuse treatment. Providing only detoxification followed by short-term inpatient care continues the revolving-door scenario that often is found among homeless persons with alcohol problems. Assistance and support for finding appropriate, affordable, and alcohol-free housing are the backbone of treatment for this special population. To accomplish even this basic goal, bridging the person's disaffiliation, distrust, and disenchantment is necessary. Overcoming a client's resistance requires a great deal of clinical skill. It also requires a great deal of patience; homeless persons with alcohol problems are among the most severely and chronically ill clients that a counselor is likely to encounter. The needs of the homeless with an alcohol problem go beyond the capacity of any single provider. Clinicians need to persist in forming coalitions with advocates, politicians, and community programs to develop adequate service systems for this population.

PSYCHOTROPIC MEDICATIONS

Neither alcohol nor other drug problems exist in a vacuum. Those with substance abuse problems can also have a variety of other problems—some physical, some psychiatric. These patients may be receiving treatment or treating themselves. The treatment may involve prescription or over-the-counter medications. The more one knows about medications in general, the more helpful one can be to a client. The group of medications of particular interest in relation to alcohol or other drug use are those with psychotropic effects. Any drug that influences behavior or mood falls into this category. Because some of these drugs have abuse potential and the ability to mimic intoxicated states, these medications are of the greatest concern to the substance abuse clinician. At the same time, they may be the most widely misunderstood.

Proprietary vs. Generic Drugs *Proprietary drugs are protected by patent and the brand name is commonly capitalized, sometimes also being accompanied by ®. Generic drugs are not protected by patent; their names indicate their chemical composition and are typically written in lowercase. Here upper- and lowercase are used to distinguish proprietary and generic drugs.*

Those with substance dependence, and particularly alcohol-dependent people, tend to seek instant relief from the slightest mental or physical discomfort. The actively drinking person may welcome any chemical relief and is at risk for using some medications in an abusive manner. The recovering person, on the other hand, may be so leery of any medication that he or she may refuse to use them when they're much needed. Thus some familiarity with the types of psychotropic medications and their appropriate use is important. Psychoactive drugs are not alike, either in terms of their actions or in their potential for abuse.

Taking a good medication history is imperative. The following are some of the questions a clinician should have in mind: "What is your philosophy about medication? What medications do you currently take? Is it prescribed, when was it prescribed, and by whom was it prescribed? Are you following the prescription? Do you take more or less than prescribed, or use a different schedule? Is the drug having the desired effects? What, if any, side effects exist? Do you have any medication allergies? Have you ever abused medication in the past?" These questions can help identify any abuse of current medications and can prevent future abuse in vulnerable, recovering individuals.

Good medicine is bitter, but it cures illness.
—Confucius

Tremendous confusion may arise from a communication tight line gap between the patient and the prescribing physician. The physician prescribes a medication intended to have a specific effect on a particular patient. The patient is sometimes unclear about (and usually doesn't question) the need for medication. There may be limited access to the physician for follow-up calls. Only feedback from the patient enables the doctor to make adjustments, if necessary. The regimen for taking a drug is important. Often, as the patient begins to feel better, he or she stops or cuts the dose of a prescribed drug. This sometimes occurs because patients assume that once the symptoms are gone they no longer need the medication, rather than realizing that it is the medicine that is keeping the symptoms under control.

Clients should be encouraged to consult with the physician before altering the way medications are taken. Because treatment requires good communication, you should help the client ask questions about the treatment and the drugs involved. Also be sensitive to the problems that the cost of medications can present for some clients. Historically those without insurance could find the cost prohibitive. This may mean that they skimp on taking medicines as prescribed to make their supply last longer. Or they may put off having a prescription refilled on schedule because their budget simply can't be stretched that far, at that time.

Every drug has multiple, simultaneous actions. Only a few of these are sought when a particular drug is prescribed. The intended effects are the drug's therapeutic effects; all the other effects are considered the drug's side effects in that particular instance. In selecting a medication for a patient, a doctor seeks a drug with the maximum therapeutic impact and the fewest side effects. Ideally the prescription of a particular drug should be a collaborative effort. Enough information must be exchanged to enable the patient to give valid consent to the doctor for the prescription. The following is a discussion of the four major categories of psychotropic medication: the antipsychotic medications, antidepressant medications, mood stabilizers, and anti-anxiety agents, as well as medications which promote sleep. Each has different actions and is prescribed for different reasons.

Common Abbreviations on Prescriptions

caps = capsules
gm = gram
gtt. = drops
mg. = milligrams
ml. = milliliter
h = hour
p.r.n. = when necessary
q.d. = once a day
b.i.d. = twice a day
t.i.d. = three times a day
q.i.d. = four times a day
q.2h = every 2 hours
q.3h = every 3 hours
q.4h = every 4 hours
q._h. = if to be taken at an hourly interval, hours between doses is inserted
a.c. = before meals
p.c. = after meals
ad lib = use as much as one desires (for "ad libitum")
p.o. = by mouth, orally
i.m. = injection, intramuscular
i.v. = injection, intravenous

Antipsychotic Medications

The antipsychotic medications, the oldest of which are sometimes referred to as neuroleptics, are drugs that relieve psychotic symptoms. In addition to the antipsychotic effect, they tend to have tranquilizing and sedative effects, calming behavior and inducing drowsiness. Antipsychotic medications have allowed many patients to live in the community rather than institutions. There are two general categories of antipsychotics, with different side effects. Those most commonly used are termed the *atypical* antipsychotics in comparison to the older *typical* or traditional group. The atypicals are used in the acute phase of mania for mood stabilization for maintenance treatment of bipolar disorder and for schizophrenia. Additionally, an antipsychotic agent may be prescribed not to relieve psychotic symptoms but for its sedative or tranquilizing properties. Such "off-label" use (using/prescribing medications in ways for which they have not been approved by the FDA) is common. The sedating effect of these drugs can be helpful for certain anxiety disorders, explosive anger problems, and insomnias. Side effects vary from medication to medication, as is true of the typical or traditional medications. Serious but reversible side effects in some of the most widely used medications in the atypical category include weight gain, increase in serum lipids, and onset of Type II (late-onset) diabetes. The potential for irreversible neurological side effects with the use of the typical or traditional antipsychotics further mandates their judicious use.

Antipsychotic medications have various side effects, making them either more or less sedating. The medication prescribed is selected on the basis of the patient's constellation of symptoms. For example, a drug with greater sedative effects might be selected for a person exhibiting manic, or agitated, behavior. Some antipsychotic drugs are currently available in a long-acting injectable form called decanoate. This form can be useful in ensuring medication compliance in clients who have a history of poor compliance. The antipsychotic medications most frequently encountered are listed in Table 12.1.

As with most medications, antipsychotic drugs interact with alcohol. A common effect of combining alcohol with sedating medications

TABLE 12.1 Antipsychotic Medications

Medication	Daily Dose Range	Overdose Danger
Atypical Antipsychotic Medications		
olanzepine (Zyprexa)	2.5–20 mg	Low
(Zyprexa Relprevv)	300–405 mg, IM q 2 weeks	
Potential side effects: sleepiness, significant weight gain, postural hypotension (a drop in blood pressure when rising after sitting or lying down), constipation, hyperlipidemia (increase of blood cholesterol or triglycerides levels), development of Type II diabetes, dizziness, muscle rigidity and weakness, possible liver enzyme elevation.		
risperidone (Risperdal)	0.5–6 mg	Low
(Respirdal consta)	12.5–50 mg. IM q 2 weeks	
Potential side effects: sleepiness, dizziness, heart palpitations, weight gain, sexual function complaints, increased fatigue, dose-related extrapyramidal effects (involuntary movements, tics, tremors).		
paliperidone (Invega)	3–12 mg	Low
Potential side effects: dizziness, lactation, heart palpitations, weight gain, fatigue, postural hypotension, cardiac arrhythmia and dose-related extrapyramidal effects.		
iloperidone (Fanapt)	12–24 mg	Low
Potential side effects: dizziness, lactation, heart palpitations, weight gain, fatigue, postural hypotension, cardiac arrhythmia and dose-related extrapyramidal effects.		
asenapine (Saphris)	10–20 mg	Low
Potential side effects: sleepiness, postural hypotension, dizziness, constipation, dry mouth, weight gain.		
lurasidone (Latuda)	40–160 mg	Low
Potential side effects: dizziness, lactation, heart palpitations, weight gain, fatigue, postural hypotension, cardiac arrhythmia and dose-related extrapyramidal effects.		
quetiapine (Seroquel)	50–800 mg*	Medium
Potential side effects: sleepiness, postural hypotension, dizziness, constipation, dry mouth, weight gain. [*Available in once-daily dose Seroquel XR. The XR indicates extended release.]		
ziprasidone (Geodon)	40–160 mg	Low
Potential side effects: possible cardiac arrhythmias, drowsiness, nausea, constipation, diarrhea, dizziness, restlessness, abnormal muscle movements, rash, cough, runny nose.		

Another Drug of Abuse

Antipsychotics aren't the first drugs that come to mind upon mention of "drug abuse." But at least one is. It is quetiapine. As alluded to, it is favored by those in prisons, it goes by the name "Jailhouse Heroin." Inmates welcome it for reducing anxiety, and creating a sense of care-lessness. It is reasonably accessible. It is not a controlled substance. Prison medical staff are far more concerned about a case of untreated schizophrenia than they are about a possible case of drug misuse.

Quetiapine abuse also occurs beyond the prison walls. Though classified as an anti-psychotic, it is also prescribed for anxiety disorders, particularly for PTSD, and for treatment of insomnia. If someone is abusing an antpsychotic drug,more than four out of five times it is quetiapine. Most of those who use it are polydrug uses. It is used to self-medicate, to counter the effects of other drug use. It is said to ease the "crash" that occurs when coming off stimulants, or treat the anxiety that accompanies a "bad trips."

Quetiapine may be taken orally, as intended. It may be crushed and snorted. Sometimes it is taken intravenously, combined with cocaine possibly along alcohol, a concoction known as "Suzie Qs".

Use extends down to adolescents. In one large study quetiapine was identified as the fourth most commonly used prescription drug. Though only fourth, nonetheless that was a quarter of all those who use prescription drugs recreationally.

TABLE 12.1 *continued*

Medication	Daily Dose Range	Overdose Danger
aripiprazole (Abilify)	5–30 mg	Low
Potential side effects: Constipation, akathisia (a mix of agitation and physical restlessness, such as pacing or rocking or fidgety leg movements), difficulty sleeping, insomnia, vomiting, lightheadedness.		
clozapine (Clozaril)	25–900 mg	High
Potential side effects: drowsiness, sedation, dizziness, headache, tremor, excessive salivation and sweating, hyperlipidemia (increase in blood lipids such as cholesterol), development of Type II diabetes, dry mouth, rapid heart rate, hypotension, fainting, weight gain, seizures. Due to multiple and potentially dangerous side effects, generally used only when other antipsychotic agents have been ineffective.		
Typical Antipsychotic Medications (Traditional)		
chlorpromazine (Thorazine)	50–500 mg	Moderate
haloperidol (Haldol)	1–15 mg	Moderate
deconate	25–100 mg IM q 2–3 wks	
fluphenazine (Prolixin)	5–60 mg	Moderate
decanoate	25–100 mg IM q 1–4 wks	
thiothixine (Navane)	5–60 mg	Moderate
perphenazine (Trilafon)	4–24 mg	Moderate
molindone (Moban)	50–225 mg	Moderate
Potential side effects: sedation, dry mouth, Parkinson's symptoms, involuntary facial movements (dyskinesias), constipation, difficulty with urination, blurred vision, muscle rigidity and weakness, weight gain (except for molindone).		

is potentiation: the two agents act in concert to exaggerate the sedative effects, which can cause problems. Alcohol can also increase the levels of neurotransmitters that these antipsychotic medications are attempting to block, leading to reduced effectiveness.

Antipsychotic drugs are much less likely to be abused than other psychoactive agents, except in certain environments such as prison, where a state of sedate oblivion can be preferable to serving time fully conscious. They are not chemically similar to alcohol and are therefore not subject to cross-tolerance or addiction. The sensations they produce are generally not experienced as pleasurable and are therefore infrequently sought out. Several of the side effects, involving involuntary movements, caused by the antipsychotic drugs are unpleasant.

Medications can be used to reduce these unpleasant side effects, including benztropine (Cogentin) and trihexyphenidyl (Artane) and medications from the benzodiazepine group of anti-anxiety medications. The latter (anti-anxiety agents) can induce pleasurable mental changes and may be abused by clients.

Antidepressant Medications

The antidepressants, another major class of psychotropic medications, are used to treat the biological component of depression. They must be taken at a high enough dose to achieve a therapeutic level. A period of regular use (often two to eight weeks) is necessary before these medications have their full effect. Therefore, a common initial complaint of patients is that the medicine isn't helping. Side effects vary according to the category of antidepressant. These are most pronounced when the person first begins taking the drug. The physician may choose to have the patient take the medication at a particular time of the day to minimize side effects. There are several types of antidepressants, grouped according to their chemical properties and how they act.

The *SSRIs*—the acronym for **S**elective **S**erotonin **R**euptake **I**nhibitors—are currently the most commonly prescribed antidepressant medications. In general, they have fewer side effects than the other categories of antidepressant medications. The most common side effects include sexual side effects (delayed orgasm, decreased libido), gastrointestinal symptoms, headache, insomnia, and agitation. In 2004 the FDA placed a warning on all SSRIs indicating that adolescents and young adults (under 25) may experience increased suicidal thinking in the first 2 weeks taking these medications.

The *tricyclic* antidepressants are an older category of commonly used antidepressants. Common side effects include dry mouth and constipation. These medications are highly lethal when taken in large doses. Given that depressed individuals are much more likely to attempt suicide, these medications have fallen out of favor.

The *SNRIs* (**S**erotonin-**N**orepinephrine **R**euptake **I**nhibitors) have actions similar to those of the SSRIs and the tricyclics. However, they have fewer unpleasant side effects and don't present the dangers associated with overdose that present with the tricyclics.

Another category, known as *MAOIs* (**M**ono**A**mine **O**xidase **I**nhibitors), requires dietary restrictions to avoid serious problems. Drugs in this category have numerous other side effects as well. They tend to be used only in severe cases of depression that have not responded to other medications.

Finally, several others do not fit into any of the preceding categories. Mirtazepine also directly affects both serotonin and norepinephrine, but it is not a reuptake inhibitor. Bupropion, another commonly prescribed antidepressant, is presently the only medication in its category and is chemically unrelated to the other antidepressants. It is *exactly* the same medication marketed as Zyban for smoking cessation. Though in the antidepressant category, trazodone is used more often for its side effect of sedation than for its antidepressant effect.

The most common antidepressants are listed in Table 12.2. There is no clear evidence that antidepressant medications invite abuse or create dependence. However, when they are used in combination with alcohol, problems can arise because of the additive effects, especially with the older antidepressants.

TABLE 12.2 Antidepressant Medications

Medication	Daily Dose Range	Overdose Danger
SSRIs (Selective Serotonin Reuptake Inhibitors)		
fluoxetine (Prozac)	10–80 mg	Low
citralopram (Celexa)	20–80 mg	Low
paroxetine (Paxil)	10–80 mg	Low
sertraline (Zoloft)	25–200 mg	Low
escitalopram (Lexapro)	10–20 mg	Low
Potential side effects: sexual dysfunction, decreased libido, nausea, headache, nervousness, insomnia, drowsiness, diarrhea, weight gain or loss.		
venlafaxine (Effexor)	75–300 mg	Low
desvenlafaxine (Pristiq)	50–100mg	Low
duloxetine (Cymbalta)	30–60 mg	Low
Potential side effects: elevated blood pressure, headache, sweating, nausea, constipation, insomnia, dizziness, anorexia, anxiety, sleepiness, difficulty with orgasm, increased liver function abnormalities, tremor.		
Tricyclics		
amitriptyline (Elavil)	10–200 mg	High
nortriptyline (Pamelor)	30–150 mg	High
imipramine (Tofranil)	30–200 mg	High
doxepin (Sinequan)	25–300 mg	High
desipramine (Norpramin)	25–200 mg	High
protriptyline (Vivactil)	15–60 mg	High
Potential side *effects:* dry mouth, increased heart rate, EKG changes, urinary hesitation, constipation, blurred vision, sedation, weight gain.		

(continued)

TABLE 12.2 *continued*

Medication	Daily Dose Range	Overdose Danger
MonoAmine-Oxidase Inhibitors (MAOIs)		
Because of the possible major interactions with foods containing tyramine and multiple medications that result in marked rise in blood pressure, use of the MAOIs requires that the patient be very diligent about diet and the use of other medications. Thus MAOIs are prescribed infrequently.		
tranylcypromine (Parnate)	30–60 mg	High
phenylzine (Nardil)	15–90 mg	High
Potential side effects: overstimulation, anxiety, agitation, mania, restlessness, insomnia, drowsiness, dizziness, gastrointestinal symptoms, headaches, rapid heartbeat. Hypertensive crisis when used with food containing tyramine or when medications with sympathomimetic effects, such as cold preparations, are taken.		
Other Antidepressant Medications		
bupropion (Wellbutrin)	100–450 mg	Moderate
Potential side effects: agitation, anxiety, dry mouth, sweating, gastrointestinal upset, insomnia, seizures, dizziness. Note: Marketed as Zyban for smoking cessation.		
nefazadone (Serzone)	100–600 mg	Low
vilazodone (Viibryd)	10–40mg	Low
trazodone (Desyrel)	50–600 mg	Low
Potential side effects: dry mouth, nausea, constipation, sleepiness, dizziness, lightheadedness, vision problems, confusion. For trazadone: hypotension, priapism (rare) in males (persistent erection in the absence of sexual stimulation).		
mirtazepine (Remeron)	15–45 mg	Low
Potential side effects: sleepiness, dizziness, increased appetite and weight gain, increased triglyceride and cholesterol levels.		

Mood Stabilizers

Mood stabilizers are used to treat bipolar (manic-depressive) disorder (see Table 12.3). A few comments on lithium carbonate are worth mention. It can be helpful in either depression or mania and is a common medication used in controlling bipolar disorder. The dose is geared to body weight, and the level is monitored periodically through blood samples. Because lithium produces no pleasant effects, it is unlikely to be abused. The opposite behavior, taking too little, is the more common problem. Feeling greatly improved, those on lithium may decide it's no longer necessary. However, maintaining stability usually depends on continuing to take the medication.

In addition to lithium, drugs initially used to treat seizure disorders are being prescribed: carbamazepine (Tegretol), valproic acid (Depakote/Depakene), lamotrigine (Lamictal), and topiramte (Topamax) are used with patients who cannot take lithium because of side effects, or they are taken in addition to lithium. Any use of alcohol with either carbamazepine or valproic acid is contraindicated because of additive effects and because there is the possibility that either of them, on its own, could cause liver damage. This would be made worse by alcohol use.

TABLE 12.3 Mood Stabilizers

Medication	Daily Dose Range	Overdose Danger
Lithium		
(lithium carbonate, Lithonate, Lithobid, Eskalith)	600–1800 mg	High
Potential side effects: hand tremor, nausea, weight gain, increased output of urine and increased fluid intake, fatigue, lethargy, hypothyroidism.		
Anticonvulsants		
A number of medications formerly used to control seizures (anticonvulsants) are now used as mood stabilizers.		
divalproex (Depakote)	500–3000 mg	High
valproic acid (Depakene)	15–60 mg per kg body weight	High
Potential side effects: gastrointestinal symptoms, asthenia, weight gain, sleepiness, dizziness, tremor, liver toxicity. Therapeutic level determined by checking blood levels. Note: Alcohol can increase risk of liver damage.		
carbamazepine (Tegretol)	400–1200 mg	High
Potential side effects: dizziness, drowsiness, unsteadiness, nausea, vomiting, skin rashes. Rare, but serious, effects on bone marrow and white blood count. Requires checking blood levels for therapeutic range. Note: Alcohol can increase risk of liver damage.		
lamotrigine (Lamictal)	100–400 mg (Adults)	Moderate to High
Potential side effects: headache, nausea, vomiting, dizziness, diplopia (double vision), blurred vision, unsteadiness, runny nose, skin rash; life-threatening skin disorders have been reported in 0.3% of adults taking Lamictal. Side effects are more common in children taking lamotrigine for epilepsy.		
oxcarbazapine (Trileptal)	600–2400 mg	Low
Potential side effects: somnolence, dizziness, vision problems, unsteadiness, speech problems, psychomotor slowing, "pins and needles" sensations, nervousness, nausea, memory problems, tremor, confusion, fatigue.		
topirimate (Topamax)	50–400 mg	Undetermined
Potential side effects: somnolence, dizziness, vision problems, unsteadiness, speech problems, psychomotor slowing, "pins and needles" sensations, nervousness, nausea, memory problems, tremor, confusion, fatigue.		

Anti-Anxiety Agents

Anti-anxiety agents are also called anxiolytic agents. The major action of these drugs is to promote tranquilization and sedation. Quite properly, alcohol can be included in any list of drugs in this class. The anti-anxiety agents have sometimes been called the minor tranquilizers. They have no antipsychotic or significant antidepressant properties and are very effective in the treatment of anxiety disorders. Short-acting forms are frequently prescribed as sleeping aids. However, their high potential for abuse and dependence makes them less likely to be the first medication prescribed for anxiety, especially in persons who have any history of abuse of alcohol or other drugs. There are two different types of anti-anxiety drugs, the benzodiazepines, and newer agents, called the "nonbenzodiazepines." The most common anti-anxiety agents are listed in Table 12.4.

The medications in the benzodiazepine class, along with barbiturates (now rarely prescribed), are most likely to present problems for those with alcohol problems. The potential for abuse of the anti-anxiety agents has become more broadly recognized. Valium, Xanax, and Ativan (benzodiazepines) are the anti-anxiety agents that have been most widely associated with abuse and dependence. In the past, Quaalude and Placidyl—which are no longer available for prescription in this country—as well as Miltown and some barbiturates led to abuse and dependence problems. Newer anti-anxiety medications, such as buspirone (BuSpar) and hydroxyzine (Atarax, Vistaril), have demonstrated far less abuse potential.

TABLE 12.4 Anti-Anxiety Agents

Medication	Daily Dose Range	Overdose Danger
Benzodiazepines		
alprazolam (Xanax)	0.25–6 mg	Moderate
clonazepam (Klonopin)	0.5–4 mg	Moderate
diazepam (Valium)	2–40 mg	Moderate
chlordiazepoxide (Librium)	5–100 mg	Moderate
lorazepam (Ativan)	0.5–6mg	Moderate
oxazepam (Serax)	10–45 mg	Moderate
Potential side effects: similar to alcohol: impaired cognitive function, impaired psychomotor performance, sedation, development of tolerance.		
Other		
buspirone (Buspar)	15–60 mg	Low
hydozyzine (Atarax, Vistaril)	25–200 mg	Low
Potential side effects: minimal; no known dependency potential.		

Beyond problems of possible abuse, there are other dangers with the benzodiazepine anti-anxiety agents and alcohol. Taken in combination, they potentiate one another. Medical ethicists and legal scholars are all familiar with the case of a 21-year-old woman named Karen Ann Quinlan, whose family was the first to have fought in court to have a family member removed from a respirator, to be allowed to die. In 1985, she had been in a coma for almost a decade. Many people are unaware that the cause of her irreversible coma was attributed to the combination of alcohol and Valium.

Because of their similar pharmacology, alcohol and the benzodiazepine anti-anxiety agents are virtually interchangeable. This phenomenon is the basis of cross-addiction and is the rationale for their use in alcohol detoxification. It is their very similarity to alcohol that makes them very poor anti-anxiety drugs for those with an alcohol problem, except for detoxification purposes.

Anti-Insomnia Agents

The final group of psychotropic medications to consider are those that promote sleep. Insomnia is one of the most common presenting problems seen in primary care settings. Several disorders, including most of the psychiatric disorders, involve insomnia. Insomnia too is rampant among those with active substance use disorders, as well as those in recovery. (See Chapter 6.) Most insomnia (especially that seen in early recovery) involves difficulty falling asleep (also called early insomnia). Difficulty staying asleep (terminal insomnia) and mid-cycle wakening (middle insomnia) can be signs of depression and/or substance use (respectively).

Often, the distress and desperation that results from sleepless nights prompts people to desire a "quick fix" rather than engaging in behavioral changes which require more discipline, consistency, and patience. Although a variety of medications are used to treat insomnia, in the long-run sleep problems tend to respond much more favorably to behavioral changes.

Early recovery is a particularly vulnerable period for clients to reach to medication to solve their sleep problems. There are some in this field who question any sedating medication for their clients, claiming these agents can increase the risk for relapse. At the very least, it is a good idea to ask clients about over-the-counter and prescribed sleeping medications and educate them about the risk of sedating medications increasing relapse potential.

Knowing that sleep will be disturbed for days to weeks early in recovery is crucial information for clients; it helps them know what to anticipate. Many times, anxiety about not sleeping leads to further insomnia, so reducing anxiety by normalizing clients' insomnia in early recovery can ultimately help restore normal sleeping patterns. If sleep does not improve after the first month of abstinence, and they do not have additional psychiatric disorders, refer concerned clients to a cognitive-behavioral therapist for sleep training. If you have any

TABLE 12.5 Insomnia Agents

Medication	Daily Dose Range	Overdose Danger
"Sleep-Specific" Benzodiazepines		
triazolam (Halcion)	0.125–0.5mg	Moderate
temazepam (Restoril)	5–30 mg	Moderate
Potential side effects: similar to alcohol, are impaired cognitive function, impaired psychomotor performance, sedation, development of tolerance		
Non-benzodiazepines		
Zolpidem (Ambien, Ambien CR)	5–20 mg	Low/Moderate
Eszopiclone (Lunesta)	1–3 mg	Low/Moderate
Zaleplon (Sonata)	5–20mg	Low/Moderate
Potential side effects: amnesia, sleep walking, tolerance, withdrawal insomnia		
Antihistamines		
Diphenhydramine (Benadryl)	25–100mg	Low
hydrozyzine (Atarax, Vistaril)	25–200 mg	Low
Potential side effects: dry mouth, constipation; no known dependency potential		
Sedating Antidepressants		
trazodone (Desyrel)	25–300mg	Low
Potential side effects: hypotension, priapism (rare) in males (persistent erection in the absence of sexual stimulation)		
doxepin (Sinequan)	25–300mg	High
Potential side effects: dry mouth, increased heart rate, EKG changes, urinary hesitation, constipation, blurred vision, sedation, weight gain		

concerns about psychiatric disorders involving insomnia, refer clients to a psychiatrist or physician with experience in addiction treatment.

In selecting medications to treat insomnia, there are several important factors to consider. In the past physicians literally traded one problem for another when they treated insomnia with highly addictive medications such as opioids, barbiturates, and (as still happens) benzodiazepines. Currently, many physicians are growing increasingly aware of the habit-forming potential of many of the so-called anti-insomnia agents, yet too little training is offered in medical curricula about treating sleep disorders in those with an active substance use disorder or those in recovery. This is why it is ideal to refer these clients either to physicians with addiction training and (assuming client consent) ensure these providers are aware of the client's history.

The medications most widely used to treat insomnia are listed in Table 12.5. They are psychotropic medications that have sedating properties as side-effects, namely those of the anti-anxiety and antidepressant groups. The non-benzodiazepines, such as zolpidem, zaleplon, and (es)zopiclone, termed the "Z-drugs," are increasingly prescribed due to their relatively lower overdose and habit-forming potential. That said, they can cause amnesia and sleep-walking in some individuals, which can be hazardous. For this reason, importance is placed on taking them immediately before climbing into bed.

In general, all medications used to treat insomnia can cause "rebound insomnia" if they are suddenly stopped, indicating they all have varying levels of habit-forming potential. The least habit-forming of the medications used to treat insomnia are melatonin (and its synthetic analogue ramelteon) and the antihistamines (diphenhydramine, hydroxyzine). Beyond prescription drugs there are also a number of over-the-counter medications available (Unisom, Sominex, Tylenol PM) to promote sleep; most of these are antihistamines. A word of caution: those in liquid forms may have a have high alcohol content as well!

On the whole, Americans are very casual about medications. Too often, prescriptions are not taken as directed, are saved up for the next illness, or are shared with family and friends. Over-the-counter preparations are treated as candy. The fact that a prescription is not required does not render it harmless. Some possible ingredients in over-the-counter drugs are antihistamines, stimulants, and—of course—alcohol. These can cause difficulty if taken in combination with alcohol or may themselves be abused. In taking a history of medications being used, don't forget to ask about over-the-counter preparations and herbal remedies, the drugs that people prescribe for themselves.

The desire to take medicine is perhaps the greatest feature which distinguishes man from animals.
—Sir William Osler, 1925

REFERENCES AND FURTHER READINGS

Davis L, Uezato A, Newell JM, Frazier E. Major depression and comorbid substance use disorders. *Current Opinion in Psychiatry* 21(1):14–18, 2008. (38 refs.)

Ecker J, Aubry T, Wasylenki D, Pettey D, Krupa T, Rush B. Predicting alcohol use and drug use among consumers of community mental health programs. *Journal of Dual Diagnosis* 8(3):188–199, 2012. (38 refs.)

Edlund MJ, Booth BM, Han XT. Who seeks care where? Utilization of mental health and substance use disorder treatment in two national samples of individuals with alcohol use disorders. *Journal of Studies on Alcohol and Drugs* 73(4):635–646, 2012. (48 refs.)

Flynn PM, Brown BS. Co-occurring disorders in substance abuse treatment: Issues and prospects (review). *Journal of Substance Abuse Treatment* 34(1):36–47, 2008. (105 refs.)

Frye MA, Salloum IM. Bipolar disorder and comorbid alcoholism: Prevalence rate and treatment considerations (review). *Bipolar Disorders* 8(6):677–685, 2006. (63 refs.)

Goldstein BI, Diamantouros A, Schaffer A, Naranjo CA. Pharmacotherapy of alcoholism in patients with co-morbid psychiatric disorders (review). *Drugs* 66(9):1229–1237, 2006. (64 refs.)

Green AI, Drake RE, Brunette MF, Noordsy DL. Schizophrenia and co-occurring substance use disorder. *American Journal of Psychiatry* 164(3):402–408, 2007. (41 refs.)

Hawton K, van Heeringen K. Suicide (review). *Lancet* 373(9672): 1372–1381, 2009. (144 refs.)

Huang DYC, Lanza H, Murphy DA, Hser YI. Parallel development of risk behaviors in adolescence: Potential pathways to co-occurrence. *International Journal of Behavioral Development* 36(4):247–257, 2012. (66 refs.)

Kelly TM, Daley DC, Douaihy AB. Treatment of substance abusing patients with comorbid psychiatric disorders (review). *Addictive Behaviors* 37(1):11–24, 2012. (148 refs.)

Mackowick KM, Lynch MJ, Weinberger AH, George TP. Treatment of tobacco dependence in people with mental health and addictive disorders. *Current Psychiatry Reports* 14(5):478–485, 2012. (76 refs.)

Mericle AA, Martin C, Carise D, Love M. Identifying need for mental health services in substance abuse clients. *Journal of Dual Diagnosis* 8(3):218–228, 2012. (65 refs.)

Mericle AA, Park VMT, Hoick P, Arria AM. Prevalence, patterns, and correlates of co-occurring substance use and mental disorders in the United States: Variations by race/ethnicity. *Comprehensive Psychiatry* 53(6):657–665, 2012. (68 refs.)

Moore THM, Zammit S, Lingford-Hughes A, Barnes TRE, Jones PB, Burke M, Lewis G. Cannabis use and risk of psychotic or affective mental health outcomes: A systematic review (review). *Lancet* 370(9584):319–328, 2007. (69 refs.)

Murthy P, Chand P. Treatment of dual diagnosis disorders (review). *Current Opinion in Psychiatry* 25(3):194–200, 2012. (46 refs.)

Ross S, Peselow E. Co-occurring psychotic and addictive disorders: Neurobiology and diagnosis (review). *Clinical Neuropharmacology* 35(5):235–243, 2012. (53 refs.)

Sacks S, Ries RK. *Substance Abuse Treatment for Persons with Co-Occurring Disorder. A Treatment Improvement Protocol, No. 42.* Rockville, MD: Center for Substance Abuse Treatment, 2008.

Schubiner H. Substance abuse in patients with attention-deficit hyperactivity disorder: Therapeutic implications (review). *CNS Drugs* 19(8):643–655, 2005. (102 refs.)

Stahl SM. *Essential Psychopharmacology: Neuroscientific Basis and Practical Applications,* 2nd ed. Cambridge, UK: Cambridge University Press, 2000.
Note: Covers the actions and uses of all psychotropic medications, with excellent cartoon illustrations of actions of medications.

Substance Abuse and Mental Health Services Administration. *Integrated Treatment for Co-Occurring Disorders: Tool Kit.* Rockville, MD: Center for Mental Health Services, Substance Abuse and Mental Health Services Administration, 2010. Available: http://mentalhealth.samhsa.gov/cmhs/CommunitySupport/toolkits/cooccurring/default.aspx.

Thornton LK, Baker AL, Lewin T, Kay-Lambkin FJ, Kavanagh D, Richmond R, et al. Reasons for substance use among people with mental disorders. *Addictive Behaviors* 37(4):427–434, 2012. (43 refs.)

Torchalla I, Nosen L, Rostam H, Allen P. Integrated treatment programs for individuals with concurrent substance use disorders and trauma experiences: A systematic review and meta-analysis. *Journal of Substance Abuse Treatment* 42(1):65–77, 2012. (70 refs.)

van den Bosch LMC, Verheul R. Patients with addiction and personality disorder: Treatment outcomes and clinical implications (review). *Current Opinion in Psychiatry* 20(1): 67–71, 2007. (36 refs.)

Vijayakumar L, Kumar MS, Vijayakumar V. Substance use and suicide (review). *Current Opinion in Psychiatry* 24(3):197–202, 2011. (49 refs.)

Wilens TE, Faraone SV, Biederman J, Gunawardene S. Does stimulant therapy of attention-deficit/hyperactivity disorder beget later substance abuse? A meta-analytic review of the literature (review). *Pediatrics* 111(1):179–185, 2003. (56 refs.)

CHAPTER 13

Drugs of Abuse Other Than Alcohol

The focus of this book has been on alcohol. An understanding of alcohol—its actions, the process of abuse, and dependence—provides a solid backdrop for considering any substance use. For those who use alcohol, other drug use is also a part of the picture. When you are trying to deal with multiple drugs, it is possible to feel overwhelmed by facts—acute effects, actions, side effects, withdrawal effects—lists, lists, lists. To help you deal with that overload, this chapter endeavors to provide a toolbox of basic concepts, which can help make sense of the phenomena that underlie drug use and help make drug effects intelligible. Discussion of the overall patterns of use and associated social problems is followed by a description of basic pharmacological concepts and an overview of the major classes of drugs of abuse. Somewhat more attention is directed to nicotine and marijuana than to other drugs due to their wider use.

DRUG USE PATTERNS

The National Institute on Drug Abuse (NIDA) conducts two regular surveys of substance use: the *National Survey on Drug Use & Health,* which samples the total population and is the source of the figures here, and *Monitoring the Future,* a survey of high school students and young adults.[1] Over the past three decades there has been a consistent decline in illicit substance use. There was an almost 50% decline between 1979 and 1992. Then there was a brief rise in use, but in 1995 use again began to fall. The other notable trend is the drop in age of first use over the past decade.

[1]The data in this chapter are from these two surveys.

TABLE 13.1 Drug Use in 2012, Age 12 and Older

Substance	Past Year (%)	Past Month (%)
Alcohol	66.7%	52.1%
Tobacco	31.9	26.7
Any illicit drug	16.0	9.2
Marijuana and hashish	12.1	7.3
Any illicit drug other than marijuana	8.2	3.4
Cocaine	1.8	0.6
Crack	0.4	0.2
Heroin	0.3	0.1
Hallucinogens	1.7	0.4
LSD	0.4	0.1
PCP	0.1	0.0
Ecstasy (MDMA)	1.0	0.2
Inhalants	0.7	0.2
Non-medical use of psychotherapeutics	6.4	2.6
Pain relievers	4.8	1.9
OxyContin	0.6	0.1
Tranquilizers	2.3	0.8
Stimulants	1.3	0.5
Methamphetamine	0.4	0.2
Sedatives	0.2	0.1

Source: Substance Abuse and Mental Health Administration. *Results from the 2012 National Survey on Drug Use & Health. Detailed Tables.* NSDUH Series H-46, HHS Publication No. (SMA) 13-4795. Rockville, MD: Substance Abuse and Mental Health Services Administration, 2013.

Table 13.1 outlines the percentage of those 12 and older in 2012 who reported alcohol, nicotine, and other drug use in the past year. Clearly alcohol and nicotine are the drugs of choice in the United States. Although other drug use and their associated problems should in no way be discounted, the fact remains that alcohol and nicotine are far and away the American favorites. Sometimes this fact gets lost in discussions of "the war on drugs."[2]

[2]In 1969 President Nixon declared a "war on drugs." The "war" has continued and escalated. It has involved military assistance to foreign countries to disrupt the drug trade, interdiction at U.S. borders, increased penalties for drug possession and drug sales, and some lesser efforts to promote treatment. An Office of National Drug Control Policy, headed by a "Drug Czar," was created in 1996 to coordinate efforts by the multiple governmental agencies involved. In 2009 the Drug Czar announced that the phrase "war on drugs" was being retired because it was counter-productive. However, this did not signal any marked policy changes.

Demographic Factors

Age

In 2008, about half of current illicit drug users were under age 26. In only four years that has dropped to 40%. For most drugs, the rates of use are higher among youth and young adults, but the differences between age groups are declining. This is attributable not to less illicit drug use among younger people; it's because the numbers are increasing among older folks. The percentages of different age groups who have used an illicit drug in the past month are presented in Table 13.2.

In contrast to those over age 25, those still in their teens (12- to 17-year-olds) have a rate one and a half times higher, and illicit drug use is three times higher among those 18 to 25 years old.

And for this The 11TH edition, to honor the 11th edition of the Encyclopedia Britannica, I have written a new Poem "Thirteen Ways of Looking at drugs of abuse other than alcohol"
with APolgies To wallace Stevens

TABLE 13.2 Past Month Illicit Drug Use by Age Group, 2012

Drug	12–17 yrs	18–25 yrs	26 yrs and older
Any illicit drug use	9.5%	21.3%	7.0%
Marijuana	7.2	18.7	5.3
Illicit drug use other than marijuana	2.3	2.6	2.8
Cocaine	0.1	1.1	0.6
Crack	—	0.4	0.2
Heroin	—	0.1	0.1
Hallucinogens	0.6	1.7	0.2
LSD	—	0.3	0.0
PCP	0.0	0.0	0.0
Ecstasy (MDMA)	0.3	1.0	0.1
Inhalants	0.8	0.4	0.1
Non-medical use of psychotherapeutics	2.8	5.3	2.1
Pain relievers	2.2	3.8	1.5
OxyContin ®	0.2	0.4	0.1
Tranquilizers	0.6	1.6	0.7
Stimulants	0.5	1.2	0.3
Methamphetamine	0.1	0.3	0.2
Sedatives	0.1	0.1	0.1

Source: Substance Abuse and Mental Health Administration. *Results from the 2012 National Survey on Drug Use & Health. Detailed Tables.* NSDUH Series H-46, HHS Publication No. (SMA) 13-4795. Rockville, MD: Substance Abuse and Mental Health Services Administration, 2013.

Interestingly, compared to other eras, the age group with the most dramatic changes in rates of illicit drug use is those in their late 50s and early 60s, i.e., the "baby boomers," the now-aging hippies. The rate of illicit drug use in that age group is considerably higher than in any time in the past.

Gender

In 2012 men continued to have a higher rate of current illicit drug use than women—11.6% versus 6.9%. But these differences are narrowing. Among those under age 18, the rate of illicit drug use in the past month was 9.6% for males and 9.5% for females. In this younger age group, females were more likely than males to be using prescription drugs for non-medical reasons (3.2% vs. 2.4%) and pain relievers (2.6% vs 1.9%)

Education

There is not a nice tidy relationship between illicit drug use and education levels. Whether in or out of college, late adolescents and young adults have similar rates of current use. However, college graduates are more likely than those who have not completed high school to have used illicit drugs at some point. But the number of those using declines, and college graduates are less likely to be current users than those with less education. Drug use patterns for those age 26 and older are sketched out below.

Illicit Drug Use	College Grad	Some College	HS Grad	< HS Grad
Current	6%	7%	7%	9%
Lifetime	51	55	47	38

Employment Status

Historically, employment status is correlated with drug use patterns. In 2012, among those 26 and older, the rate of current illicit drug use was 7% among those working full-time, 8% for those working part-time, and 14% for those who were unemployed. For those outside the labor force—retirees, students, full-time homemakers/child care providers—the rate was 5%.

A word of caution. In looking at any statistics, it's natural to think in terms of the "why" behind them. In seeing the figures above, you might conclude that those who use illicit drugs are less able to get or to hold a job, or may not even be job hunting. But during an economic downturn, if there is only one job opening for every five people who are seeking employment, might a different explanation come to mind? Is it also possible that a higher level of drug use among the unemployed may be a result of unemployment, rather than the cause? This appears to be the case with alcohol use. (See Chapter 2, page 38.)

Geographic Region

There are regional differences in drug use patterns, as well as differences between the types of communities. In 2012, the West and the Northeast have the highest rates of current illicit drug use, 11.7% and 9.6%. The lowest rate is in the South, at 7.7%. The rate in the Midwest is midway between these at 8.6%.

In terms of the total population, illicit drug use is highest in large metropolitan areas (9.9%) and declines in tandem with declines in population density. The lowest rate in the 2012 survey was in entirely rural communities (4.8%). This is true across different age groups with one exception. Among the youngest, ages 12–17, the opposite is true, with the highest rate of illicit drug use found in entirely rural areas, and the differences between different kinds of geographic characteristics is less marked.

SOCIAL COSTS

The federal government in a 2011 report estimated the annual social economic costs from illicit drug use to be in the vicinity of $193 billion. This includes health care costs ($11.4 billion), loss in productivity ($68.4 billion), as well as an array of expenses for the criminal justice system ($113.2 billion). This latter figure includes expenses related to supply reduction through international collaborative efforts with the governments of Colombia, Mexico, and Afghanistan to curtail production, as well as interdictions along the borders and the costs of incarceration in federal and state prisons and local jails. This $193 billion figure only includes the costs associated with illicit drugs. It does not include costs related to abuse of prescription drugs, sometimes termed pharmaceuticals. These represent a significant portion of substance use problems. Indeed emergency room drug-related visits are equally divided between illicit drugs and prescription drugs. In 2013, a U.S. House Committee estimated the health care costs to be more than $70 billion per year for abuse of pharmaceuticals.

A federal judge revisits the war on drugs

. . . One thing I do know is that I have spent the last thirty-six years of my life incarcerating people for violating the illicit drug laws of the United States, yet I see nothing that would lead me to conclude, even remotely, that anything that I, or for that matter, the entire "War on Drugs" machinery of the United States, have done in this interim has had any perceptible import in curbing Americans' insatiable appetite for drugs, illegal or otherwise.

– JUSTICE JR TORRUELLA, UNITED STATES COURT OF APPEALS FOR THE FIRST CIRCUIT

"One Judge's Attempt at a Rational Discussion on the War on Drugs," lecture at Colby College, 1996

The Conundrum: Mythical Numbers

One of the difficulties in sorting through the data and numbers related to drug problems is the sheer size of the numbers. But it's more than that. Numbers of this magnitude have to be *estimates;* there are those who would call this a polite word for guesses. The Gallup poll doesn't call up and ask people how many plants they are growing, or how much they expect to get for each plant they sell! So to come up with an estimate, often other estimates are used. One thing factored into this example is the number of pot plants confiscated by the authorities. It's thought that about 10% of the entire crop is seized. Also, the yield per plant also needs to be estimated. . . . You get the idea.

In respect to the drug trade, Beau Kilmer, a contributor to the book *Re-thinking the War on Drugs* discusses the notion of "mythical numbers." This refers to the phenomenon that once a statistic is put out there, it can begin to crop up everywhere; also, when numbers are repeated so often they are trusted as common wisdom. One such number is the purported size of the U.S. domestic marijuana supply. "More than 10,000 metric tons (MT) of domestic marijuana and more than 5,000 metric tons of marijuana is cultivated and harvested in Mexico and Canada and marketed to more than 20 million users in the United States." This was first included in a 2002 State Department report, next it was used by other federal agencies, from there it was included in UN reports, and finally everything came full circle. There were U.S. reports that began to use this number and credit it to the UN.

As part of the discussion of mythical numbers, Kilmer suggests that people decide if a number makes any sense. He provides an example. Going back to the figures on domestic supply and the proportion from Mexico, the numbers used imply that every past-month user in the United States had consumed 1.2 kilograms of pot in the past year. That would be enough for every single past-month user to have been stoned for every waking hour of every day for an entire year, smoking 6.7 joints per day.[3]

Crime and Incarceration

If 1 out of 10 Americans are black, why are half of the Jailed drug offenders black?
Because 9 out of 10 Judges are white?

In 2011, United States law enforcement officers made more arrests for drug abuse violations than for any other offense. These 1.53 million arrests represented around 14% of all arrests. Rounding out the top three categories of arrests, after drug violations, the next most common category was larceny & theft (1.26 million), followed by DWI (1.21 million).

Of the total number of arrests in 2011 for drug abuse violations, over half were for simple possession. They were not for dealing, not for growing, not for committing crimes related to marijuana use. In addition, the penalties fall fairly evenly; there is little distinction in sentencing based on the individual's role in the drug trade system. Users and small-time dealers have sentences equivalent to those much higher up in the pyramid. And, as one author wryly noted, the people at the bottom have no room to plea-bargain or secure lighter sentences if they turn informer. Some of the laws that contributed to the rapid rise in the prison population were the product of emotion, not reason. The most obvious was the distinction made between cocaine as a powder and cocaine in the form of crack. The differences in penalties for use of equivalent amounts were striking. A quantity of cocaine that, as powder, was handled as a misdemeanor

[3]A kilo is equivalent to 42 ounces. The number of joints this can yield was calculated by the author, drawing upon testimony by no less an authority than Robert Brown, Hawaii's Attorney General, who testified on the joints that could be made from one ounce. The headline in the next days' Honolulu paper was "One Ounce of Weed = 56 joints." So 56 joints per oz multiplied by 42 oz, amounts to 2,352 joints per the year. And in a non-leap year of 365 days, that's 6.7 joints per day.

became a felony when the drug was in the form of crack. And it involved a five-year mandatory prison term. This federal law was repealed a quarter century later (2010), under a law known as the Fair Sentencing Act. The Anti-Drug Abuse Act of 1986 had instituted a 100-to-1 ratio between crack and powder cocaine, treating one gram of crack as equivalent to 100 grams of powder cocaine for sentencing purposes. The Fair Sentencing Act lowered the ratio to an 18-to-1 ratio, fairer even if still not fair.

"More African American men are in prison or jail, on probation or parole, than were enslaved in 1850, before the Civil War began."
—MICHELLE ALEXANDER
The New Jim Crow, Mass Incarceration in the Age of Colorblindness, 2012

African Americans are a minority of those who used crack regularly, but they comprise over 80% of those arrested for use. This brings to the fore a much larger and very troubling issue, racial inequities throughout the criminal justice system. A report by the U.S. Federal Sentencing Commission noted that over a 22 month period ending in September 2011 African American males received sentences that were 20% longer than those for white males. There are questions about disparate rates of plea bargaining. New York City has been in the limelight due its "stop and frisk" policies that lead to minorities being stopped far more frequently than whites. Police need a "reasonable" basis for stopping someone. But between 85% and 90% of those minorities stopped and frisked have been proven to be totally innocent.

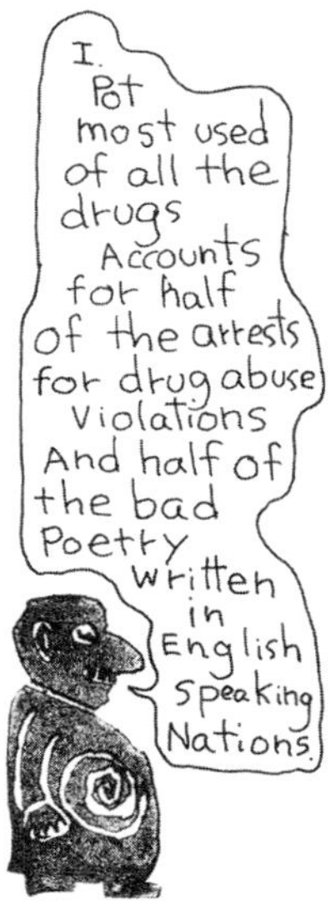

I. Pot most used of all the drugs Accounts for half of the arrests for drug abuse violations And half of the bad Poetry written in English Speaking Nations

Comparisons with Alcohol

Within the federal and state prison populations there are striking differences between the proportions and nature of crimes attributable to drinking and drug use. In general, alcohol is associated with crimes against people. Compared with other drug use, alcohol is twice as likely to play a role in homicides, 6 times as likely to be implicated in assaults, and 10 times as likely to be a factor in sexual assault. On the other hand, other drug use is associated with crimes against property. A drug other than alcohol is 8 times more common than alcohol in robberies, 10 times more common in burglaries, and 10 times more common in larceny/theft, except for auto theft, where the rate is only twice as high.

Drug arrests account for the largest portion of arrests at 13%, with DWI in the number three slot. However, if the arrests for liquor law violations and drunkenness were combined with DWI, then alcohol-related arrests would move to the number one spot, representing 24% of all arrests.

Health Problems

A host of medical problems are related to drug use. Some result directly from the drug's action. But many result from the route of administration or arise from the social circumstances that may accompany drug use.

- *Drug effects*. A variety of medical problems result from the drug's actions. (See pages 545–595 for the problems associated with different types of drugs.) Accidents and injury are more common in the presence of substance abuse, as is suicide. Overdose, too, can lead to medical problems. The combination of drugs can induce problems not associated with either alone, such as the heightened risk of rhabdomyolysis and stroke (methadone and heroin).

- *Route of administration.* Injecting drug use is related to skin infection, cellulitis, and abscess from poor injecting practices. Needle sharing is also related to increased risk of infectious disease, be it HIV, hepatitis C, or something else. In addition, intravenous use is associated with cardiovascular problems, including pseudoaneurysms and endocarditis. Drugs that are inhaled increase the risk of respiratory problems. Although admittedly not intended as a route of administration, body-packing—the ingestion of drugs as part of the drug trade to avoid detection—can lead to overdose or death if the drug escapes its packaging.
- *Illicit drug manufacture.* There are a number of problems that are associated with the manufacturing process. Methamphetamine is a prime example. Home kitchen labs are where meth is often "cooked," i.e., manufactured. The process is fraught with injury from the chemical burns from the anhydrous ammonia used, or burns that result from explosions. It presents a danger to first responders in such instances. The fumes also pollute the home and present dangers for family members, particularly children. After a home is sold, the new owners may need to decontaminate the entire house, at a cost of potentially $40,000, before it can be certified as habitable. The longer the residence was used to cook meth, the greater the contamination of wallpaper, wooden doors, woodwork, ductwork, cabinets, virtually everything in the home.
- *Social circumstances.* Sex work may be a part of the drug scene, whether to finance a drug habit or to cover basic expenses. This is associated with an increase risk of HIV, as well as an array of sexually transmitted diseases. Tattoos and body piercing are more common among drug users than among the general population. Because the practice is often a do-it-yourself effort, there is a failure to use sterile techniques, upping the odds of infection. In terms of infection, tuberculosis is most common among those with drug problems, and it is related to poor health generally, combined with poverty.

Everyone who does not live in a prostitute's bed and on a diet of cocaine snow is called an ascetic these days.
—George Bernard Shaw

PUBLIC PERCEPTIONS AND PUBLIC POLICIES

A variety of factors play a role in how the general public views drug use and drug use problems, as well as how these factors in turn influence public policy.

Legal Status

Several factors influence the way in which we view and respond to substance use. The single major factor is legal status. Perceptions of a drug's danger are tied more to its legal status than to its pharmacological properties. There are any number of ways in which we see the problems of alcohol use as belonging to "them," who are different from "us." The same is true of other drugs, but even more so. Substance use problems are often seen, erroneously, as existing primarily in urban inner cities, among minority groups, or within recent immigrant groups. There is a long historical precedent for this.

Since 60¢ of every dollar spent on drugs goes to the criminal justice system I figure every joint I smoke keeps a policeman from being laid off.

A drug's illicit status also has a major impact on how federal money is spent. A large proportion of the money spent on the war on drugs—and the use of this military metaphor should not be lost—is not for treatment or prevention. It goes to policing efforts, whether the Border Patrol, the Coast Guard, or narcotics divisions in police departments. As mentioned, in 2012, only a third of all the monies spent went for prevention and treatment, i.e., demand reduction. The majority went for supply reduction. This is a dramatic change from the early 1980s, when the expenditures for both were essentially equal, and it is matched by a dramatic rise in the prison population, attributed primarily to drug-related offenses and to mandatory sentences for drug-related offenses. Although the rise in prison population is a general area of concern, it is especially worrisome that members of minority groups are most likely to be imprisoned, despite the fact that there are not correspondingly higher rates of use among this population. This raises serious questions about disparities in policing practices and judicial responses that are based on race.

In the public health field, *harm reduction* is a very respectable approach (see Chapter 9). It is predicated on the recognition that, while preventing all use may be the long-range goal, in the interim there are steps that can be taken to reduce the negative consequences associated with use. Harm reduction has been seen as problematic when illegal drugs are involved. There is the fear that harm reduction efforts will inevitably be perceived as condoning use. One of the challenges is to create a public health response that replaces fear tactics with facts and that can see people as needing treatment and intervention rather than criminal sanctions.

Early Control Efforts

Historically, a number of drugs we now consider drugs of abuse were originally considered therapeutic agents and were commonly prescribed. The "typical" narcotic addict at the end of the 1800s was a white female who had been prescribed narcotics for the treatment of a wide variety of "female problems." Beyond physician prescriptions, many patent medicines contained an array of drugs, including drugs we now recognize as inviting abuse.

William Stewart Halsted, MD (1852–1922)

William Halsted, recognized as the father of modern surgery, entered the field when surgeons operated in street clothes, didn't believe in washing their hands, and had more in common with folk healers than modern practitioners. Halsted was the first chief of surgery at the newly opened Johns Hopkins Hospital.

He defined modern surgical principles, vis à vis the control of bleeding, anatomical dissection, sterile procedures, and wound closures. He was the first to perform a radical mastectomy, one of the first to perform gallbladder surgery (on a kitchen table in the middle of the night), and among the first to use blood transfusions. He pioneered advances for surgery of the thyroid, hernia, intestines, and arterial aneurysms. Beyond this—in his spare time—he introduced rubber gloves, created surgical instruments, made advances in use of anesthetics, created a training system for surgeons, and introduced key elements of the modern medical record.

In addition, he was addicted to cocaine for over 40 years. This addiction grew out of self-experiments conducted to explore the use of cocaine as an anesthetic and provide an alternative to ether. He entered Butler Hospital for treatment of the cocaine addiction and left with a second lifelong addiction, to morphine.

Several drugs that were originally believed to be medically useful and non-problematic turned out otherwise. For example, cocaine was initially touted as being very useful in weaning people from the opiates; thus, it was seen as effective in treating addiction. Rather quickly it became apparent that it, too, creates dependence and that the user was simply substituting one addictive drug for another.

Then there was the introduction of heroin by the Bayer Laboratory in 1898. The same pharmaceutical research team that synthesized heroin produced aspirin in the same month. Heroin was marketed as a cough suppressant and was believed—erroneously—to be superior to other available products. It was thought not merely to suppress coughs but also to improve lung function. Had this mistake not been made, in all probability heroin would never have been manufactured. Within a decade it was recognized that heroin does not promote lung function. However, by then it had taken on a life of its own.

The perceived indiscriminate use of such drugs by medical practitioners, popularly called "dope doctors," combined with the ready availability of all kinds of drugs in over-the-counter preparations, sparked the passage of two key pieces of legislation in the United States. One was the legislation that created the Food and Drug Administration in 1906. It contained what were the earliest federal provisions affecting narcotics. Any over-the-counter preparations containing opiates, cannabis (marijuana), cocaine, or chloral hydrate needed to have a label identifying these and the relative percentage(s). The other key legislation was the Harrison Act, passed in 1914, which classified certain drugs as "controlled substances." This meant that they could no longer be sold over-the-counter and could be dispensed only by physicians and used only for medical purposes.

In the earliest days of the Harrison Act, providing these drugs to addicted people was considered a legitimate use. However, that view did not prevail for very long. This led to the closing of the small number of clinics that had been established to provide drugs to existing addicts. The American Medical Association was a vocal critic of the steps that eliminated the ability of physicians to prescribe narcotics for addicted persons. The AMA's opposition was not prompted by an enlightened understanding of addiction. Rather, the point of concern was the government's interference in physicians' professional practice, in this case, by setting limits on prescribing medications.

One cannot adequately begin to summarize the subsequent decades of government drug policy. In a nutshell, following passage of the Harrison Act, the approach to drugs became increasingly punitive.

Is It Time to Rethink Prohibition as a Drug Policy?

For people in any era, it's difficult to imagine things in any way other than the way they are at the moment. "Of course the earth is flat!" "Why would any woman *want* to vote?" "Segregation really isn't discriminatory; all people like to be with their own kind."

For us living in the beginning of the twenty-first century, it is exceedingly difficult to imagine that a significant portion of the problems we see as the result of drugs might be the result of something else. That "something else" is the way in which the United States responds to drug use. A small but growing number of social historians and public policy experts point out that many of the problems and social costs associated with drugs are not the result of pharmacological effects. Instead, they result from the fact that we have made drug use illegal. (For those who think this is the dumbest thing you've ever heard, patience . . .) This does not mean adopting a laissez-faire attitude, or allowing a cocaine kiosk at the town park next to the hot dog stand. One option is to control and regulate now-illicit drugs, in the manner of legal drugs, combined with vigorous public health efforts.

While hardly a thoughtfully designed pilot public health initiative, the United States has, in effect, become engaged in a national public health experiment. It involves the legal status of marijuana. As of fall 2013, there were 19 states plus the District of Columbia that have passed laws legalizing medical marijuana. The laws differ in terms of whether they require a patient registry, allow dispensaries, specify conditions for which marijuana may be prescribed, and whether the state recognizes patients from other states.

At the same time that these actions are being taken at the state level, marijuana remains a controlled/illegal substance in the eyes of the federal government. In late summer of 2013, the U.S. attorney general announced that the federal government would *not* challenge these state laws. However in a memorandum the Justice Department identified eight situations in which the federal government would step in. These included distribution of marijuana to minors, or if any revenue from marijuana sales went to drug cartels or criminal groups, or marijuana were grown on federal lands, if marijuana dispensaries and sales became a cover for other drug trafficking, or if there were diversion of marijuana from states where it is legal to states where it is not.

In April 2012 The American Society of Addiction Medicine (ASAM) adopted a policy statement on "The Role of the Physician in 'Medical' Marijuana." It opposes medical marijuana on several grounds. One is the absence of peer-reviewed research that demonstrates marijuana is effective in treating various disorders. Related to that it has not had the usual FDA scrutiny as a medicine. Finally, the primary delivery mechanism for this "medicine" is smoking, which is a health hazard. ASAM views any physician prescribing marijuana as doing so on shaky ethical ground. It adds, "A physician should not advise a patient to seek a treatment option about which the physician has inadequate information regarding composition, dose, side effects, or appropriate therapeutic targets and patient populations."

[Members of the commission] simply state that smoking marijuana in the privacy of your home should be perfectly legal—as long as no one gave it to you [or] sold it to you or you didn't grow it yourself.
—W. WALTER MENNINGER
Report by the President's Commission on Marijuana and Drug Abuse, 1972

Another concern sometimes heard is the potential impact that the presence of medical marijuana will have on public sentiment. Will it increase the probability of more people using it, risking possible negative consequences? Adolescents are a particular concern, given the link between schizophrenia and marijuana use during adolescence. (See page 574) An interesting study sheds some light on this. It looked at adolescent marijuana use before and after in a state with legalized medical marijuana. It turns out that the level of adolescent marijuana use was not affected. As someone observed: Do you expect an adolescent to be enamored by a drug his grandmother takes?

Another twist was added when two states, Washington and Colorado, passed legislation in 2012, allowing possession of marijuana for recreational purposes.

How will all of this unfold? There is considerable speculation. Some see the federal government as wisely standing back, to see how these state-level initiatives evolve. The legalization of medical marijuana certainly does represent a trend. At some point the federal government will be compelled to take some action, to review federal laws, potentially to set national guidelines. That being the case, it would be helpful to see what works, what doesn't, and where potential problems lie. There are those, too, who are speculating about the economic aspects, namely how the tobacco companies and beverage industries may be positioning themselves. In contemplating the legalization of marijuana for recreational use, the most basic question may be what have we learned from our experience with the current legal drugs, alcohol and nicotine.

The Economic Realities

The Market Any re-thinking of drug policy requires consideration of the economic factors at play. The first thing to recognize is that there will always be a market for drugs. Making something illegal doesn't make a market evaporate. In the absence of a legal market, very rapidly, enterprising individuals figure out how to provide the desired goods. This was clear during Prohibition (see Chapter 1). One of the unanticipated consequences of Prohibition was the introduction of organized crime into American life. The potential profits were enormous. Indeed, the rate of profit was greater than had the business been legal. What happened when Prohibition was repealed? Did organized crime go away? No. It simply moved into new market niches involving other illegal activities—prostitution for one, gambling, and, later, other illicit substances.

Thank heavens for the illicit drug trade.

According to the head of the UN Office on Drugs and Crime, the approximately $325 billion in illicit drug profits that were deposited in banks kept the financial system afloat during the recent recession. In 2008, at a time when banks were dealing with huge losses from bad loans, and banks were unwilling to take a chance on each other and loan each other money. It was the illegal money in the banks that saved many of them, when lending to banks dried up.

The Profits The potential profits associated with the drug trade, as estimated by the United Nations, are almost beyond comprehension. Based on UN estimates, the global market for illicit drugs in 2011 was $411 billion. At the point of cultivation, the value is in the vicinity of $16 billion; this represents the payments to growers of poppy, coca, and marijuana.

After the completion of processing—for example, the manufacture of heroin from opium or cocaine from coca—the value increases to $120 billion. The value in terms of sales on the street is estimated to be $411 billion. The rate of profit is so great that over three-quarters of the entire world's illicit supply of drugs would have to be seized or confiscated to make the trade unprofitable. The retail value of illicit drugs globally exceeds the value of all goods and services (Gross National Product) produced by 88% of the countries of the world.

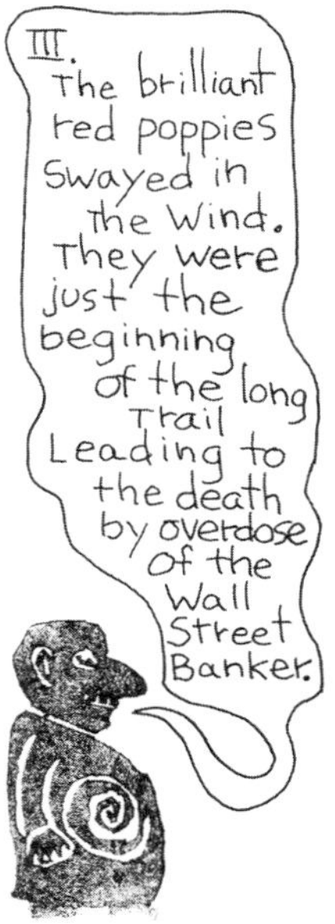

Flexibility in the Drug Trade Beyond the enormous profits, other features of the drug trade contribute to its stability. Most of the crops that underpin the drug trade can be grown virtually anywhere. So, it is possible for a country that had been only a very minor player in the production of poppy less than three decades ago to now be producing a volume of poppy that more than exceeds total global use. This is on a par with Iceland's becoming the major car manufacturer within a 30-year period! Through most of the 1970s, Afghanistan's involvement in opium production was limited, literally, to the occasional trader on camel passing through small villages, to purchase any available excess opium. That all changed when raising poppy was banned in Iran. Production simply crossed the border.

There are other examples of the drug trade accommodating to changes in circumstances. Early in the days of our war on drugs, a major concern was the amount of marijuana use. Mexico was a major supplier; the same traffickers also dealt with cocaine from Colombia, but it was a modest sideline. The seeming solution to the marijuana problem was to tighten the border in the Southwest to thwart the smuggling. Very shortly afterward, the country witnessed a rapid and dramatic increase in cocaine use, not a mere coincidence. The traffickers simply shifted their attention from marijuana to cocaine and selected an alternative point of entry, Florida.

Flexibility in Drug Production Marijuana has long been grown in northern California, in an area termed the "emerald triangle." (This is a take-off on the "golden triangle," an area of southeast Asia that was the major producer of heroin during the Vietnam War era.) Pot grown in the emerald triangle was undertaken by back-to-the-land folk, aging hippies, and small-scale opportunistic growers. However, that era is over.

To a significant degree, marijuana production in California has become the business of Mexican drug organizations. Rather than face the hassle of smuggling marijuana across the border, the Mexican gangs have imported workers to plant and tend large marijuana plots established throughout the state. California is much more than just a vast network of freeways, urban areas, sprawling suburbs, and a few valleys where veggies are grown. The state has acres of rugged, largely wilderness areas. This is where the marijuana is being grown. The areas under cultivation, known among law enforcement folks as "grows,"

Drug Seizures 2012

Cocaine	*39.7, in tons*
Heroin	*1.0*
Marijuana	*390.0*
Meth	*4.3*

Drug Enforcement Agency, <www.justice.gov/dea/resource-center/statistics.shtml#seizures>

are sophisticated operations. To prepare the site, trees are removed to allow sunlight to reach the forest floor, but retaining enough tree cover to hide the operation from aerial surveillance. The ground cover is also removed. The workforce lives on site during the growing season. They start plants, transplant, prune, build drip-irrigation systems involving an intricate array of plastic pipes to divert streams, and create fertilizing systems. Plants are culled to remove male plants, allowing the female to go unpollinated and thus prevent the buds from going to seed, which increases the THC potency and the street value.

Commandeering Public Space In California about 80% of all marijuana is grown on public lands, in national parks and national and state forests. This cultivation inflicts ecological damage. One ranger at a national park sadly commented that, "to better evade aerial surveillance, the crop is being grown on crudely terraced hillsides that erode under winter rain. [The growers] spill pesticides, fertilizer and diesel fuel used to power generators. The workers leave an ecological disaster scene; they dam creeks for water sources, plant salsa gardens, disfigure trees and leave behind tons of garbage, human waste and litter. Sometimes growers pour fertilizer right into a stream, then irrigate from it. This creates algae blooms, hurts fish and animals and contaminates downstream." In the Sequoia National Park since 2001, officers have destroyed multiple pot gardens covering over a hundred acres. But there was only enough money to clean up less than half the sites.

Substantial eradication efforts are under way, but they barely make a dent. At the conclusion of the 2006 growing season, California's attorney general reported a record number of raids and marijuana plant eradications that he said demonstrated the agency's "continued remarkable success." In 2006 the state conducted several hundred raids in more than 37 counties and seized over a million plants, with a street value estimated at close to $7 million. All of these operations only led to 27 arrests. The workers simply disappeared into the forests.

Although the use of public land to cultivate marijuana began on the West Coast, it has been moving eastward. Significant operations have been established in Colorado and recently have reached Michigan.

New Methods of Cultivation For those who don't like the outdoors, there are large indoor hydroponics farms. These can be operated anywhere. A new twist emerged in early 2007, when there was a major arrest in the Los Angeles area. The cause was transforming a rented home in a nice suburb into a hydroponics farm. No space was wasted. A maze of tubing conveyed the water; the lights were on timers. In order not to cut into the profit margin, and to avoid suspicion based on excess use of electricity, the house's electric meter had been circumvented and a direct line laid to the power grid. What aroused suspicion was the lack of activity in the home and the constantly drawn window shades. Such operations are found throughout the country.

Flexibility Among Users Those involved in the drug trade are not the only ones willing to make accommodations. People may have a preferred substance, but if it's unavailable, they will often use a different drug. An interesting example comes from Australia's 2001 "heroin draught," when, in a one-month period, there was a sudden and dramatic drop in the heroin supply. With less heroin available, injecting drug users shifted to other drugs. There was a rise in the injection of amphetamines, benzodiazepines, and opioids. In addition, there was a significant rise in the use of cocaine. When interviewed, 80% of intravenous users who had used heroin prior to the decline in availability said it was still their main drug of choice.

Facts Versus Myths Sorting through federal reports to secure information on the war on drugs is a challenge. Multiple agencies provide information on the illicit drug situation: the Justice Department, the Office of the President, the FBI, the Drug Enforcement Agency, and the list goes on. It isn't only the material that is provided; it's frequently the information that isn't provided. For example, the level of seizures in California, cited above, appears impressive. However, the "success" is less impressive when a county law enforcement agent estimates that probably 60% to 70% of plots are untouched in his county.

Suppose, if instead of judging the number of seizures, the success of marijuana eradication were measured by a different standard. How about the perceptions of high school students as to how easy it is to lay their hands on pot? Every year since 1973, more than 80% of high school seniors have reported that it is "fairly easy" or "very easy" to get pot. As a Republican member of a County Board of Supervisors in California noted, California's Campaign Against Marijuana (CAMP) is "an exercise in futility." "It's a vast expenditure of public funds that for all practical purposes does no good."

Using the total of drug arrests as a measure of enforcement can similarly be misleading. Over a several-year period, the increase in drug arrests was primarily attributable to marijuana. The bulk of these arrests were for possession, and virtually all were prosecuted as misdemeanors. One student commented, "this is like waging a war on crime and finding success in the number of arrests for jay-walking."

Societal Costs of Prohibition

When any commodity is illegal, there are societal costs for enforcing the law. There is also the loss of governmental revenue. In a report titled *The Budgetary Implications of Marijuana Prohibition,* a Harvard University economist examined the costs associated with legalizing marijuana. The report asked what would happen if it were taxed and regulated like other goods at the state and federal level. The answer is that legalizing marijuana would save an estimated $7.7 billion per year in government expenditure on enforcement of prohibition; $5.3 billion of the savings would fall to state and local governments and the remainder to the

The passage of the Volstead Act to enforce Prohibition had an immediate impact on crime. A study of 30 major U.S. cities found the number of crimes increased 24 percent between 1920 and 1921. It revealed that during that period more money was spent on police (11.4%) and more people were arrested for violating Prohibition laws (102%). But increased law enforcement efforts did not appear to reduce drinking: arrests for drunkenness and disorderly conduct increased 41 percent, and arrests of drunken drivers increased 81 percent.

—Charles Hanson Towne

The Rise and Fall of Prohibition, 1932

federal government. In addition to these savings, if marijuana were regulated and taxed at rates similar to those for alcohol and tobacco, there would be $6.2 billion annually in tax revenue. This report was endorsed by more than 530 economists, including three Nobel laureates. In their public statement they called for "an open and honest debate about marijuana prohibition," concluding, "While lost revenues are far from the central factor in determining public policy, it is one factor to be considered in any thoughtful discussion."

Cocaine Lil and Morphine Sue

Did you ever hear about Cocaine Lil?
She lived in Cocaine town on Cocaine hill,
She had a cocaine dog and a cocaine cat,
They fought all night with a cocaine rat.

She had cocaine hair on her cocaine head.
She had a cocaine dress that was poppy red:
She wore a snowbird hat and sleigh-riding clothes,
On her coat she wore a crimson, cocaine rose.

Big gold chariots on the Milky Way,
Snakes and elephants silver and gray.
Oh the cocaine blues they make me sad,
Oh the cocaine blues make me feel bad.

Lil went to a snow party one cold night,
And the way she sniffed was sure a fright.
There was Hophead Mag with Dopey Slim,
Kankakee Liz and Yen Shee Jim.

There was Morphine Sue and the Poppy Face Kid,
Climbed up snow ladders and down they skid;
There was the Stepladder Kit, a good six feet,
And the Sleigh-riding Sister who were hard to beat.

Along in the morning about half past three
They were all lit up like a Christmas tree;
Lil got home and started for bed,
Took another sniff and it knocked her dead.

They laid her out in her cocaine clothes:
She wore a snowbird hat with a crimson rose;
On her headstone you'll find this refrain:
She died as she lived, sniffing cocaine.

Anonymous, included in *Oxford Book of Light Verse*, W.H. Auden, Ed., 1938

☐ SOURCES OF DRUGS

The sources of drugs vary with the particular drug. In some instances illicit drugs are derived from plants, be they coca plants or poppy or tobacco. In other instances, the drugs are manufactured, or to borrow a slogan popularized by Dupont, providing "better living through chemistry." Then there are prescription drugs, being used for non-medical purposes. Each type of drug tends to have its own distinctive and characteristic pattern of manufacture or processing and distribution. In the cases of heroin and cocaine, large organizations commonly referred to as "cartels" are involved. In effect, these are counterparts to legal international pharmaceutical companies.

Plants: Poppies, Coca, and Cannabis Sativa

Globally the majority of *heroin* production is derived from opium poppies grown in Afghanistan. However, in the United States, the bulk of heroin is from Mexico or South America, with Mexican drug cartels playing a major role in distribution. In recent years, the heroin market was divided along the Mississippi River. Black tar and brown heroin dominated in the West, and white powder, primarily from Colombia, dominated in the East. Mexican heroin is now moving into the eastern markets, possibly made available by declining production in Colombia. *Cocaine* production, based on processing of coca leaves, which are grown in the countries of the Andes—Bolivia, Peru, and Colombia—is centered in Colombia.

Then there is *marijuana*. As described earlier, cultivation of marijuana is a sophisticated commercial operation, with Asian gangs playing the role in the East that Mexican gangs play in the West. As for value, marijuana is believed to be the country's number one cash crop, $35.8 billion, placing it ahead of corn, soybeans, and wheat. Scoring marijuana does not fit the stereotype of the drug deal. It is estimated that there are something like 400 million purchases annually. The usual purchase is small, around six or seven joints. For most users, there is no "professional" dealer in the picture. Commonly people get it from a friend or relative (89%) and for free (58%).

Illicit Drug Labs

Synthetic drugs, not prescription medications, particularly the stimulants, are manufactured in small laboratories scattered about the United States, particularly in rural areas. Of particular concern is methamphetamine production. Here a kitchen can serve as the "laboratory." The drug can be manufactured with relative ease, and the chemicals required are easily obtained. Several years ago, in an effort to make the ingredients more difficult to acquire, a federal law was passed that prohibited pharmacies from stocking cold medications with ephedrine and pseudoephedrine on open shelves; two states have passed laws requiring prescriptions for such medicines.

Beyond the dangers associated with the drugs produced, the manufacturing process itself is dangerous. Methamphetamine is a prime example. A key ingredient, anhydrous ammonia, is a dense gas that sinks rather than dispersing into the air; and it is highly flammable. It is a danger not only to the "cookers" but also to emergency or law enforcement personnel who may be called. Aside from the anhydrous ammonia, in home-based operations the fumes may be harmful to children living there.

Environmental Damage

The average methamphetamine laboratory produces 5 to 7 pounds of toxic waste for every pound of methamphetamine produced.

Methamphetamine Laboratory Identification and Hazards.Fast Facts <www.justice.gov/archive/ndic/pubs7/7341/index.htm>

Prescription Drugs

Pharmaceuticals have become a much larger part of the country's drug problem. They can be acquired by a number of routes. However, the most common means may surprise you. Over half those reporting prescription drug use for non-medical purposes identify the source as a *friend or family member*. And they are free.

The *National Survey* includes questions about the source of prescription drugs. For those acknowledging the non-medical use of pain medications, 56% said they were free and came from family or friends, 18% reported having been prescribed them by a single physician (so there was no doctor shopping), 9% reported buying them from a friend of a family member, 5% swiped them from the home of a friend or family, 4% bought them from a drug dealer or stranger, and under 1% bought them on the internet.

Of course 1% of users do not consume 1% of drugs. It's the "tale of 10 pills." When the quantity of drug needed/desired is beyond the amount that a friend or family will hand out free, and is far more than people happen to have stocked in their drug cabinet or more than would be prescribed by a single physician, what alternatives are available? One avenue is through the *diversion of legally prescribed medications*. For example, the sources of OxyContin on the street are through sales of legitimate prescriptions, prescription forgeries, and burglary of pharmacies. There are the so-called pill-mills in the Southeast United States, notorious fly-by-night pseudo-legitimate pain clinics where patients see actual doctors who prescribe high doses of opioids to virtually anyone

I will lift mine eyes unto the pills. Almost everyone takes them, from the humble aspirin to the multi-coloured, king-sized three deckers, which put you to sleep, wake you up, stimulate and soothe you all in one. It is an age of pills.

—MALCOLM MUGGERIDGE, 1962

Survey of Internet Pharmacies

To help educate the public about internet pharmacies, the National Association of Boards of Pharmacy (U.S.) wanted to create a list of recommended and non-recommended sites. The Association visited over 10,000 websites. Of note:

23% provided a physical address outside of the U.S. many provide no address
88% don't require a valid prescription
66% would provide a prescription based on an online consultation
48% offered foreign or non-FDA approved drugs

Of all the 10,0000 sites reviewed, 59 made it onto the recommended list.

The Association maintains a website with listings of approved and non-recommended internet pharmacies, including veterinary medicine sites. <www.awarerx.org/>

In a 2011 settlement with the federal government, Google agreed to pay a fine of $500 million for allowing some illegal internet pharmacies to place sponsored ads in search engine results.

In 2013, United Parcel Service paid a $40 million fine for transporting and distributing prescription drugs from illicit internet pharmacies between 2003 to 2010.

Both companies have agreed to stop doing business with such pharmacies.
—Michael Ollove

Rogue internet pharmacies: A growing danger, *Stateline*. July 10, 2013

walking in the door. A pill that costs around $4 by prescription may cost $20 to $40 on the street. Another avenue is importing drugs from countries where they are legally available. A study of persons declaring possession of prescription drugs on re-entry into the United States from Mexico found the most common drugs being brought in are those used by adolescents and young adults—benzodiazepines, including Rohypnol.

Another means of acquiring prescription drugs for non-medical use is through *internet pharmacies*. In many ways they deserve the label often applied to them, "rogue pharmacies." Largely located outside of the United States, they are unregulated. If the U.S. government uses diplomatic pressure to try to shut them down, in no time they may reappear under a new name. The danger they pose goes far beyond being a source of prescription drugs for non-medical use. The general population is turning to internet pharmacies as a means of saving money on their prescription drugs. Among the dangers associated with internet pharmacies is that they may be dispensing contaminated products, drugs that are sub-potent, super-potent, or expired, or counterfeit, or containing the wrong ingredient or no active ingredients.

Drug dealers are a major player in drug diversion. A number of techniques are used. One is to pay people for pain clinic shopping, visiting numerous pain physicians and getting multiple prescriptions. Another is to recruit a pharmacy technician or a pain clinic employee who can pilfer drugs or arrange for fraudulent prescriptions. Or they may purchase a portion of an indigent patient's or a VA patient's prescribed drugs. Finally there is blatant health care fraud, such as counterfeiting MRIs as a prop to use when doctor-shopping.

Reducing Drug Diversion

The potential for the diversion of drugs and their use for unintended purposes is especially worrisome with regard to medications having psychoactive properties. However, steps can be taken in the manufacturing process to reduce the abuse potential. Failure to have taken this into account is what caused a delay in the FDA's final approval of buprenorphine as an alternative to methadone in the treatment of heroin dependence. Buprenorphine has abuse potential, especially when crushed and injected. To reduce the likelihood of abuse, when manufactured as Suboxone, an additional drug, naloxone, not to be confused with naltrexone, is combined with the buprenorphine. Naloxone is an opiate antagonist, meaning it blocks the ability of opiates to have an effect. Of importance, this blocking ability is present *only* when naloxone is injected. If taken orally, under the tongue, as Suboxone is intended to be taken, the naloxone has no effect. However, if someone tries to inject buprenorphine and the naloxone, the latter blocks the effects of the buprenorphine. *If* someone is already on an opiate, the injected naloxone causes the person to go into immediate and very uncomfortable withdrawal. With this mixed formulation, the potential for abuse is significantly reduced. Such a formulation is not a new idea, and the pharmaceutical company that produces OxyContin has been criticized for not having anticipated the potential for abuse and used such a formulation. Of note, buprenorphine is available without naloxone (called Subutex) and is primarily prescribed to pregnant clients. During pregnancy naloxone can cross the placenta and put the fetus into opioid withdrawal if the mother is opioid dependent.

Pharmaceutical companies cannot singularly be held responsible for the abuse of their products. But it is not unreasonable to expect they will take the steps within their means to reduce the potential for abuse. It was for this reason the manufacturer of Rohypnol, Hoffman-LaRoche, made changes in its manufacturing process.

It Was a Dark and Stormy Night

Hartford Conn. AP., March 17, 2010. —Before day break, in a Hollywood-style heist, thieves scaled a brick exterior wall, cut a hole in the roof of an Eli Lilly warehouse, and rappelled inside. It's speculated that the next hour was spent putting packing boxes of prescription drugs onto pallets. These were then transferred to a large tractor trailer the thieves parked at the loading dock. Shortly after, $75 million of stolen prescription drugs were heading down the road.

Note: This heist did not involve any controlled drugs. Maybe it was just a dry run.

Rohypnol, a benzodiazepine, not approved for use in the United States but marketed in Europe and Latin America, is odorless, colorless, and tasteless. According to media accounts, it has been surreptitiously slipped into women's drinks, and the women do not realize they are consuming a drug. In combination with alcohol, there are additive effects, so intoxication occurs more quickly than with alcohol alone. In response to these reports, Hoffman-LaRoche added another ingredient to Rohypnol. This does not affect its psychoactive properties, but it does turn any liquid a milky white. So this provides a warning that something is amiss. In addition Hoffman-LaRoche took other steps. It made considerable efforts to assist date-rape victims by providing free, comprehensive testing for Rohypnol in emergency departments, law enforcement agencies, and sexual assault crisis clinics. (The pharmacological properties of Rohypnol [flunitrazepam] are discussed later in this chapter within the section "Sedative-Hypnotics.")

This raises another issue worth noting. Initial reports, in the media and elsewhere, about drug abuse and misuse may be inaccurate or incomplete. This is especially true of self-reports and the use of street drugs. There is no question about the abuse of flunitrazepam (Rohypnol). There *is* reason to question whether the level of rapes supposedly associated with its use is as extensive as has been reported. One medical center emergency department examined the results of more than 1,000 consecutive laboratory tests that were performed in cases suspected to involve flunitrazepam. The tests involved urine samples, and of the 1,077 tests performed, flunitrazepam was present in only 6 of the tests! Of all the cases, 41% of all assays were negative for all drugs tested. The remaining 59% had one or more drugs detected, including alcohol. The breakdown was alcohol (36%), marijuana (18%), all other benzodiazepines (6%), and GHB (4%).

Another study similarly raises questions about the reliability of reports of flunitrazepam use. Interviews were conducted with women who identified themselves as using flunitrazepam. However, when asked to describe the appearance of the "Rohypnol" they had taken, the descriptions being provided were not for Rohypnol but were consistent with the appearance of other benzodiazepines. Here, too, there was a wide range of other drug use reported. The substance abuse field seems to have its own versions of an internet urban myth.

As for Perdue Pharma, the manufacturer of OxyContin, sadly the criticism that has been levied is far, far less than deserved. In May 2007, Purdue pled guilty to false marketing practices. The company long claimed that OxyContin was less addictive than other opioids, that there was far less danger of withdrawal, and that the active ingredient was less easily extracted, making diversion less likely. All of these claims were false. Sales representatives used bogus scientific charts to support these points as they made their rounds of physicians' offices. The false claims continued for at least seven years *after* physicians first began raising questions in light of the high rates of OxyContin abuse they encountered, particularly in rural areas. In parts of Appalachia, some referred to OxyContin as "the hillbilly's heroin." As part of its guilty plea, the company agreed to pay a record fine of $600 million levied by the FDA. (Additional costs of over $300 million have been estimated as required to cover state and health program costs as well as to settle civil court cases.) For anyone concerned about substance abuse, hearing about this episode is likely to arouse both anger and disgust. The company's behavior is all the more reprehensible in light of Hoffman-LaRoche's response to concerns around Rohypnol.

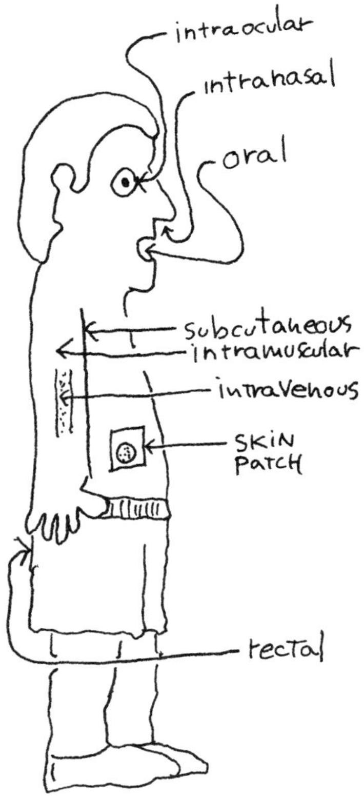

BASIC PHARMACOLOGICAL CONCEPTS

When reviewing textbooks about drugs of abuse, organized in the format of one chapter per drug, it is all too easy to feel you are drowning in facts, while remaining a little short on understanding. If this is your experience, consider a different starting point. Forget about the different drugs. Instead, begin by considering several basic, essential principles that are pertinent to understanding *any* drug.

Key constructs in considering drug use include how drugs are taken into the body; how rapidly they are delivered to the brain; how they are metabolized and the kinds of by-products produced; how rapidly they are removed; abuse potential; and how they affect the brain to produce their effects, including sites of action. The following sections discuss these key elements. With this information as background, the next task is to think in terms of different classes of drugs. All drugs in a particular class, by definition, share many features. To know to which class a drug belongs is to have considerable information.

Several of the key concepts have been discussed earlier. Here is the briefest of reviews:

- The *route of administration* refers to how a drug is taken into the body; it determines how quickly a drug reaches the brain. This, in turn, determines how rapidly its effects are felt. The route of administration also has significance in terms of the kinds of problems that can accompany drug use, be they the long-term health consequences associated with smoking or the risks of infection that can accompany injection use.

- The *site of action* refers to the particular neurotransmitters that are affected by a drug, as well as their distribution in the brain. The former determines the effects of a particular drug; the latter is associated with the types of effects as well as the possibility of lethal outcomes.
- *Metabolism* refers to how a drug is broken down and removed by the body. How a drug is metabolized and removed from the body suggests the kinds of problems that may result. As was discussed earlier (see Chapters 3 and 6), alcohol is metabolized by enzymes that are produced primarily in the liver and to a lesser degree in the stomach. One of these enzyme systems, cytochrome P450, is involved in the metabolism of other drugs as well. Thus, if different drugs are present, both requiring the same enzymes, they are in competition, and removal of both is slowed. Metabolizing any drug is typically a stepwise process, with by-products formed at each phase. Some of these by-products are benign and have no mood-altering properties. For others this is not the case.
- *Solubility in fat and/or water* is important in terms of how drugs are distributed throughout the body after ingestion.

Withdrawal

One of the defining attributes of an addictive substance is the emergence of discomfort if use is stopped or if the usual dose is substantially reduced. Some prefer the term "abstinence syndrome" rather than "withdrawal." The symptoms of withdrawal differ by drug class; however, there are several broad features. In general, the symptoms associated with abstinence are the opposite of the symptoms associated with use. Thus, for a depressant drug, one of the symptoms of withdrawal is agitation. Also, the shorter the duration of the effects of a drug, the more intense the withdrawal will be, but the duration of withdrawal symptoms will also be shorter. Conversely, longer-acting drugs have less severe withdrawal symptoms, but these symptoms persist over a longer period.

Marijuana is . . . self-punishing. It makes you acutely sensitive, and in this world, what worse punishment could there be?
—P. J. O'Rourke
Rolling Stone, 1989

Abuse Potential

Drugs vary in their potential for abuse. As discussed in Chapter 5, the speed of action and the duration of the effects are two significant determinants. For example, with cocaine or nicotine, the risk is considerable. The effects are felt very quickly and also wear off quickly, increasing the likelihood of abuse. The speed of action is related to the route of administration. As a rule, injecting a substance produces the most rapid

Cocaine, habit-forming? Of course not. I ought to know. I've been using it for years.
—Tallulah Bankhead

onset of action, followed closely by smoking, then oral ingestion. With some drugs the user has several choices in terms of how to take them. With marijuana, there is the choice of smoking or incorporating it in food, such as the well-touted marijuana brownies. With cocaine, there are the options of snorting, smoking, or injecting. As someone's drug career unfolds, it is likely that the individual will adopt more efficient routes of administration. In the wake of this, with more rapid delivery comes a more intense experience of the drug effects, a condition inviting further use.

Definitions of Medical Terms

autonomic: *elevations in blood pressure, heart rate, and body temperature; body activities not requiring conscious control.*

bruxism: *grinding and clenching the teeth.*

de-realization: *feeling detached from reality; de-personalization; common with PTSD.*

dysarthria: *speech difficulties.*

dyskinesias: *abnormal involuntary movement.*

dysphoric: *dis-ease, opposite of euphoria.*

dystonias: *muscle spasm causing cramping and stiffness.*

endocarditis: *buildup of bacteria around the valves of the heart, possible result of needle sharing.*

hypersomnia: *excessive sleep, opposite of insomnia.*

lacrimation: *shedding tears.*

nystagmus: *flickering back and forth eye movement.*

rhabdomyolysis: *breakdown of muscle tissue, from a crush injury or medication side effects.*

rhinorrhea: *runny nose.*

stereotypic: *behavior well-defined in others with a similar condition, e.g., skin scratching in heroin users.*

synthesia: *crossing sensory pathways, e.g., LSD users "seeing" sounds or "feeling" sights*

Use Patterns as an Indicator of Abuse Potential

The *National Survey* provides information on the percentage of past-year users of various drugs and the proportion of current users who are identified as meeting the criteria for abuse or dependence. The portion of past-year users who qualify for a diagnosis of abuse or dependence provides a rough measure of the likelihood that use turns into problematic use.

Drug	Users with Substance Use Disorder	Drug	Users with Substance Use Disorder
Nicotine	85.6%	Pain relievers	13.1%
Heroin	60.0	Sedatives	13.0
Cocaine	28.1	Inhalants	10.1
Marijuana	16.2	Hallucinogens	9.8
Stimulants	14.8	Tranquilizers	8.0
Alcohol	13.7		

Source: Office of Applied Studies. *Results from the 2012 National Household Survey on Drug Use and Health. National Findings.* Rockville MD: National Institute on Drug Abuse, 2013.

Based on the responses to the *National Survey* (2012), in the past year, 8.5% of those age 12 or older met the criteria for diagnosis of either alcohol or illicit drug abuse or dependence. This is equivalent to 22.1 million people. The bulk of these represent alcohol abuse or dependence. There is, however, a glaring omission in these figures. *Nicotine* is not included. It is estimated that about 23% of the population who uses tobacco are dependent. What would be a more accurate estimate of the true number of those dependent or abusing alcohol and other drugs? Rather than 22.1 million, a far better estimate of those with alcohol or drug dependence would be 62.7 million.[4]

[4]In 2012, NIDA estimated 27% of the population used tobacco in the past month and that 80% of those were dependent. Therefore, at least 21% of the population is hooked on nicotine. The comparable figure for alcohol is 6.5%, and for illicit drugs, 2.5%. A quarter of alcohol dependent people are also nicotine dependent, so add the rest of those who are nicotine dependent and the total is 62.7 million people.

Social Influences

Drugs have taught an entire generation of Americans the metric system.
—P. J. O'Rourke

Abuse potential is a pharmacological concept. It is based on the effects of a drug. However, outside of a laboratory setting social factors influence the likelihood of abuse. One is social acceptance of use. Closely linked to social acceptance is the opportunity for use. Even if a drug were ranked at the top of the list with the greatest pharmacological abuse potential, it would not be widely abused if there were little access to it. Virtually every adult of legal drinking age has the opportunity to use alcohol. Given the manner in which alcohol is used socially, for many the choice is whether to drink or not to. While it is not uncommon for a host or hostess to wander through a party with a tray of drinks for guests, this is hardly the case with illicit drugs. One does not usually find a tray with lines of cocaine or syringes with heroin being passed along with the cheese and crackers and onion dip.

The *Monitoring the Future* survey routinely asks questions about attitudes toward use as well as the students' sense of how easy it would be to get a particular drug. Similarly, the *National Survey* asks about availability and perceptions of whether obtaining a drug would be fairly or very easy. Not surprisingly, younger grade levels report drugs are less accessible. In 2011, among high school seniors 82% considered it easy or fairly easy to obtain marijuana. That's the lowest rate since the survey was introduced over 35 years ago. Even their parents can still score. Through age 50, two-thirds considered it easy to get pot.

For other illicit drugs, 53% of young adults (ages 19–22) said it was very easy or fairly easy to obtain narcotics other than heroin, followed closely by amphetamines (52%), then by cocaine (39%), ecstasy (38%), sedatives (38%), LSD (26%), heroin (21%), and tranquilizers (19%). Differences between high school seniors and young adults are negligible for most drugs. For those above age 30, there is typically a drop among those who perceive easy access. There is one notable exception, the 50-year-olds perceive cocaine as readily accessible. Steroids is the one drug that high school students consider more accessible than do all other age groups.

Problems

Many of the problems resulting from alcohol apply to other drug use. As with alcohol, the *pharmacological effects* of a given drug can lead to acute problems in the absence of dependence. Given our familiarity with alcohol, the tendency is to think that major medical problems occur only after extended heavy use. It may literally be decades of heavy drinking before irreversible liver damage or brain damage occurs. However, this is not universally true with other drugs; there is considerable variability among substances. For example, even after relatively short periods of use, inhalants can have serious medical consequences, with permanent brain damage.

With other drugs, the *presence of contaminants* as well as the *by-products of metabolism* are a concern. The potential for irreversible toxic effects was brought home in the late 1980s, in the efforts of illicit labs to produce a designer drug, a version of meperidine (Demerol). A neurotoxin was present in the drugs manufactured. This by-product, MPTP (methyl-phenyl-tetrahydropyridine), is noted for its ability to induce symptoms of Parkinson's disease. A number of users of that batch developed drug-induced Parkinson's, which is wholly nonreversible. Levamisole is a contaminant that is found in most of the cocaine being traded worldwide. Thus, it appears to be mixed with the cocaine at the point of production—and it is a white powder—to dilute the cocaine. Accordingly, the proper term for this is "additive."

Anthrax-Contaminated Heroin Still in Circulation

Health experts have warned that heroin contaminated with anthrax . . . is still in circulation in Scotland. The 39 confirmed cases of anthrax in Scotland since December 2009 have resulted in 12 deaths. . . . There is a risk of infection from both injecting and smoking the drug.

BBC News, May 12, 2010

Another concern is related to the *route of administration.* Intravenous use as a means of drug administration has special problems—namely, infection from non-sterile techniques and from the sharing of syringes. Also with injection drug use, there can be problems that simply come from inexperience and uninformed injection practices. When a drug can be taken by multiple routes, as a drug career takes hold, it is likely that the user will go from less to more dangerous routes, such as from sniffing or oral routes of administration to intravenous use.

Toxicity and Overdose

Drugs vary considerably in the risks of unintentional death from an overdose. Several measures are used in considering toxicity. One of these is known as the median *l*ethal *d*ose, the shorthand for which is LD_{50}. This term, which originated in toxicology laboratory studies, represents the amount of a drug at which half of the animals to which it is administered die. An LD_{50} doesn't represent the dose at which deaths begin to occur but is the midpoint; already 49% of deaths have occurred. Another relevant value is the median *e*ffective *d*ose, known as ED_{50}. This value indicates the dose that 50% of animals need to take to get the desired effects. In thinking about the relative safety of any drug, an important factor is the size of the window between the dose needed to get the desired effect and the dose at which death occurs. When these values are very close together, there is little margin for error. The relationship of the lethal dose to the effective dose is termed the safety ratio.

A Common Cut in Cocaine May Prove Deadly

[L]evamisole has become increasingly popular as a "cut," or diluting agent, in cocaine and possibly some heroin. It is now found in 70% of all cocaine seized in the U.S., up from 30% in 2008. Once used to treat colon cancer, [it] is now reserved for veterinary use as a medication to get rid of worms [and] can cause agranulocytosis in humans, evidenced by dead, darkened skin that looks like burns, unremitting fevers, flulike symptoms, and dangerously low white-blood-cell counts.

—Maia Szalavitz

Time Magazine, Wednesday, Jan. 20, 2010

The safety ratio and the estimated lethal dose of different drugs are provided in Table 13.3. The estimated lethal dose applies to a healthy 155 pound adult, without tolerance to the substance or without residue from any prior administrations, and in the absence of other drugs.

As is apparent, there are substantial differences in the safety ratio of different drugs. The most toxic substances have a lethal dose less than 10 times the effective dose. These substances include heroin, isobutyl nitrite, and GHB. The next most acutely toxic substances, with safety ratios from 10 to 20, include alcohol, cocaine, codeine, dextromethorphan (DXM), ecstasy/MDMA, methadone, and methamphetamine.

Remember these numbers represent averages and cannot predict the outcome for a particular individual.

TABLE 13.3 Estimated Lethal Doses of Abused Psychoactive Substances

Drug	Route of Administration	Safety Ratio	Usual Lethal Dose
Heroin	Intravenous	6	50 mg
Isobutyl nitrite	Inhaled	8	1.51 ml vaporized liquid
GHB	Oral	8	16 gr
Alcohol	Oral	10	330 g
DXM	Oral	10	1.5 g
Methamphetamine	Oral	10	>150 mg
Cocaine	Nasal	15	1200 mg
MDMA	Oral	16	2 g
Methadone	Oral	20	100 mg
Codeine	Oral	20	800 mg
Mescaline	Oral	24	8.4 gr*
Rohypnol	Oral	30	30 mg
Ketamine	Nasal	38	2.7 g
DMT	Oral	50	2 g
Phenobarbital	Oral	100	>2 g
Prozac	Oral	100	>2 g
Nitrous oxide **	Inhaled	>150	>525 l
Psilocybin	Oral	1000	6 g
Marijuana	Smoked	1000	>15 g
LSD	Oral	1000	100 mg*

*Extrapolated from animal studies.

** Never toxic if used with adequate oxygen. Non-medical doses usually 100% N_2O, and death is due to anoxia.

Source: Gable RS. Comparison of acute lethal toxicity of commonly abused psychoactive substances (review). *Addiction* 99(6): 686–696, 2004. (103 refs.)

CLASSIFICATION SCHEMAS FOR DRUGS OF ABUSE

There are a variety of ways in which drugs of abuse can be classified. The particular system used in a discussion can be more or less helpful, depending on the purpose. Whether a drug is licit or illicit certainly

makes a difference in considering the social consequences of use. However, this way of categorizing drugs usually provides little insight into the medical problems inherent with use or the risk of abuse and dependence. It certainly doesn't say much about the subjective effects that accompany use and the properties that may make the drugs attractive to some people. For those purposes, other schema will be more useful.

Licit Versus Illicit

Commonly, distinctions are made between licit and illicit drugs. On one hand are alcohol and nicotine, and on the other, everything else. Prescription and over-the-counter drugs don't quite fit into this classification scheme. While not illegal, if they are used for non-medical purposes, they are probably being abused. The licit/illicit dichotomy certainly has implications for law enforcement and societal problems. This distinction can also have health implications. Illicit drugs, by definition, are manufactured without government control or oversight and thus can be of questionable purity and strength. Heroin may have been cut many times, or barely cut at all, and thus the true dose may be higher or lower than what the user expects. Drugs sold on the street, supposedly as prescription drugs, may be just about anything. It used to be thought that prescription drugs, even if not used for medical purposes, at least didn't have the problem of adulterants or contaminants; if dispensed by licensed pharmacies in the United States, that is true. However, prescription drugs manufactured in other countries and in the absence of adequate oversight have been the source of poisonings. The problem isn't just with pet food. So, *caveat emptor* (a Latin phrase meaning "Let the buyer beware").

DEA Schedule

The Controlled Substances Act, which originated as the Harrison Act, is a federal law that identifies some drugs as controlled substances and sets forth rules and regulations about their manufacture, use, and distribution. The Food and Drug Administration (FDA) houses the administrative machinery for determining the status of a drug. Controlled substances are limited to those for which there is potential for abuse. If controlled, the drug is placed in one of five categories, depending on the assessment of its potential for abuse, potential for dependence, and current accepted medical use:

Schedule I. Any drug included here has a high level of abuse/dependence. Also, there is no accepted medical use. Included are heroin, LSD, and marijuana.

Schedule II. These drugs are essentially similar to those in Schedule I. There is evidence of the potential for abuse/dependence.

The distinguishing feature in Schedule II is that there is an accepted medical use. There are restrictions on manufacture and distribution via production quotas and import and export controls. Prescriptions are non-refillable. Schedule II drugs include methadone, morphine, amphetamines, and cocaine.

Schedule III. Drugs in this category are considered to be at moderate risk or low risk for physical dependence but at high risk for psychological dependence. There are currently established reasons for medical use. Schedule III drugs include Vicodin, Suboxone, and Tylenol No. 3 and No. 4.

Schedule IV. Drugs in this category are considered to be at low risk for physical dependence but moderate risk for psychological dependence. There are currently accepted indications for medical use. Drugs in this group include Valium, Ativan, Halcion, and Darvon.

Schedule V. Drugs in this category are considered to be at low risk for both physical dependence and psychological dependence. Again, there are currently accepted indications for medical use. Lomotil is an example.

Controlled Substance Analogs

Controlled substances are essentially identified by their chemical formulas. Several years ago those manufacturing drugs in illicit laboratories found a way around the law. They changed the drug slightly, so that the drug's chemical composition was no longer that specified by the law. For this reason these drugs are sometimes called "designer drugs." However, the changes were for the most part inconsequential in terms of the drugs' effects. A Porsche is a Porsche; it doesn't matter if it comes in charcoal gray or bright red. To plug up this loophole, an amendment was added to the Controlled Substances Act as part of the Anti-Drug Abuse Act of 1986. It created a new category—*controlled substance analog*. This is a category used for drugs that are chemically very similar to drugs in Schedule I or Schedule II. They are treated as Schedule I drugs, without any redeeming social value.

Emergency or Temporary Scheduling

To deal with the unexpected, in 1984, as part of the Comprehensive Crime Control Act, an amendment to the Controlled Substances Act was passed to allow immediate action in dealing with drugs that show up on the street and are not covered by the existing schedule. The head of the DEA has the authority to declare a drug as Schedule I on a temporary basis, until research can be conducted to ascertain the drug's properties and the appropriate schedule.

Other Drug Classification Schemes

Great Britain, under its Misuse of Drugs Act (1971), has a three-tier classification system. Level A is the category corresponding to DEA Schedule I. It includes heroin, methamphetamine, and ecstasy. Through 2004, marijuana was a Level B drug, but then was recategorized to Level C.

The Misuse of Drugs Act was amended in 2005. Two types of changes were introduced. Some are directed at changing the criminal justice process. For example, there is now the assumption of intent to supply when a defendant is in possession of a defined quantity of a controlled drug. Other changes within this criminal code are directed to promoting clinical care and professional assessment. These changes include testing of drug offenders at the point of arrest, rather than at charging; requiring those with a positive drug test to undergo an assessment by a drug clinician, and requiring drug counseling for those whose offenses are drug related.

Pharmacological Effects

Another way of classifying drugs is to group them in terms of their primary effects. This is essentially the classification schema used in the APA's *Diagnostic and Statistical Manual* and is of particular use to those working in the clinical field. This is how those who use drugs tend to think about them. This is evidenced by some of the slang such as "uppers" or "downers" used to refer to a family of drugs. People will consider drugs that have the same effects more or less an adequate substitute for one another. If someone likes to take LSD but can't get any, peyote might be an acceptable substitute. But it is far less likely a sedative will be considered an adequate alternative.

Equally important for the clinician, with a few exceptions, is that drugs in the same class share important characteristics. They are used for a particular effect, have similar effects on the brain, have similar symptoms of overdose or toxicity, and have similar withdrawal syndromes. These commonalities are also the basis for the treatment of withdrawal.

Club drug is a vague term that refers to a wide variety of drugs.
NIDA Director, 2002

Club Drugs: An Exception

These drugs do not constitute a pharmacologic class of compounds. The drugs commonly referred to as "club drugs" fall into multiple drug classes—sedatives/depressants, stimulants, hallucinogens, and dissociatives. The common denominator isn't chemistry; it's the settings in which they are commonly used—nightclubs, music festivals, dance parties, and raves, the rock concerts of this generation. Raves are commonly held in private clubs, hence the name "club drugs" for the drugs that are commonly used there. These drugs and their associated problems are discussed later in the chapter. (See pages 571–572.)

Legal Highs: Another Exception

Club drugs include alcohol, LSD, MDMA (ecstasy), GHB, GBL, ketamin (Special-K), fentanyl, Rohypnol, amphetamines, and methamphetamine.
NIDA, website, 2004

This category of drugs is a recent arrival. These drugs are clearly seen as related to illicit drugs. However, they have been synthesized to be sufficiently different to avoid being considered a controlled substance analog. Rather than being a brother or sister, these are merely cousins. Not being illegal, a number have been sold not only on the web, but also in convenience stores or delis. Among the selling points is that they are "all natural" and without "harsh chemicals." One group is the *synthetic cannabinoids* with names such as Spice, or K2, typically sold in small packets. Then there are the take-offs on the stimulants of the amphetamine class, the *synthetic cathinones*. These include "bath salts," "jewelry cleaner," and "plant food" aka "meow meow." Either mephedrone or other cathinones (related to Khat, a plant which has stimulant effects when its leaves are chewed) are the active ingredients. (See page 594). In 2012 an emergency law was passed, the *Synthetic Drug Prevention Act*; it banned 26 different chemicals thought to be used in the manufacture of these drugs.

MAJOR CLASSES OF COMMONLY ABUSED DRUGS

Nicotine

Patterns of Use

Nicotine ranks right up there with alcohol, the other licit drug, as one of the most widely used in the United States. In addition, it ranks up there as a major public health concern. Since the late 1960s, when 40% of the adult population smoked, there has been a steady decline in nicotine use. Now only 22% of the population are current smokers. For a long time, tobacco use was equated with smoking cigarettes. It is only recently that the *National Survey* began to ask questions about different forms of tobacco. In 2012, 69 million people used tobacco products in the past month. By way of contrast, in that same month, "only" 9 million people used an illicit drug other than marijuana. So for each person using an illicit drug (other than marijuana), there were eight using tobacco. Recently there has been a marked increase in the popularity of waterpipes, long used in other parts of the world for smoking tobacco. Although all the evidence suggests that this is not the case, the perception is that a waterpipe—also known as an argileh, hookah, narghile, or shisha—is less harmful and less addictive. Apparently too, waterpipes are considered more attractive, indicating a bit more class, and thus more acceptable. There has also been a rise in the use of smokeless tobacco, which too is promoted as less harmful.

A custom loathsome to the eye, hateful to the nose, harmful to the brain, dangerous to the lungs, and in the black, stinking fume thereof nearest resembling the horrible Stygian smoke of the pit that is bottomless.

—JAMES I OF ENGLAND

A Counterblaste to Tobacco, 1604

Demographics of Use

Overall, men are more likely to use tobacco than are women. However, the gender gap is disappearing. Over the years, men have quit smoking at a higher rate than women. Plus, among younger people there is virtually no difference in use patterns. When it comes to *age,* the rate of regular tobacco use rises dramatically from age 12 through 18. The percentage of smoking or using other tobacco grows rapidly, moving from 1% of 12-year-olds to 16% by age 16, to 35% by age 18. Use peaks at age 23, when 42% are smoking or using other tobacco products. At that point the proportion of users begins to decline, but the decline is much more gradual than was the rate of acquisition. You have to look to those in their mid-60s before the proportion of smokers is equivalent to the rate for 16-year-olds.

With respect to *racial/ethnic* differences, Native Americans have the highest rate of regular smokers, at 36%, followed by whites (24%), African Americans (22%), Hispanics (19%), and Asians (12%). The rates of nicotine use vary considerably among Asian people of different ethnicity. The rate of nicotine use among Korean Americans, who have the highest level of use, is essentially twice the rate among Chinese Americans, who have the lowest rate. Similarly, there are different rates among Hispanic groups.

Among adults, higher levels of *education* are associated with lower levels of tobacco use. In terms of *employment* status, the highest rate of use is among the unemployed, and the lowest rate is among "other" which includes homemakers, students, the retired, and the disabled. *Geography* is also a factor; the South is the region with the highest percentage of those using tobacco. The West has the lowest rate, followed by the Northeast and then the Midwest. The size of the community also plays a role; the highest level of smoking is found in rural areas, and the lowest rates are in large metropolitan areas.

Associated Drug Use

Smoking is strongly associated with other substance use. One of the best predictors of other drug use is smoking status. Many studies have found that those who use tobacco are more likely to use other substances—sedatives, hallucinogens, stimulants, and opioids. According to the *National Survey* (2012) data, compared with those who don't use nicotine, those who smoke are 4½ times more likely to use an illicit drug; 5 times more likely to use marijuana; 15 times more likely to use hallucinogens, and 4 times more likely to use prescription drugs for nonmedical reasons. In addition, those who smoke cigarettes are more likely to at some point to have used other drugs that are smoked. Being used to this route of administration of drugs, smokers have a greater likelihood of experimenting with other drugs that are smoked. For example, in one study, among those who entered treatment for cocaine that they'd smoked, virtually all (97%) had a history of smoking cigarettes prior to cocaine use. Also of interest, those who quit smoking cocaine stopped smoking other drugs, with one exception—nicotine. Half quit smoking marijuana and a third decreased their marijuana use when they ceased cocaine use. But only 5% quit smoking cigarettes.

Should cigarette packs carry a radiation exposure warning label?

Polonium 210 is a radioactive element, discovered by Madame Curie in the early 1900s. The tobacco companies have known for more than 40 years that this radioactive element is part of tobacco and tobacco smoke and made significant efforts to keep this information from the general public. Smoking a pack a day for one year provides as much radiation as having 300 chest x-rays a year.

American Journal of Public Health 98(9):1643–1650, 2008

The general association of nicotine use with other drug use is especially striking among teenagers. Those under age 18 who smoke cigarettes were 9 times more likely to have used an illicit drug in the past month. In terms of specific drugs, teenage smokers were 13 times more likely than their non-smoking peers to have used marijuana and 5 times more likely to have used inhalants. The use of heroin by non-smokers was so rare as to make a numerical comparison impossible.

Abuse Potential

Nicotine is a drug with a high potential for abuse/dependence. This is dramatically highlighted by the title of one journal article: "The Nicotine Addiction Trap: A 40-Year Sentence for Four Cigarettes." The authors noted that, as of 1990, the point at which the article was published, "over

90% of teenagers who smoke three to four cigarettes are trapped into a career of regular smoking which typically lasts for some 30–40 years. Only 35% of regular smokers succeed in stopping permanently before the age of 60, although the large majority want to stop and try to stop." So if people can manage to smoke three to four cigarettes and get through the initial effects—which, in fact are not pleasant (dizziness and sometimes nausea)—they will be embarking on a smoking career that statistically is likely to go on for at least four decades. The bulk of smokers begin smoking as adolescents.

Another perspective on the high rate of dependence among those who use nicotine can be gleaned by looking at the proportion of "past-year" smokers who are also current smokers, defined as use in the past month. The percentage of past-year users who are also current users is suggestive of the extent of physical dependence associated with use. How does nicotine compare with illicit drugs? For heroin and crack cocaine, the proportion of past-year users who are also current users is about 50%. The rate for tobacco is around 85%, a rate that is higher than for any illicit drug.

On tobacco

I do not think that all are equally susceptible of narcotic influence. Novices trying their first cigar are not all affected in the same degree, nor in the same way. In some, nausea will be the strongest symptoms; in others, intoxication. Some will make successive trials with little diminution of the woes that attend beginners; others seem to be fascinated almost at once. Before one has learned to tolerate use, another is already joined to his idol. I have a suspicion, too, that to live among smokers, to inhale constantly the strong fumes of tobacco, produces in some cases not only a degree of physical preparation for the use of it, but tends to implant the appetite, and urge with more or less force in the direction of indulgence. The one whose nervous system responds most promptly and fully to the intoxication will soonest be entangled in the meshes of the habit.

—J. T. Crane

Arts of Intoxication, 1870

Pharmacological Action

Different types of nicotinic receptor sites are found throughout the brain. They are present in differing concentrations, and there is considerable complexity in how they function. There is evidence, too, that the number and concentration of sites increase with the use of tobacco. The receptors appear to be located both on cell bodies and at the nerve terminals. These receptors are associated with the release of an array of neurotransmitters: acetylcholine, norepinephrine, serotonin, beta endorphin, glutamate, and dopamine, which is recognized for its rewarding properties. Nicotine also leads to the release of growth hormone, prolactin, and ACTH (adrenocorticotropin hormone) by the pituitary gland. Tolerance to nicotine develops very rapidly. The dizziness, nausea, and possible vomiting that accompany the first cigarette are diminished by the second and virtually absent after several. Research suggests that within a day of regular smoking there is also tolerance to the subjective effects and increased heart rate. Also, examination of accidental nicotine poisonings has shown that the immediate toxic effects disappear even though high levels of nicotine remain in the blood.

Tobacco and opium have broad backs, and will cheerfully carry the load of armies, if you choose to make them pay high for such joy as they give and such harm as they do.

—Ralph Waldo Emerson

Civilization, 1870

Absorption and Metabolism

When smoked, nicotine is carried by tar droplets, which are inhaled and deposited in the air sacs of the lungs. The nicotine then passes very quickly into the bloodstream, via the small air sacs in the lungs. Very rapidly, in 10 to 19 seconds, it enters the brain. Very little smoked nicotine is absorbed through the mucous membranes in the mouth, though. This is because smoked nicotine is slightly acidic, which prevents absorption. However, chewed tobacco products are slightly alkaline and are absorbed by these membranes. The speed with which nicotine reaches the brain depends on the route of administration, with smoking being the fastest. Although the nicotine is delivered quickly to the brain, the level of nicotine in the brain declines rapidly as nicotine is then distributed to tissues in other parts of the body. Between cigarettes, the level declines and provides an opportunity for the brain's nicotine receptors to be recharged.

Half-life. *The length of time for half of a drug to be removed from the body.*

Given the difference in smoking patterns, it is difficult to estimate the dose of nicotine with any precision. In one study, of a group of regular smokers, the level of nicotine per cigarette averaged 1 mg, but ranged from 0.37 to 1.57 mg. For chewing tobacco, the intake is roughly equivalent to $4^1/_2$ cigarettes if the wad is kept in the mouth for a half hour. The half-life of nicotine averages two hours; however, regular smokers often do not space cigarettes two hours apart. Consequently, with the regular administration of nicotine, the level of nicotine persists throughout the day, accumulates, and persists throughout the night. Nicotine is metabolized primarily by the liver and a much smaller amount by the lungs, and excretion by the kidneys accounts for at most 20%. The presence of nicotine "speeds up" the liver's metabolism of other medicines. Therefore, these medications may not have their intended effect. Nicotine is broken down into several compounds. The major metabolic product is cotinine. It remains in the body for a longer period than the nicotine. Its half-life is 16 hours, 8 times that of nicotine. The levels of cotinine are typically 15 times higher than the levels of nicotine. For this reason, it is often used as a marker of nicotine use. It is eventually excreted by the kidneys. It is not fully clear what the effects of cotinine are on the body. However, it does have an impact on some neurotransmitters in the brain and affects a number of enzymes. It may also play a role in withdrawal symptoms.

Assessment

The level of dependence and associated craving needs to be taken into account in undertaking smoking cessation. The *Fagerstrom Test for Nicotine Dependence* is commonly used to assess the degree of dependence on nicotine. Those with higher scores are seen as needing assistance in their efforts to stop smoking. The test is also included on numerous websites devoted to health education and smoking cessation efforts.

Fagerstrom Test for Nicotine Dependence

1. How soon after you awake do you smoke your first cigarette?
   After 30 minutes = 0, Within 30 minutes = 1
2. Do you find it difficult to refrain from smoking in places where it is forbidden, such as the library, theater, or doctors' office?
   No = 0, Yes = 1

3. Which of all the cigarettes you smoke in a day is the most satisfying?
   First in the morning = 1, Any other than the first = 0
4. How many cigarettes a day do you smoke?
   1–15 cigarettes = 0, 16–25 cigarettes = 1, More than 26 = 2
5. Do you smoke more during the morning than during the rest of the day?
   No = 0, Yes = 1
6. Do you smoke when you are so ill that you are in bed most of the day?
   No = 0, Yes = 1
7. Does the brand you smoke have a low, medium, or high nicotine content?
   Low = 0, Medium = 1, High = 2
8. How often do you inhale the smoke from your cigarette?
   Never = 0, Sometimes = 1, Always = 2

Scoring: 0–2 points indicates very low addiction; 3–4 points, low addiction; 5 points, medium addiction; 6–7 points, high addiction; and 8–10 points represents very high addiction.

Given that the Fagerstrom test score indicates the level of dependence, this score suggests the appropriate strength of a nicotine patch for those who use nicotine replacement as part of smoking cessation. Very low levels of addiction, scores of 0–2 may not require nicotine replacement. If nicotine replacement is desired, the 7 mg patch is suggested. For low to medium dependence, corresponding to a score of 3–5, the 14 mg patch is suggested. For heavy dependence, associated with scores of 6 or more, the 21 mg patch is suggested.

Treatment

There is a large body of literature on smoking cessation. Typically smoking cessation programs are offered through hospitals and community health departments or via individual physicians and health care providers. There are very few residential treatment programs for smokers. At this point, the rate of treatment success, in terms of establishing abstinence from nicotine, is in the vicinity of 15% to 25%. Commonly people try to quit smoking several times before succeeding. In general, smoking cessation programs include patient education, group supports, counseling, and increasingly nicotine replacement. When smoking cessation efforts include nicotine replacement, there is a better chance of quitting smoking. There are several forms of nicotine replacement: nicotine gum, nicotine patch, nasal sprays, and inhalers. The gum and patch are available over-the-counter. Nasal sprays and inhalers require a prescription.

If alcohol is queen,
then tobacco is her consort.
It's a fond companion
for all occasions,
a loyal friend through
fair weather and foul.
—Luis Buñuel,
Spanish filmmaker

A drug originally used for the treatment of depression, bupropion (Wellbutrin), has been found to help reduce craving among those who are quitting smoking. This drug is known as Zyban when marketed for smoking cessation and is exactly the same as Wellbutrin. The two should *not* be taken simultaneously. The prognosis for quitting increases significantly when both nicotine replacement and bupropion are used together. In 2006 a new drug, varenicline (marketed as Chantix), came onto the market. The reports thus far show higher quit rates than with either Wellbutrin or nicotine replacement products, but this medicine has been associated with suicidal ideation in some people. Thus, any client who is starting or taking Chantix should be monitored for suicidal thinking.

Of note is the substance abuse treatment field's lack of involvement in smoking cessation efforts. This is true despite the fact that no other group of health care providers has ready access to such a large proportion of smokers. The resistance to addressing smoking cessation as part of other alcohol or drug use treatment is the product of several factors: the relatively higher level of smoking among staff, the misperception that addressing nicotine dependence along with other substance use problems leads to poorer outcomes, the idea that multiple dependencies should be handled sequentially, and, most important, inadequate training in smoking cessation techniques.

If tobacco suddenly were unavailable and was as expensive as heroin and cocaine, I think that you would find that the behavior of some tobacco addicts would be very much like the behavior of some addicts of heroin and cocaine.
—C. Everett Koop
Surgeon General, 1982–1989

Summary: Nicotine

Examples:	Cigarettes, cigars, pipes, chewing tobacco, snuff.
Route of administration:	Smoked, chewed.
Absorption:	*Snorting:* absorbed through the nasal mucous membranes into bloodstream with fast onset of action. Some effect may be due to direct nerve transport of substances into brain, bypassing the blood/brain barrier. *Smoking:* molecules of vaporized drug deposit on lung air sacs and are rapidly taken into bloodstream by capillary beds nearby.
Pharmacological action:	Activates nicotinic receptors in the central and peripheral nervous systems. Primarily acts as a stimulant. Nicotine enhances the effects of many other drugs by sharing the pathways these drugs affect in the brain.
Metabolism:	Metabolized by the liver. Menthol appears to slow the metabolism of nicotine, thereby increasing the effects and the time nicotine remains in the system.
Length of action:	Approximately two hours.
Desired effects:	Relaxation, stimulation, social acceptance, image, warding off withdrawal.

Summary: Nicotine (continued)

Other acute effects:	Dizziness and nausea (in the inexperienced), increased heart rate.
Intoxication/overdose:	Uncommon. Most of the negative effects are from regular and prolonged use rather than from intoxication and overdose.
Common problems:	Dependence; the common medical problems associated with use are in large measure the result of smoking, not the nicotine per se (these include cough, bronchitis, increased respiratory infections, chronic obstructive pulmonary disease, lung cancer, and oral cancers); apparent increase in other cancers; death or injury by fire; and, among pregnant women, a higher incidence of low-birth-weight babies and an increase in spontaneous abortions.
Withdrawal symptoms:	Craving, irritability, anxiety, possible depression.
Interaction with alcohol:	Increased likelihood of use of one when the other is used; combined use increases occurrence of oral cancers.
Medical uses:	There is no FDA indication for nicotine, but some studies suggest nicotine patches can improve memory.

Nicotine	Average Amount Taken	Addiction Risk	DEA Schedule
	1 mg/cigarette	high	N/A
	4.5 mg/"wad" of chewing tobacco	high	N/A

Opiates

Historical Notes

Opium was recognized over 10,000 years ago as having psychoactive properties. The Assyrians are thought to have used it medicinally. Opium poppies were being cultivated in the area now known as Iraq over 2,400 years ago. Opium was known to the Greeks and, along with alcohol, was one of the mainstays of ancient medicine. The only improvement on either alcohol or opium alone was their combination in a preparation known as laudanum. First manufactured in 1500, it combined wine and opium with some spices; its use continued throughout the 1800s. The disappearance of laudanum was the result of passage of the Pure Food and Drug Act in 1906.

What connection might tea and opium have? In the late 1600s, the British discovered an exotic luxury, a beverage with health benefits—tea. It rapidly caught on. To meet the country's thirst, Britain began importing tea from China, the only major grower. At that time, China was attempting to limit its people's contact with the outside world. It didn't encourage trade and only had one port open to foreign countries. Britain had something it wished to buy, *tea*, but there was nothing the Chinese wished to purchase. This eventually led to a large trade deficit for the British. However, the British recognized that there was at least one item for which there would be a Chinese market. It was opium.

The Chinese viewed "opium as a poison, undermining our good customs and morality." So it passed laws making possession of opium illegal. But the British persevered. India, a British colony, was the major source of opium and was "encouraged" to trade with China. In a brief period there was an explosion in the use of opium in China. Efforts by the Chinese to enlist the British in banning the opium trade were unsuccessful. A letter to Queen Victoria requesting her intervention was not delivered. The letter questioned her royal government's moral reasoning for enforcing strict prohibition of the opium trade within England, Ireland, and Scotland while reaping profits from such trade in the Far East.

In 1839 the Chinese seized and destroyed opium stored in warehouses, laying the foundation for military intervention by the British, "to force China to open its ports to foreign trade, and to allow its citizens to have access to opium." This intervention (1839–1843) is known as the First Opium War. (The Second Opium War of 1856–1860 centered on disagreements about the prior treaty.)

What was the size of the opium trade? In 1730 the British sold an estimated 15 tons to China. Forty years later that number had grown to 75 tons; by the 1820s the figure was 900 tons per year, and by 1838 the British were selling 1,400 tons of opium to China.

The history of the drug trade and drug policy could well provide the basis for a history of racism. The willingness to sacrifice Asian people for economic ends, as is apparent in the Opium Wars, is simply one example. In America, alcohol was sold to Native Americans, often over the objections of native leaders. Much of the early hysteria over marijuana was driven by racism. More recently, race has been seen as a major factor in the disparate prison sentences for cocaine, based on whether it's in the form of crack or powder—an example of the way in which racial stereotyping acts to make persons of color significant victims of the war on drugs.

Opium Derivatives

As a general rule, any psychoactive agent that is naturally occurring in nature tends to be less potent and generally less problematic than are any derivatives created from it by processing. This is really a rather commonsense notion. Why bother going to the trouble of refining or processing if there isn't any improvement? Accordingly, distillation is required to produce alcoholic beverages above 14%. In terms of opiates, it was only in the early 1800s that opium poppies were refined to create morphine, a substance that was about 10 times more powerful. But something else had to happen before the use of morphine became widespread. The real breakthrough in terms of the administration of opiates didn't occur until 1853 with the invention of the syringe. From then on, there was the potential for delivering morphine intravenously, thereby greatly enhancing its effects. Earlier, opium smoking was introduced into the United States by Chinese laborers; however, it never caught on beyond the Chinese community, in large measure because of prejudice and racism.

Not poppy, nor mandragora,
Nor all the drowsy syrups of the world
Shall ever medicine thee to that sweet sleep
Which thou owed'st yesterday.
—William Shakespeare
Othello

The first widespread medical use of morphine was in the Civil War. It was used less than judiciously and without an appreciation of the addictive potential. A number of soldiers who lived through the war were described as having the "soldier's illness" or "army disease." The next landmark in terms of the history of opiates was the synthesis of heroin from morphine in 1898. Accordingly, heroin joined opium and morphine as an ingredient of the various tonics and medications then available. Heroin is noted for its rapid onset of action and short half-life. Both features contribute to its abuse potential. Heroin is about twice as potent as morphine—that represents a potency 20 times greater than that of opium. Appropriately, the name given this synthesized product, heroin, comes from the German word "heroisch," which means large or powerful. Its average half-life is three minutes.[5] Though heroin is metabolized quite rapidly, one of the products of its metabolism is morphine, which, of course, has psychoactive effects and stays in the system much longer. (By way of contrast, the products formed by the metabolism of alcohol are not known to have any mood-altering properties.)

Thou hast the keys of Paradise,
oh just, subtle, and mighty opium!
Confessions of an English Opium Eater, 1822

With the passage of the Pure Food and Drug and the Harrison acts, the legal and widespread supply of opium and its major derivatives, morphine and heroin, disappeared. In 1924, heroin production in the United States was outlawed. In 1942, growing opium poppies was similarly outlawed. It was in 1956 that possession of heroin was essentially made illegal, and all remaining stockpiles were to be surrendered to the U.S. government. In other countries—notably, England—heroin is still legally manufactured. England, under a policy commonly known as "The British

[5]Heroin is sometimes reported as having a half-life of around three minutes, other times the half-life is reported as around half an hour. This discrepancy apparently relates to the time required for heroin to be transformed into morphine. There is an intermediate product formed between the heroin and the morphine, 6-monoacetylmorphine (MAM), and the discrepancy is how this intermediary product is handled in the calculations. Either way, the half-life is very short. That is the important part.

System," allows prescription of heroin, referred to by its chemical name diamorphine, to those who have long-standing heroin problems and who have not succeeded in drug-free treatment or drug substitution programs such as methadone maintenance. The British System goes back to the 1920s. England is no longer alone in this approach. In 1994, Switzerland created a similar program on a trial basis. Since then other European countries have followed suit—Germany, the Netherlands, and Denmark. Pilot initiatives are under way in Canada and Belgium.

In terms of what distinguishes "opiates" and "opioids," opiates are naturally occurring or partially synthesized, whereas opioids are synthetic opiates.

Heroin Use

For many drugs, popularity waxes and wanes over time. In part this is attributed to supply but also to what is termed "generational memory." In the 1980s, heroin use was primarily associated with those described as "the dinosaurs," those in their 40s and 50s. In the early 1990s, there was a resurgence of heroin use. A new generation of users emerged, drawn from those in the 13 to 23 age bracket. This increase in use was attributed to a lowering of price, to greater purity, to the fact that cocaine street sellers in some areas began trafficking in heroin as well, and to the fact that there was no generational memory of heroin use and its problems. The new users had no experience of the problems of heroin, as they had, for example, with cocaine and especially crack cocaine.

With increasing purity, there was also the potential for other routes of administration besides IV use. Those potentially averse to IV use have not been disinclined to experiment with heroin taken in other ways. Heroin can be taken intranasally, or smoked (referred to as "chasing the dragon"), which involves not rolling a joint but lighting heroin placed on a surface such as aluminum foil and inhaling the smoke. The increased use of heroin was not restricted to urban areas but spread to the suburbs and rural areas as well. The upsurge of heroin use peaked in 1996 and then declined, though use has remained relatively stable since then.

The Basic Principles of Dealing Heroin

1. Never give anything away for nothing.
2. Never give more than you have to give. (Always catch the buyer hungry and always make him wait.)
3. Always take everything back, if you possibly can.

—William Burroughs

The Naked Lunch, Introduction, 1959

Other Opioid Use

In addition to heroin there are the synthetic manufactured opiates, the prescription drugs intended to treat pain. Drugs of this class are the most commonly abused prescription drugs. Those most frequently abused are those most frequently prescribed, and thus more available. It also happens that they are among the most potent. One study examined the levels of non-medical use: OxyContin is first, followed by hydrocodone (Vicodin), other oxycodone (Percodan and Percocet), methadone, morphine, hydromorphone (Dilaudid), fentanyl, and buprenorphine.

Detoxification

If a person has been taking opiates on a daily basis for two to three weeks, and use is stopped, expect significant withdrawal symptoms.

Compared with alcohol withdrawal, opiate withdrawal involves less medical risk. While uncomfortable, it is not associated with mortality and complications.

In the past, the most common method of detoxification from opiates was to use methadone as a substitute and then gradually taper the methadone. As mentioned earlier, buprenorphine (Suboxone) has become an alternative to methadone, and it can be used for rapid detoxification as well as for substitution therapy. It is ideal for detoxification because it controls not only withdrawal symptoms but also cravings. It can be prescribed in both inpatient and outpatient settings by physicians who have undergone training in using buprenorphine for opioid dependence. The dose can be rapidly tapered and patients can be "weaned" off opioids using this approach in a matter of days to weeks, depending on the intensity of opioid use prior to detoxification. Buprenorphine, while similar to other opioids, has several notable features. It binds so strongly to the opioid receptor that no other opioids can reach it. Thus, unlike methadone, when someone is taking buprenorphine, they cannot use other opioids to get high, which makes it an ideal medication to use on an outpatient basis. Although it binds very strongly, buprenorphine only partially activates the opioid receptor. This allows buprenorphine to help with the cravings during opioid withdrawal and means that it has no overdose potential by itself (unlike methadone).

I watched the needle take another man . . .
Every junkie's like a settin' sun.
—Neil Young
"The Needle and the Damage Done"

Other detoxification regimens have been introduced. The most controversial is known as *ultra-rapid detoxification,* accomplished under sedation. It involves administration of naltrexone, a blocking agent. By binding with the opiate receptor sites, naltrexone makes it impossible for the opiates to do so, thus causing withdrawal. This procedure has been criticized on several counts. It has been associated with several deaths and thus is a riskier procedure than other withdrawal regimens. Also, ultra-rapid detoxification is not covered by insurance and, costing up to $7,500, is seen as exploitative of patients.

I'll die young, but it's like kissing God.
—Lenny Bruce
On his drug addiction. He died at age 41.

In contrast to ultra-rapid detox is a procedure known as *rapid detoxification,* which does not require sedation or anesthesia. It also uses naltrexone, but in combination with other medications. Because chronic opioid use suppresses norepinphine (adrenaline) function, withdrawal is associated with large surges in adrenaline, which cause tremendous anxiety, insomnia, and sweating. Clonidine is a medication that can reduce the amount of adrenaline in the system and can be used as a pre- and post-naltrexone treatment. Benzodiazepines and other medications are also used, as needed for anxiety, nausea, and vomiting. Rapid detoxification takes two to three days, again, depending on the half-life of the opioid involved. This is not a simple procedure, and although it can be conducted on an outpatient basis, it requires careful medical monitoring. As with alcohol, detoxification per se is not a treatment for the dependence syndrome. It simply sets the stage for treatment of dependence.

If we burn ourselves out with drugs or alcohol, we won't have long to go in this business.
—John Belushi
Playboy interview, 1977. He died at age 33.

Summary: Opioids

Examples:	Heroin, morphine, meperidine, oxycodone, opium, codeine, hydrocodone, fentanyl, methadone, buprenorphine.
Route of administration:	*Heroin:* intravenous, snorted, "skin-popped," or smoked. *Medications:* oral, intravenous, or skin patch (fentanyl). Medications that are intended to be taken by mouth, such as oxycodone, may be crushed and injected or snorted.
Absorption:	*Snorting*: absorbed through the nasal mucous membranes into bloodstream with fast onset of action. Some effect may be due to direct nerve transport of substances into brain, bypassing the blood/brain barrier. *Smoking* (primarily heroin, chasing the dragon): molecules of vaporized drug deposit on lung air sacs and are rapidly taken into bloodstream by capillaries nearby.
Pharmacological action:	Binds to multiple opioid receptors in the central nervous system to effect changes in pain sensation, cause sedation, and provide euphoria/sense of well-being. Opioid receptors are densely populated in areas governing sensation of novelty (nucleus accumbens) and thought execution (cortex), and those near the center of dopamine release in the midbrain (ventral tegmental area).
Metabolism:	Metabolized by the liver.
Length of action:	Varies by compound. *Heroin:* 3–4 hours. *Morphine:* 3–4 hours. *Methadone:* 12 hours to days. *Buprenorphine:* 30 hours.
Desired effects:	The "rush" or "high," a feeling of intense pleasure, often described as almost "orgasmic." A state of decreased mental and physical awareness and of decreased physical and emotional pain.
Other acute effects:	Sedation, decreased judgment, decreased ability to operate vehicles or machinery, respiratory depression secondary to accidental overdose.

Summary: Opioids (continued)

Intoxication/overdose:	*Vital signs:* respiration decreased, blood pressure decreased, temperature decreased. *Physical exam:* pupils constricted, reflexes absent or diminished, pulmonary edema; possible convulsions with Demerol and Darvon (pain medications). *Mental status:* variable; possible normal mood; euphoria; sedation, possible stupor.
Common problems:	Rapidly acquired tolerance, physical dependence, respiratory depression secondary to accidental overdose, cellulitis at site of injection, sepsis (systemic infections), endocarditis, increased likelihood of exposure to HIV infection and hepatitis by sharing of needles, risk to sexual partners of IV opiate users with HIV, legal problems related to acquiring opiates illegally.
Withdrawal symptoms:	Drug craving, dysphoria and anxiety, yawning, sleep difficulties, perspiration, fever, chills, gooseflesh, abdominal cramps, nausea, diarrhea, muscle cramps, bone pain, tears.
Interaction with alcohol:	Each potentiates the effects of the other in overdose situations. Possible decreased efficacy of either when taken by an individual with tolerance to the other (cross-tolerance).
Medical uses:	Pain (morphine, meperidine, hydromorphone, methadone, oxycodone, hydrocodone); cough suppression (codeine); anesthesia (fentanyl); addiction treatment (methadone, buprenorphine); diarrhea (opium).

Opioids	Usual Therapeutic Dose/Day	Addiction Risk	DEA Schedule
Opiates			
codeine (multiple products)			
cough	5–15 mg q 4h	high	II
pain	15–60 mg q 4h		
heroin	No U.S. medical use	high	I

Oxycontin, the new gateway drug

The current heroin epidemic did not occur overnight, rising out of nowhere. But it came to attention, in large part upon the death of a public figure. Philip Seymour Hoffman. He was widely recognized as a talented actor. He was found in his apartment, dead, with a needle still sticking in his arm. Speaking of the tragic death of one individual opened the floodgates for discussion of the breadth and depth of heroin problems for individuals and communities across the country.

Oxycontin is now less available. The pill mills have been shut down. The requirements of different formulations, make it more difficult to crush pills. Prescribing patterns have changed. If originally oxycontin was a substitute for heroin, the tables have turned.

Drug use is tied to price. The cost of a bag of heroin is as little as $6. An equivalent amount of oxycontin is 10 times as much Important too, heroin is more than an adequate substitute.

Opioids	Usual Therapeutic Dose/Day	Addiction Risk	DEA Schedule
Opiates (cont.)			
morphine			
MSIR	5–20 mg q 4h	high	II
MS Contin	15–60 mg q 12h		
opium			
Paregoric	6 mg or 6 ml q 4h	high	II
Opioids			
fentanyl (Atiq, Duragesic Patch, Oral Sublimaze)	2–50 micrograms/kg	high	II
hydrocodone			
cough (Hycodan)	5–10 mg q 4h	moderate	II
pain	Limit 8/day	moderate	III
hydromorphone (Dilaudid)	1–4 mg q 4–6h	high	II
levorphanol (Levo-Dromoran)	2–3 mg q 6–8h	high	II
meperidine (Demerol)	55–150 mg q 3–4h	high	II
methadone			
maintenance	5–120 mg/day	high	II
pain (Dolophine)	2.5–20 mg q 3–4h		
oxycodone			
(Percodan, Percocet, Tylox)	1 tab q 6h	high	II
(OxyContin)	10–40 mg q 12h	high	II
propoxyphene			
(Darvon, Darvocet, Darvon-N)	One tab q 4h	low	IV
Partial Opioid Agonists			
buprenorphine			
pain (Buprenex)	0.3–0.6 mg IM or IV	low	III
maintenance (Suboxone, Subutex)	8–16 mg /day		
butorphanol (Stadol)	1–2 mg q 3–4h IM, IV, or intranasal spray	high	IV
nalbuphine (Nubain)	10 mg IM, q 3–4h	low	IV
pentazozine (Talwin)	30 mg IM, IV, or subcutaneously, q 3–4h	moderate	IV
Non-Opioid but Opioid-like-Effects			
tramadol (Ultram)	50–100mg po, q 4–6h	low	under review

*A higher dose may be needed in patients with tolerance.

Note: If amounts used are significantly higher than the recommended dose, this may signal a substance use disorder. Those with a history of substance abuse have an increased risk for excess use.

Sedative-Hypnotics (Central Nervous System Depressants)

Sedative-hypnotics constitute the category of drugs to which alcohol belongs. Accordingly, many of the drugs in this group have properties similar to those of alcohol. For this reason, some of the most serious interactions with alcohol occur with drugs in this class because they both have a depressant effect. As a result, medications in this class are used for detoxification from alcohol. In essence, they are substituted for the alcohol, with the doses then tapering off.

Cricket is basically baseball on valium.
—Robin Williams

Patterns of Use

In the general population, this is the drug class with the least difference in levels of use based on gender. Past-month use is low for all ages, under 1%.

Summary: Sedative-Hypnotics

Examples:	Benzodiazepines, barbiturates, meprobamate, chloral hydrate, GHB.
Route of administration:	Usually by mouth, sometimes by snorting, rarely intravenous.
Absorption:	*Oral:* through intestinal wall into bloodstream. *Snorting:* absorbed through the nasal mucous membranes into bloodstream with fast onset of action. Some effect may be due to direct neural transport of substances into the brain, bypassing the blood/brain barrier. *Intravenously:* directly into bloodstream.
Pharmacological action:	Typically these drugs all work by increasing the activity of the GABA neurotransmitter, which has an inhibitory effect on the brain's functions. Acute effects of this inhibition typically include decreasing likelihood of seizures, increasing sedation/sleep, relaxing smooth and skeletal muscle tissue, and causing impairment of memory.
Metabolism:	Varies by substance; primarily through liver, although some benzodiazepines are less extensively metabolized through the liver, making them safer to use for those with hepatitis (inflammation of the liver) or cirrhosis (permanent scarring of the liver).
Length of action:	Varies by substance, from 2 hours (in the case of triazolam [Halcion], a short-acting benzodiazepine used for sleep) to over 100 hours (for diazepam [Valium], one of the first benzodiazepines widely used in hospital and outpatient settings).

Sedative-Hypnotics (continued)

Desired effects:	Similar to those of alcohol, reduction of anxiety, possible elation secondary to decrease in alertness and judgment.
Other acute effects:	Sedation, impaired judgment, impaired operation of vehicles or machinery, respiratory and cardiac depression with overdose (much less likely with benzodiazepines alone).
Intoxication/overdose:	*Vital signs:* minimal changes, possibly decreased respirations, more likely with non-benzodiazepines. *Physical exam:* slurred speech, ataxia (unable to walk a straight line), stupor, coma, possible respiratory depression. *Mental status:* slurred speech, confusion, impaired judgment, delirium, coma.
Common problems:	Tolerance, physical dependence; respiratory and cardiac depression with overdose.
Withdrawal symptoms:	Similar to alcohol withdrawal. Severity and time of onset vary with half-life of drug; anxiety, elevated vital signs, sweating, tremulousness, altered perceptions, withdrawal seizures possibly leading to death (barbiturates and benzodiazepines).
Interaction with alcohol:	Potentiation of effects, especially respiratory depression; some degree of cross-tolerance.
Medical uses:	Sleep, anxiety disorders, muscle relaxation, alcohol and sedative-hypnotic withdrawal, control of seizures.

Sedative-Hypnotics	Usual Therapeutic Dose/Day	Addiction Risk	DEA Schedule
Benzodiazepines			
alprazolam (Xanax)	0.25–0.6 mg	high	IV
chlordiazepoxide (Librium)	5–100 mg	low	IV
clonazepam (Klonopin) (larger doses for epilepsy)	0.5–4 mg	low	IV
diazepam (Valium)	2–40 mg	moderate/high	IV
flurazepam (Dalmane)	15–30 mg	low	IV
lorazepam (Ativan)	1–6 mg	moderate/high	IV

Sedative-Hypnotics	Usual Therapeutic Dose/Day	Addiction Risk	DEA Schedule
Benzodiazepines (cont.)			
oxazepam (Serax)	10–90 mg	low	IV
temazepam (Restoril)	15–30 mg	low	IV
triazolam (Halcion)	0.125–0.5 mg	moderate/ high	IV
estazolzm (Prosom)	0.5–2.0 mg	low	IV
flunitrazepam (Rohypnol)*	—	high	—
Barbiturates			
butabarbital (Butisol sodium)	15–120 mg	moderate	III
butalbital (Fiornal)	1–6 tabs	moderate	III
pentobarbital (Nembutal)	100 mg	high	II
phenobarbital (Solfoton)	30–400 mg	low	IV
secobarbital (Seconal)	100 mg	high	II
Other Compounds			
chloral hydrate	250–500 mg	low	IV
meprobamate (Miltown/Equanil)	200–2400 mg	moderate/ high	IV
carisoprodol (Soma)	350–1500 mg	low	Not classified

*Not approved for use in the United States. Club drug; so-called date-rape drug.

Note: If amounts used are significantly higher than the recommended dose, this may signal a substance use disorder. Those with a history of substance abuse have an increased risk for excess use.

Gamma-Hydroxybutyrate (GHB): A Special Case

Unlike the drugs just described, GHB in the United States has an exceedingly limited legitimate use. It is marketed as Xyrem, and it was only approved in 2002 for treatment of a rare form of narcolepsy. Thus, the major source of GHB is not drug diversion but production in illicit clandestine laboratories. It is easily synthesized from readily available chemicals. Although it can be injected, it is typically consumed by the capful or teaspoonful. It is clear, odorless, and tasteless. These as well as its sedating properties contribute to its being cited in cases of sexual assault. GHB is rapidly absorbed, with peak levels achieved in 20 to 60 minutes, and it lasts no longer than three hours.

As a recreational drug, it has one major problem. There is relatively little difference between the dose that induces euphoria and the dose that causes sedation and loss of consciousness. So there is a very small margin for error. This is all the more problematic due to its illegal production; there can be considerable variability between the supposed and actual dose. (A lesser though still a potential problem is the presence of contaminants. Lye is used in its manufacture, and poor laboratory technique can mean that some of the residue of the lye remains.) There is no known antidote for GHB overdose. In cases of overdose, treatment involves responding to the life-threatening symptoms. This can entail the use of life supports to maintain respiration and heartbeat and to keep airways open. Generally, as the drug wears off, people awaken spontaneously. With regular use, dependence can occur, and the withdrawal syndrome is similar to that with alcohol.

Wacky Dust

They call it wacky dust
It's from a hot comet
It gives your feet a feeling so breezy
And oh, it's so easy to get

They call it wacky dust
It brings a dancing jag
And once it starts, then only a
Sap'll refuse to Big Apple or Shag.

Oh I don't know why it gets you so high
Putting a buzz in you heart
You'll do a marathon you'll wanna go on
Kicking the ceilin' apart.

They call it wacky dust
It's something you can't trust
And in the end the rhythm will stop
When it does, then you'll drop
From happy wacky dust

Lyrics by Oscar Levant and Stanley Adams. Recorded by Ella Fitzgerald and Chick Webb and His Orchestra, 1938

Stimulants

Stimulant drugs are given that name because of their effect on the central nervous system. In contrast to alcohol and the other sedative-hypnotics, which have a dampening effect on the central nervous system, these drugs increase levels of activity. The group includes both illicit drugs—cocaine and the illicitly manufactured methamphetamines—and prescription medications—methylphenidate (Ritalin) and amphetamines (Dexedrine, Adderall, Desoxyn). In comparing differences clinically among different stimulants, research shows that, with methamphetamines, there is a more rapid progression from first use to regular use and from first use to entry into treatment. Abuse of methamphetamine is also likely to result in more medical and psychiatric consequences. In comparing those who use methamphetamines and those who use cocaine (non-crack), cocaine use is more episodic, more expensive, and more likely to be accompanied by heavy drinking. In contrast, methamphetamine use is more likely to be daily, to be accompanied by marijuana use, to involve women, and to be accompanied by medical and psychiatric consequences.

Amphetamines

Amphetamines were widely prescribed in the middle of the twentieth century as a medication for depression and obesity. The number of prescriptions peaked in the United States in the late 1960s, with a total of 31 million. About 4% to 5% of all Americans have used amphetamines at some time in their lives, 0.4% in the past year. Amphetamines are available as pills, liquids, or powder. Oral or intravenous administration is the most common.

Methamphetamine

Although hardly ever prescribed, methamphetamine (Desoxyn and Methderine) is a prescription drug approved by the FDA for treatment of ADHD and obesity. As currently known in the substance abuse field, methamphetamine, called meth, is an illicit drug. It is easily manufactured if the essential chemicals (precursor chemicals) are available. In the United States, meth production takes place in small clandestine laboratories by a process known as "cooking." The drug was initially imported from Mexico, and its first use was centered in California. From there it spread into the Southwest and has continued to spread from west to east. With the emergence of local bootleg manufacturing, the availability of methamphetamine has grown dramatically, with the farm states of the Great Plains particularly hard struck. About 5% of the population reports some use of methamphetamine at some point for nonmedical purposes. While the small mom and pop style operation is the image we have of meth production, there too has been the emergence of super labs, as shown on *Breaking Bad*. They are based in Mexico, and beginning to provide a larger portion of the U.S. supply.

Methamphetamine can be smoked, snorted, injected, or taken orally; the most common method of meth use in the United States is injection. The drug increases the heart rate, blood pressure, body temperature, and rate of breathing; dilates the pupils; produces euphoria, increased alertness, a sense of increased energy, and tremors. High doses or chronic use have been associated with increased nervousness, irritability, and paranoia. Withdrawal from high doses produces severe depression.

Cocaine

The use of cocaine peaked in 1985, followed by a marked decline, with the levels of use dropping by two-thirds by the early 1990s. There has since been a modest rise, with use remaining fairly stable over the past decade. Cocaine use is most common among those ages 18 to 25. The highest rate of use is among 22-year-olds, with 3.3% being current use users and 8.3% reporting past-year use. Cocaine use, like marijuana use, is more common in men, with the exception of those under age 26, where women's use approaches that of men's. Racial differences are far less marked for cocaine use, although rates of use are slightly higher for Hispanic males than for other groups. Rates of cocaine use are higher in metropolitan areas, but distinctions based on geography are not dramatic.

Nobody saves America by sniffing cocaine.
Jiggling yr knees blankeyed in the rain,
When it snows in yr nose you can catch
cold in yr brain.
—ALLEN GINSBURG

Historically the route of administration was nasal inhalation. With the emergence of crack cocaine things changed. Although any method of cocaine administration is potentially lethal, the dangers increase

The shortest way out of Manchester is notoriously a bottle of Gordon's gin; out of any businessman's life, there is the mirage of Paris; out of Paris, or mediocrity of talent and imagination, there are all the drugs, from subtle, all conquering opium to cheating cozening cocaine.
—William Bolitho, 1930

dramatically with freebasing and smoking rather than snorting (intranasal administration). With freebasing, unlimited quantities can be ingested. While the level of cocaine use has been slowly but continuously declining, paradoxically there has been a marked increase in cocaine-related problems seen in hospital emergency rooms. DAWN (Drug Abuse Warning Network) is a federally supported system to track drug-related incidents by tallying emergency room visits involving drug use and the frequency of a drug being mentioned in medical examiners' (coroners') cases. Overall there has been a marked rise in drug-involved cases seen in emergency departments, with cocaine-related incidents experiencing the most dramatic rise. Between 1975 and 1985, there was a 10-fold increase, from fewer than 1,000 incidents per year to approximately 10,000. In 2010 the number was just under a half million, and represented 41% of all emergency room visits involving illicit drugs. By way of contrast, heroin accounted for under half of that. Initially the growth of emergency room visits was attributed to the emergence of crack cocaine, but the numbers have not gone down as the use of crack has declined.

Extraordinary Anesthetic for Eye Surgery—Cocaine

The author concludes this journal article with the observation, "It remains, however, to investigate all the characteristics of this substance, and we may yet find that there is a shadow side as well as a brilliant side in the discovery."
—Henry D. Noyes, MD, 1884

Summary: Stimulants

Examples:	Cocaine, amphetamines, methamphetamines, methylphenidate (Ritalin).
Route of administration:	Powdered cocaine (cocaine hydrochloride) is snorted intranasally and (rarely) used intravenously or smoked as freebase; cocaine is mostly smoked as "crack"; amphetamines are taken orally, taken intravenously, or smoked; methylphenidate is taken orally or snorted intranasally.
Absorption:	*Oral:* through intestinal wall into bloodstream. *Snorting:* absorbed through the nasal mucous membranes into the bloodstream with fast onset of action. Some effect may be due to direct neural transport of substances into the brain, bypassing the blood/brain barrier. *Smoking* example crack cocaine: molecules of vaporized drug deposit on lung air sacs and are rapidly taken into the bloodstream by capillaries nearby. *Intravenously:* directly into the bloodstream.
Metabolism:	By liver; 10% of cocaine is not metabolized but is excreted by the kidneys.

Summary: Stimulants (continued)

Pharmacological action:	Amphetamines and cocaine block the "recycling" of dopamine, causing a rapid rise in dopamine concentrations. They also stimulate dopamine and norepinephrine to be released from neurons, primarily in the novelty center (nucleus accumbens) of the brain. Cocaine blocks reuptake of dopamine, thereby prolonging dopamine effects, and may enhance dopamine transmission in mesolimbic and mesocortical areas of the brain. It depletes the neuron's dopamine supplies with prolonged use. Amphetamines and methylphenidate cause direct neuronal release of dopamine and norepinephrine and blockade of dopamine and norepinephrine reuptake to produce euphoric effects as well as various pharmacologically toxic effects.
Length of action:	*Cocaine:* smoking produces a high that lasts 20–30 minutes, half-life in plasma is approximately 1 hour, remains in the body 2–3 days. *Methamphetamines:* high lasts 8–24 hours, half-life is 6–12 hours. *Methylphenidate:* half-life is about 2 hours.
Desired effects:	Increased alertness, feeling of well-being, euphoria, increased energy, heightened sexuality.
Other acute effects:	Anxiety, confusion, irritability, possible medical problems (cardiac, central nervous system, respiratory, etc.) with potential death.
Intoxication/overdose:	*Vital signs:* increased heart rate, elevated blood pressure and temperature, decreased respiration. *Physical exam:* dilated pupils, dry mouth, cardiac arrhythmias, twitching, tremors, convulsions, stroke, coma. *Mental status:* impaired judgment, confusion, disinhibited behavior, paranoid thoughts, hypervigilance, hallucinations, elation and/or depression, suicidal behavior.
Common problems:	Dependence, tolerance; anxiety, confusion, irritability, social withdrawal; weight loss; psychosis; multiple medical problems (cardiac, central nervous system, respiratory, etc.) with potential death. With long-term, chronic use of methamphetamines there is evidence of irreversible damage to the central nervous system.

Cocaine is God's way of saying you're making too much money.
—Robin Williams

Eventually, alas, I realized the main purpose of buying cocaine is to run out of it.
—George Carlin

Bad Paint Job Arouses Suspicion

A replica of a World Cup trophy seized by Colombian authorities at the Bogota airport was made of cocaine, police said. Gold paint in "bad condition" on the trophy's surface aroused the suspicion of investigators, who sent a sample of the trophy to a laboratory for forensic testing. . . . Results revealed that the replica was made of 24 pounds (11 kilograms) of cocaine. The actual trophy is made of gold and weighs 13.6 pounds.

CNN Wire Staff, July 4, 2010

Summary: Stimulants (continued)

Withdrawal symptoms:	Depression (possibly with suicide potential), excessive need for sleep, fatigue, anhedonia (lack of pleasure), increased appetite, craving, especially with cocaine; usually not life-threatening except for suicide potential.
Interaction with alcohol:	Alcohol decreases side effects of stimulants (such as anxiety) and withdrawal symptoms; alcohol commonly used along with stimulants.
Medical uses:	*Cocaine:* local (ear/nose/throat) anesthesia. *Amphetamines and methylphenidate:* attention-deficit/hyperactivity disorder (especially in children), narcolepsy, used (though rarely) for depression unresponsive to other treatments.

Stimulants	Average Amount Taken	Addiction Risk	DEA Schedule
cocaine	Only medical use is local anesthesia	high	II
dextro-amphetamine (Dexedrin)	2.5–60 mg	high	II
methamphetamine (Desoxyn)	5–25 mg	high	II
dextroamphetamine/ amphetamine salts (Adderall)	5–40 mg	high	II
methylphenidate			
(Ritalin)	10–60 mg	high	II
(Concerta)	18–54 mg	high	II

Note: If amounts used are significantly higher than the recommended dose, this may signal a substance use disorder. Those with a history of substance abuse have an increased risk for excess use.

Hallucinogens and Dissociatives

The hallucinogens and dissociatives include both naturally occurring and synthetic preparations. While they represent different types of compounds, they are commonly combined into one category because of their shared ability to alter reality and produce hallucination-like effects. Hallucinogenic substances have played a role in human life for thousands of years. It has been recognized through the ages that a variety of plants can induce a state of detachment and precipitated visions. These have been used largely in social and religious contexts, and never became widely used and abused. These plants contain chemical compounds, such as mescaline and psilocybin, that are very similar to serotonin.

In 1935 a German pharmaceutical company began exploring the use of ergot, a compound found in rye grass, to develop new pharmaceuticals. Several years later, Albert Hofmann, one of the company's chemists, unknowingly ingested one of these compounds, LSD-25. Hofmann reported:

> [After synthesizing LSD-25] . . . I was interrupted in my work by unusual sensations. I was forced to interrupt my work in the laboratory in middle of the afternoon and proceed home, being affected by a remarkable restlessness, combined with a slight dizziness. At home I lay down and sank into a not unpleasant intoxicated-like condition, characterized by an extremely stimulated imagination. In a dream-like state, with eyes closed (I found the daylight to be unpleasantly glaring), I perceived an uninterrupted stream of fantastic pictures, extraordinary shapes with intense, kaleidoscopic play of colors. After some two hours this condition faded away.[6]

The First Acid Trip by Bicycle

Later in a self-experiment, Albert Hofmann dissolved what he thought was a prudent amount—250 millionths of a gram—in water and drank it down. It was actually a massive dose. Forty minutes later he became dizzy, observed some visual disturbance, and had a strong desire to laugh. Hofmann reported, "I asked my laboratory assistant, who was informed of the self-experiment, to escort me home. We went by bicycle, no automobile being available because of wartime restrictions on their use."

—Albert Hofmann

LSD: My Problem Child, 1980. Hofmann said it was the strangest bicycle ride of his life.

The *25* appended to the LSD refers to its being the 25th in a series of compounds that contained lysergic acid diethylamide. LSD is easily manufactured and is the most powerful hallucinogen.

The *dissociatives* include anesthetics, phencyclidine (PCP), and ketamine. They are anesthetics in that they block pain and induce loss of consciousness, but at sub-anesthetic thresholds they produce effects similar to those associated with other hallucinogens. "Dissociative" refers to an altered sense of self, of being outside of oneself. There too is a heightened awareness, be it of color or sound. Because of these hallucinogenic properties, their use as anesthetics was short-lived. Often patients became agitated, delusional, and irrational as the anesthetic effects wore off following surgery. Due to these problems, in 1965 the clinical trials of PCP as an anesthetic were discontinued. In 1963 ketamine, another dissociative anesthetic, was introduced in the United States to replace PCP; but the same problems quickly became evident. Its use in the United States is now restricted largely to veterinary practices, which are the source of most ketamine available on the streets.

I never took hallucinogenic drugs because I never wanted my consciousness expanded one unnecessary iota.

—Fran Lebowitz

PCP is produced illegally. It is a white powder that dissolves easily in both water and alcohol. It is relatively inexpensive; is active in liquid, vapor, powder, and crystalline forms; and acts on multiple receptor sites. For these reasons it is one of the most common adulterants found in psychoactive drugs and is used to cut more expensive street drugs.

Another drug in this category is MDMA, known as ecstasy. It is a designer drug, an analog of methamphetamine, and has both stimulant and psychedelic properties. Ecstasy was placed on the DEA schedule in 1985 due to the pattern of abuse and because chemically it is closely linked to another drug found to damage serotonin neurons in the brain.

[6]Hofmann A. *LSD— My Problem Child*. New York. McGraw-Hill, 1980.

Prior to this rescheduling, in addition to its being a recreational drug, it was being investigated as an adjunct to psychotherapy. Women seemingly are more sensitive to its effects. The dissociatives, along with the hallucinogens, are associated with the "rave" scene and among the substances known as club drugs (see pages 571–572).

Dextromethorphan (DXM) is a substance commonly found in over-the-counter cough medicines. It is chemically related to a morphine derivative but has activity similar to dissociatives. In small doses it acts as a cough suppressant, but in larger doses (>4 oz. of cough medicine) it produces consciousness-altering effects similar in nature to the dissociatives. It is readily obtainable and a frequent drug of choice for minors.

Summary: Hallucinogens and Dissociatives

Examples:	*LSD-like drugs:* LSD, mescaline, psilocybin, psilocin, and probably DMA, DOT, and DMT. *MDMA-like drugs:* ecstasy, a club drug. *Dissociative anesthetics:* PCP, ketamine, DXM.
Route of administration:	*LSD-like drugs:* ingested or smoked. *MDMA-like drugs:* ingested or smoked. *PCP:* smoked, ingested, or snorted. *Ketamine:* commercially available as a liquid, easily converted to a powder that is snorted; less often, dissolved in water and injected. *DXM:* commercially available in cough syrups and liquigels.
Absorption:	*LSD-like drugs:* typically taken orally, but DMT can be smoked. *MDMA-like drugs:* can be snorted, injected or taken orally. *PCP:* typically smoked but can be snorted in crystalline form. *DXM:* typically orally ingested. *Ketamine:* typically snorted.
Pharmacological action:	*LSD-like drugs:* act through stimulating serotonin 2A subreceptors in the cortex, causing changes in perception. *MDMA-like drugs:* inhibit excitatory neuron communication by blocking an excitatory neurotransmitter (glutamate) function at the NMDA receptor.
Length of action:	Varies with the substance, ranges from hours to a few days.
Desired effects:	Increased awareness of sensory input; perceptions of usual environment as novel; altered body image; blurring of boundaries between self and environment; temporary modification of thought processes, claims

Summary: Hallucinogens and Dissociatives (continued)

	of special insights, and increased empathy; hallucinations; feelings of strength, power, and invulnerability (PCP); pleasant, floating, dreamlike state (ketamine); reported sexual stimulation (ketamine).
Other acute effects:	*LSD group:* panic attacks; increased blood pressure, palpitations, tremor, nausea, muscle weakness, increased body temperature, ataxia; in some cases, accidental death (when user acts on drug-induced thought, such as belief one can fly). *MDMA group:* nausea, jaw and teeth clenching, muscle tension, blurred vision, panic attacks, confusion, depression, anxiety, paranoid psychosis, hyperthermia, cardiac arrest. *Ketamine:* frightening experience of complete sensory detachment and loss of motor control described as a "near death" experience, often referred to as the "K-hole"; paranoia; boredom; possible coma. *PCP:* psychotic reactions, bizarre behavior, outbursts of hostility and violence; feelings of severe anxiety, doom, or impending death; gross incoordination, nystagmus, hypersalivation; vomiting; fever. *Ketamine and Dextromethorphan:* hallucinations (tactile, auditory, visual), visual disturbances, paranoia, disorientation, nausea, vomiting, abdominal pain, hyperthermia ("rave-related heatstroke"), cardiac irregularities, high blood pressure.
Metabolism:	Primarily by the liver.
Common problems:	*LSD group:* flashbacks long after using, which can lead to depression, panic attacks, or in some cases suicide; hallucinogenic mood disorder; psychotic (delusional) disorders with varying courses; long-term visual changes (hallucinogen persistent perceptual disorder), a phenomenon of "after-images" or sometimes referred to as "trailing" occurring after use of LSD has stopped, sometimes for years. *MDMA group:* nausea, jaw and teeth clenching; psychotic reactions. *Ketamine:* dependence reported; hallucinations/

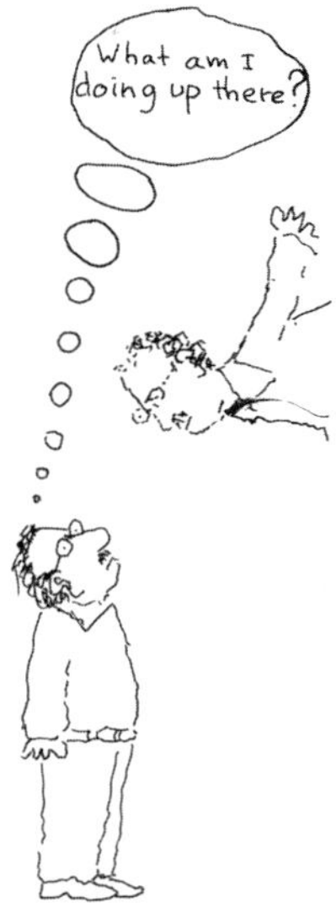

Summary: Hallucinogens and Dissociatives (continued)

	flashbacks persisting for months after use; possible memory impairment. *Dextromethorphan:* possible dependence.
Withdrawal symptoms:	*LSD and MDMA groups:* no clinical evidence of withdrawal effects when use is terminated. *PCP:* animal studies suggest withdrawal symptoms, including poor feeding, weight loss, irritability, bruxism, tremors, and preconvulsive activity. *Dextromethorphan:* insomnia, dysphoria, depression; no physical withdrawal symptoms reported.
Interaction with alcohol:	In combination with MDMA or dextromethorphan, possibly increases dehydration (especially when used at raves).
Medical uses:	Medical uses for LSD, from treating alcoholism to cluster headaches, were under investigation before it was made illegal in the 1960s; no current FDA indications. MDMA recently has been shown to improve therapy's effect on patients with PTSD. Cough suppressant (dextromethorphan). Veterinary anesthetic (ketamine).

Hallucinogens and Dissociatives	Average Amount Taken	Addiction Risk	DEA Schedule
LSD group			
LSD (acid)	10–400 micrograms	low	I
mescaline	100–200 mg	low	I
psilocybin	4–10 mg	low	I
DOM (STP)	3–5 mg	low	I
DMT	3.3–5 mg	low	I
MDMA group			
MDMA (ecstasy)	110–150 mg	moderate	I
MDA		low	I
Dissociatives/ Anesthetics			
PCP	80–500 mg	low	II
ketamine	100–200 mg	low	III
dextromethorphan	2–10 oz	moderate	over-the-counter "extra strength" cough medicines

Club Drugs: A Special Case

Club drugs is a vague term. As noted earlier, club drugs do not constitute a pharmacologic class of compounds. The drugs commonly referred to as "club drugs" fall into multiple drug classes—sedatives/depressants (alcohol, GHB [gamma-hydroxybutyrate], and Rohypnol); stimulants (amphetamines and methamphetamines); opioids (fentanyl); and hallucinogens and dissociatives (LSD, ecstasy, ketamine). The common denominator isn't chemistry but the settings in which they are commonly used: nightclubs, music festivals, dance parties, and raves. These parties involve all-night dancing, laser light shows, electronic music, *and* drugs. Attendance can range from several hundred to thousands of people. Raves originated in England and then spread worldwide.

The drugs most commonly referred to as club drugs are ecstasy, ketamine, GHB (gamma-hydroxybutyrate), and Rohypnol. They are seen as enhancing social intimacy, sensory perception, and endurance, allowing users to continue for hours on the dance floor. Although Rohypnol is commonly included in discussions of club drugs, the evidence suggests that it is uncommon, even though much discussed, (see pages 535–536).

Usually drugs are purchased at the event and bought by the capsule or the vial. Typically club drugs are cheap and conveniently distributed as small pills, powders, or liquids. Not unexpectedly, frequently the tablets or vials sold are not what they are purported to be. In the United Kingdom, common additives to GHB include cocaine, amphetamines, and morphine. In the United States, common additives are methamphetamine, PCP, and ecstasy.

In addition to the inherent problem of using unknown drugs of unknown strength, the pattern of drug use at raves introduces another problem. The usual practice is to take sequential doses of the same substance, or a sequence of different drugs, as the effects of one wear off, a practice known as "bump." This pattern of use invites problems, as the drugs vary in their rates of clearance and metabolism; also, the effects of a particular drug may vary with the dose. And if you really don't know what you consumed . . . plus judgment is impaired . . . who remembers what the supposed sequence was? Plus, alcohol use is the rule, and typically alcohol is the beverage in which these drugs are mixed. Another potential problem arises from the crowded hot conditions common on the club and rave scene. Ecstasy can cause a marked increase in body temperature, which can invite liver, kidney, and cardiovascular problems. Another problem is that ecstasy users can become dehydrated. Or fearing dehydration, folks may drink large volumes of water, inducing "water intoxication," which is potentially life-threatening as it causes disturbances in electrolyte balances.

GHB is a sedative that can lead to reduced respiration and coma when used along with alcohol. Many of the club drugs have sedative properties and, particularly when consumed along with alcohol, invite the risk of depressed respiration and coma. Over a six-year period, the number of emergency room visits involving club drugs has increased about 10-fold, from several hundred to several thousand. However, in 2002, the most recent data available, in combination, GHB and ecstasy—totaling about 7,300 emergency room incidents—represented only a tiny fraction of the 1 million–plus drug-related emergency room visits.

Cannabinoids

The cannabinoids include marijuana, synthetic THC, hashish, and hash oil. Although their psychoactive properties have long been known, use rose dramatically during the 1960s when the percentage of users among young adults went from about 3% in the beginning of that decade to 40% at the end.

Historical Tidbits

Marijuana is the most violence-causing drug in the history of mankind.
—Harry Anslinger

Director of Federal Bureau of Narcotics, 1932–1962

Cannabis, the plant from which marijuana is derived, is not native to North America. It was imported from Europe with the earliest colonists as a source of hemp, which was used for cloth and rope. It was long recognized as having psychoactive properties and was used as a medicine during the 1800s. For the most part, abuse wasn't an issue. In the first half of the twentieth century, non-medical use was restricted to "artists," "bohemians," and other marginal groups. Concerns about use were not sufficient for it to be included in the Harrison Act, passed in the early 1900s. With the passage of the Marijuana Tax Act in 1937, efforts were made to regulate marijuana. The Act was supposedly a revenue/tax measure, with individuals who distributed or dispensed or possessed marijuana required to pay a tax of $1 and, under particular circumstances, register with the government. Failure to pay the tax could lead to substantial fines and prison terms. Although use was not made illegal per se, it is evident that the tax was not created as a measure intended primarily to generate government revenues.

It was not until 1941 that marijuana was no longer classified as a medication. Interestingly, part of the groundwork for the emergence of marijuana in the 1960s was laid by U.S. government policy during World War II. Foreign sources of hemp were no longer available then, and domestic cultivation became part of the war effort. The goal was to have more than 300,000 acres in cultivation by the middle of the war. Most of this was grown in the Midwest, where wild marijuana plants can still be found.

Availability

A report issued in 2006 drawing on government data provides a number of insights. Domestic marijuana production has increased 10-fold over the past 25 years. A commonly cited statistic, and one used by the

United Nations, estimates that currently over 10,000 metric tons and an additional 5,000 metric tons harvested in Mexico and Canada are marketed in the United States. Generally, most domestically produced marijuana is used in-state. Nine states—California, Tennessee, Kentucky, West Virginia, Hawaii, Arkansas, Washington, Alabama, and (barely) Alaska—are thought to be "exporting" states. With marijuana one of the top three crops in 30 states, cultivation has become a significant element in the national economy. With the increasing attention paid to cultivation techniques, marijuana commonly has twice the THC (tetrahydrocannabinol, the psychoactive compound in marijuana) as the "backyard" varieties of the 1960s.

Potency and Danger

Whiskey or vodka, with a higher alcohol content, are more potent than wine or beer. Does this make them more dangerous? It does mean that it takes fewer ounces or gulps to feel the effect. The same is true of higher potency cannabis; it takes fewer inhalations to deliver the desired effects.

Patterns of Use

Marijuana is by far the most widely used illicit drug. Forty-three percent of those 12 or older have used marijuana at some point. In 2012, about 12% of the total population 12 and older had used marijuana in the past year, and the rate of use in the past month was a little over 7%. The 18 to 25 age group had the highest rate of use, with 19% reporting use in the past month. For those over age 25, the rate was 5%. In terms of trends, overall, use declined during the 1980s. Then, in the early to mid-1990s, there was a sharp upturn, which has since leveled off. For marijuana, as for drugs in general, there is a trend toward first use at an earlier age. In 2012, after alcohol, marijuana was the drug associated with the highest number of persons who meet the criteria for dependence or abuse, affecting 4.3 million Americans (1.7% of the population).

In terms of past month use, marijuana use is twice as common among men than women (10% versus 5%). With respect to race/ethnicity, Asian Americans have the lowest levels of current use (2.5%) and Hispanics the next lowest (6.2%); the highest level of use is among those identifying themselves as multiracial (13%) followed by Native Americans and Alaska Natives (9.4%), African Americans (9.1%), and Whites (7.4%). Use is higher for the unemployed and for those who are working full-time. In sheer numbers there are more than three times as many employed people who use marijuana. Among all age groups, use is higher in metropolitan areas than in rural areas. In terms of sections of the country, the highest rate is the West (9.4%), followed by the Northeast (7.9%), the Midwest (6.8%), and the South (5.8%).

Societal Perspectives

Despite marijuana being an illicit drug, increasingly it is distinguished from other illicit drugs. The fact is that, in some social circles, marijuana simply isn't a big issue, considered a private matter and no one else's business, if used with discretion. That includes not using in situations that invite physical risk or endanger others, such as driving. That societal attitudes have changed dramatically is evidenced by the fact that since 1996 close to half the states have approved medical marijuana and two states have approved recreational use.

I don't respond well to mellow, you know what I mean. I – I have a tendency to . . . if I get too mellow, I ripen and then rot.
–Woody Allen

In *Annie Hall,* explaining why he is passing on a party with marijuana

The problems that can occur with marijuana use simply are not in the same league as those associated with other drugs, including alcohol. Some view marijuana as essentially benign, except for the munchies. But that is to overlook the problems that can appear. Among the most significant problems is possible cognitive impairment with heavy use—impairment that interferes with learning new material, a significant issue, given the age group of most users. Another serious concern is the seeming causative role of marijuana use in some cases of schizophrenia. When the association between the onset of schizophrenia and history of marijuana use was first identified, the thinking was that marijuana did not cause this psychiatric disorder but rather precipitated its appearance in susceptible individuals. More recent evidence shows that 25% of people carry a gene that gives them a 10.9-fold risk of developing schizophrenia if they use marijuana.

Dependence can occur with marijuana. But compared to those who use many other drugs, a much smaller proportion develops dependence. Generally, the problems associated with long-term, heavier use are less dramatic than those that accompany heavy long-term drinking. On this basis, some feel strongly that the criminal sanctions that can be brought to bear are disproportionately harsh. Some people hold that marijuana's drug properties cannot be used to make the case for its illicit status. The response commonly is, "Well that may be true, but don't we have enough problems with the drugs that are legal, so why add to our problems?" The counter argument for decriminalization is that prohibition simply doesn't work and is exceedingly costly.

Clinical Issues

The person who comes to a clinician's attention due to marijuana use may be confronting the same issues as someone who is in treatment for alcohol abuse. Clearly some problems have resulted from use; otherwise, the individual wouldn't be in a clinician's office. But there may not be dependence. No one expects clinicians to be police officers. Nonetheless, the legal status of marijuana begins to cast a shadow when treatment is sought. If someone comes to professional attention, use has clearly become somewhat public. Because of the legal issues, one may question whether "moderate" marijuana use is a reasonable, realistic clinical goal. In addition, marijuana use can be problematic in the context of other drug use. When someone is stoned, the decision to drink or not to drink is hardly an informed, thoughtful one. The client needs to be engaged in the same process of self-examination that is required in the presence of alcohol abuse. Again, follow-up is required to see whether efforts to reduce risk are effective.

Medical Marijuana

According to the folk wisdom, a number of conditions can be alleviated by the use of marijuana—these include nausea and lack of appetite that can accompany chemotherapy; chronic pain; HIV- and AIDS-related problems; glaucoma; depression; anxiety; menstrual cramps and migraine headaches, as well as everyday aches, pains, stresses, and sleeping difficulties. Although this is now changing, until recently, clinical research to evaluate the therapeutic use of marijuana has been quite limited.

Over the past decade there have been concerted efforts directed at state governments to allow the use of marijuana for medical purposes. Since 1996, 19 states have enacted laws permitting use for medical reasons. There are typically several requirements—that use be recommended by a physician, that the individual register with the state, and that the individual obtain an identification card. To provide marijuana to those who meet the necessary criteria, generally regulations allow purchase through licensed dispensaries. For those who wish to grow their own, the state regulations specify the number of plants that can be under cultivation for medical use.

XIII
"All Societies use drugs." Said Professor Shultes. "And every Society Decides which are permitted and which forbidden."

These state laws are at odds with federal laws. So it's possible to be law-abiding in the state where you live, while simultaneously breaking federal laws, and therefore be open to prosecution. As of 2010, the United States Attorney General's Office announced it would not seek cases for prosecution if the basic issue involves medical marijuana. The rationale for the decision is that resources are limited, and medical marijuana is not among the government's most pressing matters. While not a solution, this does successfully skirt the issue for the time being. However, the "time being" may prove to be very short. Typically, medical marijuana is produced by a community-based not-for-profit cooperative, approved by local officials. However, in California there's been a new development. A for-profit company is seeking permission to provide medical marijuana to the local community, although it is also "willing" to sell medical marijuana statewide. It has a large industrial warehouse standing by should permission be granted. Depending on how one reads the tea leaves—or is it pot leaves?—might this group be preparing itself to become the next decade's Anheuser-Busch or Eli Lilly?

Summary: Cannabinoids

Examples:	Marijuana, hashish, THC.
Route of administration:	Smoked, taken by mouth.
Pharmacological action:	When smoked, absorbed through the lungs; produces effects through specific binding at cannabinoid receptor sites in the brain that appear to be specific for cannabinoids.

Summary: Cannabinoids (continued)

Metabolism:	Metabolized by liver. More than 55% of THC is excreted in the feces ~20% in the urine.
Length of action:	Smoking: 2–4 hours; ingestion: 5–12 hours.
Desired effects:	Sense of relaxation and well-being, euphoria, detachment; modification of level of consciousness, altered perceptions, altered time sense; sexual arousal.
Other acute effects:	Slows reaction time and alters perceptions, making it dangerous to operate machinery or drive; panic; anxiety; nausea; dizziness; difficulty expressing thoughts; paranoid thoughts; depersonalization.
Intoxication/overdose:	*Vital signs:* increased respiration rate, increased heart rate, mild increase in temperature. *Physical exam:* red eyes (conjunctival injection), mild dilation of pupils, mild tremor, decreased coordination, decreased strength, less ability to perform complex motor tasks, dry mouth. *Mental status:* feelings of depersonalization, alteration in mood, disorganization; anxiety, panic; memory problems; paranoid thoughts; hallucinations.
Common problems:	Dependence, panic, anxiety; nausea, dizziness; difficulty in expressing thoughts, paranoid thoughts, depersonalization, visual distortions, perceptual problems, motor performance may impair driving; impairment of ability to learn new material; physical effects with prolonged use include respiratory problems, possible impaired immune function, and possible reproductive problems, including low-birth-weight infants.
Withdrawal symptoms:	Craving, anxiety, irritability, nausea, anorexia, agitation, restlessness, tremor, depression.
Interaction with alcohol:	CNS depressant effects; impairment of driving-related skills.
Medical uses:	Used to reduce nausea and stimulate appetite in cancer patients, possible treatment of glaucoma. Research under way, as yet few definitive findings in respect to therapeutic use.

Cannabinoids	Average Amount Taken	Addiction Risk	DEA Schedule
marijuana	4–40 mg	moderate	I
hashish	—	moderate	I
dronabinol (Marinol)	THC/cigarette 2.5–20mg/day	low as used medically	III

Inhalants

Inhalants are substances that give off vapors or fumes, which are inhaled for their psychoactive properties. Three kinds of compounds fall into this class of drugs. The largest group of inhalants consists of common household products: paints, lighter fluid, paint thinners, other aerosols, felt-tipped pens, correction fluid, cleaning compounds, gasoline, and glue. These are termed the hydrocarbons, based on their chemical composition, and are also referred to as *volatile solvents.* Another kind, *nitrites,* take their name from their chemical composition. The butyl nitrites are found in air fresheners. Amyl nitrites, known as "poppers" or "snappers," based on the way they are packaged, were originally used to treat angina. The third kind of inhalants is the *nitrates,* which are a form of anesthetics, the most common one being nitrous oxide, known as "laughing gas."

Patterns of Use

Over the past decades, the use of inhalants increased, peaking in 1995. Since then the number of those who have ever tried inhalants has declined by a third. Unlike any other type of drug, the highest rate of inhalant use is among the youngest adolescents. Eighth-graders have the highest rate of use (6.2%), twice as high as 12th graders. Among the population as a whole, past-year use is under 1%. It is only in the past several years that inhalant use dropped from the number one spot among 8th graders, supplanted by marijuana. Inhalants, which are easily available and inexpensive, can cause permanent brain damage. This is particularly troubling because much inhalant use is a group activity, thus exposing a number of people to this danger.

Hawaii natives and Pacific Islanders have a higher rate of use, five to seven times higher than any other racial or ethnic group. The South has the highest rate of past-year use (9.5% for eighth graders), and the Northeast the lowest level (7.9%). Use is slightly higher outside of cities and the suburbs. Among eighth graders, use is virtually three times higher among those who don't expect to attend four years of college. Parental education is a predictor of use. Use is highest among those with the lowest levels of education and the rates lowest for those whose parents have the highest level of education. This is one of the few drugs in which use by females exceeds that of males.

Pharmacological Actions

Although the inhalants are a diverse group of compounds, they have several common features. Their molecules are very small, thus allowing them to be absorbed easily by the lungs. Also, their effects are very similar to those of central nervous system depressants. However, their effects seemingly are not due to their impact on neurotransmitters. Being fat soluble, they can be incorporated into cell membranes. This in turn interferes with the cell's level of excitability. The fat-soluble properties of inhalants also account for their distribution into various body organs. This is important because many inhalants and their metabolites are known to be prototypic toxins of the liver, kidneys, and nerve cells. Inhalants' toxicity on the central nervous system was first recognized in the Scandinavian countries; termed "painter's syndrome," it resulted from long exposure to paint fumes.

There are no differences but differences of degree between different degrees of difference and no difference.

Attributed to William James, supposedly while on nitrous oxide.

Summary: Inhalants

Examples:	Paints, other aerosols, organic solvents and cleaning agents, gasoline and other petrochemicals, glue; vasodilators (amyl and butyl nitrites); anesthetics (nitrous oxide).
Route of administration:	Inhalation ("huffing"). Inhalant users inhale vapor or aerosol propellant gases using plastic bags held over the mouth, or by breathing from a solvent-soaked rag or an open container.
Absorption:	When inhaled, molecules of vaporized drug deposit on lung air sacs and are rapidly taken into the bloodstream by capillaries nearby.
Pharmacological action:	*Nitrous oxide* inhibits NMDA and acetylcholine channels, and slightly potentiates GABA activity. Amyl and butyl nitrite cause vasodilation through nitric oxide activity, increasing cerebral blood flow. Exact mechanism of other volatile inhalants (gasoline and other petrochemicals) is unknown.
Metabolism:	"Avoids" liver metabolism initially due to inhaled route of administration. Metabolized by liver and removal by kidneys once in circulation.
Length of action:	Varies—several minutes to several hours.
Desired effects:	*Volatile solvents:* the "rush"; euphoria; behavioral disinhibition; sensation of floating; perceptual disturbances, including

Summary: Inhalants (continued)

	hallucinations. *Nitrites:* used to postpone or enhance intercourse, especially in gay male population; may cause euphoria. *Nitrous oxide:* euphoria, altered perceptions.
Other acute effects:	*Volatile solvents:* cardiac depression leading to "sudden sniffing death" probably secondary to cardiac arrhythmias, aspiration or respiratory depression, vehicle accidents secondary to intoxication. *Nitrites:* panic reactions, nausea, dizziness, hypotension. *Nitrous oxide:* nausea, vomiting, confusion.
Action:	*Volatile solvents:* action is not fully understood and probably varies with the substance inhaled, action on the central nervous system is similar to that of CNS depressants; may act on GABA and glutamate neurotransmitter systems, presumed that inhalants disrupt neural function; intoxication is similar to that of the CNS depressants. *Nitrites:* act by increasing cerebral blood flow, little else is known. *Nitrous oxide:* exact mechanism of action is unknown but may involve NMDA receptors.
Intoxication/overdose:	*Volatile solvents. Vital signs:* possible irregular heartbeat. *Physical exam:* ataxia, muscle weakness, dysarthria; nystagmus, diminished reflexes. *Mental status:* euphoria, giddiness, fatigue, confusion, disorientation. *Nitrites ("Poppers"). Vital signs:* decreased blood pressure, increased pulse. *Physical exam:* minimal findings. *Mental status:* minimal changes. *Nitrous Oxide. Vital signs*: increased respiration. *Physical exam:* possible asphyxiation and frostbite of nose, lips, or larynx if inhaled from tank; loss of motor control; nausea; ataxia; muscle weakness; dysarthria; nystagmus; diminished reflexes. *Mental status:* laughter, giddiness, confusion.
Common problems:	*Volatile solvents:* cardiac depressants leading to "sudden sniffing death" probably secondary to cardiac arrhythmias, aspiration or respiratory depression;

VI
Inhalants Filled the young mind with strange visions. The heart skipped a beat, started, stopped, Then started again.

Summary: Inhalants (continued)

	atrophy of various areas of brain with attendant behavioral symptoms; renal complications; vehicle accidents secondary to intoxication. *Nitrites:* panic reactions, nausea, dizziness, hypotension, negative effects on the hematological and immune systems (anemia, decreased T-cell function). *Nitrous oxide:* paranoid psychosis with confusion (chronic use), depletion of vitamin B-12 with neurological side effects (weakness, peripheral neuropathy), deficits in short-term memory.
Withdrawal symptoms:	Psychological dependence symptoms documented (craving, etc.); physical withdrawal symptoms not well established in humans; sleep disturbances, nausea, tremor, and irritability reported with volatile solvents; withdrawal seizures with nitrous oxide in rats.
Interaction with alcohol:	Varies by substance, potentiation with volatile solvents.
Medical uses:	None, except use of nitrous oxide for anesthesia.

Inhalants	Average Amount Taken	Addiction Risk	DEA Schedule
volatile solvents (commercial products)	variable	moderate	N/A
nitrites (amyl nitrite, butyl nitrite)	variable	unknown	N/A
nitrous oxide	variable	moderate	N/A

Anabolic Androgenic Steroids

Steroids are not used for their psychoactive, mood-altering properties. Drugs in this class are male hormones and are used by athletes and by people involved with bodybuilding to increase muscle development and enhance athletic performance. They have been described by some as the male chemical equivalents of breast enhancement in women. Serious physical side effects as well as behavioral problems are associated with long-term use. Anabolic steroid use is thought to cause aggression in some people; hence the term "roid rage."

The use of anabolic steroids is one of the lesser achievements of the Olympic movement. They were supposedly first used by members of the Soviet Union weight-lifting team at the 1954 Olympics. However, it was

Community-Level Drug Testing?

It is possible to monitor the water in waste-water treatment plants for the presence of drugs of abuse. A recent report discusses these efforts in Florence, Italy. The results indicated cocaine use was considerably higher than heroin use. This community drug testing is seen as useful in monitoring community drug use, and thus an aid in prevention efforts.

Forensic Science International, 2009

American ingenuity that made use more widespread. A physician with the U.S. team that year got wind of the Soviet team use and, on returning home, teamed up with a pharmaceutical company to produce what is probably the most widely known anabolic steroid, Dianabol. The use of performance-enhancing drugs was subsequently outlawed by the International Olympic Committee. At this time there is a very lengthy list of prohibited substances, and drug testing is routine. A number of these substances are included in small amounts in over-the-counter medications and in prescription drugs taken for legitimate medical conditions. So knowing what is or is not OK to use before athletic competition almost seems to require a degree in pharmacology. Ironically, the efforts to identify athletes' use of banned drugs have been the major factor leading to advancements in drug-testing procedures now available in clinical and legal settings.

VII
Oh, Soviet Weight Lifters, Could you have imagined What your use of anabolic steroids Would lead to In these many years Since the 1954 Olympics "Home-run records, Drug-fueled bicycle races, And better living through chemistry" Said UBU the ironic.

Patterns of Use

The use of steroids is relatively low. From year to year there are ups and downs, ranging from a low of 0.7% to a high of 1.9%. The *Monitoring the Future* study indicates that in 2012, 0.6% of 8th graders, 0.8% of 10th graders, and 1.3% of 12th graders had taken anabolic steroids in the past year. Originally sold over the counter as a nutritional supplement, androstenedion, a precursor of steroids, became a scheduled drug in 2005. Female use is about a quarter of the level of use by males. For males the rates for steroids or androstenedion is 1.3% for 8th graders, 2% for 10th graders, and 2.2% for high school seniors. Since 1989, with the exception of one year, the highest rate of steroid use is among high school seniors.

Another compound that could be classified as a steroid based on chemical composition is gamma-hydroxybutyrate (GHB). However, despite its chemical composition, it is classified here, as well as by NIDA in its publications, as a sedative (see pages 560–561). First synthesized in the 1960s, it was initially used as a relaxant to induce anesthesia, but it fell out of favor. In the late 1980s, prior to its gaining popularity as a club drug, GHB was being touted among bodybuilders and competitive athletes. The claims for GHB were that it enhanced strength, contributed to muscle development, and enhanced the metabolism of fat. GHB was promoted by health food stores as a dietary supplement.

Adverse reactions led to its being banned from use in nutritional and weight loss supplements in 1991. It has continued to be available through imports as well as illicit manufacture. Among athletes, this illegal status has led to a new development—the use of the easier-to-acquire "precursors," substances that when metabolized are converted to GHB and thus induce the same effects. These are becoming widely available over the internet and are marketed to adolescents and young adults as dietary supplements that increase muscle mass as well as enhance sexual performance. Their use can cause serious medical problems, including life-threatening respiratory depression.

Although I did previously deny any use of steroids, I regretfully admit that there were times when in order to fight crime in spite of age and injury...

Routes of Administration

Anabolic steroids are taken orally as tablets or are injected into the large muscles. When using steroids, athletes tend to adopt a particular regimen that entails a period of use followed by some time off or the use of different steroids in a predetermined sequence, with time off. Whatever the pattern, it is often called a "cycle." The rationale behind this, for which the medical basis is questionable, is that such a pattern can diminish side effects. The cycle of use is also coordinated with other training activities in the hope of achieving peak performance at the time of competition.

Summary: Anabolic Androgenic Steroids

Examples:	Testosterone compounds, 19-nortestosterone derivatives, orally active androgen.
Route of administration:	Orally, via skin patches, or injection into large muscles.
Absorption:	*Oral:* through intestinal wall into bloodstream. *Skin patch:* through skin into bloodstream. *Intramuscular:* absorbed through capillary beds that supply muscles over time.
Pharmacological action:	Begins when the steroid penetrates the membrane of the target cell and binds to an androgen receptor in the cell body. This hormone-receptor compound diffuses into the cell nucleus, where it either alters the expression of genes or activates processes that send signals to other parts of the cell. The effect of anabolic steroids on muscle mass is caused in at least two ways: first, they increase the production of proteins; second, they reduce recovery time by blocking the effects of the stress hormone (cortisol) on muscle tissue, so that catabolism of muscle is greatly reduced. Anabolic steroids can also decrease fat by raising the metabolism rate, as an increase in muscle mass increases the base metabolic rate.
Metabolism:	Different for various steroids: liver, kidneys, lung, skin, and breast.
Length of action:	Days to weeks.
Desired effects:	Enhancement of appearance or athletic performance with attendant self-confidence and self-esteem.
Other acute effects:	Negligible.

Summary: Anabolic Androgenic Steroids (continued)

Intoxication/overdose:	Rare; most of the negative effects are from regular and prolonged use rather than from intoxication and overdose.
Common problems:	Virilizing side effects (vary by gender); in men, increased facial hair, deepening of voice, male pattern of baldness, acne; in women, clitoral enlargement and menstrual irregularities; feminizing effects in men can include gynecomastia (breast development); reduction in HDL cholesterol; jaundice, hepatitis, liver cancer; psychiatric side effects (mania, depression, panic, and aggressive symptoms reported).
Withdrawal symptoms:	Depression, fatigue, decreased libido, muscle pain, headache, craving.
Interaction with alcohol:	Not well researched.
Medical uses:	Replacement of endogenous testosterone, to increase red blood cells and complement factor, treatment of endometriosis and fibrocystic breast disease.
Addiction risk:	Moderate.

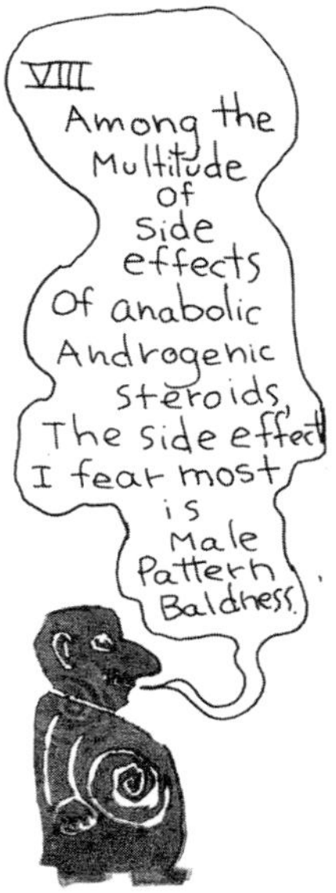

Anabolic Androgenic Steroids	Daily Dose
testosterone esters (testosterone cypionate)	equivalent of 20–2000 mg testosterone/day
19-Nortestosterone derivatives (nandrolone decanoate, nandrolone phenylpropionate)	equivalent of 20–2000 mg testosterone/day
orally active androgens (danazol, fluoxymesterone, methyltestosterone, oxymesterone, stanzolol)	equivalent of 4–200 times usual daily dose of androgens

Other Performance-Enhancing Drugs

In 1995, a poll was conducted among Olympic-level power athletes to assess their attitudes toward performance-enhancing drugs. The athletes were asked to respond to two different scenarios. The first scenario described the following situation: You are offered a banned substance with two guarantees. First, you will not be caught, and, second, by taking the substance you will win. Of the athletes asked if they would take the substance, only three said they would not. Another scenario was posed:

The best example of how impossible it will be for Major League Baseball to crack down on steroids is the fact that baseball and the media are still talking about the problem as "steroids."
—MALCOLM GLADWELL

Less money is made by biochemists working on a cure for cancer than by their colleagues struggling valiantly to hide steroid use.
—Dr. Gregory House

the same undetectable substance will enable you to win every competition entered for the next five years, but then it will kill you. More than half of those polled reported that they would still use the substance.

Typically substance abuse is thought to involve drugs that act on the brain to alter mood, perceptions, and feeling states. Substance abuse could well be defined more broadly and include substances used to alter not the brain but the body. These would be the "performance-enhancing drugs." In some instances drugs fall into both camps, as do the stimulants, the amphetamines, and caffeine.

The following overview is of substances currently outside the usual domain of the substance abuse field, but which are getting increased attention. Although professional athletes may get the bulk of attention, performance-enhancing drugs are also seen as an issue for college and high school students and even those younger. Although anabolic steroids typically receive the most attention, a number of other substances are reported to be widely used. The major groups are described below.

Human Growth Hormone (hGH)

Human growth hormone is produced by the pituitary gland. It is known to influence the body's handling of amino acids, some of the body's basic building blocks; promote the synthesis of proteins; and support growth-promoting body functions. It is a controlled substance, legally available only by prescription. Persons with an hGH deficiency tend to be short in stature. The presence of excessive amounts leads to the medical condition of giantism.

Studies are quite limited. However, the research to date seems to indicate that human growth hormone does increase muscle size, but there is no corresponding increase in performance or strength. Thus people using hGH only *look* more impressive.

Amphetamines and Stimulants

Amphetamine use is credited with increasing muscle strength and is valued for providing resistance to fatigue; especially among cyclists, it is valued for improving muscle torque and increasing lung function.

Ephedrine and Ephedra

As system-wide general stimulants, ephedrine and ephedra are claimed to increase alertness, heighten energy levels, and thus add to athletic performance. Outside the locker room, they are touted as appetite suppressants and incorporated in weight loss products. Ephedrine is the major ingredient of many cold remedies and over-the-counter decongestants. More than 40 species of plants include these compounds, including the Chinese herb Ma Huang, sometimes referred to as herbal ephedrine.

Both the Olympic Committee and NCAA have banned ephedrine, although evidence for its providing a significant performance advantage is limited. In part the ban is related to adverse effects. Among the side effects reported are irritability, rapid heartbeat, sleeplessness, and heart palpitations, as well as stroke and heart attack. Herbal weight loss products containing ephedra were banned in the United States in 2004.

Erythropoietin (EPO) and Blood Doping

Endurance athletes, such as those who run marathons or cyclists, will be aided by anything that increases the blood's capacity to handle oxygen. Hence, all kinds of training regimens, such as living at higher altitudes or sleeping in "altitude tents," have been developed with the goal of enhancing oxygen-carrying capacity. Another technique that has been devised to accomplish this is called "blood doping," the transfusion of blood, so that there is an increase in hemoglobin, the blood protein that carries oxygen. The drug EPO is a hormone produced in the kidney; it increases hemoglobin, thereby influencing the oxygen-carrying capacity of blood cells.

Studies demonstrate that these efforts do indeed increase the availability of oxygen, as well as increasing endurance. There are, however, some dangers. While the reason is not known, artificially high levels of hemoglobin are associated with stroke, heart attack, and blood clots in the lung. Therefore blood doping is a banned practice, as is EPO, although there are no easily administered tests to identify it. To reduce the possible use of EPO and doping among athletes, the Olympics has set upper limits for hemoglobin values.

Creatine

A popular nutritional supplement that has been estimated to represent a $300 million market in the United States, creatine came to attention when its use was reported in conjunction with the 1992 Barcelona Olympics, which proved to be a great marketing device.

Creatine is a naturally occurring compound made in the liver, pancreas, and kidneys and then deposited and stored in muscles. Creatine contributes to the restoration of muscles after exercise. Accordingly, the increase of creatine content in muscles enhances muscles' capacity for restoration. It is viewed as useful in anaerobic events and is reportedly used widely by college athletes, high school athletes, and persons involved in individual fitness regimens.

In studies involving an array of athletes—swimmers, cyclists, weight lifters—creatine supplementation has been shown to increase performance and endurance. For example, among sprinters, creatine has been shown to improve average sprint times by 1 to 2%. For races determined by hundredths of a second, this could be significant.

As a nutritional supplement, a product of what is sometimes termed the "neutraceutical industry," creatine is not regulated by the Food and Drug Administration. This means there is no regulation in formulating products and less pressure or opportunity for safety testing. There are no apparent problems with short-term use, but the effects of long-term use are unknown.

Beta-Hydroxy-Beta-Methylbutyrate (HMB)

The nutritional supplement HMB is marketed as an anti-catabolic. This means it supposedly suppresses the breakdown of protein after a workout and restricts the body to burning carbohydrates and fat to meet its energy requirements. Thus it is supposed to maintain and increase lean body mass. Indeed, although the basis for its function is unclear, some studies appear to support the claim that HMB supplementation does prevent exercise-induced muscle change. At best, however, the performance studies show modest improvement for persons who haven't been involved in any kind of training or conditioning. For those involved in workout and training regimens, there was no improvement.

Seemingly there are no identified negative side effects. In fact, a review of studies showed that it was associated with a lowering of cholesterol and systolic blood pressure. So it may have cardio-protective benefits even if there are no apparent performance-enhancing properties.

Androstenedione (Andro)

As mentioned above, androstenedione, upon its introduction into the United States in the mid-1990s, was treated as a nutritional supplement and sold over-the-counter. Known as Andro, it was marketed as increasing testosterone levels, and as a safe and "natural" alternative to anabolic steroids. It was thrust into the spotlight when stories surfaced that record-breaking sluggers in major league baseball were using Andro. The obvious question was whether athletic talent and hard work or drug use deserved the credit. The other question, essentially medical, was whether androstenedione was as safe as was claimed. In 2005, the FDA reclassified androstenedione from a dietary supplement to anabolic steroid. There are wide ranging significant medical consequences associated with use of androstenedione. Among men there is gynecomastia (male breast development), enlarged prostate, severe acne, reduced sperm count, infertility, and testicular atrophy. Among women there is a masculinization of features—the growth of body and facial hair, deepening of the voice, and male-pattern baldness. For both there is increased risk of pancreatic, kidney, or liver cancer/damage, as well as a reduction in HDL (good) cholesterol, glucose intolerance, blood clots, and an increased risk of heart attack..

Points for Reflection

This is far from a complete catalog of drugs associated with athletics and improving performance. Also used are pain medications that enable athletes barely able to walk off the football field to return to the game after half time or a pitcher in the World Series to continue despite a badly injured ankle requiring some temporary stitches. Drugs are even becoming available to mask the use of banned drugs.

A provocative essay in the *British Journal of Sports Medicine* raised questions worth reflection. Are "amateur" sports a notion from a bygone era? Are elite athletes as much a product of their genes as evidence of their dedication, hard work, and spirit? If an Olympic athlete has a genetic mutation that naturally provides 40% to 50% more red blood cells than average, is this an unfair advantage? Does it matter if blood counts are elevated by altitude training, by a genetic mutation, or by taking EPO, the one avenue deemed unfair?

What limits should be placed on drug use in sports? Should the emphasis be on health testing, not on drug testing? Is it better to determine a safe level of PCV (packed cell volume: that is, the proportion of blood made up of red blood cells) than worry about how a particular level is achieved, whether through training, natural maturation, or use of drugs? Realistically, can the penalties for being caught ever overshadow the benefits of winning? Is performance enhancement against the spirit of sport, or *is* it the spirit of sport?

Performance-Enhancing Drugs Beyond Sports

Anyone who's watched a sporting event or read the sports page in the past year is barely surprised by questions about the use of, misuse of, or possible permissible use of what is or is not a performance-enhancing drug. To a far lesser degree, we are aware of the use of performance-enhancing substances in other circumstances. Probably everyone is aware of students' use of stimulants to pull the infamous all-nighter before an exam. To a far lesser degree there is an awareness of the regular, if not widespread, approved use of stimulants by those in the military. These drugs are dispensed by the military out of concern for the safety of service personnel. But now it's your surgeon! As the use spreads beyond the realm of sports, the terminology changes. When it comes to medicine, the term being used is not "performance enhancement" but "neurocognitive enhancement."

Caffeine

Caffeine is the most widely used psychoactive drug in the world. Its use far exceeds that of alcohol or nicotine. It has been known and used throughout the world for millennia. It is a stimulant drug, but its effects might be considered fairly subtle. Many who use caffeine regularly are not able to easily distinguish its effects and identify mood or behavioral changes associated with use. For many it is just a beverage. However, if pushed, people might note that caffeine helps get them going in the morning or helps them stay awake if driving late at night; or they may note that they have a hard time falling asleep if they have a cup of coffee after dinner. Because coffee has psychoactive properties, there is some discussion as to whether caffeine should or should not be considered a substance of abuse.

Way too much coffee. But if it weren't for the coffee, I'd have no identifiable personality whatsoever.
—DAVID LETTERMAN

Sources of Caffeine

Caffeine isn't found only in coffee, tea, soft drinks, and energy drinks. It is also found in chocolate, cocoa, and a number of over-the-counter medications. The caffeine content of some common products follows:

Product	Caffeine Content (mg)
Coffee, decaf	4
Hershey milk chocolate bar	25
Espresso, 1-oz. cup	40
Brewed tea, 8-oz. cup	50
Coca-Cola, 20-oz. bottle	57
Red Bull (energy drink) 8.3-oz. can	80
Ben and Jerry's coffee fudge* 1 cup	85
Excedrin pain reliever, 2 tablets	130
No-Doz maximum strength* (1 pill)	200
Brewed coffee, 12-oz. cup	200
Mountain Dew, 64-oz. (double big gulp)	294
Starbucks coffee grande* (16 oz.)	550

*Added by author.

Source: Griffiths RR, Mumford GK. Caffeine: A drug of abuse? *Psychopharmacology. The Fourth Generation of Progress*. American College of Neuropsychopharmacology, 2003. <www.acnp.org>

As expected, the source of caffeine differs by age group. Soft drinks are the major source of caffeine among children and young adults. For those in middle age, it's coffee, and for the elderly, tea.

Patterns of Use

The patterns and level of caffeine consumption are changing rapidly thanks to the introduction of energy drinks. At this junction how much caffeine is being consumed by which age groups is far from certain. A survey conducted by the European Union in 2011 found that there was considerable variation in use of energy drinks among different countries. Two different use patterns were identified; the terms sound like phrases that would be used to characterize alcohol consumptions. One group was termed the "high chronic consumers," meaning a general pattern of high use, such as 4–5 times per week, and drinking an average of 4.5 liters per month. Then there were those tagged "high acute consumers" essentially the equivalent of a "binge" drinker, consuming 1 liter per session." Another finding was that energy drinks were frequently combined with alcohol among 72% of young adults and 55% of "old" adults, meaning from ages 50–65 years. The average consumption for 6- to 10-year-olds was a liter/week, which comes to four 8 oz. cans. Energy drinks then provided over 40% of their caffeine intake.

"Cocaine" Pulled from Shelves

NEW HAVEN, Connecticut—An energy drink called Cocaine has been pulled from stores nationwide amid concerns about its name. The Food and Drug Administration issued a warning letter last month that said the manufacturer was illegally marketing the drink as a street drug alternative and a dietary supplement. . . . Cited as evidence was the drink's labeling and Web site, which included the statements "Speed in a Can," "Liquid Cocaine" and "Cocaine—Instant Rush." The company says Cocaine contains no drugs and is marketed as an energy drink. "Of course, we intended for Cocaine energy drink to be a legal alternative the same way that celibacy is an alternative to premarital sex," the spokesman said. "It's not the same thing and no one thinks it is." It apparently satisfied the FDA's concerns about suggestive marketing. But it did not change its name Cocaine Energy Drink.

Associated Press, May 7, 2007

"Cocaine" Makes a Comeback

This controversial product is back on the shelves. Apparently the marketing has been toned down enough to satisfy the FDA's objections.

The Register Citizen, Torrington, CT June 12, 2012

Compared to the caffeine content of the everyday products listed above, what is the caffeine consumption of energy drinks?

Beverage	Size	Caffeine
Red Bull	16 oz	154 mg
Monster Energy	16 oz.	160
Rockstar Punched	24 oz.	160
Power Trip, extreme	16 oz.	220
NOS	16 oz.	260
5-hour Energy	2 oz.	242
DynaPep Microshot	0.14	100

It is no longer possible to simply picture a tall can of the soft drink era. 5-hour energy is described as a shot. DynaPep is a microshot, but also has a time-release formula. The options in terms of flavor seem to be growing daily. The estimated total sales for 2013 are estimated to be in the vicinity of $12 billion.

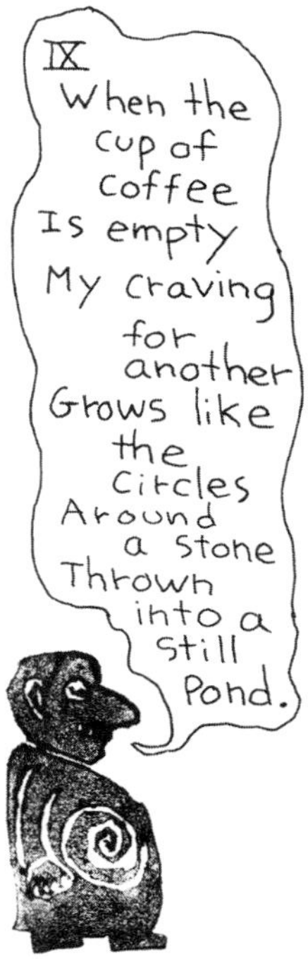

The medical community is voicing considerable concerns about the possible problems associated with energy drinks. It is quite clear to whom these drinks are being marketed: adolescents. There have been at least 13 deaths reported. Beyond the problems of acute overdose, there are questions about the potential long-term effects on adolescents. The answer is simply unknown. In addition to the caffeine content, sugar content is also a concern; two energy drinks will give you a day's quota of sugar. In early 2013, the American Academy of Pediatrics issued a warning about the health consequences. The Canadian Medical Society has issued guidelines for the maximum level of daily consumption. If you're a woman between the ages of 15 to 44 years, your quota would be provided through a serving of Ben and Jerry's coffee ice cream (1 cup), one Excedrin, and one 8 oz. cup of coffee.

Absorption and Metabolism

Caffeine is rapidly absorbed and distributed throughout the water of the body. The levels of caffeine peak between 30 and 75 minutes after consumption. Caffeine is metabolized by the liver for removal from the body. The half-life of caffeine is four to five hours. Since coffee drinkers are likely to have several cups a day, commonly there is a gradually upward rise in the blood concentration of caffeine throughout the day. Caffeine is being consumed at a faster rate than it is being removed.

Acute Effects

Caffeine acts as a stimulant by inhibiting the GABA receptors in the brain; these natural inhibitors slow communication in the central nervous system. A dose of 100–200 mg (1 to 2 cups of coffee) is associated with increased alertness, relief of drowsiness, improved thinking, and increased endurance. However, caffeine impairs fine motor coordination. With higher doses of 250–700 mg, caffeine can induce anxiety, the jitters, insomnia, nervousness, and hypertension. Levels above 1,000 mg can cause rapid heartbeat, sleeplessness, tinnitus (ringing noise in the ear), and cognitive difficulties. A fatal oral dose of caffeine can occur after consumption in excess of 5,000 mg, the equivalent of 40 strong cups of coffee taken in a very short period.

The body very quickly and rapidly accommodates to the presence of caffeine, meaning that tolerance is established. A person's response to consuming caffeine depends on several factors. For one, there are differences between people's *innate sensitivity* to caffeine. In addition, *tolerance* comes from previous use. The regular coffee drinker might have a cup and a refill and not notice much difference. For those who drink caffeine irregularly, a half of a Mountain Dew may have a far greater impact. Another factor is the *dose,* the amount of caffeine ingested. In contrast to alcohol, which we think of in particular quantities such as a can of beer, or a glass of wine, few people have any idea about the amount of caffeine they ingest. For example, someone could easily eat a chocolate bar and not long afterwards drink a cup of coffee with a half-cup refill, followed by a pain capsule, each of which would be delivering a dose of caffeine.

Various studies have demonstrated that caffeine does improve performance by increasing focus and attention and heightening the energy level. It also enhances performance in safety-critical situations that involve boring or repetitive tasks. Caffeine makes falling asleep more difficult. Not unexpectedly, people in the real world tend to orchestrate their caffeine intake throughout the day to take advantage of the enhancements in performance while avoiding the impediments.

In large measure the impact of caffeine is influenced by the person's regular level of caffeine consumption. Negative effects follow caffeine doses that are higher than usual amounts. Among the most common complaints are feeling anxious or jittery; headaches are also common.

Assessing caffeine's effects is a bit difficult. Typically tests of a drug's effects are conducted when people have been abstinent and have no drug in their systems. So imagine a regular coffee drinker being tested early in the morning, before the usual mug that is part of the routine of getting going. If that person reports a "positive" response to the caffeine, is this because a "normal" feeling state is being improved? Or is this coffee drinker actually a bit caffeine-deprived and, accordingly, the positive response is the result of treating a mini-withdrawal state?

Chronic Effects

An immediate issue in thinking about caffeine is the extent to which dependence results from use. Regular caffeine use does produce *tolerance*. This tolerance is established quite rapidly. One research study demonstrated that within a week's time, an increase in the usual amount of caffeine ceases to interfere with sleep in any way. Other studies have shown that within a couple days of higher caffeine consumption, the initial physiological changes associated with caffeine, such as increased blood pressure, fade.

Compared to other stimulants, particularly amphetamines or cocaine, caffeine ranks as a poor cousin, especially in terms of *drug seeking*. Caffeine does not produce equivalent ratings of "liking" or "euphoria" as do the other stimulants. It does not produce an equivalent change in mood states as occurs with some other stimulant drugs. In terms of ratings, its reinforcing properties were evaluated as similar to nicotine. Use may be promoted as much by what feelings caffeine can curtail (withdrawal) as by the feelings it produces.

Withdrawal is also a mark of dependence. Compared to other psychoactive drugs, the symptoms associated with caffeine cessation are relatively mild. Based on a review of about 50 studies dating back to 1833, the following withdrawal symptoms are reported, in order of descending frequency: (1) headache; (2) drowsiness along with decreased energy; (3) decreased feelings of well-being and contentment, more irritability; (4) being less sociable and talkative; (5) flu-like symptoms, aches, hot or cold spells, nausea; and (6) blurred vision. Along with these, tests typically show impairment in performance. The severity of withdrawal is proportionate to the level of the usual maintenance dose as well as the length of use. If forced to go without caffeine, approximately half of regular caffeine users experience headaches. A smaller group, about 10%, report more serious effects.

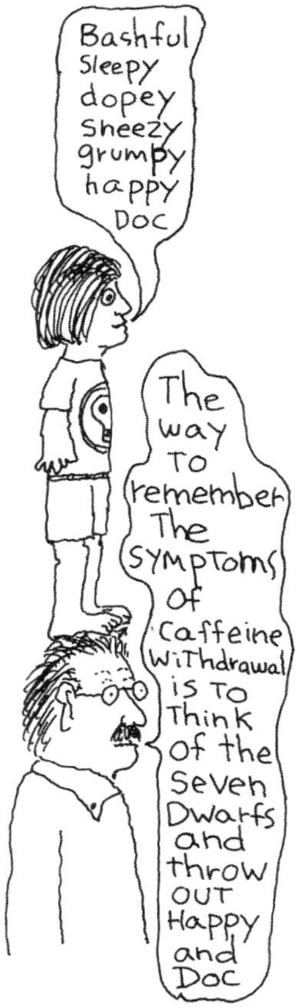

Withdrawal symptoms most typically occur from 12 to 24 hours after the last intake of caffeine. The peak of discomfort occurs between 24 and 48 hours. The duration of symptoms may range from two or three days or as long as a week until usual levels of energy and alertness return.

Significance of Withdrawal Eighty-two percent of all U.S. adults use caffeine. If even 10% experience levels of more serious withdrawal, from time to time, that represents significant numbers. The potential importance of caffeine withdrawal is due more to the sheer size of the population potentially affected than to the nature of the symptoms. At this point there are far more questions than answers as to what the impact may be. For example, what problems might caffeine withdrawal pose for a commercial airline pilot? What are the implications in the workplace or in terms of highway safety? What problems might caffeine withdrawal pose for patients after surgery? In response to the latter question, some pilot efforts have been made to infuse caffeine intravenously to reduce the likelihood of withdrawal in surgical patients.

Medical Import of Long-Term Use A significant concern with any substance is the nature of the medical conditions that may result from long-term use. It has been noted that while cutting down on caffeine may be recommended for any number of medical conditions ranging from ulcers to cardiovascular disease to cancers and anxiety disorders, the actual medical basis for this advice is rather scant. There are no medical conditions that are clearly recognized as caused or aggravated by caffeine.

Caffeine–Other Drug Interactions

As a stimulant, caffeine counters some of the depressant effects of alcohol on alertness and memory. Caffeine also reduces alcohol-induced sleepiness. However, other effects of alcohol are not tempered by caffeine. Caffeine does help with dizziness caused by alcohol, which is sometimes present with alcohol intoxication. The question has been raised whether caffeine increases alcohol tolerance in a more general fashion. There is also an interaction with nicotine. When taken with caffeine, nicotine is perceived to be more pleasurable and reinforcing and is associated with increased ratings of "liking" in laboratory settings. The liver enzymes that metabolize caffeine also play a role in metabolism of a wide variety of other drugs, from heart medications to those used for treating psychiatric illness. Having a lot of caffeine when taking higher doses of such drugs may mean these enzyme systems are overloaded, or saturated, and the rate of removal of caffeine and these other drugs will be slowed.

Alcohol-caffeine interactions Thanks to Four Loko, the effect of caffeine in conjunction with alcohol was suddenly thrust into the limelight. Available in a number of fruit flavors, Four Loko had an 11% alcohol content. Sold in 23.5 oz cans, the alcohol content was equivalent to 4–5 beers, with caffeine equivalent to 5 cups of coffee. Given the size of the drink, for a 120 pound young woman, one can was enough to produce a dangerously high blood alcohol level. In late 2010, after multiple reports of young people being rushed to the hospital and often in groups as large as 8 people, action was being taken by a number of states to ban sales of all alcoholic energy drinks. It was at this point the FDA took action and banned the addition of caffeine to any alcoholic beverage. Though alcohol is a depressant and caffeine is a stimulant, there is one thing both have in common. Both increase the level of dopamine which is associated with pleasure and which may help explain the reports of a special high attributed to Four Loco.

A Substance of Abuse?

Some point out that what is considered abuse in significant part is a social definition. Some note too that for the most part excessive use of caffeine tends to be self-limited. Of course, the same could be said for alcohol, and it is indeed the exceptions that are the concern. On the basis of applying the APA's diagnostic criteria for substance dependence, one study identified about one-third of the general population as caffeine dependent. However, within the APA diagnostic criteria, the withdrawal syndrome for caffeine is characterized as not clinically significant. Withdrawal from some other substances can be life threatening; this is not the case with caffeine.

Seemingly a small proportion of people experience severe caffeine withdrawal; they may seek medical attention for anxiety or insomnia resulting from caffeine use. Some refer to this as indicating the existence of *caffeinism.* Others, while not *denying* some instances of more marked withdrawal, seem to believe that such a term is not quite appropriate. In assessing whether caffeine constitutes a substance of abuse, a relevant question is the extent to which caffeine produces adverse effects for the individual and/or society.

Children's Use of Caffeine

Children are the segment of the population in which caffeine use is most discussed. Concerns have been raised about the possible impact of caffeine on the course of pregnancy, the impact on the newborn of prenatal caffeine exposure, and the impact on children with ADD/ADHD as well as children at large. Children, as well as adults, consume caffeine in their diets. Caffeine is consumed at least weekly by 98% of 5- to 18-year-olds, mostly in carbonated beverages. In the context of a large study of the relationship of caffeine intake and sleep among 7th, 8th, and 9th graders, the caffeine intake ranged from 0 to 800 mg/day. And yes, caffeine use at higher levels was related to sleep disturbances: less total sleep, increased awakenings, and more daytime sleep.

X
I still remember My first cup of coffee. I was seven. My babysitter was Talking with her boyfriend on the phone. I Emptyed the leftover Coffee from the Pot into a cup heated it in The microwave, added cream and a lot of sugar and quickly drank it so I wouldn't get caught. I didn't Fall asleep Till 3AM.

Of note, children too are variable in their sensitivity to caffeine. For some, caffeine is a super-stimulant. It really revs them up. They also have been found to show signs of dependence and withdrawal. If they consume, say, four times their usual dose for a week or two, they show some signs of being less alert, responding more slowly to different memory and performance tasks when they stop. However, there is no evidence of an effect either on the course of pregnancy or on infant development.

A large review study undertaken by staff of the National Institutes of Health concluded that the effects of caffeine in children seem to be modest and generally innocuous. As the word "generally" implies, this means that caffeine may be more of an issue for some children, such as those with particular sensitivity or those with anxiety disorders. Also, as tolerance develops quickly and there are some signs of withdrawal, questions are raised about the possible impact of the newer high-caffeine-containing energy drinks. Yet another question may warrant thought. If kids are drinking more sodas and soft drinks, these may be a greater danger than the caffeine content. The danger is in the calories, especially in light of what is characterized as an epidemic of childhood obesity.

Other Psychoactive Drugs Used Worldwide

Several substances, briefly noted here, are quite common in other countries. While they have been little known in the United States, that is now changing.

- *ayahuasca.* This is a hallucinogen, identified with indigenous cultures in the Amazon region in South America. It is prepared through the brewing of two plants; the psychoactive effects of one plant are inactive until mixed with the other. It has been used primarily in indigenous religious practices, consumed as a tea. This use has extended into modern religious movements, Santo Daime and União do Vegetal, which have taken root throughout the world. In the United States, the religious use of ayahuasca, initially decreed a violation of drug laws, led to a Supreme Court case. A 2006 ruling affirmed that ayahuasca tea could be used for religious purposes. (This is consistent with the Native American Church's use of peyote in its practices.) The general view is that the difficulty in producing ayahuasca makes it unlikely to become a widely used recreational drug.
- *ibogaine.* This plant is derived from the roots of a plant native to western Africa. It has been used by indigenous people to combat fatigue, hunger, and thirst and in higher doses is used in religious rituals. Over the past decade there have been reports of ibogaine's ability to promote abstinence and reduce craving among those addicted to stimulants and opiates. There are no reports of recreational use.
- *kava.* This beverage has long been common in the South Pacific islands—Fiji, Hawaii, and Tonga. The root of the plant is ground up, steeped with water, and strained similarly to a tea. The attraction is not its bitter taste or muddy appearance. It's the feeling of relaxation, which at the same time does not interfere with concentration. Kava is an ingredient in some diet supplements. Several years ago cases of liver failure were associated with use of these supplements, raising questions about kava's safety. Investigation showed that the problem compounds were not a part of the kava root, but were found only in the above-ground portion. There is some preliminary exploration of kava products as an alternative to benzodiazepines.
- *khat.* An evergreen shrub *(Catha edulis)*, found in eastern Africa and Yemen, khat has been known as a medicinal plant for centuries. The fresh leaves and twigs are chewed for their amphetamine-like effects. The juice is swallowed and the remaining portion kept in the mouth, tucked in between the gum and cheek. The active ingredient is cathinone, termed a "natural amphetamine." It is commonly used at special social gatherings but is also used by laborers, craftsmen, and other workers to keep alert and reduce fatigue. It's been long recognized to cause some gastric problems, but little research has been conducted on longer-term effects. Khat use in Western countries is primarily found in immigrant communities.

XI
My friend died In the middle of the night After chewing some strange leaf From East Africa That was supposed to get you high. I was glad I had been Too Scared To Try it.

there are varying *levels* of impairment: mild, moderate, or severe. There are 11 criteria associated with any substance use disorder. The disorder is designated as mild when 2–3 criteria are met, moderate when 4–5 criteria are positive, or severe when 6 or more criteria are positive. The other change introduced in the *DSM-5* involves the dropping of one prior criteria (recurrent legal problems) and the addition of one criteria, craving. In addition to the presence of a substance use disorder of mild, moderate or severe, there are additional diagnoses, intoxication and withdrawal.

The 11 criteria used to diagnose a substance use disorder include the following:

1. The substance is often taken in larger amounts or over a longer period than was intended.
2. There is a persistent desire or unsuccessful efforts to cut down or control substance use.
3. A great deal of time is spent in activities necessary to obtain the substance, use the substance, or recover from its effects.
4. The presence of craving, i.e., a strong urge to take the drug.
5. Recurrent substance use results in failure to fulfill major role obligations at work, school, or home.
6. Continued substance use despite having persistent or recurrent social or interpersonal problems caused or exacerbated by the effects of the substance.
7. Important social, occupational, or recreational activities are given up or are reduced because of substance use.
8. Recurrent substance use in situations in which it is physically hazardous.
9. The substance use is continued despite knowledge of having a persistent or recurrent physical or psychological problem that is likely to have been caused or exacerbated by the substance.
10. Tolerance, as defined by either of the following: *(a)* A need for markedly increased amounts of the substance to achieve intoxication or desired effect, or *(b)* Markedly diminished effect with continued use of the same amount of the substance.
11. Withdrawal, as manifested by the use of the substance (or closely related substance) to avoid withdrawal symptoms, or the presence of characteristic withdrawal symptoms.

Criteria for Diagnosis of Substance Use Withdrawal

The symptoms of withdrawal vary by substance. Recall earlier, it was mentioned that the symptoms associated with withdrawal tend to be the opposite of the effects associated with use and intoxication.

The criteria associated with withdrawal for various substances are outlined below.

Amphetamines Cessation or reduction in amphetamine or a related substance use that has been heavy and prolonged, and dysphoric mood and two or more of the following physiological changes within a few hours to days after cessation/reduction: fatigue, vivid unpleasant dreams, insomnia or hypersomnia, increased appetite, psychomotor retardation, or agitation. (Note: same as cocaine.)

Caffeine Abrupt cessation of or reduction in caffeine use, followed within 24 hours by three (or more) of the following signs or symptoms: headache; marked fatigue or drowsiness; dysphoric mood; depressed mood or irritability; difficulty concentrating; flu-like symptoms (nausea, vomiting, or muscle pain/stiffness). (Note: Although a caffeine use disorder is not included in the section of Substance Use Disorders within *DSM-5,* a withdrawal syndrome is included.)

Cannabis Cessation of cannabis use that has been heavy and prolonged (i.e., usually daily or almost daily use over a period of at least a few months), with three (or more) of the following signs and symptoms developing within approximately 1 week after cessation: irritability, anger or aggression; nervousness or anxiety; sleep difficulty; decreased appetite or weight loss; restlessness; depressed mood; physical symptoms causing discomfort such as abdominal pain, shakiness/tremors, sweating, fever, chills, or headache.

Cocaine Cessation of (or reduction in) cocaine use that has been heavy and prolonged, *and* dysphoric mood and two or more of the following physiological changes, developing within a few hours to several days after cessation/reduction: fatigue; vivid unpleasant dreams; insomnia or hypersomnia; increased appetite; psychomotor retardation or agitation. (Note: same as amphetamines.)

Hallucinogens Clinically significant withdrawal has not been well documented.

Inhalants No clinically significant withdrawal phenomenon identified.

Nicotine Daily use of nicotine for at least several weeks, *and* abrupt cessation or reduction in the amount of nicotine use, followed within 24 hours by four (or more) of the following signs: dysphoric or depressed mood, insomnia, irritability, frustration or anger; anxiety; difficulty concentrating; restlessness; decreased heart rate; and increased appetite.

Opioids Cessation of (or reduction in) use that has been heavy and prolonged (several weeks or longer) *or* administration of an opioid antagonist after a period of opioid use, *and* three or more of the following developing within minutes to several days after cessation/reduction/antagonist use: dysphoric mood, nausea or vomiting, muscle aches; lacrimation or rhinorrhea; pupillary dilation (dilation of eye pupils), piloerection (goose flesh) or sweating; diarrhea; yawning; fever; insomnia.

Phencyclidine Neither tolerance nor withdrawal has been clearly demonstrated.

Sedatives, Hypnotics, or Anxiolytics Cessation or reduction in use that has been heavy and prolonged, and two or more of the following developing within several hours to a few days after cessation/reduction: autonomic hyperactivity; increased hand tremor; insomnia; nausea or vomiting; transient visual, tactile, or auditory hallucinations or illusions; psychomotor agitation; anxiety; grand mal seizures. (Note: same as for alcohol.)

DSM-5 Diagnostic Criteria: Intoxication

The following are the criteria for intoxication for specific drugs/drug classes. In all instances it is presumed that the symptoms are not due to a general medical condition, nor are they better explained by a different psychiatric disorder.

Alcohol Intoxication

1. Recent ingestion of alcohol.
2. Clinically significant problematic behavior or psychological changes (e.g., inappropriate sexual or aggressive behavior; mood lability [mood swings]; impaired judgment; impaired social or occupational functioning) during or shortly after drinking.
3. One or more of the following signs, developing during, or shortly after, alcohol use:
   - slurred speech
   - unsteady gait (unsteady walk)
   - stupor or coma
   - lack of coordination
   - nystagmus (crossed eyes)
   - impairment in attention or memory

Amphetamine Intoxication

1. Recent use of amphetamine or a related substance.
2. Clinically significant problematic behavioral or psychological changes.
3. Two or more of the following signs, developing during, or shortly after use:
   - dilation of eye pupils
   - perspiration or chills
   - evidence of weight loss
   - elevated or lowered blood pressure
   - nausea or vomiting
   - tachycardia or bradycardia (rapid or slow heartbeat)
   - psychomotor agitation or retardation; muscular weakness, respiratory depression, chest pain, or cardiac arrhythmias (irregular heartbeat)
   - confusion, seizures, dyskinesias (difficulty in voluntary movement), dystonias (abnormal muscle tone), or coma

Caffeine Intoxication

1. Recent consumption of caffeine, usually in excess of 250 mg (e.g., more than 2–3 cups of brewed coffee).

2. Five or more of the following, developing during or shortly after caffeine use:
   - restlessness
   - excitement
   - flushed face
   - gastrointestinal disturbance
   - periods of inexhaustibility
   - psychomotor agitation
   - nervousness
   - insomnia
   - diuresis (increased urine output)
   - muscle twitching
   - rambling flow of thought and speech
   - tachycardia or cardiac arrhythmia (rapid or irregular heart beat)
3. The above symptoms cause distress or impairment in social, occupational, or other important areas of functioning.

Cannabis Intoxication

If you can remember the '60s then you weren't there.
—Robin Williams

1. Recent use of cannabis.
2. Clinically significant problematic behavioral or psychological changes (e.g., impaired motor coordination, euphoria, anxiety, sensation of slowed time, impaired judgment, social withdrawal) that developed during, or shortly after, cannabis use.
3. Two or more of the following signs, developing within 2 hours of cannabis use:
   - increased appetite
   - dry mouth
   - conjunctiva injection (bloodshot eyes)
   - tachycardia

Cocaine Intoxication

1. Recent use of amphetamine or a related substance.
2. Clinically significant problematic behavioral or psychological changes (e.g., euphoria or affective blunting, changes in sociability, hypervigilance, interpersonal sensitivity; anxiety, tension or anger, stereotypic behavior; impaired judgment; or impaired social or occupational functioning).
3. Two or more of the following signs, developing during, or shortly after use:
   - dilation of eye pupils
   - perspiration or chills
   - evidence of weight loss
   - elevated or lowered blood pressure
   - nausea or vomiting
   - tachycardia or bradycardia
   - muscular weakness, respiratory depression, chest pain or cardiac arrhythmias
   - confusion, seizures, dyskinesias, dystonias, or coma

Hallucinogen Intoxication

1. Recent use of a hallucinogen.
2. Clinically significant problematic behavioral or psychological changes (e.g., marked anxiety or depression, ideas of reference, fear of losing one's mind, paranoid ideation, impaired judgment, or impaired social

or occupational functioning) that developed during, or shortly after, hallucinogen use.
3. Perceptual changes occurring in a state of full wakefulness and alertness (e.g., subjective intensification of perceptions, depersonalization, de-realization, illusions, hallucinations, synesthesia) that develop during, or shortly after, hallucinogen use.
4. Two or more of the following signs developing during, or shortly after, hallucinogen use:
    - dilated pupils
    - sweating
    - blurring of vision
    - lack of coordination
    - tachycardia
    - palpitations
    - tremors

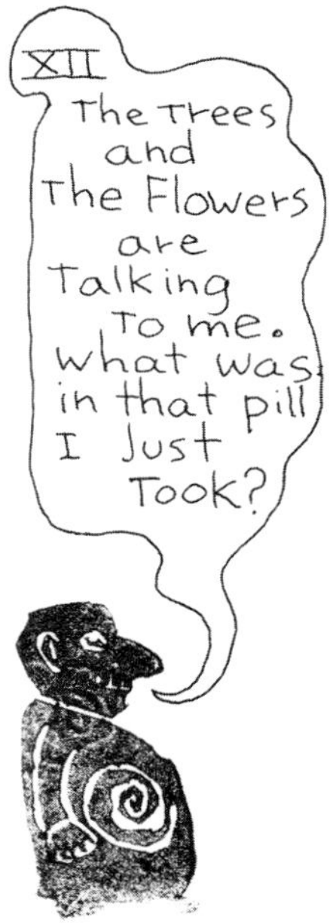

Inhalant Intoxication

1. Recent intentional use of a short-term, high-dose exposure to volatile inhalants (excluding anesthetic gases and short-acting vasodilators).
2. Clinically significant problematic behavioral or psychological changes (e.g., being belligerent or assaultive), apathy, impaired judgment, impaired social or occupational functioning after use of volatile inhalants, *or* perceptual changes occurring in a state of full wakefulness and alertness (e.g., subjective intensification of perceptions, depersonalization, de-realization, illusions, hallucinations, synesthesia) that develop during, or shortly after, hallucinogen use.
3. Two or more of the following signs, developing during, or shortly after, inhalant use or exposure:
    - dizziness
    - slurred speech
    - lethargy
    - psychomotor retardation
    - generalized muscle weakness
    - nystagmus
    - blurred vision or diplopia (seeing double)
    - lack of coordination
    - unsteady gait
    - depressed reflexes
    - tremor
    - euphoria
    - stupor or coma

Opiate Intoxication

1. Recent use of an opioid.
2. Clinically significant problematic behavioral or psychological changes (e.g., initial euphoria, followed by apathy, dysphoria, psychomotor agitation or retardation, impaired judgment, impaired social or occupational functioning) that developed during, or shortly after, opioid use.
3. Pupillary constriction (or pupillary dilation due to anoxia for severe overdose) and one or more of the following signs developing during, or shortly after, opioid use:
    - drowsiness or coma
    - slurred speech
    - impairment in attention or memory

Such writing is a sort of mental masturbation—he is always f–gg–g his imagination—I don't mean that he is indecent but viciously soliciting his own ideas into a state which is neither poetry nor anything else but a Bedlam vision produced by raw pork and opium.
—LORD BYRON

A letter commenting on Keats, 1820

Phencyclidine Intoxication

1. Recent use of phencyclidine or a related substance.
2. Clinically significant problematic behavioral changes (e.g., being belligerent, assaultive, impulsive, unpredictable; psychomotor agitation, impaired judgment, impaired social or occupational functioning) that developed during, or shortly after, phencyclidine use.
3. Within an hour (less when smoked or snorted, or used intravenously) two or more of the following signs:
   - vertical or horizontal nystagmus
   - ataxia
   - dysarthria (speech difficulty)
   - seizures
   - hypertension or tachycardia
   - muscle rigidity
   - hyperacusis (ultra acute hearing)

Sedatives, Hypnotic, or Anxiolytic Intoxication (same as alcohol)

Treatment Goals

One of the central questions in dealing with the treatment of other drug problems is the issue of treatment goals. The most troublesome question is, "In the absence of dependence, is establishing a moderate level of use an appropriate clinical goal?" Typically, trying to help someone achieve moderate use of other drugs is not generally considered an appropriate treatment goal. The potential exception is marijuana. In part this is related to a drug's illicit status, which raises the ante considerably. As a culture we do not condone recreational cocaine use or consider "a little" steroid use OK. Neither do we view "chasing the dragon" (smoking heroin) as no big deal. These judgments for the most part are not wholly arbitrary social conventions. In many instances the concern about any use reflects a drug's addiction potential. For example, with cocaine or nicotine, the risk is considerable. Consequently, establishing and maintaining a moderate, low-risk pattern of use is unlikely. In addition, with the continuing use of some substances, there is the issue of potential changes in the route of administration, which can introduce further problems. For example, to move from smoking or inhaling heroin to IV use introduces risk of infection associated with injection, as well as increasing the risk of dependence.

For some drugs, such as steroids, significant health consequences can accompany long-term use. For other drugs, potential health consequences can occur over the short haul. For example, with cocaine or inhalants, any use is considered to be risky. Accordingly, clinical efforts would be directed to helping someone stop using. Most would consider it clinically ill advised, if not downright unethical, to work with someone to achieve a moderate use.

Harm Reduction

As discussed in respect to alcohol use, although a clinician's goal may be abstinence, that may not be the client's goal. Programs and clinicians can be purists and essentially push away those clients who are not interested in adopting abstinence as the goal of treatment. However, there is an alternative possibility—harm reduction. This author first encountered the idea of harm reduction back in the late 1960s, before the term even existed. It occurred in a large city, where several free clinics had been established to serve the "flower people," counterculture, and large youth population. The foundation funding these clinics requested an evaluation of their effectiveness before providing further support. The results were far less than the organizers of the free clinics had hoped for. As one staff member plaintively noted, "We're just making drug users smarter." Those served by the clinics were not curtailing or reducing their drug use. However, there were fewer overdoses, fewer "bad trips," fewer sexually transmitted diseases, and fewer medical emergencies resulting from street drug use among the clinic's clients. The goal of the clinics may not have been harm reduction, but that was what they achieved. Creating "smarter"—meaning more informed—users yields benefits.

The goal of a harm reduction approach is to reduce the risks and harms that may be associated with use. In the United States this is such a foreign concept that it tends to rub people the wrong way or strike some as unethical. If that is your response, take a deep breath and try to set these biases aside. Dismissing harm reduction without careful thought can shortchange clients and limit your own effectiveness. The reality is that clients adopt their own goals for treatment; these cannot be imposed externally. The best that you can do is to help the client thoughtfully consider the options available. In fact, in the course of treatment, the client's goals may change.

There are a variety of harm reduction initiatives in respect to drug use. One is needle exchange programs. Another is ensuring that clients are informed about sterile injection practices and injection procedures. (Abscesses that accompany IV use are frequently due to improper injection practices.) For the young adolescent using inhalants, harm reduction might be pointing out the lesser danger of marijuana, in effect encouraging the adolescent to consider the use of a less dangerous drug. Harm reduction is at work when programs try to get the word out that there is bad dope being sold on the street. Public health departments regularly do this when there has been a rash of overdoses or medical problems due to contaminants. And, harm reduction is at work at raves, when drug testing is provided to determine if the drugs that people think they are taking are indeed those substances. Drug substitution therapies are harm reduction efforts when heroin is replaced by a safer and legal drug.

Overdose Emergency Kits

One significant addition to the array of harm reduction efforts is directed to providing emergency care for drug overdose to help avert death among opiate users. Frequently people shoot up in the company of others. If someone has overdosed, time is at a premium. Often, there simply isn't enough time to get a person to an emergency room. The only people who can respond are those who are present.

Emergency treatment consists of administering naloxone, an opiate antagonist that displaces the opiates at the opiate receptor site. Naloxone can be administered via a nasal mist inhaler or injected. Several cities have made an effort to educate injecting drug users and provided them a naloxone kit. Although there is limited formal evaluation of these efforts, the general response has been quite positive among injecting drug users and within the public health community. Another group for whom there is discussion of providing naloxone for emergencies is recently released prisoners. In the weeks immediately after leaving prison, individuals are at increased risk of overdose. Having not used while confined, their tolerance has declined, so the dose that previously was non-problematic may be lethal.

PHARMACOLOGICAL TREATMENT

Given the increasing knowledge of the changes in the brain that accompany long-term drug use, there is now the possibility for what was previously only a dream—that is, the potential to develop drugs with specific properties that may be helpful in treatment. This is different from the use of medications during withdrawal. The discussion in this chapter does not do justice to the topic but only highlights the main issues. (Please see the References and Further Readings section at the conclusion of this chapter.) In brief, there are now three major approaches to drug therapies: drug replacement, anti-craving drugs, and blocking agents.

Drug Replacement

In some instances drug replacement means substitution of a different drug; in other instances, it involves actually prescribing the drug of abuse. The goals of drug replacement are twofold. One is harm reduction. The other is the promotion of an environment in which rehabilitation efforts can gain a foothold, in which there is time to engage people in treatment, thereby creating the possibility for long-term, including abstinence-oriented, treatment. Nicotine replacement is a prime example of drug replacement. Whether the nicotine is delivered by patch, chewing gum, an inhaler, or a nasal spray, the delivery route is much safer than smoking. Another example is the use of methadone.

Methadone and buprenorphine are two pharmacological substitutes for heroin. Many of the risks of heroin are related to the route of administration. With a street drug, neither dealers nor manufacturers abide by FDA standards; thus, there is an ever-present risk of contaminants or unintentional overdose. Also, compared with these substitutes, heroin has a shorter length of action, which requires more frequent administration. On several counts, methadone is a far safer alternative to heroin. Furthermore, methadone, while pharmacologically similar to heroin, does not provide the rush that accompanies heroin use, though it does stave off withdrawal.

Buprenorphine is a newer drug available as a substitute for heroin. The major advantage of buprenorphine over methadone is that it is available for office-based use: the patient can receive a prescription to be filled in a neighborhood pharmacy and not have to travel somewhere for a daily dose of medication. Another potential advantage of buprenorphine over methadone is that it can be taken three times a week (although most clients prefer daily dosing). For either of these medications, an adequate dose must be given; if patients are under-medicated, they are far more likely to leave treatment.

Anti-craving Drugs

Craving seems to be reported as a more prominent feature of some drugs of dependence than others. Most notable are nicotine, cocaine, heroin, and alcohol. One does not typically associate a similar kind of craving with inhalants, the hallucinogens, or even marijuana. A priority in exploring new medications is to find those that will reduce craving. The first major successes with anti-craving agents were in the treatment of alcohol dependence. More recently, agents (Wellbutrin and Chantix) have been identified to deal with craving of nicotine during quit attempts. Chantix binds to the nicotine receptor sites and is thought to block the receptors associated with nicotine's rewarding effects. Research also suggests that some patients having other symptoms, particularly anxiety or depression, may respond to psychotropic medications that also can reduce craving.

Blocking Agents

Sometimes the best approach to altering substance dependence is to create chemical "walls" to keep people from using. Such medications have the effect of either blocking the substance's effects or causing adverse reactions if the substance is used. Naltrexone is a competitive opiate antagonist. That means, if present, it binds with the opiate receptors but has no activity. Therefore, if opiates are taken, they would have no effect because the receptors where they bind are already "taken." For the person who has withdrawn from all opiates, the use of naltrexone can serve as an insurance policy of sorts. If opiates are taken, there would not be the rush and high that are the motive for use.

Use of Naltrexone

Naltrexone's direct opioid-blocking effect is important in several ways. The most significant is that people can't get high; that means taking opioids is pointless. Also, a dose of naltrexone lasts about 20 hours. This dosage schedule serves as a "daily reminder" not to use. It also provides a "safety net" if people find themselves around others who are using and succumb, whether as a result of craving or others' pressure to use. Such a "safety net" can help prevent a "lapse" from mushrooming into a full-blown relapse. Naltrexone is available in two forms. One is an oral preparation, taken once a day. The other is injected (by a health care provider). It is marketed under the name Vivitrol and lasts for a month. This injectable form has the obvious advantage of skirting the compliance issues that can arise with oral naltrexone.

Many clients are hesitant to use the monthly injectable form due to concerns of pain control in case of an accident. In such emergency situations, anesthesiologists can overcome the opioid-blocking effects of both naltrexone and Vivitrol by using high-potency intravenous opioids. Clients should be assured of this prior to starting either of these medications. Many times clients who take Vivitrol carry ID bracelets or wallet cards indicating they are taking this medicine in order to alert emergency medical personnel who might treat them.

Naltrexone is usually used in the first 90 to 180 days of treatment. Longer periods are possible, as long as liver function tests are routinely performed, because naltrexone can be toxic to the liver in some people if used over long periods.

Naltrexone versus Naloxone

The names of these two drugs are very similar and both are blocking agents. So it's hard to keep straight how they differ. Naloxone (Narcan), the drug distributed in emergency overdose kits, is used almost exclusively in emergency rooms to reverse the effects of overdose. It is very potent and is administered intravenously, as it isn't absorbed very well if taken orally. Naloxone has an extremely rapid onset; that is what makes it suited to reversing overdose. This also means it has to be administered carefully, otherwise the recipient can be thrown into acute opioid withdrawal. This can lead to people jumping out of bed rapidly or flailing about very quickly after receiving naloxone. In addition, if someone has medical problems, the naloxone can cause seizures and heart attacks.

Sometimes disulfiram is referred to as a blocking agent. Certainly it serves as a disincentive to drink. Someone who uses alcohol while on disulfiram will become sick. Thus it is a blocking agent in terms of dissuading someone from having a drink. But it isn't a blocking agent in the pharmacological sense. The action of disulfiram is due to its slowing the breakdown of a by-product formed when alcohol is metabolized (acetaldehyde); it is this buildup of acetaldehyde that prompts the distress. (Interestingly, very recent research suggests it may also act as an anti-craving agent, which too may play a role in its effectiveness. This finding suggests its potential effectiveness in the treatment of other drugs of abuse, particularly cocaine.)

Looking Ahead: Vaccines

For over a decade there has been discussion within the scientific community about the potential for developing vaccines that would create a barrier for drugs of abuse to act on the brain. By prompting an immune response, a vaccine causes the body to create antibodies to the drug in question that "gobble up" the drug before it can reach the brain and cause a reinforcing high. Vaccines could be used by those in treatment, to promote recovery, and render moot the issue of compliance with other drug therapies. In addition, a vaccine could be a primary prevention effort.

Beyond the scientific hurdles, as would be expected, the notion of creating what has been referred to as a "vice" vaccine has sparked considerable discussion. What are the ethical issues around parents electing to have their children vaccinated? How about the prospect of incorporating anti-addiction vaccines into state-mandated immunization statutes? Or what if immunization were required as a condition of prison release for those incarcerated for crimes related to their drug use? Are vaccines virtually on the doorstep? If you are a doubter, you should know that the trademark *NicVAX* has already been registered for a nicotine vaccine. However, in the clinical trials to assess its performance, the result was disappointing, the quit rate was 11%. Work too is underway on a cocaine vaccine, with hopes to begin human clinical trials in the near future.

PREGNANCY AND THE USE OF DRUGS OTHER THAN ALCOHOL

Substance use during pregnancy is a major concern. Alcohol and some other drugs are teratogens, meaning that they can disrupt fetal development. Alcohol in combination with other drug use is the leading cause of preventable birth defects in the United States.

Epidemiology

Data from the most recent National Survey (2011) found that 5% of pregnant women used an illicit drug in the prior month and 1% used a prescription drug. For legal drugs, rates of smoking were lower among pregnant women (18%) than women who were not pregnant (25%). The rates of smoking during pregnancy were highest among Native American and white women. The rates of alcohol use are much lower among pregnant women (9.4%) than among non-pregnant women (55.1%). Of concern is the fact that among the 10% of the pregnant women who used alcohol in the past month, a third reported binge or heavy drinking, but that was 40% lower than two years previously.

The rate for non-medical use of prescription drugs among pregnant women was 1%. There are differences between the rates of illicit drug use for different racial/ethnic groups. The 2011 estimate of the rate of illicit drug use during pregnancy is 7.6% for African Americans, 5.3% among Hispanics women, and 4.5% among whites. In terms of absolute numbers, the largest group of pregnant women using other drugs is white women. However, these differences are not a product of race/ethnicity per se or cultural differences. The underlying factors are socioeconomic. Poverty is associated with drug use. When one takes into account age, level of education, and household income, differences in terms of race and ethnicity disappear. Another significant factor is age. The highest rate of illicit drug use is among the youngest pregnant women, at 20.9% for adolescents 15 to 17 years old. The rate declines to 8.2% for pregnant women ages 18 to 25 years and to 2.2% for pregnant women over age 25. Illicit drug use declines throughout pregnancy: the rate during the first trimester is 9.5%, during the second trimester, 4.4%, and in the third trimester, 1.8%.

The hardest thing about being a drug dependent mother is that crack houses never have changing tables.

Opiate-Exposed Infants

The medical problems encountered by pregnant opiate-dependent woman are enormous. Many of the most common problems—abscesses, ulcers, bacterial infections, and hepatitis—are due to the frequent use of dirty needles. Moreover, many opiate-dependent women are quite sexually active and have a history of sexually transmitted diseases, including gonorrhea, syphilis, herpes, and AIDS. Their living conditions are often poor, and many infections are transmitted within these settings. Because they are poorly nourished, vitamin deficiencies, such as for vitamin C (associated with nicotine and smoking) and the B vitamins (associated with cocaine use), are common. In addition, iron deficiency anemia and folic acid deficiency anemia occur during pregnancy.

The most common obstetrical complication in opiate-dependent women who have had no prenatal care is preterm birth. These infants have the expected complications seen in infants born prematurely. If the infants are born at full term, they may have pneumonia or meconium aspiration syndrome (respiratory problems from sucking feces when in the uterus or with the first breath).

The extremely high-risk environment from which pregnant drug-dependent women come predisposes them to a host of neonatal problems. In heroin-dependent women, a significant part of the medical complications seen in their babies is due to low birth weight and prematurity. The incidence of low birth weight may approach 50%. A number of conditions are known to be associated with low birth weight, regardless of its cause. Medical complications generally reflect (1) the amount of prenatal care that the mother has received; (2) whether she has suffered any particular obstetrical or medical complications, including toxemia of pregnancy, hypertension, or infection; and, most important, (3) multiple drug use, which may produce an unstable intrauterine milieu complicated by withdrawal and overdose. This last situation is extremely hazardous because it predisposes the neonate to meconium staining and subsequent aspiration pneumonia, which may cause significant problems and increase risk of death.

In both premature and term infants, withdrawal from opiates can occur (neonatal abstinence syndrome). Appropriate assessment and rapid treatment are essential to treat withdrawal in these infants so that they can recover without incident. Not all infants born to drug-dependent mothers experience withdrawal. Estimates of the percentage who have some withdrawal symptoms range from 60% to 90%. The neonatal opioid abstinence syndrome is characterized by signs and symptoms of central nervous system hyperirritability, gastrointestinal problems, respiratory distress, and vague autonomic symptoms, including yawning, sneezing, mottling, and fever. The infants initially develop tremors ("the shakes"), which are mild at first but progress in severity. A high-pitched cry, increased muscle tone, irritability, increased deep tendon reflexes, and an exaggerated Moro reflex—a reflex in newborns, a "startle response"—are all characteristic of opiate withdrawal among newborns.

In infants experiencing withdrawal, the rooting reflex—the impulse to snuggle in and nurse—is increased, and sucking either fists or thumbs is common, yet feedings are difficult and the babies regurgitate frequently. These feeding difficulties occur because of an uncoordinated and ineffectual sucking reflex. Also, the infants may develop loose stools; therefore, they are susceptible to dehydration and electrolyte imbalance. The time of onset of symptoms is variable. Following delivery, the newborn's serum and tissue levels of the drug(s) used by the mother begin to fall. The newborn infant continues to metabolize and excrete the drug. Withdrawal occurs when the level of opiates in the tissues reaches a critically low level. Because of the variation in time of onset and in degree of severity, a spectrum of abstinence patterns may be observed. Withdrawal may be mild and wax and wane; it may be delayed in onset; or there can be a stepwise pattern, with gradual, continuing increases in severity.

More severe withdrawal seems to occur in babies whose mothers have taken large amounts of drugs over a long period. Generally, the closer to delivery when a mother takes a narcotic, the greater the delay in the onset of withdrawal and the more severe the eventual symptoms in the baby. Maternal smoking in combination with opiate use further increases the severity and duration of withdrawal among infants. (Heavy

The Challenge: Post Pregnancy

Combined 2002 to 2007 data show that past month alcohol use among women aged 18 to 44 was highest for those who were not pregnant and did not have children living in the household (63.0 percent) but comparatively low for women in the first trimester of pregnancy (19.0 percent), and even lower for those in the second (7.8 percent) or third trimester (6.2 percent); similar patterns were seen with marijuana, cigarette, and binge alcohol use.

The challenge is to avoid the resumption of harmful use—whether smoking, binge drinking, or illicit drug use.

Source: Office of Applied Studies, SAMHSA. *The NSDUH Report* (May 21, 2009)

Maintaining Smoking Cessation Postpartum

Factors which reduce the likelihood of resuming smoking include:

- *encouragement and involvement of physician*
- *family meeting focused on smoking prior to leaving the hospital after delivery*
- *the presence of an active support system, with guides on how to use these supports*
- *restrictions on smoking in the home*
- *partner smoking cessation*
- *follow-up contact with a counselor or quit-line*

maternal smoking independently is associated with nicotine withdrawal syndrome.) The maturity of the infant's own systems determines whether the infant is able to metabolize and excrete the drug after delivery. Due to the variable severity of the withdrawal, the duration of symptoms may be anywhere from six days to eight weeks. Drug therapies may be used to accomplish neonatal detoxification. Although the babies may be discharged from the hospital after drug therapy is stopped, their symptoms or irritability may persist for more than three to four months.

Buprenorphine Versus Methadone Use in Pregnancy

Medical withdrawal of pregnant opiate-dependent women from methadone or buprenorphine is neither necessary nor recommended during pregnancy. For a long time methadone was the mainstay of treatment for opioid-dependent women. Daily doses typically ranged from 10 to 90 milligrams, with an average of 50 milligrams. While it was clear that methadone was safe for pregnant women, neonatal abstinence syndrome (withdrawal in the newborn) was a major problem. With buprenorphine neonatal withdrawal is far less common and less severe if it does occur. Comprehensive prenatal care is important, which can also attend to the appropriate dosage of either buphrenorphine or methadone. In the third trimester, many women need an increase in their medication dose due to various physiological changes, including weight gain at this time. If buprenorphine is used it can *only* be Subutex (buprenorphine), which does not contain naloxone, as Suboxone does. Naloxone is harmful to the fetus.

I know I shouldn't use cocaine, but I read that it wasn't so harmful during the second trimester.

If a pregnant woman has any specific medical complications, such as hyperthyroidism or diabetes, appropriate medical consultation is essential. Due to the impoverished conditions in which many of the women live, medical, social, and legal problems are common, and economic survival is tenuous.

Cocaine-Exposed Infants

Cocaine is highly soluble in both water and fat tissue; therefore, it can easily cross the placenta from mother to fetus. The fetus has a limited ability to metabolize cocaine, which may lead to its accumulation in the fetus. A binge pattern of use common with cocaine also contributes to even higher levels of cocaine in the fetus. Transfer of cocaine from mother to infant appears to be greater in the first and third trimesters of pregnancy. One of cocaine's most potent effects is the constriction of blood vessels. Constricted blood vessels in the uterus, placenta, and umbilical cord can retard the transfer of cocaine from mother to fetus. However, this constriction of blood vessels is far from being a protective device for the unborn baby. This constriction also means that there is less passage of everything else, including essential nutrients, and less ability to exchange waste products from the fetus to the mother. It is thought that this decreased blood flow may be as important as the cocaine itself in causing whatever abnormalities occur in fetal development.

Several years ago there was considerable media coverage of the detrimental effects of prenatal exposure to cocaine. However, the effects are not as clear-cut as such accounts implied. In any consideration of the effects of cocaine on pregnancy, keep in mind that women who use cocaine throughout pregnancy also have many other risk factors. These include cigarette smoking, alcohol consumption, less education, poor prenatal medical care, use of other drugs of abuse, younger age, being a single parent, and sexually transmitted diseases. In addition, problems can arise from toxic products that may be mixed with the cocaine.

The following characteristics have consistently been reported as accompanying maternal cocaine use: a greater likelihood of maternal health problems that can have an impact on the neonate (such as infections), impaired fetal growth, smaller infant head circumference, premature birth, and an increased risk of stillbirths. Cocaine use also appears to be involved with the onset of premature labor. Higher rates of early pregnancy losses and third-trimester placental abortions appear to be major complications of maternal cocaine use. However, the highly publicized behavioral problems that were supposedly characteristic of "crack babies" do not seem to be at all universal among children who have been exposed to cocaine prenatally.

Animal studies have helped provide some answers regarding cocaine's effects by using research designs that control for many of the other factors that complicate studies with humans. These studies provide evidence of growth retardation, separation of the placenta, cerebral infarctions (strokes), increased general pre- and postnatal mortality, and limb/digit reductions and eye anomalies. But the risk of such abnormalities is low in animal models and seems to require high doses. Analysis of all available studies conducted with this population suggests that cocaine is not a major source of human birth defects and that most children are likely to be normal in terms of body structure and later neurological development. The problems that are seen may be the result of other factors that are present in the lives of the addicted women, not necessarily attributable to the cocaine per se—again, these factors are poverty, inadequate pre- and postnatal care, inadequate nutrition, other drug use, and other medical problems of the mother.

Policy and Legal Issues

Being a drug-dependent mother presents many conflicts. One of the basic premises of child rearing and intervention models is that infant behavior is part of a communication system within the caregiving environment.

This is a mutually responsive system in which feedback from one partner to the other is used to regulate this system. In early work with drug-exposed infants, this complexity was not appreciated. As a consequence, it was believed that drug exposure per se led to poor developmental outcomes. If the mother was considered at all, it was thought that she could only lower the developmental outcome of the child. The Maternal Lifestyles Study, a federally funded, multicenter, prospective, longitudinal study, is now attempting to address these issues by studying the effects of prenatal drug exposure on the interplay between the neurobehavioral and regulatory capacities of the child and parenting and environmental factors. There is the belief as well that protective factors are often at work that mitigate some of the risks imposed by maternal drug use; and interventions that provide needed supports can make a difference.

Children Victims of Toxic Doses

With the increasing prescription of methadone and buprenorphin, whether for pain management or opiate addiction, there has been a significant rise in pediatric poisonings.
—E. W. Boyer

American Journal on Addictions, 2010

With respect to social policy, a variety of approaches have been suggested to protect children born to drug-dependent mothers. These include instituting systematic and massive public education and support by community leaders to stress that no drugs be used during pregnancy; giving hospitals the legal power and financial resources to care for babies until they are medically ready for discharge and the home environment is ready to care for them; placing children into foster care if drug-dependent parents cannot care for them; and facilitating the adoption process when parents anticipate little chance for improvement. Special programs for children affected by prenatal drug exposure remain limited. Such programs are needed to address and prevent any developmental disabilities; to provide supportive services to parents or other caregivers, such as foster parents or guardians, who may be caring for the child because of the mother's continued drug use; and to help parents or other caregivers cope with behavioral problems that can arise.

Who uses 80% of the world's opiates?

Americans, constituting only 4.6% of the world's population, have been consuming 80% of the global opioid supply, and 99% of the global hydrocodone supply, as well as two-thirds of the world's illegal drugs. Retail sales of commonly used opioid medications (including methadone, oxycodone, fentanyl base, hydromorphone, hydrocodone, morphine, meperidine, and codeine) have increased from a total of 50.7 million grams in 1997 to 126.5 million grams in 2007. [That's 2788,85 pounds!] This is an overall increase of 149% with increases ranging from 222% for morphine, 280% for hydrocodone, 319% for hydromorphone, 525% for fentanyl base, 866% for oxycodone, to 1,293% for methadone. Average sales of opioids per person have increased from 74 milligrams in 1997 to 369 milligrams in 2007, a 402% increase.

Source: Manchikanti L, et al. Therapeutic use, abuse, and nonmedical use of opioids: A ten-year perspective (review). *Pain Physician* 13(5):401–435, 2010. (295 refs.)

There are special considerations for children who remain in the home. Drug abuse treatment is necessary for drug-dependent mothers. Among the most alarming statistics in terms of outcome for children born to mothers addicted to cocaine are those associated with child abuse and neglect. Child abandonment is common with infants who require extended care at birth or are later hospitalized. Intoxication from crack is associated with outbursts of violence, which increases the risk for battering. In many urban areas where crack use is more prevalent, treatment programs have long waiting lists. Facilities that will accept pregnant women or women with infants are few. Unfortunately, even if treatment is provided, outcome studies suggest that, compared with alcohol and opiate dependence, individuals dependent on cocaine, especially in the form of crack, have much more difficulty maintaining abstinence. Thus, some oversight of children in the home is imperative. However, in urban areas in which child welfare systems are already overburdened, the probability of oversight to identify problems and intervene on the child's behalf is low.

INTERNATIONAL COMPARISONS

The *2013 World Drug Report,* published by the United Nations, provides information on rates of drug use and abuse worldwide, as well as information on the illicit drug trade. This particular report focused too on a relatively new topic, "New Psychoactive Substances." These are the drugs described as "designer drugs" or "legal highs" or "synthetic" versions of traditional drugs, formulated to avoid being classified as a controlled substance. They are marketed aggressively over the internet, with the names of harmless-sounding, everyday products—herbal incense, bath salts, or room fresheners. The sheer numbers of these drugs, and the speed with which they have emerged over the past five years, is unprecedented. Member countries report the appearance of these new formulations to the UN. By mid-2012, this number rose to 251, exceeding the number of substances under international control. Also possibly unexpectedly, at least in Europe, only 7% of the 15–24 year olds—the group with the highest rate of use—purchase them online. Why is the proportion so low? Possibly it's because they aren't that hard to get where someone lives. So why bother? Maybe it's because drug dealers are quite adaptable. Maybe it's because there are some things you don't want delivered to your home.

The World Report *provides information by geographical region. North America includes the United States, Canada, and Mexico. Information on North America inevitably sheds light on the United States, as it has the largest population and the highest rates of drug use. North America accounts for over half of global sales for three of the four drug classes: cocaine 62%; cannabis 55%; and amphetamine-type drugs–amphetamine 60% and ecstasy 52%. It only purchases 14% of opiates. Globally, the estimated per capita annual expenditure on drugs is $51 for those ages 15 to 65. The North American's per capita illicit drug purchase is over six times greater, $331.*

Looking Ahead

In the *2013 Report* several things were highlighted. One was the rising prominence of Africa in global substance use. For one, the drug trade is always sensitive to using the best "route" to transport drugs to minimize the risk of seizures. The trade route for cocaine was adjusted, moving through western Africa, on the way from South America to Europe. One of the effects has been to make cocaine more available in western Africa. Another conundrum is the ever growing number of "new psychoactive substances" that fall outside of the existing treaties. What reasonable steps might be taken to add these to the list of controlled substances? Another subject hinted at was how to move proactively to avoid marked increases in substance use where the rates are now relatively low. Consider China. It has one of the lowest rates of marijuana use. However, given the sheer size of China's population, this nonetheless represents over a third of all marijuana users across the globe. Even the smallest increase in the proportion using pot will have a large impact. A half percent rise in use among those between the ages of 15–65 years is five million.

The United Nation's Office on Drugs and Crime (UNODC) speaks of prevention and public health. However, the name of the Office says a lot. The dominant perspective is control, and legal constraints are used to promote prohibition. So how does harm reduction fit in? It ought to be of interest that the Netherlands—with a drug policy often viewed to be as lenient as the United States' policy is strict—ranks 38th in the rate of problems associated with marijuana use. So presumably something else is going on in Dutch society which reduces problems. Finally, there is an issue not discussed—the sheer size of the "illicit drug industry." The question boils down to how, as societies, do we wish to allocate out resources. Are there other social issues that are deemed more worthy of government expenditures than those spent on drug prohibition? A study by a Harvard economist spelled out some of the financial implications associated with legalizing drugs. The biggest item on the ledger would be savings around law enforcement estimated as $41.3 billion. The other would be new tax revenues of $46.7 billion, assuming drugs would be taxed in comparable fashion as tobacco and alcohol are now. So the new annual gain to society would be approaching a trillion dollars. The other issue requiring consideration is what the impact would be on the health and well-being of the citizenry if the legal restraints on drug use were no longer present.

REFERENCES AND FURTHER READINGS

Basic References

Arnold G. *The International Drugs Trade*. New York: Routledge, 2005.

Donovan DM, Marlatt GA, eds. *Assessment of Addictive Behaviors,* 2nd ed. New York: Guilford Press, 2007.

Galanter M, Kleber HB, eds. *Textbook of Substance Abuse Treatment*. Washington DC: American Psychiatric Association Press, 2008.

Johnston LD, O'Malley PM, Bachman JG, Schulenberg JE. *Monitoring the Future: National Survey Results on Drug Use, 1975–2011*. Volumes I and II. Bethesda, MD: National Institute on Drug Abuse, 2012.

Maldonado JR. An approach to the patient with substance use and abuse. *Medical Clinics of North America* 94:1169–1205, 2010. (126 refs.)
Note: A medical review of major substance use disorders, including syndromes of acute intoxication and withdrawal, with a review of medical management for each, and physiological underpinnings.

Office of National Drug Control Policy. *The Economic Costs of Drug Abuse in the United States, 1992–2002*. Washington, DC: Executive Office of the President, 2004. (62 refs.) (Publication No. 207303)

Ries RK, Miller SC, Fiellin DA, Saitz R. *Principles of Addiction Medicine*, 4th ed. Chevy Chase, MD: Lippincott, Williams & Wilkins, 2009.

Roffman RA, Stephens RS, eds. *Cannabis Dependence: Its Nature, Consequences and Treatment.* London: Cambridge University Press, 2010.

Substance Abuse and Mental Health Administration. *Results from the 2008 National Survey on Drug Use & Health. National Findings*. NSDUH Series H-44. Rockville, MD: Substance Abuse and Mental Health Administration, 2009. (DHHS Publication No. SMA 12-4713)

United Nations Office on Drugs and Crime. *World Drug Report 2013*. Vienna: UNODC, May, 2013.

Other Resources and Further Readings

Al-Hebshi NN, Skaug N. Khat (Catha edulis): An updated review (review). *Addiction Biology* 10(4):299–307, 2005. (112 refs.)

Anglin D, Spears KL, Hutson HR. Flunitrazepam and its involvement in date or acquaintance rape. *Academic Emergency Medicine* 4(4):323–326, 1997. (21 refs.)

Baca CT, Yahne CE. Smoking cessation during substance abuse treatment: What you need to know (review). *Journal of Substance Abuse Treatment* 36(2)205–219, 2009. (195 refs.)

Barth KS, Malcolm RJ. Disulfiram: An old therapeutic with new applications. *CNS & Neurological Disorders. Drug Targets* 9(1):5–12, 2010. (64 refs.)

Blank M, Deshpande L, Balster RL. Availability and characteristics of betal products in the US. *Journal of Psychoactive Drugs* 40(3):309–313, 2008. (16 refs.)

Britt GC, McCance-Katz EF. A brief overview of the clinical pharmacology of "club drugs." *Substance Use & Misuse* 40(9–10):1189–1201, 2005. (56 refs.)

Brouette T, Anton R. Clinical review of inhalants. *American Journal on Addictions* 10(1):79+, 2001. (66 refs.)

Carter LP, Pardi D, Gorsline J, Griffiths RR. Illicit gammahydroxybutyrate (GHB) and pharmaceutical sodium oxybate (Xyrem): Differences in characteristics and misuse (review). *Drug and Alcohol Dependence* 104(1/2):1–10, 2009. (101 refs.)

Castelli MP. Multi-faceted aspects of gamma-hydroxybutyric acid: A neurotransmitter, therapeutic agent and drug of abuse (review). *Mini Reviews in Medicinal Chemistry* 8(12):1188–1202, 2008. (141 refs.)

Caulkins JP, Pacula RL. Marijuana markets: Inferences from reports by the household population. *Journal of Drug Issues* 36(1):173–200, 2006. (37 refs.)

Centers for Disease Control and Prevention, Arant T, Henry C, Clifford W, Horton DK, Rossiter S. MMWR. Anhydrous ammonia thefts and releases associated with illicit methamphetamine production—16 states, January 2000–June 2004. *Morbidity and Mortality Weekly Report* 54(14):359–361, 2005. (9 refs.)

Cerny EH, Cerny T. Vaccines against nicotine (review). *Human Vaccines* 5(4):200–205, 2009. (38 refs.)

Copeland J, Swift W. Cannabis use disorder: Epidemiology and management. *International Review of Psychiatry* 21(2):96–103, 2009. (71 refs.)

Dasgupta N, Kramer ED, Zalman MA, Carino S, Smith MY, Haddox JD, et al. Association between non-medical and prescriptive usage of opioids. *Drug and Alcohol Dependence* 82(2):135–142, 2006. (19 refs.)

Dietze P, Miller S, Clemens S, Matthews S, Gilmour S, Collins L. *The Course and Consequences of the Heroin Shortage in Victoria. NDARC Technical Report No. 206*. Sydney, Australia: National Drug and Alcohol Research Centre, 2004. (56 refs.)

Dorsey TL, Middleton P. *Drugs and Crime Facts*. Washington DC: U.S. Department of Justice, 2010. (NCJ 165148) Available: www.ojp.usdoj.gov/bjs/pub/pdf/dcf.pdf.

Editor. *Substance Use and Misuse*. 43(6):entire issue, 2008. Special issue devoted to khat.

ElSohly MA, National Center for Natural Products Research, School of Pharmacy, University of Mississippi. *Quarterly Report, Potency Monitoring Project*, Report #87, Aug. 9, 2004–Nov. 8, 2004.

Fergusson DM, Boden JM, Horwood LJ. Cannabis use and other illicit drug use: Testing the cannabis gateway hypothesis. *Addiction* 101(4):556–569, 2006. (67 refs.)

Ferri M, Davoli M, Perucci CA. Heroin maintenance treatment for chronic heroin-dependent individuals: A Cochrane systematic review of effectiveness (review). *Journal of Substance Abuse Treatment* 30(1):63–72, 2006. (42 refs.)

Fiellin DA, Pantalon MV, Chawarski MC, Moore BA, Sullivan LE, O'Connor PG, et al. Counseling plus buprenorphinenaloxone maintenance therapy for opioid dependence. *New England Journal of Medicine* 355(4):365–374, 2006. (30 refs.)

Fuller BE, Guydish J, Tsoh J, Reld MS, Resnick M, Zammarelli L, et al. Attitudes toward the integration of smoking cessation treatment into drug abuse clinics. *Journal of Substance Abuse Treatment* 32(1):53–60, 2007. (44 refs.)

Gable RS. Comparison of acute lethal toxicity of commonly abused psychoactive substances (review). *Addiction* 99(6):686–696, 2004. (103 refs.)

Garland E, Howard MO, Vaughn MG, Perron BE. Volatile substance misuse in the United States. *Substance Use & Misuse* 46(Supplement 1):8–20, 2011.

Gartner CE, Barendregt JJ, Wallace A, Hall WD. Would vaccination against nicotine be a cost-effective way to prevent smoking uptake in adolescents? *Addiction* 107(4):801–809, 2012. (44 refs.)

Gavin DR, Ross HE, Skinner HA. Diagnostic validity of the Drug Abuse Screening Test in the assessment of DSM-III drug disorders. *British Journal of Addiction* 84(3):301–307, 1989. (23 refs.)

Gonzales R, Mooney L, Rawson RA. The methamphetamine problem in the United States (review). *Annual Review of Public Health* 31:385–398, 2010. (109 refs.)

Griffiths RR, Mumford GK. Caffeine: A drug of abuse? *Psychopharmacology. The Fourth Generation of Progress*. American College of Neuropsychopharmacology, 2003. Available: www. acnp.org/g4/GN401000165/Default.htm.

Hall W. The adverse health effects of cannabis use: What are they, and what are their implications for policy? (review). *International Journal of Drug Policy* 20(6, special issue):458–466, 2009. (165 refs.)

Heatherton TF, Kozlowski LT, Frecker RC, Fagerstrom KO. The Fagerstrom Test for Nicotine Dependence: A revision of the Fagerstrom Tolerance Questionnaire. *British Journal of Addictions* 86:1119–1127, 1991.

Howard MO, Bowen SE, Garland EL, Perron BE, Vaughn MG. Inhalant use and inhalant use disorders in the United States. *Addiction Science & Clinical Practice* 6(1):unpaginated, 2011.

Hser Y, Hoffman V, Grella CE, Anglin MD. A 33-year follow-up of narcotics addicts. *Archives of General Psychiatry* 58(5):503–508, 2001. (17 refs.)

Johnston LD, O'Malley PM, Bachman JG, Schulenberg, JE. *Monitoring the Future National Survey Results on Drug Use, 1975–2012*: Volume I and Volume II. Ann Arbor: Institute for Social Research, The University of Michigan, 2013.

Juliano LM, Griffiths RR. A critical review of caffeine withdrawal: Empirical validation of symptoms and signs, incidence, severity, and associated features (review). *Psychopharmacology* 176(1):1–29, 2004. (139 refs.)

Jupp B, Lawrence AJ. New horizons for therapeutics in drug and alcohol abuse (review). *Pharmacology & Therapeutics* 125(1):138–168, 2010. (644 refs.)

King R, Mauer M. The war on marijuana: The transformation of the war on drugs in the 1990s. *Harm Reduction Journal* 3 (article 6): 2006. (71 refs.)

Kinsey BM, Kosten TR, Orson FM. Anti-cocaine vaccine development (review). *Expert Review of Vaccines* 9(9):1109–1114, 2010. (58 refs.)

Logan DE, Marlatt GA. Harm reduction therapy: A practice friendly review of research (review). *Journal of Clinical Psychology* 66(2):201–214, 2010. (92 refs.)

Lundqvist T. Cognitive consequences of cannabis use: Comparison with abuse of stimulants and heroin with regard to attention, memory and executive functions. *Pharmacology, Biochemistry and Behavior* 81(2):319–330, 2005. (91 refs.)

Maldonado JR. An approach to the patient with substance use and abuse. *Medical Clinics of North America* 94:1169–1205, 2010. (126 refs.) Note: a medical review of major substance use disorders, including syndromes of acute intoxication and withdrawal, with a review of medical management for each, and physiological underpinnings.

Maxwell JC. Party drugs: Properties, prevalence, patterns, and problems (review). *Substance Use & Misuse* 40(9–10):1203–1240, 2005. (172 refs.)

McCance-Katz EF, Sullivan LE, Nallani S. Drug interactions of clinical importance among the opioids, methadone and buprenorphine, and other frequently prescribed medications: A review. *American Journal on Addictions* 19(1):4–16, 2010. (92 refs.)

McDonough M, Kennedy N, Glasper A, Bearn J. Clinical features and management of gamma-hydroxybutyrate (GHB) withdrawal: A review. *Drug and Alcohol Dependence* 75(1):3–9, 2004. (25 refs.)

McLaren JA, Silins E, Hutchinson D, Mattick RP, Hall W. Assessing evidence for a causal link between cannabis and psychosis: A review of cohort studies (review). *International Journal of Drug Policy* 21(1):10–19, 2010. (75 refs.)

Miron JA. *The Budgetary Implications of Marijuana Prohibition*, June 2005. Washington DC: Marijuana Policy Project, 2005. Available: www.prohibitioncosts.org/mironreport.html.

Mullins ME. Laboratory confirmation of flunitrazepam in alleged cases of date rape. *Academic Emergency Medicine* 6(9):966–968, 1999. (10 refs.)

Oei J, Lui K. Management of the newborn infant affected by maternal opiates and other drugs of dependency (review). *Journal of Paediatrics and Child Health* 43(1/2):9–18, 2007. (126 refs.)

Office of Applied Studies, Substance Abuse and Mental Health Administration. *The NSDUH Report: Trends in Nonmedical Use of Prescription Pain Relievers: 2002 to 2007* (February 5, 2009). Rockville MD: Substance Abuse and Mental Health Administration, 2009. (5 refs.)

Orman JS, Keating GM. Buprenorphine/naloxone: A review of its use in the treatment of opioid dependence (review). *Drugs* 69(5):577–607, 2009. (107 refs.)

Orson FM, Kinsey BM, Singh RAK, Wu Y, Kosten TR. Vaccines for cocaine abuse (review). *Human Vaccines* 5(4):194–199, 2009. (56 refs.)

Perron BE, Howard MO. Adolescent inhalant use, abuse and dependence. *Addiction* 104(7):1185–1192, 2009. (21 refs.)

Ray R, Schnoll RA, Lerman C. Nicotine dependence: Biology, behavior, and treatment (review). *Annual Review of Medicine* 60:247–260, 2009. (102 refs.)

Richter KP, Choi WS, Alford DP. Smoking policies in U.S. outpatient drug treatment facilities. *Nicotine & Tobacco Research* 7(3):475–480, 2005. (32 refs.)

Ritter J. Drug agents can't keep up with pot growers. *USA Today*, October 12, 2005.

Savulescu J, Foddy B, Clayton M. Why we should allow performance enhancing drugs in sport. *British Journal of Sports Medicine* 38:666–670, 2004.

Shorter D, Kosten TR. Novel pharmacotherapeutic treatments for cocaine addiction (review). *BMC Medicine* 9:119, 2011. (84 refs.)

Sinha J. *History and Development of the Leading International Drug Control Conventions*. Special report prepared for the Senate Special Committee on Illegal Drugs. Law and Government Division, Canadian Parliament: Ottawa, Canada, 2001. (21 refs.) Available: www.parl.gc.ca/37/1/parlbus/commbus/senate/com-e/ille-e/ library-e/history-e.htm.

Substance Abuse and Mental Health Services Administration, Center for Behavioral Health Statistics and Quality. (April 11, 2013). *The NSDUH Report: Nonmedical Use of Prescription-Type Drugs, by County Type*. Rockville, MD: SAMHSA, 2013.

Substance Abuse and Mental Health Services Administration, Center for Behavioral Health Statistics and Quality (January 10, 2013). *The DAWN Report: Update on Emergency Department Visits Involving Energy Drinks: A Continuing Public Health Concern*. Rockville, MD: SAMHSA, 2013. (16 refs.)

Temple JL. Caffeine use in children: What we know, what we have left to learn, and why we should worry (review). *Neuroscience and Biobehavioral Reviews* 33(6):793–806, 2009. (230 refs.)

Tobin KE, Sherman SG, Beilenson P, Welsh C, Latkin CA. Evaluation of the Staying Alive programme: Training injection drug users to properly administer naloxone and save lives. *International Journal of Drug Policy* 20(2):131–136, 2009. (14 refs.)

Tokish JM, Kocher MS, Hawkins RJ. Ergogenic aids: A review of basic science, performance, side effects, and status in sport. *American Journal of Sports Medicine* 32:1543–1553, 2004.

Warren OJ, Leff DR, Athanasiou T, Kennard C, Darzi A. The neurocognitive enhancement of surgeons: An ethical perspective (review). *Journal of Surgical Research* 152(1):167–172, 2009. (47 refs.)

Watson C, Wilkinson J. The intensive care management of common and uncommon drugs of misuse (review). *British Journal of Hospital Medicine* 72(4):211–218, 2011. (33 refs.)

Wolk BJ, Ganetsky M, Babu KM. Toxicity of energy drinks (review). *Current Opinion in Pediatrics* 24(2):243–251, 2012. (86 refs.)

Wood DM, Brailsford AD, Dargan PI. Acute toxicity and withdrawal syndromes related to gamma-hydroxybutyrate (GHB) and its analogues gamma-butyrolactone (GBL) and 1,4-butanediol(1,4-BD)(1) (review). *Drug Testing and Analysis* 3(7–8, special issue):417–425, 2011. (123 refs.)

Wu LT, Pilowsky DJ, Patkar AA. Non-prescribed use of pain relievers among adolescents in the United States. *Drug and Alcohol Dependence* 94(1/3):1–11, 2008. (38 refs.)

Zee AV. The promotion and marketing of OxyContin: Commercial triumph, public health tragedy (editorial). *American Journal of Public Health* 99(2):221–227, 2009. (70 refs.)

Odds 'n Ends

Jack Fin
e could
drink
NO Wi
ne – H
is Wif
E Could
drink
NO liquo
R – But ST
ill they both
got drunk each nig
ht – though he got d
runk much quicker...
La pauvre presse
Brattleboro, Vt.
from the Collected Do
ggerel of 18th Century
France - by J. ANZOLONE

BEYOND COUNSELING

Clinicians frequently discover that, although their formal job description is centered on serving clients, there are often other expectations and issues to consider. Such duties fall into the general area of "indirect services," an awkward phrase used to cover all the other things the clinician is often required to do. Educational activities, case consultation, and planning for community programs are just a few examples. These aspects of a therapist's work are vital to the overall success of treatment efforts.

Educational Activities

Counselors are often called on to participate in public and professional education programs. The former includes presentations to high school students or church groups or might entail being a panelist on a radio or television talk show. The latter might take the form of conducting in-service training for other professionals, supervising trainees or students, or assisting with workshops.

Do's

In any educational endeavor, plan ahead—don't just "wing it." An effective presentation takes preparation. Find out from those organizing the program what they have in mind for a topic. You may wish to suggest an alternative. Who will be in the audience, and what will be its size? How long are you expected to speak? Are there others on the program? In choosing a topic, consider what would be of interest; ask yourself what kinds of questions are likely to be on the audience's mind. Don't be overly ambitious and try to cover everything you think someone ought to know about alcohol. If your audience goes away understanding three or four major points, you can consider your presentation successful. Choose a subject about which you are more expert than your audience. A counselor might effectively talk about alcohol's effects on the body to a group of fifth or sixth graders. However, any counselor who would attempt to lecture a group of doctors about medical complications is asking for trouble. Leave time for questions, and save some of your choice tidbits for a question-and-answer period.

Feel free to develop several basic spiels and some accompanying handouts. Regardless of the topic, an annotated list of community resources and contact information is always welcome. Use audiovisual aids. They can be an excellent vehicle for stimulating conversation. Three questions for sparking a discussion afterward are "What kind of response did you [the audience] have?" "What new information did you learn?" and "What surprised you?"

If public speaking doesn't come easily, rather than trying hard to avoid such assignments or just struggling through with one eye on the clock, enroll in a public speaking course. A good place to look for such an offering is at a local community college or an adult education program.

Feel free to borrow from colleagues. One of the things that marks effective speakers is having metaphors that somehow manage to capture the essence of a situation. Remember the response to the question about alcohol-dependent people returning to controlled drinking and the metaphor of removing the spare tire.

Don'ts

Avoid crusading, personal accounts—to use AA jargon, "drunkalogs"—or horror stories. These approaches may shock your audience and titillate them, but (and it is an important "but") most audiences will not identify with what you are saying. The presentation will be unconnected to their experience. Such an approach is likely to leave those in the audience with a "That's not me!" response. There seems to be a widespread tendency to share one's personal history of alcohol or other drug use, especially when speaking with teenagers. Perhaps the motivation is to establish credibility. Perhaps it is intended to demonstrate to teenagers that, even though an adult, the speaker is in tune with the teenagers' experience. Whatever the motive, there is reason to question this approach. It is out of touch with adolescents' psychology.

Anyone who has never made a mistake has never tried anything new.
—Albert Einstein

Preaching is preaching, whatever the guise. It's also a bit presumptuous. Does the speaker really think his or her history is so compelling that the recital of past problems should motivate others to change? Furthermore, what the speaker describes as problem behavior is likely to be considered by those in the audience as escapades. There is the danger, too, that a degree of romanticism and bravado might creep into the telling. The speaker lived dangerously, at the edge, and beat the odds. Most important, however, this approach doesn't really sit well with kids or help accomplish what is intended. A middle school student, in response to a parental query as to what the mandatory drug education program was like, rolled his eyes and groaned. He recounted the "episode of the day," attributed to the teacher's "friend." The teacher, having grown up in the 1960s, managed to conjure up a succession of "close friends," each of whom had had some experience with whatever drug the class happened to be discussing. In summing up what they were learning, the student wryly noted, "I guess what we're really learning is that Mr. J. has some problems picking his friends." Whatever factual information Mr. J had intended to convey was lost. The general impression was that the sessions were contrived. The unfortunate effect, too, was to trivialize the subject.

This raises the question of the appropriateness of situations in which judges sentence DWI offenders—typically, young drivers involved in fatal accidents—to go on the "speaker circuit" to local schools or to make videotapes for such presentations. These sentences are well intentioned, but the effectiveness of such presentations needs to be questioned. There are no studies of the results of this endeavor. A judge may sentence the individual to be available to make such presentations, but the judge cannot sentence a school to use these speakers. Anyone in a situation to make a decision to accept such a presentation needs to think carefully before saying yes. Related to this are victim impact panels used in educational programs, which involve not those who caused such an accident but those who were touched by a drinking-driving event—parents, spouse, a child. Victim impact panels have been studied, and the findings are mixed. Some researchers report changes in future drinking-driving behavior among audiences composed of those who have been arrested for DWI. Others have found no change. Others have found that victim impact panels have an effect on some people—for example, those over age 35—but not on others. It is not clear what situations lend themselves to the use of victim impact panels.

Finally, clinical vignettes are usually inappropriate with lay audiences. With professional audiences, if case material is used, great care must be taken to obscure identifying information. For either audience, avoid using jargon. Instead, look for everyday words to convey what you mean or use examples or metaphors that capture what you are trying to say.

Training Others

Substance abuse professionals have a special contribution to make in training other professionals. A common complaint of many substance abuse counselors is how ill equipped some other professional helpers are to work with alcohol and drug problems. However, this situation is not likely to change unless and until the experts, such as substance abuse clinicians, begin to participate in education. Consider this a high-priority activity, even though it may take place informally.

It is especially important to stick to your area of expertise. Your single unique skill is your ability to interact therapeutically with those with substance abuse problems. Your specialized knowledge and experience are the most important things you can share. Often this is most effectively communicated by examples of the kinds of questions you ask clients and the way you respond to clients' concerns, rather than by lecturing. However, one trap you should avoid is giving the impression that what you do and know is a mystery, which others could never hope to learn. This can come across to your students in subtle ways, through statements such as "Well, I've been there, so I know what it's like" or the offhand comment "If you really want to know what alcoholism's all about, what you have to do is (1) spend two weeks working on an alcohol unit, (2) go to at least 20 AA meetings, and (3) talk firsthand to recovering people." Any or all of these might be advisable and valuable educational experiences. However, you ought to be able also to explain in very concrete terms what information such experiences can provide and why they are valuable.

A few words on supervision of trainees or students may be helpful. Do not be fooled by the notion that the arrival of a student or a trainee is going to ease your workload. It shouldn't. Doing a good job of supervision requires a big investment of time and energy. Whether the student is with you for a single day, several weeks, or a semester, serious thought must be given to structuring the time to ensure an educational experience. There are some basic questions to consider. Do you wish to impart specific skills or just have the student become "sensitized" to treatment techniques? What are the student's goals? What will prove most useful to the student later on? What is the student's background in terms of academic training and experience with alcohol problems? What clinical responsibilities, if any, are anticipated? Commonly students will sample a broad range of agency activity but also have a more in-depth, continuing involvement in selected areas.

Never be afraid to try something new. Remember, amateurs built the ark, professionals built the Titanic.
—Dave Barry

Probably the single most important thing is to allow a trainee ample time to discuss what goes on, either with you or with other staff. The idea is not to run a student ragged with a jam-packed schedule and no chance to sit down with anyone to talk about what has been observed. If a student is going to be joining you in a clinical session, be sure you set aside at least 10 to 15 minutes ahead of time as a pre-interview briefing. Also, at the conclusion, spend some time reviewing the session and responding to questions. Do not expect that what the student should have learned is obvious.

Be sure to discuss with clients the presence of trainees. Clients do not need to be provided with a student's résumé or be given a brochure describing in complete detail the nature of the training program. However, clients do need to be told who the trainees are and to be reassured that they are working with the staff in a trainee capacity. Clients have every right to be uncomfortable and apprehensive at the thought that the merely curious are passing through to observe them or that they are being used as guinea pigs. Clinicians who have worked in agencies that include trainees find that most clients do not object to being involved with students if the situation is properly presented and if they recognize they have the right to say no.

Prevention

"Prevention" is a hot topic at the national, state, and local levels. The first concerted attention to prevention appeared about a quarter century ago when the NIAAA and NIDA meshed their prevention efforts in what was then known as the Office for Substance Abuse Prevention. Several years later, the office was renamed the Center for Substance Abuse Prevention (CSAP).

Background and Terminology

Before discussing current efforts, some background on prevention and its terminology may be useful. Activities directed at preventing the occurrence of diseases are a long-standing focus of all public health efforts. This is true whether it is a program of vaccination to prevent polio or measles or efforts to prevent cholera outbreaks by ensuring that the town water supply is uncontaminated. The attention to prevention within the substance abuse field is probably most closely linked to prevention efforts in the community mental health movement during the 1950s and 1960s that drew on a public health perspective.

Public Health Model The community mental health system introduced the notion of different levels of prevention: primary, secondary, and tertiary prevention activities. What these three levels of prevention activity all have in common is that each is intended to help reduce the total number of people who suffer from a disease. Think about it for a moment. There are only three ways that the total number of sick individuals can be reduced. One way is to prevent the illness in the first place; thus no new cases develop. This is known as *primary prevention*. A second way to lower the number of sick individuals is to identify and treat those who contract the disease as quickly as possible, restoring health to those with the disease. This is *secondary prevention*. A third way to keep down the total number of cases is to initiate specific efforts to avoid relapse and maintain the health of those who have been treated. This is *tertiary prevention*.

In the earliest days of the modern alcohol movement, any discussion of prevention meant only one thing—prevention of alcoholism. Accordingly, in drawing on the public health model, primary prevention meant inhibiting the development of alcoholism. Most commonly, practitioners believed this was best accomplished through educational endeavors, whether through the mass media or presentations to the local PTA. Such efforts are what is meant by primary prevention. Secondary prevention would include all efforts to identify those with a serious alcohol problem as early as possible and to initiate treatment. An example is routine screening by physicians and referral of those with a positive result for further evaluation and/or treatment. Tertiary prevention refers to efforts to promote continuing well-being among those who have been treated and thus help them avoid relapse. In respect to alcohol disorders, this could include aftercare for those who have been discharged by a treatment program, or it could be seen as continuing involvement in a self-help group such as AA. It is interesting that in this earliest model, it was the clinician, not some specialist prevention expert, who was engaged in prevention efforts.

An ounce of prevention is worth a pound of cure.
—Benjamin Franklin

Center for Substance Abuse Prevention (CSAP) Model Another model was introduced by CSAP. Here the interest is in the target of the prevention effort. Again there are three categories or approaches. One target is the broad general population. So in terms of alcohol problems, it would be directed to drinkers and non-drinkers alike, 17-year-olds and 70-year-olds. This type of effort is referred to as a *universal approach.* Another type of prevention is more targeted and is directed toward at-risk groups; such an effort is referred to as *selective prevention.* Here the attempt is to zero in on subgroups whose members are known to have an elevated risk. These might be teenage drivers, teen athletes, college students, or the elderly using prescription drugs. The remaining level encompasses specific individuals, rather than discrete groups, who are known to be at risk, perhaps someone who grew up in an alcohol-troubled family, the person who began drinking at a young age, or the person with a history of DWIs. Initiatives of this nature are termed *indicated* approaches.

These CSAP approaches are quite similar to how those in advertising or public relations think about their work, whether it's selling a car or promoting a political candidate. Consider a political campaign. A universal approach is a TV ad or a mass mailing to every household. The hope is to get the word out to as many people as possible. Other kinds of ads are tailored to a specific group, be it union members in an urban area, farmers, the elderly, or racial and ethnic groups. These non-interchangeable ads are an example of a selective approach. The next step is to fine-tune efforts by reaching out to specific individuals, those highly likely to support the candidate and those with characteristics suggesting the odds are fairly good they're in the candidate's camp, such as those who may have volunteered in a previous campaign, made a political contribution, or belong to an organization that strongly supports the candidate. The effort to contact these specific people is an indicated approach.

Efforts Directed to the Social Systems Versus the Individual Both the public health and CSAP models involve efforts to change the behavior of individuals. Another potential target of prevention activities addresses the environment or social systems that influence the behavior of individuals. These efforts count on a ripple effect. Though environmental efforts may be seen as a less direct route, in many instances they are among the most effective. Changes in laws are among the most obvious examples of environmental/social system initiatives—whether changes in the legal drinking age or in the hours of operation of bars and retail outlets or the immediate impounding of a car after an arrest (not only upon successful prosecution) for a DWI.

Demand Reduction Versus Supply Reduction At the policy level, another set of terms is used with respect to prevention—demand reduction and supply reduction. These terms are borrowed from the field of economics. They draw on the notion of the marketplace and the fact that the availability of any commodity is dependent on two factors—one is the amount produced by manufacturers, representing supply, and the other is the level of interest consumers have in purchasing it, representing demand. If no one wants to buy a widget, fewer are made. If fewer are manufactured, there are fewer available for people to purchase. To apply this to alcohol and other drugs, demand-reduction initiatives include any activities that make these substances less attractive to potential users and thus reduce the size of the market. One obvious approach is through treatment; abstinence removes a customer. Another demand-reduction strategy is to raise taxes on licit drugs, such as alcohol and tobacco, thus increasing their cost and reducing the numbers who purchase them. Supply-reduction efforts, on the other hand, are directed at making drugs or alcohol less available. Examples of illicit drugs reduction efforts include border patrols to reduce traffic in illicit drugs or support efforts in other countries to "stamp out" the drug trade. For alcohol this may include efforts to reduce the number or package stores in a neighborhood, or to cut back on the bars' hours of operation.

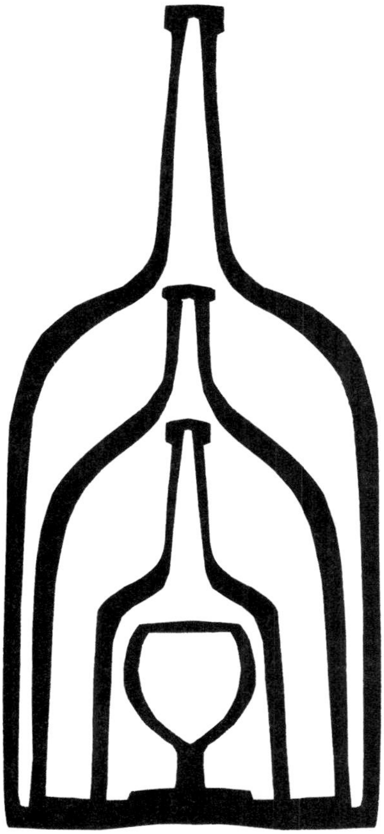

Early Prevention Efforts

As noted, the earliest prevention efforts, in the days before CSAP, were directed toward prevention of alcoholism. Gradually the goals of prevention expanded to include the serious problems that can accompany alcohol or other drug use. For alcohol, this involved efforts to prevent the negative consequences of drinking. In this context, primary prevention might be directed toward achieving low-risk alcohol use—such as "responsible drinking" campaigns. Similarly, secondary prevention can include efforts to prevent problems if/when intoxication occurs, such as designated drivers or call-a-ride.

Preventing What? It is important to distinguish between efforts to prevent an alcohol use disorder and efforts to prevent problems associated with acute use. Efforts that may be effective for preventing acute problems cannot be expected automatically to be effective in dealing with the problems of chronic use. For example, consider SADD (Students Against Drunk Driving). This program may help reduce the toll associated with teenage drinking and driving. But if the goal were preventing the development of alcohol disorders in adolescents, it would not be an effective means. To be successful, any program first has to be very clear about exactly what behavior it hopes to alter. Is it adolescent binge drinking? Is it alcohol poisonings in adolescents? The next step is to assess what kinds of activities might interfere with or reduce the behavior of concern.

Current Prevention Approaches

Prevention efforts directed at adolescents have always been a priority. As mentioned, the first wave of such efforts was largely educational. The second generation included other elements, such as providing social alternatives, or trying to build self-esteem or teach drink-refusal skills. The models now being promoted are seen as multi-pronged—for example, combining legal approaches, public education, media campaigns, and outreach efforts targeted to specific high-risk groups and individuals. Within these, greater attention is paid to the role of community organizations and their potential role in changing community norms. Community groups, too, may become involved in lobbying to change laws or in increasing local services, such as getting more police patrols.

Much is being done to mobilize parents to respond collectively to teenagers' substance use. This may involve helping parents define their collective expectations, such as those pertaining to teenagers having parties without parents or other adults present or parents' allowing alcohol to be consumed in their homes. Other activities involving parents may be organizing substance-free high school graduation parties, or post-prom events. These approaches are targeted to changing the environment and changing attitudes toward substance use. Handbooks and program guides that outline these approaches are available from CSAP.

Personnel Prevention efforts now look considerably different than they did even a decade ago. Specific programs and agencies have been created with prevention as their major mission. There is an ever-growing body of research to guide activities. As a result, prevention is emerging as a new and separate professional discipline within the substance abuse field. In terms of its evolution and development, the role of prevention specialist may be comparable to the position of substance abuse clinician a decade or two ago. The expertise required and the knowledge base required are not yet clearly defined nor agreed upon. However, one can make some educated guesses; for example, knowledge of child and adolescent development, the ins and outs of media campaigns, or the basics of health education.

Research As the prevention field has grown, there has been an increasing body of research to help guide these efforts. In general, the research findings have not been very encouraging. A variety of programs particularly directed at adolescents, often provided through the schools, involve educational efforts and alternative recreational and social activities, with efforts to build self-esteem and to teach refusal and other coping skills. Some have included a component for parents. More often than not, the results have been minimal at best. Behavior changes that may be present immediately after the program tend not to be long-lasting. Or students learn the material and have more information, yet knowledge doesn't get translated into behavioral changes.

Some programs have been well funded, popular, widely used, and well loved. Unfortunately, this doesn't make them effective. The prime example of the dearly loved but ineffective program model was D.A.R.E. (Drug Abuse Resistance Education), which has since been modified. It involved police officers coming into the schools to conduct sessions with elementary school students. Later, when D.A.R.E. students were compared to those who had not gone through the program, it was clear that D.A.R.E. simply had no impact on later substance use.

Some programs are worse than ineffective. In such cases, participants who complete the program are more likely to use alcohol or other drugs than those who did not participate! This kind of result has raised the question, not entirely with tongue in cheek, as to whether informed consent is as appropriate in the prevention arena as it is in the treatment realm. Indeed more questions are being asked about potential unintended consequences. While the party line may be that "just say no" is an approach from another era, its influence may remain. There have been several thoughtful articles raising that question. For example, is there that much difference between imploring students to "just say no" and imploring them to "make healthy choices." There have also been concerns expressed about the impact of combining drug prevention with zero tolerance for students who are identified as having used drugs and thus are expelled from school. There have been studies showing that students are not blind to what seems like hypocrisy and being needlessly punitive.

CSAP has made efforts to disseminate information about successful programs, which are described as "science-based" or "research-based," to emphasize that they are based on more than impressions on what people "believe" works. The center maintains a directory on its website, which outlines several dozen science-based initiatives, the key elements, findings to date, plus the methods used. In the 1990s, CSAP made large grants to states, termed State Incentive Grants, to promote the adoption of these science-based programs at the local level and to ensure the use of known effective approaches.

Efforts to disseminate these research-based programs proved problematic and raised important questions. In terms of the original research, was the follow-up period long enough to see how/if the early good results had staying power? Were they truly models to emulate? Plus, how realistic is it to think that others, without special resources, can replicate a demonstration project that was well funded and the recipient of technical assistance and training?

Challenges Strides have been made in prevention efforts; nonetheless there are a number of rough spots. Certainly prevention is a laudable goal. To question it may be like criticizing Mom and apple pie. Today most of the energy is being directed at adolescents and preadolescents. Unfortunately, the thrust of these programs has been the prevention of use per se—a goal of abstinence. The underlying theory may be that abstinence is the means by which other problems are ultimately reduced. Indeed, the research clearly suggests that by delaying the onset of alcohol and other drug use, there is a reduction of problems later. But adopting abstinence as a goal rather than a means can cloud thinking. All the rhetoric to the contrary, in too many cases abstinence-oriented programs sound less like public health efforts than quasi-legal policing activities.

In some ways we find ourselves trapped in a box that we have built. Yes, there continues to be discussion of "responsible use." For the drinking-age population, and especially around the holidays, there are the predictable "Don't drink and drive" messages. But when one hears the word "prevention," these are not the examples that first come to mind. It's "Just Say No." Suggestions that efforts be made to teach adolescents to recognize life-threatening alcohol overdoses engender discomfort. Such initiatives are faulted for "giving a mixed message." These objections overlook the fact that it is the non-drinking kids who, by default, are the ones in a position to act. Similarly, efforts to educate adolescents about the steps they can take to reduce the dangers of drug use at raves are criticized as "enabling." But most important, if the overriding message is abstinence, we need to recognize that we have adopted a message that has little relevance and is unlikely to reach the 40% of students who are the most vulnerable—those who are already using alcohol. Similarly, with nicotine, by 10th grade a quarter of students are regular smokers. Where are the smoking cessation programs?

Abstinence Versus Harm Reduction In the United States, there is relatively little acceptance for harm-reduction approaches around alcohol and other drug use. These include instructing injecting drug users in safe injecting practices, which can reduce infections due to shared needles, a common route of HIV/AIDS as well as hepatitis C infections, and infections due to poor injecting practices. Another approach is to train and provide heroin IV users with naloxone, a drug that is an opiate antagonist (meaning it beats the heroin to the receptors where heroin has its effects, essentially blocking heroin's actions). This can be life-saving in instances of overdose. Or harm reduction might involve testing supposed ecstasy tablets at raves to find out whether they actually are something else. Victoria, British Columbia, provides safe injection facilities through a program called InSite; such programs provide places in which drugs can be injected safely, in hygienic surroundings, under the supervision of health workers, with access to social services.

Implementation Implementing model programs is not a simple matter. The models that have been identified as research-based typically were developed in research settings. They were amply funded and adequately staffed by trained professionals. They had everything going for them. But they have to work in the real world, where things don't go so smoothly. One problem that has been identified is referred to as "fidelity." When model programs are implemented by others, how faithfully do others' efforts adhere to the original model?

The basic question is, "What differences matter?" We may know that a particular prevention program package has a known beneficial impact, but we might not know which components of the program are most critical in achieving the results. In some cases all we can do is make an informed guess. But even a guess requires some careful thinking. An example from a community prevention effort is telling. The goal was to increase parental supervision at parties kids held in their homes. One element of the program was encouraging parents to routinely contact one another when such a party was in the offing. Organized out of the local high school, a mailing went out to each family inviting parents to indicate their commitment to this kind of communication. A list was to be distributed to all families, providing the names and contact information for parents who "signed on." Unfortunately, the response rate was low; only a third of the parents responded, but the list was distributed nonetheless. Therefore, rather than showing how committed and concerned parents were, the less-than-robust list seemed to indicate the exact opposite! With a little bit of follow-up, the result probably would have been quite different.

A Difficult Question There are several models touted as science based and successful that have not lived up to the hype when others try them. One case involved the use of the social influence model. An evaluation of a school-based smoking prevention program, based on this model, found no effect. This study was conducted as perfectly as is humanly possible. There were more than 8,000 students involved, the teachers involved in the project were trained, and they rated highly on measures of how closely they adhered to the procedures that had been set. Virtually no students were lost at follow-up; 94% remained throughout the study. The students were enrolled in the third grade and followed regularly through high school and to two years post-graduation. What was the outcome? The program had no benefits. Those in the research community, with one exception, saw this as an exemplary research replication. The exception was the group promoting the model, which had reported up to 87% lower rates of substance use in schools after they had adopted this prevention program. It raised the question of whether the study described was "really" a social influence–based program. If it wasn't, then the question becomes, What was the essential missing ingredient that would explain the difference between no effect and an 87% success rate? There is a bit of skepticism about some of the dominant program models. One of the questions being asked, if quietly, is whether the evaluations tend to cast the initiative in the most favorable possible light. While not mentioned, there is also the fact that several prevention programs have generated an accompanying cottage industry, offering consultation services, providing training sessions, marketing training materials and the like. In such an atmosphere continuing to critically examine one's efforts isn't easy.

Adopting Model Programs

The earlier mentioned State Incentive Grants were for three years. Such a funding cycle is inevitably a source of problems. Essentially the first year is directed to getting up and running. The final year is directed at scurrying around to identify sources of future funding to continue the efforts that were barely under way. That leaves one year to really work on the program. In theory, the view is that such efforts provide start-up funds and that community programs, given initial support, will blossom and continue on their own, over the longer haul. This can't be presumed in the best of times and is even less likely in a period of economic downturn.

A common feature of the State Incentive Grant programs was the creation of community coalitions, which proved to be a distraction, if not an impediment. In many instances, the community coalitions formed were not coalitions at all. A true coalition is a combination of established organizations and groups with disparate goals and purposes that come together on a particular issue that happens to touch each of them, even though it may not be the primary concern of any. A true coalition is a coming together of groups with voluntary membership whose members can be mobilized. Thus a true coalition will be composed of diverse religious groups, the American Legion, unions, the Rotary Club, and other such organizations. True coalitions draw their strength from being composed of community groups who will be there tomorrow and the next day, whose activities are integral to the life of the community. A true coalition is not simply composed of different treatment agencies already involved in the substance abuse field, who come together to carve up a new pot of funding. Whom do they expect to mobilize? Their employees? Their clients? Their board members? Whatever their plans or goals, generally such pseudo-coalitions are not integral to the community. They are dependent on the funding of the moment for their existence. Unlike the religious communities, the unions, and the civic organizations who will be there tomorrow, these coalitions disappear when funding dries up. Or they try to reconstitute themselves to apply for the next round of funding to tackle the next hot issue. So the previous efforts, no longer spearheaded by anyone, flounder and are all too likely to leave little evidence of their fleeting existence.

Lessons from Fighting Back The Fighting Back program provides useful insights into the efficacy of community coalitions. The program, initiated as a major undertaking of the Robert Wood Johnson Foundation, was founded in 1988 and funded for $72.6 million, over a 10-year period. Fourteen communities were selected from over 300 applicants. The goal was to enable communities to implement a variety of anti-drug strategies to address drug problems through a community-wide approach that would involve the schools, local government, businesses, health care providers, and other community groups. Some coalitions represented an entire city; in other cases, they represented a neighborhood or borough.

The Foundation described three different types of initiatives that were undertaken. There were *environmental strategies,* designed to affect the physical and social environments that promote alcohol and drug use. These included neighborhood/graffiti clean-ups, tobacco-free school districts, community policing, workplace programs, health professional training, code enforcement, diversion programs, and sanctions for drinking and driving. There were *individual strategies* that endeavored to strengthen individuals to resist and recover from alcohol and drug use. These included parenting classes, youth mentoring, youth job referral, programs for the elderly, efforts to enhance youth self-esteem, leadership, and conflict resolution. There were before, after, and summer school programs, acupuncture, treatment services for the under-served and uninsured, and case management. The third approach was termed *supply, cost, and availability strategies*. These initiatives included such efforts as closing crack houses, opposing/closing liquor outlets in high-risk areas, banning liquor sales on Sunday, demolishing abandoned buildings, and promoting responsible beverage service.

Following a comprehensive evaluation, the Foundation presented the findings in a final report. What was found? Far less than most had anticipated or hoped. The report concluded that "despite ample technical assistance and direction, top-notch people, and sites that were pre-selected, the 10-year community-based coalition approach did not produce robust results in terms of decreasing substance abuse." This was a gentle way of saying that there was no effect. Among the findings were that those in the Fighting Back communities needing substance abuse treatment were no more likely to receive care. Crime rates were no lower. Ironically, while there was no change in opiate use, there was a decline in the number of available methadone slots. Contrary to expectations, the visibility of drug sales was not related to the levels of drug use. Of the lessons learned, a significant one is that communities are inevitably affected by decisions made at the city, state, or national level.

A central dilemma that faces community-based prevention efforts is that they are disproportionately directed at the single element that may carry the least weight—that is, the individual's psychological makeup and functioning. One writer, borrowing from the field of environmental pollution, compares this approach to "downstream" efforts in tackling pollution. Possibly this is the only thing that community-based programs can undertake. But there seems to be something wrong-minded about spending large amounts of money on efforts that, even if everything is going well, are likely to have at best a modest effect.

The Future

Prevention efforts, though not in their infancy, may still be best characterized as in their adolescence. What is apparent is that there is no single wonderful program that will do the whole thing. Many programs are available as guides, but anyone who is involved in prevention efforts needs to think critically about how to apply any program to a particular situation. If you scan the literature on the impact of different prevention efforts, whether school-based or mass-media campaigns, more often than not the conclusions include phrases such as "at best a modest impact" or "differences were not maintained" or "may be useful" or something even more blunt, such as "there was zero effect."

Insights from the European Union Given the less than robust results of prevention activities, some alternative approaches need to be considered. Efforts of the European Union (EU) and the World Health Organization (WHO) offer useful insights. A book sponsored by the World Health Organization, titled *Alcohol: No Ordinary Commodity,* was undertaken to inform public policy. The major part of the book is titled "The Toolkit: Strategies and Interventions." Different approaches designed to prevent and minimize alcohol harm are discussed. These include pricing and taxation, regulating the physical availability of alcohol, modifying the drinking context, drinking-driving countermeasures, the regulation of alcohol promotion, education and persuasion strategies, and early intervention and treatment services. The EU comprises 28 countries with very different histories and different policy approaches, which allows comparisons of different approaches and their outcomes in various circumstances.

Following a review of EU prevention initiatives which fall into six different domains, the study group rated the effectiveness of the different approaches, identified the extent of available research, and assessed the cost effectiveness of the different kinds of initiatives. This information is summarized on the facing page.

For those with a professional commitment to prevention activities, attention needs to be directed at setting priorities. If one can't do everything, what are the most pressing concerns, and what is achievable? Particularly for those in the clinical arena drawing on the World Health Organization schema, what efforts seem to be a good fit? Promoting early intervention? Providing services to high-risk groups? Increasing access to treatment? It is also important that all in the substance abuse field become informed about public policy efforts.

THE REAL WORLD

Historically the substance abuse field developed outside of mainstream medicine and the other helping professions. The very earliest alcohol treatment programs, for example, were founded for the very reason that those with alcoholism were excluded or poorly served by the traditional helping professions. The first alcohol treatment programs were often staffed by recovering people. The basic therapeutic program consisted of helping the client establish sobriety and attempting to orient him or her to the fellowship of AA.

Prevention Policy Area	Effectiveness[1]	Research Support[2]	Cost Efficiency[3]
Drinking-driving			
Lowered BAC	+++	+++	+++
Random breath test	+++	++	+
License suspension	+++	+	++
Alcohol locks	+	+	+
Lower BAC for youth	+++	++	+++
Graduated licensing	++	++	+++
Server training/liability	+	+	+
Designated drivers/ride services	0	+	++
School-based education	?/0	++	+
Community programs	++	++	+
Education and Public Awareness			
Public service messages	0	+++	++
Warning labels	0	+	+++
Alcohol education in schools	0/+	+++	+
Pricing and Taxation	+++	+++	+++
Restricting Availability			
Minimum drinking age	+++	+++	++
Govt. retail outlets	+++	+++	+++
Number of outlets	++	+	+++
Density of outlets	++	++	+++
Hours and days of sale	++	+++	+++
Advertising Controls			
Reducing volume of ads	+/++	++	+++
Control content of ads	?	0	++
Drinking Environments			
Responsible beverage service	+	+++	++
Active enforcement	++	+	+
Server liability	+++	+	+++
Enforcement of on-premise regulation	++	+	+
Public transport	?	0	++
Safer bar environments/containers	?	0	++

[1]Effectiveness: 0 = lack of effectiveness; + = limited effectiveness; ++ = moderate effectiveness; +++ = high level of effectiveness; ? = insufficient data

[2]Research Support: + = only 1 good study; ++ = 2–4 good studies; +++ = 5 or more good studies

[3]Cost Efficiency: 0 = high cost to implement and sustain; + = relatively high cost; ++ = moderate cost; +++ = low cost; ? = no information

Note: For each of these policy areas, the report includes discussion of relevant research.

Source: P. Anderson and B. Baumberg, *Alcohol in Europe.* London: Institute of Alcohol Studies, 2006. Available: http://ec.europa.eu/health/archive/ph_determinants/life_style/alcohol/documents/alcohol_europe_en.pdf.

Being a Professional Colleague

With the establishment of the NIAAA, alcohol treatment as we know it today was launched. The alcohol field is no longer staffed by paraprofessionals and is no longer functioning in isolation, separate and outside the health and human service mainstream. Tensions remain, however, because of that history. The various professions now involved in caring for those with alcohol and/or drug problems are still learning to collaborate. Being the "new kids on the block," the substance abuse professionals may need to work a bit harder at this. One of the difficulties that may go unrecognized is problems in communication. Each profession has its own distinctive language (terminology and jargon), which often is not understood by the outsider. For example, as a substance abuse clinician, you might report to the client's physician that the client has "finally taken the 'first step.'" You shouldn't be surprised if the physician has no idea what that means. In such situations, it may be tempting to get a little testy: "Well, doctors should know about AA." Of course they should, but they'll not learn if you don't use language they can understand. Remember, you expect them to use language you can understand when discussing your client's medical condition. Return the favor.

Sharing Expertise with Colleagues

Be sensitive to the fact that many other professionals have a distorted view of alcohol treatment's effectiveness. In large part, this is because they never see the successes. Those patients who come in again and again in crisis (though this may only be a very small minority of clients) are all too memorable. In fact, Vaillant found that as few as 0.5% of all the clients at one detoxification center accounted for as many program admissions as did 50% of the clients who only entered once. Of the 5,000 clients seen in a 78-month span, the 2,500 who never returned were easily forgotten, while the 25 who were admitted 60 times or more were *always* remembered. Encourage recovering clients to re-contact the physician, social worker, or nurse who may have been instrumental in their entering treatment but who has no idea of the successful outcome.

Consider making yourself available to other professionals for consultation. One of the surest ways to establish an ongoing working relationship with someone is to have been helpful in managing a difficult case. Other helping professionals may be reluctant to make a referral to an alcohol treatment program because that would imply they had already made a definitive diagnosis. Alcohol clinicians should be sensitive to the fact that in "just making a referral," the counselor, physician, or clergy member is being forced to deal with the client's denial, resistance, and ignorance of the disease. That's the hard part, especially for someone who doesn't do it day in and day out. Don't be afraid to suggest a few lines that might be used. Anything you can do to provide support, whether through consultation or being available for joint meetings, will be appreciated.

Professional Development

Being a professional also means being open to new ideas. One of the observations made about the alcohol field is that practitioners tend to keep using the familiar, rather than paying attention to new information. Over a decade ago a paper was published observing that the substance abuse field has a number of "taboo topics" that influenced the delivery of care and were not validated by research. The paper's authors furthermore suggested that these beliefs were not even open to question. The observation had some truth. The examples cited by the author included questions about the necessity of Alcoholics Anonymous for maintaining abstinence, the existence of spontaneous remission, the lack of empirical support for the addictive personality concept, the value of smoking cessation in early recovery, overuse of the addiction concept, and the lack of empirical support for the disease concept of codependency. The field has changed. Among the examples cited, some will no longer resonate. It is always easier to identify the taboos from a former era. In the future, undoubtedly, some current approaches will similarly be seen as taboo. What would you nominate as the taboo topics in the second decade of the twenty-first century? The insistence on abstinence as the central focus of prevention? The discomfort with harm reduction? A reluctance to use medications in the treatment of alcohol dependence?

I believe in evidence. I was a drunk for 22 years. I started going to AA and got sober and I've been sober for 37 years. If that's not evidence what is?

Whether the substance abuse field is more guilty of such behavior than other fields is probably not an argument worth waging. And to the extent this is the case, there may be a historic explanation. When the alcohol field was founded, care was provided in a manner that contradicted what was then the accepted mainstream way of doing things. In fact, in the early days alcohol counselors often saw part of their job to be protecting clients from the established professionals—those who, however well intentioned, didn't have a clue about treating alcohol problems. What is true is that it is always easier for any of us to continue doing what we have been doing. Don't our clients effectively remind us of this every day? Part of being a professional is evaluating new information and modifying our approaches based on the evidence.

Accordingly it is important to nurture your professional growth. This can take many forms—for example, attending workshops, going to conferences, arranging for consultation by colleagues, visiting other programs, and reading. It is important that all professionals take responsibility for their own continuing professional development. However, the adoption of evidence-based practices will not flow from staff attending a workshop or two. Such changes require a major commitment from treatment agencies to provide the education and level of supervised training required. The agency and its organizational culture are a determining factor in promoting the use of new approaches. A general surgeon doesn't go to a workshop or two and decide that next week she'll start doing open heart surgery. Nor does the substance abuse clinician attend a presentation on motivational interviewing and plan to use this technique the next day.

It has been said that the half-life of medical and scientific knowledge is eight years. This means that half of what will be known eight years from now has not yet been discovered. On the other hand, half of what is now taken as fact will be out of date. Consequently, education must be a continuing process. In the press of day-to-day work, you may find that you do not have enough time to keep up. You can find yourself having a résumé with 10 years' job experience, but it is the first year's experience repeated 9 more times.

Sources of Information As with any specialty, the daily pressures make keeping current a big problem. Get on NIAAA's and NIDA's mailing lists, regularly check their websites, read articles, and attend area or regional meetings of addiction workers of all disciplines.

Relatively little is known about counselors' sources of new information. A survey conducted in 2005 tried to gain some insights. Two types of sources were identified. One avenue might be considered broad, general sources: things such as journals, books, the internet. Counselors were also asked how frequently they used these in a year. The median was four. (Four is the midpoint in the total range of responses; half of the people used these more frequently, and half of those surveyed used them fewer than four times a year.) The other source of information was termed local sources: personal contacts, seminars and conferences, and personal experience. The median for local sources was three. Coworkers and conferences were mentioned by over 85%. Whether this is representative or not is unknown. But if it is, then the field needs to do a better job of providing continuing education opportunities for its workforce. A variety of forums are possible: speakers, case conferences (in which a clinical problem is presented and discussion focuses on possible approaches and their pros and cons), group discussions of a journal article, or a series of presentations on a particular treatment technique.

Acquiring New Skills It is important to distinguish knowledge from skills. In planning professional education programs, it is important to appreciate that while one hour may suffice to impart information, more than that is needed for acquisition of clinical skills. This is illustrated by an example of the format used to train counselors in network therapy. Training was a multisession effort. It included a didactic seminar, role playing, use of videotaped illustrations with discussion, and then clinical supervision as clinicians began to use this technique. This series of sessions resulted from the insight of program managers and administrators following their involvement in a large statewide initiative in California known as CalTOP, which was designed to gather information about treatment outcome. Furthermore, clinical training needs to be systemwide. A client's particular treatment shouldn't be dependent on luck, on the fact that the assigned counselor happened to have skills co-workers did not have.

Knowledge Dissemination At the federal level, explicit efforts are being made to promote the dissemination of new knowledge, sometimes referred to as information dissemination, knowledge transfer, or technology transfer. All fields have a certain amount of inertia. However, it seems to be particularly pervasive in the substance abuse field. The knowledge being gained through first-class research simply isn't getting down to the rank-and-file workers. A classic example is a study of the extent to which a particular counseling technique, behavioral couples therapy, had been adopted by the field at large. This technique has been widely studied and its effectiveness demonstrated in reducing substance use and improving satisfaction with the relationship. The results were disheartening. Of the almost 400 substance abuse treatment programs surveyed, only 27% offered any kind of family or couples-based treatment. Less than 5% of the agencies used any kind of behavioral therapy approach. None used behavioral couples therapy!

How do we explain this? A study explicitly looking at the dissemination process offers some insights. It involved a survey of substance abuse counselors' knowledge and attitudes toward buprenorphine, a medication that is an alternative to methadone and that was approved for use by the FDA in late 2002. The surveys were conducted over a 24-month period, before and then following the FDA action. Thus there were varying lengths of time for information to have spread through the clinical workforce. There's the good news and the bad news. For one, the proportion of counselors who were familiar with the medication did not increase over time. Therefore, we can't count on the inevitable dispersal of new information. However, certain factors appeared to determine where new information "flowed." These included the value the employing agency attaches to continuing education; access to appropriate professional expertise (for example, in the case of a medication, a physician affiliated with the program); the counselor's level of training; and the counselor's use of the internet, especially of the federal NIDA site. Two counselor characteristics were associated with lower levels of knowledge and less favorable views of the medication's effectiveness. One was greater seniority in the field; ironically, more experienced counselors were less informed. The other was the counselor's recovery status.

The above finding raises a general question about the influence of recovery on professional views about clinical care and treatment approaches. What is significant here is not that those in recovery were initially less well informed or had less positive views. What is significant is that following education and training, there were no differences in attitudes based on recovery status. Although potentially more conservative in adopting new approaches, and less likely to jump on the bandwagon of the most recent approach, those in recovery are no more closed to new approaches when provided with information and an opportunity to gain new skills.

Computer Literacy For a number of readers what follows may defy belief. Remember the average age of those in the substance abuse work force is age 52. Hopefully, agencies will begin to recognize a critically important skill found among younger workers—computer literacy. As you can benefit from clinical consultation, what can benefit older colleagues, and the agency, may be computer consultation. In the twenty-first century it is impossible to speak about professional development or professional competence and not mention computer literacy. Being somewhat, or minimally, proficient with computers and electronic communications simply isn't good enough. Even though behind other agencies, the chances are increasing that staff will be required to use a computerized record-keeping system. Colleagues will expect to be able to send you files and messages electronically or will anticipate that you can locate information on the Web. If you have just been getting by, time's up. Every community has a number of educational programs, whether provided through a local community college, or the town library, or a senior citizen's center.

No man ever reached to excellence in any one art or profession without having passed through the slow and painful process of study and preparation.
—Horace

Interdisciplinary Contacts One final factor is worth mentioning with respect to remaining current. Much of the information that the alcohol-drug counselor needs to know comes from many fields—from medicine, from psychology, from anthropology, from law, and so forth. Because of this, keeping current isn't simply a matter of time. In many instances, it means having access to an "interpreter," someone who can explain subject matter in everyday language, in a way that is easy to understand. In turn, part of the counselor's work becomes translating relevant information for clients. Beyond taking part in formal education programs, every substance abuse clinician needs to have someone to whom he or she can turn, with whom she or he is comfortable saying, "Explain this to me."

Selecting a Professional Position

In seeking and selecting professional employment, there are a number of points to consider. By analogy, accepting any employment is almost like entering into a marriage. When it works it's marvelous, but when there's a mismatch, it's quite the opposite. Many positions may have the title of "addictions counselor" or "therapist," but there is considerable variation among them, depending on the agency's setting and clientele. Beyond looking closely at the facility, it is equally important to look closely at yourself. Take a professional inventory. What are your clinical strengths, and what are areas of lesser competence? What are you most comfortable doing, and which things are more stressful? Is "routine" a comfort, or is it likely to invite boredom? Because of the differences among people, one person's perfect job is another person's nightmare.

In considering agencies, you are your own best counsel. But at the same time, consult with colleagues and use the grapevine. What should you give thought to? Among the long list of things worth considering are the following: What is the work atmosphere like? Does the agency have frequent staff turnover, or is it fairly stable? Why do people leave? Is there a sense of camaraderie? How do the various professionals on staff interact with one another? How does the counselor/therapist fit into the hierarchy? What are the opportunities for professional development, both formal and informal? How is clinical supervision handled? Does the agency support and encourage continuing education? Will the agency help cover the costs of attending conferences and workshops? What are the routes for promotion? To what are promotions tied—formal credentials, experience, certification? Is the position part of a well-established program or a new venture just getting off the ground? What kind of security does the position provide? How much security do you want and need? Where do you want to be professionally five years from now, and how will the position you are considering facilitate attaining that goal? What are the skills you would like to develop, and can they be gained in the position being considered?

Then there are always the nuts and bolts of personnel practices. Is the salary appropriate for the position, and can you live on it? Are the benefits comparable with those for other professional staff? What are the hours? Is there "on-call" or evening or weekend work? How many hours a week do comparable staff typically work? In both substance abuse and human service agencies, there is too often chronic under-staffing. So conscientious workers pitch in, work extra hours, and somehow never have the opportunity to take that time off later. Before managed care, many clinicians found themselves considering private practice. Now, with the changes taking place in health care delivery, this is a less inviting option.

A number of articles have raised questions about the ability of the nation's treatment system to meet treatment needs. This is all the more critical with the implementation of the Affordable Care Act in 2014. Substance abuse treatment is one of the 10 services that must be covered by health insurance. A report commissioned by SAMHSA looked at three major areas: the demographics of the workforce; strategies to prepare, maintain, and retain the workforce; and the anticipated workforce needs in the next five years. Here's a thumbnail sketch: The workforce is predominantly white, female, and over age 45. Nationally the annual rate of staff turnover is 18.5%. Retention strategies described include offering health care benefits, promoting a supportive workplace culture, and providing access to ongoing training. This certainly suggests what other reports confirm, that salaries and the employee benefits are not comparable to other health professions. Particularly troubling is that recruiting new staff is hindered by the lack of applicants who meet minimal requirements. (The challenges facing the field are discussed further below.)

Later Career Issues

The discussion so far has focused on those first jobs. Later in your career, different professional issues will surface. Potentially one of the most problematic centers on leaving the clinical arena for an administrative position. Among the factors to consider, the first is the obvious one—the extent of your administrative skills. While clinical skills shouldn't be a hindrance, you do need additional tools and can't respond to your subordinates as if they were clients, or to the organization as if it were a family. Management requires planning skills; an ability to consider alternatives to the way things are; and, typically, public speaking skills, preparation of reports and grant applications, representing the organization at public meetings, and more. While we recognize that education is essential for counselors, we don't always appreciate that the same is true for those in administrative roles. Among the questions to consider are, What kind of support is available when taking on this new role? Is there the possibility for a mini-internship to learn the ropes? What kind of transition period would there be and how much opportunity would there be to work with the incumbent? Is there a degree program for adult learners, with a non-traditional format that could be the source of important skills and provide further credentials?

On the surface, private practice may seem very attractive. On the other hand, it can be very lonely. Those who are in private practice need to take specific steps to develop and maintain professional contacts. (This is in addition to developing referral sources to ensure that your clients get the services they need, beyond those that you can offer.) Few of us can appreciate the extent to which our colleagues are responsible for helping us maintain our balance and are invaluable and needed resources for us. It is difficult to set any minimum length of experience before setting up a private practice, but this certainly is not the place for a newcomer to the field.

Being a Professional

What It Is

Addictions counseling is a growing profession. The professional counselor has mastered a body of knowledge, has special skills, and has a code of ethics to guide the work. Being a professional does not mean you have to know it all. Do yourself a favor right now. Give yourself permission to give up any pretense that it is otherwise. Feel free to ask questions, seek advice, request a consultation, say you don't know. Alcohol treatment requires diverse skills and talents. Treatment programs are staffed by people with different kinds and levels of training, for the very reason that no one person or specialty can do the job alone. Being a professional also means constantly looking at what you are doing, evaluating your efforts. There is always more than one approach. You cannot make people sober by grinding drunks through an alcohol treatment machine. Being open to trying new things is easier if you aren't stuck with the notion that you are supposed to be the expert. And, of course, you will make mistakes—everyone does.

What It Isn't

Overwhelming numbers of people need and ask for help. The tendency is to overburden yourself because of the obvious need. Spreading yourself too thin is a problem and a danger. You also need to develop assertiveness to resist agency pressures to take on increasing responsibilities. Both situations create resentment, anger, frustration, and a distorted view of the world: "No one else seems to care! Somebody's got to do it." It's a trap. Unless you're an Atlas, you'll get mashed.

Your personal life must be preserved—try to keep that in mind. The people who live with you deserve some of your attention too. It is hard to maintain a relationship with anyone if all you can manage is "What a day!" before you lapse into silence and soon fall asleep. Save your own space. Collapsing might give you a nice sense of martyrdom, but it won't help anybody. It's better to be more realistic in assessing just what you can do productively, devoting your energy to a realistic number of clients, and giving your best. Keep a clear eye on your own needs for time off, trips, and visits to people who have nothing to do with your work. Some compromise may be necessary between being your version of the ideal therapist and attending to your own needs.

Give some thought to handling the calls that come after working hours. Workers often have unlisted home phone numbers and don't give out their cell phone numbers. Intoxicated clients and their upset families can be notoriously inconsiderate, with "telephone-itis" setting in after a few drinks. You may think you do want to be available at all hours; if so, think about it some more. Many agencies have emergency services to handle after-hours calls. If there are situations when you decide it is important to be available to a client outside of the working day, have him or her contact the emergency service, which can in turn contact you.

You cannot take total responsibility for clients. Rarely does someone make it or not because of one incident. This does not mean that you should adopt a laissez-faire policy. However, just as you cannot take all the credit for someone who is sober and happy, neither can you shoulder all the blame when a client fails to remain sober.

Certification and Licensure

If you plan to work as a substance abuse counselor, the issue of certification and licensure is important. In the past, certification by a counselor association or licensure by a state board may have been primarily important for your own sense of professionalism. Now it is becoming a necessity. More and more frequently, a clinician's being certified or licensed is a hiring requirement. Groups that accredit treatment programs are concerned about staff qualifications as a way of assessing a program's ability to provide good care. Also, insurance companies are paying attention to the credentials of those who provide care and are making this a basis for reimbursement. Clinical agencies may be unable to bill for alcohol treatment provided by non-certified or non-licensed counselors. The same is true for counselors in private practice.

Certification and licensure are two different approaches to accomplishing the same goal. They differ chiefly in terms of the type of group that is certifying that an individual has demonstrated a minimal level of competency, or training, and is therefore qualified to do a particular line of work. "Certification" is the term used when an association or professional group confers the seal of approval. "Licensure" is the term used when an officially designated state governmental body awards the credential. Certification or licensure takes place at a state level, and each state has its own requirements. The same is true for teachers, lawyers, nurses, social workers, barbers, beauticians, and some trades people, such as plumbers and electricians. For the established professions, such as law, nursing, and medicine, there is generally reciprocity among states. In part, this is based on the fact that clear professional standards have emerged over the years. Also, there is a national examination that all states use and recognize. In addictions counseling there is much more variation among states, even though the areas assessed are similar, as can be seen in the following summary.

The temptation to form premature theories upon insufficient data is the bane of our profession.
—Sherlock Holmes

Overview of Certification and Licensure Requirements

Certifying group	The group varies by state; it is most commonly an alcohol/drug counselors' association. Some states have more than one group offering certification.
Types of certification	States typically have different types of certification available. Distinctions may be made between alcohol and other drug counselors. Some states offer an administrative or supervisory certificate as well as a clinician certificate. Levels of certification distinguish more senior clinicians from those entering the field or those in training.
Requirements	The requirements are counseling experience, education/training, and clinical supervision. The biggest differences among states are in the time requirements for each; whether there is a formula for substituting formal educational programs for work experience; and to what extent the subject area of education and training is stipulated. Several states specify clinical competencies that must be covered; several require specific educational programs in the area of ethics. States may have additional special requirements, such as length of sobriety for those in recovery.
Testing	There is generally a written examination, a personal interview, and a sample of clinical work, whether a portfolio, a case presentation, or a videotape of a clinical encounter.
Recertification	Length of certification ranges from two to four years. Recertification requires evidence of continuing education.

What the future holds for substance abuse counselors may be glimpsed by comparing state requirements for substance abuse counselors and mental health counselors. States credential both.

Almost a decade ago, the minimum state requirements for each state varied considerably. Take the area of education. Forty-nine states required a master's degree for mental health counselors. For substance abuse counselors, 22 states did not require a college degree; 4 had no minimal education requirement. Though 45 states required some credential for mental health counselors, for substance abuse clinicians, this was true in only 25 states. States required fewer hours of formal classroom instruction for substance abuse counselors. In terms of uniformity of minimal requirements for credentialing, there remains far more variation between states for substance abuse counselors than for mental health counselors. What is equally clear is that states are very sensitive to setting standards while also recognizing that substance abuse counseling is an emerging profession.[1]

A licensed social worker earns less than the manager of a fast food restaurant, and the median salary for a direct care worker in a residential treatment center was $23,000. Sticking with the fast food comparison, that's $2,500 less than the assistant manager at Burger King.

Snapshot of the Workforce

There are very little data on the substance abuse treatment workforce. The following data were drawn from a 2013 report to Congress by the Substance Abuse and Mental Health Administration on the Nation's Substance Abuse and Mental Health Workforce Issues. The request for this report was prompted by the passage of the Affordable Care Act and the Mental Health Parity and Addiction Equity Act, both of which will increase the numbers of those seeking care. The report notes that in 2011, 21.6 million citizens 12 and older needed treatment for an alcohol or drug problem; and only 2.3 million of these received treatment in a specialty program. In its introduction the report sets out factors that are recognized as significant problems. These include shortages of qualified workers, an aging workforce, problems with staff retention, and problems in recruitment. The latter two items are seen as tied to inadequate compensation. It is also noted that there is a lack of workers in rural and frontier areas, and there is a need for a more diverse workforce to reflect the racial and ethnic composition of the country. It concludes that misperceptions and prejudice often surround both substance abuse and mental health disorders, and the accompanying stigma can touch the workforce as well.

The report provides a thumbnail sketch of the substance abuse counselor workforce. The highlights are found on the next page.

[1]In light of this, most states have had provisions for grandfathering current clinical personnel, although those entering the field will need to meet a different standard.

Substance Abuse Treatment Workforce: A brief overview

Gender

Male	33%
Female	67%

Age

<35 yrs	31%
35–44	25%
45–54	23%
55–64	14%
>64	2%

Race/Ethnic Group

White	64%
Black	19%
Hispanic	11%
Native people	5%
Asian	1%

Education Level

Doctorate	2%
Masters	36%
Bachelor	24%
Associate	9%
Some college	10%
HS diploma	13%
<HS diploma	1%

Recovery Status

In recovery	34%
Not in recovery	49%
Undisclosed	7%

Certification

Licensed or certified	54%
Pursuing certification	23%
Not licensed	20%
Unknown	3%

Compensation

<$15,000	2%
$15,000–24,999	5%
$25,000–34,999	5%
$35,000–44,999	10%
$45,000–54,999	16%
$55,000–64,999	20%
$65,000–74,999	14%
>$75,000	18%
Did not disclose	10%

Employee Benefits (offered to all employees)

Paid vacation	83%
Paid sick time	82%
Life insurance	70%
Retirement plan	67%
Educational Assistance	40%

Compensation Adjustments

Time in the field	$6,400 more for over 7 years in the field
Type of credential	$3,200 more for license versus certification
	$1,900 more for certification versus no certification
Administrative	$7,100 more for those with administrative responsibilities
Type of agency	$2,200 more for private/for profit versus non-profit or public
	$5,800 more for accredited than non-accredited facility
	$6,200 more for hospital than non-hospital facility
Other	$1,000 more for men than women
	$3,300 more for whites than non-whites
	$2,300 more for those not in recovery

Source: Ryan O, Murphy D, Krom L. *Vital Signs: Taking the Pulse of the Addition Treatment Workforce. National Report, Version 1.* Kansas City MO: Addiction Technology Transfer Center National Office at the University of Missouri-Kansas City, 2012. Olmstead, TA, Johnson A, Roman PM, and Sindelar JL. What are the correlates of substance abuse treatment counselor salaries? *Journal of Substance Abuse Treatment* 29(3):181–189, 2005. (20 refs.)

ETHICS

In clinical care the most basic tool you have to help others is yourself. Therefore, how you think about the responsibilities of working with others is vitally important. Quite a few years ago, the graduation speaker for a group of counselor trainees at Dartmouth Medical School spoke on what constituted being a professional. The rhetorical question posed was, "How is a professional counselor different from the kindly neighbor who offers advice over the backyard fence?" The answer provided was that the professional counselor is able "to profess." That raised a few eyebrows, the meaning not being immediately obvious. What was being referred to as distinguishing the trained helping person from ordinary well-intentioned people is that the professional is able to state—to "profess"—what it is he or she does. A professional functions deliberately and thoughtfully. The professional doesn't rely merely on intuition or instinctive responses. The other important distinction is that the counselor or therapist has made a commitment to a set of beliefs as to how one interacts with clients. The counselor has an explicit set of ethical standards to guide helping behavior. These can be traced back to classical Greece and the Hippocratic Oath taken by physicians.

A man without ethics is a wild beast loosed upon this world.
—ALBERT CAMUS

Basic Principles

National groups and state counselor associations have adopted codes of ethics for their members. The principles that underlie these codes are the same as those for other helping professions. These codes are actually a series of statements of the most basic rules you are striving to follow in working with clients. Ethical codes are intended to serve as guidelines. They have a history and have developed from experience. The code of ethics of the NAADAC, the Association of Addictions Professionals (the acronym for its former name has been retained), addresses confidentiality, non-discrimination, interprofessional relationships, legal and moral standards, relationships with clients, the manner in which the substance abuse field is represented in public statements, issues related to payment for services, competence, and obligations to the larger society.

Integrity without knowledge is weak and useless, and knowledge without integrity is dangerous and dreadful.
– SAMUEL JOHNSON

Although commonly used, the word "ethics" nonetheless warrants a definition. One definition is that ethics encompasses the rules that define the "ought-ness" of our behavior. Ethics is a statement of how we believe we ought to behave. Those who study ethics have identified three basic principles that are germane to determining standards and values with respect to clinical work. If the clinician's behavior does not incorporate these values, there is considerable risk of doing harm.

One ethical principle for those in a helping relationship is a belief in a client's *right to autonomy*. Simply put, this refers to the belief that clients have the ultimate right to make the decisions that affect their lives. Another is the principle of *beneficence*. This represents a commitment to respect clients, compassion, a commitment to "doing good," and not behaving in a way that places the clinician's interests above those of the client. The third principle is that of *justice*. This, too, means being respectful, but it refers as well to behavior that promotes social justice, a self-imposed obligation both to be fair and to not discriminate in one's clinical work.

Even if a specific code of ethics for counselors did not exist and was not written down, these are basic ethical principles that are presumed by professional coworkers. What is required of those in helping professions is above and beyond that which may be expected of others or expected of you in other situations. It also needs to be pointed out that how these principles are put into practice is all too often neither clear-cut nor obvious. For example, consider the issue of autonomy. With respect to those who are alcohol dependent and drinking, a clinician struggles with the question of whether a client is capable of acting in his or her own self-interest. If the principle of beneficence is also factored in, it may be felt that some degree of pressure or coercion to prompt treatment is warranted, yet there are limits to the degree of coercion and how it is exercised.

Two ethical concerns deserve special comment. One is confidentiality. The other is establishing and maintaining boundaries between what is professional and personal, between work and the rest of your life, and between your professional efforts and your personal participation in AA or other self-help groups.

Confidentiality

For the alcohol professional, as for anyone in the helping professions, confidentiality is a crucial issue. Most of us probably do not consider how much of our conversation includes discussion about other people. When you think about it, it can be quite a shock. It is especially difficult when you are really concerned about someone and are looking for aid and advice. There is only one place for this in a professional relationship with a client. That is with your supervisor or therapist coworkers. It is never OK to discuss a client with a spouse, friends, or even a clinician from a different facility. Even without using names, enough usually slips out to make the client easily identified in the future. Unfortunately, the confidentiality standard is not kept all the time; there are occasional slips by even the most conscientious workers. You will do it accidentally, and you will hear it from time to time. All you can do is try harder in the first instance and deliberately forget what you have heard in the second. What your client shares with you is privileged information. That includes where the client is and how he or she is doing. Even good news is the client's alone to share.

If you have administrative responsibilities or are a clinical supervisor, it is up to you to discuss confidentiality with both administrative and clinical staff. The same is true for any volunteers working in the office. Of necessity, they have some knowledge about the people being seen, at least who they are. It must be stressed that any information they acquire there is strictly private. You do not need to get huffy and deliver a lecture, but you should make the point very clearly and set some standards in the workplace.

Confidentiality is not simply a noble idea going back to the ancient Greeks. There are laws pertaining to confidentiality and court cases that have helped to define the protections afforded patients. There are specific federal regulations with respect to confidentiality of client information and records in alcohol and drug services. Information cannot be released to any outside party without the client's permission. This means friends, physician, employer, or another treatment facility. A treatment facility is not even allowed to say whether anyone has ever been or is currently in treatment. Most agencies have a release of information form used whenever information is provided about a client. This then becomes part of the client or medical record. Similarly, if clinicians want to get information from another facility or party, they need the client's permission and a written release to forward to those from whom the information is being requested. The only exception to this occurs when the life of the client or of someone else is at risk.

E-mail and Texting One arena in which modern technology has moved at a faster pace than laws and regulations is electronic communications, e-mail and texting. E-mail was the first on the scene. Prior to the arrival of texting it had become a routine part of most people's daily lives; in many quarters it now has been replaced by texting. Indeed, both are used in communicating with patients.

When it comes to using electronic communication, there are some potential concerns. For example: How private is your client's e-mail? Is the e-mail address used only by the client or is it a family or household account? If the e-mail address is used by several people, communications are best limited to the kinds of messages that you would feel comfortable leaving on someone's answering machine, when there is the likelihood that others beside the client will hear the message. Aside from privacy, consider which communications are better handled in person, whether by telephone or in an individual session.

In both hospitals and agencies, electronic records are rapidly replacing paper records. Agencies that use electronic records have a variety of protections in place to help assure privacy and confidentiality. Chief among these is restricted access. One of the potential pitfalls associated with electronic records is the ease with which such materials can be forwarded via e-mail. For example, reports generated by such record-keeping systems can be e-mailed to others within the organization or to staff at other agencies. Interestingly, the very ease of sending such materials creates a danger that materials are sent out a bit indiscriminately. Before forwarding electronic reports, consider whether everyone on the intended recipient list *really* needs all the information included in the particular report. In addition to being overly inclusive, there is always the potential for simple error. In large organizations, material may be sent to the wrong person by selecting the incorrect Jane Smith from an in-house name directory.

Even in the presence of firewalls, and giving careful thought to whom materials are sent electronically, there is at least one other potential problem. Virtually all e-mail systems have the option of forwarding e-mail to another electronic address. People going on vacation or leaving town to attend a meeting may have their workplace e-mail sent to another account. In forwarding electronic reports via e-mail, consider whether it is something that you want going out on a large commercial system, be it Comcast, Gmail, or AOL. Indeed, some medical centers are considering placing limits on the ability to forward e-mail.

Another issue involving e-mail is the matter of authenticity. This refers to the fact that no e-mail recipient can be certain that the indicated sender is in fact accurate. Anyone can send e-mail with virtually anyone's name attached to it. The inability of e-mail to provide methods of authentication presents a possible risk to patients and health care providers. E-mail authentication has been one of the more difficult issues to address when using e-mail for medical communication. Any user of e-mail is way too familiar with spam. Beyond the unwanted advertisements, some spam involves outright scams: "Send in $20 and get some wonderful, too-good-to-be-true item." The most recent spam twist encountered by this author pretended to be from her physician: It began, "URGENT: This concerns you as a patient & we have not heard from you." This is followed by a reference to a review of my medical record, and then an offer to order a recommended weight loss product. This kind of spam suggests that it may be important to emphasize which kinds of communications a client will never receive from you and which should be viewed with suspicion.

Setting Boundaries

An ever-important and ongoing dilemma is establishing appropriate boundaries in relationships with clients. This can turn up in many forms, but ultimately the task is doing what is required to maintain a professional relationship. For example, occasionally clients will present you with gifts. While they are actively working with you, the general guideline is no gifts. This is especially true if something of great monetary value is offered. In such cases, it is important to discuss what is being said by the gift. Use your common sense, though; there are times when clearly the thing to do is accept graciously. (If you have a fantasy of a Hummer being delivered anonymously to your door, and it comes true, unfortunately, most of our experience doesn't cover that.) A bouquet of flowers from someone's garden is different from a huge bouquet from the florist. Even then, placing them in the reception area may be more appropriate than saying you can't wait to take them home.

Similarly, social engagements with a client alone or with the family are not recommended. It could be a "plot" to keep you friendly and avoid problems that have to be worked out. During office time, deal with the invitation and gently refuse.

Helping professionals are expected to avoid romantic entanglements with clients. If a romantic inclination seems to be surfacing, either for you or a client, it should be worked out—and not in bed. This is the time to run, not walk, to an experienced coworker. It may be hard on the ego, but the fact is that people with problems are as confused about their emotions as they are about everything else. They may be feeling so needy that they "love" anyone who seems to be hearing their cry. It really isn't you personally. Discuss this in clinical supervision. It is never acceptable to have a sexual relationship with a client.

The need to keep counseling and personal relationships separate does not apply only when a client is in formal treatment. It is also applicable afterward. This can be particularly difficult when the paths of a clinician and a former client intersect in other areas of life, possibly if both are members of AA or NA. However, as cruel as it may sound, former clients are forever off-limits.

It is important to keep your professional life and private life separate. Don't counsel your friends; you are likely to end up with fewer of them. If there is something that concerns you about a friend's substance use, say something about the specific behavior that was troubling. Then bite your tongue. Your friend knows what business you're in. If that person wants further information or help, he or she will ask. At that point offer the names of possible clinical services. Then it's up to your friend.

Ethical Concerns

Ethical issues that arise in alcohol and drug counseling are being more widely discussed. This reflects greater attention to medical ethics generally. There is a formal field of medical ethics. Ethics committees can be found in many institutions to help staff consider ethical dilemmas. With the alcohol field a part of health and human service fields, the issues that are raised elsewhere are now also being considered with respect to substance abuse clients.

Clinical Setting

In clinical care, several ethical issues have received particular attention. One of these concerns illicit drug use during pregnancy. How does one consider and balance the welfare of the unborn child with that of the mother? A related matter involves the ethical issues that arise when a clinician knows or suspects that a client who is a parent might be abusive or negligent. Most states have laws requiring others to report such concerns to child welfare agencies. If there is no such law, what are your responsibilities? Or what is your responsibility if your client is a family member concerned about a spouse who happens to be an airline pilot? These are situations that will require careful thought and discussion with a supervisor. Another area in which there has been increasing recent discussion involves organ transplantation. Should alcohol-dependent people be considered candidates for a liver transplant, given that the number of those who need liver transplants far exceeds the number of organs available? If so, should a period of abstinence be required to become eligible for a transplant? In that case, how long should the patient abstain? As a general rule, any medical treatment requires informed consent. For example, patients must be provided with information about a diagnosis, the stage of a disease, the prospects with/without treatment, potential complications, therapeutic alternatives, and the prognosis, before agreeing to a therapy. How does this apply to persons who are dependent on alcohol or other drugs, are in withdrawal, or are faced with punitive measures if treatment is not accepted?

Research Setting

Ethics also enters into the realm of research. Anyone who works in a setting that conducts research needs to be familiar with the guidelines for ethical research practices. Federal regulations that involve human participants are very strict. Any research project that involves human participants is required to take very careful steps to protect subjects. First, it must be demonstrated that an answer to the questions being raised requires human participants; mice, rats, or baboons wouldn't do. With that established, virtually all institutions have a committee (an Institutional Review Board) to review how the research is to be conducted. These committees are required to review the risks to those involved, to consider how it is proposed that people will be recruited, to review the steps to be taken so that potential participants understand what the research entails and what the associated risks are, and

Hippocratic Oath—Classical Version

I swear by Apollo Physician and Asclepius and Hygieia and Panaceia and all the gods and goddesses, making them my witnesses, that I will fulfill according to my ability and judgment this oath and this covenant:

To hold him who has taught me this art as equally dear to me as my parents and to live my life in partnership with him, and if he is in need of money to give him a share of mine, and to regard his offspring as equal to my brothers in male lineage and to teach them this art—if they desire to learn it—without fee and covenant; to give a share of precepts and oral instruction and all the other learning to my sons and to the sons of him who has instructed me and to pupils who have signed the covenant and have taken an oath according to the medical law, but no one else.

I will apply dietetic measures for the benefit of the sick according to my ability and judgment; I will keep them from harm and injustice.

I will neither give a deadly drug to anybody if asked for it, nor will I make a suggestion to this effect. Similarly I will not give to a woman an abortive remedy. In purity and holiness I will guard my life and my art.

I will not use the knife, not even on sufferers from stone, but will withdraw in favor of such men as are engaged in this work.

Whatever houses I may visit, I will come for the benefit of the sick, remaining free of all intentional injustice, of all mischief and in particular of sexual relations with both female and male persons, be they free or slaves.

(cont.)

to ensure that no coercion is involved. This is not as straightforward as it sounds.

Consider the situation in which the researcher, or the person requesting consent, is also the potential participant's counselor or doctor. There is an established relationship. Given the trust that is present, the client or patient may agree to virtually anything. It is not that he or she is being pressured; the client is simply apt to comply with any request because the counselor or the physician makes it. Potential research participants may not really listen to explanations, tending to do whatever is asked of them. On the other hand, the person may not be wild about the idea of participating in the research, but is fearful of the consequences of saying no. Will the counselor be angry or stop therapy? These worries may seem unfounded, but they are common.

Another source of confusion is that clients, and patients in general, assume that any research will benefit them. In an abstract way, all knowledge probably benefits all of us. But that isn't really the issue with clinical research conducted in health care settings. Clinical research is justified only when the answer to the research question is unknown: Is drug A more effective than drug B? Is the use of this counseling approach more effective than another? If the answer is clear—that is, scientifically established, as opposed to being based on hunches and impressions—then it is unethical to do research on that question. Occasionally articles appear in the newspaper referring to a research project that has been discontinued early, when it became evident that those receiving an experimental treatment were doing better than those receiving an alternative therapy, or no treatment at all. Thus the continuation of the research would have been unethical.

A number of ethical concerns arise with respect to clinical research in the substance abuse field. Should it be permissible for researchers to design a study that involves giving alcohol to research subjects who are alcohol dependent and not in recovery? If so, what safeguards are needed? What obligations exist to provide treatment after the research is completed? What are the relevant criteria in deciding who can or cannot be included in such a study? Another ethical issue centers on the role of drug testing in the workplace and the balance between public safety concerns and an individual's right to privacy.

Informed consent is obviously a concern and a challenge as demonstrated by the experiences of one research group. After describing a research study protocol to young adults with marijuana dependence—which involved random assignment to either a motivational interviewing option or to "standard" drug counseling—the research team administered a four item multiple-choice questionnaire covering the basic points. Less than half of the potential participants answered all the questions correctly. One in five didn't correctly answer the question about the

Hippocratic Oath (continued)

What I may see or hear in the course of the treatment or even outside of the treatment in regard to the life of men, which on no account one must spread abroad, I will keep to myself, holding such things shameful to be spoken about.

If I fulfill this oath and do not violate it, may it be granted to me to enjoy life and art, being honored with fame among all men for all time to come; if I transgress it and swear falsely, may the opposite of all this be my lot.

Ludwig Edelstein. *The Hippocratic Oath: Text, Translation, and Interpretation.* Baltimore: Johns Hopkins Press, 1943 right to refuse to participate. An unexpected finding, which in hindsight may seem less so, was a modest relationship between the level of drug dependence and the proportion of correct answers.

Substance Abuse Field

Beyond the ethical questions that confront an individual clinician, there are those that confront the substance abuse field. One involves the role of the beverage industry, not only in alcohol research but also in prevention or public education efforts. The alcohol field has long been wary of collaborative efforts with the beverage industry. Over a decade ago, the editors of 25 substance abuse journals adopted a set of ethical guidelines (known as the Farmington Consensus) to govern publication practices. The problems that have become evident in research funded by the tobacco industry and, more recently, by the pharmaceutical industry suggest that ongoing vigilance is justified. During the trials leading to the tobacco settlement, it came to light that the tobacco industry had stifled research findings and provided hefty compensation for expert testimony to those able to present a situation in the least negative light. More recently, the pharmaceutical industry has been recognized as engaged in the same practices. It selectively publishes research results, with one standard for positive results, while delaying reports of adverse effects. The pharmaceutical industry pays university researchers for work that can barely be termed "work." This includes presenting papers at professional meetings that have been authored by the pharmaceutical company. What are the ethical questions related to obscuring industry payments to research and clinical professionals?

Contact Me Soon!!!
Confidential, Risk-Free Opportunity!

We recently independently received an email that offered us a chance to do good and earn money for next to no work. The proposition was somewhat unethical, but the sender promised us complete confidentiality. . . . [This] was from a major university research institute, asking us to consult on a project funded by Philip Morris.

The message noted that "some scholars have decided not to take money from tobacco companies." But the writer seemed to assume that even if we were willing to take the money, we would consider it shameful; the message quickly pointed out that the compensation would be nicely laundered by the university that had received the grant from Philip Morris. Thus, no embarrassing tobacco company checks with our names on them would show up in industry document repositories.

. . . "Your name would not be associated in any way with your commentary, and you would not be mentioned in any way in any correspondence or reports of findings from the study. Once you have been paid, your name would be removed from our records". The pay? $1000 for "at most, a day and a half of work . . ."

RE Malone, EA Smith. *Tobacco Control* 18(4):249, 2009

Public Policy Domain

Ethical concerns arise in relation to public policy as well. A significant but under-recognized issue involves substance abuse treatment for prisoners. Ethical standards hold that prisoners are to be awarded the same standard of medical care provided to the general population. However, this is not the case—especially among prisoners dependent on narcotics. They are forced to undergo abrupt withdrawal whether it is from illicit drugs or legally prescribed medications, such as methadone or buprenorphine. This is true despite the fact these drugs are widely accepted and have been approved by the federal government for just this use in the United States. In addition, providing drug treatment for prisoners is the exception, not the rule. The high risk of a fatal overdose at discharge for those with a history of heroin dependence is not acknowledged, either through patient education or provision of naloxone for use in the event of heroin overdose. While in prison, inmates in the United States are rarely provided with care that would reduce the risk of HIV infection. A study of one state's correctional facilities found that over half of male prisoners at a high risk for HIV/AIDS were not tested.

Other events in the public arena raise ethical questions. Next to reproductive health and abortion, is there any other area of medicine and human services that has been subjected to more political pressure than the substance use field? A few examples follow.

- During the Reagan era, NIDA circulated a memo instructing librarians to destroy some of NIDA's own reports that had become "outdated," "misleading," and "dangerous." In that same era, NIDA circulated a "nomenclature memorandum," with a column of acceptable terms alongside a column of unacceptable terms. The unacceptable phrases were to be avoided in all agency materials, including any grant proposals submitted to the agency. One of the banned phrases was "illicit drug use." The appropriate phrase was to be "illicit drug abuse." The rationale was that if a substance were illegal, it was, by definition, obviously, "abuse."
- In the mid-1990s, the U.S. Department of State warned that U.S. agencies should avoid speaking positively about harm reduction because this was only "code for legalization." At that time, too, the United Nations was requested to clean up its language.
- In 2004, on the heels of the re-election of George W. Bush, the United Nations Office of Drug Control Policy was again requested to change its language. The costs of failing to do so were made explicit, to run the risk of losing U.S. funding. Subsequently a letter was sent to United Nations staff: "Please . . . ensure that references to harm reduction and needle/syringe exchange are avoided in UNODC documents, publications and statements."
- In 2004, ABC News had a special report on the retraction of a scientific article, an unusual response to such an occasion. The NIDA-sponsored research had purported that a single dose of ecstasy causes "severe and profound brain damage." The basic error in the study, attributed to mislabeled bottles from a supplier, was that the drug administered was methamphetamine and not ecstasy. The retraction became news as the study's findings had been very much hyped as an anti-drug message.

These instances involve what Howard Becker, a sociologist, described as "politically inconvenient scientific knowledge." Such incidents are not restricted to the United States. The opening of a supervised injection program in Vancouver, British Columbia, became a clear thorn in the side of the Canadian national government.

Cases that raise ethical concerns, whether in the clinical, research, or public policy realms, may not have clear-cut solutions. One can examine a question from different perspectives and potentially arrive at different conclusions. However, this does not relieve us from struggling with these issues.

Demands on the Profession

If you were to scan the journal literature, you would see recurring topics that can be viewed as challenges to the profession of substance abuse counseling. These challenges have less to do with changes required of individual clinicians than with the organizational climate and shortcomings that can fail both clinician and clients. One such topic of discussion is clinician *burnout* and clinician turnover. "Burnout" can mean many things, from clinicians feeling overwhelmed by multiple and unrelenting demands upon them, to a degree of cynicism that feeds a diminished sense of possibilities for clients, to feeling unsupported by agency administrators, to a pervasive weariness. Protective factors are a supportive administrative style, the presence of collegial bonds among coworkers, imparting a sense of "we're all in this together" and nourishing a sense of purpose, and the belief that one's efforts are important.

Another recurrent theme, mentioned earlier, is the need to provide opportunities for professional development that go beyond the occasional day away from an agency to attend a workshop. This discussion occurs in respect to the importance of using evidence-based treatments. Also noted is the failure to routinely provide important services. These include smoking cessation for those in treatment for substance abuse; providing screening and initiating care for infectious diseases, namely HIV, hepatitis C, and sexually transmitted diseases; and inadequate use of medications effective in alcohol treatment.

The greatest demand on the substance abuse treatment community and substance abuse professionals is infrequently discussed. It boils down to how the profession can reach out and find ways to touch the lives of the 90% of those who need treatment but who do not cross the thresholds of treatment programs. For the 10% who do, there is also a need to find ways to provide continuing care, to prevent relapse or to short-circuit that process in a manner that can reduce the future risk. This will also entail examining some hard questions. Is the disease model of addiction sometimes used inappropriately? If there are flaws in the system of care that impede access, is there a tendency to attribute this to the symptoms of addiction? The clinical enterprise cannot be viewed as the clinician doing battle against symptoms; rather, the challenge is learning how to accommodate and work around them. Whatever changes are made will require working more closely with other helping professions, being willing to experiment, and being open to possibilities that cannot now be imagined. The profession has moved far beyond requiring people to prove their good intentions by abstaining from alcohol for 24 hours before entering residential care, or failing to recognize the importance of involving family during treatment, or resisting the use of any psychotropic medications even when there is a documented co-occurring psychiatric illness. Surely, too, it can set aside the blinders that prevent exploring other options and approaches to organizing clinical care.

CLINICIANS IN RECOVERY

Many workers in the addictions field are themselves in recovery. Long before national attention was focused on alcohol treatment, for example, there were private rehabilitation centers often staffed by those then described as sober alcoholics. The days are long gone when simply being a recovering person was considered sufficient qualification for employment. Differences in philosophy or outlook among staff were evident in the early days of the substance abuse field, depending on whether the person did or did not have a personal history of substance abuse. Recovering counselors have often been described as "wearing two hats." As this term is typically used, it may suggest the presence of dual responsibilities and potentially conflicting interests.

Some thoughts for clinicians in recovery. A bind for those in recovery occurs if attending meetings of self-help programs becomes tied to their jobs more than to their own sobriety. You might easily find yourself sustaining clients at meetings and not being there for yourself. You can avoid this situation by finding a meeting to attend where you are less likely to see clients. On the occasions when clients do see you at meetings and bring up problems or questions about their treatment, gently tell them you will discuss this at your next appointment. On the other hand, if they are questioning some aspect of the meeting, introduce them to another member present.

Another problem may be the temptation to discuss your job or clients with other AA or NA members. To do so is a serious breach of confidentiality. This can be awkward if a concerned member asks you point-blank about someone. The other side of the coin is maintaining the confidences gained at self-help meetings and not reporting to coworkers what transpired with clients. Coworkers should not put you in a bind by asking. It is probably OK to talk with your AA or NA sponsor about your job if it is giving you fits. However, it is important to stick with how you feel and to leave out work details and/or details about clients.

Clinician Impairment and Relapse

Before proceeding further, it should be noted that the issue of impairment caused by alcohol and other drug use is not solely a concern for the alcohol and substance abuse field. While some professions have come further than others, virtually every professional group—physicians, nurses, social workers, psychologists—has recognized the problem and has developed policies and programs to address it. These efforts are conducted under the auspices of an impaired professionals committee, which may be affiliated with the professional association or a state licensing board. The general thrust is to encourage reporting by concerned individuals, be they family members, colleagues, or patients; to initiate a non-prejudicial review; and, where impairment is suspected, to facilitate a clinical evaluation and, as indicated, provide treatment. In many of these instances, considerable leverage is provided by the obligation to report findings to licensing boards with the prospect of disciplinary action if treatment is refused.

Every profession has members who are recovering alcohol- or drug-dependent individuals—as well as those who go untreated—but the substance abuse field is a special case. There are greater numbers of recovering people in this field, and their recovery status is more closely tied to the work they perform. Becoming a professional in no way confers immunity to relapse. However, it is not openly discussed by the profession. A search of the scientific literature identified only two articles on the topic, and one of those was 25 years ago. It has been the profession's big taboo topic. When relapse occurs, the situation has too often been handled poorly. There is either a conspiracy of silence or a move to drive the counselor out of the field. Coworkers can very readily forget everything they know, relinquish any objectivity, and function as confused, concerned family members.

Ideally, the time to address the issue of possible relapse is at the time of hiring. Both the clinician and the agency have a mutual responsibility to be alert to possible danger signs, and they should agree to address them openly. This does not mean the recovering professional is always under surveillance. It simply is a means of publicly acknowledging that relapses can and do occur and that they are too serious to ignore. If a counselor relapses, it is his or her responsibility both to seek help and to inform the agency. The job status will be dependent on evaluating the counselor's ability to continue serving clients and to participate in treatment for him- or herself. The time to agree on an arbitrator/consultant or referral is before relapse, not in the midst of it.

Some people favor an arbitrary ironclad rule: any drinking and you're out of your job. However, that seems to miss the point. There is the recovering professional, who buys a six-pack, has one or two beers, sees what is going on, picks up the phone, and calls for help. Another case is the person who "nips" off and on for weeks, who subsequently exhibits loss of control, and shows up at the office intoxicated. Though it is important not to treat the former case lightly, nonetheless the symptoms have not been fully reinstated, as they have in the latter case. What is essential is making every effort to ensure that professional care for the clinician is provided and making an equal effort to assure that the care of clients is not jeopardized.

If you are a clinician known to your clients as being in recovery, your relapse can have a profound effect on some. If you are off the job and enter treatment, you can count on the news rapidly becoming public knowledge. How this is handled with clients may vary, but it requires careful thought.

If you happen to become a coworker providing coverage for a relapsed counselor, be prepared to deal with clients' feelings of betrayal, hopelessness, anger, and fear. You will need to provide extra support. Be very clear about who is available to them in their counselor's absence. Also recognize that this can be a difficult, painful experience for you and other coworkers, who may share many of the clients' feelings. Be prepared to call on extra reinforcements in the form of consultation and supervision.

If you are a counselor who has had a relapse and you return to work after a leave, there is no way you can avoid dealing with this fact. How this is handled should be addressed in supervision and with input from more seasoned colleagues. You will be trying to walk along a difficult middle ground. On one hand, your clients do not need apologies, nor will they benefit from hearing all the details or in any way being put in the role of your therapist. Yet neither can it be glossed over, treated as no big deal and of no greater significance than your summer vacation. In short, you have to, in your own counseling, come to grips with the drinking or relapse, so that you do not find yourself working it out on the job with clients.

A similar problem is posed by clinicians who enter the field without an alcohol use disorder, but who come to recognize their own budding problem. This raises interesting questions. The accepted wisdom had long been that recovering people needed a period of solid recovery before entering the field. A period of two years was commonly cited. However, those were the days when, for many, being in recovery was *the* credential for employment. Is this approach still applicable? A far better model may be the programs for impaired professionals in other settings. Should those who have been good clinicians be expected to exit the field for a set period of time? In this situation, a "policy" cannot substitute for thoughtful consideration and the need to determine what is most appropriate on a case-by-case basis.

The foregoing may seem a very grim note on which to conclude this text. It is sobering, but it is reality too. A clinician in the substance abuse field recalled the comments George Vaillant made when he addressed her incoming medical student class. He offered two pieces of advice. First, "Select a partner who will take care of you, because your profession is based on your caring for others." Interestingly, the other word of wisdom was, "Never take anything to help you go to sleep nor anything to help you stay awake."

Maybe one of the hardest things to learn in becoming a clinician is how to take care of yourself. Like everything else, this takes practice. One aspect of caring for yourself, professionally as well as personally, is to place yourself in the company of nurturing people.

REFERENCES AND FURTHER READINGS

Issues of the Profession

Amodeo M, Lundgren L, Cohen A, Rose D, Chassler D, Beltrame C, et al. Barriers to implementing evidence-based practices in addiction treatment programs: Comparing staff reports on Motivational Interviewing, Adolescent Community Reinforcement Approach, Assertive Community Treatment, and Cognitive-Behavioral Therapy. *Evaluation and Program Planning* 34(4):382–389, 2011. (33 refs.)

Arfken CL, Agius E, Dickson MW. Clinicians' information sources for new substance abuse treatments. *Addictive Behaviors* 30(8):1592–1596, 2005. (8 refs.)

Baer JS, Wells EA, Rosengren DB, Hartzler B, Beadnell B, Dunn C, et al. Agency context and tailored training in technology transfer: A pilot evaluation of motivational interviewing training for community counselors. *Journal of Substance Abuse Treatment* 37(2):191–202, 2009. (45 refs.)

Bernstein E, Topp D, Shaw E, Girard C, Pressman K, Woolcock E, et al. A preliminary report of knowledge translation: Lessons from taking screening and brief intervention techniques from the research setting into regional systems of care. *Academic Emergency Medicine* 16(11):1225–1233, 2009. (30 refs.)

Blume SB. *Confidentiality of Patient Records in Alcoholism and Drug Treatment Programs.* New York: American Medical Society on Alcoholism and Other Drug Dependencies and National Council on Alcoholism, 1987.
Note: This pamphlet reviews the 1987 revisions of the federal regulations governing the confidentiality of alcohol and other drug abuse patient records. It addresses the records covered by the regulations; the types of communications covered; written informed consent; the application of consent to situations involving minors, incompetent persons, and deceased persons; the types of information to be released with consent; and the security of records.

Center for Substance Abuse Treatment, Addiction Technology Transfer Centers Curriculum Committee, Deitch DA. *Addiction Counseling Competencies: The Knowledge, Skills, and Attitudes of Professional Practice.* (TAP) Series 21. Rockville, MD: CSAT, 1997. (Chapter refs.)

Center for Substance Abuse Treatment. *Clinical Supervision and Professional Development of the Substance Abuse Counselor. Treatment Improvement Protocol (TIP)* Series 52. DHHS Publication No. (SMA) 09-4435. Rockville, MD: Substance Abuse and Mental Health Services Administration, 2009.

Chiauzzi EJ, Liljegren S. Taboo topics in addiction treatment: An empirical review of clinical folklore (review). *Journal of Substance Abuse Treatment* 10(3):303–316, 1993.

Dennis M. Managing addiction as a chronic condition. *Addiction Science and Clinical Practice* 4(1):45–55, 2007. (150 refs.) Available: www.drugabuse.gov/PDF/ascp/vol4no1/Managing.pdf.

Gotham HJ. Diffusion of mental health and substance abuse treatments: Development, dissemination, and implementation (review). *Clinical Psychology: Science and Practice* 11(2):160–178, 2004. (117 refs.)

Kerwin ME, Walker-Smith K, Kirby KC. Comparative analysis of state requirements for the training of substance abuse and mental health counselors. *Journal of Substance Abuse Treatment* 30(3):173–181, 2006. (24 refs.)

Kirby KC, Benishek LA, Dugosh KL, Kerwin ME. Substance abuse treatment providers' beliefs and objections regarding contingency management: Implications for dissemination. *Drug and Alcohol Dependence* 85(1):19–27, 2006. (28 refs.)

Knudsen HK, Ducharme LJ, Roman PM, Link T. Buprenorphine diffusion: The attitudes of substance abuse treatment counselors. *Journal of Substance Abuse Treatment* 29(2):95–106, 2005. (71 refs.)

McLellan AT, Carise D, Kleber HD. Can the national addiction treatment infrastructure support the public's demand for quality care? *Journal of Substance Abuse Treatment* 25(2):117–121, 2003. (26 refs.)

Mulvey KP, Hubbard S, Hayashi S. A national study of the substance abuse treatment workforce. *Journal of Substance Abuse Treatment* 24(1):51–57, 2003. (15 refs.)

Olmstead TA, Johnson JA, Roman PM, Sindelar JL. What are the correlates of substance abuse treatment counselor salaries? *Journal of Substance Abuse Treatment* 29(3):181–189, 2005. (20 refs.)

Rieckmann T, Farentinos C, McCarty D. The substance abuse counseling workforce: Education, preparation and certification. *Substance Abuse* 32(4):180–190, 2011. (24 refs)

Ryan O, Murphy D, Krom L. *Vital Signs: Taking the Pulse of the Addition Treatment Workforce. National Report, Version 1.* Kansas City MO: Addiction Technology Transfer Center National Office at the University of Missouri-Kansas City, 2012.

Stoffelmayr BE, Mavis BE, Kasim RM. Substance abuse treatment staff: Recovery status and approaches to treatment. *Journal of Drug Education* 28(2):135–145, 1998. (14 refs.)

Ethics

Babor TF. Alcohol research and the alcoholic beverage industry: Issues, concerns and conflicts of interest (review). *Addiction* 104(Supplement 1):34–47, 2009. (59 refs.)

Bruce RD, Schleifer RA. Ethical and human rights imperatives to ensure medication-assisted treatment for opioid dependence in prisons and pre-trial detention (editorial). *International Journal of Drug Policy* 19(1):17–23, 2008. (66 refs.)

Caplan AL. Ethical issues surrounding forced, mandated, or coerced treatment. *Journal of Substance Abuse Treatment* 31(2):117–120, 2006. (7 refs.)

Doyle K. Substance abuse counselors in recovery: Implications for the ethical issue of dual relationships. *Journal of Counseling and Development* 75(6):428–432, 1997. (16 refs.)

Geppert CMA, Bogenschutz MP. Ethics in substance use disorder treatment. *Psychiatric Clinics of North America* 32(2):283+, 2009. (69 refs.)

Gruning T, Gilmore AB, McKee M. Tobacco industry influence on science and scientists in Germany. *European Journal of Public Health* 15(Supplement 1):51, 2006.

Hannum H. The Dublin Principles of Cooperation among the beverage alcohol industry, governments, scientific researchers, and the public health community (editorial). *Alcohol and Alcoholism* 32(6):639–640, 1997.

Kleinig J, ed. Special issue on ethical issues of substance intervention. *Substance Use & Misuse* 39(3):entire issue, 2004.

Nunn A, Zaller N, Dickman S, Trimbur C, Nijhawan A, Rich JD. Methadone and buprenorphine prescribing and referral practices in US prison systems: Results from a nationwide survey. *Drug and Alcohol Dependence* 105(1/2):83–88, 2009. (51 refs.)

Pratt WM, Davidson D. Does participation in an alcohol administration study increase risk for excessive drinking? *Alcohol* 37(3):135–141, 2005. (18 refs.)

Reinarman C. Librarians and other subversives: Truth can be a casualty of drug wars, too. *International Journal of Drug Policy* 16(1):1–4, 2005. (9 refs.)

Rhule DM. Take care to do no harm: Harmful interventions for youth problem behavior. *Professional Psychology: Research and Practice* 36(3):618–625, 2006. (45 refs.)

Rieckmann T, Farentinos C, McCarty D. The substance abuse counseling workforce: Education, preparation and certification. *Substance Abuse* 32(4):180–190, 2011. (24 refs.)

Stenius, Babor TF. The alcohol industry and public interest science. *Addiction* 105(2):191–198, 2010. (38 refs.)

Walker R, Logan TK, Clark JJ, Leukefeld C. Informed consent to undergo treatment for substance abuse: A recommended approach. *Journal of Substance Abuse Treatment* 29(4): 241–251, 2005. (67 refs.)

Prevention

Anderson P, Baumberg B. *Alcohol in Europe*. London: Institute of Alcohol Studies, 2006.

Babor T, Caetano P, Casswell S, Edwards G, Giesbrecht N, Graham K, et al. *Alcohol: No Ordinary Commodity,* 2nd ed. Oxford: Oxford University Press, 2010.

Bennett GG, Glasgow RE. The delivery of public health interventions via the Internet: Actualizing their potential (review). *Annual Review of Public Health* 30:273–292, 2009. (162 refs.)

Brown JH, Clarey AM. The social psychology of disintegrative shaming in education. *Journal of Drug Education* 42(2): 229–253, 2012

Chun TH, Linakis JG. Interventions for adolescent alcohol use (review). *Current Opinion in Pediatrics* 24(2):238–242, 2012. (22 refs.)

Fell JC, Voas RB. The effectiveness of reducing illegal limits for driving: Evidence for blood alcohol concentration (BAC) lowering the limit to .05 BAC. *Journal of Safety Research* 37(3):233–243, 2006. (52 refs.)

Lemstra M, Bennett N, Nannapaneni U, Neudorf C, Warren L, Kershaw T, et al. A systematic review of school-based marijuana and alcohol prevention programs targeting adolescents aged 10–15. *Addiction Research & Theory* 18(1):84–96, 2010. (35 refs.)

Lynam DR, Milich R, Zimmerman R, Novak SP, Logan TK, Martin C, et al. Project DARE: No effects at 10-year follow-up. *Journal of Consulting and Clinical Psychology* 67(4):590–593, 1999. (16 refs.)

Pan W, Bai HY. A multivariate approach to a meta-analytic review of the effectiveness of the DARE program (review). *International Journal of Environmental Research and Public Health* 6(1):267–277, 2009. (48 refs.)

Tighe T, Sac L, eds. *Journal of Drug Issues* 36(2):entire issue, 2006.
Note: Devoted to the evaluation of Fighting Back program.

Wakeman SE, Bowman SE, McKenzie M, Jeronimo A, Rich JD. Preventing death among the recently incarcerated: An argument for naloxone prescription before release. *Journal of Addictive Diseases* 28(2):124–129, 2009. (29 refs.)

Wallace SK, Staiger PK. Informing consent: Should "providers" inform "purchasers" about the risks of drug education? *Health Promotion International* 13(2):167–171, 1998. (47 refs.)

Alcohol—Medication Interactions

Type of Drug	Generic Name	Trade Name	Interaction with Alcohol
Analgesics Non-opioid	salicylates	(Products containing aspirin) Bayer Aspirin Bufferin Alka-Seltzer	Heavy concurrent use of alcohol with analgesics can increase the potential for GI bleeding. Special caution should be exercised by individuals with ulcers. Buffering of salicylates reduces possibility of this interaction.
	acetaminophen	Tylenol Excedrin	With 2+ drinks per day can cause liver damage.
	diclofenac* ibuprofen*	Voltaren Advil Motrin Midol Excedrin IB Naprosyn	Increases risk of gastrointestinal bleeding.
	naproxen*	Aleve	
Opioids	buprenorphine	Suboxone Subutex	The combination of narcotic analgesics and alcohol can suppress respiratory function, potentially resulting in respiratory arrest and death.
	codeine		
	fentanyl	Duragesic	
	hydromorphone	Dilaudid	
	meperidine	Demerol	
	morphine	Avinza Kadian MSIR MS Contin Oramorph SR	
	opium	Paregoric	

*Also classified as non-steroidal anti-inflammatory drugs.

Type of Drug	Generic Name	Trade Name	Interaction with Alcohol
(opioid analgesics, continued)			
	oxycodone	OxyContin Percocet Roxicet	
	tramadol	Ultram	
	propoxyphene	Darvon Darvon-N	
	tapentadol	Nucynta	
Anti-anginal	nitroglycerin isosorbide dinitrate	Nitrostat Isordil Sorbitrate	Alcohol in combination with anti-anginal drugs may cause a drop in blood pressure—creating a potentially dangerous situation.
Antibiotics	isoniazid metronidazole nitrofurantoin	Nydrazid Flagyl Macrodantin	Certain antibiotics, especially those taken for urinary tract infections and trichomonas infections, have been known to produce disulfiram-like reactions (nausea, vomiting, headaches, hypotension) when combined with alcohol. Concurrent use of alcohol with isoniazid can cause hepatitis.
Anticoagulants	warfarin	Coumadin Jantoven	With chronic alcohol use, the anticoagulant effect of these drugs is inhibited. With acute alcohol use, the anticoagulant effect is enhanced: hemorrhaging can result.
Anticonvulsants	phenytoin carbamazepine primidone	Dilantin Tegretol Mysoline	Chronic heavy drinking can reduce the effectiveness of anticonvulsant drugs. Seizures previously controlled by these drugs can occur if the dosage is not adjusted appropriately.
	phenobarbital	Luminal	Although widely used as an anticonvulsant, phenobarbital is a long-acting barbiturate, and thus a depressant. Increased CNS depression may occur with concurrent use of alcohol, and the seizure threshold can be reduced.
Antidiabetic agents (hypoglycemics)	glimepiride glipizide glyburide insulin metformin pioglitazone saxagliptin sitagliptin	Amaryl Glucotrol Diabeta Glynase Micronase various Glucophage Actos Onglyza Januvia	The interaction of alcohol and either insulin or oral antidiabetic agents may be severe and unpredictable. The interaction may induce hypoglycemia or hyperglycemia; also, disulfiram-like reactions may occur. In combination with metformin, alcohol can lead to increased lactic acid in the blood, which is associated with increased mortality.

Type of Drug	Generic Name	Trade Name	Interaction with Alcohol
Antidepressants			
Tricyclics	nortriptyline	Aventyl	Enhanced CNS depression may occur with concurrent use of alcohol and antidepressant drugs. Alcohol itself can cause or exacerbate clinical states of depression.
	amitriptyline	Elavil Endep	
	desipramine	Pertofrane	
	doxepin	Sinequan	
	imipramine	Tofranil	
Heterocyclics	mitazapine	Remeron	
SSRIs	fluoxetine	Prozac	
	paroxetine	Paxil	
	citalopram	Celexa	
	escitalopram	Lexapro	
	sertraline	Zoloft	
SNRIs	venlafaxine	Effexor	
	duloxetine	Cymbalta	
	desvenlafaxine	Pristiq	
MAOIs	pargyline	Eutonyl	Alcoholic beverages (particularly beer, non-alcoholic beer, and red wine) as well as foods such as cheese or yogurt contain tyramine, which interacts with an MAOI to produce a hypertensive crisis (sudden sharp rise in blood pressure) as well as a hyperpyrexic crisis (sudden rapid rise in body temperature). Concomitant use of alcohol with MAOIs may result in enhanced CNS depression.
	isocarboxazid	Marplan	
	phenelzine	Nardil	
	tranylcypromine	Parnate	
Antihistamines	many cold & allergy remedies. Examples		The presence of alcohol increases CNS depression.
	chlorpheniramine	Coricidin	
	cyproheptadine	Periactin	
	diphenhydramine	Benadryl	
	hydroxyzine	Atarax Vistaril	
Antihypertensive agents			
ACE inhibitors	benazepril	Lotensin	Alcohol increases blood-pressure-lowering effects of hypertensive agents leading to postural hypotension (dizziness upon standing up, caused by a drop in blood pressure).
	captopril	Capoten	
	enalapril	Vasotec	
	fosinopril	Monopril	
	lisinopril	Prinivil	
	moexipril	Univasc	
	quinapril	Accupril	
	ramipril	Altace	

Type of Drug	Generic Name	Trade Name	Interaction with Alcohol
(antihypertensive agents, continued)			
β-blockers	atenolol	Tenormin	
	carvedilol	Coreg	
	metoprolol	Lopressor	
		Toprol XL	
	nadolol	Corgard	
	propranolol	Inderal	
	sotalol	Betapace	
Calcium-channel blockers	amlodipine	Norvasc	
	felodipine	Plendil	
	nifedipine	Adalat	
		Procardia	
	verapamil	Calan	
		Covera	
		Isoptin	
Vasodilators	hydralazine	Apresoline	
Antipsychotics			
Traditional	chlorpromazine	Thorazine	The traditional and atypical antipsychotic drugs interact with alcohol to further decrease CNS depression function, resulting in impairment of voluntary movement such as walking or hand coordination; larger doses can depress respiration. Increases incidence and severity of extra-pyramidal side effects of these drugs.
	haloperidol	Haldol	
	trifluoperazine	Stelazine	
	thioridazine	Mellaril	
Atypical	oloanzapine	Zyprexca	
	paliperidone	Invega	
	quetiapine	Seroquel	
	risperidone	Risperdal	
Anti-anxiety agents (benzodiazepines)	alprazolam	Xanax	The anti-anxiety drugs, as does alcohol, depress CNS functioning. This is the basis of possible lethal overdose when alcohol and benzodiazepines, known as minor tranquilizers, are used concomitantly.
	chlordiazepoxide	Librium	
	clonazepam	Valium	
	diazepam	Serax	
	lorazepam	Ativan	
	midazolam	Versed	
	oxazepam	Klonopin	
	temazepam	Restoril	
	triazolam	Halcion	
CNS depressants			
Barbiturate sedative hypnotics	phenobarbital	Luminal	Since alcohol is a depressant, the interaction of alcohol and other depressants further reduces CNS functioning. It is extremely dangerous to mix barbiturates and alcohol. What would be a non-dangerous dosage of either drug by itself in combination can induce coma or fatal respiratory arrest. A similar danger exists in combining nonbarbiturate hypnotics with alcohol.
Non-barbiturate sedative hypnotics	eszopiclone	Lunesta	
	flurazepam	Dalmane	
	temazepam	Restoril	
	zolpidem	Ambien	

Type of Drug	Generic Name	Trade Name	Interaction with Alcohol
CNS stimulants	amphetamines caffeine dextroamphetamine lisdexamfetamine methamphetamine methlyphenidate	Adderall Daytrana Coffee, cola, energy drinks NoDoz Stay Awake Vivarin Dexedrine Vyvanse Desoxyn Concerta Ritalin	Stimulants can blunt some of the depressant effect of alcohol, thereby reducing the subjective experience of intoxication. Stimulants do not reduce the level of impairment associated with a given blood alcohol level.
Aldehyde dehydrogenase inhibitor	disulfiram	Antabuse	Interferes with metabolism of alcohol; leads to build-up of acetaldehyde which has toxic effects on CNS. Symptoms can include headache, nausea, vomiting, convulsions, rapid fall in blood pressure, unconsciousnes, and—with sufficiently high doses—death.
Diuretics (antihypertensive)	chlorothiazide chlorthalidone furosemide hydrochlorothiazide (HCTZ) spironolactone/HCTZ triamterene/HCTZ	Diuril Thalitone Lasix Hydrodiuril Esidrix Aldactazide Dyazide Maxzide	Alcohol enhances the blood-pressure-lowering effects of the diuretic, which can possibly precipitate hypotension.
Muscle relaxants	carisoprodol cyclobenzaprine	Soma Flexeril	Increased CNS depression may occur with concurrent use of alcohol.

Based on a table prepared by: Tawnya L. Grant, Outpatient Pharmacy, Dartmouth-Hitchcock Medical Center, Lebanon NH, 2011.

Index

D

T

U

NOTES